REV. JOHN CUNNINGHAM CLYDE, D. D.
(Born October 22, 1841; died January 28, 1915.)
To whose memory this volume is affectionately dedicated by
The Northampton County Historical and Genealogical Society.

THE SCOTCH-IRISH OF NORTHAMPTON COUNTY, PENNSYLVANIA.

Published

By

THE NORTHAMPTON COUNTY HISTORICAL
AND GENEALOGICAL SOCIETY.

VOLUME

I.

1926

This volume was reproduced from
An 1926 edition located in the
Publisher's private Library
Greenville, South Carolina

All rights reserved. No part of this publication may be reproduced,
stored in a retrieval system, transmitted in any form, posted
on to the web in any form or by any means without
the prior written permission of the publisher.

Please direct all correspondence and orders to:

www.southernhistoricalpress.com
or
**SOUTHERN HISTORICAL PRESS, Inc.
PO Box 1267
375 West Broad Street
Greenville, SC   29601**
southernhistoricalpress@gmail.com

Originally published: Baston, Pennsylvania, 1926
Copyright 1926
By: Northampton County Hist'l & Gen'l Society
ISBN #0-89308-911-7
All rights Reserved.

PREFACE

The Northampton County Historical and Genealogical Society takes great pleasure in offering its initial publication to members, to descendants of the sturdy settlers of the Irish Settlements in "The Forks of the Delaware", to genealogists and students of Colonial Pennsylvania.

In this offering the Society is of the opinion that the material dealing with the religious, the educational, the civil, the military life of the Scotch-Irish of Northampton County will not only supply a long-felt need but will also indicate to what extent their achievements have served, together with the contribution of their German neighbors, to make Pennsylvania in the formative period of her history the "Keystone" of the Thirteen Original Colonies.

With the sincere hope that the volume entitled "The Scotch-Irish of Northampton County", will keep alive the valiant achievements of the Scotch-Irish pioneers, the Society herewith sends it on its worthy mission.

The Publication Committee,—

PRESTON ALEPH LAURY,
FLOYD SMITH BIXLER,
PORTER WILLIAM SHIMER,
GEORGE ALLEN CHANDLER,
HENRY FRANKLIN MARX.

January 1926. The One Hundred and Ninety-ninth of the Settlement in The Forks of the Delaware, and the Sesqui-Centennial Year of American Independence.

TABLE OF CONTENTS

	PAGE
The Scotch-Irish Immigration	1–5
Settlement of Allen Township—Pioneers—Deeds—Titles	6–12
Description of the Craig Home and Brief of Title	12–17
Description of the Hirst Home	18
The Hays' Spring	18–19
Some Worthy Trees of Bath	19–21
The Old Irish Settlement Stone Houses	22–26
The Assessment List of Allen Township, 1775	27–31
The Craig Deed—The Franklin Deed—Biddle Deed—Red Rose Deed	32–35
The Allen Tract	35–36
Copy of Deed Poll, Commonwealth of Pennsylvania to Hugh Horner	37–40
The Old Block House near Fort Ralston and Ralston Farm	41–43
Old Buildings—Fort Ralston	43–44
The Indian Forts of the Blue Mountains, H. M. M. Richards	45–51
The Historic Queen Town in the Monoquasy Valley—Bath	52–54
Genealogical and Biographical. Reprint from Clyde unless otherwise indicated	55–149
The Scotch-Irish in the Revolution—Extracts from Egle's History	150–156
List of Revolutionary Soldiers	156
Distinguished Men of the Craig Settlement, Weaver	157–159
Benjamin Franklin's Visit to the Settlement	159–161
Distinguished Men of the Settlement, Clyde	162–207
Rev. John Rosbrugh, Bulgin, Paper read before the Society	208–212
Wesselhoeft and his Bath School of Homoeopathy, McIlhaney	213–219
The Old Church in Allen, Rev. Richard Webster	220–250
The Horner Bible	250
The First Log Church	250–251
Obligation and Declaration of John Walker and Others	252–256
Deed of 1772; Deed of 1813	257–264
Clyde's History of the Allen Township Presbyterian Church	265–389
The Old Academy Repaired for a Place of Worship	390–393
The Records of the Old Academy Debating Society	393–406
Annotated List of Burials in the Scotch-Irish Settlement of Allen Township	407–423
The Scotch-Irish of the Forks of the Delaware—Hunter Settlement	424–517
Scotch-Irish Soldiers from Mt. Bethel	518–519
Scotch-Irish Soldiers from Mt. Bethel	518–520
Certificate of Names to be taxed in Mount Bethel Township	520–524
The Presbyterian Church of Mount Bethel, Foresman	576–577
Burial List in Mt. Bethel Burial Ground	577–594
A Few Scotch-Irish Families of Old Mount Bethel	525–534
The Village Poet	535–537
Temperance Dedication Hymn	538
David Brainerd	539–542
Memorial Discourse, Foresman	543–575
The Scotch-Irish Presbyterian Burial Ground, at Three Churches, Lower Mt. Bethel	576–594

LIST OF ILLUSTRATIONS

Frontispiece—John Cunningham Clyde.
Old Map of The Irish Settlement.
Map of Tracts Deeded to James Horner.
Hirst Home.
Hays' Spring.
The Horse Chestnut Tree.
The Joseph Horner Homestead.
The Hugh Horner Homestead.
The Hays' Mill.
Sheriff Scull's Return of Assessors Elected—1754.
The James Craig Home.
Facsimile of Deed to Hugh Horner—First and Last Part.
The James Kerr Home—Two Views.
The Old Block House.
Home of The First School of Homeopathy, Bath, Pa.
The James Horner, Sr., Homestead.
The Hays' Coat of Arms.
The Wolf Academy.
The Old Horner Bible—two views.
Seal of The English Presbyterian Congregation.
The Presbyterian Church at Bath.
The Old Stone Church In The Irish Settlement, and the Original Seating Arrangement.
The Old Burial Ground in the Settlement.
Brainerd Monument—Martins Creek.
The Scotch-Irish Presbyterian Burial Ground at Three Churches.

Note—The Northampton County Historical and Genealogical Society hereby acknowledges its debt of gratitude to Doctor Robert Hays Horner for the use of his photographs, and valuable information put at the disposal of the Society.

INTRODUCTION

The narratives of the Scotch-Irish Settlements in Northampton County, biographical sketches of prominent persons, lists of genealogy, of taxables, of Revolutionary soldiers and of burials together with other valuable records, have been collected from the unpublished manuscripts as well as the published writings of Doctor John Cunningham Clyde and incorporated in this volume.

The Scotch-Irish of Northampton County excelled in energy, enterprise and intelligence. The original family trees of which only a few remain, have scions in all parts of the country, and have become as important a factor in those parts as the original family trees had been in Northampton County.

The records of their achievements are now the frontier annals of frontier conditions. It was an act of wisdom on the part of Doctor Clyde to gather the information from many sources, to put it in permanent form and to publish parts of the same.

When this manuscript material came into the possession of the Northampton County Society, it was at first proposed to publish that part as a sort of a memorial to one of its energetic presidents. However, the fact that all of Doctor Clyde's publications were out of print and that a number of papers, records and other important data were at the service of the Society, it was unanimously recommended by the Executive Committee and later adopted by the Society at its regular meeting that the volume should be called, "The Scotch-Irish of Northampton County", and that the volume should not only contain Doctor Clyde's writings, but also as much of original matter, documents, and records as were accessible and obtainable.

Through the untiring efforts of Doctor Robert Hays Horner, of Horatio Gates Shull, of Asa Kinney McIlhaney, of Wilbur Lewis King and others, it was possible to include in this first volume of the Northampton County Historical and Genealogical Society, a vast amount of hitherto unpublished material. The preservation in this volume of historical material gathered from documents regarded so precious that only copies of the same were allowed to be handed to the printer, proves the wisdom of this publication and the confidence of those who submitted their documents for the use of the Society.

In presenting this copy of historical material with many illustrations of documents, homes, burial grounds and other objects, no effort was spared to retain the original form as nearly as possible. The Publication Committee knows errors were thereby transmitted, but it also knows there are errors for which the Committee alone is responsible. Regarding the work as a whole, the Committee is convinced from actual investigation that it is a reliable and trustworthy presentation of facts.

THE PUBLICATION COMMITTEE.

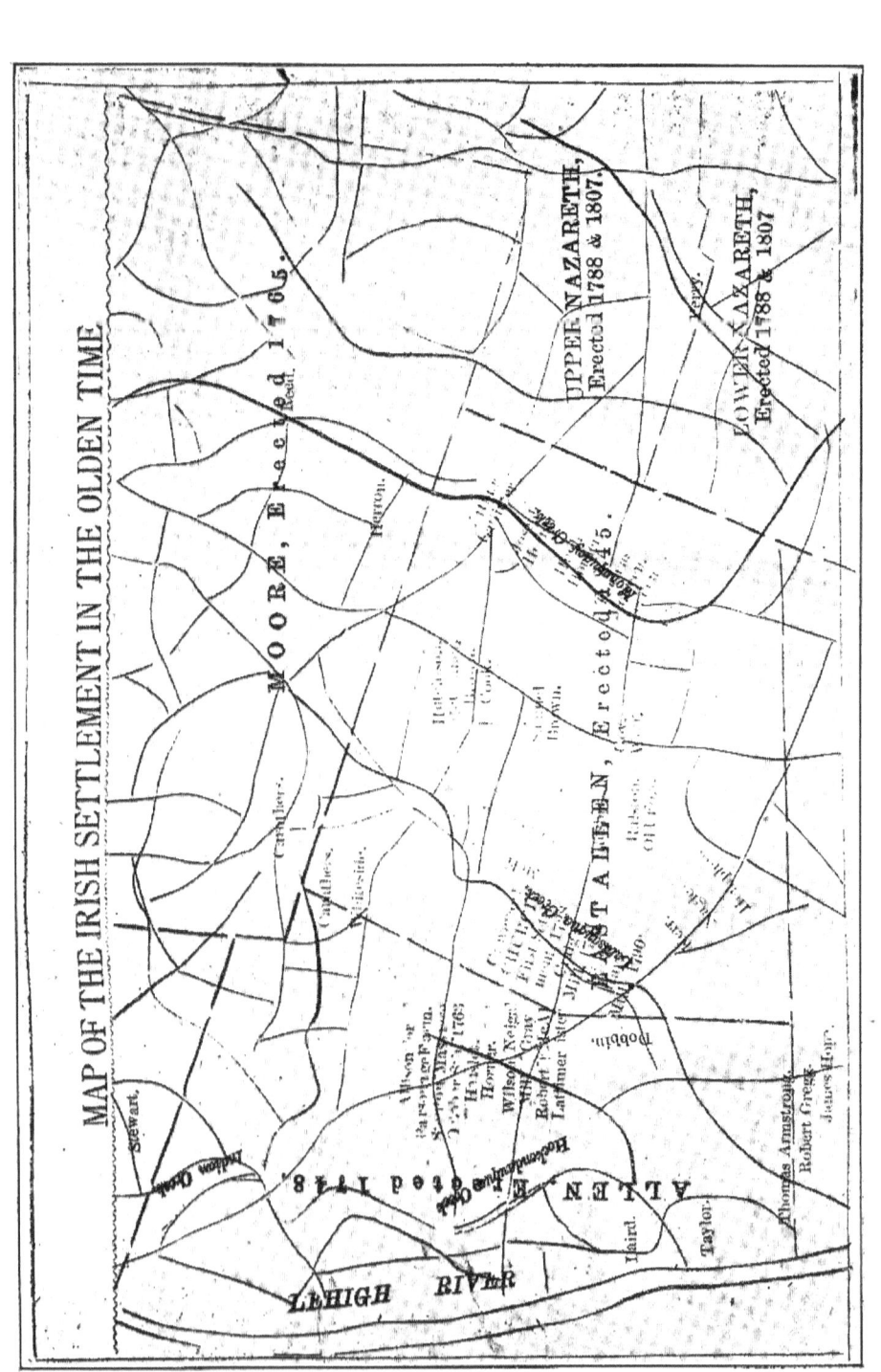

A very old and reliable map of the Irish Settlement in Allen Township. (See page 42.)

The Scotch-Irish of Northampton County, Penna.

THE SCOTCH-IRISH IMMIGRATION.

George Fisher—"Making of Pennsylvania".

THE Scotch-Irish were Scotch-English people who had gone to Ireland to take up the estates of Irish rebels confiscated under Queen Elizabeth and James I. The same James who was King of Scotland as James VI, encouraged his Presbyterian subjects to emigrate to Ireland and occupy the confiscated lands.

The migration was numerous and began in the early part of the seventeenth century, about seventy-five years before the founding of Pennsylvania. Towards the middle of the same century the confiscation of the Irish lands by Cromwell increased the emigration to still greater proportions, and after this many Englishmen joined the movement.

These people, English and Scotch, who occupied Ireland in this way, have usually been known in England as Ulstermen, and with us as Scotch-Irish, and are, of course, totally different in character as well as in religion from the native Irish. Even those who came to Ireland from Scotland were not Celtic Scotch, but people of English stock who had been living for many generations in Scotland.

They became famous in history for their heroic defense of Londonderry against James II. They were more thrifty and intelligent than the native Irish. They took the land on long leases and began to make it blossom like a garden. They were, however, soon put to a severe test by the persecution of Charles I, who after coming to the English throne in 1625, attempted to force the Scotch people in both Scotland and Ireland to conform to the Church of England. At the same time, the native Irish rose to expel the Scotch, and succeeded in killing a few thousand. So between the two persecutors, these settlers, already sturdy from their race and religion, were not without the additional discipline of suffering and martyrdom.

Many of them emigrated to America, especially when the long leases began to expire. The movement began about the year 1700, and continued for forty or fifty years. Some of them went to Maryland and a great many went to Virginia. In Virginia most of them sought the frontier, yet not all, for in Pennsylvania many remained East, many in Philadelphia. But they flourish better in the country, and best of all on the frontier. Their most striking and peculiar qualities seemed to have been developed by contact with the wilderness, and the frontier Ulsterman has become so conspicuous that his less demonstrative, though probably equally efficient, brother has been thrown into the shade.

They wanted the land as their own and would have no neighbors but their own people. When the Germans began to move into some of their settlements in Pennsylvania, it was found difficult for the two nationalities to live together, and the proprietors asked the Scotch-Irish to move farther west, a suggestion which they always eagerly accepted. They were delighted when, in 1768, the land west of the Alleghenies was opened for settlement, and they immediately began to throng through the mountain passes to reach it.

The larger part of the Scotch migration to America appears to have come by the fame of the colony for religious liberty and fertile soil. They scattered themselves to some extent all over the state, and members of the race can now be found in almost every part of it. A large number of them settled between the Lehigh and the Delaware rivers. Some went to Bucks and Lancaster counties. Many others settled in the Cumberland Valley.

Fighting had become a part of the religion of the Scotch-Irish, as peace had been a part of the religion of the Quakers, and they used the rifle to settle difficulties with the Indians which the Quakers tried to settle by treaty. They were the readiest of the ready on the battlefields of the Revolution. If they had any faults, a lack of patriotism or of courage was not among the number.

Scotch-Irish by the thousand emigrated from the North of Ireland to Pennsylvania from 1720 to 1775. For the most part the immigrants settled along the frontiers. They were excellent pioneers.

As a result of great industry and warlike zeal, the province prospered and enjoyed comparative freedom from Indian depredations.

Because of the extent of the exodus from Ireland, a bill was introduced in the Irish Parliament in 1735 restricting emigration to America. In anticipation of its passage thousands sought passage to America. In 1736, one thousand such families were in Belfast alone awaiting passage.

In "Pennsylvania History Told by Contemporaries", the editors—Messrs. Martin & Shenk—reproduce a quaint old letter written by a shipmaster to the proprietors of Pennsylvania that contains much information about the conditions existing in Ireland at that time. The letter is as follows:—

Dublin, May 3, 1736.
Hond. Sr.

"As you are the proprietor of pensilvaina & being informed of your being in London, I would beg Liberty to inform your Worship of some of the deficulty wh. poor peeple that are flying from the oppression of the Landlords and Tyths to several parts of America viz:—

When last our Irish Parlement was sitting there was a bill brought in respecting the Transportation to America, which made it next to prohibition, said Bill greatly alarmed the people particularly in the North of Ireland, and least a second should succeed greater numrs. than usually made ready but when said Landlords found it so they fell on with other means by distressing the owners & masters of the

Ships, there being now ten in the harbour of Belfast the method they fell in with first was that when anny of said Ships advertised that they were Bound for such Port & when they would be in readiness to seal & thire willingness to agree with the passengers for which & no other Reasons they esued out thire Warrants and had severall of said owners & Masters apprehended & likewise the printers of said advertisements & Bound in Bonds of a thousand pounds to appear att Carrick-fergus Assizes or be thrown into a Lowthsome Geaol & for no other reason than Encouraging his Majesty's subjects as they were pleased to cale thire indectment from one plantation to another.

But even after all this when the Assizes came on they were offread of thire Enlargement and begged very earnestly of ye judges to heave them continued upon thire Recognizes —the consequence of which may easly be seen, most of said Ships being strangers would have effectually them.

But the Judge was pleased to discharge them, nay one of the Justices gott up in Court & swore by G—d if any came to Lisburn the town in which he lived to publise an advertisement he would whipe him throw the Town. To which the Judge replied to concider if they Deserved it & if he whiped anny person to do it according to Law.

Money has been offered by some of them to swere against some of Said Ships & Rewards actually given but yett a more Hellish contrivance has been thought of & is put in practice by the Collr. Geo McCartnay of Belfast he will not now, when said Ships & passengers was just redy to seal so much as allow the poor people to carry thire old Bed clothes with them; allthow ever so old under pretence of an act of the British Parlement made in the tenth & eleventh years of the Rean of King William and repealed in ye year 1732 & said Ships being obliged to lay this affair before the Comrs. of Dublin.

Many of the seventeen or eighteen hundred souls destitute —not able to pay passage money, without houses to shelter them and dependent on Friends in America—whose reports are by Landlords regarded as forgery, Lyes & the contrivances of the Proprietors Trustees and Masters of the American Ships

    Signed by John Stewart"

Credited to "Scot in North Britain, North Ireland and North America, N.Y. 1902, Vol. II., 65—69—Charles Hanna."

SETTLEMENT OF ALLEN

Copy furnished by Dr. Robert Hays Horner

AT the time of the arrival of the first settlers, the Delaware Indians had their wigwams, and cultivated orchards of apple and pear trees near the present site of Weaversville. Indian arrows and pestles were here found in great numbers.

"The Craig or Irish Settlement" is named after the first family—James Craig—who settled, 1728, in the vicinity of the Presbyterian church near Weaversville. James Craig purchased 250 acres from William Allen, 1743,—a part of the 5,000 acre tract taken up by Thomas Penn, by warrant dated London, May 8, 1732.

In April, 1774, James Craig divided his lands among his three sons. The church, grave-yard and school-house lots were on his land and were deeded to the congregation March 4, 1770; March 11, 1772, and June 8, 1791.

The names of other prominent early settlers were: Thomas Craig (First), who was the owner of 590 acres, 96 perches, granted to him by Caspar Wister, March 28, 1739. His residence was on the farm owned by Dr. H. H. Riegel. In June, 1773, he deeded 150 acres to Andrew Hagenbuch. General Thomas Craig and Captain John Craig were sons of Thomas Craig and both served as officers in the Revolutionary war.

Thomas Armstrong's residence was on land situated near the present site of Catasauqua. The residence of John Riddle was on a farm later owned by Morgan Emaniel in Allen Township.

Widow Dobbin, a sister of William Boyd, owned 289 acres, a part of the Page tract, called the "Manor of Chawton," and her residence was on a farm owned later by Valentine Deshler. The deed dated to her bears the date April 8, 1751.

Nathaniel J. Taylor lived on the Lehigh River, a short distance above Catasauqua.

James Kerr owned a large tract, and his residence was

on a farm owned later by Isaac Miller.

Mary King's residence was on a farm owned later by David Heller.

James Hutchison, William McConnel, Joseph Brown and John Cook settled near the present site of St. Paul's church.

Samuel Brown resided on a farm owned later by M. Emaniel, but in 1777, moved to a farm where his grandson, the late William Brown, formerly resided.

Robert Gregg was the owner of 229 acres located below Catasauqua, on the Lehigh River, deeded to him by John Elliott, December 12, 1754.

James Allison lived on a farm owned later by Daniel Saeger.

James Horner emigrated to this country at an early date, resided on a farm owned later by Thomas Laubach. The wife, Jane Horner, was killed by the Indians.

James McAllster and George Gray lived in what is now Howertown.

John Hays, Sr., kept a public house on the road leading from Bethlehem to Gnadenhuetten, now known as Weisport. John Hays, Jr., his son, served in the Revolution and died in 1796.

Thomas Herron, previous to 1747, lived in Moore Township. Archibald Laird owned 210 acres on the present site of Northampton. Samuel Caruthers resided near where Seemsville now stands. Michael Clyde owned a large tract on the Monocacy Creek in Allen Township. John Boyd resided on a farm owned later by John Miller. James Hope lived near Catasauqua.

James Horner, Sr., the emigrant, was born in County Donegal in 1711; lived in County Derry in the North of Ireland, and came to the Irish Settlement (via Philadelphia) in the Forks of the Delaware, now Northampton Co., in 1728, and died May 1st, 1793.

In 1736 and 1737, the Irish Settlement commenced on the west branch of the Delaware, now called the Lehigh. The first deed to James Horner, Sr., from Allen, is dated March 5th, 1737.

The first house was a log house. The present structure, as above, was built in 1755, and is still standing today in good condition. James Horner, Sr., we believe, was one of the first grand jurors in Northampton County, and in other respects took an active part in the affairs of the county during its early history.

In 1761, he was one of sixteen subscribers to a farm, which was purchased for the Allenstown congregation in the Forks.

Mrs. James Horner, Sr., was killed by the Indians in 1763. Her maiden name was Jane Kerr, daughter of James Kerr. It is the first recorded Indian murder in the Settlement.

James Horner, Sr., was a Trustee in the Allen Township Presbyterian church.

The Franklin Society was organized in Allen Township, Northampton Co., Pa. It was also mentioned as "The Old Academy Debating Society." It was resolved to establish, promote and encourage a society of the kind, and accordingly, Mr. Henry Epple, James Horner, Sr., and John Moore were appointed a committee to draft a constitution for the government of the same, and the same gentlemen afterwards became its officers.

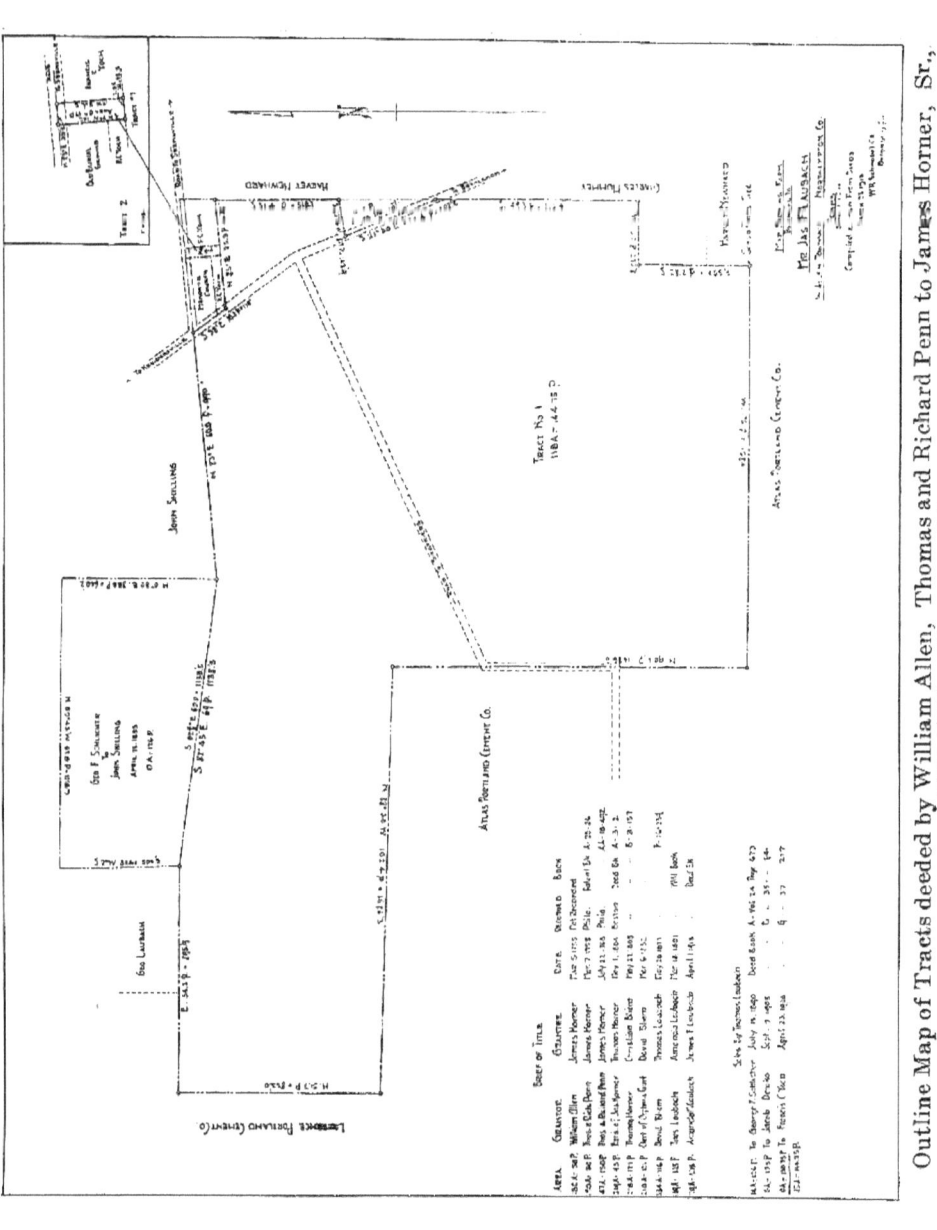

Outline Map of Tracts deeded by William Allen, Thomas and Richard Penn to James Horner, Sr., 1737-1768. (See page 9.)

Brief of Title for James Horner, Sr., Homestead.

The first deed to James Horner, Sr., from Allen, is dated March 5th, 1737.

Area	Grantor	Grantee	Date	Recorded Book
180 a— 50 p	William Allen	James Horner	Mch. 5th, 1755	Not recorded
180 a— 50 p	Thos. and Rich. Penn	James Horner	Mch. 7th, 1755	Phila. Patent Bk. A—20—26
47 a—150 p	Thos. and Rich. Penn	James Horner	July 22nd, 1768	Phila. Patent Bk. AA—10—492
219 a— 45 p	Exrs. of James Horner	Thomas Horner	May 1st, 1804	Easton Deed Bk. A—3—2
218 a—121 p	Thomas Horner	Christian Bliem	May 27th, 1805	Easton Deed Bk B—3—157
218 a—121 p	Clerk Orphans Court	David Bliem	Mch. 6th, 1832	Easton Deed Bk
134 a—116 p	David Bliem	Thomas Laubach	May 20th, 1871	Easton Deed Bk F—16—239
119 a—1.75 p	Thos. Laubach	Amanda Laubach	Mar. 18th, 1891	Easton Will Bk
119 a—1.75 p	Amanda M. Laubach	James F. Laubach	April 1st, 1913	Easton Deed Bk

Sales by Thomas Laubach.

14 a— 126 p	To George F. Schlicher	July 15th, 1890	Deed Book A—Vol. 24, page 673
0 a— 175 p	To Jacob Demko	Sept. 7th, 1905	Deed Book B—Vol. 35, page 84
0 a—130.75 p	To Francis C. Yoch	April 23rd, 1908	Deed Book G—Vol. 37, page 217

15 a—114.25 p

The above property* was the homestead of Mr. Hugh Horner. The first home was a log house, built in 1781. It was surrounded by an Indian stockade, which meant a high board, strongly-built fence, with wrought iron nails, driven in the top.

The present stone dwelling was erected in 1788. It was placed in close position to the log house, but the log house was soon removed, when the present stone addition was completed.

The land upon which this building stands was deeded to Hugh Horner in 1780, from the Supreme Executive Council of the Commonwealth of Penna. Joseph Reed was President of the Council. The purchase price was four thousand eight hundred and twenty-three pounds, fourteen shillings and four pence halfpenny. It was confiscated land, taken from Andrew Allen, the English Tory. Also additional confiscated land (adjoining) was deeded to Hugh Horner by the Supreme Executive Council, when Benj. Franklin was its President in 1786, in the tenth year of our Independence.

Hugh Horner was born Sept. 20th, 1743, and died April 15th, 1806; he married Elizabeth Wilson. He was the son of James Horner, Sr., the Emigrant.

The Presbytery of Philadelphia mentions Mr. Horner as Church Commissioner in 1780, he having presented a written application from the congregation of Allen's Town, requesting supplies from them, and also liberty to apply to some other Presbytery for the same purpose. He was a Church Commissioner in 1794, when the congregation was in a precarious condition. He was also a Trustee of the congregation when it was incorporated in 1797, under the name of the English Presbyterian Congregation in Allen Township in the County of Northampton, State of Pa., and continued after the church became a corporate body, in 1798, as its Treasurer.

On Feb. 24th, 1802, it was agreed that Samuel Sitgreaves should draw up a conveyance, transferring to the Trustees all the rights held by the contributors to the Parsonage Farm.

*Illustration facing page 38.

Thomas McKeen and Hugh Horner were appointed to bring the matter before him. This seems to have been the closing up of this intricate business.

Robert Horner's Family.

Hugh Horner, the father, died in 1806. In 1813 the two contiguous tracts of land were released to his two sons, James H. and Robert, each to receive one-half. Robert acquired the part upon which the* above building stands and lived there the balance of his life. He was born April 23rd, 1781, and died July 7th, 1844. His wife was Jane Wilson, of Tinicum, Bucks Co., Pa.

We find that he was elected a Trustee of the English Presbyterian Church of Allen Township, March 4th, 1815; also, he was made Treasurer in 1826, and was re-elected continuously for 18 years, till his death. He was a member of the Franklin Society of the Irish Settlement. He had much to do with the settlement of estates. He was a Director in the Catasauqua Bank, Catasauqua, Pa.

Hugh R. Horner's (Third) Family.

Robert Horner died July 7th, 1844, and left no will.

Hugh Horner, 2nd, was appointed administrator.

The widow, Jane Wilson Horner, and three children, Ann Horner, Jane Wilson Horner and Hugh R. Horner, 3d, were the beneficiaries. The above property was finally transferred to the son, Hugh R. Horner, 3d.

Hugh R. Horner, 3d, married Jane Elizabeth Hays, daughter of John K. Hays, of Williamsport, Pa. Their children were: Dr. Robert Hays Horner, Mary Jane Horner, John King Horner, and Joseph Allison Horner.

Hugh R. Horner, 3d, was an Elder in the Allentownship Presbyterian Church for 29 years, and a Trustee for 47 years; also a Director in the Lehigh Valley Trust Co., Allentown, Pa.

Joseph Allison Horner's Family.

Hugh R. Horner, 3d, having died in 1901, by his will his three sons were made executors. Dr. Robert Hays Horner,

*Illustration facing page 38.

John King Horner, and Joseph Allison Horner, and later Joseph Allison was made sole executor and the above property was deeded to him. He married Caroline Jane Blair, daughter of John and Emma Dawes Hemphill Blair. Mrs. Horner is a direct descendent of the Kerr family, who came to the Irish Settlement in 1728. Their children are: Ruth Blair Horner and Hugh Horner, 4th.

Mr. Joseph Allison Horner was Manager of the Nazareth Portland Cement Co. for fifteen years. He has been identified with other important cement interests, also personal and private enterprises.

Dr. Robert Hays Horner was a practicing dentist at 1128 Arch St., Philadelphia, Pa., for seven years, and at 1823 Arch St. for nineteen years, when he retired, and returning to Bath, Pa., has devoted his time to private affairs and has been living with his brother, Joseph Allison Horner.

John King Horner went to Philadelphia, Pa., in 1881; was in the wholesale hardware business for four years, as a young man; changed to the grocery business, and for the last twenty odd years has been a member of the Mitchell Fletcher Co., Importers and Grocers, Philada., Pa.

Miss Mary Jane Horner is living with her brother, John King Horner, at 129 Mt. Airy Ave., Mt. Airy, Philada., Pa.

THE JAMES CRAIG HOME.

James Craig was nearly connected by marriage with Chief Justice Allen, and had from him the gift of a farm in the "Settlement". He was a pious man. At his home Brainerd lodged and preached. In his extreme old age, and in a palsied condition, he was borne regularly into the house of God by his sons.

The property and land upon which the* above stone house stands was conveyed by deed from Wm. Allen and wife to James Craig in 1743. The family first lived in a log house when the present building was erected ten years later.

James Craig is regarded as one of the 16 Scotch-Irish

*Illustration facing page 32.

families who settled in the Forks of the Delaware (and now known as the "Irish Settlement") in 1728, and James Craig was mentioned as the leader. Hence it is sometimes called "Craig Settlement".

Brief of Title
to
A tract or parcel of land

Situate in Allen Township in the County of Northampton and State of Pennsylvania containing about 204 acres, the Estate of Lewis Audenried, Esq.

John Penn, Thomas Penn and Richard Penn, Esqrs. true and absolute Proprietors of the Province of Pennsylvania by their Warrant bearing date (at London) the 18th day of May A. D. 1732, authorized and required their Surveyor-general of the said Province to lay out unto the said Thomas Penn five thousand acres of Land in the Province aforesaid.

The said Thomas Penn by an assignment or endorsement on the said Warrant dated the 18th day of May, A. D. 1732, for the consideration therein mentioned did grant and assign unto Joseph Turner of the City of Philadelphia, Merchant, the Warrant aforesaid and the quantity of land therein mentioned, To Hold to him the said Joseph Turner his heirs and assigns forever.

The said Joseph Turner by another assignment endorsed on the said Warrant dated the 10th day of September, A. D. 1735, did grant and assign the same and the quantity of Land therein mentioned unto William Allen of the City of Philadelphia aforesaid.

Deed William Allen and Wife to James Craig in fee for a piece or parcel of land (part of the land surveyed in right of Thomas Penn, Esq. on the 8th day of April, 1734, Containing 250 acres and allowance.

Patent of confirmation Thomas Penn and Richard Penn true and absolute proprietors of the Province of Pennsylvania to James Craig his heirs and assigns forever the said 250 acres of land and the usual allowance of six per cent. for roads, &c bounded and limited as follows to wit: beginning at a corner black oak tree and extending west by John Page's land 290 perches, thence by James Gray's land north 72 perches to a white oak thence by vacant land East 147 perches to another white oak thence north 151 perches to a post thence by other vacant land East 143 perches to a hickory and thence south by land late of Jeremiah Langhorn 137 perches and land of Thomas Craig 86 perches to the place of beginning.

Enrolled the 16th of February, 1753, in Patent Book A Vol. 16 page 329 &c.

Brief of Title.

All that certain messuage or tenement and tract or parcel of land situate in Allen Township, Northampton County and State of Pennsylvania bounded and described as follows, to wit:

Beginning at a corner in center of road leading to Bath; thence along lands now or late of Absalem Reichard, north four and one-half degrees, west forty-eight and-eight-tenths perches to a stone; thence by the same and cemetery lot, north eighty-five degrees, east twenty-nine and five-tenths perches to a corner near the dam; thence along Absalem Reichard's dam, north six and one-half degrees, west eighteen and eight-tenths perches to a walnut tree; thence north twenty-one degrees, east sixteen and one-tenth perches to a post; thence by the same, north eighty-one degrees, east ten and two-tenths perches to a stone; thence by land now or late of William Jones and Harrison Danner four degrees west thirty-seven perches to a post; thence by land now or late of Robert Danner and John Roth, south, eighty-one degrees west, forty-eight and seven-tenths perches to an apple tree, thence by land now or late of John Roth, south eighty-four degrees, west one hundred and four perches to a stone in center of road to Seemsville, the Township line; thence along the centre of said road by land now or late of Sylvester Homer, south four and one-half degrees east one hundred and eighty-eight and seven-tenths perches to a corner, thence by land of and George Knapp, north eighty-six and one-half degrees, east ninety-three perches to a stone near Catasauqua Creek; thence along said creek and lands now or late of J. Kleppinger, north twenty-eight degrees, east thirty-eight perches to a post, thence along land now or late of Kleppinger crossing the creek north forty-two and three-fourths degrees, east thirteen and eight-tenths perches to a corner; thence along said Kleppinger's land, north thirty degrees, east three and two-tenths perches to a corner near tail race; thence north seventy-seven and one-fourth degrees, west twenty-three and seven-tenths perches to a stone; thence north four and one-half degrees, west twenty and eight-tenths perches to a post in center of road to Bath, thence along center of said road, north eighty-four degrees, east nine perches to the place of beginning. Containing one hundred and forty-two acres and six perches, strict measure.

Also that lot of tract of land, situate in East Allen Township, County of Northampton and State of Pennsylvania, bounded and described as follows, to wit:

Beginning at a corner of this tract with lands now or late of Samuel Koehler and Robert Koch, thence along lands now or late of Robert Koch seventy-six and three-eights degrees, east thirteen and one-tenth perches to a stone, thence along lands now or late of Robert Koch aforesaid; north sixty-two and five-eights degrees, east sixty-eight and three-tenths perches to a stone, thence along lands, now, or late of Sylvester Homer, north twenty-five degrees, west twenty and eight-tenths perches to a stone, thence along lands now or late of Dr. H. H. Riegel, south sixty-two and one-half degrees, west seventy-five and five-tenths perches to a stone, thence along lands now or late of Samuel Koehler, south seven and three-fourths degrees, east eighteen and five-tenths perches to the place of beginning.

Containing ten acres and seven perches, more or less.

Among the title papers of the present owners of the

premises we found a Brief of Title extracted from the records and papers produced by John C. Uhle, Conveyancer, of Philadelphia, Pa., and an addendum thereto in the handwriting of R. Clay Hammersly, together with a draft of a tract of land, situate in Allen Township, Northampton County, attached thereto.

The Brief is quite lengthy and appears to have been a careful abstract. We have adopted the Brief as it seems to us to be a complete record.

In checking up this Brief we had before us the following original record papers, referred to therein.

Deed

James Craig
to
Thomas Craig

Dated April 16th, 1774.
Recorded at Easton, Pa., in Book C, Volume 4th, Page 182—

Deed

James Craig
to
William Craig

Dated April 16, 1774.
Recorded as aforesaid in Deed Book C, Volume 4th, Page 184.

Deed

Robert Craig
to
William Craig

Dated February 7th, 1794.
Recorded as aforesaid in Deed Book C, Volume 4, Page 186.

Patent

The Supreme Executive Council
to
William Craig

Dated September 21st, 1786
Enrolled September 26th, 1786.

Deed

William Craig and Wife
to
Henry Epple

Dated April 1st, 1794.
Recorded at Easton as aforesaid in Deed Book B. Volume 2, Page 290.

Agreement

Henry Epple
to
Nicholas Neligh

Dated August 15th, 1803.
Recorded at Easton as aforesaid in Deed Book E, Volume 3, Page 14.

Deed

Owen Rice, the younger and
John Weaver, Administrators
of Nicholas Neligh, deceased,
Mary Neligh and Mary Epple
to
William Horner and Hugh Horner

Dated April 1, 1817. Recorded at Easton as aforesaid in Deed Book C, Volume 4, Page 322.

Deed

Joseph Horner, Committee
to
Hugh Horner

Dated March 31, 1851.

Deed

Sarah E. Horner, widow of Hugh Horner, et. al.,
to
Lewis Audenried

Dated May 11, 1864. Recorded at Easton in Deed Book F, Volume 10, Page 615.

Deed

William G. Audenried, et. al.,
to
Melchior H. Horn, Reuben A. Boyer & John Williams

Dated March 18, 1875. Recorded at Easton in Deed Book G, Volume 14, Page 577.

Deed

M. H. Horn & Wife
to
John Williams and Reuben A. Boyer

Dated June 12, 1875. Recorded at Easton in Deed Book A, Volume 15, Page 558.

Deed

Reuben A. Boyer
to
John Williams

Dated March 2nd, 1876. Recorded at Easton in Deed Book Volume 15, Page 303.

All of these record papers appear to have been carefully and accurately abstracted in the Brief referred to and will be submitted as original title papers in the possession of the present owners.—The Homeopathic State Hospital.

The Old Hirst Homestead (West of Bath)

See illustration, facing page 26.

The land upon which this log structure stands was confiscated by the State through Charles Biddle from Andrew Allen the English Tory in 1778 and sold to John Sterling. After which part of it was conveyed to Joseph Hirst and others—Ex-Governor George Wolf, was the founder of the free school system of Education of Pennsylvania, and had Joseph Hirst as his friend and staunch supporter.

The reader can easily discern in the picture a division line which is near the center of this building. This division line indicates that an addition was built to the main building by hunters and trappers for their own convenience in the early days. Jacob Hirst, a direct descendent of Joseph Hirst, who at this writing is living in Bath, Pa., and who is 94 years old, but hale and hearty with slightly deficient eyesight, can still give one tales of bygone days.

The illustration on page 54 locates the home of Dr. William Wesselhoeft who established here in 1829, the first Homeopathic School of Medicine in America and of which the neighborhood is justly proud.

The Hays' Spring

The above photo locates the famous Hays Spring—known by that name because Captain John Hays had title to the property. Benjamin Franklin going to and fro from Bethlehem to Mauch Chunk, Pa., stopped at this spring at Weaversville, Pa., many times, hence it also is mentioned as the Franklin Spring.

The first permanent settlement in what is now Northampton County, was made in Allen Township on the banks of the Hokendauqua and Catasauqua Creeks by a sturdy band of Scotch Irish in 1728. The centre of this settlement was Weaversville, Pa. Tradition has it that when the first settlers arrived one of them asked for a drink. Whereupon an Indian squaw said:—"give me a gourd and I will fetch you some;" and at that she disappeared and returned with the gourd full of cool, sparkling water. This led to the discovery of a fine spring, the finding of which led them to select the place for their future home.

This wonderful spring is producing the same excellent water today as that of 200 years ago in a Cement Region where good springs are diverted from their course because of blasting.

It is cemented up in concrete form and covered over for its preservation. The water is pumped through a pipe which passes under the stream to the upper floors of the hotel in the rear and also into a large house near-by. The present owner is Mr. David J. Snyder.

Some Worthy Trees Near Bath, Pa.

I have been greatly interested and instructed in the reading of Professor Wilson's articles on "The Romance of Our Trees." Having always been an ardent lover of nature, these excellent descriptions, with the fine illustrations, incited in me renewed affection for tree life. Consequently I take my 125 foot tape and wander over the hills to the General Robert Brown homestead, near Bath, Pennsylvania, where are many of the trees of my childhood. Like the genial poet, Dr. Holmes, I raise my hat in their presence, for here are Locust trees fifteen feet in circumference, Sycamores and Ash of fourteen feet, Sassafras of ten feet, and others nearly as large. But the noblest of all is a Horsechestnut tree that General Washington took from his Mt. Vernon estate and presented to General Brown who planted it here in front of the ancestral home—so tradition has it. Today (July 1, 1920), its base circumference is twenty feet and seven inches, and six feet from the ground its girth is seventeen feet. Its broadest expanse is eighty-five feet, and age approximately one hundred and forty years. It is as handsome in form as it is large in size and venerable in age, and it may be worth the remark that, notwithstanding all the buffeting it has received from storms, its original beauty and symmetry have not been impaired, although it has at times lost a few of its heavy branches.

To see it in full bloom, visited by thousands of bees, as I did on May 27th last, is a beautiful sight, "a pyramid of green supporting a thousand pyramids of white." Each blossom of the dense cluster has at its throat dashes of red and yellow, and the curving stamens are thrust far out of the ruffled border of the corolla. If they were rare flowers they would be admired as Orchids are now. Longfellow has beautifully immortalized another in song. But how would he have written if he could have seen this grand floral sight! These trees are the property of the Bath Portland Cement Company, and the Vice-President, Mr. F. B. Franks, is cautious for their protection. In my ramblings I thought of what some of our great American authors have written of trees. I remember that James Russell Lowell was near to nature's heart, and never lost the thrill of being out of doors. He was admirably a lover of trees, and they were the inspiration of some of his best prose and poetry. This love of trees led him to call his pleasant place of residence in Cambridge, "Elmwood." Better than any biography of Lowell are his letters, wherein are revealed his wide reading, lofty patriotism, keen wit, and gentle humor, and his fearless and unselfish devotion to what he believed to be right. Therefore, I am pleased to give you a copy of the following letter written to me many years ago, when the school children of Bath planted a Horsechestnut tree and named it in honor of the poet.

Elmwood, Cambridge, April 5, 1891.

Dear Sir:

I sympathize warmly with the gracious object for the furtherance of which Arbor Day was instituted. I have planted many trees, and every summer they repay me with an abundant gratitude. There is not a leaf on them but whispers benediction. I often think of the Scottish farmer's words quoted by Scott: "Be aye stickin' in a tree, Jock, 'twill be growin' while ye're sleepin'." In my childhood I put a nut into the earth, from which sprang a Horsechestnut tree, whose trunk has now a girth of eight feet, and sustains a vast dome of verdure, the haunt of birds and bees and of thoughts as cheery as they. In planting a tree we lay the foundation of a structure of which the seasons (without care of ours) shall be the builders, and which shall be a joy to others when we are gone.

I need not say how great a pleasure it is to me that my young friends should decorate my memory with a tree of their planting. I wish I could be with them to throw the first shovelful of earth upon its roots.

Faithfully yours,

(Signed) J. R. Lowell.

To Asa K. McIlhaney
Principal of Schools, Bath, Pa.

It is one of Lowell's last letters. Kipling calls it "delightful" and Van Dyke considers it one of the most charming bits of his correspondence.—Asa K. McIlhaney.

Northampton County Historical Society's Room contains a large photograph of the Washington Horsechestnut tree.

THE OLD IRISH SETTLEMENT STONE HOUSES,

Northampton County, Pennsylvania.

By Mary Leslie Irwin.

CHARLES WILSON (1726-68) and his wife, Margaret McNair, (1728-1823) lived in our old homestead, in the log house which stood in the clothes-yard at the corner of the garden. They probably bought the land directly from the Government (Wm. Penn), as they cleared the land and built the first log house on it.

Grandfather John Wilson (1765-1857) built the stone house now standing and owned (1911) by Henry F. Steckel, in 1815. This date is on one of the stones under the roof. Also the date and initials of John H. Wilson, Uncle John (1811-96), were carved on one of the linden trees in the front yard, visible in 1868 when we (Rev. Leslie Irwin's family) moved away from there, though grown very high above its original position. Grandfather John Wilson and wife lived in this house until they died. At that time my father and mother lived in Weaversville.

Grandmother Wilson died of a second attack of pneumonia (the first one a year previous) January 8, 1851. Her sister, Polly, took cold in going over to see her and died of the same disease January 11, and her son, Uncle William, died January 18th. His death left grandfather alone in the big house (he being then 86 years of age) with only Katie Schaefer to look after him. So Uncle Charles and family left their house to tenants (the first tenant being Dennis Riley, father of old Mr. Wm. Riley at the Blairs) and came to live with grandfather. Aunt Catharine and Uncle Charles were considering the question of educating their children, and after a visit from her uncle, Robert Steele, of Abington, moved to Hillsboro, Ohio, in 1856. My father and mother then moved from their home in Bath to take care of grandfather, until he died (1857).

Mrs. Baxter B. McClure (Sallie Ann Horner) and Jane

Horner (sister) own two farms, the Upper Farm and the Lower Farm. The Upper Farm was the Horner homestead. Its early purchase and ownership are not clearly understood, but from old deeds it seems that it was bought by Joseph Horner (1740-1835) from Margaret DeLancy in 1809, who had it from her father Wm. Allen (or from her brother Andrew Allen). Joseph Horner paid $5500.00 (£1100) for it (See old deed.) The house was built by this Joseph Horner in 1790. He, his wife (Sarah Allison), and their children lived there: James J., Jane J., Hannah, who was 'Squire James Clyde's first wife; John, who married Mary Kerr; Margaret, who died single; Sarah, died single; Samuel, died single; Joseph (Uncle Joseph), who married Margaret Wilson. Samuel Horner, a cousin from Ireland, lived with them until Aunt Jinnie's last illness.

The J's in James's and Jane's names were put there to distinguish them from the many Jameses and Janes in the Horner family. They all (the unmarried ones) ended their lives in this house, Aunt Jinnie the last. She was ill of dropsy, with Katie Schafer to attend her. Finally they brought her down to Uncle Joseph's house (the Lower Farm), eight men carrying her down through the meadow on a bed. She died very soon (Nov. 10th, 1859). After that tenants lived in the Upper House, Charles Haughawaut, etc. It was empty for several years, until Aunt Margaret, Sallie, and Jane gave the use of it to the church as a parsonage.

Dr. James lived in it for 29 years (1869-1898). Aunt Margaret had spent over $400.00 on it to fit it up for him. Then Rev. Dr. Stirling took it about Sept. (1898).

The Lower Farm was probably owned first by William Allen; second, by his son Andrew, or by his daughter Margaret DeLancy; third (in 1812) by George Nagle, who sold it for $20,000 (£4,000) in 1814 to George Levers. He was not an Irish Settlement man. He built the stone house ("new stone messuage", see old deed) and lost money on it, as it was too well built. He sold it to Sallie's grandfather, Joseph

Horner, for $24,000, in 1816. Joseph Horner left it to his sons, James and Joseph. James never married, and so the house came to Sallie and Jane.

Joseph Horner bought it while all were living at the Upper Farm and its first tenants were the Millars, the parents of Aunt Catharine.

After this came Christopher Insley, a brother of Philip Insley. Then Uncle Joseph and Aunt Margaret (Wilson) were married May 28, 1839, and came to the house to live. For one year they and the tenants had the house together, Uncle J. having the parlor, back room, and the two rooms over. It was a disagreeable arrangement. Then Uncle J. built the tenant house up the lane. The Insleys lived in it some years and then the Blairs came in April, 1845. It was thought that the Lower House was built (by Levers) the year that Aunt Sallie Horner died (1811), for Katie Schaefer, who was then living at the Hugh Horner stone house, a little girl eight years of age, tells of having been at the funeral, and as she went home, remembers seeing the workmen building the walls of the house. They all stopped work as the funeral went by. Katie Schaefer was brought up by Hugh Horner's grandfather, and lived in their family a long time.

The Hugh R. Horner stone house was built by his grandfather Hugh Horner, son of James and Jane Kerr Horner (who was killed by the Indians), and his son, Robert, lived in it and his grandson, Hugh R. Horner, until they moved to Bath in 1890.

When John Hays (1730-96) died near Meadville, Pa. (see Clyde's Genealogies, page 77) and all his sons were scattered, his wife, Great-grandmother Jean Walker, was left with her daughters Polly and Rebecca. (Her daughter Ann was Grandmother Wilson.) This grand-aunt Polly Hays is the original of the silhouette which I now have, mounted on black velvet. She lived (1786-1851.) The big house that John Hays, Sr., lived in at Weaversville was purchased from Mrs. Mary Walker King. It is no longer standing. It is replaced by a hotel. But the mill he built in 1790 is still there, and has the date in plain sight. This big house was too large for the three women, so they moved into a smaller stone house near by, which was their property. My father and mother afterwards lived in this house. It was the second one they lived in, and my brother, John Irwin, was born there, 1848. The first house they lived in was on the way over to the "Other Side Church", back off the road. I have a photograph of this second house, just as it was in old times. In the summer of 1904 an addition was built to the back of it and a large porch put on the front. By and by only Aunt Polly Hays was left. So she moved in Aunt Margaret Horner's house (the Lower house), having three rooms there and keeping house independently. Father and mother moved into the small stone house and were her tenants for one year, which must have been 1848, the year of John's birth. When Aunt Polly died, the Joseph Brown's bought the house and lot and father and mother soon bought the house in Bath (in which Belle was born) April 15, 1852, paying $1400.00 for it, a price entirely too large. And they afterwards sold it for half.

Uncle Charles Wilson's house (he lived 1805-86) was built by a German named John Hess, who lost money on the land. He thought there was coal in it. The house was bought by Grandfather Wilson and given to Uncle Charles when he was married (1836). Each son was to have a farm, Uncle John having received one at McEwensville when he was married the first time (1834), and Uncle William (1807-51) was to have the home farm. He was married (1850) to Jane Brittain and died soon after (1851). He had no desire to get well. Three of the family died in ten days.

The Snyder house was built by Hugh Wilson and the Agnew house by Abram Wilson, cousins of Grandfather John Wilson, making three Wilsons in a row, all on the same side of the creek.

The Isaac Insley house was built by 'Squire James **Ralston**, brother of Letitia, son of Samuel Ralston. (Samuel

Ralston was a brother of John Ralston). He sold it to Thomas McKeen, who also bought the Agnew house. He left the Agnew house to his niece, Mrs. Agnew. Isaac and Susan Insley bought their house from Thomas McKeen. Anthony George was living on it as tenant, and was much disappointed that it was not willed to him. Mrs. Agnew had also been a tenant.

The Philip Insley house was built by James H. Horner, (brother of Robert, who lived in the Hugh R. Horner house). James was a 'squire and the cleverest of all the brothers. He married Esther Clendenin and built this house. On his death she married James Vleit. Their daughter Henrietta married Philip Insley. (His first wife had been a Miss Barber.) They first lived in the Ann Snau house at Clyde station as Judge Kennedy's tenants, then Philip Insley bought his stone house. He and his wife and children lived in part, and Isaac and Susan in the other part, the latter farming the farm. Then Isaac and Susan bought the McKeen house and lived there.

Mrs. Nancy Boyd's house was the lowest down in the Settlement, and was built by her father, James Clyde.

Up at the old Gen. Robert Brown place. Gen. Robert Brown (1744-1823) lived in the old house (now torn down) and built the newer one for his son William. After his death William built another house on the John Lerch farm. The place first mentioned was owned by Mrs. Gulielma (Brown) Hyndman until 1904. Sold then to "The Bath Portland. Cement Co."

THE OLD HIRST HOME.
(See page 18.)

THE HAYS SPRING.

Because Benjamin Franklin, in his journeys through these regions frequently stopped here to enjoy a drink of its sparkling waters, it is also known as The Franklin Spring.

THE ASSESSMENT LIST OF ALLEN TOWNSHIP OF 1775

Certificate

The original document in possession of Asa K. McIlhaney.

OF the names and surnames of all the persons dwelling or residing in Allen Township in the County of Northampton together with an account of what tracts of land they possess as also how much of those tracts of land are improved and what parts of the same are sowed with corn, and how many bound servants and negroes with their ages, they possess, as also their stock of horned cattle, horses, mares and sheep.

NAMES	LAND	IMPROVED OR CULTIVATED	SOWN WITH CORN	BOUND SERVANTS	NEGROES	OLD	HORN CATTLE	HORSES	MARES	SHEEP
Allison, James	175	60	15	0	0	0	3	0	1	0
Brown, Samuel	100	40	10	0	0	0	3	2	0	6
Bare, Christopher	100	40	15				4	1	1	10
Bercker, Conrad	100	30	20				2	1		
Bare, Jacob	97	60	18				2	1	2	6
Boyd, Thomas	300	200	30	1	0	0	3	1	2	9
Bawl, Frederick	36	15	10				2	2		
Bartholomew, Henry	300	50	30	0	0	0	20	3	1	5
Beckel, Frederick	1526	546	10							
Bredre, Vandle	100	20	6	0	0	0	2	2	0	3
Beard, Robert	0	0	0	0	0	0	1	0	0	0
Bart, Christian	150	70	18				2		1	1
Berstler, John			30				4	2	2	6
Beil, Baltzer Henry	150	80	15				2	2		1
Brown, Samuel	200	50	20	0	0	0	0	0	0	0
Craig, Thomas	60	20								
Clippinger, Frederick	150	50	19	0	0	0	4	1	1	4
Crissler, Michael	0	0	10				3	1	2	4
Creider, Conrad	100	50	0	0	0	0	2	1	0	0
Ceiper, Michael	200	100	25				3	2	1	5
Colipinger, Henry	150	80	15	0	0	0	3	2	0	6
Craig, Robert	70	40	12				3	1		5

Crazer, Frederick	100	30	15	0	0	0	4	1	1	10
Clyd, James	100	20	10	0	0	0	1	1	0	2
Clyd, John	100	12	10	0	0	0	0	1	0	0
Craig, William	50	25	6	0	0	0	2	1	1	5
Craig, Henry	200	40	24				2	4		7
Creitz, William	100	40	12	0	0	0	4	4	0	6
Cathmann, Rudolph	270	30	24	0	0	0	4	3	0	4
Creidler, Frederick	80	20	10	0	0	0	2	2	0	2
Caster, John	0	0	0	0	0	0	1	1	0	0
Coal, Henry	100	40	20	0	0	0	2	0	2	4
Christian, Egidius	100	70	18				2	1	1	4
Carty's Widow	100	50	20	0	0	0	5	2	1	10
Coack, George	100	40	10	0	0	0	2	2	0	0
Cort, James										
Coack, Geo. and John	50	16	10				2	1	1	1
Clein, Charles										
Cleikinger, Anthony	100	30	10				2			
Doak, James							0	0		
Daniel, William	0	0	0	0	0	0	1	1	0	0
Edelman, George	200	150	20				2	2	1	1
Ellen Emich, Henry	500	30	18				3	1	3	3
Englehart, Michael										
Franck, George	100	6	0	0	0	0	1	0	0	0
Faas, George	125	60	35				3	2	1	6
Frederick, Henry	40	4	2	0	0	0	1	2	0	0
Frederick, John	200	80	15	0	0	0	5	4	0	6
Fassinger, George			36				3	4		5
Galliger, Peter								1		
Gray, Niegel	45	20	6				2	2		3
Hagenbuch, Andr.	150	50	15	0	0	0	2	2	0	0
Hays, John, Jr.	100	50	30				6	6	2	10
Horner, Joseph	0	0	0	1	0	0	1	1	0	
Hertzel, John	100	30	12				2	2		
Hower, Vandle	200	50	20				3	1	1	
Hemphill, James	100	50	10				2	2		
Horner, James	230	104	20	0	0	0	4	1	2	9
Hartman, Franz	200	50	25	0	0	0	3	3		
Hays, Robert	100	50	25	0	0	0	4	1	8	6
Hartzel, George	200	100	30				4	3		6
Horner, Hugh	150	15	8	0	0	0	0	0	8	0
Hantzkey, John	100	20	10	0	0	0	1	2	0	0
Hower, Frederick, Sen.	350	150	30				2	2	2	2
Hander, John	12	3	2	0	0	0	1	0	0	0
Hellman, Christian							1			

Haas, George	100	50	10				2	3	1	3
Hower, Frederick, Jun.	0	0	1				2			
Hartzel Jacob	100	20	10	0	0	0	1	1	0	0
Haslet William			15				1	2		
Hummel, Mathias							1			
Hower, Frederick, Sen.			40				3	2	1	
Kidd, Thomas			30				3	3		
Kerr, James, Sen.	200	120	40	0	0	0	5	2	2	10
Kerr, James, Jun.	0	0	0	0	0	0	2	0	1	0
Knauss, Paul		7	0	0	0	0	2	0	0	0
Lillie, George	100	60	10	0	0	0	2	1	1	2
Lawrence, George	100	30	18				4	3		
Lickins, Thomas	0	0	20	0	0	0	2	2	0	2
Lattimore, John	50	20	15	0	0	0	3	0	2	6
Lattimore, Arthur	180	40	0	1	0	0	3	2	0	6
Lattimore, Robert	100	50	20	2	0	0	5	2	2	10
Lazarus, Martin	200	100	30				3	2	2	6
Levan, Abraham	200	150	18	1			4	2	2	10
Lillie, Andrew	100	50	10	0	0	0	2	0	2	7
Laubach, Conrad	100	50	15				3	1	1	4
Lerch, John	150	60	15	0	0	0	3	1	1	5
Lyon, James										
Laubach, Peter	150	50	15	0	0	0	3	2	1	4
McNair, William	200	100	20	1	1	21	6	1	3	6
McNair, John	150	80	20	1			6	3		
McFadden, William	100	30	10	0	0	0	2	2	1	6
Merrich, William							1	1		
Meyer, Michael	100	30	10	0	0	0	2	2		
May, Andrew								1		
Marsteller, Freder.	200	40	20	1			2	2	1	
Musselman, Jacob	100	50	20	0	0	0	2	2	0	6
McCarty, Benjamin	100	50	25				3	1	1	12
Menich, Peter	50	20	10				1	1		2
Newhart, George							1			
Newhart, George	200	100	10				5	4		7
Neidlinger, Benedict	50	15	6					1		
Ott, Nicholas							1			
Beissel, Peter	300	100	25				5	3	1	5
Bastian, George	200	150	8				2	3		6
Bassinger, Abraham									1	
Pressin, John										
Protzman, Nicholas	100	12	10				2	1	1	3
Queer, George			10				3	3		2
Ritter, Caspar	100	30	20				1	4		3

Rivel, Bartholomew	160	50	30				4	1	1	7
Ralston, James	200	100	20				8	2	1	10
Ralston, Samuel	200	50	20		1	29	6	0	2	8
Reeves, George	50	25	10	0	0	0	1	2		0
Ralston, John	100	25					3	0		6
Ruckle, Baltzer	100	40	25				2	2		6
Rimmel, Nicholas	100	50	18				2	2	1	4
Reaber, Adam	140	80	15				2	2		
Reichart, George	75	25	18				1	2	1	4
Reiswig, Peter	100	40	10				2	1	1	
Rawdebush, George	100	50	18				4	2		6
Snyder, John	130	50	12	0	0	0	3	2	0	0
Shoemaker, Fred.	160	40	8	0	0	0	5	1	2	4
Shnyder, Andrew	100	20	10				3	1	1	
Shelp, Peter	300	80	20	1			5	2	1	8
Shearer, Henry	200	100	25				4	4		5
Sterner, Nicholas	200	60	20				3	3		4
Shnyder, Henry	50	25	5	0	0	0	1	0	0	2
Simms, George	50	20	6	0	0		2	1	1	
Sterling, John	0	0	10	0	0	0	2	1	0	0
Steinauer, Frederick	150	60	20	1			2	2	0	4
Seffrad, Philipp			20				2	3		
Shmith, John	100	50	12				2	1	0	0
Obersheimer, Peter	1	1	0	0	0	0	1	1	0	0
Sickfred, John	200	80	16	0	0	0	4	1	1	0
Sterner, John	100	25	12				2	2	0	2
Stuber, Philipp	100	40	15				2	1	1	4
Showalter, Ulrich	70	20	9	0	0	0	2	2	0	4
Springler, George	50	6	4	0	0	0	1	1	0	0
Swartz, Jacob	100	40	18				2			
Steiner, Henry	5	4	1				1			
Taylor, Geo. Esq.	300	115					3	1		4
Treisbach, Simon	120	90	10				3	2		4
Thrissel, John										
Wilson, Thomas	100	50	20				6	1	1	
Walker, John	200	100	20	0	0		4	2	0	6
Wolf, George	100	20	10				2	1		
Weaver, Jacob	150	60	16				4	4		7
Wert, John	180	80	20				2	2		4
Young, Robert	190	80								
Young, Peter	100	50	20				2	2		3
Gray, George							1	1		
Gross, Peter	120	50	20	0	0	0	1	1	1	2
Schuck, Jacob	100	50								

Crankelton, William __							1			
Class, Peter _____	200	80	30				2	2		
McHenry, Matthew __							1			
Thrissel, Joseph _____	100	40	10	0	0	0	2	2	0	2
Conrad Gies _____							1			

Probably Minors or Single.

William Kerr	Jacob Faas	Andrew Hower
Robert Brown	John Clyd	Peter Shith
Joseph Brown	James Clyd	Abraham Sterner
James Allison	James Hemphill	Jacob Narrengam
Robert Beard	John Newhart	John Mack
John Laird	Hugh Horner	Andreis McCarary
Godlieb Hapler	William Haslit	John Ruckel
John Horner	Robert Young	William Craig
Thomas Horner	Peter Galliger	Bernhard Stroub
Jacob Gilbert	Robert Gregg	John Waterson
Conrad Rieswig	John Thispin	Joseph Kidd
Andrew May	Niegel Hower	John Walker
Felix Faas	John Treisbach	

THE CRAIG DEED.
Copy furnished by Asa K. McIlhaney.

Craig's Farm of two hundred and forty-seven and a half acres of land lay in the Monoquasy valley, and included Chestnut Street and the land north of Northampton Street, Bath. "By virtue of a Warrant of the late proprietors of Pennsylvania, it was granted and conveyed to Daniel Craig, March 7, A. D. 1737, who by a Deed-Poll bearing date February 18, A. D. 1763, conveyed the same to Arthur Lattimore, who, dying, intestate, Mary Lattimore, his widow, Administratrix, and Elizabeth and Jane, their only surviving issue, and John Ralston and Robert Lattimore, Administrators, of the said Arthur Lattimore's estate, did by a Deed-Poll, bearing date April 13, A. D. 1778, convey the said estate to Peter Uppershimer, a tanner." Later the tract was transferred to the Steckels, Meyers, Siegfrieds, and Freys.

THE FRANKLIN DEED.

The land east of the Monoquasy, upon which the greater part of Bath stands, was originally the property of Chief Justice William Allen, who, in 1766, conveyed it to his son, Andrew Allen. The latter, by written Articles of Agreement, on May 1, 1776, covenanted to convey the same to John Lattimore. It comprised 159 acres and 60 perches, and was sold for £4 10s. per acre. Before Lattimore had paid all the purchase money, Benjamin Franklin, then President of the Supreme Executive Council of Pennsylvania, seized and confiscated all of Andrew Allen's land, accusing Allen of High Treason, "for having adhered to and knowingly and willingly aided and assisted the Enemies of this State and of the United States by having joined their Armies, etc." His lands were sold by the State and bought with Continental money. It should be remembered that in the Treaty of Peace at Paris, Sept. 3, 1783, it was agreed that the property of the Tories should be respected. This agreement was not kept, and the Tories were treated so badly that within a few years many of them left the country. The difficulty continued until the

THE JAMES CRAIG HOMESTEAD

Erected 1753. (See page 12.)

title thus acquired was disputed in 1809, by the heirs of Andrew Allen, and the Courts decided against the purchasers under the State, so that they had to pay for their lands a second time. This caused many of the Scotch-Irish to move away.

In 1781, John Lattimor died intestate, and at the Orphans' Court held in Easton, Sept. 20, 1782, the said tract was ordered and decreed to Robert Lattimore, the eldest son of John, for £667 3s. The precise bearings of this tract, taken from the confiscation deed, were as follows:—"Bounded by other land of the said John Lattimore, deceased, and by lands of John Wind, Conrad Best, Joseph Horner, John Sterling, Mary Lattimore and others. Beginning at a dead black-oak sapling, a corner of other land late of the said John Lattimore, deceased, thence South 128 perches and a-half to a white oak, a corner of Joseph Horner's land, thence West 226 perches to the Centre of Monackesy Creek being the corner of Joseph Horner's land, thence by the lines of John Sterling and Mary Lattimore, up the several courses of the said Creek to the smaller and upper Island to the corner of the said Mary Lattimore's land, thence South 84 degrees, East 54 perches to a Spanish oak, thence 20 degrees East 36 perches and seven-tenths of a perch, to a stone a corner of the land lately purchased of Andrew Allen, Esq., by Arthur Lattimore, then East 154 perches to the place of beginning."

In 1791, Robert Lattimore sold the tract to John Vogel, who, in turn, conveyed it to his son Jacob Vogel. The confiscation title is written on sheepskin, in a fine copper-plate handwriting, and is signed by Benjamin Franklin, in his bold hand with its chirographic curves. Attached to this instrument of writing is the Great Seal of 1780, which is two and a half inches in diameter, impressed in wax upon a pair of green ribbons, each of which is fifteen inches in length and hangs suspended from the document, and covered above and below by paper, so as to form a white paper-covered disc. The obverse of this Great Seal constitutes a shield, parted, by a fess of gold, charged with a plow which points to the great subterranean resources of the State,—also with a ship sailing upon a silver field above, symbolizing the vast net-work of commercial relations ramifying throughout the State and sending its branches out into every quarter of the globe,— and the three sheaves of wheat or garbs upon the blue fields below, typifying the splendid harvest which the State affords to the world. The whole is encircled with the words, "Seal of the State of Pennsylvania." The reverse still more eloquently symbolizes the pre-eminence of Pennsylvania in the cause of freedom and independence; for it represents Liberty as a majestic woman bearing in her left hand a wand, surmounted by a liberty cap, and in her right hand a drawn sword,—trampling upon Tyranny, personified by a lion, which lies crushed under her feet, the whole surrounded by the inscription— "Both can't survive"—and nobly has the Commonwealth demonstrated that tyranny cannot live among her liberty-loving citizens.

THE BIDDLE DEED.

The land west of the Monoquasy, and upon which the remaining part of Bath stands, was also confiscated by the State through Charles Biddle, from Andrew Allen, in 1778, and sold to John Sterling; after which it was conveyed to the Ralstons, Bergers, Siegfrieds and Hirsts.

THE RED ROSE DEED.

The land east of Bath was thrown open to settlement on the 8th of December, 1772, when it was purchased by Philip Michael, Conrad Best, and Jacob Dech. It was part of the Barony of Nazareth, originally a 5,000 acre tract of land, the property of Lady Letitia Andrey, of Worminghurst, County of Sussex, England. She was the daughter of William Penn, and was made owner and ruler of the Barony. Her title was confirmed by deed of her half-brothers, under date of Sept. 25 and 26, 1731, "on yielding and paying therefore to the said John Penn, Thomas Penn and Richard Penn, their heirs and assigns, one Red Rose, on the 24th day of June yearly, if the same shall be demanded, in full for all services and rents."

This deed is recorded in Philadelphia, in Book F, Volume 6, page 121. Authentic copies of the deed are in existence, and according to tradition, the rent was formally paid, with due ceremony, by Lady Letitia.

In 1772, Jacob Dech, of Forks Township, Conrad Best, of Williams Township, and Philip Michael purchased of Nathaniel Seidel, of Bethlehem 500 acres from the remote western end of the Barony (which reaches nearly to the borough line), for 13.40 dols. an acre, besides "yielding and paying one Red Rose on the 24th of June yearly," which is specified in the old deeds.

The land south of Bath, or of the original Lattimore farm, was originally the property of Joseph Horner and Hugh Wilson, whose descendants, Mrs. B. B. McClure and Miss Jennie Horner, still own the old homestead, and reside in the "Settlement".

THE ALLEN TRACT.

The aforesaid land titles were, however, parts of the original Allen Tract of 5,000 acres which included the "Settlement" and which, by a joint warrant of the Proprietors in 1732, was deeded to Thomas Penn, who assigned it the same day to one Joseph Turner, of Philadelphia, who transferred it three years later to William Allen, whose eldest daughter, Ann, was the wife of Governor John Penn. Another daughter, Margaret, married James DeLancey, whose home was in Bath, England, and out of respect, both to the Penn and Allen families, the name Bath was taken in honour of her English home city.

Long before the Allens gained their warrant to these lands, they had become occupied by the Scotch-Irish squatters. In 1728—antedating by many years the settlement of Easton, Bethlehem, Nazareth and Allentown—a colony of these blue-blooded Scotch Presbyterians came to this portion of Penn's wide woods, not knowing the map well enough to discover that they had settled on the manors of Chawton and Fermor, and not troubling much about the forms of law by which one comes into clear title until the time of the Allen ownership of these tracts, when conformity was yielded and settlement duly made. Meanwhile possession was worth more than parchment deeds and if the crops at first were poor, the rents certainly were cheap. But the Ulsterman has passed away, and today in this rich and delightful section abound on every side the descendants of our thrifty German forbears, who still speak, in the sixth or eighth generation, the smooth-flowing, musical and quaint Saxon dialect that the first settlers brought, over one hundred and sixty years ago, from the banks of the Rhine and the Weser. It may be said that the "Craig Settlement" is like a Celtic isle in a Saxon sea, about as large as the Galilean lake. It has maintained its distinct architectural, linguistic and religious characteristics for many generations, until, by that law of the survival of the fittest, the Saxon neighbour has, either by marriage or inheritance, or by superior ability in the paying results of agriculture, gotten possession of the once broad and rich acres of these stern and sturdy Scotch-Irish Presbyterians. The fine and proud old homesteads built spaciously of limestone in ante-Revolutionary days, by the wide-awake and epoch-making sons of Scotland, have, during the past generation or two, been filling up with the neighboring scions of Saxon origin. For it was in the Forks of the Delaware and especially on the banks of the Lehigh and Monoquasy that during the first half of the 18th century there was a strange neighbourly commingling in pioneer emergencies of four nationalities, the Indians, the English landholders, the Scotch-Irish, and the Moravian and other Germans. The nomenclature of mountain and stream was given by the Indian (Kittatinny, Lecha, Monoquasy, Hokendauqua, Catasauqua), that of the early townships, hamlets and towns by the English (Northampton, Allen, Easton, Bath, as also Reading, Lancaster and York), while the German Moravians christened their settlements with the beautiful Biblical or religious names they bear today (Bethlehem, Nazareth, Emmaus, Gnadenthal, Friedensthal, Gnadenhuetten, Christian Brunnen).

COPY OF DEED POLL

Commonwealth Of Pennsylvania

To

Hugh Horner

(For A Tract Of Land Situated In Allen Township In County Of Northampton)

Containing 150 Acres

Copy furnished by Dr. Robert Hays Horner.

THE COMMONWEALTH OF PENNSYLVANIA—To all people to whom these presents shall come greeting. WHEREAS in and by an Act of our General Assembly enacted on the fifth day of March in the year of our Lord one thousand seven hundred and seventy-eight entitled "An Act for the attainder of divers Traitors if they render not themselves by a certain day and for vesting their estates in this Commonwealth; and for more effectually discovering the same, and for ascertaining and satisfying the lawful debts and claims thereupon" Andrew Allen (among others) then or late of the City of Philadelphia late a member of the Congress of the Thirteen United Colonies, now States of America, for Pennsylvania, was strictly charged and required to render himself to some or one of the Justices of the Supreme Court, or of the Justices of the Peace of one of the Counties within this State, on or before the twentieth day of April in the year of our Lord one thousand seven hundred and seventy-eight, and also abide his legal trial for High Treason on pain that he the said Andrew Allen not rendering himself as aforesaid, and abiding the trial aforesaid, should from and after the said twentieth day of April one thousand seven hundred and seventy-eight stand and be attained of High Treason to all intents and purposes and should suffer such pains and penalties and undergo all such forfeitures as persons attained of High Treason ought to do, he the said Andrew Allen, having adhered and knowingly and willingly aided and assisted the Enemies of this State, and of the United States, by having joined their armies. AND WHEREAS the said Andrew Allen did not render himself as aforesaid nor abide the trial aforesaid and therefore persuant to the said recited Act of our General Assembly from the said twentieth day of April one thousand seven hundred and seventy-eight stands and is attained of High Treason to all intents and purposes, and all the estate real and Personal of whatsoever nature or kind soever of him the said Andrew Allen within stands and is forfeited to our use AND WHEREAS HUGH HORNER of the county of Northampton in the said Commonwealth yeoman did according to the directions of the said recited act of our General Assembly prefer his claim before the Honourable the Justices of the Supreme Court of this State, setting forth his Title to a certain Tract of Land situate in the Township of Allen in the County aforesaid, containing one hundred and fifty acres of land, formerly the property of the said Andrew Allen and which he had before his attainder as aforesaid by article of Agreement covenanted to convey to the said Hugh Horner in fee simple.

AND WHEREAS the Justices aforesaid did order and decree the said tract of one hundred and fifty acres of land and allowance situate as aforesaid to the said Hugh Horner his heirs and assigns "he the said Hugh Horner his heirs or" assigns paying to his Excellency the President and the Supreme Executive council of the said Commonwealth or to such other person or persons as they shall depute and authorize or have deputed and authorized to receive the same so much of the purchase money both principal and interest as appears by the said claim of the said Hugh Horner to remain still due and unpaid for the tract of land before mentioned" as by the said decree inrolled with the records of the Supreme Court reference thereunto being had more fully and at large appears.

NOW KNOW YE that WE, for and in the consideration of the sum of Two hundred and forty pounds lawful money

THE HUGH HORNER HOMESTEAD.

Erected in 1788. This house took the place of a log house, which had been stockaded as a defence against the Indians. (See page 24.)

of Pennsylvania to our use before the Execution hereof duly paid by the said Hugh Horner (it being the amount of the principal sum and interest ordered by the decree of the Justices of the Supreme court to be paid by the said Hugh Horner) as to our Supreme Executive Councilour Agent hath certified the receipt whereof we do hereby acknowledge and virtue HAVE granted, bargained sold released and confirmed and by force of the said recited act of our General Assembly do grant bargain sell release and confirm unto the said Hugh Horner and to his heirs and assigns the aforesaid tract or parcel of land Bounded by lands now or late of William Allen Esq., of John Clyde and James Doak.

BEGINNING at a heap of stones formerly at a white oak in the same place and in the line of said William Allen land, thence south two degrees West fifty-eight perches and eight-tenths of a perch to a small hickory, thence West four hundred and forty perches to a post, thence North two degrees East fifty-eight perches and eight-tenths of a perch to a white Oak, thence East Four hundred and forty perches to the place of BEGINNING, containing one hundred and fifty acres of land and the usual allowance of six Acres per cent. for roads and Highways. Together, with all and singular the Buildings, improvements, ways woods waters water courses rights members and appurtenances whatsoever unto the above described tract or piece of land belonging and in any wise appertaining, and the Reversions Remainders, Rents Issues and Profits thereof   AND also all the Estate Right Title Interest USE Possession Property Claim and demand whatsoever which the said Andrew Allen at the time of his Attainder of High Treason as aforesaid had or legally could or ought to have had in and to the said Premises and appurtenances.   TO HAVE AND TO HOLD the said tract or parcel of land, Hereditaments and premises hereby granted or mentioned so to be with the Appurtenances unto the said Hugh Horner and to his Heirs and Assigns, to the only proper use benefit and behoof of the said Hugh Horner his heirs and assigns forever, according to the force form and effect of the Acts of our General Assembly in that case made and provided. WITNESS HIS EXCELLENCY BENJAMIN FRANKLIN, Esquire President of our Supreme Executive council, who by virtue of certain powers and authorities in and by the above recited Act of our General Assembly to him for this purpose (inter alia) granted hath hereunto set his hand and caused the seal of the State to be hereunto affixed in the council at Philadelphia this twenty third day of June in the year of our Lord one thousand seven hundred and eighty-six, and in the TENTH year of our INDEPENDENCE.

(Signed) B. Franklin.

Attest:

"Seal of The State of Pennsylvania"
obverse—"Both Can't Survive"

Entered in the office for Recording of Deeds in and for the county of Northampton in Book F. Vol. I Page 112 and the 20th day of March 1787, which is certified under my hand and seal of this office.

(Signed) John Arndt, Recorder.

THE OLD BLOCK HOUSE NEAR FORT RALSTON

Or Place of Refuge

Copy by Dr. Robert Hays Horner.

THERE is no older building in this neighborhood. It was built in 1757 during the French and Indian war, as a house of refuge and defense against the red man. It was constructed entirely of the same character of stone from peak to foundations. It contained large fire-places on two floors. Tradition tells us there was a good spring in the cellar to provide water in case of siege, also there were port-holes in convenient places for the pioneer rifle.

Mr. Chas. A. Porter, who is Manager of the Lawrence Portland Cement Co., at Northampton, Pa., and claims title to the Ralston farm and buildings, has given the writer permission to collect a few relics from this building, which will be placed in the Museum of the Northampton County Historical and Genealogical Society, at Easton, Pa. The property having passed into the hands of cement interests, these buildings will be dismantled to make room for cement improvements, and the general advance of industrial life in the neighborhood.

Mr. John Ralston died Feb. 17th, 1795, in his sixtieth year. He was one of the delegates from Northampton Co., Pa., to frame the Constitution of 1776. He lived on the farm now owned by Chas. A. Porter. Mr. James Ralston, his father, lived on the adjoining farm. He was one of the early settlers of the Craig Settlement, was on the first Grand Jury of Northampton County, and was an Elder in the Settlement church. He died July 26th, 1775, being about seventy-six years of age. Descendants of the Ralstons are to be found at Norristown, in Chester Co., in Pittsburgh, and elsewhere.

Briefs of Title to Ralston Farm.

(Taken from original deeds.)

Thomas Craig and wife, of Allen Township,

To
James Ralston, June 25th, 1753, from the Penns.

Wm. Allen
To
John Ralston, 9th day of December, 1773.

Wm. Lattimore and James Ralston, Executors of the last Will and Testament of John Ralston
To
Robert Ralston and Samuel Ralston, 27th day of December, 1807, originally, John Penn and Richard Penn.

Deed from
Robert Ralston and Samuel Ralston, dated Oct. 31st, 1810, acknowledged same day,
To
Nicholas Kremer, entered Apl. 3rd, 1833.

Deed from
Nicholas Kremer and wife, Oct. 31st, 1810,
To
Geo. Sheffer, Senior.

Deed from
Geo. Sheffer, the elder, and wife, to Geo. Sheffer, the younger, 1825. Dated Oct. 22nd.

Deed from
Robert S. Brown and wife
To
Peter Wykoff, dated May 4th, 1839.

Deed from
Peter Wykoff and wife
To
Geo. Sheffer, Junior, dated Apl. 1st, 1842.

Deed from
Margt. Sheffer, widow of Geo. Sheffer, the younger, Harry A. Gernet and Caroline, his wife, Reuben Boyer and Rebecca, his wife,

THE OLD BLOCKHOUSE, NEAR FORT RALSTON

Erected 1757. (See page 43.)

To
Dated March 22, 1865. William Lawall, of Easton, Pa.

Deed from
Wm. H. Lawall and Mary, his wife,
To
David Shook. Dated Apl. 1st, 1867.

Deed from
David Shook and Mary, his wife,
To
Samuel Achenbach. 138 acres and 64 perches. Dated Apl. 2nd, 1877.

Samuel Achenbach and Catherine Achenbach, his wife, of the Borough of Bath, Northampton Co., Pa.,
And
Chas. A. Porter, of the City of Allentown, Lehigh Co., Pa. Dated 1924, February 15th.

The following are the names of people who rented and lived in the old Block House during the past 56 years.

Jacob Nolf, Edward Rishel, Geo. Fehnel, Geo. Clader, John Smith. At present—vacant and about to be demolished.

OLD BUILDINGS.

Fort Ralston* is the oldest structure in this locality. It was built in 1757, during the French and Indian War, as a house of refuge and defence against the red men. It was strongly built of stone, provided with immense fireplaces on two floors, and had a spring in the cellar, to provide the water, and port-holes for the trusty pioneer's rifle, while about it circled a stockade, from which defence was made. "Frontier Forts of Pennsylvania" recites a horrible tale of the bloodiest butchery that occurred in this place in 1763, when several white victims fell a prey to the savage tomahawks, and when Fort Ralston played an important part in the sad drama. Among those cruelly butchered was the wife of James Horner, whose grave is found in the old Presbyterian

*Illustration facing page 42.

church burial grounds. The inscription on her **tombstone** reads as follows:

In memory of Jane, wife of James Horner,
who suffered death by the hands of the savage Indians,
October eighth, Seventeen Hundred and Sixty-three.
Aged fifty years.

Near by this ancient place of sepulture, containing the tombs of all the worthies of this Ulster-Scot settlement, stood the first church of these devout Presbyterians. It was erected about 1731, and several times replaced by rural structures, so that the present edifice is the third in turn. The church received a charter from the Government of Great Britain, on the 12th of May, 1772. It witnessed, in its earlier days, the preaching of Revs. Gilbert Tennent, James Campbell, and David Brainerd, the celebrated Indian missionary. Rev. John Rosbrough, who was pastor during the Revolutionary War period, accompanied his flock to the front of battle as Chaplain, and fell a victim to Hessian murderers at Trenton, in January, 1777.

[Frontier Forts of Pa., 1895, Vol. I.]

THE INDIAN FORTS OF THE BLUE MOUNTAINS.

By H. M. M. Richards.

The Ralston Fort, or Brown's Fort of Northampton Co.

PROMINENTLY identified with the Indian outbreak of 1763 in Northampton County, just narrated, was the Ralston Fort, as it is frequently called. By this latter name it is given on the Historical Map of Pennsylvania, 1875.

In continuation of Mr. Mickley's map, detailing the neighborhood, especially on the west bank of the Lehigh, and in connection with which it should be consulted, I give herewith a map of the county between the Lehigh and Delaware Rivers, showing principally the details of the "Irish Settlement." I have been fortunate in securing the temporary use of an old map from Rev. D. M. James, which enables me to mark the location of many of the old settlers of the Settlement.

It will be seen that the Ralston Fort is practically in the centre of the Settlement.

It was with great difficulty I succeeded in learning the whereabouts of this defence. My first thought, when glancing at its location and name on the Historical Map,* was that it was merely an incorrect position for the Brown's Fort near Manada Gap, which has been such an enigma to historians. Nevertheless, I fully realized that it was my duty to ascertain the actual facts of the case and not merely to surmise.

Accordingly, in the first place, I entered into correspondence with very many gentlemen living within a radius of from ten to fifteen miles of the supposed locality, most of whom were men thoroughly acquainted with the history of their vicinity, but without avail. I then determined to make a personal tour of investigation, and accordingly drove through the whole country near its supposed site, but met with no more success. In addition to all my efforts, I could find no printed records of any description bearing on the sub-

*Illustration facing page 6.

ject. I had fully concluded that this fort was, beyond peradventure, a myth when, at the very last moment, I received a letter from Mr. A. H. Snyder, of Weaversville, who had been faithfully aiding me in the search, stating that he had finally succeeded in finding some one who could enlighten me, and referring me to Rev. D. M. James, D. D., of Bath, pastor of the Presbyterian Church near his place. Dr. James has most kindly placed his historical knowledge, which is probably not excelled by any one in the Irish Settlement, at my disposal, and enables me to lay most of the following facts relative to the Ralston Fort before the reader.

The first settlers in Northampton County, as now divided, were the Scotch-Irish or Ulster Scots. As early as 1728, John Boyd, who had married Jane Craig, went with Colonel Thomas Craig from Philadelphia and settled at a place on the Catasauqua Creek—known later as the Craig Settlement. (See map). They were followed by others of their countrymen, prominent amongst whom were Hugh Wilson, born in Ireland in 1689, and one of the Commissioners appointed to select the site of Easton, and Samuel Brown. By 1731 a sufficient community had gathered together to form quite a settlement, which came to be known as the "Irish Settlement." Its members were never derelict in duty towards their country. General Robert Brown and General Thomas Craig, of the Continental Army, were both natives of the Settlement. Capt. Hays commanded a company in the service of the Province during the war with the Indians, and we will presently see how greatly it suffered from them at Fort Allen. He also commanded a company in the Revolutionary War, which saw service in the battles of Long Island and Trenton. The homes of these men are shown on the map, as well as that of Governor George Wolf, the seventh Governor of Pennsylvania, who was born on August 12, 1777, and educated in the Academy established by the Presbyterians of his neighborhood in 1791 (1785) also indicated on the map. The present town of Weaversville occupies, practically, the site of these early occurrences. Near it stands the Presbyterian Church of which Dr. James is now pastor, which supersedes two others previously erected, the first having been built in 1746.

In its graveyard lie the remains of General Robert Brown, as well as those of many of the early settlers.

One of its pastors, Rev. John Rosbrough, accompanied his parishioners who enlisted in Capt. Hays' Company at the outbreak of the Revolution, as their Chaplain. The morning after the capture of the Hessians at Trenton, where the company was engaged, Mr. Rosbrough was surprised by the British while in a farm house near the village of Pennington, and cruelly put to death. He lies buried in the graveyard of old Trenton First Church.

Unfortunately, most of the lands occupied by the Scotch-Irish were owned by James Allen, a son of William Allen, the original proprietor, both of whom were loyalists. When, immediately subsequent to the Revolution, the estates of loyalist landowners throughout the Commonwealth were confiscated, many of the settlers, to avoid litigation, abandoned their farms and moved elsewhere. The Irish Settlement is now very generally occupied by Germans, but a few names of the original settlers remaining extant.

The Ralston Fort was located as indicated on the map.

The Brown property adjoins the Ralston farm. Dr. James says the fort was on the land owned by these two men, hence it was called the Ralston Fort by some and Brown's Fort by others. The old map, however, of which mine is partly a copy, seem rather to show that it stood especially on the Ralston property. The farm is now owned by Samuel Achenbach. It is distant about two miles southwest from the present town of Bath, five miles west of north from Bethlehem, four miles east of Catasauqua. It stood between the Lehigh River and the Monocacy Creek, two miles west of the latter. It is about one and a half miles east of the Allen Township Presbyterian Church graveyard near Weaversville, of which recent mention has been made.

To further aid me, Dr. James kindly entered into correspondence with Gen. R. S. Brown, a grandson of General Robert Brown of the Revolution.

I cannot do better than quote his reply in his own language. He says:

"On the Shaffer farm (now Achenbach farm) in the Settlement is or was the Block House you speak of. The first stone house in the settlement was on the Shaffer farm. I don't know whether it is still standing. About fifty yards south of the house on the farm which was my sister's, was the breastwork, and when my father bought that farm I was a boy and helped to haul away the stones behind or at the breast-works. There men awaited the enemy, the women and children were in that house; it was guarded with detachments and the house was pierced with loopholes to fire through. Such is the information I received from my father, transmitted to him by those who participated. I have no doubt of its correctness. I am glad to impart this information to you. After the lapse of a few years even this would have been gone. It is well to treasure up these facts, for in a generation or two all would have been lost."

Dr. James adds that the fort seems to have been stone in foundation seven or eight feet high, with logs on top of the walls extending like an overshot barn all around, so that an Indian could not approach without being seen. Some of its logs are still incorporated in a neighboring building.

It was undoubtedly built by the settlers, but just when is not so certain. Dr. James says it was built in 1763, but with all due deference I cannot help but think he is mistaken. We will remember that the outbreak of hostilities of 1763 was very sudden and unexpected, beginning and ending almost literally in a day's time. Under these circumstances it can hardly be possible that such a substantial defence could have been erected. It is possible, of course, that it may have been built after the danger was over with a view of preparing for future attacks, but this does not seem to be so likely. I think it is more probable that it came into existence during the earlier troubles of the Fall of 1755 when the Settlement lost so many of its people, and when the savage was almost knocking at its doors.

However that may be, it appears to have played an active part in the sad drama of 1763, very much similar to that of Deshler's Fort. At daybreak on Saturday morning, October 8th, of that year, as the savages were stealthily approaching John Stenton's house to massacre its inmates, they met Jane, the wife of James Horner, living nearby, who was on her way to a neighbor's for some coals with which to light her morning fire.

Fearing she would betray them or raise an alarm, they dispatched her with their tomahawks and then proceeded with their bloody work as already narrated. We can readily imagine the women and children fleeing to their house of refuge, when the alarm was given, and the men occupying their stations in the fort. The location of the fort so centrally in the Settlement and at some little distance from the scene of the Stenton massacre, would seem, in itself, to bear out my conjecture as to the time of its erection.

Mrs. Horner's body lies at rest in the graveyard of the Allen Township Presbyterian Church, with that of General Brown. The inscription on her tomb is as follows:

"In memory of Jane, wife of James Horner, who suffered death by the hands of the savage Indians October eighth, Seventeen Hundred and Sixty-three, aged fifty years."

It is to be regretted that we have no further record of the Ralston Fort, and yet, upon consideration, we can readily understand why such is the case. With this one exception, the Settlement was fortunately spared the inroads of the foe, and happily the history of the fort became one of passive protection rather than of active resistance. It did its duty none the less, and none the less deserves to live in the memory of mankind.

I am glad to give two photographic views of the original stone house which stood near the fort, and which was used by the women and children as a place of refuge—one view is south, the other west and north.

In my search for this fort, I had almost reached the point of despair when I learned of an old building at Kreidersville called "Fort Hannes" or "The Old Fort." I immediately drove down there.

Its position corresponded so exactly with that given of Brown's Fort that at first I could not help feeling I had discovered what I was seeking. Upon ascertaining its history, however, I found how much mistaken I had been. Even at the risk of causing a smile, I feel that the story of "The Old Fort" should be here told to prevent future liability to error, which I saw was already beginning to creep in with the lapse of years. Those in the neighborhood of whom I enquired concerning this building, all knew of it. They were unanimous in saying that it was very old, that it most likely was built prior to the Indian war, and whilst they knew nothing of its history, they thought it had probably been used as a fort at that time. It stood on the road to Siegfried's, one-half mile west of Lerch's bridge, across the Hokendauqua, at Kreidersville. They referred me, however, to Mr. Samuel Lerch, at the bridge, for more complete information. I found Mr. Lerch to be an intelligent gentleman, about 70 years old, who was more than usually well read on matters pertaining to the Indian Wars. I immediately made known my errand to him.

Yes! he was well acquainted with the story and location of "Fort Hannes," and then a smile came over his face as he added that he was certain it never played any part in the local history of the Indian troubles. He went on to explain that a couple named "Hannes" or "Hanns" lived in it when he was a boy, who did not bear very good characters and who frequently had rather rough gatherings in the house. On this account the boys, of whom he was one, nicknamed it "The Old Fort". The "boys" have grown up and died off but the name still remains, although the reason for giving it and the time when given have been forgotten. In fact, my extensive inquiry throughout the locality may have originated a belief that "The Old Fort" was indeed an old "Indian Fort". Had it not been for Mr. Lerch I would have been deceived myself, and, as I have previously said, I deem it worthy to here insert my experience as a safeguard for the future.

BATH, PENNSYLVANIA.

The Historic Queen Town in the Monoquasy Valley.

By Asa K. McIlhaney, Bath, Penna.

IN the loveliest of green valleys of Eastern Pennsylvania, like a gem in its setting, nestles Bath, an old-time municipality. It is the centre borough of Northampton County, and is eight miles north of Bethlehem and eleven northwest from Easton, the shire town. It is situated at the headwaters of the winding Monoquasy,—an Indian word meaning "stream with several large bends".

Bath was founded by the Scotch-Irish or Ulster Scots, named for an English city, and is owned and inhabited chiefly by the Pennsylvania Germans. Originally it formed part of the Craig or "Irish Settlement", and the territory was named Allen Township, in honour of Chief Justice William Allen, who became proprietor about 1740. The Craig, Ralston, Lattimore, McCord, McCook, McConnell, Brown, Sterling, Horner, and Wilson families composed the pioneer band of Ulster Scots who first settled in Bath and the immediate vicinity.

The ancestors, driven by religious persecution from their native highlands in the 17th century, the remnants of many a noble clan, sought temporary refuge in the province of Ulster, in Ireland, whence their descendants, between 1720 and 1740, set upon a new career toward a strange land. Bidding the old and feeble farewell forever, they turned their backs upon the past, and with sad hearts, leaving the green fields and flowers behind, went down from their native hills to the sea, to return no more, save in tender memories. After 1727, towards Capes Henlopen and May, that bring the tides of ocean overlapping the shores of Pennsylvania, came these Scotch-Irish emigrants. Landing in Philadelphia, they followed the course of the rivers and small streams, invariably seeking soil which could be easily cleared and which abounded in never-failing springs of pure water. Soon the hills and valleys of Pennsylvania's frontier were peopled with a sturdy, rugged race that was destined to play an important part in the formation of our national character. They were English in speech, Scotch in blood, Irish by adoption, and Presbyterian in faith. American historians are now beginning to render them justice.

As stated before, Bath was once a part of the "Craig Settlement", presumably so named on account of the Craigs, who undoubtedly were the leaders among these immigrants. Later it became known as the "Irish Settlement", a designation it bears to this day. It is a region of unsurpassed beauty, of great fertility, and, besides, so rich in historic associations. It was the first settled portion of the Forks of the Delaware, —the tract of land inclosed by the Lehigh and Delaware Rivers and the Blue Mountains. The Forks was inhabited by the Delaware Indians, who held it tributary to the Iroquois.

History has treated lightly upon the home life of those who settled here at the headwaters of the Monoquasy. Daniel Craig, the Scotch-Irish ancestor of ex-President Roosevelt, appears to have been the pioneer white settler within the limits of what is now the Borough of Bath. At the time of the formation of Northampton County (1752) he was appointed Collector of Excise for this district.

Prominent Personages.

Let us pause for a moment and take a retrospective view of Bath's prominent personages during the past century or more—Governor George Wolf, the founder of the free school system of education in Pennsylvania; Lieutenant-Governor Jacob Kern, and the Hon. Joseph Hirst, friends of Wolf, and additional supporters of the free school system; Rev. Augustus Fox, the linguist and pulpit orator; Rev. Dr. Theo. L. Seip, late President of Muhlenberg College; Dr. Wm. Wesselhoeft, who established here, in 1829, the first Homoeopathic School of Medicine in America; Surveyor-General George Palmer; General Conrad Kreider; Major Wm. G. Scott, Senator, who was instrumental in securing the charter for

Lafayette College; Senators Engelman and De Walt; Lieutenant Steckel; Captain James Ralston, who was also a surveyor, and laid out the village of Bath in 1816; Brittania D. Barnes, merchant; and Daniel Steckel, the Centenarian.

GENEALOGICAL AND BIOGRAPHICAL.

Clyde's Genealogy, 1879, unless otherwise indicated.

Abernethy.

Descendants of Hugh Abernethy and Jane Horner—a descendant of James Horner may be found in Phillipsburg, N. J., and vicinity.

Agnew.

John Agnew—a Trustee of the Settlement Church, 1856, married Mrs. Hannah, a relative of Thomas McKeen, who had a daughter, Mary Ann, married Robert Boyd.

Both Mr. John and Mrs. John Agnew are deceased. Their children were Jane; Elizabeth—married Rev. John F. Pollock; Henry—later a physician of Sherman, Pa.; and William.

Allen.

William Allen, appointed 1755 Chief Justice of the Province of Pennsylvania. He was friendly towards the Presbyterians. His portrait is to be seen in Independence Hall, Philadelphia. His name is perpetuated in the name of Allentown, the county seat of Lehigh, and the Allen Townships of Northampton County. He died in England in 1780.

Andrew, James, William and Ann were children of William. Andrew died in England. James died in Philadelphia in 1777, leaving his estate in Allentown to his children, Mrs. Grenleaf, Mrs. Tilghman and Mrs. Livingstone.

William joined the American army, but put himself under the protection of Lord Howe in 1777, and went to England.

Ann became the wife of John Penn, the Governor.

Allison.

Of the Allisons, Sarah married Joseph Horner; Mary, Joseph Hays; Jennie, William Scott, and Ann, James Wilson, who, however, was not a descendant of Hugh Wilson of the Settlement. The Blairs are descendants on the mother's side of this family.

Andress.

Charles Andress married Jane Hemphill, daughter of Moses Hemphill, and died December 21, 1837, in her fifty-second year. The only son, Charles, who resides at Catasauqua, has children: Constantine, married Gertrude Wirt; one child, Mary Jane, married Tilghman Frederick. Mary Jane; Nettie; Charles, died when 14 years of age; Albert; Cassius; Agnes, and Ida.

Jacob Andress married Mary Hemphill, a descendant of Moses Hemphill. They had one child, which died young. Mrs. Hemphill died August 22, 1853, in her seventy-fifth year.

Appleman.

Matthias Appleman married Margaret Jane Barber, a descendant of Michael Clyde through William Barber. Their children were Mary Esther, William, Philip, Clyde, George, Phineas, and an infant.

Armstrong.

Thomas Armstrong, a Coroner, and Elder of the Presbyterian Church, 1752, had a daughter, Margaret, who is supposed to have married Rev. Robert Russel.

Arnold.

Juliet Palmer, a descendant of George Palmer, was married to a Mr. Arnold.

Baldwin.

Margaret Rosbrugh, a descendant of Rev. John Rosbrugh, was married to a Mr. Baldwin. Their children were Jennie and Margaret.

Barber.

William Barber, born May 9, 1795, died September 28, 1874, lived and died at Jerseytown, Columbia County, Pa. He married Margaret Clyde, a descendant of Michael Clyde, who was born November 26, 1793, and died August 9, 1850, in her fifty-seventh year.

Their children were Wm. Finley, Elizabeth Ann, Mary, Sarah Savilla, Nancy Jane (twins), Margaret Jane.

Wm. Finley, born May 11—died July 26, 1829.

Elizabeth Ann, married Amos S. Bisel.

Mary, married Martin Girton.

Sarah Savilla, married Hiram Masteller.

Nancy Jane, born July 2, 1826, died March 18, 1831.

Margaret Jane, married Matthias Appleman, if report is correct.

Barrick.

Jane Lewis, a descendant of John Hays, through John Grier, married a Mr. Barrick. It is reported they had a family.

Barnes.

B. D. Barnes was elected a Trustee of the Settlement Church in 1834.

Lydia H., one of his children, died October 12, 1835, aged 11 months.

The family is not supposed to have been descended from the original Irish Settlement people.

Barr.

Thomas Barr, a Trustee of the Settlement Church, elected in 1844, was a friend of education, a member of the Pennsylvania Legislature and other public positions. He is reported to have died in Turbotville, Pa., in 1874 or '75.

Barrett.

Rev. John Barrett, Pastor of Pisgah Presbyterian Church, London Station, Ross County, O., married Anna Wilson, a descendent of Hugh Wilson.

Bartholomew.

Peter Bartholomew, who died July 24, 1867, is not, so far as known, a descendant of the Settlement families.

Baugh.

Louisa Ralston, a descendant of James Ralston, was married to Edwin Baugh. Their children are Fannie, Emily and Chauncey.

Berry.

Anna Ralston, a descendant of James Ralston, was married to Charles Berry.

Bisel.

Amos S. Bisel married May 31, 1843, Elizabeth Ann Barber, a descendant of James Clyde, through William Barber. Their children were Margaret, married J. J. Everett; Judith Emma, married —— Levers; William Felix, Susan Clyde, Daniel L., George S.

Bitner.

Matilda English, a descendant of Moses Hemphill through John English, married —— Bitner.

Blackmar.

A Rosbrugh descendant of Rev. John Rosbrugh married Clinton Blackmar, a resident of Cambridge, Michigan.

Blair.

James Blair, resident in the Settlement, married Martha Wilson, not connected with the Hugh Wilson family, but a descendant and connection of the Allison and Wilson families. Their children were John, married Emma Hemphill; Margaret; Robert, married a Miss Odenwelder; Joseph Horner, died April 6, 1865; Keziah; Mary; William, and Martha.

Bond.

A Miss Housel, a descendant of Robert Lattimer through Philip Housel, married 'Squire Bond, a resident of Milton, Pa.

Boyd.

John Boyd, born near Edinburg, 1690, removed from Antrim, Ireland, to America, in 1714, married Jane Craig, sister of Thomas Craig. With Thomas Craig and other families, John and Mrs. Boyd moved from Philadelphia to what became the Irish Settlement. John and Jane Boyd died about

1750. Their children were John, born 1716, died 1758; married Elizabeth Young, only daughter of Sir William Young; Elizabeth, born 1719, died 1803; children: Adam, John, William Young, James and Margaret.

Adam was born in 1746, died May 14, 1814 in his 68th year, and is buried at Harrisburg, Pa. He served three campaigns in the Revolutionary War; was in the battles of Brandywine and Germantown, went through the privations of the memorable winter at Valley Forge; was an officer and left the army chief of transportation. After the Revolution, he settled in Lancaster (Dauphin) County, Pa. In 1783, he went to Harrisburg; erected a house near the corner of Mulberry Street and River Alley; settled permanently as a farmer at Harrisburg, in 1784. In 1791 he was one of the burgesses of Harrisburg; was first President of the Town Council; was 14 years Treasurer of what is now Dauphin and Lebanon Counties; was one of the three original elders chosen in the Presbyterian Church of Harrisburg in 1794.

He married Jeanette MacFarlane of Big Spring, Cumberland County, Pa., in 1784. She was born June 23, 1764, and died December 4, 1790, at Harrisburg where she is buried.

Their children were Rosanna, Elizabeth Young, and John. Rosanna married Hugh Hamilton. See. The other two children died without descendants.

John remained single; fought at the battle of Brandywine and was killed at the battle of Germantown.

William Young fought at the battles of Brandywine and Germantown. He was born in 1749 and died in 1807 in his 58th year. He married Miss Davidson of Cumberland County, Pa. Their children were Adam, John, William Young, James, and Elizabeth. James died, leaving one daughter. William Young is living; is single, and is the last male branch of the name.

James, son of Elizabeth, was born, we believe, in 1751, and died single (1814) in his 63d year.

Margaret his sister, married Robert Sharp.—See

Jane, daughter of John and Jane, married Samuel Brown.

—See Of her sister Mary nothing definite is known.

Dr. John Boyd was no connection of the former John Boyd. He died April 5, 1837. See. He married as his first wife, Elizabeth Brown, widow of John Brown, a descendant of Samuel Brown.—See. She died Aug. 5th, 1820.

They had one son, now deceased, named William, whose family live at Washington, N. J. Dr. Boyd married as his second wife, Nancy Clyde, a descendant of Michael Clyde. They had no children. She lived to the end of her days in the Settlement upon a portion of the original Clyde estate. The following obituary notice of her appeared in the Philadelphia "Presbyterian", March 3, 1877.

"Boyd.—January 12th, at her residence in the Irish Settlement, near Bath, Pa., Mrs. Nancy Boyd peacefully fell asleep, at the advanced age of ninety-one. Though for years an invalid and sight impaired she now with undimmed vision can behold the glories of our mansions above, and again mingle with the loved ones who have preceded her. For years she was a member of the Presbyterian Church, having been born and educated in that faith. Her departure is not only mourned by the church with which she was so long connected, but by the entire community in which she lived."

Robert Boyd married Mary Ann Hannah, daughter of Mrs. John Agnew by her first husband. She is deceased, leaving a daughter who resides with Mrs. Rev. J. F. Pollock at Oxford, Warren County, N. J.

James Boyd, deceased, probably a son of John Boyd, married Elizabeth Lattimer, a descendant of Robert Lattimer. Their children were Flavel and Hervey.

Brown.

Samuel was born in 1714, died June 11, 1798, in his eighty-fourth year.

He married Jane Boyd, (?) born 1720, died March 25, 1812, in her ninety-second year. Their children were John, born 1760, died June 2, 1798, in his thirty-eighth year. Married Elizabeth Doke. Their children were Samuel, Letitia, and Mary; Samuel died recently, at Ithaca, N. Y. Letitia married James Horner, a descendant of James Horner. Mary married Joseph Price. Elizabeth, widow of John Brown, married, as supposed, Dr. John Boyd.

Robert was born 1744, (1745), died February 26, 1823, (1829), in his seventy-ninth year. He married Catharine Snyder who died in her ninety-second year.

William died in Bethlehem, 1866, in his seventy-third year. He graduated at Dickinson College. He was a member of the Constitutional Convention of Penna., 1833. He married as his first wife Susan Shimer, who died March 18, 1834, in her fortieth year. Their children were Robert S., known as General Brown, who lived near Bethlehem, served as State Senator, married Caroline Grim and had children—Oliver, Flora, Mary and Alfred, the late Dr. Alfred Brown, of Hellertown; (married Amanda Pearson); Eliza, who married Peter Wyckoff; William's second wife was Susan Ingles. They had one daughter, Gulielma, married Ed. K. Hyndman. Children, Robert and Roy.

Of William and James nothing definite is known.

Esther, married Joseph Craig.

Sarah, married James Hays, a descendant of John Hays.

————, daughter married Thomas Herron.

Joseph Brown, residing at Weaversville, Pa., married Matilda Kerr, a descendant of James Kerr. Their children were Elizabeth Kerr, Ann Fearon, and Samuel. The first two died single; Samuel married Miss Martin.

Samuel H. Brown resided at Frederick, Md., and married Sarah Jane Horner, a descendant of James Horner.

Joseph Brown, who resided at Milton, Pa., married Mary Lattimer, a descendant of Robert Lattimer.

Samuel Brown, deceased, brother to Joseph of Weaversville, Pa., married Sarah Agnes Grier, a descendant of John Hays, through John Grier.

———— Buckalew, residing at Dixon, Lee County, Ill., married Eliza Kerr, a descendant of James Kerr.

—— Buckman, married a daughter of John Horner, a descendant of James Horner.

William Burnet was a collector of salary and a Trustee of the Settlement church, 1827-1828, when he removed beyond the bounds of the Settlement.

James Cameron resided at Beaver, Pa., married, as supposed, Josephine Cunningham, a descendant of Moses Hemphill, through Hon. Thomas Cunningham.

—— Carpenter resided at Danville, N. Y., married Margaret Baldwin, a descendant of Rev. John Rosbrugh.

W. G. Case, resided at Columbia, Pa., married Sarah Scott, a descendant of Robert Lattimer through Wm. G. Scott. Their children were Howard, died single; Brainerd, married Sallie McCorkle, attorney and colonel.

David Chambers, was identified with the Settlement at an early period of its history, and was a contributor of the purchase of the Parsonage Farm.

John Church, resided at Catasauqua, Pa., married Lucinda Lytle, widow of John Lytle, a daughter of Frederick W. Nagle and a descendant of Moses Hemphill. Their children were Joseph, Emma, George, Charles, and Mary who died in 1851. The others are single.

Robert Clark, a native of Ohio, married Elizabeth Coates Clyde, a descendant of Michael Clyde. Their children were Jessie May; Frances Elizabeth, died August 11, 1874, and is buried at Dexter, Iowa.

Dr. Clark resided at Belvidere, N. J., married Jane Kennedy, a descendant of Michael Clyde through James Kennedy.

Rev. John Clark, was the third pastor of the Settlement Church. See biography of pastors in the Irish Settlement.

Adam Clendinen, died June 17, 1817, in his seventy-ninth year. He married Esther Hall of Philadelphia. She died May 11, 1816 in her sixty-second year. Their children were Jane, married Andrew Heaslet; John, died July 7, 1778; James, died March 17, 1850, in his sixty-eighth year; Margaret, died June 30, 1827, in her forty-fourth year; William, died March 5, 1827, in his thirty-ninth year; Nancy, died January 16, 1815, in her thirty-seventh year; Esther, twin sister of Robert, married as her first husband James H. Horner, a descendant of James Horner. Her second husband was James Vleit, we believe, of Bath, Pa.; Adam, died October 15, 1839, in his forty-eighth year; Robert died October 3, 1853, in his fifty-ninth year; Thomas resided in the Settlement.

Jane Clendinen died June 6, 1775. It is not known whether this was a second Jane of Adam Clendinen's or some other family.

Clyde.

CLYDE GENEALOGY

By DR. JOHN C. CLYDE.

DANIEL Clyde, the emigrant-ancestor of Windham Clydes, tradition says, was born at Clydesdale, near the beautiful river Clyde, in Scotland, in 1683. He emigrated from Londonderry, Ireland, and settled in Londonderry, N. H., in the past, which is now Windham, on the farm at present owned by O. A. Simpson.

The time of his emigration is uncertain, but tradition and circumstances seem to fix the date about 1732, or a little previous. He had a younger brother, named Michael, who subsequently followed him to America and settled in Pennsylvania, though his intention was to join Daniel at Londonderry, but landing further South, and facilities for traveling being poor and the distance considerable, he relinquished the plan and settled in one of the Scotch Settlements of Pennsylvania. Communication was kept up between the families for a time.

My investigations have shown that Michael settled in East Allen, Penna. He was born in 1710 and died May 17, 1794, in his 84th year. His wife was Bridget, who died December 15, 1786, in her 66th year. Their children were: Ann and Mary, who married and died before November 15, 1785;

John, who died in 1826, in his 81st year; James, who died in 1827; Margaret, Lettie and Elizabeth.

The children of John, son of Michael, were:—Sarah, Margaret, Mary, Elizabeth and James. The last James died in 1866, in his 84th year. He married Hannah Horner. Their son, Joseph, born April 4, 1806; is still living in Washington, Washington County, Ia. His son, John C. Clyde, preacher and author, resides in Bloomsbury, N. J.

It will be noticed here that Michael Clyde had two sons, John and James. This James, of the second generation, had three daughters and one son, John. This John died single, November 28, 1815, and so the male branch of the name in this line became extinct.

The only son of John, of the second generation, James, was the writer's grandfather, the late James Clyde, more familiarly known as 'Squire Clyde, who died, as stated, in 1866, on the old Clyde estate along the Monoquacy Creek, about a mile below Bath. The railroad station on the Lehigh and Lackawanna, called Clyde, is on these old estates.

'Squire James Clyde, after his first marriage to Hannah Horner, went to Washington County, Penna., west of Pittsburgh, previous to about 1804. Here a daughter was born, who died when but seventeen days old, December 12, 1804.

On April 4, 1806, a son, Joseph, was born. This is the Joseph Clyde mentioned by Morrison. His mother died shortly after his birth and is buried in Cross Creek Township, Washington County, Penna. The infant was carried by his father on horseback all the way from Washington County to the Craig Settlement in Northampton County, where he was reared by his mother's brothers and sisters, on the old Joseph Horner homestead, adjoining the village of Bath on the South.

After the return with the infant son in 1806 or 1807, it seems 'Squire Clyde remained in the Craig Settlement till 1810, when he went to Columbia, in Lancaster County, where he lived till about 1833. At this time he returned to the Craig's Settlement and lived there till about 1840, when he

The Famous Washington Horse Chestnut Tree, on the General Robert Brown
(See page 19.)

THE JOSEPH HORNER HOMESTEAD.
Built 1790. "Irish Settlement," Bath, Pa. (See page 23.)

again went to Columbia. Here in 1841, he married Susan Downing, and the same year returned to the Settlement, where he remained till the time of his death, in 1866.

'Squire Clyde was the life-long friend of President James Buchanan. In their early life one was a young 'Squire and the other was a young lawyer at Columbia, Lancaster County, Pa. The young lawyer was the young 'Squire's counsel. As the young lawyer's eyesight was slightly defective, the young 'Squire was accustomed to pilot him around when they went out together to attend social functions, and upon other occasions. The 'Squire paid a final visit to the lawyer when the latter occupied the White House at Washington as President of the United States in the winter of 1859-60. It is said the meeting was mutually joyous. The 'Squire was a strong pro-Slavery Democrat to the day of his death.

'Squire James Clyde, as we have seen, had but one child, who survived infancy, a son Joseph. His mother's people, who reared him, as we have seen, followed the custom of the day in seeing to it that he had the opportunity to secure some useful trade or occupation. Accordingly the young man served an apprenticeship in the tanning and the curing business with the late Anthony McCoy, whose tombstone may be seen in the Easton Cemetery, when he carried on business at Martin's Creek. At the same time and place the late George Keyser, who lived at Old Oxford, N. J., and who recently died at Belvidere, was learning his trade.

The latter has spoken to the writer upon more than one occasion of their experiences as young men together. The writer has repeatedly heard his father speak of experiences when he traveled the "River Road," between Easton and Martin's Creek.

Joseph Clyde married Ann Jamieson in 1832 at Blairsville, Penna. Her grandfather, Archibald Jamieson, raised in Glasgow, emigrated from Paisley, Scotland to America. The young couple, after marriage, went to Crawford County, Ohio, and from there, about 1836-37, came to White Deer Valley, Lycoming County, Pa.

In 1857, they removed to Logan County, Ohio, settling near Belle Centre. In 1867, they removed to Washington County, Iowa. Joseph Clyde died, June 23, 1879, and his wife at Belle Centre, December 23, 1880. They are both buried at Washington, Washington County, Iowa.

Their children were: Margaret, died September 8, 1837, aged three months and eleven days; James, died September 30, 1838, aged one month and two days. These children are buried at the Washington Church burying ground in White Deer Valley.

Henrietta married Samuel Johnston, died at Minneapolis, Minn., leaving a family.

Hannah Mary, married Hamilton Johnston, died at Cottonwood Falls, Kansas, leaving a family.

William Jamieson married Jane McClure in Logan County, Ohio. He served in the 98th Ohio Volunteer Infantry during the Civil War, was with Sherman in his "March to the Sea," was mustered out at the final review at Washington, D. C., at the close of the war; was killed by an accident at Washington, Iowa, November 13, 1873. He had one child, a daughter, Lola Winifred, who died as the wife of U. S. G. Cherry, Esq., leaving a family at Sioux Falls, South Dakota.

John C., the writer, vid. Biography of distinguished men.

James (2d) who enlisted with the writer in the 72d Reg. Ill. Inft. at Chicago, Ill., in August 1862, was taken sick at Columbus, Ky., remaining in the hospitals some four months; subsequently served under two enlistments, and was mustered out at the final review at Washington, D. C., at the close of the war.

Elizabeth Coates, married Robert Clark in Logan County, Ohio; resided with the family at El Dorado, Kansas.

Sarah Ann, married James Lambert in Logan County, Ohio, resides in Oklahoma.

Joseph married and resides with his family near Kansas City, Kan.

Samuel, born at McEwensville, died in infancy and was buried at Warrior Run graveyard, Northumberland County, Pa.

Robert married and lives with his family at Washington, Washington County, Iowa.

As the Daniel Clyde branch of the family incidentally impinges upon the subject-matter in hand, we may be permitted to make a few brief references to it.

Morrison says: "There was a company of minute-men in Windham of which Joseph Clyde was the Captain." In connection with the "Lexington Alarm," he says.—"Captain Joseph Clyde, who commanded the company of minute-men in town, was plowing in his field when tidings reached him. He left his plowshare in the mould and started immediately to head his company, each man having been notified. The women—wives, mothers and sisters of the soldiers went to work and immediately cooked a large amount of food and sent it to the front for the men."

One of Captain Clyde's brothers loaded his horse quite heavily with provisions which his mother had cooked, and followed after the company. It is not improbable that they joined the New Hampshire Militia near Boston as Captain Clyde's payroll to Cambridge, for the services of his men was £35, 8s.

Previous to this time, this son of Daniel Clyde had been "Commissioned Lieutenant of the Company, Eighth Reg't., May 3, 1770."

Subsequently to this time he was commissioned captain of a company of minute-men, with rank as colonel, February 16, 1787, and was known afterwards as "Col. Joseph Clyde."

Col. Samuel Clyde was also a son of Daniel, of him Morrison says: "He was one of the most renowned military men which Windham has given to the Country." He went to Cape Breton and engaged in the trade of ship-building; then removed to Halifax and helped construct a dock for the British navy. In 1757, he returned to Windham. He was twenty-five years of age, full of ambition and military zeal. War was raging. The great contest for supremacy in the Western world was going on between England and France, young Clyde proceeded at once to join a company of rangers and bateaux men, and was commissioned in the field as captain by General Abercrombie, May 25, 1758. He with his own company joined the army under General Abercrombie, and was in the disasterous attack on Ticonderoga July 5. The storm of the disaster was almost as sad as the repulse of General Braddock. He was present at the capture of Fort Frontenac, and afterwards passed up the lakes as far as Detroit.

He married at Schenectady, N. Y., Catharine Wasson, a niece of Dr. Matthew Thornton, the surgeon of his regiment and afterwards signer of the Declaration of Independence. She was a woman of marked character, patriotic, resolute, energetic, and had a fine education and well fitted to be the wife of a gallant soldier.

In 1762, he removed to Cherry Valley, N. Y., where he lived till his death. In 1762, he purchased a farm, ever since known as the Clyde farm, and owned (1882) by his great-grandson—Dr. James D. Clyde.

When the news of Bunker Hill reached Cherry Valley, a company was formed, July 13, 1775, with Samuel Clyde, Captain and John Campbell as lieutenant. In 1775, he was commissioned Captain by the Congress of New York. He was appointed adjutant of the regiment of which Nicholas Herkimer was Colonel. Later he became Major of a regiment which stood the brunt of the terrible battle of Oriskany, August 1777. He was struck with a clubbed musket and knocked down, but he wrested it from his assailant, and is now in possession of Dr. James D. Clyde.

At the massacre of Cherry Valley, Nov. 11, 1778, Major Clyde was surrounded by Tories and Indians. Mrs. Clyde with her eight children, on seeing the approach of the enemy, fled into the thickest of the forest, and remained there exposed to the elements until rescued and brought to the fort.

Major Clyde was commissioned Lt. Colonel and Colonel 1778-1781. He was a member of the Committee of Safety from the beginning to the close of the war. A member of the legislature, 1777; sheriff, 1785, and discharged his duties with marked ability. He closed his memorable and eventful life at the "Clyde Farm" November 30, 1790. His wife survived him many years.

Anna, a daughter of Col. Samuel Clyde, married John Thornton.

George, a son, the father of George Clinton Clyde, was born in Cherry Valley, April 25, 1802; admitted to the bar 1824, a successful practitioner, married 1829, Catharine Dorr of Chatham, Columbia County. He was a patriotic citizen, a wise counselor, a firm friend, and died December 21, 1868 and laid to rest with his fathers in Cherry Valley, where Dr. J. D. Clyde is still proprietor of the "Clyde farm."

Joseph Clyde, a grandson of Col. Samuel Clyde, through Joseph, was a member of the Constitutional Convention of 1821 in New York.

John Clyde, a grandson of the original Daniel, through Joseph Clyde, was a soldier of the Revolution.

Milton A. Clyde, a great-grandson of the original Daniel, was as Morrison says, "a self-made man, worked his way to success by unremitting energy and pluck. He was employed in laying stone along the line of the Western Railroad in Massachusetts, formed a partnership with his employer, took numerous contracts for stone-work and grading for different railroads, and later as working manager with the firm Dillon, Clyde and Co., on the Union Pacific, Lake Shore and the Central Railroad of N. J. His greatest work was the tunnelling and building of the famous underground railroad in New York City for the New York & New Haven railroad from the Grand Central depot to the northern end of Manhattan Island. While superintending this work he took a severe cold which prostrated him with congestion of the spine which terminated fatally."

John Cochron married Sarah Lattimer, a descendant of Robert Lattimer.

Orlo R. Coe, of California, married Nancy Moorhead, a descendant of Moses Hemphill.

Charles Corss, married Sarah Kennedy, a descendant of Michael Clyde through James Kennedy.

Craigs.

The Craig family (cf. Lehigh County History) are descended from William Craig, of Stirlingshire, Scotland, who, to escape the persecution of the Presbyterians by James I. settled at Dungannon, Ireland. Four of his sons and several of his daughters emigrated to America. The sons were Thomas, Daniel, James, and William. Sarah Craig, one of the daughters, born 1706, married Richard Walker, Esq., of Bucks County. She died April 24, 1784. Margaret married John Gray, died 1782, leaving two sons, John and James; and two daughters.

Jane Craig, another daughter, married John Boyd, of Allen Township, and had two sons, Robert and Thomas.

Daniel Craig and wife, Margaret, settled in Warrington Township, Bucks County, had eight children—Thomas, John, William, Margaret—married James Barclay; Sarah, wife of John Barnhill; Jane, wife of Samuel Barnhill; Mary Lewis, and Rebecca, wife of Hugh Stephenson.

Thomas, the son, took a prominent part in the Revolution, was commissioned a captain Oct. 23, 1776, and commanded a company in Col. Baxter's "Flying Camp" in the battle of Fort Washington. He served through the war and at its close was Commissioner of Purchases with the rank of Colonel. He married Jean Jamieson.

James Craig, brother of Daniel, settled in what is now Allen Township, where he purchased 250 acres from William Allen, June 13, 1743, and deeded the land for the church and graveyard to the Presbyterian congregation. He lived to an advanced age, and although palsied, was always carried to church on Sundays by his sons. His wife died previous to April 16, 1774. He had sons. William, Thomas, Robert.

William married Elizabeth Brown, sister of General Robert Brown, removed to Northumberland.

Robert married Esther Brown, leaving sons, James, Samuel, William, John, Robert and Joseph.

Thomas Craig, Esq., the founder of the Irish Settlement, after conveying 212 acres to his brother Daniel in Bucks County, he removed, 1728, to Allen Township, where he was the leading citizen for many years. In 1731 his name appears as the first elder of the Presbyterian congregation of Allen Township on the roll of the Synod of Philadelphia. He lived on a tract of 500 acres purchased from Caspar Wistar, by deed of March 28, 1739, and died in 1779 at an advanced age. His wife Mary died July 14, 1772, aged 75 years. He had sons: William and Thomas. William was the first Sheriff of Northampton County, in 1752, and had children, Thomas, Hugh, Charles, William, Mary, Sarah, Margaret and Elizabeth.

General Thomas Craig son of Thomas, was born October 26, 1739. He was engaged in farming and at the outbreak of the Revolution entered the army and rendered valuable service in the struggle for independence. He was commissioned Jan. 5, 1776, captain of a company in Col. St. Clair's battalion which saw strenuous service in the Canadian campaign. On September 7, 1776, he was promoted to Lt. Col. and on Aug. 1, 1777, to Colonel of the Third Pennsylvania Regiment. He participated in the battles of Germantown, Monmouth and Brandywine, and to use his own words, "served faithfully from the commencement of the late war to the end of it." It is said he was the first officer to protect the Continental Congress, and the first to march to Canada. He retired Jan. 1, 1783. In 1784 he was appointed Associate Judge of Montgomery County, which position he filled until 1789, when he removed to Towamensing Township, Carbon County. In 1798 he was commissioned Major-General of the Militia of the State, which position he held until 1814. Col. Craig was at Valley Forge in the winter of 1777-78 and it was through him that Mrs. Lydia Darrach conveyed to Washington the warning of Howe's expected attack at Whitemarsh, she having overheard plans discussed by the British officers at her home.

During the last years of his life he resided with a daughter, Mrs. Kramer, at Allentown, where he died, Jan. 13, 1832, aged 92 years, and was buried with military and Masonic honors. The procession marched to the cemetery to the funeral strains of the Bethlehem Band, the tolling of bells, and the firing of minute guns. After the ceremonies were over, the friends retired to the Lutheran church, the Lehigh Artillerists fired four salutes over the grave and then marched to the church, where an impressive sermon was delivered by Rev. Joshua Yeager. His remains were subsequently re-interred in Fairview cemetery.

General Craig married Dorothy Breinig, who was born 1778 (?) and died September 1, 1846. They had six children:

Charles, married Salome Beisel; Benjamin, a son, was born 1822, died Jan. 10, 1861, married Matilda Brobst. They had two children, Charles J. and Mary Alice.

Thomas, son of Thomas and Dorothy Breinig Craig, was born in Allentown, 1796. He attended the schools of his community and Wolf's Academy. For years he conducted a hotel and a general farming and lumber business at Lehigh Gap. He died in 1858 and Mrs. Craig in 1871. His first wife was a Miss Kuntz, the children were Thomas and Samuel; the second wife was Catharine Hagenbuch, daughter of John Hagenbuch, then proprietor of a hotel in Lehighton. The children of the second marriage were, Thomas, who represented his district in the House and the Senate; Eliza, wife of General Charles Heckman, an officer in the Mexican and Civil Wars; Allen, for many years Judge of Carbon County; William, who removed to Nebraska, and Robert, a captain in the regular army at Washington. John Craig, second son of Thomas and Catharine Hagenbuch Craig, was born at Lehigh Gap, Oct. 23, 1831, and became the famous "General John

Craig" of the Civil War. After the war he engaged in business, represented his district in the State Legislature, married Emma Insley, daughter of Philip Insley, of Bath.

Peter Crickmore married Frances Hemphill, a descendant of Moses Hemphill.

David Crosby married Catharine McKissick Hudders, a descendant of Michael Clyde through Archibald Hudder.

——— Culbertson married Ann McNair, a descendant of John McNair.

Hon. Thomas Cunningham, deceased, married Margaret Hemphill, a descendant of Moses Hemphill. Their children were Josephine, Lilli, Jennie, and Anna. Josephine married James Cameron, and Anna married Dr. Patrick McClain.

Dr. Smith Cunningham, deceased, married Cythia Hemphill, a descendant of Moses Hemphill. They had four children.

James Dauman married Agnes C. Forest, a descendant of John Hays through John Grier and Thomas Forest. They have three children.

Fleming Davidson married Margaret Lattimer, a descendant of Robert Lattimer.

Thomas Davis, deceased, married Elizabeth Hudders, widow of Archibald Hudders. Mrs. Elizabeth Davis' maiden name was Clyde, a descendant of Michael Clyde. They had children, Robert Whyte and Alexander Duncan; both died in infancy.

Francis Daws, deceased, married Nancy Frew Kerr, a descendant of James Kerr. The children were Elizabeth, Mary, Annie, James Kerr, and Sarah. James Kerr Daws is married and served as postmaster of Easton.

James Depue resided at Catasauqua, married Mary Jane Nagle, a descendant of Moses Hemphill. Their children were William Frederick, died in his twenty-first year; James Irwin; Moses Hemphill; Margaret, died Oct. 31, 1874; Nancy Elizabeth, and John.

Dr. E. V. Dickey, deceased, married Frances Ralston, a descendant of James Ralston.

Ebenezer Dickey married Mary Ann Ralston, another descendant of James Ralston.

Alexander and Widow Mary Dobbin were early residents of the Irish Settlement.

—— Duel married Abigail Wilson, a descendant of Hugh Wilson.

Samuel Dunlap married Nancy Hemphill, a descendant of Moses Hemphill. Their children were: Joseph, William, Walter, Lillie, Emma—married Rev. Robert Moore; Mira, Anna, Ellen, and Mary—married William Dunn.

William Dunlap married Julian Hemphill, a descendant of Moses Hemphill.

James Dunn was at one time identified with the Irish Settlement.

William Dunn married Mary Dunlap, a descendant of Moses Hemphill.

John English, deceased, married Jane Hemphill, a descendant of Moses Hemphill. One daughter, Matilda, married —— Bitner.

Henry Epple and wife, Maria Barbara, had one daughter, who married Nicholas Neligh. Maria Barbara died January 23, 1824.

Jonathan Evans married Christiana Ralston, a descendant of James Ralston.

J. J. Everett married Margaret Alice Bisel, a descendant of Michael Clyde, through William Barber and Amos Bisel.

—— Felis married Sarah Hudders, a descendant of Michael Clyde, through Archibald Hudders and Thomas S. Hudders.

Hiram B. Fish married Mary Rebecca Mulhallon, a descendant of Michael Clyde. Their children are Bertha and Clyde Mulhallon.

Thomas Forest married Jane H. Grier (born July 4, 1794), a descendant of John Hays through John Grier. Their children were: Hannah Maria; John Grier—married Elizabeth H. Horner, a descendant of James Horner; Sarah Jane—married

David West; Agnes—married James Dauman; James, deceased; William H., married twice; Joseph, deceased; S. Ralston, deceased; Robert White—married and has a family; Charles, and Louisa.

Tilghman Frederick, married Mary Jane Andress, a descendant of Moses Hemphill, through Charles Andress. Their children were Edith, George, and Charles.

——— Frew married Nancy Wilson, a descendant of Hugh Wilson.

George Frick married Rose H. Grier, a descendant of John Hays through John Grier.

Robert Fullerton married Eliza Wilson, a descendant of Hugh Wilson.

John Galagher married Isabella Grier, a descendant of John Hays.

Emeline Gardner died July 19, 1840, in her fifth year.

Rufus Gary (?) married Elizabeth Nagle, a descendant of Moses Hemphill. Mrs. Gary died April 27, 1874, and lies buried in Rochester, N. Y.

Daniel George was a collector of salary in the Settlement church and belonged to the George family who have lived for many years in the bounds of the Irish Settlement, but not descendants of the Scotch-Irish families.

——— Gerhart, deceased, married Mary Scott, a descendant of Robert Lattimer.

George Gibson and Robert Gibson were identified with the Irish Settlement at an early period of its history.

——— Gish married, it is supposed, Ellen McDowell, a descendant of Michael Clyde through Arthur E. Muhalllon.

Neigel Gray was among the early settlers.

John Gray married Jane Lattimer, a descendant of Robert Lattimer.

Martha Gray died single, June 9, 1861, in her eighty-seventh year.

Robert Gregg married Margaret ———, who died April 24, 1800, in her ninety-seventh year. They had a daughter

Margaret who married Matthew McHenry, a descendant of Rev. Francis McHenry. Mr. Gregg was one of the first three Commissioners of Northampton County and was on the first grand Jury. He died March 9, 1756, in his fortieth year.

Rev. J. N. C. Grier, D. D., married Nancy Ralston, a descendant of James Ralston. Mrs. Grier is deceased and buried at Brandywine Manor, Pa. Their children were Susan; Frances—married Thomas Happersett; Eloisa, married Richard Park; Agnes—married Washington Neligh (Neely), a descendant of Col. Nicholas Neligh.

John Grier married Jane Hays, a descendant of John Hays. Their children were (1) John Hays, born February 7 1788, married four times. First wife, Mary MacKelduff; children—John H., Elizabeth, Samuel, Mary Ann, Sarah, Agnes, Isabella and Jane; second wife Elsie Hamilton—one son, Robert; third wife, Rebecca Baily; fourth wife, Margaret Snodgrass. (2) Nathan, born June 28, 1790; (3) Agnes, married Samuel Ralston; (4) Jane H., married Thomas Forest; (5) James K, born April 22, 1796, died January 8, 1867, in his seventieth year; (6) Frances married W. Ewing Lewis; (7) Elizabeth Hays, married William W. McClure; (8) Joseph F., born January 3, 1802, known as Dr. Joseph H. Grier, deceased; (9) Mary, married James G. Long; (10) Martha married John K. Hays as his second wife, a descendant of John Hays; and (11) Isabella, married John H. Long.

William Hall, son of John Hall, and brother to the wife of Adam Clendinen, died January 20, 1813, in his fifty-fifth year.

Hugh Hamilton married Rosanna Boyd, born, 1786, died 1872, in her eighty-sixth year, a descendant of John Boyd. Their son, A. Boyd Hamilton, Esq., has a family, one son, Hugh, is Dr. Hamilton of Harrisburg; another son, Naudain, was a student of Lafayette College.

Samuel Hannon married Jane Hemphill, a descendant of Moses Hemphill.

Thomas Happersett married Frances Grier, a descendant

of James Ralston through Rev. Dr. J. N. C. Grier. Their children were Margaret; John, a surgeon; Horace; Robert; Annie; Agnes, married O. B. Kelly; Thomas, and Fannie.

——— Hart married a daughter of John Horner, a descendant of James Horner.

B. B. Hart married Letitia Horner, a descendant of James Horner.

Gilbert Hatfield married Emma Ralston, a descendant of James Ralston. Their children were Henry and Anna.

Hays

THE HAYS FAMILY

THE Hays family originated in the County Tipperary in Ireland where the first with this name was found. He lived there as early as Anno Domini 604 and was baptized by St. Patrick who introduced Christianity into Ireland. He was called at the beginning—O. Dinzal. After his baptism he was called

Polyolet Hays or Hoys

this name in the old Irish dialect means one who is promised, or specially happy or fortunate. Polyolet's descendents distinguished themselves specially by good intellect and knowledge. One of the

Ellen Hays or Hoys

was a builder of warships under the Irish King Queslo and rendered service for him. One of his sons went to Germany (and distinguished) where his descendents are still found in different parts of the country.

There are two other sons called Patrick and Hugh Hays who made a pilgrimage to the Holy Land A. D. 1096. Since then they had a coat of arms confirmed to them by King Richard of England. It is found however that they fought bravely against the English and for the liberty and independence of Ireland, and when the Constable of Chester had entered into the County of Loskommon, suffered there A. D. 1115 a great defeat, it is said that both brothers did a great deal towards gaining the victory as leaders of a troop of horsemen, Patrick however met with his death there.

Hugh had Hanna Hangle as his wife at his demise, A. D. 1145, a son was born who was called James Hays. He belonged to the highest and best nobility of the land and was County Judge in Kilkenny. He submitted to King John and had as his wife Sarah Ordoner. His estate was called Cildendrike and was situated in the mountains of Kilkenny.

The Scots entered Ireland, A. D. 1163 and devastated large stretches of land with fire and sword and with inhuman cruelty, but were defeated by the Irish near Limerick and only few escaped. James carried the principal Irish banner on this occasion and was the first to penetrate the Scottish troops.

His son Reginald Hays was a famous sea-going man and his posterity was flourishing at the time of Henry the Eighth as mariners and warriors but only ALDROVANO Hays perpetuated his race as his relations without masculine issue had died. This ALDROVANO had Martha Dugal for his wife. He was chieftain of the Irish regiment of Archers. With such a regiment he was for a long time in garrison in the Calais in France which at that time belonged to England and distinguished himself in the battle of Graveling. He had his old coat of arms and nobility renewed and confirmed by King Henry and was still living in the time of Elizabeth. He died A. D. 1589 in a duel with the Duke of Cumberland. He left four sons from whom the Hays family has spread in good numbers through Ireland and England, but not all have kept their title of nobility, although at all times they have been prominent people and have held high offices in peace and war.

In more modern days however all sure and connecting information about this family is lacking.

Record of the Hays Family
Copy by Chas. R. Stearns, per Dr. Horner.

John Hays was born about the year 1704 in the north

of Ireland in Londonderry or Donegal County. We are inclined to think that his home just before immigrating to America must have been in Donegal County, near the coast, because of a tradition in the family that some trouble with the Excise Laws was more or less the cause of his immigration. His wife, Jane Love, was born in 1705 near the same place, both being of Scotch ancestry. John Hays with his wife Jane came to this country in the year 1732*. It is said that they settled first in Chester County, Pennsylvania, where they suffered the loss of their dwelling by fire. They then made their permanent settlement in the Irish Settlement in what was then Bucks County, now Northampton County, near Weaversville, where they kept a public house, store and tannery. It is a significant fact that the Quakers settled in the southeastern part of Pennsylvania in the territory in and about Philadelphia, but they were of a very peaceable disposition and not at all prepared to meet the advance of civilization about them. On the North and South were the Phlegmatic Dutch and on the West and thus protecting the Quakers from the Indians resided the pugnacious Scotch-Irish. It has been said that William Penn placed these Scotch-Irish there, where they could satisfy their natural "Scrappy" disposition and at the same time protect the lives and property of the Quakers. John Hays that he lead a company of about thirty men known as the was evidently a leader of the settlement because we read Hays Company. Benjamin Franklin tells of stopping at Captain Hays and having been accompanied by him and his company to the scene of the Massacre at Gnadenhuetten. He also tells that on this trip Dr. Beatty, Chaplain of the company and pastor of the church at the Settlement, complained to him that the men did not attend divine worship. The Dr. told him they seemed to be regular in attendance to the commissary call twice a day to receive each one a gill of rum, and Franklin suggested the rum be dis-

---

*Another record states 1730. Moved to Northampton Co., 1732.

tributed after prayers. The Doctor accepted the suggestion, and this strange mixture of spiritual things proved satisfactory and the prayers were most punctually attended. John Hays died Nov. 16th, 1789, aged 85 years, and was buried in the burial ground at the Presbyterian Church at Weaversville. His widow lived until 1806 and died at the age of 94 years. At the time of her death she was living with her son Robert and was therefore buried in Derry Church yard, Northumberland County, Pa.

They had nine children, five sons and four daughters—John, William, Robert, James, Francis; Isabell, Jane, Mary, and Elizabeth. All the sons except William who died young, served in the Revolutionary war. Tradition says two of them were of the party left by Washington to keep up the camp fires at Trenton when Washington surprised the British at Princeton.

Children of the First John

Captain John—raised a company and marched with it as captain to Philadelphia, in Dec. 1776 and was afterward known as Captain John.

He was born in Ireland, and was two years of age when they arrived in this country. He married Barbara King, October 16th, 1760. They had 5 children—Mary, John, Jane, James and Elizabeth.

Barbara, wife of John, died August 13th, 1770.

Captain John was married again August 13th, 1771, to Jane Walker, (died Dec. 15, 1826) with whom he had six sons and four daughters, viz:—Ann, William, Isabell, Robert, Thomas, Richard, Samuel, Mary, Joseph and Rebecca.

In December 1776 he raised and commanded the company that went from the Irish settlement in answer to Gen. Washington's requisition and was present with it at the battles of Trenton, Brandywine, Germantown, and Princeton. (Egle's History of Penna. page 978.)

On June 10, 1780, the Supreme Executive Council at Philadelphia appointed John Hays, Jr., Sub. Lieutenant of the County of Northampton vice Philip Bahl resigned (Colonial Records, Volume 12, page 384). Col. Robert Lewis, the Lieutenant of Northampton County, refers to him as Col. Hays in two letters to President Reed, written from Easton and dated July 6th, and October 2d, 1781; (Penna. Archives, 2nd Series, Vol. 3, page 496, also Penna. Archives, 1st series,

Penna. Archives 1st series, Vol. 9, pages 426-428.

Penna. Archives 2nd series, Vol. 3, page 496, Vol. 14, page 594.

Egle's History of Penna. page 976.

After the war, Captain John resided in the settlement, engaged in milling, tanning and farming, etc. The Moravians wishing to exchange a large tract of land, in what is now Crawford County, for the property on which he lived, and wishing a property large enough to locate his family near each other, he undertook in company with his son William, a journey on horse-back to examine the property. While engaged in that work, he became overheated and drinking too much water from a spring he sickened and died at Meadville, Penna., Nov. 3d, 1796, aged 66.

Jane Walker, died December 15th, 1825.

Children of Captain John and Barbara King

John, eldest son of Captain John, was born Aug. 2d, 1763, married Jane Horner, May 21st, 1795, and moved to Lycoming Co., the same year, on a farm which he had bought from his father. He was elected Sheriff of the County in 1807; was elected as elder in the Lycoming Pres. church at Newberry in 1817, and died Oct. 9th, 1821, leaving one son John K. Hays. His widow died September 25th,

The following is a memorandum of the authority for the above statement filed as follows:—

Colonial Records—Vol. 12, page 384. Vol. 9, page 426

John K. Hays was born Jan. 13th, 1797. Married Jane, daughter of Thomas Hays, (his father's half-brother) on March 1st, 1827. She died Nov. 6th, 1830. They had two children Jane Elizabeth and John Walker. John K. Hays married the second time on May 31st, 1832, to Martha Grier, daughter of John and Jane Grier of Brandywine Manor. She died April 8th, 1867, leaving three children: James Grier, Martha Ann and Henrietta. John K. married his third wife, Mrs. Jane H. Teas, of Sunbury, Pa., who was a cousin and also a bridesmaid of his first wife on Sept. 24th, 1868. They resided in the old home in Williamsport, until her death Nov. 26th, 1875. John K. Hays died March 11th, 1878, aged 81 years.

Jane Elizabeth, married Hugh R. Horner. They lived in Northampton County, almost in sight of the old Homestead and have four children viz:—Robert Hays Horner. Mary Jane Horner, John King Horner, and Joseph Allison Horner. Joseph married Caroline Jane Blair. They have two children, Ruth Blair and Hugh Horner.

John Walker, married May 17th, 1855, Rachel, daughter of Charles Allen of near Williamsport. They have children, John King and Martha Jane, and have buried Georgette and Charles A.

John K. Hays, Jr., married June 25th, 1885, Sarah B. Coryell, of Williamsport, Pa. They have children, John Coryell, Walker Allen, Robert Allen, James Bingham, and Margaret C. Walker Allen and Robert Allen died in infancy and James Bingham, born Jan. 14th, 1892, died May 3d, 1907.

John Coryell married Sylvia Eliza Bowman and they have two children, John Bowman, born Oct. 14th, 1909 and Frank Carlton, born Sep. 4th, 1912.

Martha Jane married Jan. 1st, 1885, Charles R. Stearns, of same place. They have children, Rachel, Catharine, Emilie, John Walker, Martha Jane, Jr., Delphene L., George R., and Joan. John Walker died in infancy

J. Grier Hays was married in April 1873 to Emma Jarre Haines of Rock City, Illinois. They have four children, Mattie, Hettie, Mabel and James King. J. Grier Hays died on Nov. 16th, 1885. His family are living at Waterloo, Iowa.

Martha Ann, married W. H. Phillips, June 1st, 1868, and

died without children, Sept. 15th, 1875, at Milton.

Henrietta E. died single Feb. 19th, 1883.

James Hays, son of Captain John, located near Easton, and represented Northampton County in the legislature several years. He left one daughter who married John Lattimore.

Jane, married John Grier of Bucks (Now Chester County), (brother of Revs. James and Nathan Grier), and settled near Brandywine Manor. They had ten children, viz:—Rev. John H. of Jersey Shore; Dr. Joseph F. of Lewisburg, Pa.; James K. remained on the old homestead; Nancy married Samuel Ralston; Francis married Ewing Lewis; Jane married Thomas Forrest; Maria married James G. Long; Elizabeth married W. McClure; all of Chester County.

Martha married John K. Hays of Lycoming County, grandson of Captain John Hays, the oldest son of her mother's brother.

Elizabeth married Dr. E. Humphrey; they settled near Kriederville, where he followed his profession. He died there leaving five children, viz:—Mrs. Hugh Horner; John who with his two daughters went West; Dr. Charles H.; the other son located at Cherryville. (MS. omits the fifth child.)

Children of Captain John and Jane Walker

William married Lydie Temple, settled in Pittsburgh and engaged in the tanning business. He served several years in the State Senate, was elected Associate Judge of Allegheny County. He died in 1846, leaving six children, viz:—John, Robert, Henry, Charles, William and one daughter Jane, they all located at or near Pittsburgh.

Robert second son of Captain John and Jane Walker, was born in 1776 and died Feb. 1843. He went to Bellefonte about 1814 from Erie where he had been with his brother Samuel, and engaged in tanning. He was married Dec. 21st, 1819, to Eliza Henderson, a daughter of Matthew Henderson of Harris Township, Center County, Pa. She died

Sept. 9th, 1857. They had three children, viz:—

William Wallace, born June 7th, 1821, who settled in Springfield, Ill., and then at Washington, D. C., died Nov. 1895, at Bellefonte, Pa. He was married Jan. 1842 to Jane Smythe of Philadelphia, who died Nov. 1849; William was again married June 15th, 1853 to Elizabeth Magill of Danville, Pa. They had one child Ella H. who married J W Gephart of Bellefonte, Pa. They have three children, Wallace W., William W. and Mary Elizabeth.

Ellinor born Sept. 1823, died Sept. 1852 unmarried.

Alfred A., born Aug. 14th, 1826, now of Ashton, Clark Co., Mo. He was married to Rachel A. daughter of James Grier of Long Reach, Lycoming Co., Pennsylvania. She died leaving five children, viz:—

Carrie who died in 1890 unmarried.

Annie M. married to Harry C. Bubb of Williamsport, Pa.

J. Grier married Belle Seaman of Clark Co., Mo., and died in 1893 leaving two children, Raymond and Anna Belle.

William Wallace, of Chicago, Illinois.

Linn, of Ashton, Mo., who married Mary Peacock of Iowa, and they have one daughter, Rachel E.

Alfred again married a Miss Elizabeth Moran of Bellefonte, Pa., who died in 1874 leaving two children, Dr. George L. of Mercy Hospital, who married Nellie Watson of Pittsburgh, Pa., and Blanch M. of Bellefonte, Pa., who married M. Heller.

Joseph of Captain John died young, May 30th, 1795.

Ann of Captain John married John Wilson, located near Bath, and had children, John H., Charles B., William, Margaret and Jane.

Isabella of Captain John married John Ralston, settled at Brandywine Manor, had children viz.—Christiana, John, Isabella, Mary and Jane.

Rebecca of Captain John died single, April 10th, 1840.

Mary of Captain John died single January 11th, 1851.

Thomas, son of Captain John, settled in Williamsport

and married Rachel Huston, sister of Judge Huston. He filled the offices of Sheriff, Treasurer, Prothonotary, Register and Recorder of Lycoming County and died December 1846, leaving three sons, viz:—Thomas, William and Charles. They are all located in Columbus, Indiana, and five daughters, viz:—Jane, Mary, Sarah, Martha and Isabella.

Thomas Huston Hays, son of Thomas, born in Williamsport went to Indiana in 1835; engaged in contracting on the Public works located in Columbus, Indiana, and in 1840 engaged in merchandising. In 1841 he married Lucy Ann Dietz of that place. They have seven children, viz:—Rachel Anna, William, Thomas Huston, Edward Hoke, Richard Walker, Robert Dietz and Mary Elizabeth.

Richard W. died in infancy.

Mary died in infancy.

Rachel Anna, married W. H. Gold in 1868, they had two children who died in infancy. Her husband dying in 1870. In 1882 Rachel married Joseph B. Woodmansie, they have no children. He died in 1893.

William W. married Amy E. Hamilton, they have two children, Nonie and Faye.

Thomas Huston Hays, Jr., married Annie Franklin in 1867. They have three children, Carrie A., Samuel T., and Edward H. Carrie married William Rhodes in 1893. They have two children. Samuel T. married Laura W. Murphy in 1897. Edward Hays is still single.

Edward Hoke Hays, married Mattie J. Godert, they had one child, Walter O. His wife dying in 1880. Edward married Amelie J. Smith in 1882. They now reside in Needessha, Kansas.

Robert Dietz Hays, married Jennie Isaacs, 1875, they had one child, John Walker. His wife Jennie died 1884. He married Lucy D. Love, in 1891, they had two children, Basil Lloyd and Robert Love.

Lucy Ann Dietz died in 1857. After several years Thomas H. Hays married Lizzie Colgate Allen. They had four children, viz:—

Harry Colgate, who died in infancy.

Mattie, who died in infancy.

Allen M., who married Annie L. of Chicago where they now reside.

Jennie, who married Walter T. Thompson of Chicago. After living there some years they went to Orange, N. J., where they now reside. They have children, Genevieve and Barlow Hays.

Thomas H. Hays died in 1875, his widow, still living, is now with her daughter Jennie.

Mary, daughter of Thomas and Rachel Huston Hays, was born in 1811. She married William Kline of Harrisburg, 1841, at Williamsport, Pa., died 1856 leaving three children,—

Rebekah Kline, born in Harrisburg, Pa., 1843.

George Kline, born in Harrisburg, Pa., 1844, died in 1857.

Thomas Hays Kline, born in Harrisburg, Pa., 1847, died in 1875.

Charles Huston, son of Thomas and Rachel Huston Hays, was born in 1823. He married Amanda Banfill in 1851 and died in 1877. His wife died in 1897. They have two children,—

Lizzie Huston Hays, born in 1852, married Max Dalmbert in 1882. They had two children,—

Charles Hays, born in 1883.

Louis Francis, born in 1889.

Maggie Banfill Hays was born in 1859.

Charles Huston Hays died in 1877. Harriet Amanda his wife died in 1897.

Martha, daughter of Thomas and Rachel Huston Hays, was born in Williamsport, Pa., 1817. She was married in Williamsport in 1834 to E. M. Pollock of Harrisburg. She died in 1884. They had eight children,—

Edwin, born 1837, died 1885, Capt. 9th Inft. U. S. A.

Sarah Jane, born 1839, died 1896. Married Col. Caleb H. Buehler Lee, born 1863, died 1864; Schuyler C. born 1865; Jennie Louise, born 1867, died 1869; Mabel Percy born 1872.

Mary born 1841, died 1895, married George Wolf Buehler,

1862. Had one child, Martha Wolf, born 1863.

Thomas, born 1843, died 1846.

Martha Hays, born 1844, living in Harrisburg, practicing medicine.

Rachel Huston, born 1846, living in Harrisburg.

William, born 1848, died 1859.

Margaret Campbell, born 1851, married James Butler of Kirkstall Abbey, Leeds, England, 1874. They had children, —Eleanor. B. P. born 1875. John Carlton, 1878. Gerald Snowden, born 1885.

Isabella, daughter of Thomas and Rachel Huston Hays died single.

Sarah H. daughter of Thomas and Rachel Huston Hays, was born 1809. She married Charles N. Payne of Providence, Rhode Island, 1845. They had two children,—

Laura Hays, born 1846.

Thomas Hays, born 1852. He was married in 1875 to Elmira Evans and had six children,—

Charles Huston, born 1875.

Isabella Hays, born 1877.

Harry Evans, born 1879, and died in 1880.

Edwin Pollock, born 1881.

Harry Evans, born 1883.

William Hinckley, born 1886.

William, son of Thomas and Rachel Huston Hays, born in Williamsport, Pa., in ———. He settled in Columbus, Indiana, married Elizabeth Dietz. They had four children,—Charles, Henry, David and Alice. His wife dying, he married Elizabeth Gould. They had children,—Houston, William and Thomas. They now reside in Wilmar, Minnesota.

Children of Captain John—Richard

Richard the third son of Captain John and Jane Walker, born Dec. 2d, 1731. Married Christiana Ralston, daughter of John Ralston. Moved to Williamsport and went into business with his brother Thomas as hatters. After a few years he moved to a farm on Lycoming Creek about seven miles from Williamsport. They had children,—

Jane Walker, married Thomas Kerr and had children,—James Horner and Richard.

Mary Ann, married John H. Wilson and had one daughter, Annie, married A. T. Sheadle and lived at Jersey Shore, Pa.

John Ralston Hays married Sarah Hall and had children, Christianna, Mary Jane, Lettice, Richard and Elmer.

Isabella Hays married James Thomson and had children,—Samuel, Christianna, Margaret, Rose and Josephine. Samuel married Sarah Weaver. Christianna married Dr. W. R. Atkinson of Columbus, S. C. Josephine married James Farr, of Charlotte, N. C. James Thomson died Aug. 13th, 1887.

Lettice died April 1st, 1841, unmarried.

Christianna died April 4th, 1848, unmarried.

Richard Hays died October 1866. Christianna R. Hays died Feb. 13, 1854.

Samuel, son of Captain John Hays and Jane Walker, was born in 1748. He immigrated to Erie and engaged in the family business of tanning. He married Jane Bell. Their children were named,—Jane Walker, William Bell, Catharine Dorcan, John Walker, Samuel, Richard and Maria Rockwell, and two others who died in infancy.

Jane Walker was born May 28, 1814, married Samuel Kellog. They had five children,—

Kate married to Edwin Reynolds, of Meadville, Pa.

Jane married to Dr. T. B. Lachells, of Meadville, Pa.

Affie, who died single.

Mary, who died single.

Samuel married and lived in Texas.

Samuel Kellogg dying, Jane Walker married Samuel Torbert and died Oct. 13, 1899.

William Bell, son of Samuel, born June 6th, 1816, died Oct. 4th, 1900. Married Caroline Kellogg and had four children, two boys who died in infancy.

Mary married Summer Foster of Erie and has one child, William Hays.

Anna married Renaldo Clement and has two children, viz:—John H. and W. Hays.

Catharine Dorcas, second daughter of Samuel Hays was born May 18th, 1819 and married Samuel A. Law, had four children, viz:—

William L., who died single.

Samuel, unmarried.

Stephen J., who married Ella Kimball and has two children Ella F., and Catherine.

Kate, who married Pearson Church of Meadville, Pa., and has two children, Alice G. and Ethel P.

John Walker, second son of Samuel, was born Jan. 23d, 1822 and died June 24th, 1897. He married Sarah Jane and had three children, viz:—

Ida, married to H. C. McCormick of Williamsport, Pa., who has two children, viz:—

Nellie, married to Joseph Cochran and has two children.

John Hays, married to Martha Foresman, has two children. Charles, who is not married.

Sarah J. who married H. C. Bubb and had three children, John Hays, Harry Burrows and Hugh Jackson. Sarah J. Bubb died Sept. 1894.

Samuel, son of Samuel died very young.

Richard, son of Samuel died very young.

Maria Rockwell, third daughter of Samuel born 1829 was married to John A. Lew and had two children, both single, viz:—William of Meredith, New York, and Josephine of Philadelphia, Penna.

Two other children of Samuel died in infancy.

Jane Bell Hays died June 17th, 1832 and Samuel was again married to Mrs. Lattimer but had no children. He died May 25th, 1850.

Children of First John—Robert

Robert Hays was born in 1742, married Miss Mary Allison by whom he had ten children, two dying in infancy. He moved from Northampton County, in or about 1770, and settled near Warrior Run Church, where he lived nine years, then moved to a farm one mile south of what was then called Fruitstown, now Montour County, where he resided several years at which place his mother, Mrs. Jane Hays, died. From there he moved in 1806 to near what is now Dewart, Northumberland County, Pa. His place was all in woods except a small clearing on which was a cabin. He died July 1819. He was a man of strict integrity and great energy. His wife died in 1853, aged about eighty years, a woman who was highly esteemed for her amiable disposition and Christian character. He had children as follows:—

John, oldest son of Robert 3rd son of first John, born Nov. 3d, 1770, or 1773, married Margaret Falls. They had two children, a daughter who died young and James born 1799. John died in 1803. His widow married Bethuel Vincent, the father to William and Daniel of Waterford, and John H. (father to Bishop John H.) and Phoebe who married Dr. Bradley, of Waterford, and afterwards William Hinrod of Erie.

James Hays, son of John of Robert, was born in 1799. His father died when he was about four years old. After which his mother married Bethuel Vincent, as before related. He lived with the Vincent family for a short time, and then with his grandparents, until he went to Milton, Pa., to learn the trade of chair making and wheelwright. After learning his trade he located at Waterford, Erie County, Pennsylvania. He married Polly Body on December 25th, 1823. He spent the remainder of his life in Waterford, with the exception of living for a time at Millcreek Point, Pennsylvania, at the first gate out of Erie on the Erie and Waterford Turnpike, and at two other intervals on farms near Waterford. James Hays died March 1st, 1874. Polly Boyd died Nov. 18th, 1866. They had fourteen children as follows:

Lafayette S. born Sept. 23d, 1824, John V. born Jan. 18th, 1826, Duncan H., born April 3d, 1827, Charles M., born July 23d, 1828, William, born December 3d, 1829, Mary M., born Jan. 2d, 1832, Sylvester M., born Sept 2d, 1833, Lucinda B., born Sept. 2d, 1835, Irvin C., born Feb. 18th, 1837, Terrica A., born May 1st, 1841, died May 22d, 1845, Ellen D., born Oct. 15th, 1843, Celia H., born Feb. 13th, 1844, died ——————, James B., born July 22d, 1848, died Nov. 24th, 1872, and Joseph C., born May 14th, 1852.

Lafayette S. Hays, the oldest, married Mariah Stewart; they have two daughters, Emma, born June 26th, 1860, and Bell, born April 12th, 1862. Their home for some years has been Wright City, Mo.

John Vincent Hays married ———————————————. They have children, viz:—Ralph, born July 14, 1863, James, born Dec. 4th, 1865, and Madge, born May 14th, 1868. They also lived at Wright City, Mo.

Duncan Herbert, married Lucinda Dunn. They have one son, Albert, born June 29th, 1858; they live at Canyon City, Colorado.

Charles Mortimer, married Margaret L. Zimmerman; they have two (five) children, four sons and one daughter, Frank M., born Nov. 7th, 1854, William, born Feb. 4th, 1858, Joseph, born Sept. 3d, 1861, C. Boyd, born May 19th, 1868, and daughter ——————————. Their home has always been in Erie, Pa.

Sylvester Milton married Kate Thompson; they had six sons and three daughters:—Nellie, born Sept. 9th, 1859. (She married D. I. Willard and lives at Bowdie, S. Dak. 1891.)

Charles, born Feb. 18th, 1861; (he married a —————) and lives in Union City. Robert, born Dec. 24th, 1862. Ferd, born Sept. 16th, 1866. John, born June 30th, 1868. Leslie, born May 8th, 1872. Kitty, born July 17th, 1874, died———. Roger, born Nov. 11th, 1878.

Lucinda Boyd Hays married David S. Grey. Their present home (1891) is Denver, Colorado. They had eleven children:—Ida Jane, born June 4th, 1869, died May 17th,

1887, Elsworth, born ―――――, Julia Etta, born May 30th, 1863, Dwight Lincoln, born Nov. 13th, 1864, Mary Lucinda, born Nov. 25th, 1866, Hattie, born Jan. 30th, 1868, ―――――――, Laura born, ――――――, died ―――― ――, Mabel, born April 18th, 1872, David Wynn, born June 7th, 1874, Robert R., born April 18th, 1877, and Aggie, born June 15th, 1879.

Irvine Cooper Hays married Ena Barnet. They had one son, William Boyd. Ena died ――――――. Irvine Cooper afterwards married Rose Johnson. They had five children: Clarence, born April 3d, 1876, Alice, born Oct. 7th, 1878, Jessie, born Sept. 27th, 1880. These three are all dead. Ella Irvine, ――――― ――――― ―――――. Irvine Cooper Hays was a member of the 83d Reg. P. C. was wounded at the battle of Bull Run; he has always made his home at Waterford.

Ellen Dallas Hays married John Holden, they have two sons and one daughter:—Clinton, born May 31st, 1872, Fred, born July 26th, 1874, Lottie, born Oct. 16th, 1877. Their present home (1891) is on a farm near Titusville, Penna.

Celia Henrietta married Fred Bolard; **they had ten children**:—Emma, born Aug. 23d, 1865, John, born Oct. 4th, 1867, Frank, born Feb. 13th, 1871, Clinton, born Sept. 7th, 1874, Charles, born Nov. 8th, 1872, Harry, born December 17th, 1876, Laurie, born Nov. 4th, 1878, Floyd, born July 5th, 1882, Helen Celia Bolard died. Their home was at Waterford, except for a few years on a farm in Crawford County during the first year of their married life.

Jane, of Robert, born May 16th, 1774, died April 17th, 1863; she married Moses Laird, lived in Lewisburg, and had seven children, viz:—John, born Aug. 1798, Mathew, who went as a Missionary to Africa and died there. Mary, born 1801, married Dr. Dunham. Elizabeth (Mrs. Milliken) died June 1781. Robert H. born June 1806. Jane Laird died April 17, 1863. Moses Laird died ―――――――.

William of Robert, born in 1776, married Mary Wilson, they lived at Lewisburg and had nine children, viz:—

Robert, who married Emily Fields; Elizabeth, who married Thomas Chamberlain; William Wilson Hays, died aged 13 months and 26 days. Thomas, who married Mary Hulme; Mary, who married Dr. Christian Seiler; James, born May 23d, 1814; Sarah, who married Dr. Thomas Murray; William, who married Sarah Hepburn; John, born Feb. 14th, 1821.

James, of Robert, born May 31st, 1778, lived with his brother Joseph, a bachelor, until his death in 1855.

Joseph, of Robert, born in 1780, married Betty Pollock, sister to Ex-Gov. Pollock. They lived on the homestead farm near McEwensville. They had children, viz:—Robert, William, Jane and Joseph.

Robert, son of Joseph of Robert, in 1881 lived on the homestead farm, his son, W. D. lived at Grand Rapids, Mich. He had a son Thomas, and daughters, Caroline, Mary and Harriett.

William, of Joseph lived and died at McEwensville. He left children, viz:—Joseph of Lock Haven, Alfred of Muncy, W. J. of Mayville, Ind., Robert of Lock Haven, Horace of same place. John and Mary.

Joseph of Joseph, married Lucy Derrickson, her mother was a sister of John Vincent of Waterford. They lived on part of the homestead farm; their daughter, Lizzie, married a Mr. Fredericks; another daughter was Maggie.

Jane of Joseph married a Mr. Brown, from whom she separated; she made her home with her parents.

Mary of Robert, married William Walker. She was born Jan. 1st, 1782, died about 1866; they had five children.

Sarah of Robert, born May 6th, 1785; married John Simpson. They settled in Michigan near Jonesville, where she died aged between 60 and 70.

Elizabeth of Robert, born July 21st, 1788, married Thomas Brown, March 14th, 1814. They settled at Cocharntown, Crawford County, Pa., and have eleven children, viz:—William, born Dec. 24th, 1816, Robert, born March 6th, 1815, Thomas W., born Dec. 19th, 1822, James H. born August

14th, 1821, Sarah (Mrs. Jefferson) born Sept. 27th, 1826, Jane (Mrs. Loofer) born March 21st, 1818, Mary Ann (Mrs. Kellogg) born Sept. 1st, 1824, Amanda, born Nov. 22d, 1831, and Elizabeth (Mrs. Loofer) born Feb. 18th, 1823. Thomas Brown died April 23d, 1864; his wife, Elizabeth died Jan. 24th, 1884. At the time of her death she lived with her unmarried daughter, Amanda, who is since dead. Robert died May 12th, 1875. James H. died May 23d, 1823. John died April 27th, 1877. Mary Kellogg died April 12th, 1839. Joseph died _____ ____ _____.

Children of First John—Francis

Francis of first John moved to Tennessee. He visited on the West Branch in 1808, traveling the distance on horseback. Nothing has been heard from him since, except that Jack Hays, of Texas notoriety was one of his descendants.

James Hays, Lieutenant in the French and Indian Wars and Captain in the Revolution, born _____ ____ _____, died _____ ____ _____, in 1758 he went under the command of General Forbes to assist in expelling the French from the Ohio Valley, it was on this or a later expedition that he assisted in building the old Block House still standing at Frederick City, Maryland. He was afterward sent with Colonel Bouquet to rescue the captives in the Indian villages on the Ohio River. They were compelled by the terms of the treaty to leave all half-breed children and during the first night after they had secured possession of the captives several of the white mothers escaped and returned to their Indian husbands and children, their mother love proving stronger than their desire to return to civilization. Captain Hays was afterwards stationed at or near Valley Forge, where he endured great deprivation and suffering and was upheld only by his great patriotism and love and veneration for General Washington, which admiration he retained as long as he lived. He married Sarah of Jane Brown of Northampton County and after the war brought his wife and goods in a flat boat to their new home at the mouth of Beech

Creek in the Bald Eagle Valley, Penna., where they resided on a tract of land granted him by the U. S. Government for his services. Lieutenant Hays and his wife had six children, viz:—

Sarah, married to James Brown and had children, viz:—Wallace W., Samuel, of Frederick, Md., Henry and Elizabeth.

Samuel died in infancy.

John married Elsie Jackson and had children, viz:—Jackson, Samuel, Sarah, Nancy Jane and other daughters.

Mary married William Hays and had children, viz:—Sarah, William, Nelson, Eleanor, Emiline, Elizabeth and Mary.

Samuel married Susan Smith and had children, viz:—John, Elizabeth, James W., Sarah, Jane, Mary, Hannah, Charles C. and Wilson.

John of Samuel married Emeline Steaglock and had children, viz:—Mary, Samuel, D. Wilson, and Deborah. D. Wilson married Mrs. Lola M. Yeamans.

Elizabeth married Arthur Foresman.

James W. married Elizabeth Foresman and had children, viz:—Quigle, Susan and Elizabeth.

Sarah married John Dixon.

Jane married John Cook.

Mary married John McNeely, he dying, she afterwards married Constants Cooperwaithe.

Hannah married George W. Hamilton.

Charles C. married Mattie Laughrey. and had three children, Thaddeus, Sydney and Frankie.

Wilson married Mrs. Tracie Hanna and had a son Horace.

Isabella died in infancy.

Lieutenant James Hays was buried in the Hays Graveyard, at Beech Creek.

Children of First John—Jane

Jane Hays of First John married William Brown, bought

a plantation and settled where is now the city of Lynchburg. During the siege of Yorktown he used his own teams to carry supplys to the American Army. He afterwards traded his plantation for Francis Hays' farm near Dewart, Pa., but after living on the farm he and his wife both died. The family found the title defective and after a suit lost it. After the death of their parents the children were scattered, eight children having survived them.

Samuel Brown, married Ann Fearns, settled near Mackayville, Pa.

John Brown, married Esther Craig, settled near Beaver, Pa.

Thomas Brown, married Betsy Hays, settled near Franklin, Pa.

Robert Brown, born May 23d, 1776, died August 13th, 1854. He married Sarah Hays, who was born June 13th, 1783 and died August 13th, 1863. They were married by Rev. John Grier at her home at the mouth of Beech Creek, March 14th, 1813. Three children survived them, viz:—

William Wallace Brown, born Sept. 12th, 1815, married Sarah Kidd Miller.

Samuel Hays Brown, born July 16th, 1821, married Sarah Jane Horner.

Henry Clay Brown, born Jan. 11th, 1824, married Elizabeth Brown.

Joseph Brown married Mary Craig when he was an old man and he lived and died near Jerseytown, Northumberland County.

William Brown married Hannah Jackson and moved to Illinois.

Jane Brown married John Kirkwood and moved to Illinois.

Isabella Hays of First John was born in Ireland and married William Patton, settled near Bellefonte on a farm he bought of Dr. Henderson and after paying all the farm was worth was compelled to give it up, and his son then bought it and paid for it at the original price. Mr. and Mrs. Pat-

THE HAYS MILL. Erected 1790. (See page 25.)

ton are both buried in Centre County, Penna. Issue:—Samuel, Thomas, William, Sarah and Letty. Letty or Letitia moving to White Pigeon, Indiana, never married. Sarah Patton married James Grier, by whom they had Samuel Grier, of Long Reach, Miss Marie Grier and Mrs. Alfred Hays.

Mary, daughter of First John married a Mr. Gray. After his death she married a Mr. Steele.

Elizabeth, daughter of First John married Thomas Wilson, son of Hugh Wilson, one of the first settlers in the Irish Settlement and settled at Lewisburg, Pa. They had one son Hugh who was the father of Dr. William and Francis Wilson. Dr. Wilson's oldest daughter married Andrew G. Curtin who was elected for two terms as Governor of Pennsylvania. She is now residing in Bellefonte.

William, son of First John died while young.

THE HAYS FAMILY

Prepared by JOHN K. HAYS.

In accordance with the request of Rev. Clyde, of Chester County, who proposes to publish a history of the early inhabitants of the Irish Settlement in Northampton County, Pa., I have prepared the following narration of the paternal and maternal ancestors and their children, principally from tradition.

My great-grandfather, John Hays, migrated from Ireland and arrived in America when my grandfather was about two years old, he arriving in the Fall of 1796 (?) at the age of 66. I fix the date of arrival and locations 1732. He had sons—John, Robert, James and Francis—all of whom served in the Revolutionary War, two of whom were left by General Washington to keep the campfires burning in a blaze during his attack on the Hessians at Trenton. The war over, the family separating, John located in the Settlement; Robert in Northumberland County, Pa.; James at Beech Creek, Center County, Pa.; Francis in the state of Tennessee —who I have some reason to believe to be the progenitor of Jack Hays of Texas. Daughters were Isabella, Jane, Mary and Elizabeth.

John, my grandfather, married a Miss Barbara King, the sister of Mrs. Rosbrugh, and also of Mrs. J. Ralston. Hays commanded a company attached to the regiment of which the Rev. Rosbrugh was chaplain at the time of his murder by the redcoats. He and Ralston took charge of the body soon after the foul act had been perpetrated.

By this marriage he had sons, John and James. The latter located at Easton and represented Northampton County in the lower house of the Legislature; died there, leaving a daughter Maria, who married Mr. John Lattimore. Daughters—Jane, who married John Grier, of Bucks County, a brother of the Revs. James and Nathan Grier, dying early. Nathan, receiving a call to the Forks of the Brandywine Manor. His brothers, Mathew, Joseph and John, followed him and located there and died there, Jane being about 83 years of age. Her son, Rev. John H. Grier, of Jersey Shore, Lycoming County; Mrs. S. Ralston of Oxford; Mrs. Lewis and Mrs. Long, of Wainsburg, Chester County, still living. The son being about 88 and the sisters younger.

Elizabeth Hays married Dr. E. Humphrey, who settled about two miles south of Kreidersville, as practicing physician. They died there, having two sons and three daughters. The eldest married Hugh Horner, of the Settlement. John migrated West with two sisters. Dr. Charles, their youngest son, located at Cherryville as practitioner of medicine.

The first wife having died Aug. 13, 1770, my grandfather married, Aug. 13, 1771, Jane Walker, of Bucks County. They reared the following family—William, Robert, Thomas, Richard, Joseph and Samuel, daughters, Ann, Isabella, Mary and Rebecca. After his death located as follows: Mrs. Hays at Pittsburgh, Robert at Bellefonte, Samuel at Erie. These three engaged in the manufacture of leather. William represented Allegheny County four years in the Senate of Penna. Afterward elected Associate Judge. Ann married John Wilson and remained in the Settlement. Isabella married John Ralston. They located at Brandywine Manor, he as the teacher of the select school and student of theology under the Rev. N. Grier. He died early, leaving a widow and two children, who returned to the Settlement and resided with her mother, who had purchased a lot and erected a house, and resided there with single daughters, Mary and Rebecca. The grandson Ralston, having learned the tanning trade, located at Pittsburgh and took his mother and sisters with him. The mother and single daughters remained there until removed by death. Upon the death of grandfather, Thomas and Richard learned the hatters' trade, located at Williamsport. Thomas (married a sister of the late Hon. C. Huston) enjoyed the offices of Treasurer, Prothonotary and Sheriff of the county of Lycoming. Richard married Christianna Ralston of the Settlement. Dissolving the partnership, Thomas retained the business and property, Richard purchasing a farm in the vicinity. The latter was appointed a justice of the peace, which he continued to hold under election for about thirty years and married many couples.

I shall now narrate some of my recollections, derived principally from tradition of my maternal grandfather, James Horner, who occupied a farm on the northern part of the Settlement, about two miles south of Kreidersville. In the fall of 1761 a small band of marauding Indians made an attack upon the northern border of the settlement and murdered a family by the name of Stenton and burnt the house, etc., also other depredations. They were alarmed by a military company beating the reveille and turned their faces homeward. In their flight they met Miss (Mrs.) Jane Horner, who had been to the northern part of the farm to examine the spread flax and was returning with a bunch of flax in her hand to dry and to ascertain if sufficiently decomposed to separate the valuable from the worthless part. The Indians shot and scalped her in the road, supposed to be the last depredation in their hasty retreat. (cp. page 53 Northampton Co. History for different story of the massacre. Coals from a neighbor).

The foregoing first becoming public, the neighbors fled towards Bethlehem. In this retreat Mr. James Horner, (having "rapted" his dead wife in some bed covering carried her to the church), and continued his flight. His family, consisting of sons—John, Hugh, Thomas, James; daughters—Mary, Sarah and Jane (my mother). About two years after, this fright having passed away, the family continued to enjoy their homestead. Upon breaking up of the family, I find John located in Bucks County; Hugh, about a mile south of Bath—a farmer; Thomas between Weaversville and Catasauqua—a farmer; James at Pittsburgh as a merchant; Mary married a Mr. McKinstry and located near Doylestown, Bucks County; Sarah, a McNair of the Settlement, and moved to Genesee, State of New York. The above and their children, I suppose to have passed to that home from which no traveller returns, excepting Thomas, the son of Thomas, who resides at Nunday, N. Y. State.

My father, John, the eldest son of John Hays (by his marriage with Miss Barbara King), married Jane, the youngest daughter of James Horner on the twenty-first of May, 1795. My grandfather Hays had become the owner of a tract of land on the west bank of Lycoming Creek, situate in later purchase from the Indians. The Revolution over and the Indians peaceable, let the above tract under an improving lease. My father purchased the property, expecting to purchase the tenant's interest in the lease. Thither they moved in September 1795, failing to obtain the lease by permission of the tenant, drove his team to the northeast corner of the tract, then in the woods, and heavily timbered, slept in the wagon until they cleared the ground, built their cabin, then exchanged their tow for a clapboard roof, unloaded their wagon, cleared some ground and sowed some wheat, and the following harvest reaped twenty-two bushels.

On the fifteenth of January, 1797, I was born in this cabin, and had for my cradle a sap trough. I being the only edition to the family. My father John Hays, owned a large farm with gristmill and tannery attached, where four of his sons learned the trade, and three died in the business.

The Moravians of Bethlehem, owning a large body of land in Crawford County, an exchange being proposed, he having a desire to own a sufficiency of land to settle the unseated members of his family near each other, with his eldest son, William, by his second marriage, undertook the journey on horseback. And in exploring the contemplated exchange took a rash drink of spring-water, when heated by exercise, sickened and died, and is buried at Meadville, Crawford County, Pa. This occurred in the fall of 1796, he being about 66 years of age.

From this date I fix the date of the arrival of the family in America at 1732. Upon breaking up of the family, they located as heretofore narrated.

I now return to my parents, whom I left in the cabin in

the woods. The tenant seeing his inability to comply with the requisition of the lease proposed a surrender, which was accepted by my parents, moved to the better building and located on the great highway from the Susquehanna to western New York and Canada, whither many emigrants were tending. My parents, now having a small surplus of food for man and beast, found a ready market at remunerating prices to the emigrants, of whom there were many in the country north for 75 or 80 miles, without shops for man or beast. Here a supply was necessary before entering the wilderness through which a very hard road led.

About 1797 they felt themselves able to erect a saw-mill on a run on the western part of the farm, where a portion of the better part of the surplus timber was converted into lumber, which found a market in the vicinity.

They, now having many acres cleared and production, in 1806 erected a commodious stone dwelling. I believe the first in the late purchase, and exchanged their clapboard for a shingle roof.

In the fall of 1807 my father was elected and commissioned sheriff of Lycoming County, then embracing Sullivan, Bradford, Tioga, Potter, McKean, and parts of Clearfield and Clinton. He appointed a janitor for the jail and deputies for the far-off districts. He resided and managed the farm in clearing and culture until October 9, 1821, when it pleased Providence to remove him by death. Mother and I ran the concern until Sept. 23, 1824, when she also was called.

I then was compelled to hire all my help indoors and out, but I continued to run the farm in this way until the first of March, 1827 when I married Jane the daughter of Thomas Hays of Williamsport.

A cousin thought I had sown a sufficiency of wild oats, I proposed to kick the world before me and retain a share, or as much as Providence would allow me. I rebuilt my saw-mill. This season with farm operations gave me an active life. Farm operations being over for the season, I turned my attention to preparing stone and lumber for the erection of a new barn which the farm needed, and commenced in Spring of 1830 and had it ready for clover hay.

November 6, 1830, it pleased Providence to remove my wife by death, leaving with me two children, who were kindly cared for in the family of their grandparents. I let the farm to croppers, I retaining stock and fixtures. On the thirty-first of May, 1832, I married Martha, the daughter of John and Jane Grier, of Chester County. I resumed possession of the farm the following Spring and cleared about fifty acres of land. The health of the wife failing and the older children wanting school facilities, the location did not afford help in and out. Consequently the balance sheet did not show an extensive margin. These reasons with others induced me to abandon the farm, which I still own.

We moved to Williamsport in the Spring of 1842 with five children, who had arrived to maturity. My second wife died April 8, 1867. In the meantime my eldest daughter had married H. R. Horner, of the Settlement, and occupied a part of the farm on which his grandfather had located near Bath. His brother, J. W. Hays, married, located in Williamsport and engaged in the stove and tinning business and is still engaged in it. I and my three children—James E., Martha Ann and Henrietta lived together. The two latter took charge of the house, the eldest having found some person with whom she was disposed to unite, induced me to seek a helpmate. I married a Mrs. Jane Teas, widow of Dr. Teas of Northumberland, a cousin and bridesmaid of my first wife. Our marriage occurred on September 24, 1868. The son of J. G. Hays read medicine and located in Daratae, near Beloit Co., Iowa. Daughter Martha Ann married W. H. Phillips, a partner of brother J. W. Hays and located here. Their business being unremunerative, supposing their means sufficient to carry on two shops, dissolved partnership, Phillips moving to Milton, Pa. Her health failed and died there Sept. 15, 1875, leaving no children. My youngest daughter, Henrietta, had spent her time principally with her sister and had returned home when it pleased Providence to visit me with the rod of affliction in removing my third wife by death, which occurred on the twenty-fifth of November, 1875.

This leaving me as it were alone in my eightieth year with my youngest daughter as housekeeper and nurse of the family, (self, daughter) and kitchen help when obtainable.

May I be enabled to be very grateful to Divine Providence for his many blessings and mercies unto me in casting my lines in pleasant places and having in each a sufficiency of this world's blessing of food and raiments. May this chastisement which he has laid upon me be a means of weaning me from the improper cares of this world and fixing them on those things that will prepare me for an inheritance amongst those. He has located on His Right hand in His upper Kingdom, through that atonement and sacrifice which has been made by His only Begotten and well-beloved Son. And in whose merits may I be enabled to put my trust for the salvation of my immortal and never-dying soul, and may His merits be as the shadow of a great rock to my eternal welfare.

Colonial Dame Services.

Lieut. John Hays, Sr.

John Hays, Sr., was born in Ireland, ——— ——— in 1704. Was a citizen of **Northampton Co., Pa., and** died in Weaversville, Pa., Nov. 16, 1789, at 85 years. His services upon which my claim to eligibility to membership is based are as follows:

Lieutenant 13th Co., of 23 New Companies of Penna. Regiments. May 1758. Joseph Shippen, Jr., Brigade Major, Swatara Township, Lancaster Co., Pa.

Penna. Archives, 5th Series, Vol. 1, p. 174. Frontier Forts of Pa. Vol. 1: 180, 188, 190, 191, 196, 197, 221, 224, 225.

Reference to Authorities for Line of Descent

1. Egle's Penna. Genealogies 2nd Ed. p. 262.
2. Ibid.
3. Clyde's Irish Settlers, p. 58.

Egle's Notes & Queries 1899-189-190.
Egle's Penna. Genealogies, 2nd Ed. p. 262.
4. Egle's Notes & Queries 1899, p. 189-190.
Clyde's Irish Settlers, Page 58.
5. Egle's Notes & Queries, 1899. p. 189-190.
Clyde's Irish Settlers, 390, 391, 54, 56, 168, 356.
6. Egle's Notes & Queries, 1899. p. 189-190, 167.

Certified copies of Bible records for first three generations.

JOHN HAYS, JR.

My ancestors' services in assisting in the establishment of American Independence during the War of the Revolution were as follows:

On May 22, 1775, he was appointed committeeman for Allen Township, Northampton Co., by the Committee of Correspondence. (Penna. Archives, 2nd Series, Vol. 14, p. 594.)

In December, 1776, he raised and commanded the company that went from the Irish Settlement in answer to General Washington's requisition, and was present with it at the Battles of Trenton, Brandywine, Germantown and Princeton. (Egle's History of Penna. p. 976.)

On June 10, 1780, the Supreme Executive Council at Philadelphia appointed John Hays, Jr., Sub-Lieutenant of the County of Northampton, vice Philip Bahl, resigned. (Colonial Records, Vol. 12, p. 384.)

Colonel Robert Lewis, the Lieutenant of Northampton Co., refers to him as "Col. Hays" in two letters to President Reed, written from Easton, and dated July 6, and Oct. 2, 1781.

(Penna. Archives, 2nd Series, Vol. 3, p. 496.)

(Penna. Archives, 1st Series, Vol. 9, p. 426.)

(On the other side, under "The following is a memorandum of the authority for the above statement" fill in as follows:—

Colonial Record, Vol. 12, p. 384.
Penna. Archives, 1st Series, Vol. 9, pages 426-428.
Penna. Archives 2nd Series, Vol. 3, p. 498—Vol 14, p. 594.
Egles' History of Pennsylvania, p. 976.)
Captain Thomas Huston—(1739-1824.)
First Lieutenant on the "Franklin," September 2, 1775.
Captain of the "Warren," March 11, 1776.
Captain of the "Convention," August 17, 1778.
Pennsylvania.

Record found in Archives of Pennsylvania, also Register of the Penna. Society, Sons of the Revolution.

Thomas Huston was a native of Bucks Co., his parents having emigrated from Ireland. At the time of the Revolution he resided in Newtown, Pa., 22 miles out of Philadelphia.

Was married to Jennett Walker—result of union nine children, Charles, Jane, Mary, Elizabeth, Rachael, Martha, Hugh, Sarah and Thomas.

To the National Board of Management of the Daughters of the American Revolution

I, Mary Jane Horner, being of the age of eighteen years and upwards, hereby apply for membership in the Society by right of lineal descent in the following line from James Horner, who was born at Donegal Co., Ireland, on the —— day of 1711 and died in Scotch Irish Settlement, Northampton Co., Penna., on the first day of May 1793. His place of residence during the Revolution was Scotch Irish Settlement.

I was born in Scotch Irish Settlement, County of Northampton, State of Pennsylvania.

I. I am the daughter of Hugh R. Horner, born Oct. 13, 1827, died Dec. 24, 1902, and his legal and lawful wife, Jane Elizabeth Hays, born Nov. 26, 1826, died Oct. 14, 1907, married at Williamsport, Penna., May 6, 1856.

Their children 4, born 4, died ——, married first.

II. The said Hugh R. Horner was the son of Robert Horner, born April 23, 1780, died July 4, 1844, and his legal and lawful wife Jane Wilson, born —— 1779, died May, 1855, married in Tinicum, Bucks Co., 1819. Their children 6, died 6, married one.

III. The said Robert Horner was the son of Hugh Horner, born Oct. 20, 1743, died April 15, 1806, and his legal and lawful wife Elizabeth Wilson, born ———, 1748, died Dec. 22, 1835, married in Northampton Co., Penna., 1778. Their children 8, born 8, died 8, married 4.

IV. The said Hugh Horner was the son of James Horner, born 1711, died May 1, 1793, and his legal and lawful wife, Jane Kerr, born 1713, died Oct. 8, 1763, married 1740. Their children 7, born 7, died 7, married 7.

Andrew Heaslet married Jane Clendinen daughter of Adam Clendinen.

Moses Hemphill, married Agnes Sharp a native of Ireland.

Mr. Hemphill died February 16, 1822 in his seventy-second year. Mrs. Hemphill died April 2, 1817 in her sixty-seventh year. Their children were James, married Cynthia and had children; Julian married William Dunlap; Caroline, deceased; Margaret married David McClay; Cynthia, deceased; John, deceased; Moses, deceased. Joseph married Miss Wilson, had children—James, Cynthia, Nancy, Jane, Thomas, Ellen, Mary, Sharp and Margaret. Thomas was married and had a family. Mary married Jacob Andress. Nancy married Thomas Wilson, a descendant of Hugh Wilson. Elizabeth married James Kerr, a descendant of James Kerr. 1st Margaret died without descendants. 2nd Margaret married Frederick W. Nagle. Jane married Charles Andress.

Thomas Herron, married ——— Brown, a descendant of Samuel Brown. Mr. Herron died October 4, 1772 in his sixty-third year. Their descendants are in Ohio.

Joseph Harvey married Ann Horner, a descendant of James Horner. They settled in Bucks county.

George Hice was a trustee in the Settlement church in 1821.

E. K. Hindman married Gulielma Alabama Brown, a descendant of Samuel Brown.

Rev. Brogan Hoff—see sketch in Clyde's Irish Settlement. Mrs. Caroline Clay wife of the late Rev. B. Hoff died November 20, 1876 in New York City, aged 67 years.

Horner

Record of the Horner Family.

Copy furnished by Dr. Robert Horner.

Great-Great-Grandfather.

James Horner, Sr., born 1711; married Jane Kerr.

Jane (Kerr) Horner, born 1713; killed by the Indians, October 8th, 1763.

Record of James Horner, Sr., Family.

Hugh Horner, 1st, born Sept. 20, 1743; married Elizabeth Wilson.

John Horner, born Oct. 1st, 1747; married Susan Darrah.

Thomas Horner, born Nov. 1st, 1749; married Jane Patterson.

Sarah Horner, born Dec. 12th, 1751; married William McNair.

Mary Horner, born Jan. 5th, 1754; married Samuel McKinstry.

James Horner, born May 14th, 1757; married; went to Pittsburg.

Jean Horner, born Oct. 20th, 1759; married John Hays.

Record of Hugh Horner's (First) Family.

Great-Grandfather.

Jean Horner, born Feb. 27th, 1777; married Samuel Abernethey.

James Horner, born Jan. 1st, 1779; married Esther Clendinen.

Robert Horner, born April 23d, 1781; married Jane Wilson.

Judith Horner, born April 28th, 1784; died at 12 years of age.

William Horner, born May 31, 1786; died; never married.
Hugh Horner, 2d, born April 21st, 1788; married Sarah E. Humphreys.
Elizabeth Horner, born May 28th, 1790; never married.

Record of Robert Horner's Family.

Grandfather.

Ann Horner, unmarried, departed this life Feb. 3d, 1879, aged 50 years.

Jane Wilson Horner, departed this life, Sept., 1904, aged 78 years, unmarried.

Elizabeth Wilson Horner, departed this life, Dec. 29th, 1834, 13 years old.

Mary Long Horner, departed this life Oct. 4th, 1847, aged 16 years.

Hugh R. Horner, 3d, born 1828, Oct. 13th; died 1901, Dec. 23d, aged 73 years, 2 months, 10 days.

Robert Wilson Horner, departed this life Jan. 20th, 1825, aged 4 days.

Record of Hugh R. Horner's (Second) Family.

Father.

His wife was Jane Elizabeth Hays.

Robert Hays Horner, unmarried.
Mary Jane Horner, unmarried.
John King Horner, unmarried.
Joseph Allison Horner, married.

Dr. Robert Hays Horner has been for a number of years and still holds the office of Elder and Trustee in the Walnut Street Presbyterian Church, Bath, Pa.

Joseph Allison Horner's Family Record.

His wife was Caroline Jane Blair.

Ruth Blair Horner.
Hugh Horner, 4th.

Record of Thomas Horner's Family.

Thomas, son of the Emigrant James Horner, married Jane Patterson.

Sarah Horner, born Jan. 19th, 1785; married Nathan Kerr.

Jean Horner, born Jan. 12th, 1787; died Jan. 20th, 1791.

James Horner, 2d, born July 30th, 1789; married Lettuce Brown.

Jane Horner, born Feb. 12th, 1795 never married.

Anna Horner, born May 31st, 1797; married Joseph Harvey.

Thomas Horner, born 1800; married Cassandra Anderson

P. C. Hosmer married ——— Rosbrugh, a descendant of Rev. John Rosbrugh.

A. D. Hosmer married ——— Rosbrugh, a descendant of Rev. John Rosbrugh.

Philip Housel married Ann Lattimer, a descendant of Robert Lattimer.

Their children were a daughter, married Esq. Bond; and a son William who became Dr. Housel of Brooklyn, N. Y.

Joseph Howell elected trustee of the Settlement church, 1842, and served in other capacities. John Howell was elected trustee 1848. The Howell family is supposed not to be descended from the Settlement people.

The three Hudders—John, Thomas S. and Archibald were natives of Chester county, Pa.

John married Mary Clyde, a descendant of Michael Clyde. Their children were John; Ann married Isaac Speer.

Thomas S. married Mary Hudders, a descendant of Michael Clyde through Archibald Hudders. Their children were Elizabeth married James Olsen; Sarah married ——— Felis; Thomas Jefferson and three others who died in infancy.

Archibald Hudders married Elizabeth Clyde a descendant of Michael Clyde. He died October 10, 1824, and she, February 12, 1831, as Mrs. Thomas Davis.

Their children were Eliza Ann, married John H. Wilson, a descendant of Hugh Wilson; Sarah Clyde married James Johnson; John married Esther Prichard; Mary married

Thomas S. Hudders; Margaret married Archibald Woodside; Catharine McKissick married David Crosby, and Rachel Davis Johnson married William McIntyre.

Edward Humphrey married Elizabeth Hays, a descendant of John Hays—He died December 5, 1847, she, January 27, 1844 in her seventy-fourth year. Their children were John H. married Mary Ann, died July 20, 1845 in her thirty-ninth year, had a daughter Elizabeth Ann, died August 25, 1839; Sarah E. married Hugh Horner, a descendant of James Horner; Mary K. married John (?) Lyle; **Charles H. is Doctor** Humphrey of Cherryville, Northampton County, Pa. His family consists of the following children,—Charles—Dr. Charles Humphrey, Bethlehem, Pa.; Ellen; Sarah Jane; William; Robert; Thomas, deceased; Jane married Michael Weitzel.

William Hunter married Elmira Moorhead, a descendant of Moses Hemphill.

Dr. Hunter married ―――― McNeil, a descendant of Samuel McNeil.

James Hutchison lived in East Allen Township.

Philip Insley married Henrietta Horner, a descendent of James Horner. They have seven daughters, four of whom are married.

George Insley married Maria Horner, a descendant of James Horner.

Isaac Insley was a collector of salary in the Settlement church, 1844; married a relative of James Vleit. They had children,—Henry, and Lillie married a physician of Chapmanville, Northampton County, Pa.

Rev. Leslie Irwin, born July 22, 1806, died November 16, 1873 at Quincy, Ill.

Married Mary Ann Wilson, a descendant of Hugh Wilson. See sketch of Rev. Irwin in Clydes "Irish Settlement."

The following obituary notice of Mrs. Irwin's death September 13, 1877, appeared at Quincy, Ill:—Mary Ann Irwin, relict of Rev. Leslie Irwin, died September 13, 1877, aged 63 years and 11 months.

Deceased was a daughter of John Wilson, Esq., who was for 42 years a ruling elder of Allen Township Presbyterian church. She was a child of the covenant, and in early life publicly recognized the baptismal vows which had been assumed for her. She was married to the said Rev. Leslie Irwin by Rev. Richard Webster of Mauch Chunk, Pa., November 11, 1845, and for more than a quarter of a century was a faithful and efficient co-worker with her husband in the Lord's great vineyard. She has now gone to share with him the rewards and crown which he has been enjoying for nearly four years past. He has doubtless given her a glad welcome in their new eternal home. He often bore testimony to her great worth and her admirable qualifications in the discharge of her duties in the very delicate and difficult position of a pastor's wife. He often spoke of the most excellent gift which the Lord had given him in her that she co-operated quietly, though effectively, with him in every good word and work; that she contributed largely to the domestic peace of the household and congregation, and that in this respect no one had been more highly favored than he had been. She leaves in the church militant a son and two daughters to mourn over their loss, but to rejoice that the same is her infinite gain. D.—Presbyterian.

Their children were Samuel Hays, born May 16, 1850, died December 4, 1854 in his fifth year. John married Miss McIntyre. Isabella and Mary reside at Quincy, Ill.

Rev. David M. James is the present pastor of the Settlement church, see sketch in Clyde's "Irish Settlement." He is married and his children's names are David and Hattie.

James Johnson married Sarah Clyde Hudders, a descendant of Michael Clyde. Their children were Franklin, married Mary McKissick, a descendant of Michael Clyde. After her decease, her husband married a second time. Thomas married Miss Strickland—They had one child. He married a second time, has a family. William is married and has a family. Margaret, Ann, and Rachel were living in Wilmington, Del.

O. B. Kelly married Agnes Happersett, a descendant of James Ralston, through Rev. Dr. J. N. C. Grier and Thomas Happerstett.

James Kennedy was the late Judge of Northampton County, Pa. He died in the Settlement, November 2, 1872 in his eighty-fifth year. He married Jane Clyde, a descendant of Michael Clyde. She died December 30, 1854 in her seventy-first year. One child, a son, Clyde, who married Henrietta Sherrard of New Jersey. Their children were,— Jane married Dr. Clark. Sarah married Charles Corss. Samuel is Dr. Kennedy of Stewartsville, N. J.

———— Kern married Mary Palmer, a descendent of George Palmer. Their children were Elizabeth, married Dr. John Mulhallon; George P. is Dr. George P. Kern, of Bath, Pa., is married and has children,——Alice and Palmer, who is Dr. Palmer Kern of Bath, Pa.

Kerr

James Kerr was one of the early settlers in the Irish Settlement.

He was married and had children,—

James, married Jane McInstry (?). Children:—Joseph, married Margaret Hagenbuch. The husband died, July 23, 1833; the wife, November 15, 1824; James married Elizabeth Hemphill, a descendant of Moses Hemphill; John married Sally Kennedy; Nathan married Sarah Horner, a descendant of James Horner, and Mary married Samuel Stewart.

The children of James and Elizabeth Hemphill Kerr were Caroline, married Thomas Hemphill; Nancy Frew married Francis Daws; Matilda married Joseph Brown; William died February 20, 1815; John died January 20, 1824; James died in the fourth year of his age.

The children of John and Sally Kennedy Kerr were so far as known, Mary and James.

The children of Nathan and Sarah Horner Kerr were Eliza, Lavinia and others whose names could not be obtained.

William was married probably three times. He moved to Washington County, Pa., Mary, one of his children, married John Horner, a descendant of Joseph Horner. David, married Letitia Clyde, was born April 1, 1758, died November 23, 1845.

Elizabeth married James Clyde, a descendant of Michael Clyde.

Thomas Kerr married Jane Hays, a descendant of John Hays. Their children were James Horner Kerr—Rev. J. Horner Kerr, pastor of Rural Valley Presbyterian Church, Rural Valley, Armstrong County, Pa.; Richard, of whom little if anything is known.

Ann Carr whose connection is unknown, died April 29, 1832.

THE GENEALOGY OF JAMES KING

of the Scotch-Irish Settlement

By Wilbur L. King

James King was one of the early settlers in the Scotch-Irish settlement in Allen township, Northampton county, Penna., and one of its prominent citizens. He married Mary Walker.[1] Both he and his wife came to America from the

---

1. The brothers and sisters of Mary Walker were John, an assessor in Northampton County, a ruling elder in the Presbyterian church in the Settlement, and a pious and worthy man who died June, 1777, age 61 years; Robert, who died unmarried in 1758, age 58 years; Richard, a man of property, usefulness and high respect, and a captain in the Revolutionary army; and Christiana, who married John McNair, who died 1762, age 72 years.

north of Ireland, presumably as early as 1728, with a band of home-seekers led by Col. Thomas Craig.[2] Mr. King died April 30, 1745, age 38 years, and his wife died January 9, 1790 age 78 years. Both are buried in the Irish settlement graveyard,[3] Mr. King's grave stone being one of the very oldest in the county. The family were members of the Presbyterian church and we find Mary King and her son-in-law, John Ralston, on the list of contributors toward the purchase price of the Presbyterian parsonage in the settlement in 1761. She was evidently a woman of deep religious convictions as we find that she made provision in her will that all her grandchildren should be given a new Bible. On December 4, 1750, she purchased from Evan Patterson of old Broad street, London, William Allen of Philadelphia and William Webb of Chester county, Penna., a tract of land containing 217 acres and 29 perches with allowances of six per cent for roads, etc., situate "upon a creek or small branch of the west branch of the Delaware river, commonly called or known by the name Calisuka."[4] The children of James and Mary King were.

  a. Gabriel, died May 28, 1758, age 21 years. He is said to have been "eminent for his piety."[5]

  b. Anna, commonly called Nancy. She was living at the time of her mother's death.[6] She married Robert Lattimore and had children: 1. William, a general in the Revolutionary war, died Nov. 11, 1833, age 70 years; 2. James; 3. Jane, wife of John Gray; 4. Sarah married John Cochran; 5. Mary married Joseph Brown; 6. Margaret married Fleming Davidson; 7. Elizabeth married James Boyd; 8. Anne married Philip Housel.

---

2. History of Northampton Co., Penna., by Wm. J. Heller, Vol. 1, page 42.
3. Genealogies, necrology and reminiscences of the Irish Settlement by Rev. John C. Clyde.
4. This farm is located on the Catasauqua Creek near the present site of Weaversville.
5. History of Northampton County, Penna., by Rupp, page 17.
6. Volume 2, page 79, Register of Wills, Northampton County, Pa.

c. Barbara married Captain John Hays, Jr., a son of John Hays, Sr.,[7] on Oct. 16, 1760, died Aug. 11, 1770, age 30 years and is buried in the Irish settlement graveyard. He was born in Ireland, was a soldier in the Revolutionary war, and died while absent from home at Meadville, Pa., Nov. 3, 1796. They had issue: 1. Mary died Sept. 9, 1776; 2. John who married Jane Horner May 21. 1795, and in 1807 was elected sheriff of Lycoming county and died Oct. 9, 1821; 3. James who represented Northampton county in the Legislature for several years; 4. Jane who married John Grier of Bucks county and settled in Chester county; 5. Elizabeth married Dr. E. Humphrey.

Capt. John Hays. Jr., was again married Aug. 13, 1771 to Jane Walker who died Dec. 15, 1825 and with whom he had issue: 1. Ann born 1772, married John Wilson of Bath; 2. William born 1774, served four years in the Senate of Penna., elected Associate Judge of Allegheny county and died 1846; 3. Isabella married John Ralston; 4. Robert, a tanner, died Feb. 15, 1843; 5. Thomas who filled the offices of Sheriff, Prothonotary, Treasurer, Register and Recorder of Lycoming county and died 1846; 6. Richard, a Justice of the Peace, died Oct. 8, 1856; 7. Samuel, a tanner, died May 27, 1850; 8. Mary died Jan. 11, 1851; 9. Joseph died March 30, 1795; 10. Rebecca died April 10, 1840.

d. Sarah died Feb. 27, 1784, age 41 years; married Samuel

---

7. John Hays, Sr., born 1704, and wife Jane (nee Love) came with the early emigrants to Allen Township from West Donegal, Ireland, in 1732. He lived on the main road leading from Bethlehem to the Moravian mission at Gnadenhutten, north of the Blue Mountains, where he kept a public house. He died Nov. 16, 1789, leaving a widow who died at Derry, Northumberland County, in 1860. They had nine children: Francis, James, Robert, William, John, Isabel Patton, Mary Gray, Jane Brown, and Elizabeth Wilson.

Ralston (8) who died Oct. 13, 1785, age 55 years. Both are buried in the settlement graveyard. Their children were, Samuel died Jan. 11, 1795, age 24 years; James died Jan. 20, 1836; Isaac; Gabriel; Mary; Letitia died Sept. 30, 1848; and Sarah.

e. Christiana died Dec. 2, 1826, age 82 years; buried at Brandywine Manor, Chester county, Penna. She married John Ralston,[8] one of the delegates from Northampton county to frame the constitution of 1776. He was a member of the Provincial Congress during the Revolutionary war, a captain and paymaster in the militia and a worthy man and an elder in the Presbyterian church. He was the son of James and Mary (Cummock) Ralston and died Feb. 17, 1795, age 60 years. Had issue: Mary; Letitia married Capt. Benj. Wallace who was taken prisoner with Gen. Brown by the British at Long Island in the Revolutionary war; Jane; Ann; Christiana; James who surveyed for the plan for the village of Bath; John a student in theology died Oct. 5, 1804; Robert; and Samuel.

---

8. He was the son of James Ralston, who died July 26, 1775, age 76 years, and his wife Mary, who died July 23, 1774, age 74 years. James Ralston was one of the early settlers in the Irish Settlement, an elder in the Settlement church, and was one of the first Grand Jury of Northampton County. Their children were: Mary, died Nov. 20, 1748; Samuel, died Oct. 13, 1785; John, who married Christiana King; and Jane, who married Rev. John Rosbrugh.

———— Kline married a daughter of Thomas Hays, a descendant of John Hays.

Neill Kurtz married Mary Jane Long, a descendant of John Hays, through John Grier.

Franklin Lafever married Amelia Scott, a descendant of Moses Hemphill through Alexander Scott.

Archibald Laird at one time collector of provincial taxes lived where the town, Northampton now stands. He purchased 210 acres June 6, 1766 and sold the same in 1771 to

B. Beil, the progenitor of the Beil family of Allen Township, Northampton County, Pa.

James Lambert married **Sarah Ann Clyde, a descendant** of Michael Clyde. Their children were Learna Clyde and Annetta Blanch.

Arthur Lattimer a brother of Robert owned land on which the town of Bath now stands. He was born in Ireland, 1710, and died in 1777 in the sixty seventh year of his age. His wife, a native of Ireland in 1780 about sixty-five years of age, a Mrs. J. W. Abbot of Tamaqua is a great-granddaughter. Mrs. Henrietta Gearhart of Danville, Pa., and Miss M. A. Lattimer, Pittsburgh, are descendants. Dr. Clyde believes they are descendants of Robert Lattimer.

Robert Lattimer lived about a mile from the Settlement church. He married Nancy King, a descendant of James King. Their children were,—William, known as General William Lattimer who died November 11, 1833 in his seventieth year. He married Mary Walker. Their children were John, married Miss Hays; William married Mary Ralston; Robert, deceased. No descendants. After his death, his widow married Charles Green of Easton; James, died April 18, 1843, in his fifty-fifth year; Samuel was married, left descendants; Ralston Monroe, died November 22, 1822 aged 11 months and 7 days; Christiana married John Ralston; M—— A—— Nancy and one more of whom nothing is known.

James, married ———— Walker. They had among other children, a daughter who married Mr. Erwood.

Jane married John Gray.

Sarah married John Cochran.

Mary married Joseph Brown.

Margaret married Fleming Davidson.

Elizabeth married James Boyd.

Anne married Philip Housel.

Obituary Notice in the "Presbyterian".

Lattimer—In Tamaqua, Pa., November 10, 1875, Mrs. Catharine widow of James Lattimer in her eighty-first year.

Rev. Daniel Lawrence, pastor of the Settlement church from April 2, 1747 to May 21, 1752—See sketch Clyde's "Irish Settlement."

——— Leaming married Jane Rosbrugh. Their children were Jefferson, died single; and James R. is Dr. Leaming of New York City.

Dr. Andrew Ledlie was surgeon of the Twelfth Pennsylvania Regiment.

———Levers married Judith Emma Bisel, a descendant of Michael Clyde through William Barber and Amos Bisel.

W. Ewing Lewis married Frances Grier, a descendant of John Hays through John Grier. She was born April 27, 1798. Their children were,—John married Martha Barr, and have four children; William; Martha; Victoria, married John Morton, and James K.

———Lewis brother to W. Ewing Lewis, married Elizabeth Grier, a descendant of John Hays through John Grier. They had two children William and Jane.

Mary Likens, died June 16, 1733 in her eighteenth year.

William Line married Mary Scott, a descendant of Moses Hemphill through Alexander Scott.

John Loder has children buried in Settlement burying ground.

John H. Long married Isabella K. Grier, a descendant of John Hays through John Grier. Their daughter married Neill Kurtz.

James G. Long married Mary Grier, a descendant of John Hays through John Grier. She was born July 29, 1803 and died January 2, 1868 in her sixty-fourth year. Their children were John Flavel, married and has a family; William T. married, has a family; James A. married and has a family; Thomas S. is Rev. Thomas S. Long, pastor of Greenwich Presbyterian church, in N. J., married Catharine Ayers. They have a family and reside near Bloomsbury, N. J.; Jane E. and Mary A. both are single.

John Lyle was a collector of salary in the Settlement

church in 1844 and in other respects served it. He married Mary K. Humphrey, a descendant of Dr. Edward Humphrey.

John Lytle married Lucinda Nagle, a descendant of Moses Hemphill. Their children were—Mary; Margaret married William Mote; John Henry lived at Catasauqua; Frederick married Mary Esch. They have one child and resided at Catasauqua; George died single in 1874, and is buried in Catasauqua.

Andrew Mann was early identified with the Settlement. It is presumed he was the Mann connection into which the McNairs and others of the Settlement married.

William Marsh married Amanda Horner, a descendant of James Horner.

Thomas Martin, originally a native of Mount Bethel, Northampton County, married Letitia Ralston, a descendant of James Ralston.

An amusing incident transpired when Samuel, Jane, Christiana and Mary Ann Ralston paid a visit to friends in Virginia. Having reached the terminus of the R. R. which was at Staunton, Va., they procured a hack to convey them fifteen miles. Mr. Ralston knew where his sister, Mrs. Berry, lived and on arriving in the evening, asked permission to stay over night, whereupon, Mrs. Berry, being a widow, replied she did not like to entertain travelers (strangers) when her son was absent. Mr. Ralston said he was accompanied by three ladies and as they had some knowledge of each other, it would, perhaps be pleasant for both parties.

He informed her he was her brother, to which she replied: "If you are, you have a mark on one of your temples," and upon examination, found the proof. Several minutes elapsed before either could speak. The others, who till now, remained in the carriage, were soon brought into the house.

The same evening a messenger was dispatched to apprise the other sister, Mrs. Martin, who resided about a half a mile distant, but the inclemency of the weather, and the advanced age of Mrs. Martin (over eighty) forbad her making the trip then, but as early as eight o'clock next morning found her with her Pennsylvania friends, she went on horseback. Each of the sisters had large families and a son of each were elders at the same time in the Presbyterian church of New Providence, Va., where a remnant of the families is still found.

Hiram Masteller married Sarah Savilla Barber a descendant of Michael Clyde through William Barber. Their children were Thaddaeus Clyde and Sarah.

James McAllister lived in what is now Howertown, Northampton County.

Dr. Patrick McCain married Anna Cunningham, a descendant of Moses Hemphill through Hon. Thomas Cunningham.

David McClay married Margaret Hemphill, a descendant of Moses Hemphill.

Dr. James L. McLain married, October 27, 1875, Anna Ralston, a descendant of James Ralston.

The following obituary notice appeared in the "Presbyterian" August 11, 1877,—"McLain—At Urbana, O., July 8. Robert Alvin, infant son of Dr. James L. and Anna Ralston McLain, aged 4 months and 18 days."

William W. McClure, died August, 1874, married Elizabeth H. Grier, a descendant of John Hays through John Grier, born January 22, 1800 and is deceased. Their children were,—Agnes, married Dr. N. G. Thomson; Caroline; James Grier, married Eliza Mackelduff, their children were—Elizabeth J., Emma M., Helen G. and an infant; Baxter B. married Sally Ann Horner, a descendant of Joseph Horner; Clarissa G. The family resided in and around Brandywine Manor.

William McConnel lived in East Allen Township.

Robert McDowell married Sarah Mulhallon, a descendant of Michael Clyde. Their children were Rebecca, married David McKenna; Ellen, married Mr.———Gish; Elmira;

Nancy Clyde married Lt. J. Moser of the U. S. Navy; Robert Murray married, (October, 1875) Stella E. Lilliendahl.

Rev. Francis McHenry, licensed to preach the Gospel in Ireland, arrived in America in 1737. The following year he was ordained and installed pastor of "Forks of Neshaminy" church and Deep Run, which he served until his death January 23, 1757. He was identified with the "Old Side" party in the disruption of the Presbyterian church in 1741.

He married Mary Wilson, a descendant of Hugh Wilson—They had one son, Matthew, surgeon on board the Provincial ship, Montgomery, April 13, 1776. He died December 13, 1783 in his fortieth year. He married Margaret Gregg, a daughter of Robert Gregg. She died, March 17, 1796 in her forty-third year. Their children were,—Ann, died October 18, 1818 in her forty-first year; Elizabeth, died June 8, 1831 in her fifty-seventh year, and Matthew who died at Mount Holly, N. J., if correctly informed.

Samuel McInstry married Mary Horner, a descendant of James Horner.

William McIntyre married Rachel Davis Johnson Hudders, a descendant of Michael Clyde through Archibald Hudders. They had two children both of whom died in infancy.

Thomas McKeen was a trustee of the Settlement church and treasurer from 1802-'04. He kept store about a mile below Bath on the Monoquacy Creek.

John McKelvy married Jane Ralston, a descendant of James Ralston.

They resided in Pittsburgh and have a family.

David McKenna married Rebecca McDowell, a descendant of Michael Clyde through Robert McDowell.

John McKissick married Sarah Clyde, a descendant of Michael Clyde.

She died 1867 and is buried in Columbia, Pa. Their children were James Clyde, died January 20, 1852 aged 35 years and 30 days. He married a Miss McCormick now deceased. They had children John and Lillie; Eliza; Mary, married

Franklin Johnson, a descendant of Michael Clyde through Archibald Hudders, and James Johnson.

John McNair and wife Christiana were natives of Scotland. They emigrated to Ireland, 1690, from there to America with widowed mother of John McNair and settled in Irish Settlement in 1736-7. The farm on which they lived is now owned by Robert Weaver.

John died in 1762 in his seventy-second year; Christiana his wife, January 27, 1782 in her eighty-second year. Their children were William, born in Ireland, 1727, he owned one or more slaves. He emigrated to Western New York about eighteen hundred and there died an old man. His first wife was Margaret Wilson, a descendent of Hugh Wilson, died July 20, 1783 in her forty-ninth year. They had children—John, Hugh, Charles, William, Christiana and Margaret. His second wife was Sarah Horner, a descendant of James Horner. She was born December 12, 1751 and died and was buried in Livingston County, New York. Their children were—James, Andrew, Robert and Jane. John was born in the Settlement, 1738, and died in Western New York. He married Margaret Denny March 20, 1764. She lived in Western New York about 1804. Their children were,—John; William, died August 2, 1769; Samuel, father of Samuel McNair; David, father of John L. McNair; James; Robert; Sarah, died February 16, 1788; Christiana, and Margaret. Robert and Andrew were lost overboard while crossing the Atlantic. Margaret, married Charles Wilson, a descendant of Hugh Wilson. Ann married ———— Culbertson, many of the McNairs are Presbyterians and officers in the church.

Samuel McNeill married Mary Palmer, sister of George Palmer. She died July 17, 1810 in her fifty-eighth year. Their children were,—Palmer, died December 15, 1819 in his twenty-eighth year; Elizabeth; Sarah, married, and one of her daughters became, we believe, the wife of Dr. Hunter.

Charles Meloy was elected trustee of the Settlement church in 1802.

Elizabeth Miller died April 10, 1824 in her twenty-eighth year. As a descendant she lived at James Clyde's.

Alexander Miller married Eliza Ann Mulhallon, a descendant of Michael Clyde through Arthur E. Mulhallon. She died April 15, 1868 in her sixtieth year. Their children were Eliza R. (?), died December 10, 1831 in her fifth year; Clyde married, had a family and lived in the South; Arthur is married, has a family and lives in Slatington, Pa.

William Moffat died December 25, 1831 in his eighty-sixth year. Mary his wife died October 6, 1829 in her eighty-third year. There are no descendants.

Charles G. Moore married Adaline Moorhead, a descendant of Moses Hemphill.

Rev. Robert R. Moore, pastor of Fourth Presbyterian church, Pittsburgh, married Mary Dunlap, a descendant of Moses Hemphill through Samuel Dunlap.

——————— Moorehead, deceased, married Mary Hemphill, a descendant of Moses Hemphill.

Their children were Nancy, married Orlo R. Coe; Catharine; Mary; Elmira, married William Hunter; Josephine married Jesse Reed; Adaline, married Charles G. Moore; Matilda, James and William.

Lt. J. Moser, U. S. N., married Nancy Clyde McDowell, a descendant of Michael Clyde through Arthur E. Mulhallon.

William Mote married Margaret Lytle, a descendant of Moses Hemphill through Frederick W. Nagle. Their children were William and John.

John Morton married Victoria Lewis, a descendant of John Hays through John Grier. There are no known descendents.

——————— Mulhallon married Sarah Wilson, a descendant of Hugh Wilson. The following are supposed to be descendants,—Sarah W. Landers, Mary Lewis, **W. W. Mc**Henry—all of Iowa; Henry McHenry, Sarah Sufferen, Mrs. William Petrie, William Mulhallon and George Magee of New York State; the Mulhallons of Monroe, Michigan are also descendants.

Arthur Mulhallon died September 18, 1826 in his forty-second year. He married Rebecca Clyde, a descendant of Michael Clyde. She died April 12, 1868 in her eighty-third year. Their children were, John who was Dr. Mulhallon of Bath, Pa., who married Elizabeth Kern, a descendant of George Palmer. They had one daughter; William was the late Dr. Mulhallon of Brooklyn, N. Y. He left a wife and family; Eliza Ann, married Alexander Miller; Elmira Bleckley died single, September 17, 1835 in her twenty-second year, and Sarah, married Robert McDowell.

Frederick Nagle, died December 6, 1864 in his seventy-third year. He married Margaret Hemphill, a descendant of Moses Hemphill. She died February 14, 1864.

Their children were,—William Frederick; Nancy; Mary Jane, married James DePue; Catharine died August 1, 1835 in her nineteenth year; Elizabeth, married Rufus Gary; Margaret, married Henry Raup; Caroline September 14, 1838 in her thirteenth year, and Lucinda, married first John Lytle, second, John Church.

John Neal married Susanna Dobbins, a descendant of widow Dobbins,—a sister of William Boyd and perhaps a member of the John Boyd family. She resided on the "Page Tract" otherwise known as the "Manor of Chawton," she died in 1766. Her children were,—Alexander, Leonard, William, James, Susanna and Elizabeth, who married William Perry.

John Nicholas Neligh died June 15, 1816 in his forty-eighth year. He kept a store on a farm now owned by John Williams, and married the only daughter of Henry Epple. One of their children, Henry died November 20, 1798. Another son—married Christiana (?) Ralston.

Their children were Washington, married Agnes Grier, a descendant of James Ralston, through Rev. J. N. C. Grier, D. D. Their children were Oletha, Nathan Neander; John, married and resided in Philadelphia; Robert, married Christiana Ralston, a descendant of James Ralston.

William Oliphant and wife Susanna had a daughter Margaret, died May 12, 1778 in her sixteenth year. The mother died March 11, 1778 in her fifty-eighth year.

James Olsen married Elizabeth Hudders, a descendant of Michael Clyde through Thomas S. Hudders.

Henry Orr, a supposed relative of John Agnew, died August 9, 1850 in his twenty-ninth year.

———— Paine married Sarah Hays, a descendant of John Hays.

George Palmer, surveyor-general of Pennsylvania lies buried in the Settlement burying ground. He married as his first wife a sister of Col. Thomas Craig. Their children were John and Eliza. John died June 14, 1813, and Eliza married James Ralston, a descendant of James Ralston. George Palmer married as his second wife Mary Conrad, a supposed relative to Mrs. William Brown. She is buried in the Settlement burying ground.

Their children were Charlotte, died March 20, 1810 in her fourth year; Deborah, died April 9, 1810, in her second year; Mary married ———— Kern; Sarah, married Dr. Wesselhoeft; Harriet, married Dr. Reynolds; Juliet married ———— Arnold; Thomas was married and left a family, we believe.

Richard Park married Eloisa Grier, a descendant of James Ralston through Rev. J. N. C. Grier, D. D. Their children were Bowen, married Ellen Black. There were other children whose names we have not learned.

———— Pattent married a daughter of John Hays; another Pattent (Patton) married Mary Ralston, a descendant of James Ralston.

Rev. Francis Peppard, fifth pastor of the Settlement church, vid. sketch in Clyde's "Irish Settlement."

Joseph Perry, died June 26, 1766 in his fifty-fifth year.

William Perry married Elizabeth Dobbin.

William Philips married Martha Ann Hays, a descendant of John Hays.

Rev. Thomas Picton was at one time Principal of the Academy in the Settlement.

Rev. John F. Pollock, pastor of Oxford Presbyterian church, N. J., married Elizabeth Agnew, a descendant of John Agnew.

──────── Pollock, married Martha Hays, a descendant of John Hays.

Joseph Price married Mary Brown, a descendant of Samuel Brown. She died May 4, 1834.

Dr. Pursell married ──── Scott, a descendant of Robert Lattimer through William G. Scott.

Thomas F. Quay married Matilda Horner, a descendant of James Horner.

James Ralston was one of the early settlers, an elder in the Settlement church. He died July 26, 1775, about 76 years of age. He married Mary in Ireland, who died July 23, 1774 in her seventy-fourth year. Their children were,—Mary, died November 20, 1748; Samuel, died October 13, 1785 in his fifty-fifth year, married Sarah King, a descendant of James King. Sarah died February 27, 1784 in her forty-first year. Their children were Samuel, died January 11, 1795. Married Letitia Rosbrugh, a descendant of Rev. John Rosbrugh, who died at nearly ninety and was buried in Danville, N. Y.; James, known as Squire Ralston, died January 20, 1836, in his sixty-ninth year. He married Eliza Palmer, who died February 13, 1808 in her twenty-eighth year; Isaac, was married and left one daughter Christiana, married ────────── Neligh, a descendant of Nicholas Neligh; Gabriel; Mary married ──────── Pattent (Patton); Letitia, died September 30, 1848 in her sixty-eighth year.

John son of James, died February 17, 1795 in his sixtieth year. He was one of the delegates from Northampton County to frame the Pennsylvania Constitution 1776. He lived on a farm now owned by S. Achenbach. He married Christiana King, a descendant of James King. Their children were, Mary, married William Lattimer, a descendant of Robert Lattimer; Letitia married Thomas Martin; Jane, married Thomas Walker; Ann, married Charles Berry; Christiana married Richard Hays, a descendant of John Hays; James, married Frances Grier, a sister of John Grier. Their children were Nancy wife of Rev. J. N. C. Grier, D. D. Christiana, and John married Jane Buchanan. Their children were Francis, James, John, Catharine, Robert, Mary Ann, Sarah Jane and Eloisa; James, son of James, son of John and Francis Ralston, was married twice. As his first wife Margaret Happerstett. Their children were John, James, Frances, Agnes, Louisa, Thomas and Rees. As his second wife, James married Mary Martin. Their children were,—Emma, Robert, Henry, Anna and Helen.

John, son of John and Christiana King Ralston married Isabella Hays, a descendant of John Hays. She died in March, 1855 in her seventy-ninth year. Their children were Christiana and John. The former married Jonathan Evans and the latter Christiana Lattimer. They had children Isabella, Mary and Jane, who married John McKelvy.

Robert, son of John and Christiana King Ralston, married Mary Rosbrugh. They had one daughter, Christiana who married Robert Neligh.

Samuel, son of John and Christiana King Ralston, married Agnes Grier. Their children were James Grier Ralston, (Rev. James Grier Ralston, D. D.) who married Mary Larrimer. They had children Anna, Ella, Carra; Chistiana; Jane E. married William Robinson; Mary Ann, Frances, the former married Ebenezer, the latter Dr. E. V. Dickey; John K. married Anna Fries, whose children were Samuel, Margaret and Isabel; Agnes is single.

Jane married Rev. John Rosbrugh. She was the daughter of the first James and Mary Ralston.

Henry Raup married Margaret Nagle, a descendant of Moses Hemphill through Frederick W. Nagle. Their children were William, married Ellen Keck; Mary Margaret: Nancy C.; Samuel; Laura Jane; Elizabeth C.; Joseph, and Ebzena. (?).

This Indenture Made the first day of October in the Twenty eighth year of the Reign of our Sovereign Lord George the Second by the Grace of God of Great Britain France and Ireland King Defender of the Faith &c: Annsque Domini 1754, *Between* Nicholas Scull Sheriff of the County of Northampton in the Province of Pennsylvania of the one Part And Daniel Brodhead Aaron Dupui James Horner Joseph Levis Jacob Mowry Nicholas Tunston Freeholders of the County and Province aforesaid of the other Part *Wittnesseth* That According To law and the Charter of the Said Province we with meny others Did meet the First day of October at Easton in the aforesaid County the Place by law appointed For Elections and Did then and there Elect and Choose George Kustard Joseph Everhart Robert Lyle George Rea John Walker ~~~~ Boughman of the County aforesaid To be Assessors For the said County, For the year Ensuing In Wittness whereof we have Set our hands and Seals hereunto the day and year First above written

        Nicholas Scull Sheriff (RED SEAL)

        Joseph Levis (RED SEAL) Dan'l Brodhead (RED SEAL)

        Jacob Mowry (RED SEAL) Aaron Dupui (RED SEAL)

        Nicholas Tunston (RED SEAL) Jas Horner (RED SEAL)

The Northampton County Sheriff's Return of Assessors—1754.
Nicolas Scull, sheriff.
See page 27—Return of an Assessment made in 1775.

———————— Reed married Louisa Scott, a descendant of Robert Lattimer through William G. Scott.

Jesse Reed married Josephine Moorhead, a descendant of Moses Hemphill.

Timothy Reed and son lived near Chapman's Quarries, Northampton County, Pa.

Dr. Reynolds married Harriet Palmer, a descendant of George Palmer.

George Richie, was a collector 1821, and a trustee 1822 in the Settlement church.

James Riddle and John Riddle were identified with the Settlement at an early period.

William Robinson married Jane E. Ralston, a descendant of James Ralston.

Timothy Rogers of the Settlement was a member of the Third Pa., Regiment during the Revolution.

ROSBRUGH, WILLIAM

Going back to the family history in the old country, we find that they left Scotland about the year 1720, and settled in the vicinity of Innes Killen, Ireland, where the parents died. In the family there were at least three children.— William, John and Sarah. These immigrated to America about the year 1740. Of the sister's history, we have not been able to learn anything. It seems they settled near what is now Dannville, Independence Township, Warren County, New Jersey. The homestead is now, we believe, a part of, or adjoining, the property owned by the Crane Iron Company, of Catasauqua, Pa., and leased by Mr. William Vreeland, of Dannville.

It was here doubtless that Rev. John Rosbrugh spent his early life, and here that he married and buried his first wife. Here also his elder brother ended his days. The exact date of the death of William Rosbrugh we have not been able to learn. It was, however, some time previous to 1776, a fact which is revealed by the provisions of Rev. John Rosbrugh's will with reference to his (William's) sons.

He married Jane Christie, who had a brother in Philadelphia engaged in mercantile pursuits. They both died a few years after their marriage, leaving three children, who were placed under the guardianship of their uncle, Rev. John Rosbrugh. Those of the Rosbrugh connection, who died whilst residing in New Jersey, were most likely buried in the old Moravian graveyard near Hope, in Warren County.

Second Generation

The children of William Rosbrugh were Sarah, Robert and John.

Of Sarah there seems to be nothing known. She probably died young, and unmarried, an assumption which would seem to be substantiated by the fact that whilst the uncle, Rev. John Rosbrugh, their guardian, makes a bequest in his will to both Robert and John, no reference is made to their sister Sarah.

Robert married Isabella Carney or Karney.

John married Mary Carney, sister to Robert's wife.

When arriving at man's estate, the two brothers engaged in the milling business in what is now Hope township, Sussex, now Warren County, N. J. This property, we believe, is now known as Townsburry's mill on the Pequest river, owned by Mr. John Green. They became possessed of considerable property, partly by inheritance, but principally through their own industry.

Unlike their uncle, Rev. John Rosbrugh, they sympathized with the mother country in the Revolutionary struggle. At the commencement of the conflict, fearing the consequences of the course taken by the American people, and to protect themselves from the stringent measures adopted against such sympathizers—a few which are hinted at in the foregoing pages—they sold all their property. The price was paid in Continental money, which became well-nigh worthless at the close of the war.

Robert moved South about the year, 1783, and settled, it is supposed, in North Carolina. All trace of this branch of the family has been lost by those of the connection living in the North.

John's first wife, Mary Carney, died young, September 6, 1786, leaving three children. He married, February 5, 1789, as his second wife Susanna Thatcher, granddaughter of Samuel or Elijah Thatcher, who is said to have been very wealthy and who died in the city of Philadelphia.

The old Thatcher homestead was in the Pohatcong Valley, Warren County, N. J., eight or nine miles from Easton, Pa. In the early days the Thatcher family were ardent adherents of the Methodist church, and the old homestead was long famous as a place for holding camp-meetings. A stone church and the Thatcher burial ground were near by.

The original Elijah or Samuel Thatcher had at least one son, whose name was Thomas, and whose wife's name was Susanna. Thomas and Susanna had two sons,—Thomas and Elijah and four daughters,—Sarah, Susanna, Clorinda, and a fourth whose name has not been discovered.

The tombstone inscription of Thomas Thatcher, Jr., and wife are as follows: "Sacred to the memory of Thomas Thatcher, son of Thomas and Susanna Thatcher, who departed this life April 13, 1830, in the 77th year of his age."

"Sacred to the memory of Aner Thatcher, wife of Thomas Thatcher who departed this life in August, 1845 in the 87th year of her age."

Sarah married, we believe, Garret Howel, who resided near the Delaware Water Gap. They emigrated, 1801, to Canada, where their numerous descendents now reside.

Susanna became the second wife of John Rosbrugh, a nephew of Rev. John Rosbrugh.

Clorinda died single. Her tombstone inscription is:

"In memory of Clorinda Thatcher, who departed this life January 28, 1826, in the 67th year of her age."

The fourth daughter married Andrew Kitchen, but we have learned nothing definite about the family.

Elisha married, October 25, 1796, Mary Coleman, who was born February, 1765. Tombstone inscriptions are as follows:—

"Sacred to the memory of Elisha Thatcher, who was born February 23, 1769, and departed this life, November 13, 1845, aged 76 years, 8 months, and 20 days."

"In the memory of Mary Thatcher, wife of Elisha Thatcher, who departed this life, April 28, 1843, in the 79th year of her age."

Of Samuel, who was born October 20, 1801, the inscription is as follows:

"In memory of Samuel, son of Elisha and Mary Thatcher, who died September 19, 1802, aged 11 months."

Of Aaron— "In memory of Aaron, son of Elisha and Mary Thatcher, born March 16, 1810."

Of Susanna—"Susanna, daughter of Elisha and Mary Thatcher, who departed this life August 23, 1820, aged 12 years, 4 months and 13 days."

Of Mary Ann—"In Memory of Mary Ann, daughter of Thomas and Elizabeth Thatcher who died February 19, 1830, aged 18 days.

Tradition has it that certain inducements were held out by the British authorities for persons to remove from the United States to Canada, and that it was through this that John Rosbrugh removed his family thither in 1800.

Third Generation

The three children of John Rosbrugh by his first wife, Mary Carney, were William, born February 4, 1781, settled in Waterloo County, Canada; Sarah, born June 22, 1783, married Mr. Griffin; Jane, born January 21, 1785, married Mr. Turner and settled at Erie, Pa.

The children of John Rosbrugh of the second generation, by his second wife, Susanna Thatcher were:—

Clorinda, born April 4, 1792, married Thomas Armstrong, settled in Canada; John Christie, born September 7, 1793; Thomas, born October 9, 1795, married Joanna S. Mulholland, settled in Canada; Robert, born January 14, 1797, settled in Canada; Samuel, born May 4, 1798; Abner, born July 31, 1800; Mary, born November 13, 1802, became the wife of Joseph Lyons; Susanna, born May 15, 1805 and became the wife of Hiram Hawkins, settled in Canada.

Fourth Generation

The children of William Rosbrugh of the third generation are,—William, John, Enos, Hiram, Mary Ann, Susan, Sarah, and Jane.

The children of Mr. and Mrs. Sarah Rosbrugh Griffin of the third generation are Mrs. William Buchanan. If there are others, their names have not been learned.

The children of Thomas Armstrong and Clorinda Rosbrugh are Thomas, of Pontiac, Michigan; John, of Canada; Benjamin, of Canada; Samuel, of Middleville, Michigan.

The children of Thomas and Joanna S. Mulholland Rosbrugh of the third generation are,—William of Rosbrugh's Mills, N. C.; John, M. D., Hamilton, Ontario, Canada; Abner, M. D., Toronto, Canada; Eliza, who became Mrs. Knox residing at Oakland, California; Eunice, who became Mrs. Sylvester Smith, residing in Austin, Minnesota; Mary, wife of Mr. M. C. Moe, residing at Rochester, Minnesota; Annie, wife of C. C. Wilson, residing at Rochester, Minn.; Susanna, residing at Fayetteville, N. C.

Children of Robert Rosbrugh of the third generation are,—Hiram, William, Mrs. Hill, Mrs. Collins, Mrs. McKay and Mrs. Lorilla.

Children of Samuel of the third generation are, George, Rachel, Mrs. Quackenbush, Emerson, Daniel and Mrs. Susanna Thatcher.

Children of Abner of the third generation are,—Frank and Melvin.

Children of Joseph and Mary Rosbrugh Lyons of the third generation are,—Sarah, wife of Jarvis Bronte, James, Susan, wife of Henry Englehart, John, Ellen, wife of Hector

Holmes, Jane, Harker and Elsie Ann, wife of Daniel Vaughan.

The children of Hiram and Susan Rosbrugh Hawkins of the third generation are—Hiram, of Bradford, Pa.; Joseph L. of Ottawa, Kansas, Mrs. William Fonger, Mrs. W. H. Howard, Mrs. W. H. Robinson, Mrs. Edson Marlatt.

Fifth Generation

Children of Thomas Armstrong of the fourth generation are,—Alfred, Charles, Eunice, wife of Mr. Collingswood, Pontiac, Mich., Clorinda, wife of Mr. R. Furniss of Clifton, Niagara Falls.

The children of John Armstrong of the fourth generation reside in Canada. So do the children of Benjamin Armstrong.

The surviving children of Mr. and Mrs. Eliza Rosbrugh Knox of the fourth generation are,—George W. of California; Thomas R. Oakland, Calf.

The children of Mrs. Jarvis Bronte are James, Milton, Charles, William, Mrs. M. Richardson, Mrs. Amos Cassidy, Mrs. Samuel Magill, all living in the vicinity of Hamilton, Canada.

The only child of Mrs. Sylvester Smith is Fay Smith, Austin, Minn.

Rev. John Rosbrugh

After Chaplain Rosbrugh was laid in his narrow bed, Cornwallis, when he retired to rest on the evening of the ill-fated January 2, 1777, expected an easy victory, but the next morning events proved the opposite. For Washington, seeing the swollen river behind was practically impossible in case of a retreat, planned to out-general Cornwallis by moving stealthily around to the rear of the enemy, and move on and capture the stores at New Brunswick. The plan succeeded. A few of the members of the Hays' Company kept the camp-fires burning brightly till toward dawn.

When the British commander awoke in the morning he

could see no enemy but he heard the sound of artillery in his rear. The British were not only prevented from crossing over to the Pennsylvania side of the river on their way to Philadelphia, but were unable to hold Princeton.

In this, the company which Mr. Rosbrugh led out, felt that their duty had been performed, and they accordingly left the army to return to their peaceful avocations until the necessities of the country's cause should call them again to enter the ranks with their compatriots. They reached their homes, via Bethlehem, on January 19, 1777.

Their return, whilst gladdening the hearts of many, was the beginning of sorrows for Mr. Rosbrugh's family. Though possessed of some means, before the Revolutionary struggle was concluded, the family was reduced well-nigh to destitution through the loss of their natural protector and supporter. In the depreciation of the Continental currency, the family lost heavily, but the funds intended for the relief of the distressed were not used until the family were well-nigh driven to despair.

The Provincial Assembly provided that the Committee of Associators should have the disposition of funds for the relief of families unable to maintain themselves in the absence of the providers engaged in the service of their country, yet Mrs. Rosbrugh was from time to time refused aid, though she had received an order upon the proper authorities.

Only after Mrs. Rosbrugh had petitioned His Excellency, John Dickinson and the Honorable Executive Council, did she, February 14, 1785, receive word from John Dickinson that "The case of Mrs. Roseborough and her family entitles them to such relief—— and that the overseers of the poor should certify the necessity of granting them such support."

From this source therefore she received from time to time various sums, the amount of which, up to 1789 is shown by the action of an Orphans' Court held that year.

The amount in June, 1789 was 355 pounds; for September, 1789, 156 pounds, 17 shillings and 6 pence.

John Arndt, Clerk, records that the Court had decreed

and directed an order to be drawn on John Craig, Esq., Lieutenant of the County, directing him to pay Jean Rosbrugh, the widow of the Reverend John Rosbrugh, deceased, the sum of 156 pounds, 17 shillings and six pence to be considered in full for the several allowances heretofore made her by this court to the seventeenth day of May, 1788.

Such were some of her trials consequent upon the death of her husband. She lived more than thirty-two years after his decease. Upon her tombstone there is the following inscription:—

"In memory of Jane Rosebrugh, who departed this life March 27, 1809, aged seventy years, relict of Rev. John Rosbrugh, formerly pastor of this congregation, who fell a victim to British cruelty, at Trenton, January 2, 1777."

"My flesh shall slumber in the ground
Till the last trumpet's joyful sound;
Then burst the chain with sweet surprise,
And in my Saviour's image rise."

Thus passed away the first generation, and it now behooves us to turn our attention to the descendants of Mr. Rosbrugh.

The Second Generation

Rev. John Rosbrugh's children were—James, Letitia, Mary, Sarah and John.

John was born, probably in the year 1776. He never married, and remained a resident of the Irish Settlement, Northampton County, Pa., at least down to 1810. The date of his death, it seems, is lost. Nothing definite either, appears to be known, as to the place of his burial, though tradition has it that he lies somewhere in Chester or Lancaster county, Pennsylvania.

Sarah, never married. She removed to Western New York in the latter part of the eighteenth or early part of the nineteenth century.

She died at the age of seventy-six years and lies buried near Dansville, Livingston County, New York.

Mary married Robert Ralston, her cousin, who was the son of her mother's brother John, the member of the Continental Congress. They had an only child, whom they called Christiana.

Letitia, born April 12, 1769, married Samuel Ralston, her cousin, son of her mother's brother Samuel. We believe they have no descendants. Her husband died January 11, 1795, in the twenty-fourth year of his age. She never married a second time, but removed to Western New York, whither her brother, Judge James Rosbrugh, had gone, in the latter part of the eighteenth century. After living in widowhood about fifty years she died at the advanced age of nearly ninety and was buried near Dansville, Livingston County, New York.

James, born April 24, 1767, at Mansfield Woodhouse, now Washington, Warren County, New Jersey, is the only one of Rev. John Rosbrugh's children by whom the name in his branch of the family has been preserved. He remembered the scenes in Allen Township connected with his father's raising the military company and their departure for the seat of war, and dictated these with other things, to one of his sons, before his death, by which means we have written testimony from him in regard to them.

When he had grown to manhood, he felt the need of a better education than was afforded by "The Settlement," in which he lived, and began to look around for the means of obtaining the same. He could not leave his mother with his three sisters and a young brother to go to a distant school. Consequently he must endeavor to establish a superior school in his own vicinity. It was necessary to build a house and hire a teacher. He went among his neighbors and friends and succeeded in getting the means for building a commodious stone structure, known to this day as "The Academy." An accomplished teacher was employed and the project was a success, many receiving within its academic walls such advantages in learning as before could only be had by going away from home to a distant city. Many of its scholars were fitted for usefulness—some became distinguished—among others George Wolf, the celebrated Governor of Pennsylvania. When he went to old Mr. Wolf to get a subscription for the building and teacher, and to get him to promise to send George to school, he first met with a refusal. Mr. Wolf said George had already as good an education as he had, and he had done well enough. But, said young Rosbrugh, "Don't you want to give George a chance to rise in the world? If he has an education, he may become Governor of the State." Mr. Wolf laughed at the idea of his George being Governor, but he subscribed. George went to the school and became one of its best graduates. Having studied law, he became a member of the Legislature and subsequently Governor.

October 18, 1792, James Rosbrugh married Margaret, daughter of Charles and Margaret McNair Wilson, of the Irish Settlement. Mrs. Margaret Wilson Rosbrugh was born May 15, 1768 and died January 21, 1857.

In the year 1795 the family removed to what was called the Genesee Country in Western New York, arriving at what was afterwards their home—now Groveland, Livingston County, about the fourth of July.

Mr. Rosbrugh became naturally a leader among the people, acting as the Justice of the Peace, and representing the great County of Ontario—which covered all the territory west of Cayuga bridge—in the State Legislature at Albany. During the war of 1812, he went home from Albany and raised a company among his neighbors as volunteers, was elected Captain and went with them to the frontier under proclamation of General Smith, who proposed an immediate invasion of Canada. Strange as it may seem, he here met, enlisted under the banner of the enemy, his cousin John Rosbrugh—William's son—who had visited him in his home in Western New York, twelve years before, as he journeyed with his family from New Jersey to take up his abode in Canada.

He continued to perform his legislative duties at Albany, after the war closed, and was elected a member of the Convention for the revision of the organic law of the state in 1821. When Livingston County was formed out of Ontario, he represented it in the Legislature—was one of the county judges, and also the first Surrogate, which latter office he held for many years, and which terminated his public life. He died, November 18, 1850, in Western New York.

Third Generation

Aside from Judge James Rosbrugh's children, it seems that Rev. Mr. Rosbrugh had grandchildren only through his daughter Mary, who married Robert Ralston. This daughter had an only child Christiana. She married Robert Neely. When she died, or where she was buried we have not been able to learn.

The grandchildren through Judge James Rosbrugh were as follows:—

Jane, born November 17, 1793, married William Leaming, May 25, 1819.

John, born October 28, 1795, married Mary Gohene, September 7, 1818.

Charles W., born May 22, 1798, married Maria Miles, June 6, 1821.

Hugh W., born June 15, 1800.

James Ralston, born July 24, 1803, married Christiana Kelly, February 16, 1831.

Ezra, born June 10, 1807, married Charlotte M. Bloss, February 3, 1836.

Margaretta, born June 25, 1809, married Nathaniel A. Baldwin, May 30, 1830.

Fourth Generation

The great-grandchildren of Rev. John Rosbrugh, so far as we have been able to learn their names, are as follows:—

The Neelys—If we have been correctly informed the children of Robert and Christiana Ralston Neely were as follows:—

Washington, of Findley, Hancock County, Ohio, who married Agnes Grier, the daughter of Rev. J. N. C. Grier,

D. D., of Brandywine Manor, Chester County, Pa., and whose children are Oletha, Nathan and Neander.

John, of Philadelphia.

Robert, of Brandywine Manor, Pa.

The Leamings.—The children of William and Jane Rosbrugh Leaming were:—

James R., born February 25, 1820. He is Dr. Leaming of No. 160, W. 23rd street, N. Y.

Margaret, born March 23, 1822.

Sarah, born December 1, 1824.

Letitia Ralston, born June 23, 1827.

Thomas J., born May 6. 1829.

Jane R. born March 4, 1833.

The Baldwins—The children of Nathaniel A. and Margaret Rosbrugh Baldwin,—

Martha M. born March 16, 1831.

Margaret R. born August 19, 1835.

Henry A. born September 30, 1838.

Jane R. born September 30, 1840.

The Rosbrughs—The family of John and Mary Gohene Rosbrugh of Tecumseh, Lenawee County, Michigan, were as follows:

Amanda, James, Sarah, Anna M., Charles W., Francis A., Margaret B., Patience E.

Amanda, born March 6, 1819.

James, born September 6, 1820, resided at Amboy, Lee County, Ill.

Sarah, born February 13, 1824.

Anna M. born July 13, 1826.

Charles W. born August 12, 1831.

Francis A., born May 8, 1835.

Margaret B. born May 20, 1838.

Patience E. born December 14, 1842.

The family of Charles W. and Maria Miles Rosbrugh of Freeport, Ill., were Henrietta, born September 8, 1823.

Caroline, born October, 28, 1825.

Letice R., born August 6, 1827.

Ezra, born May 1, 1835.

The family of James R. and Christiana Kelly Rosbrugh were,—

Moses K. born March 23, 1833; Studied law, married and settled in Ohio where he died.

Benjamin F. born February 9, 1835.

Daniel K. born January 31, 1840.

Christiana H. born September 12, 1847.

The family of Ezra and Charlotte M. Bloss Rosbrugh, Brighton, Monroe County, N. Y.:——

Amy Celestia, born July 15, 1837; died May 7, 1841.

Emma Jane, born August 10, 1842; died August 17, 1842.

Sarah Frances, born August 6, 1846; died July 31, 1853.

Such are the links by which the present generation are bound to the Clerical Martyr of the Revolution and the scenes connected with the dark page of American History.

THE ROSBRUGH FAMILY

(From Clyde Ms.)

Of his three daughters, Sarah, Letitia and Mary, it may be said the first, Sarah, never married, the second, Letitia, married Samuel Ralston, who died at the early age of twenty-four years. She never married again but removed to Western New York, whither her brother, Judge James Rosbrugh, removed in 1796. After living in widowhood about fifty years, she died at the advanced age of nearly ninety and was buried near Dansville, Livingston County, New York.

The third, Mary, married Robert Ralston, whose only child, Christiana, we believe, became the wife of Robert Neely, of Chester County, Pa.

Of his sons, James and John, the former only, left descendents, the latter dying single. There still remains in the Craig Settlement a monument of James Rosbrugh's energy and consideration for the welfare of the community. The "Old Academy," erected in 1785, in which some of our forefathers for so many years studied, and subsequent to 1813 worshipped, sitting upon the hardest of pine benches, still stands, though dismantled and devoted to humbler uses.

The late James McKeen, of Easton, and the writer's father went to school together there. To James Rosbrugh perhaps more than to any other was the community indebted for the erection of this building.

In his undertaking, it is said, he called upon a German by the name of George Wolf for aid, but was refused at first, though Mr. Wolf afterwards helped to build the academy. But in the course of the conversation, Mr. Rosbrugh told him that his sons, George and Philip, would have the advantage of an education, and that his son, George, might be Governor of the State some day. The sequel of the matter was that George Wolf got his English education in the Old Academy, and after his election as Governor of the State, it all came to the mind of Mr. Rosbrugh, who took pride in telling it.

A significant fact is that Governor Wolf is recognized as being the Father of the Pennsylvania Public School System. At the High School building on Second Street, Easton, Penna., there has been erected a memorial to Governor Wolf.

On October 18, 1792, James Ralston was married to Margaret, daughter of Charles and Margaret McNair Wilson. Their first child, a daughter, Jane, was one-year-and-a-half old when the young family, with all their effects started for the "Genesee Country," as Western New York was then called—the "El Dorado" of those seeking new homes in the wilderness. They moved in covered wagons, driving their herds and flocks with them, encamping wherever night overtook them as they journeyed through the almost trackless wilderness. After some weeks they arrived at their destination, the Genesee Valley, which extends from Lake Ontario about sixty miles southward.

Mr. Rosbrugh was the first white settler in Groveland Hill but there was a flourishing village at Williamsburg, founded by Colonel Williamson; the Wadsworth brothers were at Big Tree, now Genesee, and these were his white neighbors. Soon others came in and villages sprang up as by magic.

Mr. Rosbrugh became a leader among them naturally. He was the local Justice of the Peace, and he represented the great County of Ontario, which covered all the territory west of Cayuga bridge—in the legislature at Albany.

During the War of 1812, he went home from Albany and raised a company of his neighbors as volunteers; was elected Captain, and went with them to the frontier under the proclamation of General Smith, who proposed an immediate invasion of Canada.

Mr. Rosbrugh continued his legislative duties at Albany after the war had closed, and was elected a member of the Committee for the revision of the organic law of the State of New York in 1821.

When Livingston County was formed out of Ontario, Mr. Rosbrugh represented it in the Legislature; was one of the County judges and also first Surrogate, which office he held for many years, and this terminated his public life.

Evenly and happily his life wore on until November 18, 1850, when he passed to a better life.

Mrs. Rosbrugh survived him a few years, even coming back to the Craig Settlement in Northampton County to visit her aged brother John Wilson.

———————— Rote married ———————— Brown, a descendant of Samuel Brown.

———————— Russel married Lavinia Kerr, a descendant of James Kerr.

Rev. Robert Russel, sixth pastor of Settlement church. See sketch in Clyde's "Irish Settlement." He was in his seventieth year when he died. He married Margaret Armstrong, a descendant of Thomas Armstrong. She died April 10, 1824. Their children were,—Thomas Boyd, died February 5, 1827 in his twenty-fourth year; Susan, died March 10, 1862 in her sixty-fourth year; Sarah; Robert, both died without descendants.

Alexander Scott married Ellen Hemphill, a descendant of Moses Hemphill. Their children were Amelia, married Franklin Lafever; Mary, married William Line; Thomas; James, and Alexander.

William Scott married Jennie Allison.

William G. Scott married Nancy Lattimer, a descendant of Robert Lattimer.

Their children were,—Jane Walker, died September 6, 1836 in her second year; Sarah, married William G. Case; Mary, married ——— Gerhart; Louis, married ——— Reed; daughter married Dr. Pursell; Anna Eliza, and William Lattimer.

——— Sharp married Mary Wilson, a descendant of Hugh Wilson.

Robert Sharp married Margaret Boyd, a descendant of John Boyd. There is one known child—Thomas Sharp of Newville, Cumberland County, Pa.

——— Sheldon married Mary Kerr, a descendant of James Kerr.

——— Shelmire married a descendant of James Horner.

Isaac Speer married Ann Hudders, a descendant of Michael Clyde through John Hudders.

Samuel Stewart married Mary Kerr, a descendant of James Kerr.

Alexander Stewart married Mary Ann Grier, a descendant of John Hays through John Grier. They have one son, who is married and has a family.

Charles Stewart, probably a descendant of Samuel Stewart, was married to Mary Kerr, a descendant of James Kerr.

Patrick Stewart was early identified with the Settlement. William and Robert Stewart are supposed to be descendants.

James Taylor married Frances Ralston, a descendant of James Ralston.

Nathaniel J. Taylor resided on the Lehigh River above Catasauqua.

Dr. N. G. Thompson married Agnes McClure a descendant of John Hays through John Grier and William W. McClure.

James Thompson married Isabella Hays, a descendant of John Hays. They have a family.

———— Van Zant married a descendant of James Horner.

James Vleit married as his first wife Esther Horner, widow of James H. Horner, descendant from James Horner. Her maiden name was Esther Clendinen, a descendant of Adam Clendinen.

Rev. Eleazer Wales was the first preacher of the Settlement church—See sketch in Clyde's "Irish Settlement."

The Walker Family of Pennsylvania

Among the Ulster Scotts who settled on the Neshaminy in Warrington Township, Bucks Co., between 1720 and 1725, was William Walker and Ann, his wife, with children, John, Robert, Richard, Christiana and her husband John McNair, Mary Ann, and her husband, James King.

Of these John Walker, John McNair and James King removed to Bath, now Northampton Co., and formed the Craig's Settlement there.

William the Elder died in Warrington, Bucks Co., 1738 aged 66 years, and his wife Ann died there 1750 aged 70 years. Both are buried in Neshaminy Church yard.

John, the youngest son, born in Ireland about 1717, came to Bucks Co., Pa., with his parents about 1724, and removed to Northampton Co., about 1752. He married Mary Ann Blackburn, born 1717.

John Walker was a prominent man in the affairs of Northampton County during the Colonial times, a soldier in the Provincial forces during the French and Indian War, and was an Associator at the outbreak of the Revolution. He died June 7, 1777; his wife died April 14, 1773. Children:

William, born 1746 died 1804. Jane married Aug. 13,

1771, Capt. John Hays, whose first wife was her cousin, Barbara King, daughter of James and Mary Ann (Walker) King. Ann born 1750, died 1826, married Col. Joseph Grier, of Bucks Co. Mary Ann married Robert Lattimore. John Jr., married Mary Darrah.

Ref: Pennsylvania Colonial and Revolutionary Families pp. 1212-1213.

Service of James King: Officers of two Regiments, New Castle Co., Pa., 1747-8: John Vance, Captain; James King, Lieutenant; Samuel Alricks, Ensign.

Ref: Pa. Archives, 2nd Series, 5th Series, 1:27.

No Colonial Dames Services so far found for John Walker. I cannot verify the above statement that John Walker was an officer in French and Indian War.

(Signed) Eleanor M. Bamford.
July 1, 1920.

Robert Walker was married to Mary Ann Blackburn who died April 14, 1773 in her fifty-sixth year. He died in February 1758. Their children were,—John who married Mary, died June 15, 1793, in her thirty-third year. Their children were Thomas, died June 4, 1871, husband of Jane Ralston died November 22, 1827; Mary Ann died single, May 16, 1862, aged about 65 years.

John Walker, probably a brother of Robert Walker, died June 7, 1777 in his sixty-first year. Rev. Richard Walker of Allentown may be a descendant.

Charles Warman, a collector of the Settlement church, and the family by the same name were not descendants from the early Settlement families.

Hiram B. Warner married Harriet Horner, a descendant of James Horner.

Joseph Weaver, late of Bethlehem, was married to Mary Hemphill, a descendant of Moses Hemphill.

John Weidner, died May 13, 1821.

Michael Weitzel married Jane Humphrey, a descendant of Dr. Edward Humphrey. Their children were Sarah Jane, died February 25, 1850 in her sixth year; Elizabeth and Edward.

John Wells, M. D., married Agnes Ralston, a descendant of James Ralston. Their children were John, Franklin, Harrie, Taylor and Agnes.

Dr. Wesselhoeft married Sarah Palmer, a descendant of George Palmer. They had a son Robert Palmer who is buried in the Settlement church graveyard.

David West married Sarah Jane Forest, a descendant of John Hays, through John Grier and Thomas Forest. They have three sons and three daughters.

James Whiteside, native of Ireland, died April 18, 1823, aged 43 years. His wife———died in September, 1823. Their descendants are scattered.

Joseph Wilver married Elizabeth Horner, a descendant of James Horner.

Wilson

Alexander Wilson was collector of salary in the Settlement church in 1804.

Hugh Wilson was appointed Justice of the Peace of Northampton County, June 9, 1756. He was born in Ireland, 1689, died in the Settlement in 1773 in his eighty-fourth year. He married Sarah Craig in Ireland and were among the earliest of the settlers in the Irish Settlement. Their children were—Samuel, whose children were Hugh, born in 1761 and died November 30, 1830 in his seventieth year. Married Elizabeth Osman. Abram, died January 30, 1840 in his seventy-fifth year—married Mary Young. Their children were Samuel, Hugh Osman, John, Eliza Ann and infant. Thomas and Samuel died single; Sarah married ——— Mulhallon; Abigail married ——— Dual; Mary married ——— Sharp; Elizabeth married ——— Winters.

Charles, second son of Hugh and Sarah Craig Wilson, born 1726, died August 20, 1768 in his forty-second year. Married Margaret McNair, born 1728 and died November 25, 1823 in her ninety-fifth year. Their children were,—Sarah, born, 1757, died December, 1778 in her twenty-first year; Hugh, married; Christiana, married William Lattimer; John, born 1766 and died January 1, 1857 in his ninety-first year, married Ann Hays,—born August 9, 1772, died January 8, 1851 in her eightieth year,—children were,—Charles, married Catharine Miller—Children, Anna—married Rev. John Barret; Mary Jane; Charles—married and has a family; Margaret; Samuel; Elizabeth; John Alexander and Robert Steele, died July 20, 1843. Jane died, October 18, 1826; William McNair, born July 18, 1806, died January 18, 1851, married Jane Britain, no descendants; Margaret married Joseph Horner, a descendant of Joseph Horner; John H. married as his first wife Eliza Ann Hudders. As his second wife, he married Mary Ann Hays. They have one daughter Annie; Mary Ann, married Rev. Leslie Irwin.

Francis died single; of James nothing is known.

Thomas the fifth child of Hugh and Sarah Craig Wilson, married Elizabeth Hays—a son, Thomas, married Nancy Hemphill who had children—James, John, Thomas, Joseph—was Col. Wilson of the Union army, Craig, Franklin, William, Nancy, Jane, Mary Ann, Eliza—married Rev. Francis McHenry. Margaret—married William McNair, and Elizabeth married William Craig. (The original Wilson homestead lay northwest of what is now Howertown. Hugh Wilson was possessed of nearly seven hundred acres of land in that locality.)

There was a Mary S. Wilson who died February 3, 1828, but her connection can not be traced.

Another Wilson family incidentally connected with the Settlement was composed of the following members,—Mary, Sarah, Esther—married Samuel Abernethy; Elizabeth—married Hugh Horner, a descendant of James Horner; James—married Ann Allison, a sister to Sarah Allison, who married Joseph Horner.

——————— Winters married Elizabeth Wilson, a descendant of Hugh Wilson.

Wolf

George Wolf was born in what is now East Allen Township in August 12, 1777. He received his English education at the Academy on the Monoquacy Creek in the Settlement about a mile below Bath. He studied law with John Ross, Esq., of Easton, Pa., and was elected to the State Legislature in 1814. He represented his district in Congress from 1824-29, and was Governor of the State from 1829-1835. Died March 11, 1840.

The father, George Wolf, at first refused to contribute towards the erection of the Academy but after some consideration of its value to his sons George and Philip, he not only contributed but also assisted in its erection. The father saw his sons attending the Academy, and one of them Governor of Pennsylvania.

Archibald Woodside married Margaret Hudders. Their children were Mary, Amanda, William and three others who died in infancy.

Peter Wyckoff married Eliza Brown. They had one child, a son, who died in childhood.

Sir William Young was an Ulster Baronet. He had only one child, a daughter, Elizabeth, who married John Boyd.

THE SCOTCH-IRISH IN THE REVOLUTION

AFTER the defeat of the Americans on Long Island, in November, 1776, Washington and his forces retreated through New Jersey to Pennsylvania. From his headquarters in Bucks County, under date of December 22, 1776, the General writes to Col. John Siegfried, of Allen township, as follows:—

'Sir: The council of safety of this state, by their resolves of the 17th inst., empowered me to call out the militia of Northampton County to the assistance of the Continental army, that by our joint endeavors, we may put a stop to the progress of the enemy, who are making preparations to advance to Philadelphia as soon as they cross the Delaware, either by boats or on the ice. As I am unacquainted with the colonels of the militia, I have taken the liberty to enclose you six letters, in which you will please insert the names of the proper officers, and send them immediately to them, by persons in whom you can confide for their delivery. If there are not as many colonels as letters you may destroy the balance not wanted.

'I earnestly entreat those who are so far lost to a love of country as to refuse to lend a hand to its support at this time, they depend upon being treated as their baseness and want of public spirit will most justly deserve.

'I am your most obedient servant,

George Washington'.

"A number of companies of militia of the county, upon this requisition, immediately marched and were engaged in the battles of Trenton, Brandywine, and Germantown. One of the earliest of those to take the field was a company Captain Hays enlisted in the Craig Settlement in Allen Township. The Rev. John Rosbrugh, their pastor, accompanied the patriots of his flock in the capacity of chaplain, and with them reported for duty on the banks of the Delaware, near Coryell's ferry, Bucks County. Having taken part in the capture of the Hessians at Trenton, the first action in which they participated, the next morning, Mr. Rosbrugh, while in a farm-house near the village of Pennington, was surprised by a scouting party of British horse, and cruelly put to death. He lies buried in the graveyard of the Old Trenton First Church." Page 976, Egle's History.

"In the Revolutionary War the Scotch-Irish of Northampton were among the first to take up arms in defense of their adopted country's liberties, and Captain Hays' Company saw service at the Battle of Long Island (?) and at Trenton. General Robert Brown and General Thomas Craig, both officers in the Continental army, were natives of the Irish Settlement." Page 988, Egle's History.

Most of the Northampton troops, says Ellis, which were in the field, took part in the battles of Trenton and Princeton. The Rev. Mr. Rosbrugh, a Presbyterian clergyman of the Irish-Settlement, in Allen township, lost his life in the first engagement. Intensely brave and patriotic, he knew that the Commander-in-Chief had need of men, and that was sufficient to show him that it was his duty to heed his country's call, and to come up to her help against the mighty. He took the most active part and the liveliest interest in the organization of Captain Hays' Company, which was raised, at a fews hours' notice among the liberty-loving covenanters of the Irish settlements, and, doffing the sacred vestments, he shouldered his musket, and, with unfaltering faith, advanced into the field of battle, where God had mustered the hosts for war.

"The company of Captain Hays, after Trenton and Princeton did not enter into winter quarters with the army in New Jersey, but returned to their homes for the time passing through Bethlehem on the 19th of January. This was not on their part a retirement from service, but they simply took winter quarters at home in the bosom of their families, instead of the comfortless cantonments at Morrisburg, for they could at two days' notice, rejoin their companions in arms when the return of spring should place the army of Washington again in the field. Page 59, Ellis History.

The following is a list of Captain Rundio's Company from Northampton County which fought in the battles of Long Island, Fort Washington, and in which General Robert Brown was their First Lieutenant:

"Robert McFerren, William Young, Philip Burwin, Jacob Holser, Samuel Jones, Samuel McFadden, Adam Sly, Daniel Murray, John Handelong, Samuel Been, Pharo McGee, Conrad Waltman, Jacob C. ———, Michael ———, George Marsh, Melchior ———, John Hunter, George Beelign, Jacob Warner, John France, Jacob Hance, Jacob Nyhart, Michael Longbrich, John Galloway, Isaac Shimer, John McGee, Robert Miller, James Grim, Benjamin Schwartzwood, Patrick White, Peter Zink, Conrad Becker, John Boyd, John Dull, John Christian, Jacob Moritz, John Dieffenderfer, Ned Lafferty, Michael Clase, Lundovic Moser, Jacob Strole, Peter Longberich, William Weals."

Some of these will be recognized as Scotch-Irish origin, and the Boyds and others perhaps members of the same families as those inserted in the genealogies.

The following will show how General Brown, together with his men, was made a prisoner of war at the surrender of Fort Washington:

"Nov. 15, 1776, General Howe sent a flag demanding the surrender of Fort Washington, or all to be put to the sword—an answer to be returned in two hours."

Col. McGraw, commanding on the Island, having called the Field officers together, a council was held, and it was unanimously agreed to return for answer that we were determined to hold the Fort to the last extremity, and to rely on General Howe's clemency in being put to the sword.

"Nov. 16th an attack having begun early in the morning, continued until about 3 o'clock in the afternoon, whom (when) the Hessians, being in possession of the hill on the north, the British, Scotch and Hessians on the east and the south, General Howe sent a second flag with the following summons,—

"The Commander-in-Chief demands an immediate and categorical answer to his second summons of Fort Washington. The garrison must immediately surrender prisoners of war and give up their arms and ammunitions and stores of every kind, and send two Field officers to these quarters, as hostages. In so doing, the General is pleased to allow the garrison to keep possession of their baggage and the officers to have their swords.

"Agreed to: J. Patterson, adjutant General; Robert McGraw, Col. of the Fifth Pennsylvania Battalion, Commanding at Fort Washington."

The following list will show who died in imprisonment from General Brown's company, December, 1776:

John Christian, Dec. 25; Jacob Moritz, 28th; John Dieffenderfer, 29th; Benjamin Swartwood, Jan. 30, 1777; Ned Lafferty, do 4th; Pharo McGee, do 9th; Jacob Warner, do 9th; John Handelong, do 11th; Isaac Shimer, do 14th.

Signed, John McDowell, Ensign, 30th.

Endorsed: A list of Captain Rundio's Company, by Andrew Boyd.

The following is General Brown's parole to the British General, Clinton.

"We whose names are hereunder written do pledge our faith and Honor to General Clinton that we will not depart from ye house we are plaised in by the Commisary of Prisoners; nor go beyond the Bounds Prescribed by him, and farther that we will not do or say anything contrary to the Interest of his Majesty or his government.

Robert Brown.

"On Board ye ship Judith, December 10, 1777," p. 275.

Under date of October 20, 1875, General Robert S. Brown of Bethlehem, Pa., grandson of General Robert Brown of the Revolution in speaking of these privations, says:—

The Brown family of the Settlement, are Scotch-Irish Covenanters, who fled the old country from the persecutions of Cromwell.

"Though possessed of a large landed estate in Northampton County, Samuel Brown, the ancestor, compelled all his sons to learn and serve regular apprenticeship to trades upon the plea that he did not know but what they might want them some day. Professional men these days were few and far between—in the Revolution they were patriots."

"The Flying Camp, the elite of Washington's army were officered by men from the Settlement, of whom my grandfather was one. When Washington was driven out of New York, this force was put into Fort Washington with orders to hold it to the last extremity—it was the forlorn hope. After fighting from sunrise to sunset—their ammunition being all expended—being surrounded by ten thousand Hessians and English, and after giving them the clubbing of all their guns, they surrendered. It was an alday fight by two thousand against ten thousand.

"Those that survived were put into an enclosure, and for three days and four nights got nothing to eat or drink. From their exposure, sickness and starvation, they died like sheep in the shambles. On the fourth day, a mess of men, composed of six, received a handful of worm-eaten crackers.

"Some time after this the officers were paroled. General Brown, being master of a trade, worked at that, and with the proceeds bought bread for his men and thus saved many a life. This fact the veterans were not slow in giving publicity to, and it gave him such a hold upon them and the community, that it served as a carte blanche from them to him during his life and he was continued by them, against his wishes in public life to near the end of his days.

"General Robert Brown, a prominent citizen of what was at present East Allen Township, was a Lieutenant in Colonel McGaw's Regiment, Flying Camp, and was captured at the surrender of Fort Washington, November 16, 1776. There he and his companions fought for forty-eight hours, without food or water, and when completely exhausted and when their ammunition was gone they surrendered, but not before. They were then driven like cattle to a church, fitted up for a prison in New York."

"Of the two thousand soldiers, closed in that one building, two or three hundred died, and were dragged out, many of them still breathing, while being taken for burial. A handful of wormy crackers were given to each man several hours after they had been shut up."

"Robert Brown was let out on parole, with some others of the officers, after being incarcerated in that loathsome place for three days. After this he was confined in New York and received supplies from Mr. Pintard and from Commissary-General Skinner."

He was exchanged at Elizabethtown, January 25, 1781, and returned to his home in Northampton County. The title of General he received from holding that office in the militia. His old commissions from Gov. Findley and McKean are very antique looking papers. He was elected to the first Senate of Pennsylvania and represented the county in the legislature from 1783-1787. He was in 1796 sent as a representative to Congress, in which office he remained for eighteen years in succession, when he finally positively refused to allow his name to be used again, on account of old age, and bodily infirmaties, Thomas J. Rodgers of Easton was his successor.

His valedictory address, to his constituents in 1812, was excellent and might well be patterned after, by many public men of our day, whose advantages of education have been much greater than were his.

"Robert Brown's correspondents were among the first men in the nation:—Such as Samuel Sitgreaves, Easton; Albert Gallatin and Colonel Rohn of Virginia; Henry Clay, John Calhoun, Richard M. Johnson and many other political men; then there were Bishop White and his brother John White; there are letters to him from all these. When Mr. Sitgreaves was a member of the Convention to form the first Constitution of this State, he wrote to General Brown, almost every day to keep him informed as to the progress of the debates." Page 240, Ellis.

Scotch-Irish Soldiers of the American Revolution from Allen Township.

[Compiled by Asa K. McIlhaney]

Gen.—Thomas Craig
    Robert Brown
Lieut.—Timothy Reed
    Wm. Caruthers
    John Reed
Chaplain—Rev. John Rosbrough
Capt.—John Craig
    Neigal Gray
    John Ralston
    Wm. Craig
    Samuel Craig
    Andrew Clendenin
    Robert Harp
Major—James Boyd
Surgeon—Matthew McHenry
Private—Arthur Lattimore
    Samuel Wilson
    James Hemphill
    Robert Craig
    Daniel Black
    Hugh Horner
    John Sterling
    William Lattimore
    Abraham Wilson
    Joseph Horner
    James Horner
    Mark Sterling
    Daniel McGinnis
    Edward McGinnis
    James Brown
    James Kerr
    Thomas Horner
    James Clyde
Private—John Hays, Jr.
    Thomas Herron
    John Brown
    Robt. Lattimore
    John McNair, Sr.
    George Gray
    Hugh Wilson—(Son of Thomas)
    Robt. Brown
    John Gray
    Wm. Kerr
    Timothy Rodgers
    Moses Campbell
    John Clyde
    Robt. McNealy
    Hugh Wilson—(Son of Charles)
    Hugh Wilson (Son of Samuel)
    Samuel Ralston
    Joseph Chambers
    Thomas Campbell
    John McNair, Jr.
    Thomas Boyd
    James Allison
    Robt. McFerron
    John Walker
    Alexander Boyd
    Wm. Congleton
    James Lattimore
    Wm. Moffit
    John Currie
Ensign—Thomas Horner
Adj.—Thomas Boyd

From: "Penna. Archives," Fifth Series, Vol. 8.

DISTINGUISHED MEN OF THE SETTLEMENT

Paper by John D. Weaver—a Native of Weaversville, Pa.

Read at the meeting of the Society

THE object of this paper is not to delve minutely into the past associations of the neighborhood, but rather to advocate making well-known what is little known concerning the heroism of the men who lived in these parts prior to, during and after, the Revolutionary War. Allow me to assure you that distinguished personages in this great nation-creating event hailed from the country round about today's meeting place, but even right here on their home ground only a small number of the inhabitants of the present time are able to mention the names of the Generals, the Captains and Colonial Delegates from these surroundings who fought on the battlefields or deliberated in legislative halls in a united effort to sever the yoke that held them as vassals of foreign kings and potentates. Instilling the names and deeds of these valorous Northampton county soldiers and statesmen in the minds of home people and the country at large is what I advocate. To do so is a patriotic duty. It is a labor of love for patriots to champion and a work that historians can proudly record. The zeal of these men made us; to the impregnable future we cast the hope that the fame justly due them will be recognized.

Ladies and gentlemen, inspiring deeds occurred in this immediate locality, but the trackless past and the inertia of the average citizen have deprived these parts of your county of much of its rightful heritage. During the Revolutionary war the very arteries of the Nation extended to and vibrated in unison with this community. Valor and patriotism verily permeated the air of it. Centering at and around the spot on which you are gathered today, no other ten-mile strip of country in all America supplied, proportionately, as many men and officers in the contest of 1776 as did this section of Northampton county. Were the sleeping patriots in yonder cemetery to appear at present and relate the sacrifices they made in behalf of freedom, Allen and East Allen townships would immediately be elevated to towering heights. The swarthy Pennsylvania German and the alert Scotch-Irish from roundabout here emblazoned the Revolutionary firmament and rendered effective service to the then hardpressed, struggling Colony. These men did more to found our Nation than is accorded them by the modern press and the fact-passing public, but it is nevertheless the opinion of the writer of these words that, were records to be readjusted and the truth made known, the pages of history would rightly illumine the Pennsylvania German and the Scot and dim the prominence and credit thrust upon New England. As an example of the heraldry of the men from this section, I will briefly point to one— Rev. John Rosbrugh, pastor of the old Presbyterian Church, a mile from this spot, at the time the Revolutionary War was raging. Closing his Bible and going to the front with many members of his congregation, he proceeded to Trenton and there, on Jan. 2, 1777, died—a victim of "British cruelty," as carved in marble in the old Presbyterian Church cemetery near Weaversville. Men from this threshold of infant Americanism died for their country and their faith in it, but their memory is unsung and unhonored by the country at large. Right over there, only three short miles from here, another illustrious son of Northampton county—Gov. George Wolf— came into this life, in 1777, but his achievements no longer diffuse conversation, nor the printed page. George Wolf, Congressman, Comptroller of the United States Treasury and Governor of this State, was the father of Pennsylvania's free school system, and as such we owe to him, educationally, all that we are. Men of this calibre should be permanently honored—and not forgotten.

An active subject for discussion at today's meeting of the Northampton County Historical Society would be devising means to permanently attest the memory and accomplishments of her famous sons. Without doubt these parts have supplied their share. Descendents from the Pennsylvania German-Scotch-Irish stock hereabouts include one of the world's most prominent men, ex-President Theodore Roosevelt, a direct descendent of Daniel Craig, of the original Scotch-Irish who settled on lands between Weaversville and Bath in 1728. Simon Cameron, United States Senator and Secretary of War during Lincoln's first term as President; Jeremiah Black, celebrated Judge; Edwin Forrest, famous actor; the Hon. Henry Lattimore, United States Minister to Germany; Gen. Robt. Brown of Bethlehem, and the Hon. Andrew Reeder of Easton, born in 1807 of a Pennsylvania German mother, are among other stalwarts whose ancestors lived and died on the historic soil on which this meeting is being held today.

The Great Benjamin Franklin On The Spot Where You Are Gathered This Day.

While the incident may be known to members of the Northampton County Historical Society, I will take occasion to reiterate and impart family lore handed down from generation to generation in connection with the over-night stay made by the great Benjamin Franklin on the very spot where you are now assembled. Franklin, the recognized genius of his time, was the Postmaster-General of the English colonies in 1756. As such he came here in the interest of post roads, post offices and the postal service in Northampton county and beyond. When he came here he was accompanied by his little daughter Sally, who, as the story goes, rode on a saddle horse and the father in a light carriage. On reaching this point, darkness overtook them and so remained here over night with John Hays, a prominent man, who owned and lived in the dormer-windowed stone house that at that time stood on the present site of the Weaversville Hotel. In that old house, standing right here on this venerated ground, Franklin was the guest of and enjoyed the hospitality of John Hays. The next morning, after breakfast, the Postmaster-General wandered around the home of his host, plucked a few flowers, and then with Sally continued his circuit of inspection. After leaving it was said that a "more satisfactory" arrangement had been made at Bethlehem whereby the inhabitants of this section would be given "improved" postal service. (This meant one mail a week instead of one every other week!)

Relative to Benjamin Franklin ever having been in Weaversville, considerable doubt and surprise is expressed nowadays, but to dispel this doubt and authenticate the fact the statement will be made that Mrs. Michael Weaver (nee Magdalene Fatzinger), wife of the founder of Weaversville, was a little girl eight years of age when the Hays family still lived in the old homestead and, having frequently gone there, throughout her life she often told her relatives and friends the incident (as related to her by the Hays) of Franklin's visit with them. Years later Mrs. Weaver personally informed her grandson, William T. Weaver, of the famous Franklin's sojourn at Weaversville, and subsequently William T. Weaver conveyed the information to his son, John D. Weaver, the writer of this sketch.

When John Hays died, Michael Weaver, son of John Weaver, living on a large farm near the old Presbyterian Church, purchased the Hays property. Magdalene Fatzinger, the little girl friend of the Hays family, became the wife of Michael Weaver and together they lived in the house where Franklin stopped, Mrs. Weaver, who survived her husband, having resided therein for a period of sixty years. To her family and interested persons she pointed out the very room, as told to her, that Franklin occupied the night he was there in 1756. Thus little doubt can be entertained that America's leading citizen, Benjamin Franklin, patriot, philosopher, diplomat, scientist, Governor of Pennsylvania, member of the Constitutional Convention, Signer of the Declaration of Independence, thinker, author, editor, printer, tallow-chandler, and one of very few men in all history who had genius and common sense combined in the same personality, tarried in Weaversville—on the appropriate spot where Northampton

Facsimile of Deed to Hugh Horner, 1786, Tenth Year of Our Independence, Signed by His Excellency, Benjamin Franklin, Esq., President of the Supreme Executive Council. (See page 37.)
I. Beginning.

Facsimile of Deed to Hugh Horner, 1786, Tenth Year of Our Independence, Signed by His Excellency, Benjamin Franklin, Esq., President of the Supreme Executive Council.

county's historians of the present are gathered together today. Of the above enumerated appellations given to one of the foremost Americans of the past and present, Franklin preferred to be referred to as "Printer." In proof of this statement it will be said that among his papers one was discovered after his death, in 1790, directing that the following simple words should be used in designating his last resting place: "The body of Benjamin Franklin, Printer, lies here."

As to what became of the old house that sheltered the great printer at Weaversville, the information is herewith given that in 1859 Samuel Weaver, son of Michael, razed it to the ground and erected on its site what was then said to have been the largest private brick residence in Northampton county. The structure is now the Weaversville Hotel. An almost exact duplicate of the old Hays house can be seen at the road corner (opposite the former Weaversville Academy building) a few hundred yards up the hill from the hotel.

My paper has exceeded limitations and expectations, but let me yet suggest that the Northampton County Historical Society inaugurate a movement to erect a monument at Weaversville commemorating the wonderful Franklin and his visit there. This would not only be a tribute to the chivalrous man, but also a monument to the honor and credit of the Northampton County Historical Society.

DISTINGUISHED MEN OF THE SETTLEMENT

[Dr. J. C. Clyde]

"We cannot pause, 'tis not for human will
  To check the pen or shun its solemn trust;
But living souls discerning good and ill,
  May leave their records beautiful and just."

THE Province of Pennsylvania was granted by the Crown to William Penn in 1681. At William Penn's death in 1718, his sons, John, Thomas and Richard, became the proprietors. On the 18th of May, 1732, by a joint warrant of the Proprietaries made at London, the Surveyor General was directed to lay off a tract of five thousand acres for the personal use of Thomas Penn. This was done and it included lands which had been occupied by at least some of the families who originated the Craig Settlement, as transfer deeds show.

The warrant for these five thousand acres was immediately transferred to Joseph Turner, of Philadelphia, and by him to William Allen in 1735. William Allen deeded part of this tract to James Craig in 1743, he being one of the first settlers.

From this it appears there were no surveys until 1732. But the first settlers were on the ground previous to this time. The records of the Synod of Philadelphia seemed to show that the Elder Thomas Craig represented the church of the Craig Settlement in the Synod 1731. The Scotch-Irish were here, therefore, previous to this date, and family records show us that that they came and squatted upon the unoccupied land in 1728. Of this, Dr. Egle, in his history of Pennsylvania says:—

"The Proprietary Land Office having been closed from 1718 to the year 1732, during the minorities of Richard and Thomas Penn, emigrants seated themselves without title on such vacant lands as they found convenient. The number of settlers, of this kind, entitled them to consideration. Their rights accruing by priority of settlement were recognized by the public and passed with their improvements through many hands in confidence that they would receive the Proprietary sanction.

"Much agitation was produced when the Provincial Proclamation required all who had not obtained and paid for warrants to pay to the Receiver General within four months, the survey due for their lands under the penalty of ejectment. As a consequence great difficulties arose. The Assembly sought to compromise the matter, payment for the purchase money being postponed for several years longer."

The names associated with the earliest history of the Craig Settlement and whose memories reach even to the present day, were William Allen, Thomas and James Craig, John Boyd, Hugh Wilson, James Horner, Joseph Horner, Thomas Armstrong, Robert Gregg, John Hays, James Kerr, James King, Arthur and Robert Lattimer, John McNair, James Ralston, John and Robert Walker.

HONORABLE WILLIAM ALLEN

William Allen, who became Chief Justice of Pennsylvania in 1750—a portrait of whom may be seen in Independence Hall, Philadelphia,—we believe, was associated with the Penn family. His daughter, Ann, became the wife of Governor John Penn. Through his intimacy he became possessed of large tracts of land, and among others the five thousand acres already referred to. Branches of the family have remained near the Craig Settlement to within a comparatively recent period, as in the case of the Greenleafs of Allentown, whose old home, we believe, is now or was recently occupied by the late Judge Albright. The name of Allen Township and Allentown is in perpetuation of his name.

THOMAS ARMSTRONG

Of Thomas Armstrong, the History of Northampton County, published in 1877 says:—

Thomas Armstrong's residence was on land now owned by Samuel Koehler, in Lehigh County, near Catasauqua. He was commissioned coroner October 4, 1755, and was an elder in the Presbyterian congregation as the following certificate will show:—

"The bearer, James Young, hath lived in the congregation for several years and always behaved himself soberly and honestly, and now, at the time of his removal from us, is a single person, free from all public scandal, known to us, is certified at the Forks of the Delaware, this fourth day of August 1752. Thomas Armstrong, Elder."

His daughter, Margaret, became the wife of Rev. Robert Russel, who was pastor of the Settlement Church from 1798 to 1827. A portrait of Mr. Russel is still extant within the bounds of the Craig Settlement.

Rev. Richard Webster in Rupp's history, says Mr. Armstrong removed to Fagg's Manor, Chester County, Pennsylvania.

ROBERT GREGG

One of the first three commissioners of Northampton County was Robert Gregg. He also was on the first grand jury. He died March 9, 1756, in his fortieth year. His daughter, Margaret, married Dr. Matthew McHenry, who was appointed surgeon on board the Provincial Ship Montgomery, April 13, 1776, whose father was Rev. Francis McHenry, pastor at the Forks of Neshaminy and Deep Run, Bucks County, in 1738, and whose mother was Mary, daughter of the original Hugh Wilson, of the Craig Settlement.

THE CRAIGS

Of the Craigs there seem to have been two brothers, Thomas and James, and a sister Jane. Thomas seems to have been an elder in the church. Benjamin Franklin, writing to Governor Morris, speaks of Elder Craig from the Irish Settlement.

Among the elders present at the meeting of the Synod of Philadelphia, September 15, 1731, was Thomas Craig. We suppose the Thomas Craig of the Craig Settlement was the one referred to.

He was one of the original Commissioners appointed at the erection of Northampton County 1752, to purchase the site and erect the court-house and jail at Easton. He was one of the first justices of the County.

He was the owner of more than five hundred acres of land, granted him by Caspar Wister, March 28, 1739. His residence was on the farm owned by Dr. H. H. Riegel. In June 1773, he deeded one hundred and fifty-five acres to Andrew Hagenbuch of Berks County.

General Thomas Craig and John Craig were sons of Thomas Craig, and both served as officers during the Revolutionary War. The former served as Colonel of the Third Pennsylvania Regiment, and as Brigadier General * * * *.

He died in Allentown, Lehigh County, January 20, 1832, when upward of ninety-two years of age and was buried with military and Masonic honors.

John Craig was commissioned December 2, 1778, and served as a Captain in the Fourth Regiment, Pennsylvania Light Dragoons, and was pronounced by General Washington, the best horseman in the army. From 1793 to 1796, he was Sheriff of Northampton County.

The first James Craig, if we are correct in the family genealogy, was appointed Constable for Allen township, June 16, 1752.

He seems to have had three sons—William, Thomas and Robert. Of these, the former, if we are correct as to the family relations, took an active part in the division of Bucks County by which Northampton County came into existence 1752, and was elected the first sheriff of the new county. He was recommended by the court June 16, 1752, to the Governor for a license to keep a public house, and seems to have been the progenitor of the many Craig hotel keepers.

John Craig, of which branch of the family we are unable to say, was on the grand jury in Lehigh County, which indicted John Fries for treason in 1799.

One branch of the family removed to Ohio in 1815 or '16, where their descendants may be found and with whom we have had correspondence during the past few years. As within the memory of this generation members of the family will be recognized in General Thomas Craig of Lehigh Gap, Honorable Allen Craig of Mauch Chunk, and others.

Jane Craig, sister to the first Thomas and James, was the wife of John Boyd, one of the original settlers and of whom we will now speak.

JOHN BOYD

The subject of this sketch was born in or near Edinburg, Scotland, 1699. He removed with his father's family to Antrim, Ireland, in 1700. From thence he removed to America when twenty-four (fourteen) years of age in 1714, settling in Philadelphia. In 1715 he married Jane Craig, sister of Thomas Craig. She was born in Scotland in 1695.

John and Jane Boyd removed with Colonel Thomas Craig and other families from Philadelphia in 1728 and formed what has since been known as the Craig or Irish Settlement in Northampton County. The farm on which they lived was owned in 1879, we believe, by John Miller.

As the family records were burned during an Indian incursion into the Craig Settlement, 1756, the date of the birth and death of John and Jane Boyd are not definitely known. As near as we can learn John Boyd died on his farm near Bath in 1750, aged about sixty years. Jane Boyd outlived her husband several years. They had several children, the names of whom, except that of John, Mary and Jane, have been lost. There is even some doubt about Jane.

The first of these, John, was born in Philadelphia in 1716 and went to the Craig Settlement with his father, and in 1744 married Elizabeth Young, only daughter of Sir William Young. He died in 1758 in his forty-sixth (second) year. Their children were Adam, John, William Young, James and Margaret. Of these John remained single, fought at the battle of Brandywine and Germantown. His son, William Young, was living in 1879, was single and the last of the male branch of the name.

Adam was born in 1746 and died May 14, 1814, in his sixty-eighth year, and is buried at Harrisburg. He served three campaigns in the Revolutionary War, was in the battle of Brandywine and Germantown; went through the privations of the memorable Winter at Valley Forge; was an officer and left the army Chief of Transportation. After the Revolution, he settled in Lancaster (Dauphin) County, Pennsylvania. In 1783, he went to Harrisburg, erected a house near the corner of Mulberry Street and River Alley; settled permanently as a farmer at Harrisburg in 1784.

In 1791, he was one of the burgesses of Harrisburg; was first president of the Town Council; was fourteen years treasurer of what is now Dauphin and Lebanon counties, Pennsylvania; was one of the three original Elders chosen in the Presbyterian church of Harrisburg, 1794. He married Jeanette McFarlane of Big Spring, Cumberland County, Pennsylvania in 1784. Their children were Rosanna, Elizabeth Young and John. The last two died without descendants. Rosanna married Hugh Hamilton. Their son was A. Boyd Hamilton, Esq., recently of Harrisburg, one son, Hugh is Dr. Hamilton of Harrisburg. Naudain, another son, lately pursued his studies at Lafayette College, Easton, Penna.

HUGH WILSON

One of the first, Hugh Wilson was appointed Justice of the Peace, June 9, 1756. He was born in Ireland, 1689, and died in the Craig Settlement, 1773, in his eighty-fourth year. The original Wilson homestead lay northwest of what is now Howertown in Allen Township. By two deeds, bearing date March 7, 1737, and June 29, 1738, respectively, the original Hugh Wilson became possessed of nearly seven hundred and thirty acres of land in that locality.

His wife was Sarah Craig, whom he married in Ireland. Whether or not she was a sister of the first Thomas, James and Jane Boyd, we are unable to state positively, but we presume there was a relationship.

The Wilsons by some branch of the family have always

been identified with the Craig Settlement. Hugh Wilson's grandson John lived and died, 1857, in the Settlement in the ninety-first year of his age. His daughter, Mrs. Margaret Horner, lived until within a comparatively recent period, dying in her home near Bath.

Honorable Robert E. James, President of the Easton Trust Company, is one of Hugh Wilson's descendents through Rev. Francis McHenry and Robert Gregg, already alluded to.

Another descendant is Miss Mary Irwin, of Columbia College Library, New York City. She is the only surviving child of the late Rev. Leslie Irwin, so long pastor of the Settlement Church.

JAMES KING

One of the early settlers in the Settlement was James King, who died April 30, 1745, in his thirty-eighth year. One of his children, Gabriel, died May 28, 1758, in his twenty-first year. Rupp in his History of Northampton County says that he was "Eminent for his piety."

David Heller is said to have lived on the property owned by James King.

ROBERT WALKER

Robert, who died 1758 in his fifty-eighth year, was the father of John Walker, one of the first to serve on the grand jury in Northampton County. John Walker, probably a brother of Robert Walker, died June 7, 1777, in his sixty-first year. Rev. Richard Walker, late of Allentown, is supposed to have been a descendant of the Settlement Walkers. A number of tombstones in the Old Brandywine Manor burial ground, Chester County, Penna., mark the last resting place of other members of the Walker family.

JAMES KERR

The descendants of James Kerr, one of the early settlers of the Craig Settlement, are scattered far and wide throughout the country. One of these is Rev. John Kerr, recently of Parnassus, Pa., Presbytery of Allegheny. Whilst this is the case, representatives of the blood have remained in the bounds of Northampton County to this day. Of these we might mention Mrs. John Blair, lately of Bath, and Mrs. Joseph Weaver, lately of Bethlehem, who descended from him through the Hemphills; and also Mr. Samuel Brown of Bethlehem, and James Kerr Dawes, Esq., who was Postmaster at Easton, and whose sisters are still residents of the same place.

Transcript of a letter from Robert Kerr, Crosses, April 30, 1792.

Addressed to "M. Daniel Craig, Care of Robert Smith, Hatter in High Street, Philadelphia."

Sir:

America! America! like the sound of Babylon's fall has roused the slumbering world, and put it into motion. The disputes of Mr. Burk, and your great and justly esteemed political genius—hath opened the eyes of many nations. Not long since the majority of mankind saw their rights only through the fals mediums of Lords, Dukes, Earls, Princes, Kings and ministers, and secretaries, of Star chamber and privy council and I don't know what. Titles invented to impose on the populace; to keep them in awe, and which neither make a man good, great, nor useful. Much people now wish to imitate the example of America; and think they may assert the privilege of men without being guilty of treason.

Here we sigh for the extensive fields and boasted freedom of America. But the ties of regard for our first best country are bound round our hearts strong almost as the magnet of enchantment.

The accounts we receive of your country from those who have seen it are various and different as the people themselves. How to account for this I know not. Ignorance of the country; or the desire some have of amusing their audience, or imposing on them; or the different dispositions of others to lessen or aggrandize what they have seen may be the reason. Or what is more likely every one speak of it according as they have prospered in it without ever comparing it with the other countries and weighing the advantages and disadvantages peculiar to each. This makes the credit of all suspected; and leaves us in uncertain lies.

In order that you may bring Ireland and America into competition and judge whether or not, by probability it would be advantageous for us to remove to America I will give you as minute an account of the state of our family and nation as possible.

My father Henry Kerr (Son to William your mother's brother who with his wife died about the time my father wrote last to you), is none of the greatest favorites of fortune nor insolently trampled on by her. He has the necessaries without many of the luxuries of life. He possesses a farm containing about 20 acres Irish plantation measure. Small you will say but if report says true better than 100 in America. That you may know whether or not. Through the year it will support six or eighteen people and six cows and two horses. For this he pays 80 pounds yearly rent and about 2 pounds and 10 schillings of tythes, hearthes, ussos?

Farther my father is the only surviving life of his lease which makes it less worth staying by and the more difficult to part with to advantage. Lands in common sell here from 20 to 30 shillings per acre.

My father has but three children. His eldest Mary is married. His youngest son is about fifteen years of age and I about twenty-two. To me he gave a classical education. I have acquired a tolerable knowledge of the Latin and the Greek tongues, and studied one season in the University of Glasgow in Scotland. This considerably affected me. I came home in April, 1791 and in May took a lingering fever under which I languished more than 50 days much of the time without hope of life. For this and other reasons I resolved never to go back to college.

Now I much wish to know from the mouth of truth what sure encouragement I would meet with to teach the Latin and Greek and to speak, read, and write the English tongue, in some measure of propriety, emphasis and grammar.

Here victualing is cheap. Oatmeal about 12 per Cwt. Flour, from 15 to 20. Beef about 25. Butter 50 per Cwt. ————— Able men services may be had through the year for 5 pounds. Women for half the money. It is said that taxes with you are weighty servants, high and money hard to get.

Government now seems inclined to favor every religious denomination of people. From it the County is augmented to the amount of near 30 per annum to each Presbyterian and dissenting clergyman.

The papists these four or five years have raised much disturbance in the north of this kingdom. With drums beating and the French flag flying, bodies of them come into our fairs and places of public concourse and proclaim a reward for a Protestant. Several lives have been lost in both sides and we think the gentle men have not been alert to suppress them. This makes them the more insolent. Notwithstanding, this year they got a bill brought in to the house demanding all the immunities and liberties of Protestants. But except three or four articles it was rejected.

Satisfy me by writing to me immediately and defer it not. Direct to the care of William Robert Buckley, Mill Street, Monaghan. I shall make no excuse for troubling you with a letter. I wish to cultivate an acquaintance with my most distant friends. Nor shall I apologize for the length of it. Considering the distance we are at, I have not time to make it shorter.

The young man who carries this is Mr. James Galbraith, a most genial and well-behaved young man. I wish I could say anything in his favor that would recommend him to you. If you could but serve him by a good advice or an information of the country.

But I haste and detain him whilst I subscribe myself your sincere friend.

Crosses, April 30th, 1792.

Robert Kerr.

JOHN McNAIR

Mr. McNair and his wife Christiana were natives of Scotland. They emigrated to Ireland about 1690 on account of persecution and settled in Parish Taboyn, County Donegal. Thence they emigrated to America with the widowed mother of John McNair, and in 1736 or '37 located on a farm in the Settlement, later owned by R. Weaver.

John McNair died in the Settlement 1762 in his seventy-second year. His wife Christiana died January 27, 1782 in her eighty-second year. Their children were William, John, Robert, Andrew, Margaret and Ann. Of these William, born in Ireland 1727, kept slaves at a time when Pennsylvania was still a slave state. He with his family removed to Western New York about 1800 where he died in old age.

His first wife Margaret Wilson, daughter of the original Hugh Wilson, died July 20, 1783 in her forty-ninth year. His second wife, Sarah, daughter of James Horner, died and was buried in Livingstone County, New York. The McNairs in Western New York became very numerous, and are now scattered all over the country.

ROBERT LATTIMER

About a half a mile from the old church in the Settlement, Robert Lattimer had his place of residence. He married Nancy King, a daughter of James King. Of this union there were the following children:—William, James, Jane, Sarah, Mary, Margaret, Elizabeth and Anne.

William who became General William Lattimer, died November 11, 1833 in his seventieth year. Arthur was a brother of Robert Lattimer. He is supposed to have owned the land on which the town of Bath stands. He was born in Ireland 1710, and died, 1777, in the Settlement aged sixty-seven years.

The wife of Mr. J. W. Abbot, recently cashier of the First National Bank, Tamaqua, is a great-granddaughter of Arthur Lattimer. In the "Presbyterian" of December 11, 1875, the following obituary notice appeared:—

"Lattimer—In Tamaqua, Pa., Nov. 10th, Mrs. Catharine, widow of James Lattimer, in the 81st year of her age."

Descendants of the Lattimers, may be found scattered far and near throughout our country.

JAMES RALSTON

James Ralston was one of the early arrivals in the Craig Settlement. He had the office of Elder in the old church and served on the first grand jury of Northampton county. He died July 26, 1775, when he was about seventy-six years of age.

His grandson Samuel married Letitia daughter of Rev. John Rosbrugh, pastor of the Craig Settlement church, and so cruelly murdered at the Battle of Trenton, 1777.

Descendants of the Ralstons are to be found at Norristown, in Chester county, in Pittsburgh and elsewhere.

JAMES HORNER

Among the oldest of the Scotch-Irish families was that of James Horner. He and his wife, Jane, came from Ireland. He also was one of the first grand jurors in Northampton county. He took an active part in the affairs of the county in its early history. He died May 1, 1793, in his eighty-second year.

His wife, Jane, was killed by the Indians October 8, 1763, in her fiftieth year while she was returning from an errand.

Their children were Hugh, Jane, Thomas, Sarah, Mary, James, and John. Some members of the family have ever since resided in the Craig Settlement and have always manifested a keen interest in matters of the church, the country and business. The Eldership and Corporation of the church for five generations had representatives of the family in that office, of whom Hugh R. and Robert Hays, are noted examples. While the Horners were noted as successful farmers, the success attending their business adventures have brought them distinction in that field of endeavor. The brothers Joseph A. and Robert Hays Horner are the most noteworthy examples.

JOSEPH HORNER

Another branch of the family is represented by Joseph Horner. He died and was buried in the old burial ground 1835, at the age of ninety-five years. The last male representative by the same name of this branch of the family died in 1866. The homestead is occupied by Miss Jane Horner. The grandmother of Dr. John Clyde who has done so much in collecting and arranging the material relating to the Scotch-Irish of Northampton county was a sister of the late Joseph Horner.

JOHN HAYS

One of the first arrivals in the Settlement, John Hays departed this life in his eighty-fifth year, November 16, 1789.

The descendants are scattered along the Susquehanna. Some of them, at least till a comparatively recent period, might have been found near Watsontown, Northumberland County. Another branch was represented in the late John K. Hays of Williamsport. The late Doctors Humphrey of Cherryville and Bethlehem traced their ancestry to John Hays. So did the late Mrs. Hugh R. Horner and the late Mrs. Margaret Horner of the Settlement.

A singular incident connected with the Hays family and for which the family is not to be held responsible was the production of the notorious out-law,—Texas Jack. He had been a well-known fighter during the Mexican war, and conspicuous in the early history of California. His bravery made him the terror of the Rio Grande. He held the office of sheriff in San Francisco, California. He fell into disfavor with the Vigilance Committee and of late years had lived in retirement. He died in 1883.

A nephew of "Col." Jack Hays the Texas Ranger, Major Hammond, was appointed 1885, Surveyor General of California; thus giving the Craig Settlement the credit of furnishing the State of California with a Surveyor General as well as a "Texas Jack."

SAMUEL BROWN

In continuing our sketches we find the names of Rosbrugh whose life is more fully described in a part of Clyde's work reprinted in this volume. The Clyde family will have a separate treatment. It remains to consider briefly Samuel Brown, born in 1714 and died June 11, 1798. He married Jane Boyd, a daughter of John Boyd. Among the children was Robert, born 1744, died Feb. 26, 1823, an active participant in the Revolution as First Lieutenant in Captain Rundio's Company. He fought bravely in the battles of Long Island and at Fort Washington where he was taken prisoner in November, 1776.

When he was paroled, he worked hard at his trade and gave great assistance and relief to his suffering fellow-soldiers. He was exchanged as a prisoner of war in 1781. In recognition of his valuable services, his fellow-citizens made him General of Militia. The commissions from Governors Findley and McKean have been preserved.

He was elected to the first Senate of Pennsylvania and represented the County in the Legislature from 1783-1787. He was sent, 1796, as a Representative to Congress in which office he continued for eighteen successive years and which he positively refused to serve after that on account of age and bodily infirmities. His son Robert married Cath. Snyder.

He had an only child—a son William who died in Bethlehem, January 10, 1866 in his seventy-third year. He was a graduate of Dickinson College and a member of the Constitutional Convention of Pennsylvania, 1833. He married as his first wife Susan Shimer. Robert Shimer and Eliza were the children of this union. His second wife was Susan Conrad, (Ingles), of Maryland. Their one daughter, Gulielma Alabama, married Mr. Edward K. Hyndman, who had children—Robert and Roy.

Robert S. was the late General Brown residing near Bethlehem. He served as State Senator in 1863 and was a prominent politician. He also served in the responsible position of Jury Commissioner of Northampton County.

Additional names of early settlers which should be sketched but which, would require more space than we have at our command, are the following: Dobbin, Epple, Hemphill, Hudders, Humphrey, Insley, Irwin, Kennedy, McDowell, McHenry, McKissic, McNeil, Moffat, Moore, Moorhead, Mulhallon, Neligh, Russel, Whiteside, Wyckoff, Young and many others. The following, however, will be of interest.

John K. Hays, "Presbyterian," March 30, 1878

Died in Williamsport, Pa., on the morning of March 11th, 1878, in full assurance of a blessed immortality, John K. Hays, in the eighty-second year of his age. He was the son and only child of John Hays, Esq., formerly High Sheriff of Lycoming County. Sheriff Hays was from Northampton County, Pa., and was married, on the 25th of May, 1795 to Miss Jane Horner, of the same county, and soon after migrated to Lycoming County, where he had previously purchased a farm on the west side of the Lycoming Creek, about five miles north of Williamsport. There he settled, and there John K. Hays was born January 15, 1797. At a suitable age he was sent to the Classical School of Rev. Thomas Hood of Buffalo Valley, Pa. Among his fellow students were Dr. James S. Dongal, of Milton, and Dr. William Wilson, Flavel Clingan, Thomas T. Smiley, and other noted men in Pennsylvania; and afterwards finished his education under Rev. Dr. J. F. Grier, of Reading. Under such influences young Hays was educated, and the seed thus sown in his early childhood a rich, ripe harvest bore in after years.

Descended from a stock in whose breast glowed an indomitable love of liberty, his ancestors espoused the cause of civil freedom in this country. His grandfather, John Hays, Jr., was an elder in the Presbyterian Church of the Forks of the Delaware (now Allen's town,) in which the lamented Rev. John Rosbrugh officiated. The manly piety and heroic devotion to the cause of liberty induced this reverend pastor, with his elders and the members of his church, to organize a company, and at the appointed time shouldered their muskets and proceeded to Philadelphia. Their pastor went in the capacity of a private soldier. During the retreat of our army through New Jersey this heroic pastor was most inhumanly murdered by a drunken British soldier, and left weltering in his blood. John Hays soon found the mangled body of his beloved minister, and at the risk of his life, with a saddened and moistened eye, consigned it the next day to the grave in an obscure place, within the limits of the City of Trenton.

The writer of this article was well acquainted with John K. Hays for forty years. He was a worthy descendent of such a noble ancestry. Through his long life he maintained a reputation for strict, honest and sterling integrity; a most intelligent student of God's Word, and at the same time not neglectful of the solid and substantial literature of ancient and modern times. He was a Presbyterian from conviction and education, and to the writer frequently, during his illness, expressed his full confidence in the finished righteousness of Christ as the sole foundation of his hope for a blessed immortality beyond the grave. He frequently rendered thanks to God for the mercies vouchsafed to him in early youth, for his pious ancestry, and above all, for the great love of his blessed and glorified Redeemer, whose rod and staff comforted him as he was about to enter the dark valley and shadow of death. S. P.

McKeen

James McKeen was for a longer or shorter period, during his early life, identified with the Irish Settlement. We believe he studied for a time in the Old Academy. The greater portion of his life was spent at South Easton, Pa., where he resided until his death 1871. He was an elder in the Brainerd Presbyterian church of Easton from its organization in 1854, and paid one-half of the original cost of the church building and contributed largely to its support. He was for many years, 1852-1871, a generous trustee of Lafayette College. The central dormitory building of the college, erected at a cost of $25,000.00 bears his name. He was thrice married. His first wife was a sister of Mr. Levi

Bennet, we believe, of Easton. Their children were Major Thomas L. and Elizabeth. His second wife was ———— Armstrong. Their children were Helen, and Sarah. His third wife was Eliza Craig who is deceased without descendants.

Thomas L. succeeded his father in an extensive iron and lumber business and resides in Easton. He married Elizabeth Steward of Easton. They have a family, the eldest daughter married Edward Chidsey, Esq., of Easton.

Elizabeth married William C. Cattell, D. D., LL. D., President of Lafayette College.

Helen married William Calvin Ferriday. Children are Lizzie, Harry, James.

Sarah died single in 1868.

Colonel Thomas McKeen died November 25, 1858 in the 96th year of his age. The following notice of his death appeared in the papers at the time,—

"The Patriarch of Easton is gone. He left us for the spirit-land yesterday at 3:30 o'clock, p. m. full of years and ripe for heaven. Col. Thomas McKeen was born in the North of Ireland, June 27th, 1763; emigrated to this country in 1783, a short time before the ratification of the articles of peace, and after living a long, active and useful life, died on the 25th of November, 1858, in the 96th year of his age.

In religion he was a Presbyterian and in politics, a Democrat, and in both though determined and straight forward, yet conciliating and conservative, as willing to concede to as to demand from others, the exercise and expression of an honest judgment in matters civil and sacred. He was a Christian without desiring to occupy a high seat in the synagogue, and a politician who did not desire place.

In 1844, he removed from Allen Township to this place, to take charge of the cashiership of the Easton Bank, in which he remained until the decease of the late Samuel Sitgreaves, Esq., when he was elected President, and in which office he remained until within a few years, when through the monitary of age and piety, he determined to seek repose in the bosom of his family and friends. Temperate in all things, his end was peace, literally peace, dying in the hope of a blessed immortality. We conclude this brief and hasty notice, by commending his life as a pattern, both in Church and State, to all who survive him." He was active in the Franklin Society at the Old Academy in 1808.

"The remains of the venerable Col. Thomas McKeen were this day committed to the silent tomb. The funeral services were conducted at the house, by Rev. Drs. Gray and Steel, and consisted of the reading of the 103 Psalm by Dr. Gray and a prayer by Dr. Steel. The funeral cortege left his late residence in Spring Garden Street at 11:30 o'clock and proceeded to the Easton Cemetery, where his remains were deposited in the handsome family vault which he some time since caused to be erected. On placing the remains in the tomb a prayer was made by Dr. Gray, and the tomb was closed and the long procession of carriages returned to Easton."

"The funeral sermon will be preached at the First Presbyterian Church on next Sabbath morning by Rev. Dr. Gray."

"We saw in the procession the officers of the Presbyterian Church, the clergy of the place, the officers of the Easton Bank and the Delaware Bridge Company. The deceased was 95 years and 5 months old."

THOMAS McKEEN

Thomas McKeen was a trustee of the Settlement Church, (1799-1801), and treasurer from eighteen hundred and two (?) to eighteen hundred and four. We believe he left no descendants. He kept store for many years about one mile below Bath on the Monoquacy Creek.

JOHN CUNNINGHAM CLYDE

The Cyclopedia of American Biography has the following:
"Clyde, John Cunningham, clergyman and author, was born in White Deer Valley, Lycoming County, Pa., October 22, 1846, son of Joseph and Ann (Jamieson) Clyde, and a descendant of Michael Clyde, a Scotchman, who landed in

America, presumably about 1735 and became a member of the Irish Settlement in Northampton County, Pa. The line of descent is through his son John and his wife Elizabeth; their son James and his wife Hannah, who were the grandparents of John C. Clyde.

He attended McEweneville Academy and the Geneva Hall College and Lafayette College. but lost two years at the latter on account of the war. Enlisted as a private, August 7, 1862 in Co. E. 72nd regiment-Illinois Volunteers from Chicago; he was soon after made a deputy provost-marshal at Columbus, Ky., in the following spring he combined with his duties those of clerk of the military post and in this capacity served under Col. George E. Waring; for disability developed in military service, he was honorably discharged July 12, 1863. He was graduated at Lafayette in 1866 delivering the Latin Salutatory. From the same institution he received the degree of A. M. in 1869. In the same year he was graduated at Princeton Theological Seminary, having been previously licensed to the ministry by the 2nd Presbytery of Philadelphia at Catasauqua, Pa. He was ordained to the full work of the ministry by the Presbytery of Chariton, at Centreville, Ia., was Stated Supply at Centreville, Ia., in 1869-70 and at Shenandoah, Schuylkill County, Pa., in 1870-72; pastor of East-Whiteland congregation at Frazer, at which place he built a new church edifice, acting as treasurer of the building committee; pastor at Bloomsbury, Hunterdon County, N. J., during 1879-1901, when he removed to Easton, Pa. He still preaches, (1907), most of the time in churches of his own and other denominations.

The degree of Doctor of Divinity was conferred by Maryville College, Tenn., in 1885.

Dr. Clyde is the author of the "History of the Allen Township Presbyterian Church," (1876); "Genealogies, Necrology, and Reminiscences of the Irish Settlement," (1879)—sequel to the former work; "Rosbrugh A Tale of the Revolution," or "Life and Labors and death of Rev. John Rosbrugh," (1880); "Life of James H. Coffin, LL. D." (1881);

"History of the First Presbyterian Church of Bloomsbury, N. J.," (1884); "Guide to Non-Liturgical Prayer," (1885); "A time to Dance" Sermon, (1887); "Mohammedism a Pseudo-Christianity," (1889); "The Christian Temper and Scientific Thought," (Reprint from Christian Thought), (1889).

He has been for many years a trustee and treasurer of the corporation of Newton Presbytery of which he is a member; he is a member of the American Institute of Christian Philosophy; The Academy of Political and Social Science; The National Geographic Society; and the Victorian Institute, or Philosophical Society of Great Britain; beside various positions of trust and administration of local character.

Dr. Clyde was married at Easton, Pa., October 26, 1869 to Martha Hollock, only surviving daughter of Prof. James H. Coffin, LL. D. of Lafayette College. Of three children born to them, only one survives infancy, Margaret Horner Clyde. He is the oldest living male representative of the Michael Clyde branch of the family. Died.

CULBERTSON

Tecumseh, Michigan, Feb. 19, 1880

Rev. John C. Clyde:

A member of the Rosbrugh family handed me your circular and in looking over it I see by your special request that I am able to add something to the History of the Irish Settlement.

I am a member of the Culbertson family, mentioned in your work, and am in possession of some papers that have a good deal of historical value.

1. A commission given to my grandfather James Culbertson by the Hon. William Denny, Lieutenant governor and Commander-in-Chief of the Province of Pennsylvania and counties of New Castle, Kent and Suffolk on the Delaware, to raise a company on foot to serve in the French and Indian War, dated in the thirty-first year of His Majesty's Reign, A. D. 1758, which was done and he served until the close of that war.

Also a secret circular issued by the officers of the Battallion to petition His Majesty to give them a grant of land, which was done. Land located on the James River in Virginia.

Said James Culbertson and oldest son John enlisted in the Revolutionary War. Served a term of six months, came home and were both killed by the Indians at their home in Allen Town and must have been buried in the Church burying ground.

Although I find that James Culbertson and Anna, his wife, were granted letters in 1769, he came from the Church in Chester County in 1760. His letter signed:—Thomas Brown, John Culbertson, Samuel Allen, David Denny, Elders.

But I cannot tell where they removed to. Their letter is dated April 20th 1769—Signed by James Ralston, James Craig, John Walker.

I can find no further record of their church relations, but I find my father's letters of dismissal, dated Allen Town, February 14, 1797, signed by Hugh Horner, William McNair, John McNair, Elders, (cf. Page 181, The Irish Settlement), which states that he has lived within the bounds of that congregation from infancy.

I find a receipt given to the widow of James Culbertson for the payment of five pounds and ten shillings, it being the price of a gun said James bought of a certain Edward ——————— (name not clear), for which the husband of Ann Fleming became security from date of receipt August 10th 1778—(no town named). There is a tradition that they had lived in Allen Town until 1797, when the widow and a part of the family came to Western New York, where she died.

I also have a letter written by John Culbertson, directed to James Culbertson, in the Forks of the Delaware, written May 26, 1766, Chester County.

The writer is James' father and is the John Culbertson who was one of the Elders of the church that dismissed James in 1760.

All of these papers are in a good state of preservation.

The Commission is on parchment. These I found among my father's papers after I grew to manhood. I wish you could see the originals. There is no question about them, as they have been in my possession for thirty-five years and have been in the possession of the family since his death, which occurred in May 1831.

I have the family record of my father's family and know where they are buried. C. W. Culbertson.

John Rosbrugh, Clerical Martyr of the Revolution

John C. Clyde, D. D.

Early Life

In order that his name may be correctly quoted and written by future generations, we first will settle its orthography. This has been in the minds of some an unsettled question for many years. In the minutes of the Synod of New York and Philadelphia, between the years 1761 and 1777 it is spelled once "Roxburrow," once "Roxborough," and nineteen times "Rosborough." In the records of the College of New Jersey it is spelled "Rosbrough." Mr. Headley in his papers "The Clergy of the Revolution" under date of August 12, 1875, in the New York Observer," wrote of him as "Rev. John Rossburgh." Rev. D. X. Junkin, D. D., in the same paper, August 26, attempting to correct Mr. Headley's orthography spelled it "Roseborough." In Ellis' History of Northampton County, we find it "Rosebury." From letters signed and his autograph in the records of the Allen Township Presbyterian Church, of which he was pastor at the time of his death, it is ascertained the correct spelling is "Rosbrugh." The name in later years is by his descendants and other branches of the family, spelled "Rosebrugh" and so pronounced.

John Rosbrugh was not a native-born American but belonged to that sturdy class known as the Scotch-Irish, who have furnished so large a proportion of the brains, backbone, and muscle which have been indispensable in shaping and maintaining our nationality. He was of the number of those who, for conscience sake, left Scotland and went to the North of Ireland, and who have made that part of Erin's Isle present socially, religiously and politically so marked a contrast with its more southerly portion. He was born in the year 1714, shortly before the family left Scotland, or shortly after they arrived in the North of Ireland, the exact date of the migration not being now obtainable. Of the family to which he belonged we have no definite information further than that he had an older brother William. It seems that the same impulse which constrained the family to migrate from Scotland to the North of Ireland, impelled this William Rosbrugh, together with his brother John—though the latter was young in years—to take their departure for a land more inviting beyond the sea, in America.

Just when they came to America is not now definitely known. Collateral circumstances however, would point to the probable time at which they came. It was doubtless at the time those Scotch-Irish Settlements were formed in the Middle States which figured so prominently in colonial history and the early history of our nation.

They settled in New Jersey, but in what particular part we are unable to decide. John's first marriage took place about the year 1733, when he was nineteen years of age. His wife's Christian name was Sarah, but the surname has been lost. He has no descendants by this marriage, the wife dying at the birth of their first child which also died at the same time.

For the next twenty-seven or twenty-eight years we have very little information with regard to the family. The elder brother William died, leaving two sons, Robert and John. The latter after his father's death and until he was of age, made his home with his brother (uncle) John for whom he was called.

Abner A. Rosebrugh, M. D. of Toronto, Canada is a descendant of William, the brother of the subject of this sketch.

Preparation for the Ministry

What private advantages Mr. Rosbrugh had for obtaining an education is now unknown. He however, pursued his studies in the College of New Jersey, at Princeton, graduating, as the records show, in 1761 in the class with David Cadwell, Lawrence Van Derver, David Gillespie, Isaac Handy, Thomas Henderson, William Janney, Nathan Ker, John Lefferty, Thomas McCracken, David Rice, Samuel Sloan, Jacob Thompson, Jaheel Woodbridge.

What incentive constrained him to seek the Christian Ministry will now perhaps never be known, but that his attention was so directed the sequel shows. It seems also he was not possessed of sufficient pecuniary means to obtain that thorough education which was required of those who would enter the sacred office in his day. But there was a beneficiary fund in connection with the College of New Jersey, and to this he turned for aid. The conditions upon which aid could be obtained from this fund settled the question as to the beneficiary's character and qualifications. On the afternoon of October 3, 1755, Gilbert Tennent and Samuel Davies presented the following report to the Synod of New York, convened in the City of Philadelphia.

"To the Reverend Synod of New York,

"The annual interest of the following donations was appropriated by the donors, for the education of such youth for the ministry of the gospel, in the College of New Jersey, as are unable to defray the expenses of their education, who appear, upon examination, to be of promising genius, Calvinistic principles, and in the judgment of charity, experimentally acquainted with a work of saving grace and have a distinguished zeal for the glory of God, and salvation of men."

Following this was a list of thirty-four names, showing a subscription amounting to £. 357-4s. 6d., the donors being residents of the mother country. This fund was placed in the hands of the officers of the College of New Jersey at Princeton, and the Synod by Committee from year to year examined beneficiaries and disbursed the interest of the fund. From 1758, the year in which the Synod of New York and Philadelphia united, till 1765 no regular report was made to the United Synod of the disbursements of the interest of the fund. In this year, however, the committee in charge of the same, made a report covering the whole period. The record is as follows:—

"The committee appointed to dispose of the money in the hands of the treasurer of New Jersey College, appropriated for the education of the poor and pious youth, brought in a state of their accounts since the year, 1758 which is as follows:—

1758, Nov. 23,	Paid by the treasurer to Mr. William Tennent for the use of Mr. Leslie _____ £	13	0	0
	for Mr. Carmichael _____	14	15	1
	To Mr. Carmichael _____	10	0	0
1760, June 11,	To President Davies, for use of Mr. Blair _____	20	0	0
1761, Aug. 3,	To Mr. Rosborough per order	30	0	0
1762, May 25,	To Mr. Rosborough per order	14	0	0
1763, Aug. 16,	To Mr. Robert Cooper, per order _____	20	0	0
1764, July 5,	To Mr. Robert Cooper, per order _____	13	0	0
Nov. 13,	To Samuel Leak, per order _	40	0	0

£ 174 15 1

Thus we see John Rosbrugh at Princeton College in 1761 and 1762—though well on in years—classed as a poor, pious, promising Calvinistic young man, giving evidence of a work of grace in the heart and having a distinguished zeal for the glory of God and the salvation of man.

Having been received under the care of Presbytery, May 22, 1762, as a candidate for the ministry, by August 16, 1763, he had so far progressed in his theological studies that the Presbytery of New Brunswick saw their way clear to license him to preach the gospel. This fact appears also in a subsequent record made with reference to it. On the forenoon of May 17, 1764, there was inserted in the minutes of the Synod of New York and Philadelphia, convened at Elizabethtown the following:—

"The Presbytery of New Brunswick report that since our last, ———— they have ordained to the work of the ministry, the Rev. Messrs. Amos Thomson, Jacob Kerr, and Nathan Kerr, who being present took their seats in the Synod; and that they licensed Messrs. David Caldwell, Francis Pepper and John Roxburrow to preach the gospel."

It is probable Mr. Rosbrugh further pursued his studies after his licensure, and at the same time exercised his gifts as a preacher. By December 1764, the Presbytery was so well satisfied with his qualifications that they proceeded to his ordination. A reference to the minutes will show that this took place December 11, 1764. It was reported to the Synod of New York and Philadelphia, convened in Philadelphia, on the afternoon of May 15, 1765, as follows:—

"The Presbytery of New Brunswick report that they have ordained Messrs. James Lion and John Roxborough to the work of the ministry, and that they have licensed Simon Williams."

The place at which Mr. Rosbrugh was ordained was the old Greenwich Church, now within the bounds of the Presbytery of Newton, Warren County, New Jersey.

Field of Labor in New Jersey

In referring to the old Greenwich Church, formerly known in the neighborhood as the Tennent or Brainerd Church, we must not confound the building and locality with the present Greenwich Presbyterian Church, though the latter has occupied its present site for more than a hundred years. The spot where Mr. Rosbrugh was ordained was a half or three-fourths of a mile to the south or southwest. Leaving Phillipsburg for New York by the Central R. R. of N. J., the traveler is brought by a journey of about five miles to the Pohatcong Creek. As he passes over the high embankment by which the cars are carried over the bed of the stream, if he will look to the southeast, his eye will rest upon the site of the original Greenwich Church which is but a few hundred yards distant. It stood upon what is known as the Reily farm, now owned by Hon. H. R. Kennedy. If the traveler will go upon the spot, he will behold a scene of marvelous beauty. To the south he will see the Musconetcong range of mountains, with the stream of the same name flowing at its base. To the southwest and west he will see a broken range of hills, stretching far away across the Delaware into Pennsylvania. To the northwest and north, across Pohatcong Creek, will be spread out the fertile valley of the Delaware in Warren County, New Jersey, and Northampton County, Pennsylvania, the whole circumscribed by the Kittatinny or Blue Mountain range twenty miles or more away. To the northeast and east will appear the valleys of the Pohatcong and the Musconetcong creeks with the range of hills which separates them. Such was the scene that met the eyes of John Rosbrugh in December, 1764, when he repaired to the Old Greenwich Church to receive ordination to the Christian ministry. Nothing remains of the log church in which he reverently knelt except the foundation stones, which have been built into a lime-kiln, which may now be seen near by.

It is probable that at the time of his ordination, Mr. Rosbrugh entered upon regular pastoral labors in the congregation of Greenwich, Oxford and Mansfield Woodhouse. Although there had been more or less preaching at one or other of these points by various clergymen as missionaries or supplies by appointment of ecclestical courts for perhaps twenty-five years previous, Mr. Rosbrugh seems to have been the first settled pastor at least of the Presbyterian order—north of Musconetcong mountains in the bounds of what is now Warren County, New Jersey. These three points of his charge seem to have been the earliest localities in the region from which the principles of the Christian religion were disseminated. By following the early records from 1739 on, it will be found that preaching was supplied from time to time at Mr. Green's—then Green's Ridge—then Grenidge—then Greenage,—and finally Lower Greenwich, which meant the place where Mr. Rosbrugh was ordained.

Likewise preaching was provided at the same time at Mr. Barber's neighborhood, near "Musconnekunk," "Mr. Barber's" was supplanted by name "Mansfield Woodhouse," doubtless to correspond with the name of the township in which it was located, or to designate it as being at a particular woodhouse in Mansfield Township. This was some eleven or twelve miles above Lower Greenwich, and like it in the Musconetcong Valley. The traveler taking the cars of the Delaware, Lackawanna and Western Railroad, at Hampton Junction on the Central Railroad of New Jersey, and riding toward Washington, passes through the bounds of the old Mansfield Woodhouse congregation. As he leaves the station, he will see the valley below, surrounded by white tombstones, the present Musconetcong Valley Presbyterian Church, which is one of the daughters of the original Mansfield Woodhouse church. As he sweeps around the point of the hill a half a mile further on he will see across the valley upon the hillside, two or three miles distant, the white tombstones in the graveyard where once stood the mother church. On arriving at Washington, he will see as one of the most prominent buildings of the place, the present First Mansfield or Washington Presbyterian Church, which is the other daughter. Repairing to the old graveyard just indicated, now lying a half a mile south of him, he will see all that remains to call to remembrance the labors of the Revolutionary pastor there. No stone, we believe, now chronicles the burial of the parishoner or friend during his ministry, but the western part of the burial ground is filled with nameless graves, by the side of some of which he doubtless stood and performed the last rites of Christian burial for the departed,

Standing here upon the side of the hill which separates Musconetcong and Pohatcong valleys, a beautiful prospect is spread out before the eye. To the south and southwest three or four miles away, is seen the irregular range of the Musconetcong mountain beyond the stream of the same name, whilst in the immediate landscape are seen fertile fields, comfortable farm-houses and inviting groves.

Oxford, the other part of the charge was near Belvidere, the county seat of Warren. In early days it was known as "Greenwich upon the Delaware," "Upper Greenwich," or "Oxfords," which name may still be seen in the burying ground and heard in the community—and finally "Oxford." It is now known as the First Oxford Presbyterian Church, Presbytery of Newton. Two miles from Belvidere upon a little eminence, just where a small stream flows out from among the northern spurs of Scott's Mountain, we find the site of the original Oxford Church. Standing at the modern church amid the graves of past generations, to the southwest, west and north, stretch out beautiful hills and vales in upper Northampton County, Pa., and Warren County, N. J. Following the range of the Kittatinny mountains as they are seen projected against the sky, the Delaware Water Gap soon comes prominently into view to the right, whilst the New Jersey foot-hills stretch away to the east in broken profusion. Little or nothing remains at the site of the church to call to remembrance the first pastor and the days of the Revolution. Thus we see Mr. Rosbrugh in 1764, practically in charge of all the interests of the Presbyterian church in that large and prosperous region now known as Warren County.

Ministry in New Jersey

It was at Mansfield Woodhouse that Mr. Rosbrugh made his home, whilst occupied with the regular duties of his charge, he was appointed from time to time to supply neighboring congregations. On April 10, 1765, Presbytery appointed him to supply two Sabbaths between that date and the third Tuesday in October at Upper and Lower Hardwick—now Yellow Frame and Hackettstown respectively in the Presbytery of Newton, Warren County, N. J. On May 29th, of the same year, he was appointed to supply two Sabbaths at Deep Run near Doylestown, Pa., twenty-five miles distant. On October 16, 1765, he was again appointed to supply two Sabbaths at Upper and Lower Hardwick—twenty to thirty miles distant. On April 16, 1766, he was appointed to supply one Sabbath at Upper Hardwick and one at Bedminster—in Somerset County, twenty-five to thirty miles distant.

Having entered upon the full work of the ministry, he felt that he ought to take to himself again a wife. Belonging to the class known as the Scotch-Irish, it was most natural for him to seek a helpmate from among those who were of similar origin. Some twenty miles away in Allen Township, in "Forks of the Delaware," now Northampton County, Pa., had been for nearly forty years, a settlement of the Scotch-Irish. To the Irish or Craig Settlement, as it was called, therefore he looked for a wife. It was not long till he had found and won the object of his desire. He became intimate with the family of James Ralston, an elder in the Irish Settlement, or Allen Township Presbyterian Church. The family was composed of the following members, we believe, viz: Samuel, John, Mary, Jane and Letitia. As living descendants of this family, among others, we might mention Rev. John Grier Ralston, D. D., Norristown, and the Ralston families of the Old Brandywine Manor Presbyterian congregation, Chester County, Pa., wife of the venerable Rev. J. N. C. Grier, D. D., for forty years pastor of Brandywine Manor was also a descendant.

Mr. Rosbrugh married the daughter Jane of this family, and took her to their home in the bounds of the congregation at Mansfield Woodhouse. The time at which the marriage took place we have not been able to learn, but conjecture it was in the early part of 1766. He was absent from the meeting of Synod, which convened in New York, May 21st of that year. We conjecture he silently rendered his excuse, whilst absent in the words of Nehemiah 6:3, "I am doing a great work, so that I cannot come down."—I am getting married. In Philadelphia, May 20, 1767, he gave to Synod his reasons for the previous year's absence, and for ought we know, gave them as here indicated.

On the 24th of April, 1767, there was born to him a son, whom he called James, doubtless for his wife's father, James Ralston. Between the time of his marriage and the birth of a son, we find him engaged in numerous labors beyond the bounds of his own charge. On October 21, 1766, he was appointed to supply at Upper and Lower Hardwick the first Sabbath of December, 1766, the first Sabbath in January and February, 1767. April 21, 1767, he was appointed to supply two Sabbaths in May at Lower Hardwick, fourth Sabbath in July, Upper Hardwick, and fourth Sabbath in September at Bedminster. These labors in May, outside of his own charge, together with the journey to and attendance upon the meeting of Synod in Philadelphia the same month, show the arduousness of the service he rendered.

We find Mr. Rosbrugh was a man careful to obey the behests of the ecclestial courts which had jurisdiction over him. The Synod of New York and Philadelphia had taken steps to secure a fund for the propogation of the Gospel among the poor. They had enjoined upon the members to make collections for the purpose. On the afternoon of May 22, 1767—the Synod then being in session in Philadelphia—the members were called upon to render an account of their faithfulness in the matter. When the list had been completed, the following minute was made, viz:

"The Synod are obliged to declare that it is a matter of real grief to them to find that so many of their members have paid so little regard to the authority of Synod, enjoining a liberality for so pious and important a purpose."

Mr. Rosbrugh, however, escaped this censure, for among the reports from the Presbyteries, the following came from the Presbytery of New Brunswick, to which he belonged, viz:

THE JAMES KERR HOMESTEAD
Oldest House in Weaversville—Front View.   (See page 168.)

Of New Brunswick Presbytery,

Mr. Reed	£ 1	10	0
Mr. Hanna	1	0	0
Mr. Kirkpatrick	2	17	1
Mr. Rosborough	1	0	0
	£ 6	7	1 Pro. cur."

Thus he appears as one of the four in his Presbytery who were faithful under the injunctions laid upon them.

On the 28th of May, he obtained leave of absence for himself and elder, John Maxwell from further attendance upon the sessions of the Synod at that meeting, and started upon his journey homeward. Having returned to his duties at home, he doubtless in connection therewith, performed the extra service in July and September, to which he had been appointed by Presbytery in the spring. We find that at the Fall meeting of Presbytery on October 20, 1767, he was appointed to preach, one Sabbath at Upper Hardwick and one at Smithfield—the latter being now within the bounds of Lehigh Presbytery in Monroe County, Pa., beyond the Kittantinny range of mountains, twenty or thirty miles distant. We present these details of labor that an adequate idea may be formed of the arduous and patient services rendered by the subject of this sketch. Mansfield Woodhouse and Oxford were each ten or twelve miles from Greenwich and five or six ——— from each other. Remembering this, and also that in addition to the labor of serving those congregations under such circumstances, he traveled far and preached much in the regions beyond, we have some forecast of the indomitable courage, perseverance and devotion to duty that manifested itself in severer trials in after years. In all this work there was doubtless little encouragement, at least in a worldly point of view. The discouraging phase of his experience is reflected in a representation which he made of his charge to Presbytery on April 19, 1768. The record is as follows:

"Mr. Rosbrugh represented to the Presbytery, that Mansfield Woodhouse, one branch of the present charge, through the removal of sundry of his members out of the congregation, and by other means were now become so few and weak as not to be able to contribute their quota towards his support, and that sundry of them had consented to his leaving them. And that seeing the other branches of his charge were not able to make up the deficiency of that now mentioned, and as his circumstances are straightened and necessitous, these things laid him under the disagreeable necessity of asking to be wholly dismissed from his present charge."

The consideration of this matter was laid over till the next day. It then came up and the following record was made with regard to it:

"Mr. Rosbrugh's request for a removal from his present charge, came under consideration, and the Presbytery after hearing and considering the reasons for said motion, do judge that the matter is not yet ripe for proceeding to his removal, as it does not appear to us that Mansfield Woodhouse, the branch of the congregation which it seems is most deficient in supporting Mr. Rosbrugh, have been formally notified of Mr. Rosbrugh's design at this time to sue for a dismission from them; neither is there any one here to represent Oxford congregation, which is another branch of his charge, and as the removal of a minister is a weighty matter, and not to be rashly done, we would proceed with all possible tenderness and caution in it. We therefore think proper to defer this matter till the fall Presbytery, and in the meantime order that Mr. Rosbrugh give due notice to the people of Mansfield Woodhouse that unless they discharge their arrears and pay their quota as usual, his labors shall be taken from them, and should they decline to bear their part as before, then Mr. Rosbrugh is to preach one-half of his time till next Presbytery, at Greenwich, and a third part at Oxford, and the remainder at discretion."

Such was the status of his affairs in April, 1768. At the same meeting of Presbytery when the above action was taken, he was appointed to supply one Sabbath at Smithfield and one at Allentown in the Irish Settlement, Northampton County, Pa., and preach as often as he could at Upper and Lower Hardwick, between that time and the spring meeting of Presbytery. At the fall meeting of Presbytery, October 18, 1768, the report was brought in that Mansfield Woodhouse had failed to make up their quota of Mr. Rosbrugh's salary and that he had accordingly preached one-half of his time at Greenwich, and one-third at Oxford. The Presbytery adjourned to meet at Oxford on the third Wednesday of November to further consider the case. At this meeting it seems some arrangement was made and certain conditions specified upon which Mr. Rosbrugh was to remain in charge of Greenwich and Oxford. At the spring meeting of Presbytery, however, April 18, 1769, it was reported that Oxford and Greenwich had failed to comply with the conditions upon which he was to remain with them, and he was accordingly dismissed from all parts of his charge.

The Transition to Allen Township, Pennsylvania

The foregoing circumstance would seem to indicate that the immediate future was dark and uninviting to the churchless pastor. But such was not the case. Within a week previous to the meeting of the Presbytery at which he was released from his pastoral charge, his heart was cheered by the birth of a daughter. This happy event occurred April 12th. He called his daughter Letitia doubtless after the mother's sister, Letitia Ralston. With the little boy James, two years old and the babe, we may suppose he spent many happy hours. But another circumstance added much to the dispelling of any misgivings which he may have had for the future. At the same meeting of Presbytery when he was released from his pastoral charge, a call was presented to him to take charge of the Allen Township Presbyterian Church in connection with Greenwich. Thus he was to be provided with a home in the Irish Settlement, Northampton County, Pa., among the Scotch-Irish, the stock from which he himself had sprung as well as his wife. He was now called to the congregation in which his father-in-law, James Ralston, was an elder, and his wife's family were members.

This matter had well been forwarded before the meeting of Presbytery which convened to dissolve the pastoral relation at Oxford and Greenwich, March 29, 1769. The Allen Township people asked permission of the First Philadelphia Presbytery—to which they belonged—to present a call to Mr. Rosbrugh of the New Brunswick Presbytery; showing that they had decided at that time, to call him. They were advised to secure, in connection with Mt. Bethel, as much of his time as they could. Mr. Rosbrugh had expressed his willingness to accept their call, as early as April 3rd and the following record was made in their church book, viz:

"The Rev. John Rosbrugh accepted the call to Allentown Congregation, the 3rd day of April, 1769; that is to allow the congregation two-thirds of his time for * * * pounds per annum."

The completed arrangements then doubtless was to give to Greenwich one-third, and Allen Township two-thirds of the minister's time. With this arrangement in view, the matter was brought before the Presbytery of New Brunswick, where it was duly considered, April 18, 1769, and it was decided to make such arrangement, provided the Allen Township Church was "regularly set off" to the Presbytery of New Brunswick, it having been under the care of the Presbytery of Abington from 1751 to 1758, and from that time on, under the First, or old Presbytery of Philadelphia. In pursuance of the stipulation of the Presbytery of New Brunswick, the Allen Township people petitioned the Synod of New York and Philadelphia, convened in Philadelphia, to set them off to New Brunswick Presbytery. The petition came up for consideration on the afternoon of May 23, 1769, and the following action was taken:

"A petition from the congregation of Allentown, in the Forks of Delaware, to be taken from under the care of the First Presbytery of Philadelphia, and to be put under the care of the Presbytery of New Brunswick, was brought in and read. After the committee in behalf of the congregation and both Presbyteries concerned were heard, it appeared not expedient for the present to grant the prayer of the petition. But the Synod order the First Presbytery of Philadelphia to inquire more particularly into the state and connection of that congregation, and empower said Presbytery to set them off to the Presbytery of New Brunswick if it should appear expedient; or if it should appear more expedient to set off the congregation of Greenwich to the First Presbytery of Philadelphia, the Presbytery of New Brunswick are empowered to set them off."

Notwithstanding this delay, Mr. Rosbrugh doubtless devoted his time thereafter almost exclusively to Allen Township and Greenwich. This is confirmed by a record made October 19, 1769, by the Presbytery of New Brunswick which is as follows:

"That Mr. Rosbrugh be a constant supply to the people at Greenwich and Allentown, except 3rd Sabbath to Mt. Bethel till our next."

At the spring meeting of his Presbytery, on April 17, 1770, he was appointed to supply one Sabbath at Mt. Bethel, one at Oxford, one at Basking Ridge, at Lower Hardwick one and administer the Lord's Supper, in addition to his regular labors at Allen Township and Greenwich. In accordance with the action of the Synod in 1769, the matter of the transfer of the Allen Township Church to the Presbytery of New Brunswick, came up on the afternoon of May 21, 1770, in the Synod of New York and Philadelphia, convened in New York, when the following action was taken:

"The First Presbytery of Philadelphia reported that in compliance with an order of Synod last year, they had, in conjunction with the Presbytery of New Brunswick, inquired particularly into the state and connections of the congregation of Allentown, in the Forks of the Delaware, and it is the unanimous opinion of both Presbyteries that it is at present most subservient to the interests of religion in those parts, for the Presbytery of New Brunswick to take under their care not only the Congregation of Allentown, but also the Congregation of Mt. Bethel both which are in the Forks of Delaware, and both which have been under the care of the First Philadelphia Presbytery. The Synod therefore order the Presbytery of New Brunswick to take both the said congregations under their care for the future."

The conditions upon which Mr. Rosbrugh was to be allowed to accept the call to Allen Township and Greenwich were thus met. Notwithstanding this, he did not at that time express to Presbytery his acceptance of the call. This may have been owing to troubles which arose about this time in the Mt. Bethel Church, which was doubtless to constitute a part of his charge. In October, 1771, he was appointed to supply this place on the fourth Sabbath of that month and administer the Sacrament of the Lord's Supper, and preach three more Sabbaths at his discretion. At the spring meeting of Presbytery, April 15, 1772, he expressed his acceptance of the call to the Allen Township church, but for some reason no preparations were made for his installation. If we mistake not, Greenwich was not included in the call as accepted by Mr. Rosbrugh in 1772. On October 13, 1772, the Allen Township people renewed their request for his installation, which was "cheerfully complied" with. It took place October 28, 1772, at 12 o'clock. Rev. John Guild presided and preached the sermon. The other members of the committee of installation were Rev. John Hanna, Rev. Jacob Van Arsdalen and Rev. Samuel Kennedy.

Ministry in Allen Township

At what particular time Mr. Rosbrugh removed his family to the bounds of the Allen Township congregation is now not known, but it was most likely shortly after the dissolution of the pastoral relation between himself and the churches to which he ministered in New Jersey. It is not probable that he remained long in the bounds of the Mansfield Woodhouse Congregation after the unhappy state of affairs which we see existed there in the latter part of 1768. The most natural place to which we would expect him to remove as soon as he conveniently could, would be the Allen Township congregation, where his wife's people lived. There we may suppose he took up his abode therefore, in 1769 or 1770. After his removal there were born to him two daughters, one of whom he called Mary, doubtless after his wife's sister, Mary Ralston, who had died, a blooming girl of sixteen, November 20, 1748, and whose body lies in the Allen Township burying ground. The other he called Sarah, perhaps in memory of the deceased wife of his youth. Another son was born to him here also, whom he called John, doubtless after his wife's brother, John Ralston.

If the traveler will go to a little hamlet near Weaversville in Northampton County, Pa., he will be surrounded by the scenery amid which Mr. Rosbrugh spent the closing years of his life. The purling brook still flows by. The old mill-site is still there. The rocky ascent of the highway up which he marched with his parishioners when starting to the seat of war, is still there. The old Allen Township stone church, erected in 1812 and '13—now hidden by the wooden encasement—is there, within a hundred yards or so of the site of the building in which Mr. Rosbrugh preached. Just up the stream a few steps, is the old burying-ground where lie the remains of his wife, by the side of Barbara Hays, Mary Craig, Thomas Herron, Mary Ann Walker, Mary Lykens, Hugh Wilson, Mary Ralston,—his own mother-in-law,— Jane Clendinen and Mary Hays, together with others whom he laid in the grave during his ministry there. Leaving the church and going eastward, the traveler finds himself up on the elevated highway along which Mr. Rosbrugh traveled week after week as he toiled in the work of the Master. Away to the southeast, south and southwest may be seen the Lehigh mountains with the river of the same name flowing at their northern base. Here and there as the eye wanders over the landscape may be seen ascending at Catasauqua, Allentown, Bethlehem and other places, the smoke of the iron furnaces of the Lehigh Valley. To the east and west stretch out the fertile and beautiful hills and vales of Northampton and Lehigh counties; whilst away to the north against the skies, may be seen the symmetrical range of the Kittatinny or Blue Mountains. Having gone a mile perhaps, a sharp descent in the road brings the traveler to Reuben Beavers. This was the home of Rev. John Rosbrugh in 1776, and the home of his sorrowing family after his death. Just below it was the old Ralston estate, and the blockhouse or fort for the defence of the settlers prior to and during the French and Indian war. Such were the surroundings of Mr. Rosbrugh after he removed from New Jersey to Pennsylvania.

From his installation in 1772 onward for several years, he seems to have been quietly occupied with his ministerial labors. He attended the meeting of Synod in Philadelphia in May, 1774. He attended the meeting of his Presbytery at Bound Brook, April 23, 1776, and was chosen Moderator. He also attended the meeting of the Synod in Philadelphia in May of the same year. On October 9, 1776, Presbytery appointed him to supply two Sabbaths at Mt. Bethel, and one at Greenwich. This however was the last opportunity his Presbytery had of assigning him to duty.

Before proceeding however to the darkest and saddest part of his career, let us take a glimpse at the bright and cheerful characteristics of his nature. Mr. Rosbrugh was fond of mirthfulness, and was accustomed to entertain his friends with such anecdotes as the following:

At the first meeting of Synod in Philadelphia, two young clergymen attended on horseback from Virginia. On the way arriving at a village, near night, they inquired for a Presbyterian, hoping to find lodging for the night. They were directed to the principal man of the place, the owner of a mill at which many were employed. He gladly received them—showed them great attention—had their horses taken care of and supper prepared for themselves. After a long evening talk, instead of asking the young ministers to lead in devotions, he thought it would be a good thing to show them how good he could do it himself. His method was patriarchal. He first read a chapter in the Bible, which he explained to the family, then a version of the Psalms—lining it in singing—before prayer. This night the chapter in course was the fourth of Numbers, the fifth and sixth verses of which are as follows:

"And when the camp setteth forward, Aaron shall come and his sons, and they shall take down the covering vail and cover the ark of testimony with it: and shall put thereon the covering of badger skins, and shall spread over it a cloth wholly blue and shall put in the staves thereof."

For "badger skins," he read beggar skins. When he had finished reading, he turned to the family and said:—There is nothing of particular importance in this chapter, it merely goes to show the blessedness of the gospel dispensation, for now each man can enjoy his religion under his own vine and fig tree, but then just as soon as a man becomes too poor to pay his tithes, off went his skin to be used in covering the articles in the tabernacle.

Mr. Ralston in making his pastoral visits, once came to a widow living alone. He found her at her devotions and did not disturb her until she was through. She read the Scripture, then lined a Psalm as she sang it, before prayer. He asked her why she lined the Psalm, as there were none to hear her when she was alone. "Ah!" she said, "it is so quiet I fain would 'dight my gab twice wi'it."

Incentives to Patriotism

These were Revolutionary times, and Mr. Rosbrugh was filled with the spirit of freedom. It was the heavy yoke, politically and religiously, which the mother country had imposed upon her people that drove him and many of his class from the heather, hill and dale of Scotland, to their new home in America. That the same yoke should be imposed upon them in their new home, seemed to him like the pursuit and oppression of the innocent and suffering by a natural enemy. Aside from this general incentive which fired his zeal, there were special reasons why he should be intensely interested in his country's welfare. The Synod of New York and Philadelphia to which he belonged, at its meeting in New York on May 20, 1775, had sent out by pastoral letter, burning words of Christian advice and patriotism to all her ministers and congregations in view of the disheartening aspect of political affairs. Beside urging recognition of God in all the trials of the hour, and to duly repent of transgressions; to respect their allegiance to the British crown so far as might be consistent with the securing of their just rights, politically and religiously; to abstain from lawlessness and excesses in social life, they said:—

"Suffer us then to lay hold of your present temper of mind, and to exhort especially the young and vigorous, by assuring them that there is no soldier so undaunted as the pious man; no army so formidable as those who are superior to the fear of death. There is nothing more awful to think of,—than that those whose trade is war, should be despisers of the name of the Lord of hosts, and that they should expose themselves to the imminent danger of being immediately sent from cursing and cruelty on earth to the blaspheming rage and despairing horror of the infernal pit. Let, therefore, everyone, who from generosity of spirit, or benevolence of heart, offer himself as a champion in his country's cause, be persuaded to reverence the name, and walk in the fear of the Prince of the Kings of the earth, and then he may, with unshaken firmness, expect the issue either in victory or death."

"Be careful to maintain the union which at present subsists through all the colonies. Nothing can be more manifest than that the success of every measure depends on its being inviolably preserved and therefore we hope that you will leave nothing undone which can promote that end. In particular as the Continental Congress, now sitting at Philadelphia, consists of delegates chosen in the most free and unbiased manner, by the body of the people, let them not only be treated with respect, and encouraged in their difficult service, not only let your prayers be offered up to God for his direction in their proceedings but adhere firmly to their resolutions and let it be seen that they are able to bring out the whole strength of this vast country to carry them into effect."

Thus Mr. Rosbrugh would feel that he was under moral obligation, with all Presbyterians to lend his aid to repel what seemed to him an unjust demand on the part of the Mother Country.

In the minutes of the Council of Safety, September 24, 1776, we read: "An order was drawn on Robert Trowers, in favor of Messrs. Jacob Stroud, Neigal Gray, Abraham Miller, Simon Dreisbach, John Ralston, Jacob Arndt and Peter Burkhalter, members of the Convention of Northampton County, 3,000 pounds powder, 600 pounds lead for the use of said county."

The following names with others are found connected with the Revolution from the Irish Settlement, viz:—Major George Nagle; Lt. Robert Gregg; Ensign William Craig; John Craig, John Boyd, Andrew Boyd, William Young, William Weals, Henry Epple, Gen. Thomas Craig and Robert Brown, afterwards known as General Brown. Captain Benjamin Wallace, who married Letitia Ralston, Mr. Rosbrugh's sister-in-law also entered the conflict on the field of battle. At Fort Washington a number of these fell into the hands of the enemy.

With the fall of Fort Washington, the "Flying Camp" was formed, to which the Irish Settlement gave her quota. By November an express rider had been sent out "To Northampton and Bucks counties to request the commanding officers of the militia to hold themselves in readiness to march to this city at an hour's warning." The following letter to Colonel John Siegfried of Allen Township where Mr. Rosbrugh and his congregation were located aroused the people to a high pitch of patriotism.

"Sir:

"The Council of Safety of this state by their resolves of

the 17th inst, empowered me to call out the militia of Northampton County, to the assistance of the Continental army, that by our joint endeavors, we may put a stop to the progress of the enemy, who are making preparations to advance to Philadelphia as soon as they cross the Delaware, either by boats or on the ice. As I am unacquainted with the names of the Colonels of your militia, I have taken the liberty to enclose you six letters in which you will please insert the names of the proper officers, and send them immediately to them by persons in whom you can confide for their delivery. If there are not as many Colonels as letters you may destroy the balance not wanted, I earnestly entreat those who are so far lost to a love of country as to refuse to lend a hand to its support at this time, they depend upon being treated as their baseness and want of public spirit will most justly deserve.

I am sir, your Most Obedient Servant:

George Washington."

This letter caused Mr. Rosbrugh to assemble his congregation and read to them the call for reinforcements. He preached a sermon Judges 5:23, "Curse ye Morez, saith the angel of the Lord; curse ye bitterly the inhabitants thereof, because they came not to the help of the Lord, to the help of the Lord against the mighty." He declared he was ready to die in full faith of what he preached and intended to go with them in his proper capacity as Chaplain, if they would consent to march to the country's rescue. The people expressed their willingness to go if he would be their commander. This was a position he had not thought of occupying. He desired therefore to consult his beloved wife before acceding to the people's desire.

With her brother John, a prisoner, what would become of him, of her and the little ones? But the country called and none should refuse. As the people desired him to go not as Chaplain but as commander, she said "Then go."

Mr. Rosbrugh counted the cost and after making his will

he was ready to go. The morning dawns, the people again assemble in church. He told those who felt it their duty not to enlist, to go home and take care of their affairs as well as look to the interests of those who went. To those who felt as he did, that duty called to the country's rescue, to follow him. He put the musket to his shoulder and marched out to the highway and all fell into line and followed him. They marched eastward to Jacksonville, then southward, crossing the Lehigh at Bethlehem, and followed the "Old Bethlehem" road to Philadelphia, where they arrived about December 24, 1776.

On the 26th he received the commission as Chaplain of the 3d Battalion of Northampton Militia. Thus he was relieved of the command of the company which he mustered and led to the seat of war. Captain John Hays assumed the responsibilities of that position. Mr. Rosbrugh's duties were now those of Chaplain not simply to the company which he raised, but to all troops from Northampton County, known as the 3d Battalion of Militia.

While the foregoing circumstances were transpiring at Philadelphia, there were important operations going on at Trenton. The British did not attempt to cross the Delaware filled as it was with floating ice, to pursue further their flying foe. They waited for the flood to subside and the waters to freeze. This delay to them was dangerous.

Washington stationed one body at Morrisville and the other at Bristol. The plan was for them to cross the Delaware at their respective places while he would cross at McKonkey's ferry. The two other bodies failed, but Washington carried out his part of the plan and made the whole undertaking a success. He had under his command on the evening of the 25th twenty-four hundred brave and resolute men and twenty pieces of artillery. As the shades of night closed in and shrouded their movements from view, these commenced to cross to the New Jersey side. It was nearly four o'clock, owing to the ice and other impediments, before all the men and artillery were safely landed. He gave words of encouragement to his trusty followers and took up his line of march for Trenton.

The enemy finding themselves surrounded in Trenton, surrendered. The commander, Captain Rahl though mortally wounded, surrendered his sword to General Washington. The result of the undertaking was a great success, which greatly elated and encouraged the dispirited Continental army.

Meantime, Captain Hays with Rosbrugh and his company were sent in haste from Philadelphia to Bristol. Mr. Rosbrugh on horseback wrote his last letter in broken sentences to his wife, stating that he is well, but that it may be the last letter the family shall receive.

The British chagrined at their failure immediately reformed their ranks and rushed to the charge. The victory was again on the side of the Americans. Night came on and the two armies ceased the strife. Lighting their campfires they awaited the fortunes of war upon the morrow.

It was the conflict of this evening, January 2, 1777, at the battle of Assunpink, that Mr. Rosbrugh lost his life. There are several versions of the sad event. "The heroic pastor was surprised in a farmhouse near Pennington," another, "Having taken part in the capture of the Hessians at Trenton, the next morning while in a farm-house near the village of Pennington—was cruelly put to death." The most trustworthy account is that which was given by Captain Hays, who buried the body, which states that unconscious of danger, he came to a public house in Trenton. He entered to obtain some refreshments. While at table he was alarmed by hearing the cry, "The Hessians are coming." Hastening out, he tried to make his escape by the bridge, but found it guarded. He turned his steps down the stream toward the ford. On arriving there, he found it impossible to make his escape. He turned back into a grove of trees where he was met by a small company of Hessians. Seeing escape was impossible he surrendered himself a prisoner of war. He begged for his life, but they prepared to put him to death. Seeing this, he knelt at the foot of a tree, and it is said, prayed for his enemies. Now seventeen bayonet thrusts were made in his body, and one bayonet was left broken off in his quivering frame. Sabre lashes were made at his devoted head, three of which passed through the horse-hair wig which he wore.

So died the "Clerical Martyr of the Revolution," at the age of sixty-three.

It was not long until Captain Hays was apprised of the death of his pastor, upon which he hastily wrapped the body in a cloak and buried it where it lay, being under necessity to hurry forward with the rest of the troops in the night march which precipitated the battle of Princeton in the morning.

Sometime after, Mr. Duffield, a brother Chaplain took up the body and reburied it. There are various traditions as to the place where the body rests. A common one is that it lies in the burying-ground at the Old First Presbyterian Church in Trenton. Another that he lies buried in Father Cooly's graveyard, a few miles from Trenton. Some of his descendants believe that the body was taken to Philadelphia, but where buried they have no means of ascertaining.

April 22, 1777, the Presbytery of New Brunswick made the following record:

"Rev. Messrs. Tennent and Rosbrugh have deceased since our last Presbytery." In like manner the Synod of New York and Philadelphia of which he had been a member, placed on record May 21st.

"New Brunswick Presbytery reports that Rev. Mr. William Tennent departed this life, March 8, 1777, and that Rev. Mr. John Rosbrugh was barbarously murdered by the enemy at Trenton on January second."

Thus his record disappears from the records of the church militant.

Rev. John Rosbrugh—Clerical Martyr of the Revolution

By Rev. Fred G. Bulgin, Bath, Pa.

In 1728, a band of Scotch-Irish or Ulster Scots, led by Col. Thomas Craig and John Boyd of Philadelphia, sought their abode in the "Forks of the Delaware" the common designation in early times of what is now Northampton County, Pennsylvania, and settled at a place on the Catasauqua creek known later as the Craig Settlement.

In 1731, these people organized the Allen Township Presbyterian Church. The first house of worship was a rude log structure erected in 1746 on the south side of the road in Craig's Meadow, near what is now Weaversville. This was succeeded by a second log building on the north of the road. These two buildings served the people sixty-seven (67) years, until 1813 when the present stone house was erected, which was enclosed in weather boards in 1870. In the same year—1870—the congregation erected a fourth church edifice in the borough of Bath. The graveyard adjoining the old church was occupied for burials as early as 1745, as the oldest stone bears that date in the name of James King.

This congregation has never been very large but it has been composed of families generally well to do, thrifty and united. It is a church of historic interest for good in this vicinity, and there is much reflection in that it has remained so united for one hundred and ninety (190) years, having survived for nearly two centuries in the best civilization of the best period of the world's history.

In connection with the ministry of this church in its early history, we find the names of the Revs. Gilbert Tennent, James Campbell and David Brainerd, the last of whom preached for some time to the Indians.

The frequent calls upon the records of Presbytery for supplies of preaching abundantly attests the important place that religion had in this settlement. They looked to the education of their children. It was a typical Presbyterian colony, and visitors today are soon reminded by the people of Northampton County of the points of interest in what they are proud to claim as the home of what is this day spoken of as "THE IRISH SETTLEMENT."

In 1769, there came to serve them as supply a Scotch minister, the Rev. John Rosbrugh. Of the early life of this man scarcely anything is known. Probably he was born in Scotland in 1714. His parents left for Ireland shortly after this son was born. Be it remembered, that those were days when Presbyterians did not have things made exceedingly pleasant for them. And some years after, the Rosbrughs joined the procession across the seas in search for a wider place and a freer air, where they might worship their God without molestation.

When past forty years of age, John Rosbrugh turned his thoughts towards preparation for the gospel ministry, graduating from the college of New Jersey in the class of 1761. The records of the Presbytery show that he had a rather difficult time passing his examinations for licensure, but at last he reached his goal, when Presbytery ordained him, Dec. 11th, 1764, pastor of Greenwich, Oxford, and Mansfield Woodhouse (now Washington) churches. He had for a parish what is now Warren County. He did not have an easy time of it. How could he with so large a territory? The Presbytery released him from this charge in 1769.

Then he began supplying in the Forks of the Delaware. He was not unknown in the Allen Township Church, for some years before he had found favor in the eyes of Jane Ralston, daughter of James Ralston, the leading ruling eldei in the church. In 1772 Mr. Rosbrugh was installed pastor, and in this field all went happily.

April 23rd, 1776 Presbytery met in Bound Brook and the Rev. John Rosbrugh was chosen moderator.

The Presbytery met again, in the intervals of Synod, at Philadelphia, May 23rd, 1776, and the records show that the following were present—"Mr. Rosbrugh, the moderator; the

Rev. Dr. Witherspoon, William Tenent, Elihu Spencer, John Debow, Jeremiah Halsey, Elder John Walker."

This was the last meeting of Presbytery that Mr. Rosbrugh attended.

That Fall the news from the Army threw a gloom over everybody in the "Forks of the Delaware." Things seemed to be going from bad to worse.

Then one Sabbath morning the pastor appeared in his pulpit with a letter from the front, which he read. It was a cry for help from Washington in his headquarters in the Keith House, Upper Makefield Township, calling for the immediate mobilization of the Northampton County Militia. The pastor preached a sermon from the text "Curse Ye Meroz, saith the Angel of the Lord; curse ye bitterly the inhabitants thereof, because they came not to the help of the Lord against the mighty."

Such was the magnetism of the preacher and such the spirit of his people that a company marched away from this parish, reporting at the front within eight days from the date of Washington's letter. It is declared that during the Revolutionary War practically every able bodied man in the Allen Township Presbyterian Church served in the cause of the struggle for independence.

It was this sort of spirit ever rallying to Washington's side, that enabled him to win the victory.

Reaching the front Rosbrugh gave up the command and received appointment as Chaplain of the Third Battalion of Northampton County Militia.

On January 2nd, 1777, Washington made a demonstration against the enemy, marching out as far as Maidenhead. As the British appeared in force the patriot army retreated upon Trenton. It had been a muddy day, but suddenly toward night a sudden change came. The ground hardened. Washington withdrew all his forces to the south side of the Assanpink Creek, where a portion of his army was already intrenched,

Chaplain Rosbrugh, unacquainted with military ways was left behind. He was eating his supper in the "Blazing Star Tavern," which stood where the Mechanics Bank now stands, when he was apprised that the enemy was upon him. Rising, his horse was gone; he tried to cross at the bridge, but could not. He turned to the ford, which was near what is now Warren street, only to meet disappointment again. He turned back, was overtaken by a company of Hessians, who bayoneted "the rebel parson to death," crying for mercy and praying for his captives.

During the evening, Captain Hays, of his own congregation hunted up the body of his pastor, and gave it hasty burial on the spot. The American cause was trembling in the balance, and having performed his task, he hurried away for the midnight march upon Princeton.

The next Monday, the Rev. George Duffield, a Chaplain of Congress, who served also in the Army as he was able, hearing of the death of his friend, hunted for the grave and had the body taken up to inter in the burying ground. The death of Rosbrugh made a profound impression. All sorts of stories became current. Some reported he was killed in Pennington, some that he was buried in Philadelphia.

Some years ago Rev. George Ingrim, Stated clerk of the Presbytery of New Jersey found a clipping in the Presbyterian Historical Society that sent him to the files of the Pennsylvania Evening Post of the issues of April, 1777, where, running through several numbers is a report of a committee appointed by Congress to investigate alleged atrocities committed by the enemy. Reference is made to the murder in Trenton of a minister of the gospel and then follows an affidavit of the Rev George Duffield afterward pastor of the Pine street Presbyterian Church, setting forth the facts of the death and burial of Chaplain Rosbrugh, which in substance has been given above.

Those who have carefully looked into these facts agree that the churchyard of the first Presbyterian Church, Trenton is the resting place of this patriot.

And now, after one hundred and forty (140) years have passed since the bullets flew over Trenton and the gallant Rosbrugh was gone to his death, the Presbytery of New Brunswick, with the co-operation of their friends unveiled a monument in that revolutionary churchyard in memory of this patriot pastor.

And here in this historic section and in his own parish, may there be erected another Rosbrugh memorial which will tell the story of service, heroism and sacrifice of the brave men who risk their all in the cause of American Independence.

Wesselhoeft and His Bath School of Homoeopathy

By Asa K. McIlhaney, Bath, Pa.

"Dr. William Wesselhoeft, the distinguished pioneer of homoeopathy in Pennsylvania, was born Sept. 1st, 1794, in Chemnitz, Germany.

"He was the second son of Karl Wesselhoeft who, with his brother-in-law, Frederick Fromman owned the largest publishing house in the University town of Jena, during the palmy days of Saxe-Weimar. When four years old, his father moved from Chemnitz. At ten years of age, the poet Goethe took a kindly interest in his education, and gave him pencils and paper and friendly advice, in order to foster a love for drawing, for he believed that art was an essential to early education, and he himself excelled in it. Nor did Karl, his father, stint these educational advantages, though impoverished by the wars with Napoleon. He had residing in his family as private tutor to his children the celebrated DeWette, afterwards professor of theology at Berlin, and later at Basle; and after DeWette, Grossman who became Superintendent of the Lutheran churches at Leipsic.

"This family consisted of William, his brothers Edward and Robert, his sister Wilhemina, and a ward of his uncle Fromman, Minnia Herzlied, celebrated in the "Memoirs of Goethe," as one of the ladies who for a time held the sentimental poet's heart.

"In 1809, William Wesselhoeft became a pupil at the Real-Schule of Nuremburg, then under the direction of G. H. von Schubert the great natural philosopher and psychologist, in whose autobiography may be found frequent mention of young Wesselhoeft. Here besides studying Latin and Greek, he began his profound studies in the natural sciences, including anatomy, of which he was very fond, becoming very expert in anatomical drawings. His botanical studies also were extensive, and he prepared a valuable hortus siccus, a written explanation of every plant. During his student life, he was in the habit of making extensive tours for the purpose of exploration in botany, mineralogy and geology, and his collection of minerals and geological specimens were given to Dr. Adolph Donai for the benefit of the students in the Perkins Institution for the Blind.

"Our young savant also studied transcendental physics under the celebrated Oken. In 1813, when nineteen he entered the University of Jena, graduating there seven years afterwards as doctor of medicine, having perfected his general and medical education at the Universities of Berlin and Wurzburg, at each of which he resided for a season, and at which he passed the second and third examinations necessary in Germany to obtain a license to practice medicine. Wesselhoeft was not only a scholar of parts but also an attractive man of the world. At this time, Goethe was much interested in meteorology, and Wesselhoeft enjoyed making observations of the clouds for him at the University at Jena.

"Wesselhoeft was in sympathy with the patriots who had returned from German Army service, in which struggle Koerner fell in 1806.

"When in Berlin, in 1819, he became intimate with Old Jahn who invented the modern system of gymnastics, and had in Berlin, a gymnasium as early as 1811. It was the time of the Burschenschaften, in Germany, secret political societies to promote nationality; and William and Robert Wesselhcoft who were students at Jena, were very active in promoting these organizations. These Burschenschaften were betrayed by a traitor, and many were arrested, among them William and Robert Wesselheoft. William who was at the time pursuing his studies at Berlin, was thrown into the political prison, and Robert was confined in the fortress at Magdeburg. William escaped after a two month's imprisonment, and was for a long time, concealed in his father's house at Jena. Then young Dr. Wesselheoft wished to go to the assistance of the Greeks, who were struggling for freedom. He became surgeon to the German Philhellen, and started well equipped with surgical appliances. Indeed, so ample was the quantity of lint and of bandages prepared by his sister Wilhemina, his friend Ferdinanda, and others in the secret, that it is said to have lasted him all his life. When he arrived at Marseilles, an injunction was laid on the vessel and no more volunteers could go to Greece. From Marseilles he went to Switzerland, where his friends, Follen and Beck, and De Wette who had found positions in the University of Basle where Wesselheoft also found employment as demonstrator of anatomy and assistant oculist. He remained there two years, and spent his vacations in tours among the lofty mountains, not only for love of natural science but for the picturesque. During the later years of his life, he often talked of revisiting Switzerland, and the last picture he purchased was a sketch of the Alps, painted by Leutze, where the needlewood pines seem to whisper of the solitude, and as he said, reminded him of his own youth.

"But there was interference by the allied powers with the German refugees, driving Drs. Follen and Beck from Switzerland, and compelling Wesselhoeft, to leave for America, at the same time. Some letters showing his sympathy with Follen had fallen into the hands of the despots. He sailed from Antwerp, and was four months on the voyage. On his arrival, he went to Lehigh County, Pa., where lived a German family he had known at home. From there, in 1824, he went to Northampton county, seeking a place to practice, and settled in Bath, where the population then was largely German. Follen and Beck, who also came to America, made efforts to induce him to go to Massachusetts. In 1825, Tickner wrote asking him to take charge of the gymnasium at Cambridge and Boston, but already a large practice occupied him at Bath, and he refused.

"In 1824, his father became much interested in Homoeopathy, and importuned his son to make a trial with Homoeopathic remedies, of which he sent a supply with Hahnemann's Organon, and the Materia Medica Pura. William Wesselhoeft read the Organon, but it did not convince him. He looked upon this teaching as the other extreme to the prevailing drugging and blood-letting of that time. He had devoted himself mainly to surgery, or as much as offered itself among the agricultural population of this locality. After a successful operation for cataract on an old woman who had been blind for many years, his fame rose. He soon did much of the surgical work of Eastern Pennsylvania. Before he left his native country, he devoted much of his leisure time, and his exceptional mechanical skill, to learning the art of making surgical instruments. Many of the instruments he brought with him were the work of his own handicraft. His son, Dr. William Wesselhoeft of Boston, lately deceased, a leading surgeon of this country, had part of a set of eye instruments in his possession which shows the skill he had attained in this branch of mechanical work.

"In the beginning of 1828, a girl with a very offensive Ozoena came under his care. She had been treated by many Allopathic physicians before, without success. Then he thought he would look into his Homoeopathic Materia Medica, and see if there were any remedy there which corresponded to the symptoms of her case. With the usual luck of a beginner, he hit upon Pulsatilla, but was ashamed to give it in the thirtieth potency, therefore gave it in the sixth.

"A tremendous aggravation of symptoms took place, which lasted for many days, and he was on the point of being discharged as having poisoned the girl, when he entreated the parents to give him a little more time. He recognized that this was what Hahnemann called Homoeopathic aggravation, and consequently became intensely interested in this,—the first experiment. He stopped all meditation and waited; in less than three months the case was cured.

"This was the entering wedge to more experiments, and in six months, as he expressed it, "I stood like a cow before a new barn door." He now began to work, abandoned as much as possible his practice, and made a vow that he would never give another Allopathic dose. He gathered about him a few physicians and intelligent laymen. These physicians were:—Drs. Romig, Detwiller and Freytag, and some intelligent clergymen of the Moravian, Lutheran and Reformed faiths,—Revs. Becker, Helfrich, Fuchs and Waage.

"At this time, he was engaged to Sarah Palmer, (daughter of Surveyor-General George Palmer of Bath), whom he was soon to marry. He told her that she would have to wait; that he had found a new truth, and during his studies to perfect himself in its practice he would lose much of his income, and would not be in a position to marry her for a year. To all of this she readily assented. Wesselhoeft now devoted himself almost exclusively to the study of the Meteria Medica Pura, and some of his neighbors remarked afterwards that they never saw his light go out during the nights. He arranged repertoires from thirty or forty polychrests. With these he armed the members of the little associations of physicians and laymen whom he had interested in the new art. Every week these men reported to him the success of their remedies, and at each meeting he gave them new food for thought and work. This was the beginning of Homoeopathy in Pennsylvania.

"In 1829, an epidemic of an intestinal character occurred in Northampton county and at that time Dr. Wesselhoeft had given up the old practice and devoted himself entirely to Homoeopathy. For a year he treated free all cases that came to him wishing to learn more thoroughly the new Materia Medica. He established offices in Bath and surrounding places, where he invited the sick to come for treatment, and he devoted a part of each day to these clinics.

"Previous to 1830, Wesselhoeft furnished all the medicines and books, most of which came from his friend Dr. Stapf, Hahnemann's first and beloved pupil, but in that year Dr. Detwiller received books and medicines from Dr. Siegrist of Basle.

"To Dr. Wesselhoeft belongs the honor of starting the first Homoeopathic School of Instruction in America. This was in Bath, Pa., and continued from 1829 to 1835.

"To him in Bath, as medical students, came Joseph H.

Pulte, a graduate of the University of Marburg, later author of medical books, founder of Pulte Medical College in Cincinnati, and later U. S. Minister to Austria; J. C. Gosewisch, of the University of Gottingen, the first to introduce homoeopathy in the state of Delaware; Gustav Reichelm, of the University of Halle, who carried the new science across the Alleghanies and settled in Pittsburgh; John H. Floto, a university graduate and Lutheran minister, who made his home at first in the South, but later in California; besides these were Ferenthiel, a nobleman, usually called Herr von Fahventheil, Wolford, Humphrey, Rhoads, Nagle and others

"By April, 1835, the number of converts had so increased that Wesselhoeft with Freytag, Detweiler and Romig and the aforenamed pioneers had the courage to go upon society organization and found a college of homoeopathic medical instruction properly chartered by the state, under the name of "The North American Academy of the Homoeopathic Healing Art." It was established in Allentown, and was the first institution of its kind in the world, having its inception in the Bath school and in the Homoeopathic Society of Northampton County. Sometime previous to this (1833) Dr. Constantine Herring had begun the practice in Philadelphia. He was induced to come to Allentown and be president of the new college. He accepted under the conditions that his salary should equal that paid to a clergyman. Partly through the treachery of one of the trustees, and the financial panic following the closing of the United States Bank, Dr. Herring's salary was discontinued, and he returned to Philadelphia in 1839.

"Wesselhoeft with Romig, Detweiler and Freytag, and a few others, kept on with the work for a year or two longer, until finally the mortgages on a property were foreclosed.

"Although the institution was destined to a brief existence (1835-1841), yet some of its best elements were utilized in forming the Hahnemann's Medical College, Philadelphia. From these institutions has sprung the Homoeopathic State Hospital for the Insane at Rittersville, the cornerstone of which was laid in the presence of the Governor and many other prominent men, June 27th, 1904.

"In 1841, Wesselhoeft with his family removed to Boston. In a very short time his successes were recognized, especially in the scarlet fever epidemic which was at that time prevailing in that city; and in a few years he had established himself firmly in the nurseries of Boston. It soon became evident to the community that a larger field was his, in the treatment of chronic diseases and in a short time he had an exceptionally large office practice.

"There is no doubt that Dr. Wesselhoeft had the most agreeable expectations with respect to society, in removing from the interior of Pennsylvania to Boston; as he had not been insensible to the immense changes from Saxe-Weimer to Northampton County, where though the population was friendly and respectable, yet it left the scholar to sigh occasionally for the circles of his youth, which Goethe had graced with front sublime as Jove, and where Jean Paul Richter poured out his rich and beautiful humor.

"During the last year of his life, he became aware that he was overtaxing his constitution. He went for a vacation to the country; but a cold brought him back to the city. He sent to Philadelphia for Herring, refusing to see all others that he might have strength to talk to him. However, he died a few hours before his old friend arrived on Sept. 1st. 1858.

"History, like charity, should begin at home. It should not end there. There are many people who have visited the historic localities of Europe, but have never been to the interesting localities at their very doors. We should see and know our own first. I hope the Northampton County Historical Society will recommend to the proper state authorities the advisibility of marking the historic sites in the county with appropriate memorials and that No. 9 Chestnut Street, Bath, where in 1829 the first Homoeopathic School of Medicine was established in America, will be one."

THE OLD CHURCH IN ALLEN

A Sketch of the Irish Settlement in the Forks of the Delaware

By REV. RICHARD WEBSTER,

Pastor First Presbyterian Church, Mauch Chunk, Pa.

Copy from sketch in the "Presbyterian," 1847—loaned by Miss Jane Horner, Bath, Pa.

The purchase of William Penn was understood to include all the land from Duck Creek, Delaware, to the Lehigh hills, and to be bounded east by the river Delaware, and west by the Susquehanna. By the Lehigh hills, was designated the range called Musconetcong in New Jersey, and Conewago on the Susquehanna; it is commonly styled now the South, or Second Mountain, to distinguish it from the Kittatinny or Blue Mountain.

The Forks of Delaware is the tract inclosed by the Lehigh and Delaware rivers, and by the Blue Mountain. It was inhabited by the Delaware tribe, but they held it as tributary to the Iroquois. Long before the settlement of the Middle States from Europe, this confederacy held supreme sway over all the Indians in our country. The terror of their arms had been felt by the Pequots in New England, the Wyandottes beyond Lake Huron, and the Cherokees, Catawbas, *and Powhatans in Virginia and the Carolinas. There were originally five tribes, Onandagas, Mohawks, Oneidas, Cayugas, and Senecas. In 1712, the Tuscaroras emigrated from the South, and were admitted to the union, and from that time they were called by the English, when spoken of as one people, the Six Nations; they were not called so by themselves, but Mengwe, or Konushionis; by the French Aquanushionis and Iroquois. These sovereigns had their council fire at Oswego, New York and their residence was chiefly on the head waters of the Hudson, the Delaware, and the Susquehanna, and along the chain of the Great Lakes.

In 1732, an old claim was revived by the Pennsylvania proprietaries that all the land that could be gone over by a man walking for a day and a half, should be given them. Advertisements were issued for the best walkers, and five hundred acres of land and five pounds promised to the one who would go over the largest space in the appointed time. In 1733 the walk was performed, and in such a manner that the proprietors' line was run as high as Shehola in Pike county, and they to have all land lying south of a direct line thence to the Susquehanna.

Surveyors immediately began to locate the patents that were issued, although the Indians had not left the country. Penn had given by will to his grandson, William Penn, ten thousand acres, to be laid out in whatever part of the province might be most for his advantage. William Allen, the father-in-law of Thomas Penn, purchased this grant, and procured it to be laid out in the Minisinks, above the Delaware Water Gap, in the fine richlands, occupied by the Shawnese Indians. In 1734, the proprietors sat up a lottery to dispose of one hundred thousand acres, and many who drew prizes, took up lands in the Forks, although it was full of Indian dwellings.

In 1736 and 1737, the Irish Settlement commenced on the west branch of Delaware, now called the Lehigh; the date of the deed from Allen to Hugh Wilson is 1737; his deed to James Horner is dated March 5, 1737. Others may have purchased a few years earlier.

The removal of the Irish Presbyterians to this country was for the purpose of accumulating property. Speculators in land sent to Great Britain the most exaggerated descriptions, and the desire to emigrate became an epidemic disease, hurrying immense multitudes hither. There they were tenants, holding their land by lease, and many of them having no prospect of ever rising above the condition of hired laborers; here they might acquire land, and hold it in fee. The tide began to set in as early as 1718; large numbers of Irish Presbyterians settled in Massachusetts, New

Hampshire, and New York. In Pennsylvania the number of Irish congregations increased in number so greatly from 1725 to 1731, that Donegal Presbytery was erected for the accommodation of the ministers settled on the Susquehanna in Lancaster county, and this Presbytery reached, before 1740, far down in western Virginia, and to the frontiers of Pennsylvania.

There were two Irish settlements in the Forks; one on the north branch at Mt. Bethel, called Hunter's Settlement, or Forks North; the other Craig's Settlement, in Allen's town, on the west branch. They do not appear to have been molested by the Indians for ten or fifteen years; and may we not infer justly that the usual complaints made against the Presbyterians are wholly unfounded?

In 1737, the Indians confirmed the sale of the land in the Forks, but still complained that it had been taken by fraud, and refused to remove. In 1738, Whitefield bought of Allen the manor of Nazareth, lying between the Irish settlements, and commenced building; he abandoned his plan, and sold the property to the Moravians. In 1741, the proprietaries invited the Six Nations, as masters of the Delawares, to interpose and compel them to retire; and in 1742 no less than two hundred and thirty Indians came to Philadelphia on this business, and in the most insulting manner commanded the Delawares to retire to Wyoming. They obeyed; of course many remained. The neighborhood of Cherryville was known as the Indian land, and the peach trees in their clearings near Bath, were still fruitful, sixty years ago.

The first settlers were Thomas Craig, James Craig, Hugh Wilson, with his three sons, Thomas, Samuel, and Charles, Thomas Armstrong, Robert Gregg, James King, John McNair, John and Robert Walker, James Ralston, John Hays, Arthur Lattimore, James Horner, and James Kerr.

The Craigs were not related. James Craig is believed to have been connected with William Allen by marriage; he was probably the oldest man of the company; his two sons, Robert and James, were grown up before their father came to the Forks. In the family of James Craig, came Timothy Reed and his wife; they lived to an advanced age, and their son, John Reed, a very intelligent, well informed man, with an excellent memory, is now living, at the age of ninety-five, in Moore township, Northampton county. Thomas Craig was advanced in life, his only son, William, being in the vigor of manhood. Hugh Wilson, before coming to this country, had a daughter married to the Rev. Francis McHenry, of Deep Run, Pennsylvania, and a son in business in New York. James King and John McNair, with John Walker, whose sisters they married, left their wives while they prepared new homes for them, under the hospitable roof of their brother-in-law, Capt. Richard Walker, of Neshaminy, an elder, and a firm supporter of his minister, William Tennent. The names of these men, and of all the first settlers, came down with a good report.

The farms sold to them lay on the slate lands, on the Hoquendoquy and the Collasaque,* on toward Kreiderville and the mountains. The limestone land on the Monocacy was not sold until after the Revolution.

The nearest place of worship was at Tehicken, in Bucks county. They were not the people to remain long without the means of grace, especially when their relatives at Tehicken, Deep Run, and Neshaminy were well supplied. They made application to New Brunswick Presbytery, then recently organized, in August, 1738, and Gilbert Tennent was directed to visit them in the fall. In May, 1740, the Rev. James Campbell, (who spent the close of his life in North Carolina), was sent to supply them, and in the fall he and William Robinson, (so eminently successful in labour), then just licensed, were sent. In May, 1742, Forks and Greenwich supplicated for the Rev. Charles McKnight, but Robinson was sent, and Campbell was charged to give one-fourth of his time to Forks. In August, Forks again asked for McKnight, but Campbell was required to divide one-half of his time between Greenwich and Forks. In October, the Rev. William Dean was licensed, having been received as a candidate in the preceding August, and he was sent to Neshaminy and Forks. In the next May, Forks, with Brandywine and Cape May, presented calls for Mr. Dean, and Newcastle Presbytery requested that he might be joined to them. He declined the three invitations, and the Presbytery sent him to Forks and Pequea. In the fall of 1743 Campbell and Beatty of Neshaminy, went as supplies to Forks, and the latter, with Dean, went thither in the ensuing summer.

William Dean settled in Newcastle Presbytery, and was sent by the Synod in 1746, with Mr. Bryam, on a mission to Virginia. President Davies says there was an extensive revival under their labours in Augusta county; Mr. Dean, just before his death, in 1747, was called to Timberridge and Forks of James river. What congregation enjoyed his pastoral services is unknown to the writer; Davies connects him in honourable mention with Robinson, as one of our most useful ministers.

It was in May, 1744, that the man of God, David Brainerd, journeying through the Highlands and Minisinks, came wet and fatigued of a Saturday to a settlement of Dutch and Irish people, twelve miles above the Forks of Delaware. This is the neighborhood of Milford, Pennsylvania; he spent two Sabbaths with the whites and the Indians there. He then proceeded to Newark, and was ordained by the Presbytery of New York, and soon after took up his abode at Mount Bethel, in the Forks. On Monday, the 23rd of July, he rode fifteen miles south-west, to a settlement of Irish people, and preached near night from Matt. V. 3, with some degree of freedom and fervency. This was in James Craig's meadow, in front of the meeting house in Allen township. The next day he rode seventeen miles west over a hideous mountain, and preached to thirty Indians; and having preached on Wednesday to them, he returned to the settlement, where a numerous congregation assembled to hear him, and there was a considerable appearance of awakening.

In the autumn, with the Rev. Eliab Byram, of Rosciti-

THE JAMES KERR HOMESTEAD
Oldest House in Weaversville—Rear View. (See page 168.)

cus, now Mendham, New Jersey, he travelled to the Susquehanna, visiting the Indians; returning, they reached the settlement on the 9th of October, and both of them preached. On the Sabbath Brainerd preached. "God was gracious to me, and I was much assisted in preaching. I know not that ever God helped me to preach in a more close and distinguishing manner, for the trial of men's state. Through the infinite goodness of God, I felt what I spoke, and was enabled to treat the truth with uncommon clearness." On the last Lord's day in the year he preached from Mark VIII, 34, with very great freedom and clearness, and in the afternoon especially, with considerable warmth and fervency. "In the evening also had great clearness while conversing with friends on divine things, and I do not remember ever to have had more clear apprehensions of religion."

On the 17th of February, of a Lord's day, he preached on the sunny side of a hill on which the church of Mount Bethel stands, with the grave-yard at its foot. He preached from John VIII, 37, some of the people having come twenty miles. "In the afternoon it pleased God to grant me great freedom and earnestness, and like Jesus, I stood and cried. I was scarce ever able to offer the free grace of God to perishing sinners, with greater liberty and fervency. Afterwards, I was enabled earnestly to invite the children of God to come renewedly, and drink of the fountain of the water of life. It was a comfortable time to me. There were many tears in the assembly, and I doubt not the Spirit of God was there, convincing poor sinners of their need of Christ. O, that I could forever bless God for the mercy of this day, when he answered me in the joy of my heart." February 24th, he preached to a few white people from John, VI. 67, and on April 14th, from Ezek. XXXIII. 11, with considerable freedom, to people gathered from all parts round about.

He went to Philadelphia to obtain leave of the Six Nations to settle in Wyoming, and April 28th, he preached, with considerable assistance, at the settlement. In May, he went to the Susquehanna, and travelled from Harrisburg up to Wyalusing, and saw seven or eight tribes. Returning, he preached at the settlement, from Isa. lvii. 10, with some success, some being awakened. President Edwards says, that the account of Brainerd's labours and success among the Indians in the Forks, he omits, because Brainerd had printed it in his public journal. I have not had the satisfaction of seeing it; it is in the Philadelphia Library, and is entitled Mirabilia Dei, the wonders of God in the wilderness.

On the 4th of September he went to the settlement, and preached from Luke xiv. 22, "God was pleased to afford me some tenderness and enlargement in the first prayer, and much freedom as well as warmth in the sermon. There were many tears. God's people seemed to melt, and others to be in some measure awakened."

He went to Shamokin, where Shikellimy, an Onondaga Indian, the agent of the Six Nations, resided; and September 20th, returned to the Settlement, visited dear Christian friends, and spent the time profitably. On the 21st of February, 1746, he was at the Forks; divers white people were awakened, and he preached to them daily through the week.

Brainerd died at Northampton, Massachusetts, October 9th, 1747, aged thirty. His life was published in 1749. We may judge of the esteem in which he was held in the Forks, from the fact that there were sixteen copies of the first edition subscribed for there; viz. Rev. Daniel Lawrence, James Craig, Thomas Craig, William Craig, Mary Dobbin, James Horner, William Heslet, Mary Knight, James Kerr, John McNair, James Ralston, Hugh Wilson, John Walker, William Young.

There was a log church at this time, in the meadow, between the mill-race and the Hoquendoquy, on James Craig's land. After Brainerd preached, the people would retire weeping to pray among the hazle bushes, which then grew all around, and he would come and comfort them. The oldest stone in the grave-yard is to the memory of James King, who died in 1745, and the next oldest bears the name of his only son Gabrial; these died in faith. Mrs. King was left a widow with four young daughters; she would take a child in her arms, and ride to Mount Bethel, to hear Brainerd preach in the open air. Mr. Congleton built a room or "lean-to," for Brainerd's accommodation, that he might always have a place of retirement, when he desired to be alone.

He seems never to have preached to the people on the West branch, without observing special attention, and signs of good. There he had Christian friends, and while conversing with them, his apprehensions of divine things became clearer than ever they had been before, and never, in his preaching, had he opened the truth so distinctly, and applied it so searchingly to try the state of their souls, as at the Forks, on October 9th, 1744.

Such were the first ten years of the church in Allen township.

---

*In 1742, Zinzendorf met at Ostonwakin Indians speaking several languages, and Europeans leading Indian life. He went to the dwelling of old Madame Montour, a French lady, who had married an Indian. Her husband, a chief, had been shot in the war against Catawhees (Catawbas?) She wept on seeing him, professed to be tired of Indian life, and asked baptism for her children. Zinzendorf declined. Her children were Roland and Catharine Montour—the celebrated "Queen Easter," we presume—a merciless foe.

*The following towns in Massachusetts were settled from Ireland: Worcester, in 1718; Lunenburg, in 1728; Palmer, before 1730; Coleraine, in 1734; Blandford, Greenwich, Pelham, Oakham; in New Hampshire, Londonderry, in 1718; Chester, Bedford, Windham, Antrim, Litchfield, and Derry; and Orange county in New York.

*Absurdly enough, the village and Post office at the Crane Iron Works, on the Collasaque, are styled Catasauqua.

The earliest record to be found is "the Count Book of the congregation on the west branch of Delaware in the Forks. The first entry is as follows:

"Received from the congregation of the West Branch the sum of 40£ in full payment of the year 1747, I say, received by me, this 30th day of January, 1749-50.

Daniel Lawrence."

Mr Lawrence was a pupil of the Rev. William Tennent, and had been educated at the Log College. He was taken on trial as a candidate by New Brunswick Presbytery on the 11th of September, 1744, and was licensed May 28, 1745, and appointed to supply the Forks. In September he had calls offered to him by the Presbytery from Newtown and Bensalem, Hopwell and Maidenhead, and Upper and Lower Bethlehem. He did not accept, and in May, 1746, Hopewell and its associates renewed their request, and Forks asked that he might be sent to them for a year as a candidate for settlement. In October they made him out a call, and he was ordained and installed on the 2d of April, 1747, by a committee of Presbytery. The Rev. Richard Treat, of Abingdon, presided, and the other services were performed by the Rev. James Campbell, the Rev. James Davenport, and the Rev. James McCrea, of Lamington, New Jersey.

Mr. Lawrence served both the settlements in the Forks, and he complained to the Presbytery that his salary was not paid, and that he had an uncomfortable debate with one of his hearers. ("Debate" is used in the old records for disagreement, difficulty, or contention. "Ye fast for strife and debate.") In 1751, Mr. Lawrence's health failed, and the Synod directed him to spend the winter and spring at Cape May, the people being in necessitous circumstances. He did so, and found his health much improved. The Synod of New York divided New Brunswick Presbytery, and constituted out of that part that lay in Pennsylvania and west Jersey, the Presbytery of Abingdon. At the first meeting of the new Presbytery, held in Philadelphia on the 20th of May, 1752, Cape May supplicated, that in case Mr. Lawrence was liberated from the Forks, he might come to them on trial for settlement. The Presbytery, judging that as Mr. Lawrence was languishing in health, with discouraging symptoms, and frequently disabled from attending to his duty in the Forks, and as there was a prospect of his recovery by changing his residence, unanimously dissolved the pastoral relation. Mr. Thomas Armstrong was the elder present at this meeting; he afterward removed to Fagg's Manor. At the next meeting of Presbytery, Mr. Lawrence was called to Cape May, and he remained there till his death, April 13, 1766. A faithful, zealous minister, and not behind his early associates in the Log College, in the purity of his character. and his diligence in his work. His grandson, the Rev. Samuel Lawrence, was for many years the pastor of Greenwich, Cumberland county, New Jersey, and his great grandson, the Rev. D. L. Hughes, is the pastor of Little Valley, in Huntingdon Presbytery.

Bucks county originally included the Forks, but on March 11, 1752, Northampton county was erected, embracing besides its present limits Pike, Wayne, Monroe, Lehigh, Carbon, and part of Schuylkill. The legislature at the same time directed Thomas Craig, Hugh Wilson, Thomas Armstrong, of the Settlement, James Martin of Mount Bethel, and John Jones, to purchase land on the Lehicton (or the Bushkill), and lay out a county town, and erect suitable buildings. They were ordered to raise, by tax, for this purpose, 300£. The first court was held on the 16th of June, 1752. "The Justices of our Lord and King" were Thomas Craig, Timothy Horsefield of Bethlehem, Hugh Wilson, James Martin, and William Craig. Sixteen licenses were granted to keep public houses, one of which was to William Craig. It was through his exertions the county had been erected, and the next year the commissioners allowed him 30£ to reimburse the expenses he had incurred. On the grand jury, in October, 1752, were James Ralston, Robert Gregg, James Horner, and John Walker. Robert Gregg was one of the commissioners, and James Ralston and John Walker were assessors.

While Mr. Lawrence was absent for his health in 1751, his place was supplied by the Rev. Benjamin Chesnut, afterwards pastor of Woodbury and Timber Creek, New Jersey. Mr. Lawrence was directed by the Presbytery to spend two Sabbaths in the Forks, and in the fall, after his dismission, the congregation supplicated that he might be among the supplies. He was ordered to spend four Sabbaths, Campbell and Beatty each two, and the Rev. Evander Morrison to supply at discretion. In May, 1753, Lawrence, Chesnut, and Martin of Newtown, were appointed supplies, and in the fall Chesnut went four Sabbaths, and leave was given to the congregation to ask supplies from New Brunswick Presbytery. In April, 1754, Martin, and Andrew Hunter of Greenwich, were appointed supplies, and in the fall the Rev. Benjamin Hait came as supply to the Forks. In May, 1755, they made out a call for Mr. Hait, as did also Fagg's Manor and Amwell. He accepted the call to Amwell.

From 1750 to 1760, the perils of Indian warfare were dreaded, prepared for and felt all along the Pennsylvania frontier. In 1746, the Moravians had established themselves at the confluence of the Mahoning Creek with the Lehigh, and Gnadenhutten soon became a very regular and pleasant town; the church stood in the valley, and the Indian houses in a crescent on the rising ground. The Six Nations renewed, in 1750, the order for the Indians to remove to Wyoming, and nearly all the Delawares left the Forks. But Gnadenhutten lay beyond the Forks, and the Christian Indians, who had emigrated from New York, had each their separate plantations, supporting themselves. In 1752, the population was about 500.

At this time, the Six Nations were in secret league with the French, and they used every method to persuade the government of Pennsylvania that they were devoted to the interests of Great Britain. Their agent, Shikellimy, at Shamokin, enjoyed the highest confidence of the Pennsylvania authorities, and through him the Six Nations were kept acquainted with all the affairs of the province. Gnadenhutten lay on the Warrior's path from the Delaware to Wyoming, and in 1752, about 1,000 Indians, principally Nanticokes, who had been removed by the Six Nations from Maryland to the North branch of the Susquehanna, came apparently as friends to visit the Christian Indians, and invite them to settle in Wyoming. Accordingly about 80 Indians with Tadeuscund, a Delaware chief who had been baptized, left the Lehigh and settled in the valley. In 1753, Paxinos, a Shawnese chief, with 23 Indians and three ambassadors from the Six Nations came to the Mahoning, and desired the whole settlement to follow Tadeuscund. They refused, and were told that if they did not obey, their ears would be cleaned with a red hot iron. Few things could have been more offensive to the Christian Indians, or more trying to the missionaries. The former on account of the impoverished state of their badly worked lands, had moved their houses to the north side of the Lehigh, where Weissport now stands. The Moravian Society took the charge of cultivating the Mahoning lands, and turned the old church into a dwelling; a new church with a bell was erected in 1754, at Weissport, and a Synod held there. The Indian threat was terribly fulfilled; the French war broke out on the Western frontier, and in July, 1755, Braddock was defeated. Soon after the Indians fell on the settlement at Shamokin, killed fourteen white persons, but spared the Moravian missionaries. On the 24th of November, 1755, the mission house at Gnadenhutten was attacked at night, and consumed by fire, with eleven missionaries. The Christian Indians immediately proposed to pursue the murderers, but Shebosh, the only remaining missionary, forbade them. They fled to the woods, but returned the next day, and in consequence of an assurance from the government that they should be protected, they remained. Hays, with his company from the Irish settlement, was immediately sent thither, and fortified the dwellings. The men seeing no Indians for a long time, amused themselves by skating, and occasionally they saw an Indian or two on the ice, a party went to surprise them, and was drawn on, till suddenly they were surrounded, and scarcely one escaped unhurt. Again the soldiers became secure, and while on New Year's day they were hauling wood, without any apprehension, suddenly the Indians appeared, dispersed them, set fire to the Indian dwellings, and destroyed the fortification and the plantations.

Immediately Franklin was sent with 500 men to defend the frontier; and the government desired the Rev. Mr. Beatty, of Neshaminy, to go with the forces. When Franklin approached Bethlehem, December, 1775, he met wagons and a number of persons moving off from the Irish settlement, and also from the German neighborhoods in Lehigh township, being terrified by the defeat of Hays' company, and the burnings, and the murders on New Year's day. Soon after his arrival at Bethlehem, the principal people of the Irish settlement, as Hugh Wilson, Elder Craig, and others, came and threatened if he did not add 30 men to Craig's company for their safety, they would one and all leave their country to the enemy. Hays' company was reduced to 18 men, partly by the loss of Gnadenhutten and partly by desertion, and were without shoes, stockings, blankets, or arms. Trump and Aston had made but small progress in erecting the first fort, complaining of the want of tools. Wayne's company was posted at Nazareth. Franklin immediately directed Hays to complete his company, and he went down to Bucks county with the Rev. Mr. Beatty, who promised to assist him in recruiting. His lieutenant was lying unfit for action, lame with frozen feet, and the ensign with 18 men were posted among the inhabitants to give some satisfaction to the settlement people, for Franklin refused to increase Craig's company. He also threatened to disband and remove the companies already posted, unless the people staid in their places, behaved like men, and assisted the province soldiers. Their alarm was not unreasonable, for all the settlers lived west and north of the church, towards Kreiderville and beyond it. John Hays lived first near the slate quarry in Whitehall, and at that time, lived where the road crosses the creek by the mill in Kreiderville.

Franklin posted Lieutenant Davis at Nazareth, sent

Trump and Wetterholt to defend Lynn and Heidelberg; he sent 30 men to Upper Smithfield, and in order to proceed more swiftly with the fort, he raised another company under Captain Foulk, and detached him and Captain Wayne to that service. He also ordered Arndt to come up with his men from Rockland, Bucks county.

Franklin left Bethlehem, January 15th, with Wayne's and Foulk's companies, and 20 men of McLaughlin's, to lay out the intended fort and get it despatched. "I hope," says he, "to get this done soon, but at this season it seems like fighting against nature."

On the 16th he came to Hays' quarters, and on his way there reviewed Craig's company.

The next day he passed cautiously through the Lehigh Gap, "a very dangerous pass," and came to Uplinger's, about a mile up the creek from Craig's tavern. The next day he rested because it was rainy, and on the next, the Sabbath, reached Weissport at two, and inclosed the camp with a strong breast work, musket proof, with boards brought from Dunker's mill. Monday was dark and foggy; Tuesday he selected a site for the fort, began to cut timber for stockades, and to dig the ground; the logs were cut and hauled, and in another day, the building was inclosed, and the next, the stockades were finished. Saturday the flag was hoisted, a salute fired, and the fort named "after our old friend Allen." Three houses were erected in Fort Allen. Franklin's command consisted of twelve companies and two detachments; Hays had forty-five men, Craig thirty, and Martin of Mount Bethel thirty.

It is curious that there is no mention of any murders in the settlement; it is believed that several families were left homeless, and lost some of their members. Spangenberg, a Moravian bishop, thought the Indians in greater danger of being hurt in the Irish settlement than anywhere else in the province. In June the bishop wrote to the Governor that Jo Pepy and Nicodemus, (whom he styles good for nothing, faithless creatures), were coming to Bethlehem, and that Jo had lived among the Presbyterians, and being treacherously gone from them, they are exasperated in the highest degree. There was such a rage in the neighborhood against them that he feared they would mob the Indians and the Moravians, and therefore besought the governor to remove the vagabonds. In July Governor Morris met the Indian chiefs at Easton; Tadeuscund, and fourteen others of the Six Nations were there, and Jo Pepy was one of the interpreters. A treaty of peace was made, and assurances given by the Six Nations that the murders at Gnadenhutten, and elsewhere had not been committed by their consent. In 1757, there was an Indian council at Easton; another in 1758, when five hundred Indians attended; another in October, 1759, and another in 1761.

In 1757 and 1758, the Rev. Thomas Lewis, of Bethlehem, New Jersey, supplied frequently, and from 1758 to 1761, Mr. Martin, Mr. Chesnut, Mr. Siminton, and Mr. Latta occasionally. In 1759, the name of the second pastor of the congregation, the Rev John Clark, appears. He graduated at New Jersey College in 1759, and was taken under the care of New Brunswick Presbytery, November 20. 1759. Then licensed May 9, 1760, he was sent to supply Tehicken, Allen's town, and Mount Bethel. In the October following, he was called to Tehicken, and also to Allen's town, and he took the matter under consideration. The Presbytery, believing it would be of great service to the interest of religion, ordained him as an evangelist at Bethlehem, New Jersey, April 29, 1761, and directed him to supply Oxford, New Jersey; Smithfield, Pennsylvania, and the Forks. He was dismissed on the 28th of May, and joined Philadelphia Presbytery, August 12, 1761, and was called to the Forks, but did not accept until the next meeting on November 17, when opposition was made to his settlement, and the dissatisfied persons were heard in Presbytery. The commissioners were then asked if the congregation could support him without the aid of the dissentients and being informed that they were, they had leave to prosecute the call. Mr. Clarke was installed Wednesday,

October 13, 1762, over the two congregations in the Forks with a salary of 80 £ and a parsonage. Troubles occurred and were brought before the Presbytery, October 22, 1766, and the Presbytery advised that the matter be dropped. Mr. Clark then gave his reasons for desiring to be released from the pastoral charge of Mount Bethel, eighteen persons having signed a paper accusing him of misrepresentation. The Presbytery pronounced the paper disorderly, and refused to release him. In April following, some of the signers renewed their attack, and asked Presbytery to have Mr. Clark tried; they refused, there being no sufficient cause, and sent Mr. Beatty and the Rev. William Ramsey of Fairfield, New Jersey, as a healing committee.

Before his settlement, the Old and the New side united, and the Synods of New York and Philadelphia were merged in one; the New-side Presbytery of Abingdon, and the Old-side Presbytery of Philadelphia were amalgamated under the name of Philadelphia Presbytery. The two congregations in the Forks came under its care; and the one on the West Branch was weakened probably in 1761, by the formation of an Associate Presbyterian church. The seceder ministers came to Pennsylvania in 1754, in answer to the earnest supplications sent by the Rev. Alexander Creaghead of Middle Octorara, Pennsylvania, to Scotland. They had a congregation at Deep Run, Pennsylvania, and they built a meeting house near Howertown in the settlement. They never had a minister, but enjoyed occasional supplies, and to the close of their existence, the Rev. Mr. Marshall of Philadelphia, visited them; for while many of the Associate ministers and churches joined with the Reformed Presbyterians in constituting the Associate Reformed body, the faithful remnant in the Forks would not come under "the little constitution." They for the most part removed soon after the Revolution to Western Pennsylvania, and the old log church is gone, and the graves around it are overgrown with trees. There were three families of the Boyds, Samuel Brown, (father of General Robert Brown) David McClean,

Michael Clyde, John Clendnin, Thomas Sharp, (the ancestor of the Rev. Alexander Sharp of Big Spring, Pennsylvania) John Clendenin, and George and James Gray.

The following entry in the count book marks the state of things:—"August 21, 1759,—This day, as some people of the congregation have for some time wanted convenient seats, it is unanimously agreed to allow one long seat on each side; and it is agreed that the above mentioned seats be only for the present, till other accommodations be made."

Was Governor Robert Hunter Morris, the deistical Chief Justice of New Jersey previously, who sought to rob Brainerd's Indians of their lands?

In 1761 some of the congregation purchased eighty-two acres of Samuel Wilson for 202£ and erected a house on it for the use of the minister. The land had belonged to Morgan Jones of Pencader. The money was raised by the following individuals: James Craig and James Ralston paid each 12£; Thomas Armstrong, Arthur Lattimore, Charles Wilson, Samuel Wilson, John Walker, James Kerr, William Heslett, and Thomas Herron, of Moore township, each 11£; Robert Lattimore, 8£; James Horner, John McNair, and William McNair, 5£; Alexander Lobbin, 6£; John Riddle, David Chambers, John Ralston, and Mary King, 3£.

During Mr. Clark's ministry occurred the only Indian murders in the settlement of which we have any record or tradition. In 1758 a great Indian Congress was held at Easton; on his way thither Tadeuscund, the Delaware chief who had left Gnadenhutten at the bidding of the Six Nations, met the chief who had commanded the expedition in 1755, and destroyed the Moravians on the Mahoning. They quarrelled, and Tadeuscund struck the murderer with his hatchet and killed him on the spot. No notice was taken of this at the time. Tadeuscund was the chief speaker in the council, and his assumption of authority greatly offended the Six Nations. In each succeeding council they complained that the Governor recognized him as their king, though he was their subject. On the 19th of April, 1763, they sent some of their people to

Tadeuscund in Wyoming; they were received as friends, and that night he was burned alive in his hut and twenty dwellings of his people consumed. On the 8th of October following, fifteen or twenty Indians attacked the house of Nicholas Martz, in Whitehall township; he fled to Adam Fashler's, where were twenty men under arms. They went immediately in pursuit, and found in one place a boy and a girl dead, and in another a man, his wife, his three children and a girl dead; another girl scalped, and another wounded; returning, they found a woman and a child dead in the road. The same day the Indians came to John Stinson's, near the present residence of Dr. Humphrey, and the Mennonist church, near Kreiderville; they demanded liquor, were refused, and went away. At this time there were twenty ———— in the house under Captain Wetherholt, ready to go to Fort Allen the next day. Early in the morning, the servant, going for the Captain's ———— was shot dead, Wetherholt was ———— in the door, and his sergeant, in attempting to draw him in, was dangerously hurt. The lieutenant then advanced, but an Indian, springing on the dead bodies, put a pistol to his breast. He thrust it over his shoulder, drew the wounded men in, and shut the door. The Indian then went to the window, and shot Stinson as he was rising from bed. His wife and children escaped, unhurt, to the cellar. Captain Wetherholt killed, from the window, an Indian who was attempting to fire the house, and the rest fled, bearing off the dead bodies of their companions. Mrs. Jane Horner, the wife of James Horner, of the Settlement, on her way to Stinson's that morning, was shot by the roadside and left dead. A son of William Heslett, while working in the field, was killed and scalped.

Mrs. Horner was a native of Ireland; her maiden name was Kerr, and she was in her fiftieth year. She came with her husband to America in 1734, and after a short residence in Tinicum, settled among the first in Allen township.

Throughout the settlement all was terror; the bodies were carried to the church, and the women and children hurried to the fort, and every precaution was taken. Fifty men assembled on the Lehigh to surprise the Christian Indian village of Nain, but they soon retired. Word was sent from the Settlement to Bethlehem, and the Indian villages of Nain, on the Lehigh, and Wequetauk, near Nazareth, that if an Indian should be seen in the woods, he would be shot. The Indians were all removed to Philadelphia about the 8th of November, and lodged in the barracks.

The blow fell principally on the German settlements in Lehigh county; in six townships eighteen persons were murdered. The Governor sent a message to the legislature, and soldiers were sent from the neighborhood of Harrisburg, to drive the Indians out of Wyoming and destroy their supplies. They found the Valley deserted by the Indians. A few New England people had settled there, having sown the land in the fall of 1762. On the 20th or 21st of October they were all but one murdered, after being barbarously tortured, by the Indians. The troops buried the remains. Scouts professed to have traced the murders on the Lehigh and the Susquehanna, to the cabins of the Indians near Bethlehem and Conestoga. The Rev. John Elder, of Paxton and Derry, was a colonel in the Provincial service, and had charge of the block-houses from the Susquehanna to the Delaware, and his soldiers were thoroughly trained as scouts and rangers. He wrote to the Governor in September, 1763, to remove the Conestoga Indians, because they harbored murderers; and he promised, that if this were done, and a garrison placed there, the frontier could be kept in safety. He was disregarded, and his rangers prepared, on a Sabbath morning in December, to destroy the Indians. Mr. Elder then mounted his horse, and rode before them to dissuade them. They replied, "The blood of the murdered cries for vengeance; we have waited long enough for the government; the murderers are within our reach; they must be destroyed." Mr. Elder conjured them to remember that they could not distinguish the innocent from the guilty. The reply was, "Can they be innocent who foster murderers?" He then commanded them, as their minister and their officer, to desist; but they turned from him, and destroyed the Indians at Conestoga and Lancaster.

Lazarus Stewart, the captain of the Rangers, was proclaimed a murderer, and a reward set on his head. His minister besought pardon for him, representing him as a patriotic, humane, liberal, and religious man, and setting forth the provocations which roused him to this deed of retribution. Stewart published a manifesto in his own defense, and retired, with forty of his men, to Wyoming, and settled the town of Hanover, Luzerne county, under the Connecticut claim. He was slain in defending his country against the British, Tories, and Indians, in the battle of Wyoming, July, 1778. A Presbyterian church was formed, and a meeting-house built at Hanover at an early day; but harassed by the Pennimites, and wasted by war and migration, it declined, and was without a minister after the departure of Rev. Andrew Gray, some forty years ago. It now enjoys the ministrations of the gospel, through the aid of the Board of Missions.

Of the Rev. John Clark no traditions exist in the Settlement; a very few aged persons remain who were baptized by him. He resigned the pastoral charge November 3, 1767, on account of bodily weakness, and soon after went to labour in Newcastle Presbytery. He was called December 27, 1769, to Bethel, in Upper Node Forest, in Baltimore county, Maryland. The congregation first appears on the records of the Newcastle Presbytery, 1761, and is styled Nodd's Forest and the Head of Winter's Run. The pastoral relation was dissolved in 1775, but he remained at Bethel as supply till 1781, when he removed to Western Pennsylvania. He settled at Bethel and Lebanon in Redstone Presbytery (now in Ohio Presbytery), and died there on the 13th day of July, 1790. It is stated in Day's Historical Collections of Pennsylvania, that when an attack was made with five hundred whiskey insurgents on Gen. Neville's house, in July, 1794, Mr. Clark, a venerable clergyman, besought them to desist, but in vain.

He was one of the original members of Ohio Presbytery, at its erection in September, 1793.

The Rev. John Rosbrugh accepted the call to the Forks, on the third Tuesday of April, 1769; two-thirds of his time being given to Allen township, and one-third to Mount Bethel. Mrs. Lattimore, nearly connected with him, told me that he lived in Tinicum, and buried his wife and child there before preparing for the ministry. On the records of the Synod is the following account: "Paid by the treasurer of New Jersey College to Mr. Rosbrugh, August 3, 1761, 30£; and May 25, 1762, 14£." The fund out of which this money was paid was given to Gilbert Tennent while in Great Britain, by some benevolent persons, to aid indigent youth in preparing for the ministry. Mr. Rosbrugh pursued his studies while the admirable Samuel Davies was at the head of the College; he graduated in 1761, and studied divinity with the Rev. John Blair. He was taken under care by the New Brunswick Presbytery, May 22, 1762, and after much delay was licensed, August 18, 1763. His first field of labour was Hardwick, Oxford, and Mansfield-woodhouse, and to this was added west branch of Blackriver. In April, 1764, Oxford, Mansfield-woodhouse, and Greenwich petitioned that he might preach to them as a candidate; he did so, and they called him in October. He accepted the call, and was ordained at Greenwich on the 11th of December, 1764. Four years passed, and in April, 1768, he asked to be dismissed, the people failing to support him; the Presbytery deferred the matter, but bade him inform the worshippers at Mansfield-woodhouse, that unless they discharge the arrears, and pay their due proportion of the salary, he should give all his time to the other two. This admonition had no effect, and Mr. Rosbrugh abandoned Mansfield, and asked leave to give up the other two. The congregation of Greenwich opposed the request, and promised to arrange matters with Oxford for his regular payment and furnishing him with a house. They failed, and he was dismissed April 18, 1769, and on the same day the Forks in conjunction with Greenwich, made him a call. The Presbytery consented to his receiving the call, if the Forks were placed under their care. In May, 1770, the Synod transferred the two congregations in the Forks from the First Philadelphia to the New Brunswick Presbytery. He was called April 14, 1772, and was installed at Allen's Town October 28. He married, for his second wife, Jean, the daughter of James Ralston, one of the ruling elders of the church of Allen township. The congregation flourished, and the church was enlarged in size. He was an able, eloquent preacher, although a defect in his speech sometimes caused him to stammer.

The province of Pennsylvania was endeavoring, at this period, to dispossess the Connecticut people, who, having purchased of the Six Nations in 1754, had, in 1769, established themselves in Wyoming. They were driven away, but still they returned. In 1770 Capt. Ogden, with six companies, proceeded thither; one of them was from the Settlement; and commanded by Captain Thomas Craig. Ogden proceeded from Philadelphia to Fort Allen, and along the Warrior Path, through the Shades of Death, (now Rockport and Whitehaven) till, in September, he entered the valley at Solomon's Gap. The settlers did not know that they had arrived, and when, in parties of three or four, they went to their work, they were seized, secured, and sent to Easton jail. They fled to the Fort, wholly unaware where the foe was posted, or in what strength. The fort was suddenly stormed, and Captain Craig, advancing to the sentinel, spoke as a friend, and then knocking him down, gave the people the first alarm by jumping in among them. Turning suddenly, he saved the life of Capt. Butler, who was about to be bayoneted.

The French war had trained the troops of the province to skill and firmness, and of the young men of the Settlement, several had distinguished themselves as privates and officers. The Revolution drew on, and the Forks resounded with the grievous wrongs done to the colonies. When Montgomery led his men to the attack on Canada, Captain Thomas Craig was with him; he was at Germantown and Monmouth, and at the surrender of Cornwallis. He rose by the merit of perfect discipline and tried bravery, to the command of a regiment. He was brave and impetuous, and Lindley Murray, in one of his "Mark Bancroft" sketches, says he required his men to reserve their fire till they could see the white of their enemies' eyes. He died in Allentown in 1833, aged 93; he took pleasure in the fact that he was baptized by David Brainerd.

In September, 1776, a company was raised in the Settlement and vicinity, commanded by Captain Peter Rundio. This company was in the battle of Long Island, and, after the evacuation of New York, was left in Fort Washington, on the Hudson, under Colonel Magaw of Chester county. On the 15th of November Sir William Howe invested the fort, and demanded an immediate surrender, and after a day of hard fighting, Colonel Magaw surrendered his 2,000 men to Howe with 7,000. Rundio's men were imprisoned in a church, and left for days without food; many died, and it was not till thirteen months after that the lieutenant of the company, afterwards Gen. Robert Brown, was released on parole. He remained a prisoner three years, and, by working as a blacksmith, nobly supported himself and preserved his men from perishing for want of food.

By the fall of Fort Washington and Fort Lee a great blow was given to the hopes of many. Washington retreated through New Jersey before the Hessians; the militia of Pennsylvania was called out. Those from the Settlement were led by Capt. Hays, and Mr. Rosbrugh, though an elderly man, went with them as chaplain. Washington had abandoned New Jersey, and lay west of the Delaware, but on Christmas evening, with Mifflin's and Knox's brigades, he crossed the river, defeated the Hessians, and killed their commander, Col. Rahl. On the 27th of December, 1,800 Pennsylvania militia, under Col. Cadwalader, moved to Crosswicks, and with 1,800 under Gen. Mifflin, to Bordertown. Lord Cornwallis assumed the command and marched toward

Trenton; and on the 2nd of January, 1777, Washington crossed the Assunpink Creek. Mr. Rosbrugh, while our army passed rapidly through Trenton, delayed, it is said, to rest himself and his horse; John Hays remained to feed his beast and bear him company. The Hessians coming suddenly upon him barbarously murdered him, stabbing him again and again, and mangling his face. Hays buried the body in the road, and returned home with the sad tidings to the widow. Her brother, John Ralston, was a member of the Provincial Congress then sitting in Philadelphia, and he wrote at once to confirm the news, and to comfort her with Christian consolation. Mr. Duffield, a merchant of Philadelphia, went at once to Trenton, and caused the body to be taken up and decently interred in the grave-yard—I suppose of Trenton Old House, now the first church in Trenton at Ewing. Mrs. Rosbrugh hastened thither, accompanied by her husband's friend, the Rev. Alexander Mitchell of Tinicum, and saw the body lifted from the ground; but the face was so mangled by bayonet thrusts and other ill usage, that she could not recognize the least resemblance to her husband, although she fully identified it by a scar on the back, out of which a wen had been cut, so large that it was noticeable under his coat.

One son of Mr. Rosbrugh survives, at East Groveland, New York, and two daughters at Dansville, New York; his daughter, Mrs. Ralston, of Chester county, died within a year.

In May, 1777, the Synod, at the request of the congregation, placed it under the care of the First Philadelphia Presbytery, and for four years the Rev. Alexander Mitchel was the frequent and welcome supply for a fourth of his time.

The Rev. Dr. James Sproat, of the Second Church of Philadelphia, in April, 1778, offered to the Presbytery to supply the Forks, the British then occupying the city; he lived in the parsonage, and preached twenty Sabbaths at Allentown, and probably as many at Mount Bethel.

In July, 1779, the Rev. Alexander Mitchel made application in behalf of Liberty Hall, North Carolina, and received 50 £. This, I suppose, was the institution at Charlotte, North Carolina, founded by the Rev. Joseph Alexander, and to which, at that period, Dr. McWhorter, of Newark, had been called, and of which, for a time, he was the head. On the 22d of August following, the people were gathered on a Saturday to hear the Rev. James Grier preach, preparatory to the Lord's supper, when a stranger entered, and Mr. Grier, welcoming him with great cordiality, insisted he should preach. It was the Rev. William Graham of Virginia; he preached and administered the sacrament, and received 60 £ for Liberty Hall, Virginia, now Washington College. This was Continental money.

The supplies, till 1788, were Mr. Mitchell, Dr. Richard Treat of Abingdon, James Grier of Deep Run, Dr. Isaac S. Keith, afterwards of Charleston, South Carolina, and his brother, Robert Keith, (they were related to the McNairs of the Settlement), John Debon, afterwards of Eno and Haw-fields, North Carolina, Dr. Nathan Grier, of Brandywine, and Dr. Nathaniel Irwin of Neshaminy.

After the Revolution, an entire change took place in the situation of the congregation; originally all the farms lay west of the road from Bath to Allentown; but the lands on the Monocacy being confiscated, because the Allens (except James) had espoused the royal cause, they were sold by the State and bought with Continental money. The title thus acquired was disputed, and the courts decided against the purchasers under the State, and the lands were paid for a second time, or passed into other hands. In some instances the legislature granted relief to those who had purchased of the State. Defective title caused many of the early settlers of Mount Bethel to move away, and may have been among the reasons why so many left the Settlement to seek new homes in the Redstone country.

In 1783, the Rev. Francis Peppard became the minister, and remained till May, 1795. He was a native of Ireland. He graduated at New Jersey College in 1762, was licensed by New Brunswick Presbytery in 1763, and ordained in 1764, by the New York Presbytery, pastor at Mendham, New Jersey. He left there in 1769, and joined New Brunswick Presbytery in 1773. The Forks, in October, 1780, asked leave of the First Philadelphia Presbytery to seek supplies from New Brunswick Presbytery. Leave was granted, and in April, 1781, Captain John Ralston, as their commissioner, requested that they might present a call to New Brunswick Presbytery for Mr. Peppard. This was granted, and the Forks, and also Lower Smithfield, called him, April 24, 1781. He accepted the former, and was dismissed to First Philadelphia Presbytery, which, however, he did not join till May, 1783. He was installed on the second Tuesday of August after. Several things contributed to make his situation uncomfortable. A number of the congregation, residing on the Monocacy, purchased land, and erected a large stone building, greatly superior to the church, for an academy; they established a library and a debating society. Mr. Peppard viewed this as preparatory to setting up altar against altar, and dividing the congregation. His course did not conciliate the good will of those who were interested in the undertaking. For a while a classical school was taught in the academy; Mr. Leo, Mr. Andrews, and the Rev. Thomas Picton, now of Bedford Presbytery, were successively the teachers. Under Mr. Andrews, the late Governor Wolf, a native of Allen township, was educated. The academy was built on ground to which no good title could be given, and it was recovered from the purchasers by suit at law. The land was purchased by Thomas McKeen, Esq., then a member of the congregation, but for many years the cashier and president of the Easton Bank. Through his kindness, it has been used as a chapel for many years, being spacious, airy, and commodious. Mr. Peppard, in August, 1794, asked to be dismissed from his charge, because the salary had not been paid, and he was dismissed in November. He removed to Hardwick, New Jersey, and died, March 30, 1797. His grandson, the Rev. Mr. Kerr, is one of our Indian missionaries.

In 1797, the congregation was incorporated. During the vacancy, the supplies were Michael Arthur, Jacob Lake of Mansfield, John Hanna of Bethlehem, Asa Dunham of Mount Bethel, Peter Wilson of Hackettstown, (then called Independence) and afterwards of Cincinnati, Dr. Finley of Baskingridge, and Dr. Irwin of Neshaminy. The prominent candidates before the congregation were Robert Russel and Uriah Dubois; the old people preferred Mr. Russel, and overruled the counsel of the young men who admired Mr. Dubois. Mr. Russel was a native of Fagg's Manor, and had married the daughter of Thomas Armstrong, formerly an elder in the Settlement. He was ordained and installed by Philadelphia Presbytery in 1798; Dr. Green preached the sermon, and Dr. William M. Tennent, of Abingdon, and Dr. Irwin, gave the charge to the pastor and people. Mr. Dubois settled at Deep Run and Tinicum. Early in the present century the congregation dwindled by many removals; the McNair family to Western New York, the Hays to Pittsburgh and the West Branch, the Ralstons and the Walkers to Chester county, the Wilsons to Union county, the Erwins to Painted Post, the Craigs to Lehigh county, the Greggs, Hemphills, Sharps, and Boyds to Western Pennsylvania and Ohio.

The old version of the Psalms was always sung till Mr. Matthew Duncan became the clerk; his mother, Mrs. Margaret Duncan, left by will funds to erect the Associate Reformed church in Thirteenth street, Philadelphia; his son is the Rev. J. M. Duncan of Baltimore.

In 1813, the site of the present house of worship was purchased, and a stone church erected. The original church lot was given by James Craig. The parsonage farm was subsequently sold, and the proceeds invested in stock of the United States, Northampton, and Easton Banks; by the failure of the two first named concerns, the greater part of the church fund was lost. Mr. Russel died December 16, 1827, a worthy minister of Jesus Christ.

He was succeeded by the Rev. Alexander Heberton, who remained five or six years; to him is due the credit of having opened a sessional record, and prepared a sketch of the history of the congregation. His labours were not without fruit, nor were those of the Rev. Brogan Hoff, who remained a short time. The Rev. William McJimpey was the stated supply for one or two years. In 1835, the Rev. Leslie Irwin began to labour in the Settlement, and was ordained, December 25, 1835, by Newton Presbytery, to which the church had been attached in Mr. Russel's time. A steady growth in numbers, and in contributions to our Boards, has been seen in the church during eleven years; and the solemn scenes which marked its infancy have been at times graciously renewed by our blessed Saviour.

Brief notices of the early settlers will close these sketches.

James Craig was nearly connected by marriage with Chief Justice Allen, and had from him the gift of a farm in the Settlement. He was a pious man; at his house Brainerd lodged and preached. In extreme age and palsied, he was borne regularly into the house of God by sons. He had four; Robert and William moved to Northumberland county, Samuel served under General Wayne, and John was in the Light-horse during the Revolution.

Thomas Craig is said to have come from Dublin; an upright, pious man, the stone he erected to the memory of his wife is the only one in the grave-yard bearing the name of Craig. His only son, William, married a daughter of Hugh Wilson; one of his sons was General Thomas Craig; another son, Hugh, died young, when about to prepare for the ministry.

Hugh Wilson was born in 1689, at Cootehill, near Coleraine. He died in 177—. He was a pious man, retiring daily to a secret place, and, prostrate on the ground, pleading with God. In his dying hour he united with his family in singing the fortieth Psalm: "I waited for the Lord, my God." His sons: Thomas early removed beyond the Allegheny; one of his sons is living, a ruling elder, and formerly an associate judge; Samuel died in the Settlement, and Charles also. William was in business in New York, and Francis was an Episcopal clergyman in South Carolina. His daughters married the Rev. Francis McHenry of Deep Run, William Craig, and William McNair.

John and Robert Walker were brothers of Captain Richard Walker, who married a relative of the   , and was a man of property, usefulness, and high respectability. Robert Walker died unmarried, in 1758, aged fifty-eight years. John Walker died in June, 1777, aged sixty-one years, a pious, worthy man, and a ruling elder. His son, John, removed to Chester county; the Rev. Richard Walker, of Allen town, is his descendant. One of John Walker's daughters married John Hays, the maternal grandfather of the Rev. John Hays Grier, of Pine Creek, Pennsylvania; another married Joseph Grier, the father of the Rev. John W. Grier, United States Navy.

John McNair, a brother-in-law of the Walkers, was an excellent man, and a ruling elder. He died in 1762, aged seventy-two years. His son, William, married a daughter of Hugh Wilson, and their son, Judge Hugh McNair, of Sparta, New York, died in 1845, aged eighty-five years, a worthy man, and a faithful ruling elder. A daughter of John McNair married Charles Wilson, son of Hugh; she was early left a widow, but bore up patiently and bravely. She lived to an advanced age, blessed with seeing her children fulfilling her precepts, and walking in the truth. Her oldest son, Judge Hugh Wilson, of Union county, died in 1845; one of her daughters is living, the wife of Mr. Rosbrugh, of East Groveland, New York; her youngest son, baptized by the Rev. Mr. Clark in 1765, remembers to have heard Mr. Rosbrugh preach, and to have seen most of the first settlers of these broad lands descend to the grave. Still vigorous, he has good possession of his faculties, and is a regular attendant on the house of God, in which so long as clerk and ruling elder he has served his generations. It was the melancholy duty of the writer to stand with him by the grave of his father and grandfather, while the earth was opened to receive the last of his grandsons.

"God of his childhood, be the God
Of his declining age."

James King died in 1745, aged thirty-eight years, a good man. His widow, Mary Walker, was a woman of an excellent spirit, who looked well to her household, and trained up her children in the fear of God. Her four daughters married Robert Lattimore, John Ralston, Samuel Ralston, and John Hays, Jr.

James Ralston was a man of great enterprise, real worth, and piety. He died, July, 1775, aged seventy-six years. His son, John Ralston, was a member of the Provincial Congress, a worthy man, and a good ruling elder. He died in 1795, aged sixty years.

John Hays died, November 16, 1789, aged eighty-five years. His son, John, married, first the daughter of James King, and then the daughter of John Walker.

James Horner was born in the county Derry, Ireland, in 1713, and died, May 1, 1793. His sons, Hugh and Thomas, lived to advanced years, serving as magistrates and ruling elders.

Arthur Lattimore, born in 1710, died in 1777, he was a pious, excellent man; his only children were twin daughters, deaf and dumb. He had two brothers in the Settlement; John, and Robert the father of General William Lattimore.

Samuel Brown died in 1796, aged eighty-four years. His son, Gen. Robert Brown, represented Northampton county for several years, in Congress, and died in 1823, aged seventy-eight years.

Michael Clyde died in May, 1794, aged eighty-four years.

The earliest school teacher was Mr. Carruthers, who had served under the distinguished Colonel James Gardiner, a competent and faithful teacher, and a good citizen.

The average length of life is remarkable. In fifty years, but two men are known to have died as young as thirty-eight. It throws light on their habits of life, and their merciful deliverance from Indian barbarities illustrates God's providential care of them, and their own freedom from the sin of provoking or oppressing the Indian.

K. H. (Mauch Chunk).

The Horner Bible

This Bible was published in Edinburgh, in 1746, by Richard Watkins, His Majesty's Printer. While it is not an old Bible it has a hair-hide cover, which is unusual. It was the property of James Horner, Sr., the emigrant, who came to the Irish Settlement in 1728. It is believed this Bible was closely associated with the first log church (Presbyterian) in the Settlement, which was erected in 1746. It was in the hands of Hugh R. Horner for many years and is now in possession of Miss Mary J. Horner, his daughter, of Philadelphia.

First Log Church

In 1736 and 1737, the Irish Settlement commenced on the west branch of the Delaware, now called the Lehigh. Others may have settled there a few years earlier.

There were two Irish Settlements in the Forks, one on the north branch, at Mt. Bethel, called Hunters Settlement or Forks North; the other Craig's Settlement, in Allen's town, on the west branch.

The first settlers in the Craig Settlement were Thomas Craig, James Craig, Hugh Wilson with his three sons, Thomas, Samuel and Charles, Thomas Armstrong, Robert Gregg, James King, John McNair, John and Robert Walker, James Ralston, John Hays, Arthur Lattimore, James Horner, and James Kerr.

The Craigs were not related. James Craig is believed to have been connected with William Allen by marriage. The nearest place of worship at this time was Tehicken in Bucks County. In 1738 the congregation at the Forks made application to New Brunswick Presbytery for supplies.

In July, 1744, that man of God, David Brainerd, came to the Settlement and preached to the people in James Craig's meadow.

When David Brainerd returned to Forks in 1746, there was a log church at this time in the meadow, between the Mill-race and the Hoquendoquy, on James Craig's land.

After Brainerd preached, the people would retire weeping to pray among the hazle bushes, and he would come and comfort them. He seemed never to have preached to the people at the West branch without observing special attention and signs of good.

Such were the first ten years of the church in Allen Township.

The earliest record to be found is "The Count Book of the Congregation," on the west branch of the Delaware in the Forks.

The first entry is as follows:—

"Received from the congregation of the West Branch the sum of 40£ in full payment of the year 1747. I say received by me this 30th day of Jan. 1749-50.

David Lawrence."

OBLIGATION & DECLARATION

Of John Walker and others in Trust to The Members of Allen Township Congregation

Copy furnished by Dr. Robert Hays Horner

TO ALL PEOPLE to whom these presents shall come, We John Walker of Allen Township in the county of Northampton, in the Province of Pennsylvania Yeoman, Arthur Lattimore of the same place Yeoman, Robert Lattimore of the same place Yeoman, John Ralston of the same place Yeoman, John McNair of the same place Yeoman, and William Craig of the same place Yeoman, SEND GREETING, WHEREAS James Craig of Allen Township in the county of Northampton, Yeoman, in and by two certain Indentures bearing date the day next before the day of the date hereof under his hand and seal, duly executed, for the consideration of forty shillings, twenty thereof being mentioned in each of said Indentures, Did Grant and convey unto us the said John Walker, Arthur Lattimore, Robert Lattimore, John Ralston, John McNair and William Craig TWO CERTAIN LOTS or pieces of ground, situate in Allen Township aforesaid, (the one lot for a Meeting House seat and the other for a burying ground) the Meeting House lot beginning at a post placed for a corner by the side of the great road leading from Allen Township aforesaid to Mt. Bethel Township in Northampton County aforesaid, and thence extending South eighty-eight degrees West five perches six feet to stones for a corner, thence by the said James Craig's land the three courses and distances next following, Viz: North twenty-six degrees East nine perches two feet to a stone for a corner, North eighty-three Degrees East four perches to a stone for a corner, and South fifteen degrees West eight perches six feet to the place of Beginning, containing thirty-seven perches of land. AND THE OTHER LOT FOR THE BURYING GROUND about twenty perches North distant from the Meeting House lot BEGINNING at a hickory grub on the side of the said James Craig's mill race, thence extending South twelve degrees West nine Perches four feet to a hickory sapling at a corner, Thence West eight perches to a stone at a corner, thence North nine perches to a stone at a corner, thence ten perches to the place of BEGINNING containing eighty-one perches, AND IS surrounded on all sides by land of the said James Craig TOGETHER with the appurtenances to hold to us the said John Walker, Arthur Lattimore, Robert Lattimore, John Ralston, John McNair and William Craig, our heirs and assigns for ever, as in and by the said recited Indentures relation being thereunto had more at large appears. AND WHEREAS a large building hath been erected on the first of the said described lots or pieces of ground for a church or meeting house therein to perform Divine Worship according to the Methods ways and usage of the Presbyterians AND WHEREAS the end intent and purpose of the aforesaid Indentures and the conveyances thereby made, was to set apart and Vest in Us and our heirs the said Building and lots or pieces of ground for a church or House of Religious worship, and for a burying place for the use and service of the members of the Presbyterian Congregation residing in and near Allen Township aforesaid, whereof for the time being the Rev. John Rosbrugh, is Minister, and such other persons as now are or shall or may be joined unto them in communion and Church Fellowship forever hereafter, who do hold or continue to hold the system of Doctrine contained in the Westminster confession of Faith and Directory, agreeable to the present interpretation of the Synod of New York and Philadelphia, to which they are now united, yet under and subject never-the-less to the following provisoes, conditions and Limitations,—that is to say PROVIDED Always that no person shall be deemed to belong to the said congregation unless he hath statedly attended upon the Publick Worship of God in the said congregation for the space of twelve months, and shall have regularly contributed to the support of the Ministry and other charges attending the same according to the usage of Presbyterians, nor shall any one be deemed longer a member thereof than he continues to hold and conform to the Westminster confession of faith and directory aforesaid, and shall continue to attend statedly in an orderly manner upon the Publick worship of God in the said congregation and be in communion with the said Synod as aforesaid expressed PROVIDED also and it is hereby agreed that neither we nor any person whatsoever succeeding us in this Trust who shall hereafter fall from or change his or their Religious principals aforesaid, or shall separate from the said Synod or depart from the said congregation, or who shall refuse or neglect to contribute towards the support of the Ministry, shall be capable to execute this trust, or stand siezed of the premises to the use aforesaid, nor have any right nor interest in the said described pieces or lots of ground, or in the Buildings thereon erected, or to be erected, as aforesaid, while he or they shall so continue, But in such case, as also when any of us or any other person or persons succeeding us in the trust aforesaid, shall happen to depart this Life, that then it shall and may be lawful for the said congregation from time to time, and as often as occasion shall require to make choice of others to manage their Trust instead of such as shall so fall away withdraw themselves or depart this Life, which choice shall be made by a majority of votes consisting of the Adult male members of the aforesaid congregation convened by due and publick notice for that purpose given (in which publick conventions the Pastor of the said congregation for the time being when there shall always preside as Moderator) or else by a committee of their number chosen for that purpose, AND IN ORDER TO PREVENT LAWSUITS in case it should be disputed in time to come whether any particular persons are actually members of the aforesaid congregation or not, or if any controversies shall arise in relation to the pews in the said house of worship, that then the said controversies and all other matters of a civil nature respecting the said lots of land and House of Worship shall be finally determined by a majority of votes of all the Adult Male Members of the aforesaid Congregation in the manner as above prescribed. NOW THEREFORE KNOW YE that we the said John Walker, Arthur Lattimore, Robert Lattimore, John Ralston, John McNair, and William Craig, being desirous to preserve the Estate in the Premises so conveyed unto us and our heirs, by the said recited Indentures in Trust to and for the several and respective uses, ends, intents and purposes aforesaid, DO HEREBY DECLARE and own that the aforesaid Indentures or conveyances of the premisses's was so made and executed unto us for those very ends, intents and purposes aforesaid and none other, and that we permitted our names to be made use of in the said recited Indentures at the special instance and request of the said James Craig and the rest of the Adult Male members of the said Congregation AND WE the said John Walker, Arthur Lattimore, Robert Lattimore, John Ralston, John McNair and William Craig, do hereby covenant promise and grant for ourselves severally and respectively, and for our several respective heirs to and with the said James Craig, and his heirs and the rest of the Adult Male members of the Aforesaid congregation that we, and every of us, and every of our heirs, shall and will stand siezed of the Premises and every part and parcel thereof with the appurtenances to the several and respective uses, ends, intents and purposes aforesaid, and to and for no other use intent or purpose whatsoever, and FURTHER THAT WE and every of us and our Heirs respectively shall and will from time to time and at all times hereafter as often as occasion shall require at the proper costs and charges in the Law of the aforesaid congregation, make do, acknowledge and suffer or cause to be made done acknowledged and suffered, all and every other such further and other reasonable act and acts, deed or deeds, Devee or Devices in the law whatsoever for the conveyance of the Premisses to the several and respective uses, ends intents, and purposes herein before mentioned, limited and declared, and to and for no other use, end intent or purpose whatsoever, as by council learned in the law shall be reasonably Devised, Advised or required. IN WITNESS whereof we the said John Walker, Arthur Lattimore, Robert Lattimore, John Ralston, John McNair and William Craig, have hereunto set our hands and seals the twelfth day of March in the twelfth year of the reign of our Sovereign Lord GEORGE the third, by the grace of God King over Great Britain etc., AND in the Year of our Lord one thousand seven hundred and seventy-two, and FURTHER we the above said Trustees do hereby bind ourselves, our Heirs, assigns and successors that no person or family upon any pretence whatsoever shall have liberty or be permitted to reside or dwell in any house already built or shall or may be built on any of the above described Lots or pieces of ground, as their place of dwelling or residence after the above said date, forever, by these presents

  John Ralston (Seal) John Walker (Seal)
  John McNair (Seal) Arthur Lattimore (Seal)
  Wm. Craig (Seal) Robert Lattimore (Seal)

SEALED AND DELIVERED

  in the presence of us:—

  John Rosbrugh John Hays William Carruthers

The twelfth day of March 1772, before me, Hugh Wilson, Esq., one of the Justices of the Peace for the County of Northampton came the above named John Walker, Arthur Lattimore, Robert Lattimore, John Ralston, John McNair and William Craig, and acknowledged the above written obligation and Declaration to be their act and deed and desired it might or may be recorded as such.

In witness whereof I have hereunto set my hand and seal the day and year above written.

            Hu: Wilson (Seal)

ENTERED in the office for Recording of Deeds in and for the County of Northampton in Book B Vol. 1 Page 423 etc., the 25th day of May Anno 1773. Witness my hand and seal of Office at Easton the day and year above said.

            Lewis Gordon, R. D. (Seal)

Home of the First School of Homeopathy, Established by Dr. William Wesselhoeft, in 1829. Bath, Pa., (See page 53.)

1772

DEED

James Craig to John Walker and Others for 81 Perches of ground in Allen Township, Northampton County.

THIS INDENTURE made the eleventh day of March in the year of our Lord one thousand seven hundred and seventy-two, being the twelfth year of the reign of our Sovereign Lord George the Third, by the grace of God, King over Great Britain etc., BETWEEN James Craig of Allen Township in the County of Northampton in the Province of Pennsylvania, Yeoman of the ONE PART, AND John Walker of Said Allen Township, Yeoman, Arthur Lattimore, of said Township Yeoman, Robert Lattimore of the same place Yeoman, John Ralston of the same place Yeoman, John McNair of the same place Yeoman, and William Craig of the same place Yeoman, OF THE OTHER PART. WHEREAS John Penn, Thomas Penn and Richard Penn Esquires, true and absolute Proprietaries of the said Province of Pennsylvania, by their Warrant bearing date at London the eighteenth day of May 1732 did authorize and require their then Surveyer General, of the said Province to lay out to the said Thomas Penn five thousand acres of land in the Province aforesaid, AND WHEREAS the said Thomas Penn by an assignment or Indorsement on the said warrant dated on the day aforesaid for the consideration there within mentioned did grant and assign unto Joseph Turner of the City of Philadelphia, Merchant, the warrant aforesaid and the quantity of land therein mentioned. To hold to him his heirs and assigns forever, and WHEREAS the said Joseph Turner by another assignment indorsed on the said warrant, dated the tenth day of September Anno Dom. 1735 Did grant and assign unto William Allen of the city of Philadelphia aforesaid, Merchant, the said warrant and quantity of land aforesaid AND WHEREAS the said William Allen for the consideration therein mentioned hath sold and made deed bearing date the thirtieth day of June Anno Dom.

1743, unto the aforesaid James Craig for two hundred and fifty acres of the aforesaid land situate in Allen Township aforesaid, as will more fully appear by having recourse to said deed. WITNESSETH that the said James Craig, for and in consideration of the sum of twenty shillings lawful money of Pennsylvania, to him in hand well and truly paid by the said John Walker, Arthur Lattimore, Robert Lattimore, John Ralston, John McNair and William Craig at or before the sealing and delivery hereof, the receipt whereof the said James Craig do hereby acknowledge, and thereof do acquit, and forever discharge the said John Walker, Arthur Lattimore, Robert Lattimore, John Ralston, John McNair and William Craig their heirs and assigns, By These Presents have granted, bargained sold released and confirmed, and by these presents do grant bargain sell release and confirm unto the said John Walker, Arthur Lattimore, Robert Lattimore, John Ralston, John McNair and William Craig their heirs and assigns A CERTAIN PIECE OR LOT OF GROUND situate in the aforesaid Allen Township, being part of the above said deeded land, and converted into a Burying ground, BEGINNING at a hickory grub on the side of the said James Craig's mill race thence extending South twelve degrees West nine perches four feet to a hickory sapling at a corner, thence West eight perches to a stone at a corner, thence North nine perches to a stone at a corner, thence ten perches to the place of BEGINNING, containing eighty-one perches, and is surrounded on all sides by land of the said James Craig. TOGETHER Also with all and singular the Buildings improvements, ways woods waters, Water courses, Rights Liberties, privileges hereditaments and appurtenances whatsoever unto the hereby granted premisses belonging, or in any wise appertaining, and the Reversions and Remainders thereof TO HAVE AND TO HOLD the said above described piece or lot of ground hereditaments and premises hereby granted or mentioned to be granted, with the appurtenances unto the said John Walker, Arthur Lattimore, Robert Lattimore, John

Ralston, John McNair and William Craig, their heirs and assigns to the only proper use, and behoof of them, the said John Walker, Arthur Lattimore, Robert Lattimore, John Ralston, John McNair and William Craig, their heirs and assigns forever AND THE SAID James Craig and his heirs the said above described piece or lot of ground hereditaments and Premises hereby granted or mentioned to be granted with the appurtenances unto the said John Walker, Arthur Lattimore, Robert Lattimore, John Ralston, John McNair and William Craig, their heirs and assigns, against him the said James Craig and his heirs and against all other person and Persons whatsoever lawfully claiming or to claim, by from or under him, them or any of them SHALL AND WILL WARRANT AND FOREVER DEFEND by these presents and the said James Craig for himself his heirs executors and Administrators, doth covenant promise and grant to and with the said John Walker, Arthur Lattimore, Robert Lattimore, John Ralston, John McNair and William Craig, their heirs and assigns, by these presents, that he, the said James Craig and his heirs and all and every other person and persons whatsoever having or lawfully claiming any Estate, Right, Title, or Interest of in or to the hereby granted premises, or any part thereof, by from or under him, them or any of them shall and will from time to time, and at all times hereafter upon the reasonable request and at the proper cost and charges in the law of the said John Walker, Arthur Lattimore, Robert Lattimore, John Ralston, John McNair and William Craig, their heirs or assigns, Make, Execute and Acknowledge, or cause to be made executed and acknowledged all and every such further and other reasonable act and acts deed or deeds, conveyances or assurances in the law whatsoever, for the further and better conveying and assuring of the premises aforesaid unto the said John Walker, Arthur Lattimore, Robert Lattimore, John Ralston, John McNair and William Craig their heirs or assigns, as by them or their council learned in the law shall be reasonably Devised, Advised or required. IN WITNESS

WHEREOF the said parties to these presents have Interchangeably set their hands and seals hereunto dated the day and year first above written.

James Craig (Seal)

Sealed and delivered
in the presence of us:—
        Jno Rosbrugh
        John Hays
        William Carruthers.

Received the day of the date of the within written Indenture of the within named John Walker, Arthur Lattimore, Robert Lattimore, John Ralston, John McNair and William Craig the full sum of twenty shillings, it being the consideration money within mentioned. I say received by me.

James Craig

Witnesses at signing
        Jno Rosbrugh
        John Hays
        William Carruthers.

The eleventh day of March 1772 before me Hugh Wilson, Esq., one of the Justices of the Peace for the county of Northampton came the within named James Craig and acknowledged the within written Indenture to be his act and deed and desired the same may be recorded as his act and deed. In witness whereof I have hereunto set my hand and seal the day and year aforesaid.

Hu. Wilson

Entered in the office for Recording of deeds in and for the county of Northampton in Book B Vol. 1 page 419 etc., the 20th day of May Anno 1773. Witness my hand and seal of office at Easton the day and year abovesaid.

Lewis Gordon, Recorder.

DEED

Nicholas Neligh and Wife to The Trustees of the English Presbyterian Congregation of Allen Township for 128 perches of land in said Township. Year 1813.

THIS INDENTURE made the thirty-first day of March in the year of our Lord one thousand eight hundred and thirteen Between Nicholas Neligh of Allen Township of the county of Northampton and Commonwealth of Pennsylvania, Esquire and Maria his wife (daughter and heir at law of Henry Epple late of Allen Township Deceased) of the one part and John Wilson, James Horner, Sr., John Boyd, John Clyde, Jr., James Kerr, Jr., and Edward Humphrys, Trustees of the English Presbyterian Congregation of Allen Township aforesaid of the other part WITNESSETH that the said Nicholas Neligh and Maria his wife for and in consideration of a small lot of land in said township whereon the meeting house belonging to said congregation lately stood, and which is now about to be conveyed to the said Nicholas Neligh his heirs and assigns forever, and also the sum of five shillings lawful money as it now passes current in Pennsylvania to them in hand well and truly paid by the said John Wilson, James Horner, Sr., John Boyd, John Clyde, Jr., James Kerr, Jr., and Edward Humphrys the receipt whereof is hereby acknowledged, and they the said Nicholas Neligh and Maria his wife fully satisfied and paid, HAVE granted, bargained and sold aliened enfeoffed released and confirmed and by these presents DOTH grant bargain and sell alien enfeoff release and confirm to the said John Wilson, James Horner, Jr., John Boyd, John Clyde, Jr., James Kerr, Jr., and Edward Humphrys and their successors, Trustees of said congregation for the sole purpose of erecting a meeting house for said congregation and other necessary buildings for the use of the same and none other: all that Tract and lot of land situate laying and being in the said township of Allen Aforesaid, BEGINNING at a post and stone near the mill race thence by the School House lot South eighty-five degrees West seven perches to a stone, thence by other land of said Nicholas Neligh North five degrees West seven perches and six-tenths to stones, thence North eighty-five degrees East eight perches and eight-tenths to stones thence North twenty-one and three-quarter degrees East fourteen perches to stones thence North six and three-quarter degrees East thirteen perches and six-tenths to the Graveyard Wall thence along said wall South eighty-eight degrees East three perches to a corner near the mill race, thence down said race South eleven degrees West fifteen perches to a corner and thence by said race South twenty-two and three-quarters degrees West twenty-one perches and one-tenth to the place of Beginning, containing one hundred and twenty-eight perches strict measure (It being part of a tract of land which William Craig and Elizabeth his wife did by their Indenture bearing date the first day of April in the year of our Lord one thousand and seven hundred and ninety-four for the Consideration therein mentioned sell convey and assure unto Henry Epple and to his heirs and assigns forever, as in and by said Indenture recorded in the recording office at Easton in Book B Vol. 2 Page 290 etc, relation being thereunto had will more fully and at large appear, and the said Henry Epple being so thereof siezed died intestate leaving a widow and one daughter, the above mentioned Maria Neligh, party to this Indenture, and the said widow by her release duly executed, and recorded in the recording office at Easton in Book F Vol. 3 page 179 hath released all right or claim of Dower of into or out of the said plantation, or any part thereof, leaving the said Nicholas Neligh and Maria his wife heirs of the same without encumbrance for claim of Dower or otherwise). Together with all and singular the Buildings and improvements, ways woods waters water courses rights liberties privileges hereditaments and appurtenances, whatsoever thereunto belonging or in any wise appertaining, and the reversions and remainders, rents, issues and profits thereof and also all the Estate right title interest use trust property claim and demand, of them the said Nicholas Neligh and Maria his wife in law equity or otherwise. TO HAVE AND TO HOLD THE SAID lot of land with the appurtenances unto them, the said John Wilson, James Horner, Sr., John Boyd, John Clyde, Jr., James Kerr, Jr., and Edward Humphreys and their successors for the uses above mentioned forever, and the said Nicholas Neligh and Maria his wife for themselves, their heirs Executors and Administrators doth hereby covenant promise grant and agree to and with the said John Wilson, James Horner, Sr., John Boyd, John Clyde, Jr, James Kerr, Jr., and Edward Humphrys and their successors, against them the said Nicholas Neligh and Maria his wife, and against all and every other person or persons lawfully claim or to claim the same, or any part thereof by through or under them or either of them, shall and will warrant and forever defend by these presents. In witness whereof the said parties to these presents have hereunto interchangeably set their hands and seals the day and year first above written.

         Nics Neligh (Seal)
         Mary Neligh (Seal)

Sealed and delivered
in the presence of us:
  Thos. McKeen
  Robert Russel

RECEIVED on the day of the date of the above written Indenture, of the above named John Wilson, James Horner, Sr., John Boyd, John Clyde, Jr, James Kerr, Jr., and Edward Humphrys five shillings etc., the consideration above mentioned. I say received by us.

            Nics Neligh.

Northampton County SS: On the 31st day of March 1813 personally appeared before me, Thomas McKeen one of the Justices of the Peace in and for the said county, the above named Nicholas Neligh and Maria his wife, and acknowledged the above Indenture to be their act and deed, and desire the same might be recorded as such, she the said

Maria being of full age separately and apart from her said husband by me examined and contents being first made known unto her, she voluntarily consenting.

Witness my hand and seal the day and date above written.

Thomas McKeen. (Seal)

It is agreed and he the said Nicholas Neligh within mentioned doth hereby convey as far as in him lies all right and title of the west side of the Mill Race and adjoining the school house lot to the great road for a road to pass and repass from said great road to the within granted land if such right is now vested in said Nicholas. Witness my hand and seal the 31st March 1813.

Nics Neligh (Seal)

Witness: Tho McKeen.
Robert Russel

Recorded in the office for Recording of deeds at Easton in and for the county of Northampton in Book B. Vol. 1 Page 98, etc., the 20th day of May Anno Domini 1814.

Witness my hand and the seal of the said office.

Nath. Michler, Recorder.

(A Reprint)

HISTORY OF THE
ALLEN TOWNSHIP PRESBYTERIAN CHURCH

And the Community which has sustained it, in what is known as the Irish Settlement, Northampton County, Pa.

By John C. Clyde, A. M.

Whose ancestry have been identified with the Settlement from its infancy,

Philadelphia:
Published By The Presbyterian Historical Society.
R. Magee & Son, Printers.
1876

Preface

IN the summer of 1866, the author's attention was directed to the subject of preparing a History of the Irish Settlement. At the time he commenced the collection of materials for the purpose. The original plan was to prepare a history in two parts: one to treat of the religious, and the other of the secular affairs of the community. It soon became apparent that the collection of the material for the secular part would be a formidable undertaking. In the face of insuperable difficulties, as it seemed, this feature of the work was dropped. A manuscript History of the Church, however, was completed in 1870, but without any definite purpose of publishing the same. At the earnest solicitation of friends, that manuscript, re-modeled, revised, re-written, and amplified, we have presented in the following pages.

It was the author's original intention to include in this volume two additional chapters, relating more particularly to the secular affairs of the community. By this means he hoped to interest the descendants of the old families of the Settlement, in order to secure their co-operation in obtaining material for a companion volume to the present one, treating of the secular affairs of the Settlement. One of the Chapters omitted was a necrology, being a transcript of all the inscriptions upon the tombstones in the old burying ground. The other was composed of genealogies and reminiscences. It was a source of regret to the author to find when ready to go to press, that these chapters could not be included. It is the present intention, that any disappointment arising from this source shall only be temporary in its character. The author hopes that, in no distant day, he will be able to present a secular history of the Settlement as a companion to the present volume, in accordance with his original design.

The genealogies omitted, though nearly two hundred and fifty in number, and to a high degree satisfactory as regarded the generations of the old families between their arrival in this country and 1876, were necessarily incomplete in some particulars. In the secular volume we hope to include the necrology and make the genealogies perfect as far as possible down to 1876. We invite all, therefore, who have not yet already done so, to furnish us with perfect genealogies of their families, so far as they can, together with reminiscences of the Settlement or individuals. The professional and public career of individuals in Church or State, their religious beliefs, etc., are solicited, together with any other matter which would be interesting to posterity. The author would be thankful, if persons who know of sources of information relative to the Settlement or its people, would make known the same to him. Thus may be constructed a permanent record of what our ancestors have done to assist in securing the present prosperity of our nation. Whilst the secular chapters have been omitted from this volume, the history of the Church has been retained complete, which includes much of the secular affairs of the Settlement.

In the preparation of these pages we have been indebted to many descendants of the Old Settlement families, both within and without its bounds. We have been assisted by the present pastor and officers of the church in no small degree.

We would also acknowledge the kindness shown us by Rev. Amzi L. Armstrong, Stated Clerk of the Presbytery of New Brunswick, and Rev. H. C. McCook, Custodian of Philadelphia Presbytery minutes, in furnishing extracts and permitting us to peruse the early minutes of these Presbyteries for records bearing upon the early ecclesiastical affairs of the Settlement Church.

We have also consulted Rupp's History of Northampton County, Henry's History of the Lehigh Valley, Dr. Charles Hodge's and Webster's Histories of the Presbyterian Church, Dr. D. X. Junkin's Historical Discourse at the Semi-centennial of the Presbytery of Newton, etc.

It is hoped what we have written with reference to the Church will be found to be in the main, correct and trustworthy. If some of the names are not spelled, in all cases, as the present generation would spell them, we would say we have given them as they are found in the old records.

Frazer, Pa, November, 1875.   J. C. C.

Contents

Chapter I. 1728-1760.

First Settlers. The Allen Purchase. First Pastorate, Rev. Eleazer Wales. David Brainerd's Preaching. First Church Building. Second Pastorate, Rev. Daniel Lawrence.

Chapter II. 1761-1783.

Rev. John Clark's Ministry, Parsonage Farm. The Seceder Church. Rev. John Rosbrough's Ministry. Deeding of Church and Grave yard lots. Rev. Francis Peppard's Removal to the Settlement.

Chapter III. 1784-1812.

Rev. Francis Peppard's Pastorate. Incorporation. Rev. Robert Russel commences Ministry. Affairs of the Parsonage Farm. Building Grave Yard Wall. Sale of Old Church.

Chapter IV. 1813-1825.

New Location and New Church Building. Origin of Alteration in services,—

Chapter V. 1826-1835.

Unfortunate Investments. Failure of Northampton Bank. Rev. Robert Russel's Death. First Sessional Records. Pastorate of Rev. Brogan Hoff.

Chapter VI. 1836-1869.

Rev. Leslie Irwin's Pastorate. First Preaching at Catasauqua. Preaching in Bath. Grave Yard re-modeled,—

Chapter VII. 1870-1875.

Rev. D. M. James' Ministry. Causes of Settlement's Decline. Auspicious Circumstances in Community. New Church at Bath. Re-modeling of the Old Church at Weaversville,—

Chapter VIII.

Sketches of Pastors, Eleazer Wales, Daniel Lawrence, John Clark, John Rosbrough, Francis Peppard, Robert Russel, Brogan Hoff, Leslie Irwin, D. M. James,—

Chapter IX.

Church Officers—Elders, Trustees, Officers of Board Collectors, Ecclesiastical Connections.

1728-1738—(?) Presbytery of Philadelphia.
1738-1751—Presbytery of New Brunswick.
1751-1758—Presbytery of Abington.
1758-1770—Presbytery of Philadelphia (1st).
1770-1777—Presbytery of New Brunswick.
1777-1821—Presbytery of Philadelphia.
1821-1851—Presbytery of Newton.
1851-1870—Presbytery of Philadelphia (New 2d).
1870-1876—Presbytery of Lehigh.

IRISH SETTLEMENT: CHAPTER I.—1728-1760.

In 1728, John Boyd, who married Jane Craig, went with Col. Thomas Craig from Philadelphia to the Forks of the Delaware and settled in what was afterward known as the Irish Settlement. At or about the same time, Hugh Wilson, Samuel Brown, and probably a few more went thither and settled. In 1731, there had accumulated a sufficient community to assume the name of the Craig Settlement.

If the record from which we derive our information is correct as to dates, and that it is so is substantiated by the best of evidence, we find these families followed the example of the Scotch-Irish in other parts of the country, in occupying vacant lands not yet open to settlers. The Craig or Irish Settlement was in existence before the Allens, whose name is identified with it, became possessed of the land which it occupied. The Allens came into possession in the following manner: In 1681, Charles II. of England, granted the province of Pennsylvania to William Penn. At the death of William Penn in 1718, his sons, John, Thomas, Richard, became Proprietaries of the Province of Pennsylvania. By a joint warrant of the Proprietaries, dated at London, May 18, 1732, the Surveyor General of the Province was directed to lay off a tract of five thousand acres for the personal use of Thomas Penn. This was done, and the tract thus laid off included the Craig or Irish Settlement, as we shall presently see. The same day (May 18th, 1732) on which the warrant was dated, Thomas Penn made an assignment of the tract of land to Joseph Turner of Philadelphia. At this point the Allens came to notice. William Allen, Esq., of Philadelphia, in 1750, was an intimate friend of the Penn family. His daughter, Ann, became the wife of Gov. John Penn. Through this intimacy, William Allen acquired large landed estates in the Province. Among others, he became possessed of the five thousand acre tract set off for the personal use of Thomas Penn. The warrant for the land which had passed into the hands of Joseph Turner, May 18th, 1732, was by him transferred to William Allen, September 10th, 1735. That this tract embraced the Craig or Irish Settlement is made clear from the following facts: June 13th, 1743, William Allen deeded over to James Craig two hundred and fifty acres of the five thousand acre tract. These two hundred and fifty acres acquired by James Craig were in the immediate vicinity of the present church building at Weaversville, as the church and grave yard lots were deeded over to the congregation by James Craig. Thus we see the Irish Settlement came under the auspices of the Allen family in 1735. From William Allen, or his heirs, the early settlers received the titles for their land, a fact which proved disasterous to many of them, as the Allens espoused the royal cause in the American Revolution, and their lands, we believe, were forfeited.

It is not unlikely that the families removed to the Settlement between 1731-1735, when William Allen became possessed of the land. But when Mr. Allen assumed control there doubtless was a new incentive to the Scotch-Irish people to emigrate to that part of the country. Although he was a friend of the Penn family, he was also friendly to Presbyterianism. In 1755, when the Synod of Philadelphia provided a fund for the relief of the widows and children of deceased ministers, Hon. William Allen became the trustee of the same. In 1763, when the Synod of New York and Philadelphia desired to present an address to the King of England, Hon. William Allen was chosen with others to bear the same to His Majesty. He presented one hundred acres of land to the Deep Run Presbyterian Church as a parsonage farm. By these and other acts of consideration for Presbyterianism, we may justly infer that the Scotch-Irish were induced to settle upon lands owned by him that they might thereby secure the favor of one who was not averse to the religious principles held by them. By the year 1737, the Settlement had grown to considerable proportions. By this time we find the following families living there:

Thomas Craig, John Boyd, Hugh Wilson, James Horner,

Thomas Armstrong, Robert Gregg, John Hays, James Kerr, James King, Arthur Lattimer, John McNair, James Ralston, John Walker, and Robert Walker.

These with a few others perhaps, may be regarded as the early settlers. With the influx of Scotch-Irish families the Settlement gradually came into notice as the Irish Settlement, instead of the Craig Settlement so called from its founder.

Having the principles of Scotch-Irish Presbyterianism within them, we may truly say they carried the Gospel with them into the wilderness. Although not absolutely positive, collateral evidence perhaps justifies us in making the statement that the Settlement Church was organized by the Philadelphia Presbytery, under the ministry of Eleazer Wales, as early as 1731, and that Thomas Craig, if not the original Elder, was at least a member of the first Session.

It will be noticed that the names of Rev. Eleazer Wales and Elder Thomas Craig appear upon the roll of the Synod of Philadelphia for the first time, we believe, in 1731. It would seem the Settlement Church had been organized by that time, and these representatives were present at Synod in performance of their duty. Assuming this to be the fact, we find this pastorate continued until 1734. In this year, however, "by the records of the Presbytery of Philadelphia, it appears that the Rev. E. Wales resigned the pastoral charge of Allentown" (cf. Webster, in Rupp p. 482.) From 1734 to 1738, the church seems to have been in an unsettled condition. In 1738, however, they sought supplies from the Presbytery of New Brunswick instead of Philadelphia.

It appears that their application came up before the Presbytery for consideration July 31st, 1739, as they were convened at New Brunswick. In answer thereto, it was "agreed that Mr. Gilbert Tennent preach at the Forks sometime this fall." It seems Mr. Tennent fulfilled his appointment, and visited the Settlement in the latter part of 1739. In the spring of 1740, they again applied to the Presbytery for a supply of preaching. The matter came up for consideration May 31st of that year. The following action was taken with reference thereto:

"In compliance with the afore-mentioned supplication for supplies, the Presbytery doth appoint as follows: That Mr. Robinson supply the Forks the first Sabbath in July; that Mr. Campbell supply Tehicken half his time, and Newton and the Forks the other half equally between them."

The Presbytery convened in New Brunswick again that year, August 2d., at which time it was reported that the foregoing appointments had been complied with. The same day "a call was presented from the Forks of the Delaware for Mr. McKnight's labors." The call seems not to have been accepted. Two days later, at the same meeting of Presbytery, (August 4th, 1740), the people again petitioned for preaching. We find a reference made to it, under the date, in the following record:

"A petition from the Forks of the Delaware and Mr. Green's being presented to the Presbytery, in compliance therewith they thought proper to advise Mr. Campbell to supply them as often as he shall judge proper, till our next."

How often, or just what length of time Mr. Campbell continued to preach under this appointment, does not appear. He ceased, however, before the spring of 1742. On May 29th, 1742, we find the people petitioning again for preaching. This time they petitioned in conjunction with Greenwich. We are unable to decide from the records whether this petition from the Forks was from Mt. Bethel people to the exclusion of the Settlement; or from the Settlement to the exclusion of Mt. Bethel; or from them both conjointly. There is little doubt, however, but that the application was at least shared by the Settlement people. The minister they desired to have sent to them was Rev. Charles McKnight. The application came up before Presbytery on the above date, as the Presbytery was convened in Philadelphia. Whether Mr. McKnight was secured or not does not appear. If he did go it was but for a short time, for October 12th of this year we find the people again asking for supplies. In answer to this application the Presbytery appointed Mr. Campbell to devote one-third of his time to them. For immediate supply of the pulpit we find the following appointments by Presbytery: Rev. William Dean was appointed to preach next Sabbath (i. e. next after October 13th, 1742) at Neshaminy, and then three Sabbaths at the Forks of the Delaware. After this he was to supply Cohansie and Cape May until within three Sabbaths of the next meeting of the Presbytery which was to be on the fourth Tuesday of May, 1743. These three Sabbaths were to be spent in the Forks of the Delaware.

With Mr. Campbell devoting one-third of his time to the Settlement and Greenwich, in addition to these six Sabbaths of Mr. Dean, the Settlement must have enjoyed a good supply of preaching from October 12th, 1742, to the latter part of May, 1743. At the meeting of Presbytery in Philadelphia, on the fourth Tuesday of May, (May 26th) 1743, three calls were presented for the services of Mr. Dean. One from the Forks of the Delaware, one from the Forks of Brandywine, and one from Cape May. Mr. Dean not being prepared to decide whether he would accept one or any of these calls, was granted till the next meeting of Presbytery to consider the matter. In the meantime Presbytery directed Mr. Dean to supply the Forks of the Delaware until their next meeting; at the same time preach as much as was convenient at Pequea. The Presbytery next convened August 12th, 1743, at which time Mr. Dean, by letter, signified that he was not yet ready to declare his acceptance of any one of the calls which had been presented to him, but was willing to continue to supply under the then existing arrangement. Presbytery directed him to continue to supply in the Forks of the Delaware, and instead of preaching at Pequea and Forks of Brandywine, as was intended, devote that time to preaching at Tehicken and Bethlehem, N. J. At a meeting of Presbytery held October 12th, 1743, Mr. Dean declared his non-acceptance of any of the calls that had been presented to him. It now seems his labors ceased in this locality until the next year. We find the next day, October 13th, 1743, Mr. Campbell is permitted by Presbytery to supply Tehicken and Bethlehem which had been assigned to Mr. Dean. If he had been devoting one-third of his time to the Forks of the Delaware and Greenwich, as by appointment October 12th, 1742, which does not clearly appear, he now ceased to devote so much time to the Settlement as formerly. Presbytery simply requested him to supply the Forks of the Delaware sometimes. At the same meeting of Presbytery, October 13th, 1743, Rev. Charles Beatty was ordered to supply in the Forks of the Delaware sometimes. At the spring meeting of Presbytery, 1744, we find the people asking supplies. The Presbytery considered their petition May 26th, and accordingly sent Mr. Dean to supply the Forks till the next meeting which was on September 12th. There being no record to the contrary it is presumed Mr. Dean fulfilled the appointment. Whether he devoted his whole time to the Settlement or not does not appear; at all events we find during this summer of 1744, David Brainerd, the celebrated missionary to the Indians, made his first recorded visit to the Settlement. From Mr. Brainerd's diary we learn that he preached there July 23d, 1744, and from Matt. V, 3:

"Blessed are the poor in spirit, for theirs is the kingdom of heaven."

On the 4th of the following September, he again preached there. His text was, Luke XIV. 22:

"And the servant said, Lord it is done as Thou hast commanded, and yet there is room."

Presbytery convened September 12th, 1744, at which time Mr. Dean's appointment in the Forks having closed, the people renewed their application for supplies. In accordance with this application Rev. Eleazer Wales, their old pastor, was appointed to supply them the two last Sabbaths of September, and the first Sabbath of October.

Mr. Beatty was also appointed to supply one Sabbath, and Mr. Dean as much as he could until the next meeting of Presbytery. We find however, that Mr. Dean did not preach in the Settlement in accordance with this appointment, as he was dismissed by the Presbytery of New Brunswick, October 4th, of this year, to connect himself with the Presbytery of New Castle. In the latter part of October of this year, we find David Brainerd again visiting the Settlement. He speaks of making a journey from the Susquehanna to the Forks of the Delaware. At the end of the second day's journey he says he and his party came to the Irish Settlement. The distance from the Susquehanna to the Settlement being about two day's journey on a direct route to the Forks of the Delaware at Easton, there is little doubt but that this and the Irish Settlement spoken of in Mr. Brainerd's diary, are identical. On this journey the Rev. Eliab Byram, member of the Presbytery of New York, accompanied him. They arrived at the Settlement on Saturday evening, and the next day preached to the people.

On the 14th of April, 1745, we find in the diary of Mr. Brainerd the following record:

"Was disordered in body with fatigue of the late journey, but was enabled, however, to preach to a considerable assembly of white people gathered from all parts round about, with some freedom from Ezek. XXXIII: 11.

This was at Mt. Bethel or Easton, some doubt existing as to which of these places was the scene of Mr. Brainerd's missionary labors. However, some of the white people referred to were doubtless from the Irish Settlement.

On May 19th, 1745, the Presbytery met, and the Settlement people made their usual application for preaching, accompanying it with a request for the administration of the Lord's Supper in their midst. From the records of this meeting of Presbytery we learn that Mr. Daniel Lawrence preached at the Forks and Greenwich on the last Sabbath of June.

Presbytery convened September 20th, 1745, at which time two calls were brought in for pastoral services of Mr. Daniel Lawrence. The one was from the two Bethlehems and the other from Maidenhead and Hopewell. Mr. Lawrence not being present at the meeting of Presbytery, consideration of these calls was deferred until the next meeting. Under the circumstances, Mr. Lawrence was directed to supply two Sabbaths at Maidenhead and Hopewell, and then he was to repair to the Forks of the Delaware. He was to supply two-thirds of his time in the Forks, and devote the other third to the two Bethlehems.

In the early part of 1746, we find David Brainerd again at the Settlement. In his diary, under date of February 18th, 1746, we find the following record: "Preached to an assembly of Irish People nearly fifteen miles distant from the Indians." This distance being about the same as that from Easton to Weaversville, there is little doubt but that this sermon was preached in the Irish Settlement, near the latter place. This was near the end of Mr. Brainerd's earthly labors, as he died in 1747.

About the year 1746, the first church building was erected in the Settlement. It was a rude log structure and stood a little to the southeast of the present church building.

The grave yard was occupied for burial purposes about the same time, or perhaps a little earlier. The oldest stone is in memory of James King, one of the first settlers, and bears the date of 1745.

July 21st, 1746, Presbytery convened. At this meeting there was a supplication from the congregations of Maidenhead and Hopewell, requesting the labors of Mr. Lawrence until the next meeting of Presbytery, by way of trial, with a view to his settlement among them. Also a similar supplication from the Forks of the Delaware, for his services for one year with a view to his settlement there. Likewise a supplication from the Bethlehems for the same purpose. Some people from Oxford Furnace also supplicated that they might share the labors of Mr. Lawrence in case he should be appointed to supply the Forks of the Delaware. It seems in the midst of this clamor, as it were, for the services of Mr. Lawrence, the Presbytery returned him to his labors in the Forks with instructions to preach every fifth Sabbath at

Tunis Quick's (?) in the Forks of the Delaware. Thus things seem to have remained until the meeting of Presbytery October 16th, of this year. At this meeting, the people in the Forks renewed their call for Mr. Lawrence to undertake the pastoral charge among them. The matter being proposed to him by Presbytery, he signified his acceptance of the call; Presbytery thereupon appointed a committee to ordain and install him. This committee was composed of Rev. Richard Treat, Rev. James Campbell, Rev. James Davenport, Rev. James McCrea and Rev. Charles Beatty. Rev. Richard Treat was to "Preside over the whole affair." Mr. Lawrence was given John iii. 18, from which to preach a popular sermon as part of trial for ordination. He was also directed to prepare a Latin Exegesis and hand it in to the committee, in the Forks of the Delaware, on the first day of April, 1747. The committee having assembled in the Forks at this time, and these requirements having been complied with on the part of Mr. Lawrence, Presbytery directed the committee to proceed to his ordination and installation if the way should be found in all other respects clear.

The ordination and installation was to take place April 2d. The instructions of Presbytery were carried out, as we learn from the following report:

"FORKS OF DELAWARE, APRIL 2d, 1747.

"The Committee appointed by the Presbytery to attend to the ordination of Mr. Daniel Lawrence, viz: Mr. Treat, Mr. Davenport, Mr. McCrea, Mr. Campbell, (Mr. Beatty for good reasons not attending), did, according to appointment, meet at the place, and having yesterday heard him preach a sermon on John iii. 18, and received his Exegesis (upon the question assigned), both to good satisfaction, and there appearing no objection in the way, they proceeded this day according to appointment, with fasting and prayer and imposition of hands, to ordain Mr. Lawrence to the Gospel ministry over this people. Concluded with prayer and blessing. Then and there it was agreed by the representatives of the two settlements that they have and desire to be united; that so long as Mr. Lawrence shall continue to be minister to them both that he shall preach two-thirds of his time at the western settlement, and the other one-third part at the northern without any alteration except by judgment of Presbytery."

Thus did Mr. Lawrence commence his pastoral labors at the Settlement, April 2d, 1747, devoting to them two-thirds of his time. On account of some difficulty with the people, as well as ill-health, he spent the winter of 1747, and spring of 1748, at Cap May.

At a meeting of the Synod of New York, convened at Maidenhead, May 18th, 1748, we find the following record: At the sitting of the Synod on the forenoon of May 19th, "motion was made to the Synod in behalf of Cape May, in order to have some provision made for the settlement of a minister there. ————— The Synod proceeded to consider the motion respecting Cape May, and in order to the relief of that people, the Synod doth recommend to the Presbytery of New Brunswick to send down Mr. Lawrence immediately for a few Sabbaths."

Thus it would seem Mr. Lawrence, by his sojourn at Cape May during the winter opened the way for his return thither in the spring, as above indicated. How long he remained there at this time does not appear. It was probably, however only for the few Sabbaths indicated. Returning to the Settlement he seems to have continued his labors until the spring of 1752.

In the meantime the Synod of New York organized a new Presbytery called Abington. This occurred in 1751. The new Presbytery was to be composed of those members of the Presbytery of New Brunswick who lived in Pennsylvania, and those who lived in New Jersey, "to the southward of Philadelphia, bordering upon Delaware."

Thus the Church in the Settlement with its Pastor came under the jurisdiction of the Presbytery of Abington.

The first meeting of the Presbytery, by direction of Synod,

was on the third Wednesday of May, (20th), 1752, in the city of Philadelphia. At this meeting, "Cape May supplicated that Mr. Lawrence might be sent unto them on trial for settlement, in case he be liberated from his present charge." The matter of the dissolution of the pastoral relation between Mr. Lawrence and the Church in the Settlement, came up for consideration in Presbytery the next day. After hearing Mr. Lawrence and the commissioners from the congregation, the Presbytery finally dissolved the pastoral relation, assigning as a reason for doing so, the feeble health of Mr. Lawrence and the prospect of his recovery by removing to some other field of labor. Thus the Church became vacant May 21st, 1752.

During Mr. Lawrence's ministry, we find the following names as being at least financially, connected with the church: John Boyd, William Young, George Gibson, Robert Gibson, James Hope, John Riddle, Widow Dobbin, James Kerr, Widow King, James Craig, William Craig, Thomas Craig, James Ralston, Joseph Perry, James Egleson and Andrew Mann.

These are the first names entered in the first account book extant of the congregation. We find the following inscription written upon the (inside) cover of this book:

"The account book of the congregation of the West Branch of Delaware in the Forks, January 9th, 1749. The payments to commence May 1st, 1749, and continue according to terms."

The Church during its early history, was designated by the name of "Forks of Delaware," as well as Allentown. After Mr. Lawrence left the congregation, in 1752, till 1761, they were supplied principally by Presbytery.

As appears from the records of the Presbyteries, these supplies were as follows: Immediately upon the dissolution of the pastoral relation, the commissioners from the congregation present at that meeting of the Presbytery, May 21st, 1752, asked for supplies. In answer to this request Mr. Lawrence was to supply two Sabbaths, Mr. Charles Beatty, two; Mr. James (?) Campbell, two; Mr. Thomas Lewis, one.

Further, provisionally, Mr. Beatty, Mr. Lewis, Mr. Campbell, and Mr. Richard Treat were to supply them, each one Sabbath in addition. At the meeting of Presbytery at Philadelphia, September 19th, 1752, supplies were asked for.

Mr. Lawrence was appointed to preach four Sabbaths; Mr. Beatty, two; Mr. Campbell, two; and "if Mr. Morrison be at liberty he is desired to supply this winter between Tehicken and the Forks."

At Presbytery in Philadelphia, May 16th, 1753, supplies were asked for. Mr. Lawrence was appointed to supply "two or three times" at the Forks.

June 20th, of this year, preaching was again applied for, and Mr. Henry (?) Martin was sent to preach four Sabbaths.

At Philadelphia October 4th, 1753, "Application was also made from both settlements in the Forks of the Delaware for supplies, and the North Branch particularly desire leave to apply to the Presbytery of New Brunswick, or any other Presbytery belonging to our Synod, for the same purpose."

The next month, November 21st, there was a meeting of Presbytery in Philadelphia at which time Mr. Benjamin Chestnut was appointed to preach four Sabbaths, and Mr. Henry Martin four. At the meeting the Presbytery said:

"The Forks of the Delaware have full liberty to make application to any Presbytery belonging to our Synod for as much supply as they can afford."

At the meeting of the Presbytery at Newton, April 9th, 1754, Mr. Martin reported that he had preached two of the Sabbaths of his appointment at the "Forks," but had failed the other two for reasons which were sustained by Presbytery.

At this meeting appointments were made for the Settlement, as follows: Rev. Andrew Hunter, third and fourth Sabbaths of September; Mr. Chestnut, four Sabbaths; Mr. Martin, two; Mr. Beatty, two. These appointments were subsequently reported complied with.

Philadelphia, November 5th, 1754, Mr. Hunter was appointed to supply three Sabbaths; and Mr. Martin, two; which were complied with.

Philadelphia, May 28th, 1755, Mr. Lawrence was sent to supply the first Sabbath of October; Mr. Martin, two Sabbaths; and Mr. Chestnut, two. At this meeting of the Presbytery, "the congregation in the Forks of the Delaware" asked permission to present a call to a "candidate," under the care of the Presbytery of New Brunswick, and if he did not accept, asked for what supplies the Presbytery might be able to give them.

This request was acceded to, but who the call was made out for does not appear. That it was not accepted is manifest from the fact that the congregation remained vacant for several years after.

Philadelphia, October 21st, 1755. Mr. Beatty, Mr. Chestnut and Mr. Martin were appointed to supply each one Sabbath and fulfilled their appointments.

Philadelphia, September 21st, 1756. Mr. Beatty appointed to supply three Sabbaths; Mr. Chestnut, three; and Mr. Martin, two, before the next (May) meeting of Presbytery.

Philadelphia, May 24th, 1757. Rev. William Ramsey appointed to supply the last Sabbath in June and the first two in July; Mr. Martin, two; before next meeting of Presbytery; Mr. Chestnut, the first two Sabbaths in August; and Mr. Beatty, the first Sabbath in September.

Philadelphia, October 4th, 1757. Mr. Martin appointed to preach four Sabbaths; Mr. Beatty, one; and Mr. Chestnut, the second Sabbath of November.

Philadelphia, November 31st, 1758. Mr. Chestnut appointed to preach two Sabbaths in the fall and two in the spring; and Mr. Martin to preach four Sabbaths, two of them to be in the winter.

Philadelphia, May 15th, 1759. Rev. James Latta appointed to preach the fourth and fifth Sabbaths in September; Mr. Chestnut, four Sabbaths, two of them being the last Sabbath in July and the first in August; Mr. Beatty, two Sabbaths; and Mr. Martin, "as much as he can."

Philadelphia, October 2d, 1759. Presbytery appointed that Mr. Martin preach four Sabbaths; Mr. Chestnut, four; Rev. John Simonton, two; and Mr. Beatty, two.

Philadelphia, May 14th, 1760. Rev. Joseph Montgomery to preach one Sabbath; and Mr. Latta, two.

Philadelphia, August 20th, 1760. Mr. Latta to supply two Sabbaths.

Philadelphia, November 20th, 1760. Mr. Latta, to supply two Sabbaths before the next meeting of Presbytery; and Mr. Chestnut, two Sabbaths in March. Thus is completed the list of supplies for this long vacancy.

In addition to these supplies, furnished by the Presbyteries of Abington and Philadelphia, under whose jurisdiction the Church was during this vacancy, we find, from evidence preserved in the bounds of the congregation, that Rev. Benjamin Hait, of the Presbytery of New Brunswick, preached in 1758; and Rev. Thomas Lewis, of the Presbytery of Suffolk, preached in 1759.

Notwithstanding this long vacancy in the pastorate, the congregation seems to have been in a prosperous condition, as the following record goes to show:

"August 21st, This day, as some people of this congregation hath for some time past wanted convenient seats, it is unanimously agreed to allow one long seat on each side, viz: one before William Hazlet, to John Hays and son, and one on the other side to John Clendinen. Also, it is proposed to set one short seat on the upper side of the pulpit. It is agreed that the above-mentioned seats are only to accommodate people for the present, till other accommodations be made."

CHAPTER TWO—1761-1783.

In 1758, the Old Side and New Light parties in the Presbyterian Church united. This made some changes necessary in the arrangement of Presbyteries. Accordingly the Presbytery of Abington, which had belonged to the New Light party, was merged into that of Philadelphia. The

Church in the Settlement, therefore, now came under the care of the Presbytery of Philadelphia.

At a meeting of this Presbytery, in Philadelphia, August 13th, 1761, Rev. John Clark presented his credentials from the Presbytery of New Brunswick and was received a member of the Presbytery. The same day a call was presented to him from the "Forks of Delaware." He took the matter under consideration until the next meeting. In the meantime he was directed to supply "at the Forks of Delaware in the following manner, viz: two Sabbaths at Allentown and one at Hunter's Settlement, interchangeably, except two Sabbaths at Tehicken."

Here, it will be observed, the church began to assume the name of Allentown, to more clearly distinguish it from the other church in the "Forks," Mt. Bethel, at Hunter's Settlement.

For some reason, which does not clearly appear, the congregation became divided upon the subject of calling Mr. Clark. At the next meeting of the Presbytery, November 17th, 1761, both parties appeared, to press their views in the matter. The one party did not wish the Presbytery to permit Mr. Clark to accept the call which he had under consideration; the other insisted upon their right to call him. The Presbytery inquired of the commissioners from the congregation, who favored the calling of Mr. Clark, whether they thought they were able to support him as promised in their call, in case the opposing party declined to assist. If they thought they could they were granted liberty to prosecute their call, leaving the opposing party to act according to their own judgment. It seems the friends of Mr. Clark expressed their ability to fulfil their promises to him, as, at a later hour of the same day, "Mr. Clark signified to the Presbytery his acceptance of the call from the Forks of Delaware, in which they promise him, during his continuance with them as a regular Gospel minister, the sum of ———— pounds per annum and the use of a parsonage."

At this meeting of Presbytery, Mr. Latta was appointed

to preach at the Settlement three Sabbaths in March; and Mr. Chestnut, the last Sabbath of November. It would seem the dissatisfied ones in the congregation were not disposed to acquiesce in the settlement of Mr. Clark, as we find that at the meeting of Presbytery in Philadelphia, April 6th, 1762. "A few people in the Forks of Delaware applied for preaching." It seems there were criminations and recriminations. The installation of Mr. Clark had been deferred up to this time, probably on account of the difficulties in the congregation. Now, however, a request was preferred for his installation. The request was acceded to by Presbytery, but the time for the installation was to be fixed at the next meeting. Accordingly, May 18th, 1762, at Philadelphia, the Presbytery fixed Wednesday following, October 13th, as the day for Mr. Clark's installation. Rev. Richard Treat was to preside and preach the sermon. Rev. Henry Martin, Rev. James Latta, and Rev. Charles Beatty, were to assist in the other parts of the service.

This committee reported to Presbytery, November 9th, 1762, that they had installed Mr. Clark according to appointment. Thus the church came under the care of a regular pastor again, October 13th, 1762.

In order that the ecclesiastical connections of the church may be properly traced, it should be remembered that during this year, 1762, the Presbytery of Philadelphia was divided. The two Presbyteries were designated respectively First and Second Presbytery of Philadelphia. The church in the Settlement was under the care of the First Presbytery. It should be remembered also, that Mr. Clark was installed pastor of two congregations, Allentown and Mt. Bethel. It seems the troubles in the Settlement Church well nigh, if not wholly, subsided after the installation of Mr. Clark. Apparently things moved along smoothly in the pastoral charge until 1766. October 26th, 1766, however, difficulties in the Mt. Bethel Church were brought to the attention of Presbytery. Mr. Clark desired to be released from his pastoral charge. This was not acceded to by the Presbytery, but all parties were counseled to exercise Christian forbearance, and settle their difficulties in an amicable manner. Thus things were quieted down until the next spring. April 7th, 1767, however, the Mt. Bethel people asked Presbytery to appoint a committee to inquire into their affairs, and call Mr. Clark to account upon some charges which they desired to prefer against him. Mr. Clark made a satisfactory explanation to Presbytery in regard to the matters, and Rev. Charles Beatty and Rev. William Ramsey were sent to Mt. Bethel as a healing committee. Notwithstanding this, May 21st, 1767, commissioners from Mt. Bethel reported to Presbytery that there was no hope of peace and reconciliation among them; whereupon Rev. Richard Treat, Rev. Enoch Green and Rev. Benjamin Chestnut, from the First Philadelphia Presbytery, were added to the committee already appointed, and Rev. John Hanna, Rev. William Kirkpatrick, and Rev. John Rosbrough, of the Presbytery of New Brunswick, were invited to meet with them at Mt. Bethel on the third Tuesday in June, and endeavor to settle the difficulties. November 3d, 1767, ths committee reported that some of them had fulfilled the duties of their appointment, but as there was not a quorum present, they had taken no decisive action. They had, however, endeavored to allay the existing animosities.

The next day, however, November 4th, owing to the gloomy aspect of affairs and the bodily weakness of the pastor, Presbytery released Mr. Clark from his pastoral charge. Thus the church in the Settlement became vacant again, November 4th, 1767.

It was during Mr. Clark's ministry that we have the first recorded Indian murder in the Settlement. The victim was the wife of James Horner, one of the early settlers. Her remains lie in the old church yard. Having traced the pastorate of this period to its close, we return to the secular affairs of the congregation. In 1761, the congregation purchased a piece of land from Samuel Wilson, containing about eighty-two acres, for a parsonage farm. The transfer was made in the name of Thomas Armstrong and James Ralston, as contributors to the purchase price. They were to hold it in trust for the congregation. These eighty-two acres were a part of the two hundred and fifty acres purchased by Samuel Wilson from Zechariah and David Jones of "White Clay Creek Hundred, (?) in the county of New Castle, upon Delaware". David and Zechariah Jones, here spoken of, were the heirs and executors of the will of their father, Morgan Jones, of "Hundred of Pecander, in the county of New Castle, upon Delaware." The assignment made by them to Samuel Wilson, of the eighty-two acres, was on March 2d, 1761.

The purchase price was two hundred and two pounds. The situation of this parsonage farm was perhaps a half-mile or a mile north of the present village of Howertown. As the property was simply held by Thomas Armstrong and James Ralston, in trust for the congregation, it was deemed necessary to make some public declaration as to whom the property in reality belonged; and what the original intent was in its purchase; and also to bind those who might come after them in trust, so that the property thus belonging to the congregation might not be squandered and the trust abused. Accordingly, in 1767, Thomas Armstrong and James Ralston made a declaration, the purport of which was as follows: The property, although deeded over to them in person, did not belong to them exclusively, but they were only contributors to the purchase price, together with others. Their names were only used in the transfer, at the special request of other contributors. The names of the other contributors were James Craig, Arthur Lattimore, Charles Wilson, John Walker, James Kerr, William Heaslet, James Horner, John Riddle, David Chambers, John Ralston, Mary King, Robert Lattimore, William McNair, John McNair, and Alexander Dobbin, of Allen township, and Thomas Herron, of Moore Township.

Samuel Wilson, from whom the property was purchased, was himself a contributor. The trustees could not sell the property without the consent of the majority of the contributors, or their heirs. This consent had to be given in writing, and signed by the contributors or their heirs. In case any one of the original contributors died before such consent might be required, his or their heirs had the right to vote instead. The heirs, however, could only cast one vote, and this was by the oldest living son. If no son happened to be alive to cast the vote, then the eldest living daughter had the right to vote. If there was no daughter, then the principal heir mentioned in the will of the deceased contributor. And if such heir was not alive, then the oldest son or daughter of such heir was to vote, as in the case of the son or daughter of the contributor himself. This consent being thus obtained, the trustees had the right to sell the property and make a deed for the same. They also had the right to sue for any portion of the sale price, if it was necessary. The price of the property was to be divided among the contributors, or their heirs, in proportion to the amounts respectively contributed. A list of the contributors, with the amounts contributed, was given to determine the pro rata of distribution, if it ever should be needed. If the price of the property was received in payments, the trustees were to divide each payment in the proper proportion. They were to bear not more than their proper proportion of the expenses attending the sale of the property or the collection of the money for which it was sold. They were not bound to proceed to the collection of such money without the direction of the contributors or their heirs, and not then until money was furnished them to defray the expenses of such collection nor were they responsible for the loss by bankruptcy or any other case over which they had no control, or any part of the price.

Such was the jealous care with which the interests of the church and the people were watched over.

About this time the congregation in the Settlement became weakened probably on account of the formation of the Associate Presbyterian Church. The seceded ministers came to Pennsylvania in 1754. They had a congregation in Deep Run. They built a church in Howertown, but never had a minister. The Rev. William Marshall, of Philadelphia, Clerk of the Associate Presbytery, however, visited them from time to time. Many of the Associate ministers and churches joined the Reformed Presbyterians in forming the Associate Reformed Presbyterian body. The faithful "remnant in the Forks" would not acquiesce, and removed to Western Pennsylvania. The old log church is gone and the graves near it are overgrown with trees.

The vacancy in the Settlement Church was not of long duration, after Mr. Clark left. From time to time supplies were granted by Presbytery. The next spring after Mr. Clark left, the Presbytery, May 28th, 1768, sent Rev. Alexander Mitchell to supply two Sabbaths, and again, November 23d, to supply one Sabbath.

March 29th, 1769, the Settlement people asked permission of Presbytery to present a call to Rev. John Rosbrugh, of the Presbytery of New Brunswick. They were advised to secure, in connection with Mt. Bethel, as much of Mr. Rosbrugh's time as they could. As Mr. Rosbrugh was connected with the Presbytery of New Brunswick, the people thought it would be to their advantage to be transferred from the care of the First Philadelphia Presbytery to that of the Presbytery of New Brunswick.

They, therefore, petitioned the Synod, convened at Philadelphia, May 23d, 1769, to transfer them to the care of the latter Presbytery. The committee from the congregation and both Presbyteries concerned were heard, after which the Synod deemed it not expedient at that time to accede to the request. They, however, directed the First Presbytery of Philadelphia to inquire more particularly into the circumstances of the congregation, and if they found it expedient, they were empowered to transfer them according to their desire.

The Presbytery did inquire into the matter. In the meantime, November 9th, 1769, Mr. Mitchell was sent to preach one Sabbath in the fall, and Mr. Boyd one Sabbath in the spring.

THE HAYS COAT OF ARMS. (See page 77.)

At the same time Presbytery expressed the hope that a part of the time of Mr. Rosbrugh might be secured. They also suggested the propriety of Mr. Rosbrugh's connecting himself with the First Philadelphia Presbytery.

In pursuance of the action of 1769, we find the following minute made by the Synod, May 21st, 1770, while in session in New York:

"The First Presbytery of Philadelphia reported that, in compliance with an order of Synod last year, they had, in conjunction with the Presbytery of New Brunswick, inquired particularly into the state and connections of the congregation of Allentown, in the Forks of the Delaware, and it is the unanimous opinion of both Presbyteries that it is at present most subservient to the interests of religion in those parts, for the Presbytery of New Brunswick to take under their care, not only the congregation of Allentown, but also the congregation of Mt Bethel, both of which are in the Forks of the Delaware, and both which have been under the care of the First Philadelphia Presbytery, The Synod, therefore orders the Presbytery of New Brunswick to take both the said congregations under their care for the future."

Thus was the church returned to the care of the New Brunswick Presbytery, from which it was separated by the erection of the Presbytery of Abington in 1751.

While these matters were going on in the Synod, and First Philadelphia Presbytery, corresponding movements had existed in the Presbytery of New Brunswick which were calculated to lead Mr. Rosbrugh to the pastorate of the church in the Settlement. April 19th, 1768, that Presbytery had directed him to preach one Sabbath at the Settlement before the spring meeting of the Presbytery. April 18th, 1769, he was released from his former pastoral charge, and the same day received a call to the church in the Settlement, in connection with the church at Greenwich. He was granted permission to accept this call upon condition that the Allentown Church should be transferred to the care of the Presbytery of New Brunswick. This accounts for the presentation of the petition by the Allentown people to the Synod, on the 23d of May following, for the transfer of the congregation. Mr. Rosbrugh had been at the Settlement and had expressed his acceptance of their call, April 3d, previous to its presentation to him in Presbytery on the 18th of the same month. This is made explicit by the following record in the books of the congregation:

"The Rev. John Rosbrugh accepted the call of the Allentown congregation the 3d day of April, 1769; that is to allow the congregation two-thirds of his time for ——— pounds per annum."

Having expressed his acceptance to the people, and learned the conditions upon which the Presbytery would allow him to accept it, it was natural for the people to seek to fulfil the conditions, viz: the transfer of the congregation. From the time Mr Rosbrugh expressed his willingness to accept this call, his time was doubtless largely if not exclusively devoted to the Settlement and Greenwich.

The petition for the transfer of the congregation not being granted in 1769, as we have seen, the Presbytery of New Brunswick appointed Mr. Rosbrugh, October 19th, 1769, "constant supply to the people of Greenwich and Allentown" until the next meeting, except three Sabbaths, which he was to devote to Mt. Bethel. As we have seen, the Synod transferred the Church in the Settlement to the care of the Presbytery of New Brunswick, May 21st, 1770. The conditions upon which Mr. Rosbrugh might accept the call being fulfilled he expressed his acceptance of the same April 15th, 1772. It was probably on account of the unsettled state of the ecclesiastical connections of the Settlement Church, that caused the neglect of completing the pastoral relations during the two years which transpired between the transfer and installation. Even when the matter was agitated and the call was accepted, the installation was deferred until the fall of 1772. October 13th, 1772, however, the people renewed their request for Mr. Rosbrugh's installation. The Presbytery thereupon appointed October 28th, at noon, as the time for the services. Rev. John Guild was to preside and preach the sermon. The other members of the committee were Rev. John Hanna, Rev. Jacob Vanarsdalen, and Rev. Samuel Kennedy.

Thus the Settlement Church came again regularly under the care of a pastor, October 28th, 1772. From this time till 1776, affairs moved along quietly and satisfactorily in the congregation. But, in 1776, the spirit of American independence roused the Settlement people along with their fellow countrymen. A company of soldiers was recruited in the Settlement which marched to the seat of war under the command of Captain Hays. Mr. Rosbrugh accompanied them as Chaplain. When at Trenton, January 2d, 1777, he was overtaken, when comparatively alone, by a company of Hessians, and brutally murdered. Thus, in so tragic a manner, the church again became vacant. It should be recorded to the lasting credit of the Church in the Settlement, that they continued Mr. Rosbrugh's salary while he was connected with the army, and after his death honorably paid all dues to his widow.

During the pastorate of Mr. Rosbrugh, the church and grave yard lots were deeded over to the congregation. They were both upon land owned by James Craig, and by him deeded to the congregation, March 17th, 1772.

The property was made over in trust to John Walker, Arthur Lattimore, Robert Lattimore, John Ralston, John McNair and William Craig. The burying ground contained eighty-one perches, and the church seat, thirty-seven perches of land. (Vid. Obligation & Declaration & Form of Deed).

As in the case of the parsonage farm, the trustees made a declaration with regard to the original intent in conveying the property to them. The declaration was made March 12th, 1772, the import of which was as follows: The church was for the use of the Presbyterian congregation of Allen Township; and the burying ground for the use of its members. Certain requisites were necessary to constitute a person a member of the congregation. He must hold to the principles of the Westminster Confession of Faith and Directory, as interpreted by the Synod under whose care the congregation at the time was. He must have attended upon Divine worship in the congregation for at least twelve months, and contributed regularly to the support of the Gospel, in order to have any interest in or claim to the property belonging to the congregation. A person was no longer considered a member, if he departed from the principles of the Westminster Confession of Faith and Directory; or did not continue to attend in an orderly manner upon Divine worship. No one who changed his religious views, separated from the Synod or congregation, or refused or neglected to contribute to the support of the church, could succeed to the trust, or have any interest in the property. If any one died, while in the trust, the congregation could choose another to succeed him. This choice was made by a majority of votes of all the adult male members of the congregation. In meetings called for this purpose, the Pastor of the congregation, if present, was, at all times, to preside as Moderator.

If it was not convenient for the choice thus to be made it might be done by a committee appointed by the congregation for that purpose. In order to prevent lawsuits or troubles arising with regard either to the pieces of ground or the pews in the church, the decision of a majority of the adult male members of the congregation was declared to be final in all such cases. No person was allowed to occupy as their place of residence, any building or buildings which were then upon the premises, or that might be erected thereafter. Thus we see again the care with which the rights and interests of the congregation were regarded.

After the death of Mr. Rosbrugh, January 2d, 1777, the congregation desired to be returned to the care of the First Philadelphia Presbytery. They sent a supplication on this subject to Synod, convened at Philadelphia, May 21st, 1777, which came up for consideration on the 23d. The supplication was granted as shown by the following minute of the Synod under that date:

"By the committee of overtures, a supplication from the congregation of Allentown, in the Forks of Delaware, requesting that they might be set off from the Presbytery of New Brunswick, and put under the care of the First Presbytery of Philadelphia, to whom they formerly belonged, was brought in and read. The Presbytery of New Brunswick freely concurring, the Synod granted the supplicant's request, and the First Philadelphia Presbytery is ordered to take said congregation under their care."

The congregation being vacant, supplies were required. April 8th, 1777, the congregation asked supplies of the First Presbytery of Philadelphia. They requested that Rev. Alexander Mitchell might be sent to them one-fourth of his time as stated supply. This request was granted.

At Deep Run, June 17th, 1777, further supplies were asked, especially for one-fourth of Mr. Mitchell's time. Mr. Mitchell was sent to preach one Sabbath, and Rev. Nathaniel Irwin to preach one Sabbath, and Rev. James Grier one Sabbath, until the next meeting of Presbytery.

The first Presbytery of Philadelphia, met again at Deep Run, April 7th, 1778, on account of the presence of the British Army in Philadelphia at that time. At this meeting "A commission from the congregation of Allentown, in the Forks of Delaware, appeared before Presbytery and represented that the Rev. Mr. Sproat, a member of this Presbytery, in consequence of an invitation from the congregation, had come into the society, and agreeably to their earnest desire, expressed a willingness to supply them till the way should be clear for his returning to his own congregation in Philadelphia. The Presbytery are well pleased with this proposal, and recommended it to Mr. Sproat to supply the said congregation as long as may be convenient for him, and on such terms as he and they agreed."

Mr. Sproat was pastor of the Second Church of Philadelphia, and was absent from the city on account of the presence of the British there. While in the Settlement he lived in the parsonage, and preached twenty Sabbaths, at least, for the people. At Neshaminy, September 1st, 1778, Esquire McNair, commissioner in behalf of the congregation, asked for supplies. In answer, Mr. Mitchell was sent to preach one Sabbath in October, and one more at discretion. Presbytery met at Newton, November 3d, 1778, at which time the people asked that Mr. Isaac Keith, if licensed, might be permitted to supply them regularly until the next meeting of Presbytery.

Presbytery, however, appointed Mr. Mitchell to preach the first and second Sabbaths in February. Mr. Irwin to preach one Sabbath before the next meeting, and Mr. Robert Keith and Mr. Isaac Keith each seven Sabbaths before the next meeting. At Pittsgrove, April 9th, 1779, Robert Keith was appointed to preach two Sabbaths. May 21st, 1779, Captain Ralston as commissioner asked particularly for the services of Mr. Isaac Keith. Mr. Mitchell was appointed to preach three Sabbaths in July and three in August, and administer the Lord's Supper; Mr. Irwin was to preach the third Sabbath in October.

At New Providence, November 2d, 1779, Rev. Alexander Mitchell, in behalf of the congregation asked for supplies. Mr. Irwin appointed to preach the third Sabbath in March; Mr. Grier the fourth Sabbath in November, and first and second Sabbath in March; and Mr. Mitchell was to preach six Sabbaths before the next meeting of Presbytery.

During the year 1779, Rev. Joseph Treat, of the Presbytery of New York, and Rev. William Graham, of the Presbytery of Hanover, preached one or more Sabbaths.

The Presbytery of Hanover occupied Southern territory, and Mr. Graham seems to have visited the congregation in quest of funds for a Southern institution of learning. Upon the church books stands the following record: "July 28th, 1779, application was made to this congregation from Liberty Hall College, North Carolina, for the charitable benefactions; and in consequence the congregation raised a collection amounting to 50 pounds, ten shillings and 6 pence for the use of said college." We also find Mr. Graham's receipt for this collection as follows:

"August 23d, received of Allentown congregation the sum of sixty-eight pounds, thirteen shillings and six pence for the use of Liberty Hall Academy, in Virginia, by William Graham."

These records doubtless refer to the same thing. Some member of the congregation seems to have made the record of the collection, calling the institution a college in North Carolina. Mr. Graham seems to have received an additional contribution, and gave his receipt for the whole amount, properly calling the institution an Academy in Virginia.

At Neshaminy, April 4th, 1780, William McNair, Esq., as commissioner, asked for supplies. Mr. Mitchell was sent to preach four Sabbaths in April, Mr. Boyd one Sabbath in September, Mr. Grier, third Sabbath in April, and first in July, and three Sabbaths in August. Mr. Isaac (?) Keith was to preach the fifth Sabbath in April. At Philadelphia, May 19th, 1780 Mr. Mitchell was appointed to preach two Sabbaths in Newton. October 17th, 1780, we find the following record made by Presbytery:

"A written application of Allen's Town was presented by Mr. Hugh Horner, their commissioner, requesting supplies from us, and also liberty to apply to some other Presbytery for the same purpose. Presbytery cheerfully grant them that liberty, and recommend to them to apply to the Presbytery of New Brunswick as most likely to favor their design."

Presbytery, at this meeting, appointed Mr. Mitchell to preach the fifth Sabbath of October, the second Sabbath of December, and the second Sabbath of February, Mr. Irwin, the first Sabbath in January, and Mr. Grier the first Sabbath in April. In addition to these we find that, during the year, Rev. John DeBow, of the Presbytery of Orange, preached one or more Sabbaths. Also Mr. Frederick Stiner, who does not seem to have been in connection with the Presbyterian Church.

It would seem the people improved the permission granted them to apply to the Presbytery of New Brunswick for supplies, as we find them asking permission of Presbytery convened at Neshaminy, April 17th, 1781, to present a call to a member of the Presbytery. The following record, under that date, is sufficiently explanatory:

"Mr. John Ralston, a commissioner from Allen's Township, requests supplies for that congregation, and also that they may be permitted to prosecute a call before the Presbytery of New Brunswick for Rev. Mr. Peppard, a member of that Presbytery."

At a later stage of the meeting, "The congregation of Allen Town are permitted to prosecute the call for Mr. Peppard before the Presbytery of New Brunswick, agreeably to their request."

At the same meeting, April 17th, 1781, the Presbytery appointed Mr. Mitchell to preach the fifth Sabbath of April, and the fourth Sabbath of August, Mr. Boyd the first Sabbath of September, and Mr. Irwin the fourth of September.

The call presented to Mr. Peppard was accepted by him, but at what time does not appear. He removed to the bounds of the congregation, but took no immediate steps for the transfer of his ecclesiastical relations. His residence among the people and preaching to them without being installed, was in due time taken notice of by the First Presbytery of Philadelphia, under whose care the church was.

In the minutes of Presbytery, convened in Philadelphia, October 15th, 1782, the following record may be found:

"Presbytery were informed that the Rev. Francis Peppard, a member of the New Brunswick Presbytery, has accepted a call from the congregation of Allen Township, in the Forks of the Delaware, and has for some time, resided among that people as their minister, but as the congregation has not applied to this Presbytery to have him installed, nor has Mr. Peppard offered to join himself to us as a member, the Presbytery appoint Mr. Mitchell to write to Mr. Peppard and the congregation on that affair, and make report at our next."

At a meeting of the Presbytery, May 23d, 1783, Mr. Peppard presented his dismission from the Presbytery of New Brunswick, and was received a member of the First Philadelphia Presbytery. The commissioners of the congregation, at the same meeting, applied for the installation of Mr. Peppard. Accordingly, Rev. Alexander Mitchell was appointed to preside at the installation, which was to take place on the second Tuesday of August.

Rev. James Grier was to preach the sermon, and Rev. Nathaniel Irwin was to give charge. We find the following report of this committee to Presbytery, at Philadelphia, October 21st, 1783:

"The committee appointed to install Mr. Peppard in the congregation of Allen Township, in the Forks of the Delaware, report that they attended upon and performed that business on the thirteenth of October. Their reasons for not attending the day appointed sustained." Thus the congregation, on October 13th, 1783, came again regularly under the care of a pastor.

CHAPTER III.—1784-1812

That the ecclesiastical connections of the congregation may be followed, it should be remembered that during Mr. Peppard's pastorate, in 1786, the First and Second Philadelphia Presbyteries united, forming that of Philadelphia. From this time forward the church in the Settlement was under the care of this Presbytery.

The pastorate of Mr. Peppard does not seem to have been the pleasantest in the history of the congregation. Several things conspired to make his situation unpleasant. Among other things, several families on the Monoquacy creek purchased a piece of ground and erected a building called the Academy. They collected a library and started a debating society. This building was far superior to that in which the people worshipped. Mr. Peppard thought this was setting up altar against altar. He therefore opposed it. The ground on which the building was erected had no good title, and was recovered by suit at law. The land was purchased by Mr. Thomas McKeen. In addition to the troubles with regard to the Academy, difficulties arose involving church discipline. Mr. Peppard seems to have been very zealous in endeavoring to preserve the purity of the church. When derelictions in duty occurred he had the offenders brought before the Session. The matter did not always stop there, but was sometimes carried up to the Presbytery. One of these cases was brought before Presbytery in Philadelphia, December 22d, 1791, and drew forth extended admonitory resolutions addressed to the Session, congregation, and aggrieved party.

An unhappy state of affairs continued until October 21st, 1794, at which time Mr. Peppard asked to be released from his pastoral charge on account of some difficulty with reference to the payment of his salary. The Presbytery cited the congregation to appear before them, in Philadelphia, November 17th, 1794, by commissioner to show reason why Mr. Peppard should not be released. Accordingly, Mr. Hugh Horner appeared in behalf of the congregation and protested against the dissolution of the pastoral relation. Notwithstanding this, Presbytery released Mr. Peppard the same day.

Thus the church, November 17th, 1794, became again vacant. Immediately upon the release of Mr. Peppard from the pastoral charge, the congregation, by their commissioner, asked for supplies. It does not appear that any were appointed at this meeting, which may be accounted for by the fact that Mr. Peppard did not cease his labors in the congregation until May, 1795. Although the pastoral relation had actually been dissolved November 17th, 1794, the Philadelphia Presbytery reported to the Synod, May 25th, 1795, that Mr. Peppard was in the pastorate at Allentown at that time. About this time, however, his labors ceased there, being dismissed in April from the Philadelphia Presbytery to connect himself with the Presbytery of New Brunswick. In April

1795, Presbytery appointed Rev. Daniel Jones to preach the fifth Sabbath of November, the fourth Sabbath of February and the first Sabbath of March. During this year also, Rev. Jacob Lake, Rev. Michael Arthur, Rev. Nathaniel Irwin and the Rev. John Hanna preached. In April, 1796, Rev. James Boyd was sent to preach the first Sabbath in October, and Rev. John Gemmel the first Sabbath in August. In October of this year, Presbytery appointed Rev. Daniel (?) Jones to preach the first and the second Sabbaths in December; Rev. Uriah Dubois, the second Sabbath of November, and the first and second Sabbaths of March, and Rev. Nathaniel Irwin, the fifth Sabbath of October. In addition to these, during this year, Rev. Robert Russel, Rev. Asa Dunham, Rev. Francis Peppard, Rev. John Hanna, Rev. Peter or James Wilson and Rev. Robert Findley preached. In 1797, we find Rev. Asa Dunham, Rev. Uriah Dubois, Rev. George or Archibald Scott, Rev. Robert Russell, Rev. Nathan Grier, and Rev. Nathaniel Irwin preached.

After the close of the American Revolution the congregation became weakened on account of frequent removals. This was occasioned by the Allens (except James) espousing the royal cause in the struggle for liberty. Their lands were confiscated we believe. This caused difficulties in the titles of the property. Some paid for their property the second time, while others removed on account of the difficulty.

With the year 1797, however, began as it were, a new era in the history of the congregation. They had previously carried on the affairs of the church by means of officers appointed by themselves, but who had no power to defend the rights or enforce the claims of the congregation. Difficulties arose from time to time with regard to the renting of the pews in the church. The management of the parsonage farm also was a source of trouble. The affairs of the congregation being in an unwieldy condition, it was deemed expedient to have it incorporated. Accordingly, Messrs. John McNair, Hugh Horner, James Ralston, Joseph Horner, Thomas Horner and William Lattimore, as trustees of the congregation, petitioned for an act of incorporation. This petition was granted and the congregation was incorporated under the name of the "English Presbyterian Congregation," in Allen Township, in the County of Northampton, State of Pennsylvania.

They were allowed to control property whose income should amount to any sum not exceeding two thousand pounds lawful money of the State of Pennsylvania. The following rules were adopted to govern the Society under their charter:

"First. All those who have or may hereafter subscribe these rules, and contribute towards the support of the Society, shall be considered members in common; but those only who are admitted to sealing ordinances are members in full communion.

"Second. The spiritual government of this Society shall be by a minister and at least three regularly ordained elders, who shall constitute a Session, and have power to hear and try all cases respecting their members, that may orderly come before them, so far as they are warranted by Scripture and our church standards, and decide thereon in the first instance with liberty of appeal.

"Third. That six Trustees shall be chosen from said Society, two of whom shall vacate on the first day of January next, and two in each successive year, and their places be filled up by a new election; whose business it shall be to settle accounts with the Treasurer on the same day yearly; to have charge of all money belonging to the Society; all pews or seats in the church to be taken from and given up to the Trustees; and those who attempt to give or receive seats without their consent, shall be deemed inimical to the interests of the Society, and meet a serious rebuke in Session at a future day.

"Fourth. The Trustees may, at any time when the concerns of the Society require it, on previous notice stating the design, convene the members, a majority of whom shall be decisive in all matters that shall orderly come before them.

"Fifth. All donations, bequests to the Society, and all possessions, effects, and property whatsoever, shall, and at all times and forever, be and remain appropriated, secured and made use of for the Society.

"Sixth. Every member of the Society renounces herewith expressly all and every claim to the property of the Society, and promises that in case any part of said property shall come into his hand, put upon his name in trust, he will in no manner abuse such confidence, nor make for himself or his heirs claim or pretension thereto; and that he will do with it agreeably to the disposal of the Society, and faithfully and punctually observe their orders.

"Seventh. All those who shall emigrate from other Societies and bring with them a certificate or testimonial of their good morals, shall be admitted to equal privileges with others in like standing."

The congregation being incorporated, its affairs were carried on in a systematic manner. The Trustees elected a President and Secretary from their own number from time to time, and their proceedings were carried on according to parliamentary rules. The minutes of the Trustees' meetings were carefully recorded in a book provided for the purpose. From this book may be learned the whole internal affairs of the Society from that time. As specified in the provisions of the charter, two new Trustees were elected annually to fill the places of those whose term of office expired on the first of January of each year. Those whose terms of office thus expired were a committee to settle with the Treasurer for the previous year.

At the time the congregation was incorporated, it was without a pastor.

As we have intimated, in 1796 and 1797, among others, Rev. Robert Russel preached in the Settlement. In 1796, Rev. Uriah Dubois also preached. When the question of the election of a pastor came up, both these gentlemen were candidates.

The younger members of the congregation were in favor of Mr. Dubois, but the older members preferred Mr. Russel. When the question came to a vote, the younger members were overruled, and Mr. Russel was elected pastor. Having elected Mr. Russel, the people proceeded to settle him among them. The course pursued by them is pointed out in the following minute made by the Presbytery of Philadelphia, December 2d, 1797:

"It appeared to Presbytery that application had been made by the congregation of Allen Township, in the State of Pennsylvania, to a committee of this Presbytery sitting at Deep Run, in the month of August last, for directions as to the method in which they might prosecute a call to Mr. Robert Russel, then a licentiate under the care of the Presbytery of New Castle, and that the aforesaid committee considering that the prevalence of a contagious fever in the city of Philadelphia then did, and for a considerable time probably would prevent a regular meeting of the Presbytery, certifies these circumstances to the Presbytery of New Castle, that if a regular call should be offered through them to Mr. Russel, no exception would, in the judgment of the committee, be taken to this procedure by the Presbytery of Philadelphia, which certificate was offered to the Presbytery of New Castle and they judged it sufficient to authorize them in presenting said call to Mr. Russel, which they accordingly did and on his acceptance of the same, dismissed him to join this Presbytery as already stated. Whereupon Presbytery heard Mr. Russel deliver a popular sermon and examined him on experimental religion and systematic divinity, as parts of trial for ordination, and agreed to sustain the same."

The Presbytery, or a committee thereof, repaired to the Settlement, April 17th, 1798, and there further examined Mr. Russel in Systematic Theology, Ecclesiastical History, Church Government and the Arts and Sciences. All these parts of trial were sustained. The next day Mr. Russel preached a popular sermon, and was ordained and installed. In these services, Dr. Ashbel Green of Philadelphia, preached the ordination sermon, Dr. William Tennent of Abington, and Rev. Nathaniel Irwin of Neshaminy delivered the charges.

Thus April 18th, 1798, the church again came under the care of a regular pastor. The first meeting of the Trustees after the incorporation that we have any account of was June 11th, 1798. At this meeting all the original Trustees, viz: Hugh Horner, John McNair, Thomas Horner, William Lattimore, James Ralston, Joseph Horner were present. In addition, Adam Clendinen, William Kerr, James Clyde, John Walker, James Kerr, James Hays, and Henry Epple. As the charter required two of the Trustees to vacate on the first of January of each year, there probably was an election previous to this time to fill the two vacancies occurring January 1st, 1798. If this was not the case, the election must have taken place at this meeting, June 11th, 1798, as we find Mr Epple among the number of Trustees at this time, and elected President of the Board for the year. Mr. William Lattimore was at the same time elected Secretary. Mr. Hugh Horner had been Treasurer previous to the incorporation and was continued in that office. The President and Secretary were to hold their office for one year. Thus was the Board of Trustees under the charter fairly organized, and went forward from year to year to transact the business of the corporation.

At this meeting, June 11th, 1798, the Trustees appointed a committee to settle with Messrs. William Kerr, John Walker, Thomas Horner, and James Kerr, respecting the affairs of the parsonage farm. These gentlemen probably had the direct oversight of the parsonage farm at the time, and the settlement referred to was doubtless with regard to the sale of the property. Although we have not the means at hand to determine the exact time at which it was sold, collateral evidence goes to show that it was on or about April 10th, 1797, as Jacob Bear's bonds for the purchase of the same bore that date. In accordance with this, October 13th, Jacob Bear applied to the Trustees to know if they would receive a part of the interest due April 10th previous, on the sale of the parsonage farm. The money for this property was paid to the Trustees from time to time, and was invested largely in United States Stock, in Northampton and Easton banks. The Northampton bank failed and the greater portion of the money was lost.

Although the congregation had been weakened by removals, it still remained pretty strong at the time of its incorporation. A ledger account was opened in the latter part of 1798. The names of over fifty persons were entered as financially, at least, connected with the congregation or society. How many of these were regular members of the church does not appear, but probably the greater part.

As an act of incorporation required a settlement each year with the Treasurer, the Trustees, January 7th, 1799, made it a standing rule that the two Trustees who went out of office each year were to be a committee to make such settlement.

A singular custom prevailed in the congregation at this time. It was that the Elders and Trustees were each to pay tweny-five cents every Sabbath as collection money. This custom becoming burdensome or inconvenient was done away in 1799.

Early in the present century the congregation became much weakened on account of many families removing to other parts of the country. The McNairs removed to Western New York; the Hays to the West Branch of the Susquehanna, and Pittsburgh; the Ralstons and Walkers to Chester county; the Wilsons to Union county; the Craigs to Lehigh county, the Greggs and Hemphills, Sharps and Boyds to Western Pennsylvania and Ohio. From this period we may perhaps properly date the decline of the Settlement. The church, however, kept on its course, sustaining the ordinances, and carrying forward its secular affairs under the guidance of its Board of Trustees.

Up to the year 1800, although the Trustees had elected their officers and transacted their business as a body, they had not formally organized themselves into a Board. This formation of what was called the "Board of Trustees," was effected January 25th, 1800.

After the formation, the Board assumed the direct responsibility in the affairs of the society. The papers belonging to the congregation were put into their hands. Among these were the bonds for the payment of the price of the parsonage farm, and the securities for other moneys belonging to the congregation held by different persons, the charter of incorporation, the deed of the parsonage farm from Thomas Armstrong to the congregation, and the deed for the same from Samuel Wilson to Thomas Armstrong. Thomas McKeen and Henry Epple were appointed a committee to draft rules for the government of the Board in their proceedings. They drafted a set of rules, the first of which defined the times of meeting which were to be on Saturday after the annual election of Trustees, for organizing the Board; and on the last Saturday of March, June and September. It also prescribed a fine for non-attendance. The second defined the duties of the President. The third, those of the Treasurer. The fourth, those of the Secretary. The fifth, the duties of the members. The sixth the time and manner of making out duplicates for the collection of pew rent. It may now be said the Board was fully organized. They had a constitution in the charter of the congregation, and had now adopted a set of by-laws. As they were fully organized, and had entered upon the executive duties of their office, they were prepared to take decisive action with regard to the disposal of property belonging to the congregation, subject to the provisions of the charter. One of the first and most difficult things they had to do was to straighten out the affairs pertaining to the parsonage farm. It had been formally sold, but no deed had been made to the purchaser. How to make a good title to the property under the circumstances was the question. In order to clear the way, January 31st, 1800, those who had contributed to the original price, or the heirs of such as had done so, handed into the Trustees the written consent to the sale of the same, as required by a previous arrangement between the purchasers, already referred to. This paper was submitted to Thomas Long, Attorney at Law, in Easton, for his opinion as to its legality. What opinion was expressed does not appear. However, it is evident from the nature of the paper that time and trouble had been taken in order to have matters so arranged as to give the Trustees complete control of the church property. The drawing up of the paper was in 1797, the year the church was incorporated, but did not come before the Trustees regularly until in January, 1800. It was not ratified by law until February 15th, 1802, at which time it was recorded in the office for the recording of deeds, in Northampton county, at Easton.

However, March 29th, 1800, the Trustees unanimously agreed to apply to the proper civil authorities to grant them power to make a title to the property which had been sold on or about April 10th, 1797. They appointed Thomas McKeen to draw up a petition for that purpose. May 3d, Mr. McKeen reported that he had not drawn the petition and suggested that the whole matter be put into the hands of an attorney. It was accordingly referred to John Ross, Esq., of Easton, to be by him arranged and brought before the proper civil authorities. From some cause or other the matter was not adjusted by Mr. Ross, for January 9th, 1802, Hugh Wilson and James Clyde were appointed to confer with Samuel Sitgreaves, Esq., presenting to him all the papers relative to the parsonage farm, and get his written opinion as to making a title for the same. If the papers were of sufficient authority, they were instructed to employ him to draw up the title. Even this arrangement did not bring the matter to an issue, for February 24th, of this year the congregation assembled for the purpose of consulting as to the best means to adopt in order to make a deed for the property. It was agreed that Samuel Sitgreaves should draw up a conveyance transferring to the Trustees all the rights held by the contributors to the same. Thomas McKeen and Hugh Horner were appointed to bring the matter before him. This seems to have been the closing up of this intricate business. The transfer of the contributors' rights to the property was recorded, as we have intimated, February, 15th, 1802.

In the minutes of a trustee meeting held March 28th, 1801, we find a rather novel and interesting record. We insert it here as it embraces casual information from which to determine the situation of the original church building. It is as follows:

"Whereas great inconvenience is found to result to Mr. Epple from members of the congregation tying their horses to the fences near the meeting house, and it being the wish of the Trustees to remedy the same; therefore be it Resolved, that James Hays and Samuel Morrison be a committee to contract with some persons to put up posts and rails, (for the purpose of tying horses to), on the south side of the road, between the meeting house and the creek, on the public grounds northeast of the meeting house, and on the vacant ground near the school house; and to superintend the doing of the same."

Those familiar with the locality will perceive that the incidental description of the church property here given, cannot be made to apply to the site of the present church building near Weaversville. It must be referred to the north side of the public road near the creek.

At this time it was not definitely known where the deeds of the church and graveyard lots were. James Kerr was appointed to make inquiry through the congregation for them. After some delay he procured them and presented them to the Board of Trustees. In 1803, there seems to have accumulated in the treasury considerable money. This perhaps was owing to the sale of the parsonage farm. March 5th of this year, the Trustees lent out for three years to various persons about $2,550. The money was to draw six percent. interest, and be secured by judgment bond and approved security. When money was thus lent out by the Board they took every precaution to secure the same, and were very positive in their requirement of its payment when it became due. They appear to have exercised freely their power as a body corporate. Frequent records are made in which the civil law was called in to enforce the collection of moneys due the congregation. Notwithstanding, the congregation seems to have had considerable money at their disposal, the arrears reported by the collector, on the duplicates of 1804, go to show that the support of the congregation was to some degree falling away. During the next three or four years various expedients were devised or proposed for the relief of the waning fortunes of the congregation. In 1808, extra duplicates were issued to bring up arrears. Notwithstanding the fortunes of the congregation were waning, we find them still ready to do their share in helping along others who seemed to be more needy than themselves. This is shown from the following record, which explains itself: Received of Allentown congregation, by the hands of John Walker, thirteen dollars and ten cents, as a donation to Harmony congregation, toward paying for building their meeting house. I say received by me in behalf of said congregation, December 27th, 1809.

(Signed) Garnet A. Hunt,
Greenwich, New Jersey.

N. B.—Harmony congregation will pay the above money to Allentown congregation when they build a meeting house.

About this time the graveyard was enclosed with a stone wall. The following record is made incidentally with reference to it:

"It is further agreed that the Trustees of congregation are to collect and settle the accounts between the Treasurer and Managers of the burial ground." In connection with this we find the following:

"June 15th. At a meeting held the day aforesaid, per order of the President, to make settlement with the acting manager of the building of a stone wall of the English Presbyterian burial ground in Allen Township, present,—Dr. Edward Humphrey, President, James Kerr Trustee, William

Lattimore, James Horner, Sr., Nicholas Neligh, Secretary, and after examining the accounts, find Thomas Horner has a credit coming to him of ———."

This was in 1811. On the same day as the foregoing, action was taken with regard to the sale of the old church building, which stood on the north side of the public road. This appears from the following record:

"Where and by them it was agreed that the old meeting house should be sold, and on taking consideration it was unanimously agreed that the said Nicholas Neligh should have the meeting house, and to take the same away and clear the premises between this time and 27th May, 1812, by paying on that day sixty dollars, Pennsylvania currency."

During the year 1811, we find the pecuniary support of the congregation continuing to decline. November 26th of that year the Trustees took the following action: "It was unanimously agreed that duplicates be made out to the amount of ————, a sum necessary to be raised in order to assist in the payment of Mr. Russel's salary." This explains itself. Pecuniary difficulties seemed to thicken around the congregation. As the contributors to the support of the church seemed to be falling away, the Trustees apparently felt the necessity of making most of the invested property belonging to the church. They sought additional security from those who held the money in order to further secure the interests of the church. In this they were met by opposition as the following record shows:

"The Trustees then took into consideration the propriety of demanding bond and security from the present money holders, and having called on Mr. ———— for his bond and security, he refused in a peremptory manner, and said he would not have anything more to do with the congregation. Whereupon it was unanimously agreed that his name be erased from the list of supporters."

Notwithstanding the prospects of the congregation were not of the brightest character, they felt they must go forward in the work of the Lord. The old church building had been sold and was to be removed in the early part of 1812. This year, therefore, they must take definite action with regard to a new church. To this work they accordingly addressed themselves.

CHAPTER IV. 1813-1825

In 1813, the present church building near Weaversville, was built, or at least commenced. As we have stated, the old church had been sold. Whether the new one should be built on the same ground or not, became a matter of consultation. Out of this consultation grew the record of how and why the church was removed from the old lot, and placed where it now stands. The following is the record—it bears date of January 11th, 1813:

"The Trustees met on the ground formerly occupied as a meeting house lot, the corners of which not being easily discovered, Mr. Neligh agreed to give the same quantity of ground anywhere the Trustees should point out. Whereupon a lot of the same dimensions was surveyed, which not joining the great road immediately, Mr. Neligh promised to enter into an agreement never to put any fence whatever between said lot and great road." Although the question of changing the site of the church was considered in the meeting held January 11th, 1813, we find it was not settled at that time. The matter came up again in a meeting held in March. We insert the record of that meeting's proceedings, as it makes the whole matter clear and satisfactory.

"Academy, March 15th, 1813.

"At a meeting of the English Presbyterian Church, of Allen Township, at the Academy, on Monday, the 15th day of March, 1813, convened agreeably to public notice for the purpose of ascertaining the will of said congregation, whether a meeting house was necessary to be built for the use of said congregation, and where said meeting house should be erected, Rev. Robert Russel was unanimously appointed Chairman and John Boyd, Secretary.

"A motion was made and seconded, that with a view to

unite the two sections of the congregation, a house should be erected on a lot of James Dunn's, joining the lands of Adam Clendinen, and lost, only two or three rising in its favor. A motion was made and seconded, that the Academy should be fitted up for a house of worship, and a new house built at or near where the old meeting house formerly stood, jointly, by the congregation, which was negatived. Another motion was made and seconded, that the Academy should be fitted up for a house of worship, and a new house built on or near the old spot, the former by that part of the congregation on or near the Monoquacy (Creek), and the latter by that part of the congregation adjacent to the old meeting house, so that each side respectively completes its own meeting house; but when finished that both houses shall belong to the congregation in common; that is to say, the people on the east side of the congregation to have an equal right in the house which shall be built on the west side with the said western people themselves; and the people on the west side to have an equal right in the house built on the east side with the people on the east side themselves; so that it is fairly understood that both houses shall be owned by the congregation in common in as full and ample a manner as if there was only one house built at the joint expense of the whole congregation. Carried by a large majority in the affirmative.

"Another motion was then made and seconded, that the Trustees of the congregation be empowered to exchange the old meeting house lot, for some other piece of ground more convenient for the site of the church, if the said Trustees should see proper so to do. Leave unanimously given to exchange."

This record sufficiently explains itself. Those who are acquainted with the situations of the two houses of worship will readily perceive the cause of the disagreement with reference to a house of worship in common. To those who may not be acquainted with the situations of the two houses, a word of explanation here may not be inappropriate. The building called the Academy stands near the Monoquacy Creek, perhaps a mile south of the village of Bath. This places it in the eastern portion of the congregation. The old church stood near where the present one stands, making it perhaps three miles west of the Academy, and within half a mile of the village of Weaversville. This placed the church building proper in the western half of the congregation.

We venture an explanation (without positive knowledge on the point) of the disagreement manifested in the record of the church meeting above given, and also the cause of the final agreement in regard to the matter. This final agreement would seem at first sight, to throw the burden of building a new church upon the western half of the congregation.

It will be remembered, however, a number of families on the Monoquacy Creek combined and independently erected the then substantial stone building called the Academy. This was large enough, and sufficiently well adapted, to accommodate the congregation as a house of worship. The persons who owned the Academy were doubtless members of the congregation. Having the interest of the congregation at heart, we may suppose they munificently offered to donate the Academy building to the congregation for a house of worship, since the old log church had been sold and had been, or was about to be, torn down. This would save the expense of a new house of worship. This, however, would give the eastern half of the congregation the ascendancy, besides confining the preaching exclusively to that neighborhood. This would necessitate the western half of the congregation to always go three miles, more or less, to church. It is easy to see then how a difficulty would arise to prevent the acceptance of the Academy building, exclusively, by the congregation, as a house of worship. On the other hand, since the eastern half of the congregation offered to gratuitously provide a house of worship for the whole congregation, they could not be expected to assist in building a house of worship in the western half of the congregation, which would necessitate them always to go three miles, more or less, to church. A compromise therefore would naturally be expected. This seems to have been effected. The eastern side of the congregation seems to have donated the Academy building to the whole congregation, and beside, fitted it up for a house of worship. The western half of the people seem to have taken the old church lot, or its equivalent, and erected a church building, also for the whole congregation. This put both sides upon an equal footing as regarded the furnishing of houses of worship. There now being two churches belonging to the congregation, they made a positive agreement that each half of the congregation should have equal rights in the building furnished by the other half.

Such, we conjecture, were substantially the circumstances which originated the two houses of worship in the congregation, and the alternation in the services held in the two houses, which has existed for so many years. As to exchanging the old church lot for a more desirable one, we have the following record:

"Session Room, March 19th, 1813.

"At a meeting of the Trustees of the congregation at their room, for the purpose of exchanging the old meeting house lot for ground which would be more suitable for building a meeting house on, agreeably to a vote of the congregation, it was unanimously agreed that the old lot should be exchanged for one on the west side of Mr. Neligh's run, and adjoining the old burying ground."

The exchange was made and the new lot deeded over by Mr. Neligh to the congregation, March 31st, 1813. It was part of the tract of land sold to Mr. Henry Epple, by William Craig. At Mr. Epple's death he left but one daughter, who became heiress to the property. This daughter was the wife of Mr. Neligh, by whom the deed of the lot was made. The transfer was in the name of John Wilson, James Horner, Sr., John Boyd, John Clyde, Jr., James Kerr and Edward Humphrey, Trustees of the congregation. Such were the circumstances attending the selection of the site where the church building, near Weaversville, now stands. The old site, as we have intimated, was southeast of the present one and north of the public road.

About this time there seems to have been considerable irregularity and commotion in the secular affairs of the congregation. For some time previous to 1813, the Trustees do not seem to have been sufficiently strict in the observance of the rules adopted for their guidance in 1800. This matter had been noticed by some members of the Board. A motion was therefore made to remedy the neglect, as appears from the following record:

"Session Room, March 10th, 1813.

"Trustees met agreeably to appointment, when the by-laws made on the 31st of January, 1800, for the government of the secular affairs of the church and Trustees being read, a motion was made and seconded that they should be adopted by the subscribers, whereupon they were unanimously agreed to. Witness our hands, the day and year above written.

(Signed) James Horner, John Clyde, Ed. Humphrey, John Boyd."

One provision of these rules was, that the two retiring Trustees each year should be a committee to settle with the Treasurer. This matter of settling with the treasurer seems to have been neglected, but after the re-adoption of the rules, their provisions in this regard were observed as formerly.

With the year 1813, Edward Humphrey and James Horner, Sr., went out of office. Accordingly we find it recorded in 1814, that

"Edward Humphrey and James Horner, Sr., were appointed to settle with the Treasurer, and they are authorized to call on the Secretary for the necessary accounts to enable them to complete said settlement."

These irregularities adjusted in 1814, we find commotions attending the election of Trustees at the opening of the year

1815. January 2d, of this year, James Kennedy and Nathan Kerr were elected to the office of Trustee. The members of the Board were, after this election, as follows:

"John Boyd, James Clendinen, James Kennedy, John Clyde, James Horner, Nathan Kerr. This election of Trustees, however, was subsequently overturned, and the composition of the Board considerably changed. We find the following record bearing upon the subject:

"At a meeting of the English Presbyterian Church, of Allen Township, on Saturday, the 4th of March, 1815, (public notice having been duly given), in order to choose two new Trustees in the room of Nathan Kerr and James Kennedy, who were declared illegally elected; and by a meeting of the congregation called for that purpose, three other Trustees, two of whom resigned, and the third was conceived by the same meeting not duly elected; James Clyde and John Wilson were unanimously appointed judges of said election; when, upon counting the votes at the close of the poll, it appeared that James Kerr, Sr., was duly elected in the room of James Clendinen, resigned, Hugh Wilson in the room of John Clyde, resigned, James J. Horner, re-elected. James Kennedy and Robert Horner for three years from the first Monday in January last."

By this action, therefore, the membership of the Board became as follows: John Boyd, James Kerr, James Kennedy, Hugh Wilson, James J. Horner, Robert Horner. From the year 1815 forward, for several years, the prospects of the congregation seem to have brightened somewhat. We find no evidence that the congregation was pecuniarily straightened, although they had been engaged in constructing a new house of worship as well as fitting up the Academy for Divine services. The number of supporters increased from 38 in 1812 to 56 in 1818. The brightening up of affairs may perhaps be attributed in part to the impetus which the new church building gave to the affairs of the congregation.

It will be remembered the new church building was erected upon the newly acquired lot. The church lot was open to the public road. This seemed to the congregation not desirable, and they therefore, in May, 1819, took steps to have it enclosed. Special directions were given as to how it was to be done. The fence on the north and west sides was to be post and rail, and on the south and east sides board.

There was to be a gate on the south side having an entrance of five feet in the clear. We insert these particulars that those who may be familiar with the locality may be enabled to draw a picture of the church and surroundings, as they appeared fifty years ago.

In 1823, we have revealed incidently some of the inner workings of the congregation by the death of the Treasurer. This officer was the custodian of the books and valuable papers of the corporation. For these he gave his receipt, at length, when entering upon the duties of his office. When he left it he took a receipt for the same from his successor. James H. Horner was elected Treasurer in 1815.

April 1st, 1816, he gave his receipt for the books and papers of the congregation. He was their custodian until 1823. October 11th, of this year, he resigned, and John Wilson was elected in his stead. The Trustees appointed Abram Wilson and James J. Horner to settle with the late Treasurer, and deliver the books and papers of the congregation to the newly elected Treasurer. Between October 11th, when this appointment was made and November 8th, James H. Horner died. At the time of his death, the books and papers of the congregation had not been turned over to the committee, as will appear by the receipt we insert below. As stated, James H. Horner had given his receipt for the books and papers, April 1st, 1816. In the minute book, where the list of books and papers is given, just underneath James H. Horner's name we find this receipt:

"Received, November 8th, 1832, of Robert Horner, administrator of the estate of James H. Horner, the above books and papers, or others in lieu thereof.

(Signed) Abraham Wilson
Hugh Horner
James J. Horner."

In connection with this we find John Wilson's receipt for the papers and books. We insert the list of these here in order to preserve a record of them for future reference in case it should ever be found necessary to recall them. The receipt and list is as follows:

Received, November ——, 1823 of the Trustees of the English Presbyterian congregation of Allen Township, the following books, bonds, deeds, etc.:

1) A book of accounts of the congregation.

2) One bond against   for $ with interest since May 1st, 1823.

3) One bond against   for $ with interest since May 27th, 1823.

4) One bond against   for $ with interest since November 27, 1822.

5) One bond against   for $ with interest since May 27th, 1823.

6) One bond against   for $ with interest since May 27th, 1823.

7) One note against   for Lbs.   with interest since January 7th, 1823.

8) A deed of conveyance from Nicholas Neligh to Trustees of the English Presbyterian congregation of Allen Township, for 128 perches of land in said township.

9) A deed from James Craig to John Walker and others.

10) An obligation and declaration of John Walker and others.

11) The act of incorporation.

"Received the above books and papers, which I promise to keep in safety, and deliver to the Trustees of said congregation when called for, and receive all moneys now due or may hereafter become due on said obligations, and pay the same to the order of the Board of Trustees.

(Signed) John Wilson."

This list of bonds and so forth, the figures of which we have omitted gives consolidated statement of the assets of the congregation at the time. Mr. Russel's receipt for salary, given November 12th of this year, is in keeping with the foregoing. It is as follows:

"Received of James H. Horner, late treasurer, at sundry times subsequent to the 22d day of January 1823, the sum of   dollars, and of James H. Horner and Hugh Horner. Trustees, the sum of   dollars, making together the sum of   dollars, in payment of salary due from the congregation, November 12th, 1823.

(Signed) R. Russel."

And we have intimated, the prospects of the congregation, seemed to be brighter for a number of years after the erection of the new church building near Weaversville. The number of supporters seemed to keep up remarkably well, considering the drain upon the community caused by removals and deaths. It is apparent, however, that formerly the names of contributors represented whole families, whilst latterly they represented more frequently only individuals.

In 1825, the depletion of the community began again to make itself felt. Although for several years previous to this, the number of supporters appears in no appreciable manner to have been diminished, the actual support, financially considered, was manifestly waning. March 26th of this year, several members of the congregation met with the Trustees to consult in regard to the affairs of the church. Considerable amounts had been returned, for several years previous, on the duplicates as arrears. The salary of the pastor was with difficulty made up. A committee was appointed to confer with the pastor and represent to him that the congregation was unable to make up the salary they had promised to pay him, and obtain an abatement on his part, if possible. An agreement was effected whereby Mr. Russel relinquished a part of his salary. In this agreement it was intimated that it was possible the circumstances of the congregation might become still more straightened, and against this precautions were taken.

Although it was with difficulty they did so, we find the congregation fulfilling all their pecuniary obligations to Mr. Russel up to the end of the year 1825. Such was the state of affairs in the congregation, therefore, at the opening of the year 1826.

CHAPTER V. 1826-1835.

In 1821, the church came under the care of the Presbytery of Newton. With the year 1826, there would seem to commence a new era in the history of the congregation. There is nothing of special importance to record concerning this date, but there seems to be a dividing line between the early and the latter church. The old time-worn books of record were now full and laid aside. With the blackened leather covers of those old books, and a small bundle of papers equally antiquated, lay the data from which, to a large degree, the early history of the congregation was to be deduced. Yet who, from looking at these old records, tangled and incongruous, which had been made from time to time, during a period of seventy-five or eighty years, would suppose that there was material in them for a connected narrative—something pertaining to nearly every year of that long period? Who would suppose that from those old smoky and blackened pages, whereon were records in juxtaposition, telling of events which were separated by perhaps twenty, thirty or forty years of time, an intelligible idea of the church's history could be deduced? But time and patience in deciphering those almost illegible lines, which had been placed there by various and unsteady hands at different times during a period of three-quarters of a century previous, the facts of the foregoing pages, for the most part, have been snatched, as it were, from oblivion. These facts it is hoped, have been preserved to the descendants of those early settlers, and to the church which has been one of the way-marks in the progress of Presbyterianism in America.

But having gleaned from these musty pages, as we hope, the greater part of their interesting matter, we lay them aside, as did the church of 1826, and look to the subsequent records.

We have endeavored so far to give such statistics as might enable the reader to observe the fluctuations in the fortunes of the congregation; their periods of brightening prospects and those of shadow and decline. We are now called upon to record a period of shadow. It may have been noticed that although there were periods of brightening, the general tendency was toward decline. This was doubtless owing to the drain which other parts of the country were constantly making upon the supporters and resources of the congregation. Many were removing to other parts of the country, and those who took their places were not naturally affiliated with the people who supported this church. In addition to this cause of decline another misfortune about this time overtook the congregation. It was the unfortunate investment of its funds. We have inserted a schedule of the assets of the congregation in a previous chapter. Whilst there we left the amounts, in detail, in blank, it may not be improper here to state, that the schedule showed the aggregate assets of the congregation to be, exclusive of the church and grave yard properties in use, about $3,400.00. It seems a considerable portion of this money became available in 1827. We have before spoken of this property, belonging to the congregation, and of its disposal, and how a large portion of it was lost by the failure of the Northampton Bank. We have in 1827, the records of how this investment came to be made. We have spoken of Mr. John Wilson becoming treasurer in 1823. We find he was succeeded in that office by Mr. Robert Horner, in 1826. The funds of the congregation were therefore in the hands of Mr. Robert Horner in 1827. We find that January 11th, 1826, he receipted for the books, papers and funds enumerated in the schedule, just referred to,

THE OLD WOLF ACADEMY

Erected in 1785. Also used as a place of worship from 1813. (See page 141.)

Accordingly, under date of September 3d, 1827, we find him directed to purchase stock in the Northampton Bank. The record is as follows and will explain itself:

"A motion was made and carried that the money belonging to the congregation in the hands of Robert Horner, be put to the use of purchasing stock in the Northampton Bank, in case stock can be had at par."

Thus it would appear that there was an amount of the capital of the congregation or corporation, now in the treasury. This money was expended for the purpose indicated, as shown by the certificates of stock of the Northampton Bank which may be seen among the papers of the congregation. As we have before said, the money was lost by the failure of the Bank at the time so many banks failed under the old National Banking system. Although this calamity did not fall immediately upon the church, it was the more severe when it did come, from the fact that at the very time they were unconsciously making a bad investment, other causes were weakening them. By an agreement made April 6th, 1825, to which we have referred, the pastor relinquished a portion of his salary. From that day forward he receipted for his salary in full only on the ground of the agreement into which he had entered. In his receipts he referred from time to time to the agreement. The congregation were enabled to come up to their engagements until May 27th, 1827.

August 5th, 1827, Mr. Russel gave a receipt in full up to that date. But the people now became conscious that they would not be able to meet their engagements, even though the pastor had relinquished a part of his salary. They could not consistently ask him to make any further abatement, and the next best thing, they thought, would be to retain him but for a portion of his time. Accordingly, a meeting was called in October of this year, to consult with reference to this matter. We have the following record in the minutes of this meeting:

"A motion was made that a committee be appointed to wait on the Rev. Russel, and to inform him that the congregation was willing to give him ———— dollars for one-half of his time from the 27th of November."

But this was not long to effect the aged servant of God. The congregation, though they felt their troubles increasing, were soon to be called on to endure still greater trials. He who had ministered to them in spiritual things for nearly thirty years was soon to be taken from them. He who had grown gray and venerable in their service was soon to be called home to his Father's house in heaven. The last official act performed by him, of which we have any record, is the following:

"Received ———— December 11th, 1827, of Robert Horner, Treasurer, the sum of   in part of my salary due on the 27th November last.
(Signed) R. Russel."

Five days after this, on December 16th, 1827, he bid adieu to the cares of earth. Having fought the fight of faith, and having finished his course, he ascended to receive his crown of glory. A plain marble stone in the church yard, with the following inscription, marks the last resting place of the revered and good man:

"Sacred to the memory of Rev. Robert Russel, A. M., late of the English Presbyterian Congregation of Allen Township, who departed this life December 16th, 1827, in the seventieth year of his age, and the thirtieth of his ministry. He was a man full of the Holy Ghost. How well he taught them many a one will feel unto their dying day, and when they lie on the grave's brink unfearing and composed, their speechless souls will bless the holy man whose voice exhorted, and whose footsteps led unto the path of life."

The final act in which Mr. Russel's name appears in connection with the church, is in the following receipt given by his son, who was his administrator:

"Received, January 3d, 1828, of Robert Horner, Treasurer, the sum   it being the amount in full of salary due from the English Presbyterian Congregation of Allen Town-

ship, to my father until the day of his death.
(Signed) Robert Russel, Administrator."

Thus closed the extended ministry of this servant of God. He had entered upon his ministry in the Settlement, April 18th, 1798. It was his first pastoral charge. In it he remained for nearly thirty years, and was removed therefrom only by the hand of death.

Thus the congregation, December 16th, 1827, became vacant. Under the circumstances it was necessary to make some provision for supplying the pulpit. Accordingly, a meeting was called, January 7th, 1828, to consider the matter. We insert a part of the minutes of that meeting, as it explains itself and gives us the information desired:

"At a meeting of the English Presbyterian Congregation of Allen Township, in the church, the 7th of January, A. D., 1828, for the purpose of selecting a pastor to fill the vacancy occasioned by the death of the Rev. Robert Russel, a motion was made and seconded that the congregation proceed to take the question whether they should employ the Rev. Alexander Heberton to supply the vacancy occasioned by the death of the Rev. Russel, until the 27th of November next."

The motion was carried, and Mr. Heberton accepted the terms offered by the congregation, and commenced his labors among them. He continued to preach until the next fall, at which time, October 6th, the congregation again assembled to invite him to continue as stated supply for one year after November 27th. The invitation was accepted and he continued his labors. This year we again find the people unwittingly involving themselves in financial difficulties. Again money had accumulated in the hands of the treasurer. Again we find him directed to invest the same in stocks which proved valueless. A minute of the meeting of the Trustees held October 6th, is as follows:

"At a meeting of the Trustees present it was resolved that the moneys now in the hands of Robert Horner, belonging to the congregation, be laid out in the purchase of United States Bank stock."

The receipts for the purchase made by this order may still be found among the papers of the congregation. Having begun the purchase of United States stock we find the people continuing it. On January 22d, 1829, we find the Trustees again directing the purchase of this kind of stock. It would seem the prospects of the congregation brightened up for a time under the ministry of Mr. Heberton. The number of contributors in 1828 was seventy-seven against forty-eight in 1827. The prospect of advancement under Mr. Heberton's ministry seems to have induced the people to make efforts to have him continue with them. Accordingly, on September 25th, 1829, they again appointed a committee to confer with Mr. Heberton with reference to his continuing still another year as supply after November 27th. An agreement was effected and his labors were continued.

There seems to have been a desire on the part of the congregation, at this time, to purchase the property on which Mr. Russel was living at the time of his death. What the reasons were for this does not appear. It may have been thus securely to invest the money of the congregation. But this would not seem probable, for their funds had been similarly invested previously, and the caring for the property was attended with so many difficulties and inconveniences that it was sold so as to make the funds more serviceable. Whatever may have been the reason, the fact is attested by the following record in the minutes of the meeting held September 7th, which is as follows:

"On motion it was resolved, that a committee of four be appointed, who, in conjunction with the Trustees of the church, are to view the premises of the late Rev. Robert Russsel, with a view of purchasing the same."

What was the result of this appointment does not appear. We call attention to these financial transactions of the church, that it may be known that the cause of decline has been such as could not be foreseen, and that those faithful men who have administered the trust committed to them by our fathers, have not been negligent in the performance of their duty. We have inserted them that all may see through what vicissitudes the heritage of our fathers has passed, what its ultimate fate has been, and what effect that fate has produced upon the welfare of the church and the community.

The congregation met September 4th, 1830, and appointed a committee to solicit Mr. Heberton to remain still a third year from the 27th of November ensuing. The committee reported his acceptance, and his labors continued. This arrangement, however, was not to continue for any great length of time.

Mr. Heberton received in the early part of 1831, a call to the Presbyterian Church of the present city of Allentown. He accepted the call and was released by the congregation in the Settlement. This appears from the following record in the minutes of a meeting held February 21st, 1831, and is as follows:

"Whereas, The Rev. Alexander Heberton, having received an invitation to the pastoral charge of the First English Presbyterian Church in the borough of Allentown, he considering it to be an incumbent duty to accept of the same; we the congregation agreeably to his request, resolve to release him from his present engagement with us, after the first of April next."

Having thus been released from his engagement, his connection with the congregation soon ceased, and his name disappears from its records. Before we proceed to the events which transpired under the ministry of Mr. Heberton's successor, it may not be inappropriate here to refer to a matter which seems rather strange in the history of the congregation. From the commencement of the records of the church, by its proper officers, about 1749-50, to about 1827-8, a period of nearly eighty years, in common with the great mass of our churches, during their early history, there was no record kept of the Sessional proceedings. If this record was ever kept, it seems to have been long since lost, as no traces of it appear in the congregation at the present day. Who and when the many persons whose names appear upon these secular records, became communing members of the church, lies buried in impenetrable darkness. We are therefore unable to ascertain the true numerical power of the congregation at any period during this time. It is true we have endeavored to present in some approximate degree by giving the number of names attached to the collector's duplicates from year to year. But this does not give the number of communicants, as some at least who were pecuniary supporters of the church are known not to have been communicants.

To what extent this prevailed we are unable to decide. This was more especially the case after the congregation became an incorporated body. Had this record been kept it would doubtless have unfolded a great volume of interesting matter pertaining to this old congregation, but which is now irretrievably lost.

This omission, however, was remedied by Mr. Heberton, when he became stated supply to the congregation. The interesting items found in this book, as now used by the Session of the church, makes us feel more keenly the loss occasioned by the omission of this Sessional record previous to 1827.

With this advance, therefore, on the part of Mr. Heberton, his successor entered upon the duties of supplying the congregation. Mr. Heberton having finished his labors with the people, a meeting was called to take measures to have the pulpit supplied until the next meeting of Presbytery. This meeting was held May 9th, 1831. A motion was made in order to get the sense of the congregation as to obtaining the services of Rev. Mr. McJimsey as stated supply until the meeting of Presbytery. The motion was carried, and Mr John Wilson and Mr. James Kennedy were appointed a committee to confer with Mr. McJimsey to see if he would agree to the terms of the congregation. Mr. McJimsey accepted the terms offered and commenced his labors. He continued his labors during the early part of the summer of 1831, and his services being acceptable, a meeting of the congregation was held August 27th of this year to consider the propriety of having Mr. McJimsey continue as stated supply during the year. A motion was made to this effect and carried. Mr. McJimsey accepted and continued his labors. September 1st, 1832, the people again invited Mr. McJimsey to remain with them another year. He accepted the invitation and continued to labor among them. He, however, did not continue with the people through the year. Although we have no direct statement of the fact, it is apparent that he left the congregation on or before the first of April, 1833. The following receipt is the last record we have of him in connection with the Settlement Church:

" Received, March 30th, 1833, of Robert Horner, Treasurer, ———— dollars seventy-five cents in full of salary until the first of April. (Signed) Wm. McJimsey."

Here closes the record of Mr. McJimsey's labors among this people. Little appears concerning him except that he was a member of the Presbytery of Albany, New York, when he came to the congregation; and it does not appear that he ever changed his ecclesiastical connections to that under which the Church in the Settlement was during his ministry there. It appears that after Mr. McJimsey's departure, the Rev. Brogan Hoff, as agent for the S. S. Union, visited the congregation. This was in May of this year. The congregation having heard him, prepared to give him a call. The call was accepted and he was installed pastor, but at what precise time does not appear. It would seem he did not enter immediately upon the pastoral duties of the congregation, for during this year we find as supplies, the names of Mr. Vandiveer, Mr. John Gray, Mr. Love, Mr. Talmage, Mr. Wolf and Mr. Comfort.

The congregation now began to devise means to increase the minister's salary. For this purpose they met November 22d, 1833, and decided to this end the pews should be rented out. The actual renting of these took place December 4th.

In the selection of pews, those who had contributed to the building of the church had the preference.

In 1834, in addition to the preaching of Mr. Hoff, we have the single name of ———— Galloway as supply one Sabbath. Early in the year 1835, the pastoral relation between Mr. Hoff and the congregation was dissolved. This appears from the minutes of a meeting held March 4th. The record is as follows: "The object of the meeting being stated, viz: that the Rev. Mr. Hoff requested that the connection between him and this congregation be dissolved, this congregation agrees that this request be granted."

Thus ended the pastoral relation between Mr. Hoff and the congregation. The following names appear as supplies during the remainder of 1835. Mr. McCollough, Mr. Berg, Mr. Helfenstein, Mr. Love, Mr. McCook, Mr. Adam, Mr. Carpenter, Mr. Sloan, Mr. Junkin, Mr. Vandiveer and Mr. Hawthorn. This brings us down to the pastorate of Rev. Leslie Irwin.

CHAPTER VI. 1836-1869

The congregation convened October 3d, 1835, and appointed a committee to confer with Mr. Leslie Irwin, in regard to his supplying the pulpit of the Settlement Church for six months. An agreement was affected, through this committee between Mr. Irwin and the church upon which he seems to have immediately entered upon the duties of stated supply. His services having been satisfactory to the congregation, on April 18th, 1836, they extended an invitation to him to continue his services until the meeting of Presbytery in October of that year. This offer was accepted and he continued his labors as stated supply. Before this term was completed, the congregation became so well pleased with him that they met August 13th, and resolved to extend a call to him to become their pastor. After some delay he accepted the call, and was ordained and installed in June, 1838.

The affairs of the congregation now moved along smoothly until 1841, when the old enemy, the failing support of the congregation, made its appearance. This year the deficiency was made up, not as formerly by an additional duplicate, but by the private subscriptions of the remaining supporters. A large deficiency appeared again in 1842, and also in 1843. It was made good in each case by private subscriptions as before. It seems, special efforts were made to increase the number of supporters in order to obviate this inconvenience of a deficit in the support of the congregation. It will be noticed that the number of names from the collector's duplicates increased to sixty-five in 1843, against forty-three in 1841.

In 1844, it was found that the grave-yard fence, which had been erected in 1811, had become somewhat dilapidated. Accordingly, August 13th, of this year, measures were taken to have repairs made thereon. At the same time directions were given to have the floor of the church repaired, and the pulpit lowered. These had remained, it seems, as constructed in the new church building more than thirty years before, in 1813.

At a meeting of the Trustees at which these repairs were ordered, which were made necessary by the destroying hand of time, they were called upon to repair a breach which had been made by the hand of death. In 1826, they had elected Mr. Robert Horner their Treasurer. From year to year they re-elected him for eighteen years. But at this meeting, August 13th, 1844, they had the sad duty of electing a new Treasurer, to fill the place of one who had for so many years held this office by successive re-elections. That he should be thus elected from year to year for so long a time, is the best proof of fidelity and propriety with which he discharged the duties of the office. Robert Horner died in July of this year. There may be seen in the old churchyard a marble slab bearing the following inscription:

"In memory of Robert Horner, who departed this life July 7th, 1844, aged sixty-three years, two months, and fourteen days."

It will be remembered the two places of preaching regularly were at the Church near Weaversville, and at the Academy, below Bath. Sometime previous to 1845, Mr. Irwin deemed it proper to preach at the Crane Iron Works, or Catasauqua, as it is now called, as there was a growing population there which was within the bounds of his congregation, and there seemed to be a need for religious instruction among the people. This was upon the extreme western border of his charge. In like manner he perceived a need for religious instruction in the town of Bath, which was likewise in the bounds of his charge on the east.

On account of this division of Mr. Irwin's time into four instead of two parts, as is not uncommon under such circumstances, the regular members of the church manifested dissatisfaction with the new arrangement. A meeting was called November 1st, 1845, at which time notice was given of this dissatisfaction in the congregation. It was stated to exist mainly in the eastern portion of the charge. The ground of the complaint was said to be the unequal portion of time allowed them for morning service at the Academy. They claimed as a matter of right and justice that the morning service should alternate between the Church near Weaversville, and the Academy. They expressed their willingness, however, for the afternoon service to be held at the church, so long as the pastor continued to preach at Bath and Catasauqua.

The dissatisfaction was of so decided a character that several persons gave notice that they should reduce their subscriptions if their just claims were not complied with. Such, in brief, was the trouble which arose in the congregation at this time, but which after a time subsided without producing apparently any damaging commotion among the people. Mr. Irwin continued to preach at Bath and Catasauqua. In 1847, we find the latter place rendering some pecuniary support to the congregation. Mr. Frederic W. Nagle appears to have been the collector of salary from the western part of the charge. Of the $215.67 collected by him, $68.75 was from Catasauqua. This then may be considered the first pledge of Presbyterianism in Catasauqua, which has so wonderfully increased since that time. In 1848, it contributed $50.00, and the same amount in 1849, thus continuing the good work. This enlargement of the labors of the pastor seems to have relieved somewhat the pecuniary affairs of the congregation.

In 1848, 1849, 1850, 1851, 1852, 1853, 1856, 1857, and 1858, the income was greater than was necessary for the expenses, and in consequence, one-fourth of the stipend was thrown off each year. In 1854 and 1855, one-third was thrown off.

With the year 1851, there seems to have been a general renovation of the church property. The graveyard had either become too much crowded, or change in regard to it was deemed expedient. Accordingly, a portion of ground on the west side was exchanged for ground situated south of the old graveyard. This will best appear from the following record found in the minutes of a meeting held June 14th, 1851:

"At a meeting of the congregation held at the church on the 14th, day of June, 1851, convened agreeably to public notice, for the purpose of taking into consideration the propriety of enlarging the graveyard, and to effect the same by exchanging that portion of the enclosed church ground on the west side of the graveyard wall with Absalom Reichard, for lands lying on the south side of the graveyard, the meeting was organized by calling James Kerr to the chair, when a motion was made that the Trustees of the congregation be authorized to make the exchange of said lands. The question being put, it was unanimously agreed to."

Such is the record of the decision in regard to the matter. The Trustees carried out the instructions given by the congregation, and the exchange was made, as appears from the minutes of a meeting held November 1st.

We make the following brief extract bearing on this point:

"Deeds of conveyance for the exchange of ten perches of land, with Absalom Reichard and wife, were made, adjoining the graveyard."

The deed of conveyance made by Absalom **Reichard to**

the Trustees, was in trust for the congregation. The names of the Trustees inserted were Joseph Brown, Hugh Horner, William Brown, Thomas Clendinen, Robert McDowel and Philip Insley. It bears date November 1st, 1851. Thus, at this time and in this manner, was the burying ground enlarged to its present proportions.

This year also it was found necessary to put a new roof on the church near Weaversville, which seems to have stood without repair since the church was built in 1813, some thirty-eight years. A new roof being found necessary on examination, Joseph Horner and John Horner, at the meeting held November 1st, were appointed a committee to circulate subscriptions to defray the expenses of the new roof. The committee reported at a meeting held November 27th, and orders were given for the putting on of the roof. During this year the church was transferred to the care of the new Second Presbytery of Philadelphia.

We have previously spoken of the care with which the Trustees watched over the interests of the church in the early days of the corporation, appealing at times to the civil law to enforce their just claims. Although there does not seem to have been occasion for them to exercise their power for a number of years previous to 1854, in this year we have a record which shows that the spirit of the fathers had descended to their children. There had been a dereliction on the part of one of the collectors for a previous year. The collector had not made a final settlement with the Trustees. He was by them ordered to make such settlement within ten days under penalty of being prosecuted. In such manner, therefore, we find the latter day Trustees watching over the rights and claims of the church. Their firm action secured the end in view, for November 27th, of the same year, the Treasurer reported the settlement of the duplicate in question.

Matters now passed along in the congregation for a number of years without any apparent deviation from the quietude which characterized the church during the greater portion of her history. But whilst all seemed quiet and satisfactory, further trouble was insidiously working itself to the surface. This seems to have originated in the old arrangement of the pastor, whereby part of his time was occupied at Catasauqua. As we have intimated, the Catasauqua people had supported the pastor of the old Settlement Church in part, through the Trustees of the corporation. As we have pointed out, the pecuniary affairs of the old church seemed to be relieved somewhat whilst this was going on. But in 1859, the Settlement people again found themselves straightened for funds to meet their obligations to the pastor.

A meeting was called November 12th of this year, to consider the matter of the support of the congregation. One-fourth and sometimes one-third of the stipends had been thrown off during several years previous. This must be discontinued. Upon mature deliberation it was decided to increase the assessments to what they were in 1843, in order to meet the liabilities of the congregation. The trouble thus adjusted was but the beginning of a series which terminated in the dissolution of the pastoral relation between Mr. Irwin and the congregation. The portion of the people living in and near Catasauqua had formed themselves into a separate congregation and had built a house of worship. Mr. Irwin had removed to Catasauqua in order that he might supply the people there as well as at the old church and Academy.

Dissatisfaction arose, from one cause or another, among the members of the old congregation. Pecuniary difficulties harassed the Board of Trustees. Troubles appeared to be rising on all sides. Under the circumstances, a meeting of the congregation was called July 21st, 1860, in which the minutes of which we find the following record bearing on this subject:

"The object of the meeting having been stated that, whereas there has been a large falling off of the members of the congregation by deaths, removals, and otherwise, thereby disabling the Trustees to raise the pastor's salary; it was, on motion resolved that a committee be appointed to call on the pastor, the Rev. Leslie Irwin, and ask for a reduction of his salary." This deficiency in the salary took definite proportions November 14th, at which time the amount of the deficiency being ascertained, Mr. ———— and Mr. ———— were appointed to take up subscriptions through the congregation to meet the deficiency. At the same time Mr. ———— was appointed to confer with Mr. Irwin upon the embarrassing state of affairs in the congregation. This conference resulted in an agreement between Mr. Irwin and Mr. ———— as set forth in a loose note among the papers of the congregation containing a memorandum of the same in the following words:

"November 15th, 1860. It is understood and agreed upon between Rev. L. Irwin and Mr. ————, that Mr. Irwin is to preach as usual for the sum of ———— dollars, for one year from the 27th inst., and after that time if necessity, or change of circumstances should require any reduction, he (Mr. Irwin) is willing to make it."

Such in brief are the circumstances of the church in 1860.

We now pass on to 1863. In this year it was found that repairs were again needed upon the church building near Weaversville, as well as upon the wall of the burying ground. A meeting of the Trustees was held November 6th, at which time it was resolved to have the roof of the church and the graveyard wall repaired. The subject was again brought up in the meeting held November 14th, at which time it was decided that the roof on the north side of the church should be slate, and the graveyard wall should be protected by boards laid lengthwise, until the spring of 1864, when further action should be taken in regard to the matter. These seem to have been the last repairs of any consequence, put upon the old church building previous to that general renovation of which we shall speak hereafter.

In 1845, Joseph Horner was elected Treasurer of the Board of Trustees. From year to year he was re-elected for twenty-one years. In January, 1866, he was as usual elected to that office, but this was for the last time. He was soon to bid adieu to earth and all its sorrows. As with his predecessor, the best evidence of the fidelity with which he discharged the duties of the office is in the confidence manifested by the Trustees from time to time in re-electing him to the office. As a man he had few equals in kindness. Although the words he spoke were few, he manifested the nobleness of his heart by that which speaks louder than words, praiseworthy actions. All who knew him only knew him to speak well of him. None could say they had an enemy in him, for those with whom he had most to do, and who were most likely to complain, could not say less than, "That man was my friend," or "I loved that man."

Under the trials of a lingering illness and fatal disease, he exercised the greatest patience and resignation, never uttering a murmuring word, or making complaint against the hand of Providence. In peace he breathed his last, dying, as far as mortal eye could see, the death of the Christian.

Appropriate to the character of the man, the following simple inscription may be seen upon his tombstone in the old burying ground, where his remains lie in peace, beyond the cares and turmoil of this world:

"In memory of Joseph Horner; born October 24th, 1790; died January 27th, 1866."

A meeting of the Trustees was held at the house of Mr. John Agnew, March 7th, to elect a new Treasurer. At this meeting Mr. Joseph Brown resigned the office of President of the Board, which he held at the time, and Mr. Thomas Clendinen was chosen in his place. Then Mr. Brown was elected Treasurer, which office he has continued to hold to the present time (1875).

The Trustees in session, January 7th, 1867, took into consideration the unattractive appearance of the old burying ground. It was uneven and infested with weeds and briers, which though cut down from year to year, as often grew up again, and made the appearance of the grounds forbidding. In order to improve the appearance of the place, the following resolution was offered by Mr. Joseph Brown in regard to the matter:

"On motion of Joseph Brown, a resolution was passed to employ some suitable person to fix the graves and level the ground in the graveyard; the necessary expenses to be paid out of the treasury."

This resolution was carried into effect, and the old burying ground thoroughly renovated. The inequalities in the surface of the ground have, to a large extent, been removed. The graves have been properly filled up; old and tottering tombstones have been reset; some of the older people have put neat and substantial railings around the graves of their ancestors; and evergreens have to some extent been planted. These, with the green sward that now meets the eye on entering, in contrast with the former brambles, give the old burying ground an inviting aspect; and show the care which the present generation are bestowing upon the place where lie the ashes of our ancestors. The whole is protected by a substantial stone wall, kept in suitable repair. Those who live far away from those scenes which surrounded their ancestors, may be assured that the resting places of these are properly cared for.

We have alluded to the difficulties which arose in the congregation in 1860, and how they were adjusted. This, it seems, was but a temporary accommodation of affairs of the congregation which were in a very discouraging condition. As we have previously intimated, Mr. Irwin, for a number of years, lived in Catasauqua, preaching to the old congregation and new one at the same time. The division of his time in this manner gave grounds for dissatisfaction on the part of the members belonging to the old congregation. From some cause or other, be it more or less clearly defined, Mr. Irwin deemed it expedient for him to remove from Catasauqua to his farm, perhaps a half-mile below Bath. This he did in 1864. Having given up his charge in Catasauqua, he now ministered exclusively to the old congregation, preaching alternately at the church near Weaversville, and at the Academy near Bath. Now living among his people, in the eastern part of the congregation, he endeavored to stay the decline of the church, which had become so manifest. Whether it originated in the old dissatisfaction or was based upon some other cause we are not prepared to state; at all events the pastor did not seem to command that co-operation of his people which was so essential to success in the existing state of affairs. Many of the children in the congregation had not been baptized in infancy. Those who had been, and had grown up to be young men and young women, did not seem to be coming up to the responsibilities of church membership, as might properly have been expected of them. The pastor agitated the subject of erecting a new church building in the town of Bath. The members of the church seemed to feel that this project would not be successful under the circumstances. At all events they do not seem to have responded to the suggestions of the pastor in as full and prompt a manner as was calculated to make the project successful. Thus matters went on for a year or two previous to the spring of 1868. Some time before the meeting of Presbytery, (Second of Philadelphia), in April, 1868, Mr. Irwin left the congregation. Mr. Joseph Brown and Mr. John Horner appeared at the meeting of Presbytery at Catasauqua in April, as commissioners from the congregation, in accordance with the appointment of a meeting held March 28th. In view of the state of affairs the congregation having consented thereto, the pastoral relation was dissolved. Thus the church became vacant after enjoying the pastoral services of Mr. Irwin for more than thirty years.

From the meeting of Presbytery in 1868 to November 1869, the congregation was vacant. During this time the pulpit was supplied by various persons from various sources. Occasional sermons were preached by members of the Second Presbytery of Philadelphia. Other ministers would preach for the people as occasion would direct. From September, 1868 to April, 1869, numerous supplies went from the Theological Seminary at Princeton, N. J. Among these, from the class of 1869, may be mentioned Mr. W. W. Heberton, son of Rev. Alex. Heberton, former stated supply to the congregation. The Rev. W. W. Heberton is now (1875) pastor at Elkton, Md. Mr. L. W. Eckard, since Missionary to China, but now pastor at Abington, Pa., Mr. Andrew H. Parker, pastor at East Kishoquillas, Pa. Mr. John Murdock, for a time since pastor at Islip, L. I., Mr. A. P. Kelso, now Missionary to India, Mr. Jacob Krewson, pastor at Forrestville, Bucks county, Pa., Mr. William G. Cairns, pastor at Cream Ridge, N. J., Mr. R. P. Gibson, pastor at Silver Spring, Pa., Mr. Charles S. Wood, of Richwood, O., Mr. W. S. C. Webster, of Elizabeth, N. J., and perhaps a few others, supplied the pulpit upon one or more occasions. The writer of these pages also preached a few times whilst visiting among the people.

The congregation were so well pleased with the services of Mr. Jacob Krewson, that they extended a call to him to become their pastor, in the spring of 1869. This, however, was declined on the part of Mr. Krewson. From the class of 1870 in Princeton Theological Seminary, Mr. John Turner, now pastor at Thompson Ridge, N. Y., Mr. John D. Hewitt, pastor at Ringoes, N. J., and Mr. W. W. Curtis, of Silver City, New Mexico, may be mentioned as supplying the pulpit upon one or more occasions.

Mr. Curtis was the regular supply during the summer of 1869. His preaching was greatly blessed to the people. To his labors at this time may largely be attributed the improved temporal and spiritual condition of the congregation since. He has many warm friends among the old Settlement people, and has been the means of interesting them in benevolent enterprises beyond their own bounds since his sojourn among them.

Many have been the needy Christians in the missionary fields of the west who have been clad and encouraged by benefactions from the Settlement, drawn forth through the solicitations of Mr. Curtis. Mr. Curtis not having completed his theological studies, left the people in the fall of 1869, and returned to Princeton. Thus we are brought down to the present pastorate.

CHAPTER VII. 1870-1875

With the re-union of 1870, the church came under the care of the Presbytery of Lehigh. During the summer of 1869, the Rev. David M. James, pastor of the Mt. Olive Presbyterian Church, N. J., visited the Settlement and preached for the people. The congregation perceived in him the proper qualifications of mind and heart to make a suitable pastor for them. They without delay extended a call to him. Notwithstanding the temporal and spiritual condition of the church was not of the most inviting character at the time, be it said to the lasting credit of Mr. James, he did not decline to enter upon the work to which God by his Providence seemed to be calling him. He accepted the call of the people, and the Presbytery proceeded to make arrangements for his installation.

This took place November 9th, 1869. We cannot do better than give the words of one who was an eye-witness of and participated in the interesting services of Mr. James' installation, which were so auspicious for the future of this old historic church. We find them in the "Presbyterian" of November 27th, 1869, as follows:

"Messrs. Editors:—The Rev. David M. James was installed pastor of the Allen Township Presbyterian Church on the afternoon of the 9th inst. The Rev. Mr. Banks of Easton, Pa., presided and preached; the Rev. Mr. Kerr delivered a very appropriate charge to the pastor, and the Rev. Mr. Fulton of Catasauqua, Pa., the charge to the people. The exercises were throughout of an interesting and impressive character. We congratulate this congregation upon their happy selection of a pastor. Mr. James is an alumnus of Lafayette College, and a graduate of Princeton Theological seminary. He has been for a number of years the efficient pastor of Mt. Olive Church, N. J. He now comes to a church of historic interest. Although its membership has been largely reduced by removals, those very changes which have been its loss, have been great gain for the cause of Christ, and of Presbyterianism in many other parts of the country, particularly in the middle and western states. For more than one hundred and thirty years the descendants of a respectable and thoroughly indoctrinated Scotch-Irish ancestry have been maintaining and propagating the faith of their fathers in this region, and sending forth an element and influence that shall live and last and operate in the Presbyterian Church, where perhaps much of a present, but ephemeral notoriety will be unheard of. In connection with the ministry of this church, either of regular pastorate or supply, we find the names of Revs. Gilbert Tennent, by whom the church was organized in 1738; James Campbell, 1740; Beatty, 1743; David Brainerd, 1744; Lawrence, 1747; John Clark, 1762; John Rosbrugh, 1769; Alexander Mitchell, 1777; James Sproat, 1778; Francis Peppard, 1783; Robert Russel, 1798; Alexander Heberton, 1827; William McJimsey, 1831; Brogan Hoff, 1833; and Leslie Irwin, 1835. Of these are men of God whose praise still lives in the churches, and whose record shall be forever on high. Mr. Leslie Irwin served this church for about thirty years, and since his removal to the west in 1868, the church has been without a regular pastor until now, although many acceptable supplies have filled the pulpit; in particular, Mr. Curtis, now of the Theological Seminary, Princeton, whose labors here during the past summer have been greatly blessed to the people. Mr. James now enters upon this charge under very favorable circumstances. He enjoys their merited confidence, while they are much united and revived under his ministry. At their last communion season, twenty persons were united to the membership of the church. They have now concluded to erect a new church at Bath. And from the need of a new Presbyterian church, particularly at this point, from the ability of the people, and from the interest they now manifest in this worthy enterprise, we are persuaded the good work will soon be accomplished. And also that a rich blessing is yet in store for the descendants of those fathers who consecrated this ground with their tears, when they retired to weep under the hazel bushes, with the message of Jesus from the burning lips of David Brainerd in their hearts." "Lehigh."

We have intimated that at the time Mr. James was called to the pastorate of the church, her prospect temporally and spiritually were not of the most encouraging character. We might say they were exceedingly discouraging. It was about that time the foregoing pages were written, substantially as the reader here finds them. With the circumstances of the congregation vividly before the mind we then wrote as follows: We cannot turn from the records of these events, simple and comparatively unimportant as some of them may seem, without reflecting upon the mutability of all things here below. Those who founded and who were for many years the staunch supporters of the church, have all passed away. We open those old records and read name after name whose counterpart we find upon many a tombstone in the old graveyard. Here too are the monuments which were raised to the memory of the dead when we had no national existence. When we walk through this old city of the dead and read the names of those who were laid low in the tomb a hundred years ago, and then look out upon the splendor of our nation which has risen since those were laid there, we pause and ask ourselves, can all this have transpired in so short a time? There attach themselves to these sacred spots, which seem as links to bind us to a former age, such hallowed associations as make the passer-by pause and consider, when and under what circumstances in the distant future some one may pay the same tribute of respect to his memory. Here are the evidences of work performed by our ancestors when those beautiful surrounding hills and vales were covered with the primeval forests. Here are designated the last resting places of those who encountered the trials of an early settler's life, braved winter storms and a savage foe in an age gone by. When we consider, too, the various estates which in that early day were held by our Scotch-Irish ancestry, and now see so many of them possessed by those of another nationality, we ask ourselves, shall this course of disintegration and decay continue? Shall that name which has for nearly a hundred and fifty years designated this beautiful region to which so many in various parts of our broad land are pleased to trace their ancestry, be lost in oblivion? Shall we hear no more of the Irish Settlement? Shall those old buildings where the praises of God have been celebrated for the last half or three-quarters of a century, be deserted and desolate? Shall those old pews, which speak of better days, be empty and forgotten? Shall those walls decay, totter and fall, no more to rise? Shall these, like the forms of those who reared them to the service of God, sink beneath the sod? Alas, we fear such must be their fate. Decay and desolation seem to be written upon those old walls. Yet this change from brightness to shade in the prospects of the old time honored church, is not attributable to the faithful few who continue to resort there for worship. Those old walls are as dear to them as were the walls of a once magnificent Jerusalem to the Jews. It is a higher and mightier hand than man's that is working. If the praise of God cease to be celebrated in these sacred retreats, by those of the nationalities which instituted His praise there, let it be remembered that from these have gone out streams to make glad the city of our God. As a church God has been, and "is in the midst of her; she shall not be moved; God shall help her, and that right early."

Such was the feeling which the circumstances of the congregation created within our mind at the commencement of the pastorate of Mr. James. Whilst we expressed that feeling, since five or six years have rolled by we find we quoted the words of the sacred writer in a wonderfully prophetic manner. We declared that God has been and was in the midst of the old church, and that he would help her, and that right early. This has been proven to be emphatically true. God did help her, and that right early, as we shall presently see.

Before we speak of the present prosperity of the church, let us make a brief resume of the circumstances which apparently led to the decline and threatened the extinction of the congregation.

Allen and East Allen Townships were the center of what was known in earlier days as the Irish Settlement. After the Settlement was commenced in 1728, and grew under the auspices of the Allens, who were friends of Presbyterianism, people of Scotch and Irish extraction, and imbued with the principles of Presbyterianism, immigrated thither. The surrounding country at that time was to a large extent a wilderness. Thus it can be clearly seen how all the circumstances in the early days of the Settlement were conducive to the prosperity of the church. Her star was then in the ascendant. As families moved into the neighborhood, and the children grew up, the church was proportionately strengthened. But there was a limit to this tide of fortune. The time came when immigration to the Settlement to a large degree, if not wholly, ceased. The surrounding country began to be filled up with that thrifty and substantial class of people known as the Pennsylvania Germans. There was no room for the Settlement to grow in proportions, and no new supply of material from abroad to make it grow. Thus we can see how the Settlement and her church was brought to a standstill, so far as her prosperity was concerned. But coming to a standstill was but to begin a retrograde movement. The families of the old settlers growing up, must be provided for. There was no inviting and economical mode of providing for them in the bounds of the old Settlement. Necessity, therefore, compelled the people to look beyond the Settlement for homes for their children. In addition to this natural cause of emigration, difficulties with regard to land titles, growing out of the results of the American Revolution, tended in the same direction. The question now arose as to whether the children in the families should seek homes in the newer portions of the country, or whether the whole families should emigrate and settle where all could live in close proximity to each other. The latter plan seems to have been to a large degree adopted. This emigration of families from the Settlement to other parts of the country, has been insidiously going on, to a greater or less degree, for more than seventy years. Through this, the descendants of the old settlers may be found today scattered along the banks of the Susquehanna, in Centre county, in Chester county, in Pittsburgh and vicinity. Hosts of these descendants may be found in the Genesee country, in western New York; in fact they are scattered all over the Middle and Western States, to the latter of which they have gone as by a second emigration. They have carried Presbyterianism with them, so that it may truly be said that from the old Settlement have gone forth streams which have made glad the city of our God.

This constant removal of families, as we have endeavored to point out in the foregoing pages, wrought its legitimate effects upon the old mother church. She was slowly dying from disintegration. The question may be asked why the community which has ever been populous in the Settlement, did not supply material for the church in place of that which was lost by emigration? This question may be answered by calling attention to the fact that it was almost universally the case that when a Scotch or Irish family removed, their property fell into the hands of a Pennsylvania German. In fact, this substantial class of our citizens have for many years been pressing hard upon the precincts of the old Settlement. Their inclinations so far as church relations are concerned, have been toward the Lutheran and German Reformed denominations. They have ever gone upon the assumption, apparently, that they were not expected to take an interest in the old Settlement Presbyterian Church. On the other hand, the Scotch-Irish element, apparently, went upon the assumption that it was their mission to conserve the interests of Presbyterianism in the community. Whilst ready enough to extend the hand of fellowship to a German brother-Christian, they do not seem to have made any strenuous efforts to enlist the sympathies of these people in the affairs of the old Settlement Church. Thus we can see how death and emigration would work their ravages upon the church, with comparatively nothing to counteract their influence. Under the influence of these and other causes, we may truly say the church was threatened with utter extinction. So it seemed about the time the pastorate of Mr. James commenced. The old church near Weaversville, had in appearance fallen far behind the age. There was still the high, narrow pulpit with its winding stairs at one side, just as they had been built, for aught we could learn, more than sixty years ago. There were the old fashioned straight high backed pews in which the members of the church had sat from infancy to old age. There were the old posts, placed to support the joined wooden ceiling long before the recollection of the Younger members of the church. There was the old communion table, with its beautifully carved legs, telling of an age gone by. The old walls were stained and begrimed through the leaking of the decaying roof. Such was the old church near Weaversville. Nor was the Old Academy, the other place of preaching, much more inviting. It had been built for school purposes, but when the waning fortunes of the Settlement divested it of its importance as an institution of learning, it was accommodated to the use of public worship. But there remained the old platform, extending across the entire southern end of the room. In the middle of this was the semi-circular railing which supported the pulpit board. Time had made an indelible impression upon the old leather covered Bible, and had riddled the old cloth screen upon the railing, putting it in sad contrast with the brass headed tacks which held it in position and which grew brighter and brighter as furbished by the vestments of the men of God from year to year.

In front of the minister's face, and where he could almost touch it with his hands as he proclaimed the word of truth, was the old fashioned stove with its pipe rusting through under the corroding hand of time. Upon the minister's right were the benches, apparently made only for temporary use many years before, upon which sat the male portion of the congregation. On the left were similar benches occupied by the females The walls and ceiling were discolored and unsightly. In short, the whole appearance of the house of worship was uncomfortable, uninviting, and out of date.

This aspect of the buildings and the depleted resources of the congregation, made us, as the descendant of one of the old families, tremble for the ark of God in the Settlement. It was under these influences we penned the picture which we have inserted above. But it has been truly said, the darkest hour is just before dawn. So it proved to be in this case. The people were not deceived in their estimate of Mr. James when they called him to the pastorate, in 1869. A man of experience in the pastorate, and knowing how to win the hearts of those outside of the church as well as in it, he was the right man in the right place, to accomplish a good work for God and Presbyterianism within the bounds of the old Settlement.

We must now call attention to the result of a quiet work which has been going on among our Pennsylvania German citizens, and which has so favorably manifested itself in the bounds of the old Irish Settlement. The present generation have been under the influence of our common school system. The result of this has been to introduce the English language to a large extent among the German population. It perhaps may be truly said, that the younger generation of Germans in Northampton and other counties, now generally use the English language in ordinary conversation. This being the case, it would be natural for them to have a desire to listen to English preaching, by ministers who always had spoken the English language This has manifested itself in the town of Bath, whose population is almost exclusively Pennsylvania German. The younger people speak, generally, the English language. They have enjoyed suitable church privileges under the ministry of the Lutheran and German Reformed Churches where the German and English languages have been used interchangeably. But whilst they have been appropriately indoctrinated in the great fundamental principles of Christianity in this way, they have manifested a desire for English preaching.

Mr. James, and the remnant of the old Settlement people, were quick to discover this auspicious change in the sentiments of their worthy neighbors, and take advantage of it for the welfare and advancement of the Presbyterian Church. Another auspicious circumstance was the spiritual awakening among the people, apparently through the instrumentality of the Rev. Mr. Curtis, just previous to Mr. James' entrance upon his pastorate. We learn that at the sacramental occasion previous to Mr. James' installation, twenty persons connected themselves with the church. Thus were the people spiritually enlivened and strengthened for the work which was before them. Another auspicious circumstance was the fact that whilst God by his providence had depleted the ranks of the old Settlement people, he had granted a goodly portion of this world's goods to those who remained.

Under these circumstances it was decided that the time had arrived for building a Presbyterian Church in Bath. The members of the church resolved to do their part, and seek the aid and co-operation of others in the community, and especially of those living in Bath. Be it said to the lasting credit of all, the old Settlement people responded liberally when called upon for this purpose, and the Bath people, as well as others more distant, heartily seconded their efforts. Of those who did so in the congregation we might mention the names of Mrs. Margaret Horner, wife of the late Joseph Horner, who so long and so faithfully served the church as Treasurer, together with her two daughters; the late Judge James Kennedy, whose name for many years was familiar in the church; Mrs. Dr. Boyd, daughter of James Clyde, whose name appears frequently among the Trustees of the congregation; Mr. Joseph Brown; Mr. John Horner, son of Hugh Horner, whose name is prominent among the Trustees of former days; Mr. Hugh R. Horner, son of Robert Horner, who so long and so faithfully served the congregation as Treasurer; Thomas Clendinen, and others whose names would not sound so familiar to those who now live beyond the bonds of the Settlement.

Of these outside of the congregation we might mention the names of James Vleit, Esq., Dr. Shull, of Bethlehem, William Chapman, and others. In seeking a location in Bath the people desired one sufficiently central and still appropriately retired. Upon the road leading from Bethlehem to Bath, upon a beautifully shaded portion of the street, not more than two squares from the business portion of the town, they found and secured a lot combining admirably the requisite qualifications. The lot was purchased Monday, January 31st, 1870. Here, under the superintendence of Mr. Hugh R. Horner, and James Vleit, Esq., in 1870, the people erected a neat and commodious house of worship. The building stands back from the sidewalk ten or fifteen feet, and is on the west side of the street. It is a substantial brick structure thirty-eight by sixty feet. From the main entrance, out of the vestibule, a step or two down leads into the Sabbath school and lecture room. Here may be found a cheerful and attractive place of worship. Maps, charts and other modern appliances are at hand for the proper instruction of the children and people. To remind all of "the hole of the pit" whence they have been dug, the old seats from the Academy, altered and made more comfortable, are made to do service in seating the congregation. Here are the large heaters by which the main audience room above is warmed. Here the people hold their fairs, festivals, and enjoy many social occasions.

Ascending to the main audience room we find all the surroundings cheerful and inviting. The pulpit is neat and of the latest and most approved pattern. In the rear of the pulpit may be seen richly carved and upholstered chairs, the gift of Mrs. Margaret Horner. In front may be seen a beautiful table, the gift of Mrs. Webster, of Mauch Chunk. In the opposite end of the room may be seen a conveniently constructed choir gallery, in which may be found a suitable church organ, the gift of the Misses Sallie and Jennie Horner. Upon the pulpit board is a beautiful Bible, the gift of Miss Maria Insley. The pews are sixty-three in number and are calculated to seat comfortably three hundred and fifty persons. They are ash, oiled and finished with walnut scrolls and tops. The windows are stained glass. The room is made comfortable in winter by heaters in the basement. The building is surmounted by a symmetrical and attractive spire. In the tower has been placed a suitable bell which calls the worshipers together from time to time. This whole munificent gift of some $8,000 or $10,000 value was dedicated to the service of Almighty God on Thanksgiving day, November 24, 1870

"In the morning, at eleven o'clock, the dedicatory services were conducted by the pastor, Rev. David M. James, assisted by Rev. D. S. Banks, who preached an appropriate sermon. In the evening addresses were delivered by Revs. J. W. Wood, of Allentown, William Fulton, of Catasauqua, and D. S. Banks, of Easton. "Two venerable members, Judge James Kennedy, and Mrs. Nancy Boyd, who contributed so liberally and who have expressed such earnest desires to see the church completed, were both present, though past eighty years of age, and enjoyed the services with all the fervor of former years."

Such are the extracts from the report of the dedicatory services, made at the time. In this new building Mr. James preaches from time to time to the interested and largely increased audiences, composed to a gratifying degree of the citizens of Bath.

The Old Academy has been sold and dismantled. Whilst the exterior presents the same general appearance, little remains within to remind the beholder of days gone by when Governor Wolf, Thomas McKeen and their compeers, frequented it. Ere we bid the old building farewell, we may be permitted to insert here a reminisence of her beginning, communicated to us by Mr. Samuel McNair, of Broadheads. Wisconsin. We give it in his own words. "Rev. John Rosbrugh was the father of James Rosbrugh who used to tell an anecdote connected with the history of the building of the Academy at Bath, which was as follows: He with a number of other young men wanted the advantage of something better than a common school education, and they took measures to build by subscription. He called on George Wolf for aid, but Mr. Wolf refused by saying, 'That this edecation and things make rascals.' He refused at first, but afterwards he did help to build it. But in the course of the conversation Mr. Rosbrugh told him that his sons, George and Philip would have an advantage of an education, and that his son George might be Governor sooner or later. 'Well then when my son George is Governor there will be queer times!' The sequel of the matter was that George Wolf got his English education in the Old Academy, and after his election (to the Governorship of the state), it all came to the mind of Mr. Rosbrugh, who used to take pride in telling it."

Thus we see the beginning and the end of the old Academy which served the people as a place of worship for nearly sixty years. We cannot speak of the old church near Weaversville, the other place of preaching, as we have spoken of the Academy. Ever since the old Academy was decided upon as a place of preaching, in 1813, it may emphatically be said there have been "two sides" in the congregation. Each side has manifested; from time to time, a lively concern lest the "other side" should become possessed of undue advantages in church accommodations. The new church being erected in Bath, and the old Academy abandoned, the east side had obtained a great ascendancy over the west side. The people on the west side perceived that unless something was done, and that speedily, at the old location, there was great danger that the old church would be deserted and fall into decay, being eclipsed by the new building in Bath. Accordingly, the people of the west side urged the entire renovation of the old church building, erected in 1813, near

Weaversville. The work was undertaken simultaneously with the erection of the new church in Bath. It had been the custom to enter by two doors on the south side of the building. These were masoned up and a new one opened at the east end of the building; over this a substantial frame vestibule was erected. All the old exterior stone wall was hidden by being encased in a wooden siding which was painted white. Instead of the rusty old stone building which had stood for nearly sixty years, it was made to wear the appearance of a neat frame structure. Internally, all was changed. The old high, narrow pulpit, with its winding stairs at the one side, which stood at the north side of the room, was removed. In its stead, at the west end of the room, a modern, comfortable and attractive pulpit and platform were erected. The old supporting posts in the middle of the room were removed, and the ceiling strengthened by a truss in the attic.

The old high-back pews were removed, and modern and more comfortable ones put in their place, facing to the west instead of the north. An elevated platform was erected in the rear of the audience, near the new entrance, for the choir, and an organ was provided for their use. The walls and ceiling were divested of their smoke and stains, and arrayed in pure white. In short, the whole building was thoroughly renovated and rejuvenated. The old school house, which stood between the church and the road, was removed. A neat pale fence was built around the church lot, and the grounds put in appropriate order. All was made to wear the appearance of comfort and convenience. It was re-occupied for divine service, December 4th, 1870. Thus has the old Church in the Settlement renewed her youth.

Under the pastorate of Mr. James they are moving along harmoniously and doing a good work for God and Presbyterianism in the community. The English speaking portion of the German community of Bath and vicinity, seem to be interested in the new life of the old Settlement Church. The

Settlement people are extending the hand of Christian fellowship to their worthy friends and neighbors, and they are responding to a commendable degree by pecuniary support and substantial Christian work. The church, amid the new circumstances into which she has come, is laboring to make all feel in the community that they are welcome to all her privileges and blessings. It is hoped, also, by all who feel an interest in the church outside of as well as within the precincts of the old Irish Settlement, that those who occupy the places once filled by the Scotch and Irish people, will take up and sustain the good old heritage of Presbyterianism which has been handed down from generation to generation in their midst. That they will do this we have every reason to believe, judging from the disposition already shown on their part in the matter. We are rejoiced to be able to take up and re-echo, upon the eve of the Centennial of our American Independence, the words of an encouraged pastor in the old Irish Settlement Church, that,

"There is as good a prospect for a Presbyterian Church to continue a hundred years to come, as there was a hundred years ago," when the pastor of the church, Rev. John Rosbrugh, was murdered by a relentless British foe, as he did his part to secure our National Independence.

CHAPTER VIII. SKETCHES OF PASTORS

Rev. Eleazer Wales

The first pastor of the Settlement Church seems to have been Rev. Eleazer Wales. What the ecclesiastical antecedents of Mr. Wales were, previous to 1731, we have not been able to learn. That year, however, his name appeared, we believe, for the first time, in the minutes of the Synod of Philadelphia. Although we have not positive evidence in the case, it is to be presumed he became pastor of the Settlement Church about that time. At all events, that year Thomas Craig appeared in Synod as an elder. We presume this was the same Thomas Craig who, in 1728, started what was af-

THE JAMES HORNER, SR., HOMESTEAD.
This building, erected in 1754, took the place of the log house, built in 1737.
(See page 38.)

terwards known as the Craig, or Irish Settlement. The presumption that Mr. Wales was pastor and Mr. Craig elder in the Settlement Church, in 1731, becomes almost certain when we observe that this pastoral relation is alluded to and dealt with shortly after. We are informed by the minutes of the Presbytery of Philadelphia, that the pastoral relation between Mr. Wales and the Settlement, or Allentown congregation, was dissolved in 1734. We find that during each meeting of the Synod from 1731 to 1735, Mr. Wales was present. In 1736, he is marked absent. In 1737 and 1738, we believe his name does not appear at all. In 1739, he is reported as a member of the Presbytery of New Brunswick. It seems after leaving the Settlement Church he became pastor for a short time, of the Middle Smithfield Church. Dr. D. X. Junkin, in his Historical Discourse at the Semi-Centennial of the Presbytery of Middle Smithfield, says:

"A little log church was built about 1725.——— It is supposed that Rev. Azariah Horton, before mentioned as David Brainerd's forerunner preached the first sermon in English, in 1741, or '42. He preached in the little log church.——— A Rev. Mr. Wales, from Allen Township seems to have been the earliest settled pastor. A Rev. Mr. Rhodes was also a laborer in that field, with much success; both of them between 1750 and the opening of the War of the Revolution."

We suppose Dr. Junkin had good authority for making this statement with reference to Mr. Wales, though he has erred in assigning labor to him between 1750 and the Revolution. Mr. Wales died previous to November 7th, 1750.

From all the data, we infer that Mr. Wales was dismissed from the Presbytery of Philadelphia in 1735, or '36, and connected himself with the Presbytery of New York. When the brethren assembled at New Brunswick, on the afternoon of August 8th, 1738, for the purpose of constituting the Presbytery of New Brunswick, Mr. Wales was one of the members, being received from the Presbytery of New York.

Thus he is regularly reported to Synod in 1739, as a member of the New Brunswick Presbytery.

At the first meeting of Presbytery, August 8th, 1738, "Upon a supplication made by Joshua Nicholas, in behalf of the people of Pepack, and other adjacent parts, desiring some supplies of preaching, agreed that Mr. Wales preach at John Frasier's upon the third Sabbath of this inst.; upon the Monday following at Edward Barber's; and upon the Tuesday at Amwell Meeting House."

He may have been, previous to this, or now became pastor at Smithfield for a short time, as suggested by Dr. Junkin. But during the greater part of his time in connection with the Presbytery at New Brunswick, he was pastor of the church of Kingston, near Princeton, N. J.

While in this charge, in 1743, he supplied at Freehold the first Sabbath in February, April and May. In 1744, he supplied the Settlement Church the last two Sabbaths in September and first in October, as we have seen in the History of the Church. In 1746, he was appointed to supply two Sabbaths at Hopewell and Maiden Head. It was represented to Presbytery, May 16th, 1750, that he was too infirm and weak to attend to ministerial duties in his congregation, and supplies were sent to the people. Shortly after this he died. At a meeting of Presbytery, November 7th, 1750, the following simple record is made: "Mr. Eleazer Wales, one of our members, has been removed by death since our last."

Rev. Daniel Lawrence

The Rev. Daniel Lawrence was the second pastor in the Irish Settlement. He was a pupil of Rev. William Tennent, and pursued his studies at the "Log College". On the 12th of September, 1744, he appeared before the Presbytery of New Brunswick and was received under their care as a candidate for the Gospel ministry. His parts of trial were assigned him at this meeting of Presbytery. At a meeting held in Philadelphia, October 2d and 3d, 1744, he was examined on his parts of trial and his examinations sustained. At the

Spring meeting, held in Philadelphia, May 28th, 1745, he appeared before Presbytery and was licensed; he preached the next month (the last Sabbath in June, 1745,) at the "Forks of Delaware," or Irish Settlement and Greenwich. Presbytery convened September 20th of this year, at which time two calls were brought in for the pastoral services of Mr. Lawrence. The one was from the two Bethlehems, in New Jersey; the other from Maiden Head and Hopewell. Mr. Lawrence not being present at the meeting, consideration of these calls was deferred until the next meeting. Under the circumstances he was directed to supply two Sabbaths at Maiden Head and Hopewell, and then repair to the "Forks of Delaware." He was to supply two-thirds of his time in the Forks, and devote the other third to the two Bethlehems. At a meeting of Presbytery, July 21st, 1746, a supplication was sent in from the congregation of Maiden Head and Hopewell, requesting the labors of Mr. Lawrence until the next meeting of Presbytery, by way of trial, with a view to his settlement among them. Also a similar supplication from the "Forks of Delaware," for his services for one year with a view to his settlement there. Likewise a supplication from the two Bethlehems in N. J., for the same purpose. Some people from Oxford Furnace, also, supplicated that they might share the labors of Mr. Lawrence in case he should be appointed to supply the "Forks of Delaware." In the midst of this clamor, as it were, for the services of Mr. Lawrence, the Presbytery returned him to his labors in the Forks, with instructions to preach every fifth Sabbath at Tunis Quick's, (?) in the "Forks of Delaware." Thus things remained until the meeting of Presbytery October 16th, of this year. At this meeting, the people in the Forks renewed their call for Mr. Lawrence to undertake the pastoral charge among them. The matter being proposed to him by Presbytery, he signified his acceptance of the call. Presbytery thereupon appointed a committee to ordain him. This committee was composed of Rev. Richard Treat, Rev. James Campbell, Rev. James Davenport, Rev. James McCree, and

Rev. Charles Beatty. This committee was to meet in the "Forks of Delaware," April 1st, 1747, at which time Mr. Lawrence was to preach a trial sermon from John iii, 18, "He that believeth on him is not condemned; but he that believeth not is condemned already, because he hath not believed in the name of the only begotten Son of God." At the same time he was to hand in a Latin exegesis. All parts of trial being sustained, the committee proceeded the next day, (April 2d, 1747), to ordain him to the work of the Gospel ministry, and install him pastor of the two churches in the Forks, viz: Allentown and Mt. Bethel. On account of ill health and other causes, he spent the winter of 1747 and the spring of 1748 at Cape May. By direction of the Synod of New York, given May 19th, 1748, the Presbytery of New Brunswick returned him again in the spring of 1748 to supply a few Sabbaths at Cape May. Having fulfilled the mission of the Presbytery he returned and continued his labors in the Settlement until the spring of 1752. At this time he was connected with the Presbytery of Abington, which had been erected the previous year. At the first meeting of the Presbytery after its constitution, May 20th, 1752, the church at Cape May applied to it for the services of Mr. Lawrence, in case he was released from his charge in the Forks, which he was seeking for at the time.

The next day, May 21st, 1752, the pastoral relation between him and the churches in the Forks was dissolved. Mr. Lawrence accepted the call to Cape May in 1752, and commenced his labors there as pastor in that year. He continued to labor in this pastorate for fourteen years, until 1766, only laying down the work with his life. He died at Cape May, April 13th, 1766.

Rev. John Clark

The third pastor of the Settlement Church was Rev. John Clark. Mr. Clark was licensed to preach the Gospel by the Presbytery of New Brunswick in the latter part of 1759, or early part of 1760. Having been licensed, he was appointed by the Synod of New York and Philadelphia, to supply the pulpit of Rev. Charles Beatty, the first and third Sabbaths of July, 1760. He was ordained to the full work of the ministry, by the Presbytery of New Brunswick, in the latter part of 1760, or early part of 1761. He was dismissed from the Presbytery of New Brunswick, and connected himself with the Presbytery of Philadelphia, August 13th, of that year. At this meeting of Presbytery, a call was presented to him from the "Forks of Delaware." He took the matter under consideration until the next meeting of Presbytery. In the meantime he was directed to supply "at the Forks of Delaware in the following manner, viz: two Sabbaths at Allens Town, and one at Hunter's Settlement, (Mt. Bethel), interchangeably, except two Sabbaths at Tehicken." November 17th, 1761, Mr. Clark expressed his acceptance of the call to the Forks of Delaware. He was installed pastor of the Settlement Church, October 13th, 1762. Rev. Richard Treat presided and preached the sermon. Rev. Henry Martin, Rev. James Latta and Rev. Charles Beatty assisted in the installation services. Mr. Clark continued in the pastorate for four years, till 1766, at which time troubles arose in the Mt. Bethel portion of the charge. He then asked for a dissolution of the pastoral relation, which was not granted. The troubles, however, culminated in a dissolution November 4th, 1767. Mr. Clark remained in connection with the Presbytery of Philadelphia for several years, but came under the care of the Presbytery of New Castle in 1772. (?) Here he remained till 1783, at which time he was dismissed to the Presbytery of Redstone. He remained in connection with this Presbytery till 1794, during a portion of which time, at least, he was pastor of the Lebanon and Bethel Churches. In 1794, the Presbytery of Ohio was formed out of that of Redstone, and Mr. Clark became a constituent part of the new Presbytery. Here we lose sight of Mr. Clark. Where or when he died we have not learned.

Rev. John Rosbrugh

The fourth pastor of the Settlement Church was Rev. John Rosbrugh. He was of Scottish descent, and was imbued with the principles of Scottish Presbyterianism. He pursued his studies in the College of New Jersey, at Princeton, from the year 1760-3, under the care and assistance of the Synod of New York and Philadelphia. In the latter part of 1763, or early part of 1764, the Presbytery of New Brunswick licensed him to preach the Gospel. Within a year after his licensure he was ordained to the full work of the ministry by the same Presbytery. This took place at the Greenwich Presbyterian Church, New Jersey, December 11th, 1764.

After his ordination, he shortly entered upon the duties of his pastorate at Oxford and Mansfield Woodhouse. Whilst attending to the duties of this pastorate he performed a large amount of labor in other fields. He preached repeatedly at Upper and Lower Hardwick, also at Bedminster, Deep Run and Smithfield. Difficulties, however, arose in his charge in 1768. April 19th, of this year, Mr. Rosbrugh represented to the Presbytery that ——————, one branch of his charge, through the removal of members beyond the bounds of the congregation, and from other causes, had become so weakened as not to be able to raise their proportion of the salary. Some of the people had expressed their willingness, under the circumstances, for the pastoral relation to be dissolved. As the other branches of his charge were not able to make up the deficiency, and as his circumstances were straightened, he expressed himself as under the disagreeable necessity of asking for a dissolution of the pastoral relation. His request came up for consideration the next day, (April 20th). The Presbytery decided that it was not expedient to grant the request at that time. This was because it did not appear that ———— had been apprised of Mr. Rosbrugh's intention to resign at that meeting of Presbytery. In fact, no representative was there from any portion of the charge. Accordingly, further consideration of the matter was postponed till the fall meeting of Presbytery. In the meantime Mr. Rosbrugh was directed to notify the people of ————
that unless they came up to their pecuniary obligations, his

services would cease among them. In case they did not, he was directed to preach one-half of his time at Greenwich, one-third at the portion of his old charge which had not been delinquent, and the remainder at discretion. When he received these instructions, he was also directed to supply one Sabbath at Smithfield, and one at Allentown, (Irish Settlement), before the spring meeting of Presbytery. October **18th, Mr. Rosbrugh** reported that he had failed to accommodate matters at ——————, and had devoted one-half of his time to Greenwich, and one-third to Oxford as directed. Presbytery adjourned to meet at Oxford on the third Wednesday of November, to further consider the troubles in Mr. Rosbrugh's charge. The result of this meeting was to direct him to labor at Oxford and Greenwich upon certain specified conditions. These conditions not being complied with, Presbytery, April 18th, 1769, released him from his charge there.

The same day a call was presented from the "people of Allentown, in the Forks of the Delaware, requesting him to take the pastoral charge of them, in connection with Greenwich." The Presbytery agreed that Mr. Rosbrugh might accept the call, provided the Allentown Church was put under the care of the Presbytery of New Brunswick, it having been under the care of the Presbytery of Abington from the formation of that Presbytery, in 1751, till its absorption by the Presbytery of Philadelphia in the union of 1758, and after that time, under the Presbytery of Philadelphia till 1769, when this stipulation was made.

Mr. Rosbrugh had been at the Settlement and had expressed his acceptance of the call April 3d, 1769, just previous to its coming up in Presbytery on the 18th. From this forward, his time was largely, if not exclusively, devoted to the Settlement and Greenwich. He attended the meeting of Synod in Philadelphia, in May of this year, and prosecuted the petition for the transfer of the Settlement Church to the Presbytery of New Brunswick.

The petition not being granted until the spring of 1770,

Mr. Rosbrugh was appointed by his Presbytery, October 19th, 1769, "constant supply" to the people of Greenwich and Allentown until the next meeting, except three Sabbaths, which he was to devote to Mount Bethel. April 17th, 1770, he was appointed to preach one Sabbath at each of the following places: Mt. Bethel, Oxford, Basking Ridge and Lower Hardwick, at which place he was to administer the Lord's Supper. The Synod, May 21st, 1770, granted the petition of the previous year, and transferred the Settlement Church to the care of the Presbytery of New Brunswick. The conditions upon which he might accept the call to the Settlement, in conjunction with Greenwich, having been fulfilled, April 15th, 1772, Mr. Rosbrugh expressed his acceptance of the call, but was not installed at that time. October 13th, 1772, the Settlement people renewed their request for his installation, which was granted. This took place October 28th, 1772, at twelve o'clock. Rev. John Guild presided and preached the sermon. The other members of the Committee of Installation were Rev. John Hanna, Rev. Jacob Vanarsdalen, and Rev. Samuel Kennedy. Mr. Rosbrugh becoming permanently identified with the Settlement, married as his second wife, Miss Jane Ralston, a daughter of Mr. James Ralston, a ruling elder in the congregation.

From his installation in October, 1772, until 1776, he was occupied with his pastoral duties in the Settlement. He attended the meeting of Synod in Philadelphia, in May, 1774, and also the meeting in May, 1776, at which time his elder, Mr. John Walker, accompanied him. These were Revolutionary times, and Mr. Rosbrugh imbibed the spirit of independence, along with his fellow countrymen. A company of soldiers was recruited in the Settlement, and Mr. Rosbrugh accompanied them to the seat of war as chaplain. When at Trenton, January 2d, 1777, he was overtaken by a company of Hessians, when comparatively alone, and by them brutally murdered. Captain Hays, from the Settlement, hastily buried his body by the wayside. It was subsequently disinterred by Rev. George Duffield, D. D., pastor of the Old Pine

Street Church, Philadelphia, and buried in the graveyard at Trenton.

Rev. Francis Peppard

The fifth pastor of the Settlement Church was Rev. Francis Peppard. He was licensed to preach the Gospel by the Presbytery of New Brunswick in the latter part of 1763, or early part of 1764, at the same time with Rev. John Rosbrugh, his predecessor in the pastorate. He was ordained to the full work of the ministry by the Presbytery of New York, in 1764-5, and continued in connection with that Presbytery till 1772-3, when he became connected with the Presbytery of New Brunswick. These were his ecclesiastical relations in 1781, when the congregation in the Settlement extended a call to him. He now commenced his labors there, and continued them, without being installed, for about two years. On account of this irregularity, the Presbytery of Philadelphia, in the fall of 1782, inquired into the matter. Accordingly, Mr. Peppard secured his dismission from the Presbytery of New Brunswick, and connected himself with the First Philadelphia Presbytery, May 23d, 1783. At the same time the congregation, by their commissioners, applied for the installation of Mr. Peppard. The time for his installation was to be the second Tuesday of August. Rev. Alexander Mitchel was appointed to preside. Rev. James Grier was to preach the sermon, and Rev. Nathaniel Irwin was to give the charge. The services did not take place in August, as appointed, but were duly attended to by the committee, October 13th. The pastorate of Mr. Peppard in the Settlement, was not a very pleasant one to him.

James Rosbrugh, son of Rev. Mr. Rosbrugh, with some other young men, desired better educational advantages than were afforded in the common schools. They procured a lot of ground on the Monoquacy creek, in the eastern portion of the congregation, and proceeded to erect an academy. From some cause, Mr. Peppard thought this would be a detriment to the welfare of the congregation, and accordingly opposed it. This raised animosities in the congregation toward him, and rendered his situation unpleasant. In addition to this he felt himself called on to exercise church discipline in certain instances, which tended to widen the breach between himself and some of his people. Further difficulties arose growing out of the payment of his salary. An unhappy state of affairs continued until October 21st, 1794, at which time Mr. Peppard asked for a dissolution of the pastoral relation. All parties were cited to appear before Presbytery at Philadelphia, November 17th. At this time the commissioner from the congregation protested against a dissolution of the pastoral relation. Notwithstanding this Presbytery released Mr. Peppard from his charge. Although the pastoral relation was dissolved, Mr. Peppard continued to minister to the people till May, 1795. His labors having ceased in the Settlement in April, 1795, he was dismissed from the Presbytery of Philadelphia to connect himself again with the Presbytery of New Brunswick. This was but a little less than two years before his death.

He died March 30th, 1797, and was buried at the Hardwick, or Yellow Frame Church, N. J.

Rev. Robert Russel

The sixth pastor of the Settlement church was Rev. Robert Russel. Mr. Russel was licensed by the Presbytery of New Castle (?) some time previous to 1797. He preached in the Settlement in 1796 and 1797. The congregation being vacant, and being well pleased with his ministerial qualifications, resolved to give him a call. The church, however, was under the care of the Philadelphia Presbytery, whilst Mr. Russel, was a licentiate under the care of the Presbytery of New Castle. In August, 1797, a contagious fever in Philadelphia prevented a regular meeting of Presbytery, and it was uncertain when a meeting could be held. At this time the Settlement people were desirous of prosecuting their call for Mr. Russel. As they could not obtain instructions how to proceed from Presbytery in regular session, they applied to a committee of the same, sitting on Presbyterial business in the month of August, at Deep Run. This committee represented the state of affairs to the Presbytery of New Castle in behalf of the Settlement congregation. Thereupon that Presbytery presented the call to him, and upon his signifying his acceptance of the same dismissed him to connect himself with the Presbytery of Philadelphia. This he did December 2d, 1797. Mr. Russel having been received, the Presbytery proceeded with his trial for ordination. They heard him preach a popular sermon, examined him on experimental religion, and systematic divinity, as parts of trial. These being sustained, Presbytery deferred further trials until the time of ordination and installation within the bounds of the congregation where he was to labor. Presbytery convened, or a committee thereof, in the Settlement, April 17th, 1798. Mr. Russel was further examined in systematic divinity, ecclesiastical history, church government, and the arts and sciences. These examinations having been sustained, the next day Mr. Russel preached a popular sermon and was ordained and installed. In these services **Dr. Ashbel** Green, of Philadelphia, preached the ordination sermon, Dr. William Tennent, of Abington, and Rev. Nathaniel Irwin, of Neshaminy, delivered the charges. This was Mr. Russel's first and last charge. Passing through the scenes spoken of in the foregoing historical sketch, between 1798 and 1827, he ended his days with the people of his first charge. After serving nearly thirty years in the pastorate, he died December 16th, 1827.

He was buried in the old burying ground near Weaversville, where the stone erected to his memory may still be seen.

Rev. Brogan Hoff

The seventh pastor of the Settlement Church was Rev. Brogan Hoff. Mr. Hoff was born at Harlington, Somerset county, New Jersey, in 1794. He graduated at Queen's College, New Brunswick, in 1815, and from the Theological Seminary, at New Brunswick, in 1818. The same year he was licensed to preach the Gospel by the Classis of New Brunswick, and became pastor of a Dutch Reformed Church in Philadelphia. Here he remained until 1824. June 10th, 1824, he was installed pastor of the Presbyterian Church, of Bridgeton, New Jersey. Here he labored until April, 1833, at which time the pastoral relation was dissolved. In the following May, he came to the Settlement as an agent of the American Sunday School Union. The congregation being pleased with him, gave him a call, which he accepted, and was installed November 12, of that year. He remained in the Settlement until the spring of 1835, at which time the pastoral relation was dissolved, and he was dismissed to the Classis of Green, March 24th. From the Settlement he went, in 1835, to the United Reformed Churches of Leeds and Kiskatom, (?) near Catskill, N. Y. Here he remained until 1842, when he removed to Germantown, New York. In the charge of Germantown, he remained until his resignation in 1850. This seems to have been his last charge, as he was without charge in 1869. Since 1869, he died of apoplexy, at his home in Germantown, New York.

Rev. Leslie Irwin

The eighth pastor of the Settlement Church was the Rev. Leslie Irwin. The following sketch of Mr. Irwin's life and labors has been furnished by his family:

"Rev. Leslie Irwin was born at Ballibay, County Monaghan, Ireland, July 22d, 1806. His parents were truly Christian people. He breathed a pious atmosphere from childhood to manhood. He obtained a liberal education, commencing at the age of ten years the study of the classics, at an academy in his own native town. At the age of fourteen he was prepared to enter college, having the Christian ministry in view at this early period of life. He was taken under the care of Monaghan Presbytery, and received a certificate of admission to college, after having passed a rigid examination by said Presbytery, as is customary for all candidates for the ministry in Ireland. Entering the Royal Belfast College, he completed his collegiate and theological course in six years. As the Synod of Ulster, (for at that time there was no General Assembly in Ireland), did not allow their candidates to be licensed till one year after completing their Theological course, Mr. Irwin engaged in teaching, and was elected principal of a Classical Academy, which his own pastor, Rev. James Worrell, founded for the purpose of giving a thorough education to young men in that section of the country. He retained this situation for six years, and labored with great fidelity and success. In this connection the fact ought not to be omitted, that his salary, £30 a year, was given to his parents, while he supported himself with the sums received for supplying vacant churches, he having been licensed to preach by the Synod some time in the second year of his position as principal of the Academy. He was a thorough linguist and, in the strict acceptation of the term, a fine scholar in general. In fact, he was qualified to fill almost any chair in the best institutions of learning in this or any other land, but his modesty kept him comparatively unknown. On resigning his position in the Academy, Mr. Irwin came to America in 1834. This he did, believing he would have a more extensive sphere of usefulness in this land. He found true friends in the Rev. Messrs. William L. McCalla and Winchester, Dr. Green, and James and William Latta. Through their agency he was invited to supply the pulpit of the Ninth Presbyterian Church of Philadelphia, Pa., for one year, in the absence of the pastor. In July, 1835, he was introduced to the Presbyterian Church in Allen Township, Northampton Co., Pa., and after preaching to them with great acceptance for a year, he was ordained and installed pastor in the autumn of 1836, on a salary of $500 a year. Some time in the years 1839-40, the iron works at Craneville, now Catasauqua, were established, some seven miles distant. As the result of earnest personal labor, and visitations from house to house on his part, a church was soon formed of over one hundred members. He then assumed charge of both churches, that at Allen Township and the newly formed church at Catasauqua, and performed an almost incredible amount of labor for both of them, riding fourteen miles every Sabbath besides attending four services, prayer-meeting and lecture combined, each week. In 1845, Mr. Irwin was married to Miss Mary Ann Wilson, daughter of John Wilson, Esq., a ruling Elder for forty-two years of the Allen Township Church. Mrs. Irwin, and three out of their four children, still survive him. He often congratulated himself as having been favored in his domestic relations and used to say that but for this he could not have sustained the great amount of labor which he performed.

After a pastorate of thirty-three years' duration he removed in May of 1868, to South Bend, Indiana, and finally to Quincy, Ills., in July of same year. Instead of feeling himself at liberty to desist from active labor on account of his enfeebled health, his heart warmed toward the people at Ellington and Burton, six and nine miles distant from his home. To these he labored, rain or shine, with untiring devotion. He aided these churches largely out of his own pocket to enable them to get a house of worship. The Presbytery of Schuyler have therefore upon their roll, the "Memorial Presbyterian Church of Ellington, and of Burton". Both are in a flourishing condition and have more than tripled their membership.

His great desire was that after his departure these churches would be in a condition to support a pastor.

For days before his decease he prayed frequently for these churches, that God would build them up and glorify Himself through them.

Early on the Sabbath morning, (November 16th, 1873), agreeably to his desire, he fell asleep in Jesus. The funeral took place on November 18th from his residence, and his remains were laid in the family vault at Ellington Home Cemetery, near the church he loved so well."

June 14th, 1925, the Walnut Street Presbyterian church of Bath, celebrated their 195th anniversary Sunday morning at ten o'clock. Rev. Raymond C. White, pastor of the Bridge Street Presbyterian Church, of Catasauqua, preached the sermon.

At the close of this service, a tablet was placed on the walls of the church by his daughter, Miss Mazie Irwin, of New York City, in honor of her father, who was pastor of this church from 1835 to 1868, and while pastor there organized the Bridge Street Church at Catasauqua in 1850 and preached there for a number of years.

Mr. Irwin was received by the Presbytery of Newton as a licentiate of Presbytery of Philadelphia, December 22d, 1835, and was ordained an evangelist.

Rev. David M. James

The ninth and present pastor of the Settlement Church is Rev. David M. James. Mr. James is a native of Cumberland Co., New Jersey. He pursued his preparatory studies for college at Easton, Pa., and entered Lafayette College there, graduating in 1852.

He studied theology at the Theological seminary, Princeton, N. J, and was licensed to preach the Gospel by the Presbytery of Passaic, July 3d, 1854. October 4th, 1854, the same Presbytery ordained him to the full work of the ministry and installed him pastor of the Mount Olive Church, N. J. Here he labored until 1869, when he became pastor of the Settlement Church, in which pastorate he continues to labor with success. A tablet to his memory has been erected in the church.

Ministers

Reverend Eleazer Wales 1731-1734.
Reverend Daniel Lawrence 1745-1752.
Reverend John Clark 1761-1766.
Reverend John Rosbrugh 1772-1777.
Reverend Francis Peppard 1783-1795.
Reverend Robert Russel 1798-1828.
Reverend Brogan Hoff 1823-1835.
Reverend Leslie Irwin 1835-1868.
Reverend David M. James, D. D., 1869-1898.
Reverend Thomas C. Sterling, Ph. D., 1898-1905.
Reverend Seth Russell Downie, A. M., 1905-1910.
Reverend H. H. Henry, D. D., 1910-1916.
Reverend H. H. Henry, D. D., Sept. 18th, 1916.—Pastor Emeritus.
Reverend Raymond S. Hittinger 1916 (Nov. 16th), 1919.
Reverend Fred G. Bulgin 1919 July 14th 1922.
Supplies since 1922,—Chamberlain and ———— Couliard.

CHAPTER IX.—CHURCH OFFICERS.

ELDERS.

During the early history of all, or nearly all, the Presbyterian Churches of America, it was customary to keep no sessional records. The church in the Irish Settlement was no exception to this rule. It passed through about one hundred years of its history without making any permanent record of who its spiritual rulers were, or who were admitted to sealing ordinances. The names of the eldership are, therefore, almost entirely lost. We can only determine who a few of them were by references incidentally made to them in the general affairs of the church and community.

It would seem Thomas Craig was one, at least, of the original elders. His name appears as an elder in attendance at the meeting of the Synod of Philadelphia, in 1731. In 1756 Dr. Franklin, in a letter to Governor Morris, speaks of "Elder Craig," of the Irish Settlement. We suppose he referred to Elder Thomas Craig.

In 1769 we know James Ralston, father-in-law of Rev. Mr. Rosbrugh, was an elder. He died in 1775. Also, we know that John Walker was an elder in 1775. He was reported as Mr. Rosbrugh's elder at a meeting of Presbytery, held at Mt. Bethel that year. He died in 1777. Who succeeded these we have not been able to learn. We know, however, that John Wilson was an elder. He was born in 1766, and died in 1857, having served in the eldership forty-two years. The late Judge James Kennedy was an elder. He was born in 1787, and died in 1872. The present eldership are Hugh R. Horner and John Horner. This is about all we have been able to learn with regard to the eldership in the Settlement Church.

SUCCESSION OF TRUSTEES UNDER THE CORPORATION.

The church, having been organized in 1728, carried on its secular affairs for about sixty years by means of officers chosen by the people. The records extant, belonging to that period, are in such a condition as to render it impossible to give an intelligent account of who looked after the secular affairs of the church. Names appear upon the books in an official capacity; but who were in office from year to year cannot be determined. This confusion, however, disappears with the year 1797. At this time the church became incorporated. The third rule adopted to govern the congregation under the charter of incorporation, was as follows:

"That six Trustees shall be chosen from said society, two of whom shall vacate on the first day of January next, and two in each successive year, and their places to be filled up by a new election, whose business shall be to settle accounts with the Treasurer on the same day yearly; to have charge of all money belonging to the society; all pews and seats in the church to be taken from and given up to the Trustees; and those who attempt to give or receive seats without their consent, shall be deemed inimical to the interests of the society, and meet a serious rebuke in Session at a future day." We subjoin the Trustees under this rule, from 1797. The third couplet shows the persons elected for the year.

1796.
Joseph Horner.	James Ralston,	Thos. Horner,
Wm. Lattimer,	Adam Clendinen,	William Moffat.

1797.
James Ralston,	Thomas Horner,	Hugh Horner,
Jos. Horner,	Wm. Lattimer,	John McNair.

1798.
Thos. Horner,	Hugh Horner,	Henry Epple,
Wm. Lattimer,	John McNair,	Joseph Horner.

1799.
Hugh Horner,	Henry Epple,	James Hays,
John McNair,	Joseph Horner,	Thos. McKeen.

1800.
Henry Epple,	James Hays,	James Ralston,
Joseph Horner,	Thos. McKeen,	Samuel Morison.

1801.

James Hays,	James Ralston,	John Clyde,
Thos. McKeen,	Samuel Morison,	James Kerr.

1802.

James **Ralston,**	John Clyde,	Hugh Wilson,
Samuel Morison,	James Kerr,	Charles Meloy.

1803.

John Clyde,	Hugh Wilson,	Edw. Humphrey,
James Kerr,	Charles Meloy,	John McNair.

1804.

Hugh Wilson,	Edw. Humphrey,	Hugh Horner,
Charles Meloy,	John McNair,	Joseph Horner.

1805.

Edw. Humphrey,	Hugh Horner,	Joseph Kerr,
John McNair,	Joseph Horner,	(?)

1806.

Hugh Horner,	Joseph Kerr,	John Wilson,
Joseph Horner,	(?)	Thomas Horner.

1807.

Joseph Kerr,	John Wilson,	Adam Clendinen,
(?)	Thomas Horner,	Robert Ralston.

1808.

John Wilson,	Adam Clendinen,	John Rosbrugh,
Thomas Horner,	Robert Ralston,	Jas. Horner, Jr.

1809.

Adam Clendinen,	John Rosbrugh,	Nicholas Neligh,
Robert Ralston,	James Horner,	James Clyde, Jr.

1810.

John Rosbrugh,	Nicholas Neligh,	James Kerr, Sr.,
James Horner,	James Clyde, Jr.	Wm. Lattimer.

1811.

Nicholas Neligh,	James Kerr, Sr.,	Edw. Humphrey,
Jas. Clyde, Jr.	Wm. Lattimer,	Jas. Horner, Sr.

CRAIG'S SETTLEMENT IN ALLEN TOWNSHIP. 371

1812.
James Kerr, Sr.,	Edw. Humphrey,	James Kerr, Jr.,
Wm. Lattimer,	Jas. Horner, Sr.	John Wilson.

1813.
Edw. Humphrey,	James Kerr, Jr.,	John Boyd,
Jas. Horner, Sr.,	John Wilson,	John Clyde, Jr.

1814.
James Kerr, Jr.,	John Boyd,	James Clendinen,
John Wilson,	John Clyde, Jr.,	Jas. Horner,
		(Son of Thos. Horner).

1815.
John Boyd,	James Clendinen,	James Kennedy,
John Clyde, Jr.,	James Horner,	Nathan Kerr.

The elections were overturned this year. Some trustees resigned. A new election resulted as follows:

John Boyd,	James Kerr, Sr.,	James Kennedy,
Hugh Wilson,	James Horner,	Robt. Horner.

1816.
James Kerr, Sr.,	James Kennedy,	James J. Horner.
James Horner,	Robert Horner,	A. E. Mulhallon.

1817.
James Kennedy,	Jas. J. Horner,	Edw. Humphrey,
Robert Horner,	A. E. Mulhallon,	Joseph Kerr.

1818.
James J. Horner,	Edw. Humphrey,	John Wilson,
A. E. Mulhallon,	Joseph Kerr,	Wm. Horner.

1819.
Edw. Humphrey,	John Wilson,	James Kennedy,
Joseph Kerr,	Wm. Horner,	Robert Horner.

1820.
John Wilson,	James Kennedy,	Edw. Humphrey,
Wm. Horner,	Robert Horner,	James Kerr.

1821.
James Kennedy	Edw. Humphrey,	George Hice,
Robert Horner,	James Kerr,	Hugh Horner,

1822.

Edw. Humphrey,	George Richie,	James J. Horner,
James Kerr,	Hugh Horner,	Abram Wilson.

George Hice, elected in 1821, resigned, and George Richie was elected to fill his place in 1822.

1823.

George Richie,	Jas. J. Horner,	Joseph Kerr,
Hugh Horner,	Abram Wilson,	Thos. Horner, Jr.

1824.

Jas. J. Horner,	Joseph Kerr,	A. E. Mulhallon,
Abram Wilson,	Thos. Horner, Jr.	William Horner.

1825.

Joseph Kerr,	A. E. Mulhallon,	James Kennedy,
Thos. Horner,	Wm. Horner,	Joseph Horner.

1826.

A. E. Mulhallon,	James Kennedy,	Jas. Kerr, Jr.,
Wm. Horner,	Joseph Horner,	Robt. Clendinen.

1827.

James Kennedy,	James Kerr, Jr.,	Joseph Kerr,
Joseph Horner,	Robt. Clendinen,	Charles Wilson.

1828.

James Kerr, Jr.,	Joseph Kerr,	James J. Horner,
Robt. Clendinen,	Charles Wilson,	William Burnet.

1829.

Joseph Kerr,	Jas. J. Horner,	Thos. Horner,
Charles Wilson,	William Burnet,	J. H. Humphrey.

Shortly previous to the election for this year, which came on January 5th, Mr. Burnet removed from the Settlement, and his place was supplied at this election by the name of James Kennedy.

1830.

James J. Horner,	Thos. Horner,	William Brown,
James Kennedy,	J. H. Humphrey,	Hugh Horner.

1831.

Thos. Horner,	William Brown,	Joseph Horner,
J. H. Humphrey,	Hugh Horner,	Charles Wilson.

Shortly previous to January 3d, 1831, when the annual election occurred, Thomas Horner removed from the congregation, and Thomas Clendinen was elected to fill the vacancy.

1832.
William Brown, Joseph Horner, Thos. Clendinen,
Hugh Horner, Charles Wilson, Chas. Humphrey.

1833.
Joseph Horner, Thos. Clendinen, James Kerr,
Charles Wilson, Chas. Humphrey, James Kennedy.

1834.
Thos. Clendinen, James Kerr, James Clyde,
Chas. Humphrey, James Kennedy, B. D. Barnes.

1835.
James Kerr, James Clyde, Hugh Horner,
James Kennedy, B. D. Barnes, Thos. Clendinen.

1836.
James Clyde, Hugh Horner. James J. Horner,
B. D. Barnes, Thos. Clendinen, Thos. Horner,

1837.
Hugh Horner, James J. Horner, Charles Wilson,
Thos. Clendinen, Thos. Horner, William Brown.

1838.
James J. Horner, Charles Wilson, Hugh Horner,
Thomas Horner, William Brown, Thos. Clendinen.

1839.
Charles Wilson, Hugh Horner, James Kerr,
William Brown, Thos. Clendinen, Joseph Horner.

1840.
Hugh Horner, James Kerr, William Wilson,
Thos. Clendinen, Joseph Horner, William Brown.

1841.
James Kerr, William Wilson, Fred W. Nagle,
Joseph Horner, William Brown, Hugh Horner.

1842.
William Wilson, Fred W. Nagle, Joseph Howell,
William Brown, Hugh Horner, Philip Insley.

1843.

Fred W. Nagle,   Joseph Howell,   James Kennedy.
Hugh Horner,   Philip Insley,   Charles Wilson.

1844.

Joseph Howell,   James Kennedy,   Hugh Horner,
Philip Insley,   Charles Wilson,   Thomas Barr.

1845.

James Kennedy,   Hugh Horner,   Joseph Brown,
Charles Wilson,   Thomas Barr,   Philip Insley.

1846.

Hugh Horner,   Joseph Brown,   William Brown,
James Kennedy,   Philip Insley,   Thos. Clendinen.

This year James Kennedy was elected to fill the place of Thomas Barr, who had removed from the Settlement.

1847.

Joseph Brown,   William Brown,   Robt. McDowell,
Philip Insley,   Thos. Clendinen,   Hugh Horner.

1848.

William Brown,   Robt. McDowell,   John Howell,
Thos. Clendinen, Hugh Horner,   Charles Wilson.

1849.

Robt. McDowell,   John Howell,   Philip Insley,
Hugh Horner,   Charles Wilson,   Joseph Brown.

1850.

John Howell,   Philip Insley,   Hugh Horner,
Charles Wilson,   Joseph Brown,   Robt. McDowell.

1851.

Philip Insley,   Hugh Horner,   Thos. Clendinen,
Joseph Brown,   Robt. McDowell,   William Brown.

1852.

Hugh Horner,   Thos. Clendinen,   Charles Wilson,
Robt. McDowell,   William Brown,   Joseph Brown.

1853.

Thos. Clendinen, Charles Wilson,   Hugh Horner,
William Brown,   Joseph Brown,   Philip Insley.

1854.

Charles Wilson,	Hugh Horner,	Thos. Clendinen,
Joseph Brown,	Philip Insley,	William Brown.

1855.

Hugh Horner,	Thos. Clendinen,	Joseph Brown,
Philip Insley,	William Brown,	Charles Wilson.

1856.

Thos. Clendinen,	Joseph Brown,	John Agnew,
William Brown,	Charles Wilson,	Hugh Horner.

1857.

Joseph Brown,	John Agnew,	Thos. Clendinen,
Charles Wilson,	Hugh Horner,	Philip Insley.

Hugh R. Horner elected for one year to fill vacancy caused by the removal of Charles Wilson. (?)

1858.

John Agnew,	Thos. Clendinen,	Hugh R. Horner,
Hugh Horner,	Philip Insley,	Joseph Brown.

1859.

Thos. Clendinen,	Hugh R. Horner,	H. Horner, Esq.,
Philip Insley,	Joseph Brown,	John Agnew.

1860.

Hugh R. Horner,	H. Horner, Esq.,	Thos. Clendinen,
Joseph Brown,	John Agnew,	Philip Insley.

1861.

H. Horner, Esq.	Thos. Clendinen,	Joseph Brown,
John Agnew,	Philip Insley,	Hugh R. Horner.

1862.

Thos. Clendinen,	Joseph Brown,	John Agnew,
Philip Insley,	Hugh R. Horner,	John Horner.

1863.

Joseph Brown,	John Agnew,	Thos. Clendinen,
Hugh R. Horner,	John Horner,	Philip Insley.

1864.

John Agnew,	Thos. Clendinen,	Joseph Brown,
John Horner,	Philip Insley,	Hugh R. Horner.

1865.

Thos. Clendinen,	Joseph Brown,	John Howell,
Philip Insley,	Hugh R. Horner,	John Agnew.

1866.

Joseph Brown,	John Howell,	Thos. Clendinen,
Hugh R. Horner,	John Agnew,	Philip Insley.

1867.

John Howell,	Thos. Clendinen,	James Blair,
John Agnew,	Philip Insley,	Hugh R. Horner.

John Horner elected for one year to fill place made vacant by the removal of John Agnew. (?)

1868.

Thos. Clendinen,	James Blair,	Joseph Brown,
Philip Insley,	Hugh R. Horner,	John Horner.

1869.

James Blair,	Joseph Brown,	Thos. Clendinen,
Hugh R. Horner,	John Horner,	Philip Insley.

1870.

Joseph Brown,	Thos. Clendinen,	James Blair,
John Horner,	Philip Insley,	Hugh R. Horner.

1871.

Thos. Clendinen,	James Blair,	John Horner,
Philip Insley,	Hugh R. Horner,	Joseph Brown.

1872.

James Blair,	John Horner,	Thos. Clendinen,
Hugh R. Horner,	Joseph Brown,	Philip Insley.

1873.

John Horner,	Thos. Clendinen,	James Blair,
Joseph Brown,	Philip Insley,	Hugh R. Horner.

1874.

Thos. Clendinen,	James Blair,	John Horner,
Philip Insley,	Hugh R. Horner,	Saml. T. Brown.

1875.

James Blair,	John Horner,	Thos. Clendinen,
Hugh R. Horner,	Saml. T. Brown,	Philip Insley.

1876.

James R. Blair,	Hugh R. Horner,	Thomas Clendinen,
Philip Insley,	John Horner,	Samuel T. Brown.

1877.

John Horner,	Samuel T. Brown,	Philip Insley,
James R. Blair,	Hugh R. Horner,	Thomas Clendinen.

1878.

Thomas Clendinen,	Philip Insley,	John Horner,
Samuel T. Brown,	James R. Blair,	Hugh R. Horner.

On motion, Isaac B. Insley was chosen to fill the vacancy on Board of Trustees caused by the death of Philip Insley.

1879.

Hugh R. Horner,	James R. Blair,	Thomas Clendinen,
Isaac B. Insley,	John Horner,	Samuel T. Brown.

May 20, 1879, Theodore Howell was elected Trustee to fill the unexpired term of Thomas Clendinen, deceased.

1880.

John Horner,	Samuel T. Brown,	Hugh R. Horner,
James R. Blair,	Theodore Howell,	Isaac B. Insley.

1881.

Samuel T. Brown,	Isaac Insley,	John Horner,
Theodore Howell,	Hugh R. Horner,	James R. Blair.

1882.

James R. Blair,	Hugh R. Horner,	Theodore Howell,
John Horner,	Samuel T. Brown,	Isaac B. Insley.

1883.

Baxter B. McClure,	Samuel T. Brown,	James R. Blair,
Hugh R. Horner,	Theodore Howell,	Isaac B. Insley.

1884.

Isaac B. Insley,	Theodore H. Howell,	Baxter B. McClure,
Samuel T. Brown,	James R. Blair,	Hugh R. Horner.

1885.

Hugh R. Horner,	John H. Blair,	Isaac B. Insley,
Theodore Howell,	Baxter B. McClure,	Thomas Worman.

Thomas Worman elected to fill the unexpired term of Samuel T. Brown.

1886.

B. B. McClure,	Thomas Worman,	Hugh R. Horner,
John H. Blair,	Isaac Insley,	Theodore Howell.

1887.

Isaac B. Insley,	Levi Worman,	B. B. McClure,
Thomas Worman,	Hugh R. Horner,	James R. Blair.

1888.

Hugh R. Horner,	John H. Blair,	Isaac B. Insley,
Levi Worman,	B. B. McClure,	Thomas Worman.

1889.

B. B. McClure,	Thomas Worman,	Hugh R. Horner,
John H. Blair,	Isaac Insley,	Levi Worman.

1890.

Isaac B. Insley,	Dr. J. O. Berlin,	B. B. McClure,
Thomas Worman,	Hugh R. Horner,	John H. Blair.

1891.

The minutes of the congregational meeting for this year could not be found.

1892.

B. B. McClure,	Thomas Worman,	Isaac B. Insley,
Dr. J. O. Berlin,	Hugh R. Horner,	John H. Blair.

1893.

Isaac B. Insley,	Dr. J. O. Berlin,	B. B. McClure,
Hugh R. Horner,	John H. Blair,	Thomas Worman.

1894.

Hugh R. Horner,	John H. Blair,	Isaac B. Insley,
Dr. J. O. Berlin,	B. B. McClure,	Thomas Worman.

1895.

B. B. McClure,	Thomas Worman,	Hugh R. Horner,
John H. Blair,	Isaac B. Insley,	Dr. J. O. Berlin.

1896.

Isaac B. Insley,	B. B. McClure,	Hugh R. Horner,
Dr. J. O. Berlin,	Thomas Worman,	John H. Blair.

1897.

Hugh R. Horner,	Isaac B. Insley,	B. B. McClure,
John H. Blair,	Dr. J. O. Berlin,	Thomas Worman.

1898.

Thomas Worman,	B. B. McClure,	Hugh R. Horner,
John H. Blair,	Isaac B. Insley,	Dr. J. O. Berlin.

1899.

Isaac B. Insley,	Dr. J. O. Berlin,	Thomas Worman,
B. B. McClure,	Hugh R. Horner,	John H. Blair.

1900.

Hugh R. Horner,	John H. Blair,	Isaac B. Insley,
Dr. J. O. Berlin,	Thomas Worman,	B. B. McClure.

1901.

B. B. McClure,	Thomas Worman,	Hugh R. Horner,
John H. Blair,	Isaac B. Insley,	J. O. Berlin.

1902.

Frank L. Worman,		Dr. J. O. Berlin,
B. B. McClure,	Thomas Worman,	James K. Worman.

Alfred Whitesell was elected for one year to fill the unexpired term of Mr. Hugh R. Horner.

1903.

Frank L. Worman, J. Allison Blair, B. B. McClure.
James K. Worman, Thomas Worman,

Chas. I. Berlin was elected to fill the unexpired term of his deceased father.

1904.

Thomas Worman,	Chas. I. Berlin,	James K. Worman,
B. B. McClure,	J. Alison Blair,	Frank L. Worman.

1905.

R. Kenedy Worman was elected to fill the unexpired term of his deceased father.

Chas. I. Berlin,	David M. James,	B. B. McClure.
J. Alison Blair,	James K. Worman,	

1906.

James K. Worman,	J. Alison Blair,	R. Kenedy Worman,
Chas. I. Berlin,	David M. James,	B. B. McClure.

1907.
R. Kenedy Worman, B. B. McClure,   James K. Worman,
J. Alison Blair,   Chas. I. Berlin,   David M. James.

1908.
Dr. Franklin J. Hahn, David M. James, R. Kenedy Worman,
James K. Worman, J. Alison Blair,   B. B. McClure.

1909.
James K. Worman, J. Alison Blair,   Dr. Franklin J. Hahn.
R. Kenedy Worman, David M. James,

1910.
B. B. McClure,   R. Kenedy Worman, James K. Worman,
J. Alison Blair, David M. James,   Dr. Franklin J. Hahn.

1911.
Dr. Robert Hays Horner was elected to fill the unexpired term of B. B. McClure of 2 years.
D. M. James,   Dr. Franklin J. Hahn, R. Kenedy Worman,
James K. Worman, J. Alison Blair,

1912.
James K. Worman, J. Alison Blair,   Dr. R. H. Horner,
D. M. James,   Franklin J. Hahn,   R. Kenedy Worman.

1913.
Dr. R. H. Horner, R. K. Worman,   James K. Worman,
J. Alison Blair, D. M. James,   Dr. Franklin J. Hahn.

1914.
John S. Worman was elected to fill the unexpired term of his brother, R. K. Worman (for 2 years).
Dr. Franklin J. Hahn, David M. James, James K. Worman.
Dr. R. H. Horner, J. Alison Blair,

1915.
James K. Worman, J. Alison Blair,   John S. Worman,
David M. James, Dr. Franklin J. Hahn, Dr. R. H. Horner.

1916.
John S. Worman,   Robt. Hays Horner, James K. Worman,
J. Alison Blair, David M. James,   Dr. Franklin J. Hahn.

1917.
Dr. Franklin J. Hahn, David M. James, John S. Worman,
Dr. R. H. Horner, James K. Worman,   J. Alison Blair.

1918.

J. Alison Blair, Frank Harding, Dr. Franklin J. Hahn,
David M. James, Dr. R. H. Horner.

Clarence Graver was elected to fill the unexpired term of John S. Worman, Trustee.

1919.

Clarence Graver, Geo. F. Hutchison, J. Alison Blair,
Frank Harding, Dr. Franklin J. Hahn, David M. James.

1920.

D. M. James, Dr. Franklin J. Hahn, Clarence Graver,
Geo. F. Hutchison, J. Alison Blair, Frank Harding.

Dr. Robt. H. Horner was elected to fill the unexpired term of Clarence Graver.

1921.

J. Alison Blair, Frank S. Harding, Dr. R. H. Horner,
D. M. James, Dr. Franklin J. Hahn, Geo. F. Hutchison.

1922.

Edgar P. Miller, Geo. F. Hutchison, J. Alison Blair,
Dr. Franklin J. Hahn, Dr. R. H. Horner, D. M. James.

1923.

Dr. Franklin J. Hahn, David M. James, Edgar P. Miller,
Geo. F. Hutchison, J. Alison Blair, Dr. R. H. Horner.

1924.

Dr. R. H. Horner, J. Alison Blair, Dr. Franklin J. Hahn,
David M. James, Edgar P. Miller, Geo. F. Hutchison.

1925.

Edgar Miller, Geo. F. Hutchison, Dr. Franklin J. Hahn,
David M. James, J. Alison Blair, Dr. R. H. Horner.

[Copy furnished by Dr. Robert Hays Horner]

ELDERS.

Thomas Craig,	1731	John Horner,	1872–1882
James Ralston,	1769–1775	John M. McIlhaney,	1883–1907
John Walker,	1775–1777	Baxter B. McClure,	1883–1911
John Wilson,	1815–1857	David M. James, Jr.,	1905–
James Kennedy,	1828–1872	Peter E. Kreidler,	1905–1916
Chas. Wilson,	1842–1857	Chas. I. Berlin,	1905–1907
Hugh R. Horner,	1872–1901		

1906.
Peter E. Kreidler, Baxter B. McClure, John M. McIlhaney,
Chas. I. Berlin, David M. James,

1907.
Peter E. Kreidler, Baxter B. McClure, John M. McIlhaney,
Chas. I. Berlin, David M. James,

1908.
Peter E. Kreidler, J. T. Lerch, A. Lambert,
Baxter B. McClure, David M. James, J. B. Allen.

1910.
Peter E. Kreidler, Daniel F. Worman, J. T. Lerch,
B. B. McClure, David M. James, J. B. Allen.

1911.
J. T. Lerch, Robt. O. Stradley, Peter E. Kreidler,
Daniel F. Worman, David M. James, J. B. Allen.

1912.
David M. James, J. B. Allen, J. T. Lerch,
Peter E. Kreidler, Daniel F. Worman, Robt. O. Stradley.

1913.
Daniel F. Worman, Peter E. Kreidler, Wm. D. Worman,
David M. James, J. T. Lerch, Robt. O. Stradley.

1914.
Robt. O. Stradley, J. T. Lerch, Daniel F. Worman,
Peter E. Kreidler, Wm. D. Worman, David M. James.

1915.
D. M. James, Wm. D. Worman, Robt. O. Stradley,
J. T. Lerch, Daniel F. Worman, Peter E. Kreidler.

1916.
Peter E. Kreidler, Daniel F. Worman, D. M. James,
Wm. D. Worman, Robt. O. Stradley, J. T. Lerch.

1917.
J. T. Lerch, Daniel F. Worman, D. M. James,
Wm. D Worman, Robt. O. Stradley, Dr. Franklin J. Hahn.

1918.
David M. James, Wm. D. Worman, J. T. Lerch,
Daniel F. Worman, Robt. O. Stradley, Dr. Franklin J. Hahn.

1919.

Daniel F. Worman, D. M. James, Wm. D. Worman,
Dr. Franklin J. Hahn, F. D. Harding, Clarence Graver.

1920.

Dr. Franklin J. Hahn, Frank S. Harding, Daniel F. Worman,
W. D. Worman, D. M. James, Clarence Graver.

1921.

D. M. James, W. D. Worman, Dr. Franklin J. Hahn,
F. S. Harding, Daniel F. Worman, Clarence Graver.

1922.

D. M. James, D. F. Worman,

1923.

Daniel F. Worman, Dr. Franklin J. Hahn, Asa K. McIlhaney,
Dr. R. H. Horner, David M. James, Wm. D. Worman.

1924.

Asa K. McIlhaney, Daniel F. Worman, Dr. Franklin J. Hahn,
Wm. D. Worman, Dr. R. H. Horner, David M. James.

1925.

Dr. R. H. Horner, Asa K. McIlhaney, David M. James,
Daniel F. Worman, Dr. Franklin J. Hahn, Wm. D. Worman.

OFFICERS OF THE BOARD.

	PRESIDENTS.	SECRETARIES.	TREASURERS.
1797.	J. McNair, (?)	J. Ralston, (?)	Hugh Horner.
1798.	J. McNair, (?)	J. Ralston, (?)	Hugh Horner.
1799.	Henry Epple,	J. Ralston, (?)	Hugh Horner.
1800.	Henry Epple,	Sam. Morrison,	Jas. Ralston.
1801.	James Kerr,	Sam. Morrison,	Jas. Ralston.
1802.	James Kerr,	Sam. Morrison,	Tho. McKeen.
1803.	James Kerr,	E. Humphrey,	Tho. McKeen.
1804.	John McNair,	E. Humphrey,	Tho. McKeen.
1805.	J. McNair, (?)	E. Humphrey, (?)	Tho. McKeen.
1806.	Jos. Horner,	Jos. Kerr,	Tho. McKeen.
1807.	Thos. Horner,	Jos. Kerr,	Tho. McKeen.
1808.	John Wilson	Jas. Horner, Jr.,	Tho. McKeen.
1809.	A. Clendinen, (?)	J. Horner, Jr., (?)	Tho. McKeen.

PRESIDENTS.	SECRETARIES.	TREASURERS.
1810. Jas. Kerr, Sr.,	Nich. Neligh,	Tho. McKeen.
1811. Ed. Humphrey	Nich. Neligh,	Tho. McKeen.
1812. Jas. Kerr, Sr.,	Jas. Horner, Sr.,	Tho. McKeen.
1813. John Wilson,	John Boyd,	Tho. McKeen.
1814. Jas. Kerr,	John Clyde,	Tho. McKeen.
1815. Robt. Horner,	John Boyd,	J. H. Horner.
1816. Robt. Horner,	Jas. Kennedy,	J. H. Horner.
1817. Jas. J. Horner,	Jas. Kennedy,	J. H. Horner.
1818. Ed. Humphrey,	Wm. Horner,	J. H. Horner.
1819. Ed. Humphrey,(?)	Wm. Horner,(?)	J. H. Horner.
1820. John Wilson,	Wm. Horner,	J. H. Horner.
1821. Ed. Humphrey,	Hugh Horner,	J. H. Horner.
1822. Ed. Humphrey,	Hugh Horner,	J. H. Horner.
1823. Abram Wilson,	Hugh Horner,	J. H. Horner.
1824. Jas. J. Horner,	Wm. Horner,	J. H. Horner.
1825. Jas. Kennedy,	Wm. Horner,	J. H. Horner.
1826. Jas. Kerr, Jr.,	Jos. Horner,	Robt. Horner.
1827. Jas. Kennedy,	Jos. Horner,	Robt. Horner.
1828. Jas. Kerr, Jr., (?)	Chas. Wilson, (?)	Robt. Horner.
1829. Jas. J. Horner,	Chas. Wilson,	Robt. Horner.
1830. Jas. J. Horner,	Wm. Brown,	Robt. Horner.
1831. Hugh Horner,	Wm. Brown,	Robt. Horner.
1832. Hugh Horner,	Wm. Brown,	Robt. Horner.
1833. Jas. Kennedy,	T. Clendinen,	Robt. Horner.
1834. Jas. Kennedy,(?)	T. Clendinen, (?)	Robt. Horner.
1835. Jas. Kennedy,	T. Clendinen,	Robt. Horner.
1836. Jas. J. Horner,	Thos. Horner,	Robt. Horner.
1837. Jas. J. Horner,	Thos. Horner,	Robt. Horner.
1838. Jas. J. Horner,	Thos. Horner,	Robt. Horner.
1839. Wm. Brown,	Hugh Horner,	Robt. Horner.
1840. Wm. Brown,	Hugh Horner,	Robt. Horner.
1841. Wm. Brown,	Hugh Horner,	Robt. Horner.
1842. Wm. Brown,	Hugh Horner,	Robt. Horner.
1843. Jas. Kennedy,	Hugh Horner,	Robt. Horner.
1844. Jas. Kennedy,	Hugh Horner,	Robt. Horner.
1845. Jas. Kennedy,	Hugh Horner,	Jos. Horner.

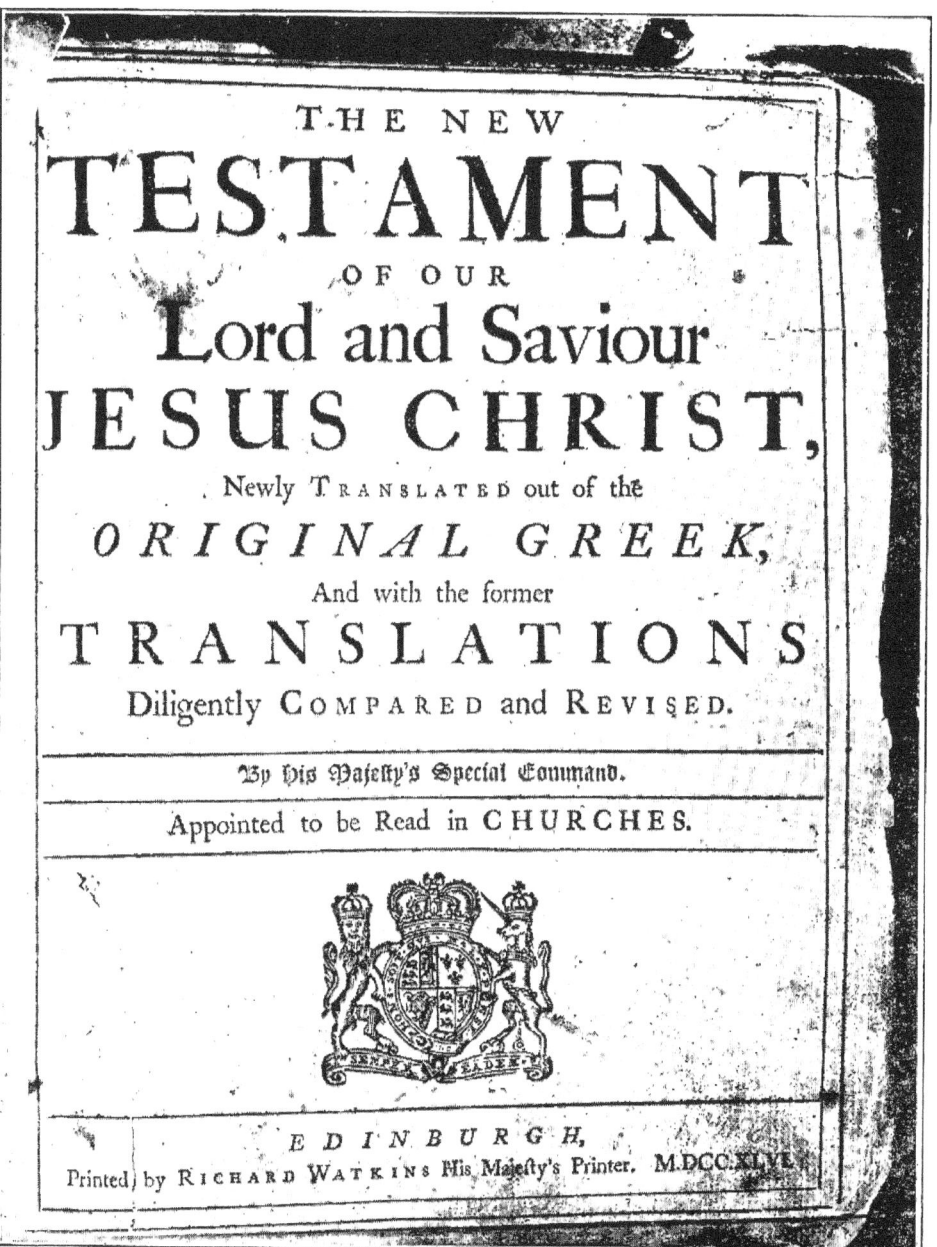

This is a Facsimile of the Title-Page of the James Horner Bible. (See page 250.)

This Illustrates the Hair-hide Cover of the Horner Bible. (See page 250.)

PRESIDENTS.	SECRETARIES.	TREASURERS.
1846. Wm. Brown,	Hugh Horner,	Jos. Horner.
1847. Wm. Brown,	Hugh Horner,	Jos. Horner.
1848. Wm. Brown,	Hugh Horner,	Jos. Horner.
1849. Jos. Brown,	Hugh Horner,	Jos. Horner.
1850. Jos. Brown,	Hugh Horner,	Jos. Horner.
1851. Jos. Brown,	Hugh Horner,	Jos. Horner.
1852. Wm. Brown,	Hugh Horner,	Jos. Horner.
1853. Wm. Brown,	Hugh Horner,	Jos. Horner.
1854. Joseph Brown,	Hugh Horner,	Jos. Horner.
1855. Joseph Brown,	Hugh Horner,	Jos. Horner.
1856. Jos. Brown, (?)	Hugh Horner, (?)	Jos. Horner.
1857. Joseph Brown,	Hugh Horner,	Jos. Horner.
1858. Joseph Brown,	Hugh Horner,	Jos. Horner.
1859. Joseph Brown,	Hugh Horner,	Jos. Horner.
1860. Joseph Brown,	Hugh Horner,	Jos. Horner.
1861. Joseph Brown,	Hugh Horner,	Jos. Horner.
1862. Joseph Brown,	Jno. Horner,	Jos. Horner.
1863. Joseph Brown,	Jno. Horner,	Jos. Horner.
1864. Joseph Brown,	Jno. Horner,	Jos. Brown.
1865. Joseph Brown,	H. R. Horner,	Jos. Brown.
1866. Thos. Clendinen,	H. R. Horner,	Jos. Brown.
1867. Thos. Clendinen,	H. R. Horner,	Jos. Brown.
1868. Thos. Clendinen,	H. R. Horner,	Jos. Brown.
1869. Thos. Clendinen,	H. R. Horner,	Jos. Brown.
1870. Thos. Clendinen,	H. R. Horner,	Jos. Brown.
1871. Thos. Clendinen,	H. R. Horner,	Jos. Brown.
1872. Thos. Clendinen,	H. R. Horner,	Jos. Brown.
1873. Thos. Clendinen,	H. R. Horner,	Jos. Brown.
1874. Thos. Clendinen,	H. R. Horner,	Jos. Horner.
1875. Thos. Clendinen,	H. R. Horner,	Jos. Horner.

[By a glance at the list of the members of the Board of Trustees and those of the Session, it will appear that James Horner (Emigrant 1728) and his descendants for five generations in direct line were represented either in the Board or in the Session. The present representative is Elder Robert Hays Horner, of Bath, Pa. Such a record is unusual, as well as commendable.]

PRESIDENTS.	SECRETARIES.	TREASURERS.
1876. Thos. Clendinen,	Hugh R. Horner,	Jos. Brown.
1877. Thos. Clendinen,	Hugh R. Horner,	Jos. Brown.
1878. Thos. Clendinen,	Hugh R. Horner,	Jos. Brown.
1879. Sam'l T. Brown,	Hugh R. Horner,	Jos. Brown.
1880. Sam'l T. Brown,	John Horner,	Hugh R. Horner.
1881. Sam'l T. Brown,	John Horner,	Hugh R. Horner.
1882. Sam'l T. Brown,	John Horner,	Hugh R. Horner.
1883. Sam'l T. Brown,	B. B. McClure,	Hugh R. Horner.
1884. Isaac B. Insley,	B. B. McClure,	Hugh R. Horner.
1885. Isaac B. Insley,	B. B. McClure,	Hugh R. Horner.
1886. Isaac B. Insley,	B. B. McClure,	Hugh R. Horner.
1887. Isaac B. Insley,	B. B. McClure,	Hugh R. Horner.
1888. Isaac B. Insley,	B. B. McClure,	Hugh R. Horner.
1889. Isaac B. Insley,	B. B. McClure,	Hugh R. Horner.
1890. Isaac B. Insley,	Dr. J. O. Berlin,	Hugh R. Horner.
1891. Minutes for this year were not to be found.		
1892. Isaac B. Insley,	B. B. McClure,	Hugh R. Horner.
1893. Isaac B. Insley,	B. B. McClure,	Hugh R. Horner.
1894. Isaac B. Insley,	B. B. McClure,	Hugh R. Horner.
1895. Isaac B. Insley,	B. B. McClure,	Hugh R. Horner.
1896. Isaac B. Insley,	B. B. McClure,	Hugh R. Horner.
1897. Isaac B. Insley,	B. B. McClure,	Hugh R. Horner.
1898. Isaac B. Insley,	B. B. McClure,	Hugh R. Horner.
1899. Isaac B. Insley,	B. B. McClure,	Hugh R. Horner.
1900. John H. Blair,	B. B. McClure,	Hugh R. Horner.
1901. John H. Blair,	B. B. McClure,	Hugh R. Horner.
1902. Alfred Whitesell,	B. B McClure,	James K. Worman.
1903. Dr. J. O. Berlin,	B. B. McClure,	James K. Worman.
1904. Chas. I. Berlin,	B. B. McClure,	James K. Worman.
1905. Chas. I. Berlin,	B. B. McClure,	James K. Worman.
1906. David M. James,	B. B. McClure,	James K. Worman.
1907. David M. James,	B. B. McClure,	James K. Worman.
1908. David M. James,	B. B. McClure,	James K. Worman.
1909. David M. James,	B. B. McClure,	James K. Worman.
1910. David M. James,	B. B. McClure,	James K. Worman.
1911. David M. James,	Dr. R. H. Horner,	James K. Worman.

PRESIDENTS.	SECRETARIES.	TREASURERS.
1912. David M. James,	Dr. R. H. Horner,	James K. Worman.
1913. David M. James,	Dr. R. H. Horner,	James K. Worman.
1914. David M. James,	Dr. R. H. Horner,	James K. Worman.
1915. David M. James,	Dr. R. H. Horner,	James K. Worman.
1916. David M. James,	Dr. R. H. Horner,	James K. Worman.
1917. David M. James,	Dr. R. H. Horner,	James K. Worman.

(Temporary Secretary)

1918. David M. James,	Robt. H. Horner,	James K. Worman.
1919. David M. James,	Frank S. Harding,	James K. Worman.
1920. David M. James,	Frank S. Harding,	Clarence Graver.
1921. David M. James,	Dr. R. H. Horner,	Geo. F. Hutchison.
1922. David M. James,	Dr. R. H. Horner,	Geo. F. Hutchison.
1923. David M. James,	Dr. R. H. Horner,	Geo. F. Hutchison.
1924. David M. James,	Dr. R. H. Horner,	Geo. F. Hutchison.
1925. David M. James,	Dr. R. H. Horner,	David M. James

was elected until Jan. 1st, 1926

COLLECTORS OF SALARY UNDER THE CORPORATION.

The sixth rule for the government of the Board of Trustees, adopted by them January 31st, 1800, was as follows:

"The Board shall, at the meeting on the last Saturday of September, in every year, (as appointed in rule first,) make out duplicates for pew rent for the then present year, and deliver them to collectors to be then appointed, with a warrant from the President annexed, authorizing them to collect the same. Each collector will be expected to collect his own duplicate, or show cause why he cannot."

Under this rule the following collectors were appointed:

	Names of Collectors.		No. of Contributors.
1800.	James Horner, Jr.,	Robert Hays.	48
1801.	John Clyde, Jr.,	James Kerr, Jr.	48
1802.	James Clyde, Jr.,	James McNair.	44
1803.	Thomas Horner,	William Moffat.	39
1804.	Alexander Wilson,	Nathan Kerr.	41
1805.	Edward Humphrey,	James Rosbrugh.	33
1806.	Robert Ralston,	Thomas Horner.	36

	Names of Collectors.		No. of Contributors.
1807.	James Horner,	James Kerr.	37
1807.	(Extra) James Clyde,	Thomas Horner.	28
1808.	(Regular) Jas. Clendinen,	Edw'd Humphrey.	36
1809.	Samuel Ralston,	James Horner.	36
1810.	Abram Wilson,	John Lattimer.	44
1811.	Robert Horner,	Joseph Kerr.	(?) 37
1812.	John Clyde,	James (T.) Horner.	38
1813.	John Lattimer,	William Horner.	39
1814.	Joseph Horner, Jr.,	William Clendinen.	40
1815.	James Lattimer,	Hugh Horner.	42
1816.	Arthur E. Mulhallon,	Thomas Horner, Jr.	52
1817.	Samuel Horner,	James Kerr, Jr.	53
1818.	George Hice,	William Clendinen.	56
1819.	Hugh Wilson,	Hugh Horner.	50
1820.	Joseph Kerr,	Joseph Horner, Jr.	50
1821.	George Richie,	Thomas Horner.	51
1822.	John Wilson,	Thomas Clendinen.	55
1823.	James Kennedy,	John Humphrey.	53
1824.	John Boyd,	James Kerr, Jr.	53
1825.	Charles Wilson,	Charles Humphrey.	52
1826.	William Wilson,	Hugh Horner.	53
1827.	William Burnet,	Thomas Horner.	48
1828.	James Kennedy,	John H. Humphrey.	77
1829.	Thomas Clendinen,	Joseph Horner, Jr.	71
1830.	Joseph Kerr,	William Wilson.	67
1831.	Charles Humphrey,	John Wilson, Jr.	55
1832.	James Kerr,	Daniel George.	58
1833.	(No record of Collectors.	Pews rented out Dec. 4th.)	
1834.	Hugh Horner,	Charles Wilson.	41
1835.	William Brown,	Frederick W. Nagle.	47
1836.	Robert Clendinen,	William Wilson.	44
1837.	James Kerr,	Joseph Horner.	43
1838.	Thomas Horner,	John Wilson.	43
1839.	Thomas Clendinen,	Philip Insley.	44
1840.	James Kerr,	James Kennedy.	43
1841.	William Wilson,	Robert Clendinen.	43

	Names of Collectors.	No. of Contributors.	
1842.	Frederick W. Nagle,	Joseph Horner.	58
1843.	James J. Horner,	Thomas Clendinen.	65
1844.	John Lyle,	Isaac Insley.	54
1845.	William Wilson,	Robert Clendinen.	57
1846.	Robert McDowell,	James Kerr.	50
1847.	Frederick W. Nagle,	Charles Wilson.	48
1848.	John Horner,	Charles Stewart.	43
1849.	James Blair,	Thomas Clendinen.	44
1850.	Hugh R. Horner,	Joseph Brown.	46
1851.	Robert Clendinen,	Isaac Insley.	43
1852.	John Horner,	Charles Wilson.	44
1853.	John Agnew,	Thomas Clendinen.	44
1854.	Joseph Brown,	Hugh R. Horner.	46
1855.	Isaac Insley,	John Horner.	41
1856.	Philip Insley,	Thomas Clendinen.	42
1857.	Thomas Barr,	John Agnew.	43
1858.	Joseph Brown,	Isaac Insley.	42
1859.	Thomas Clendinen,	James Blair.	43
1860.	John Horner,	Hugh R. Horner.	34
1861.	Thomas Clendinen,	Philip Insley.	34
1862.	Joseph Brown,	James Blair.	32
1863.	William Agnew,	John Horner.	30
1864.	Hugh R. Horner,	Thomas Clendinen.	26
1865.	Joseph Brown,	Philip Insley.	28
1866.	Thomas Clendinen,	Hugh R. Horner.	27
1867.	James Blair,	John Horner.	24
1868.	(No duplicates, being without a pastor.)		
1869.	Thomas Clendinen,	Hugh R. Horner.	28
1870.	Samuel T. Brown,	John H. Blair.	29
1871.	John Horner,	Charles Warman.	42
1872.	Robert Blair,	Samuel T. Brown.	35
1873.	Thomas Clendinen,	Hugh R. Horner.	50
1874.	John Horner,	Thomas Warman.	52
1875.	(Appointed in November.)		

Subscriptions Towards Repairing the Old Academy "for a Place of Worship"

"On demand we promise to pay John Wilson and James Kennedy, the sum annexed to our names for the purpose of repairing what is called the Old Academy in Allen Township.

John Wilson _____$50.00	John Steiner _____ 2.00
James J. Horner ____ 50.00	Rebecca Mulhallen . 20.00
Robert Horner _____ 50.00	James Clyde _____ 25.00
James Kennedy _____ 50.00	William Boyd _____ 5.00
R. D. Barnes _____ 20.00	James Otul (?) _____ 5.00
Jacob Kern _____ 20.00	Philip Insley _____ 3.00
Jacob Snyder _____ 5.00	Abram Wilson _____ 20.00
Daniel Steckel _____ 5.00	
M. G. Scott _____ 5.00	1819-20

James Kennedy collected 210.00

200.00 paid Robert Horner

10.00 paid J. J. Horner

September 5th Robert Horner paid one hundred dollars _____$100.00

September 20—Paid R. Horner fifty dollars_ 50.00

September 24—Paid R. Horner twenty dollars 20.00

$170.00

October 8—Paid R. Horner thirty dollars ____ 30.00

$200.00

Copy of Resolutions re Old Academy.

At a meeting of a number of members of the English congregation of Allen Township held in pursuance of public notice at the Academy on Saturday the 29th of April, 1820 for the purpose of adopting measures preparatory to fitting up and making more comfortable the said Academy for a house of public worship.

The Rev. Robert Russel was appointed chairman and J.

Ralston Sec'y, when the following resolutions were unanimously adopted:—

1st Resolved, That Hugh Wilson, James Kennedy and James J. Horner be a committee to take, or procure subscriptions—and collect and furnish sufficient funds for the purpose of repairing and fixing up said Academy in such manner as shall hereafter be directed for a house of public worship.

2d Resolved that William Moffat, John Wilson and Doctor John Boyd be a committee to superintend, arrange and direct the repairing of the Academy for a House of Worship as aforesaid, by placing therein a sufficient number of comfortable seats or benches, and erecting a temporary pulpit in the north end of the house, and also, to repair as far as they conveniently can the windows and roof thereof.

3d Resolved that the first mentioned committee are hereby required and directed to pay over to the second, or committee of arrangement the necessary funds which by their appointment they are required to collect for the execution of the second resolution.

By order of the meeting,

J. Ralston, Sec'y.

The Old Academy.

"In 1785, an Academy was erected in Allen Township, (now East Allen), on the Monocacy Creek, about a mile south of the borough of Bath, in the center of what is known as the 'Irish Settlement'. A number of the citizens in the settlement were anxious that their sons should have better advantages of acquiring an education than the schools of that time in the neighborhood afforded. In view of which they raised money for the erection of the building by voluntary contributions. The school was commenced immediately after the completion of the building, with Robert Andrews, A. M., a graduate of Trinity College, Dublin, as principal.

In this Academy, among others, George Wolf, who subsequently became Governor of this State, and the unflinching friend of the present school system, received a classical education. A debating society was also connected with the school, and it is said that George with a number of young men who came out from Easton, on horseback, took an active part in the debates. On relinquishing his studies under Mr. Andrews, he acted as principal in the Academy with credit."

"The old Academy was, in 1826, abandoned for school purposes. It had, however, exerted a potent influence upon the people of the entire community, and impressed on them the importance of a higher education. It was under Presbyterian control, and its influence had not a little to do with the establishment of Lafayette College, in 1826. This academy is still standing, although it has been dismantled, but the substantial exterior, with moss-covered roof presents nearly the same appearance it did over a century ago when frequented by such men as George Wolf, Thomas McKeen and others who have since occupied prominent positions in the world."

The old Academy was definitely set apart for a house of worship in 1813. As the author's father, born in 1806, attended school during the latter days in which it was used for such purpose, it would indicate that it was used for school as well as church purposes as late as 1823.

Under date of Feb. 16, 1878, he says, "As regards the Academy, I can remember going to school in it. I think the little frame school house, (near by and to take the place of the Academy for school purposes),was built when I was about seventeen years old. I studied grammar in it (Academy) under Thomas Moffat, I think, when I was about that age. I can give you the names of some of the teachers who taught in the Academy before that:—William G. Scott, who married Miss Lattimer; William Boyd, brother of Dr. Boyd; Mr. Kellog, from Bucks County, and Mr. Price, who married Miss Brown, daughter of Dr. Boyd's first wife. These are all I can remember. It was, however, nothing more than a common school. It had ceased to be used as an academy before my day. I think I can remember to have heard that it was procured from Thomas McKeen, but in what way, I do not remember to have heard. I remember there was a tolerably good library there when I was a boy, and it was removed to John Wilson's. I remember that I borrowed some books out of it while it was at Mr. Wilson's, but I do not know what became of it."

It is said the Old Academy Library was sold at auction.

Records of the "Old Academy Debating Society".

Constitution of the Franklin Society, with the By-Laws, Minutes, &c. Allen Township, Northampton County, December 26, 1807.

J. Moore, Secretary.

Proposition.—Whereas we, the subscribers, having taken into view the advantages resulting from a well regulated **Polemical Society,** as it has a tendency to incite members to reading and meditation, to improve in them, that useful and ornamental art of eloquence, by a free and liberal discussion of various interesting subjects of debate, of a moral, political, and philosophical tendency; now therefore, we in order to avail ourselves of these as well as the many other advantages arising therefrom, do form ourselves into a society of the foregoing description, under the name and style of Franklin Society; and do ordain and establish the following rules and regulations as the constitution of government for the same. Witness our hands:—

Members' Names.

Honorary Members:—Henry Epple, Thos. Horner, Joseph Horner, Michael Weaver, John Weaver.

Members:—

James Horner, Sr.	Joseph Kerr	Robert Horner
James Horner, Jr.	Charles Wilson	John Clyde
John Moore	Hugh Wilson	Robert Ralston
James Horner	James Clyde	John Kerr
Andrew Hagenbuch	John Rosbrugh	John Wilson
Thos. McKeen	D. M. MacGregor	James Ralston

Constitution similar to those of that period.

By-Laws.

Article First—Of Order.

Section 1st. The speaker on any subject under discussion in the society, shall address his discourse to the President.

Section 2d. The Respondents and Opponents shall take their seats according to the direction of the President, and in the order in which they were chosen.

Section 3d. All motions must be seconded, and no vote shall be taken on any motion until the previous question is taken.

Section 4th. No member shall be interrupted while he is speaking except it shall be to call him in order, or to explain a mistake.

Section 5th. No member shall be allowed to smoke segars after the house is called to order, until adjourned.

Section 6th. The following shall be the order in which the business of the society shall be done:—

1st. The Secretary shall call the roll.
2d. The minutes of the preceding meeting shall be read.
3d. Delinquent members shall make their excuses.
4th. New members, if any, to be elected.
5th. A new subject to be chosen.
6th. A Respondent and Opponent to be appointed.
7th. The Committee to produce new subjects of debate at the next meeting, to be appointed.
8th. The President shall call for new motions.
9th. The debate, to be opened by Respondent.
10th. The decision.
11th. Adjournment.

Section 7th. That no member shall speak more than three times on the subject of debate, without leave of the President.

Article Second—Of Fines.

Section 1st. The meetings of the society shall be held every Saturday evening; and any member who shall not attend at any of the stated meetings of the society, shall pay a fine of three cents; but the President shall have the power to remit the fines of absentees, if their excuses for their absences are satisfactory to him.

Section 2d. If any member shall commit any breach of order, and shall, after being called to order by the President, repeat or continue the disorderly conduct, he shall pay a fine of twelve and a half cents.

Section 3d. The Honorary members must be subject to all the laws of the society while attending, and they may be fined for misconduct, as other members.

Section 4th. That nothing shall be taken as an excuse for the absence of a member, at any stated meeting, but sickness, or his being at the distance of ten miles from place of meeting at the time the society meets.

Article Third—Of Expulsion.

Section 1st. That any residentiary member who shall neglect to attend the meetings of the society, for four meetings successively, without he shall first have obtained leave of absence of the President, shall be considered as having relinquished his right of membership; and his name shall accordingly be erased from the roll of the society.

Section 2d. That any member who shall willfully and intentionally offend against any of the rules of the society, and after being admonished by the President, shall still continue to offend, he shall be expelled from the society.

Section 3d. That Honorary members shall not be expelled for any other cause than that mentioned in the second section of this article.

Section 4th. That if any person shall be elected a member of this society and shall neglect to come forward and sign the constitution and pay his entrance, on either of the two succeeding meetings to that of his election, he shall be considered as having forfeited his right of membership.

Minutes.

Saturday Evening, Dec. 19th, 1807.

A number of gentlemen having met in the Collosaucon school-house, for the purpose of forming themselves into a Polemical Society, Mr. John Weaver was chosen Chairman, and John Moore appointed Secretary. The meeting after maturely considering the business, were of the opinion that it was laudable and commendable, and not only so, but highly useful—to the young gentlemen in particular—as it is a means of acquiring learning and information, and the best method of dispelling the fear and awkward bashfulness which some men are troubled with in speaking before a public assembly.

They therefore resolved to establish, promote and encourage a society of the kind; and accordingly appointed Mr. Henry Epple, James Horner, Sr., and John Moore, a committee to draft a Constitution for the government of the same, who were directed to report at the next meeting. A motion was made that a committee of two persons should be appointed to produce a written question of debate at the next meeting which was agreed to, and Mr. Henry Epple and Mr. John Moore were appointed the committee. A motion was made to adjourn, and to meet again on the evening of the 26th. Agreed and adjourned.

John Moore, Secretary.

Saturday Evening, December 26th, 1807.

A number of gentlemen having met in the Collosaucon school-house, agreeably to appointment, for the purpose of forming themselves into a Polemical Society, chose the Rev. Mr. Russel as Chairman, and John Moore, Secretary. The committee that was appointed to draft a Constitution was then called upon, who reported a Constitution containing fifteen articles, which were read, separately considered and adopted. The members then agreeably to the Constitution, proceeded to the election of a President, Vice President, and Secretary, and after counting the votes, it appeared that the following gentlemen were chosen for the first three months:

Henry Epple, President.
James Horner, Sr., Vice President.
John Moore, Secretary.

D. M. MacGregor was appointed Assistant Secretary. The following question was then chosen for discussion the first meeting at the Academy:—Which is the most censurable: the merchant who brings slaves, or the farmer who buys them?

Debators, Respondents—D. M. MacGregor, John Moore, John Rosbrugh, Thomas Horner, James Horner, Sr., William Randal.

Opponents—John Weaver, James Horner, Jr., Robert Horner, James Clyde, Andrew Hagenbuch and James Horner.

The following question was chosen for the next meeting at the Collosaucon school-house:—Which has the greatest influence over men, women or wine?

A motion was then made that no spectators should be admitted in the meetings of the society, which was agreed to.

John Weaver, D. M. MacGregor, and John Moore were appointed a committee to draft a code of By-Laws for the regulation of the society, and ordered to report at the next meeting. James Horner, Sr., D. M. MacGregor were appointed to produce each a written question to debate, at the next meeting at the Academy. James Clyde and Thomas Horner were appointed to produce subjects at the next meeting at the Collosaucon school-house. The following persons were then nominated as new members of the society:

John Clyde, nominated by James Clyde.
Hugh Wilson, nominated by James Horner, Sr.
Col. Thomas McKeen, nominated by James Horner, Sr.
John Wilson, nominated by James Horner, Sr.
Robert Ralston, nominated by Robert Horner.
Joseph Carr, nominated by Thomas Horner.

John Carr, nominated by Thomas Horner. Adjourned.—John Moore, Secretary.

Academy, Saturday Evening, January 2d, 1808.

The society met agreeably to appointment, and proceeded to business by reading the minutes of the preceding meeting, which were approved. The following gentlemen were then regularly admitted as members of the society, viz:—John Clyde, John Wilson, Joseph Carr, Col. Thomas McKeen, Robert Ralston, and John Carr.

The following question was then chosen for the next meeting at the Academy:—Whether is war or luxury, most prejudicial to a nation or people? Respondents, Thos. McKeen, D. M. MacGregor, James Horner, Jr., James Horner, Sr., Robert Ralston, John Carr, Robert Horner, James Horner, Thomas Horner. Opponents, James Clyde, John Moore, Joseph Carr, John Weaver, John Clyde, John Wilson, John Rosbrugh, Andrew Hagenbuch, William Randal.

Thomas McKeen and John Rosburgh were appointed to produce each a written question at the next meeting at the Academy. The committee that were appointed to form a code of By-Laws were then called upon, who reported a code containing three articles. Adopted. The following gentlemen were then nominated as new members, viz:—Dr. Edward Humphrey, Capt. James Ralston and Joseph Horner.

The question chosen for this meeting was then debated, and decided that the merchant was the most censurable by a majority of three votes.

A motion was made and seconded that authors may be quoted in the speeches of the members, but that their speeches shall not be wholly made up of the words of the author—which motion carried.

A motion was made that no member should be permitted to read a written piece on the subject of debate, also carried. Adjourned.

John Moore, Secretary.

Collosaucon, January 10, 1808.

At a meeting of the Franklin Society held in the Collosaucon school-house, Saturday evening, January 10, 1808, the Secretary called the roll and it appeared that the following gentlemen were absent: John Weaver, D. M. MacGregor, William Randal, John Clyde, and Thomas McKeen, who stand accountable for their absence.

The society then went into election of new members, and the result of the election was that Dr. Edward Humphrey, Capt. James Ralston, and Mr. Joseph Horner were admitted as honorary members by a unanimous vote. The following question was chosen for debate at the school-house, viz.: Whether has the discovery of the Continent of America been an advantage or disadvantage to mankind in general?

10 Respondents and 10 Opponents selected —(names omitted).

Joseph Carr and John Clyde were then appointed to produce each a question at the next meeting at the school-house. A motion was then made that the members shall, on debate first speak as they were chosen, and afterward they may speak promiscuously, and adopted.

Capt. Michael Weaver, Abraham Wilson, Charles Wilson and Abraham Levan, Jr., were nominated as new members. The question, viz:—Whether has women or wine the greatest influence over men, was then debated with much eloquence and by a majority of thirteen out of fourteen it was decided that women have the greatest influence.

J. Moore, Sec.

At a stated meeting of the Franklin Society, held at the Academy, on the 16th day of January, 1808, the following were present: Thomas McKeen, Esq., James Horner, Jr., Robert Horner, Andrew Hagenbuch, James Horner, and D. M. MacGregor. The President and Vice President being absent, D. M. MacGregor was chosen President pro tem. After the house was called to order, Col. Thomas McKeen voluntarily paid his fine of three cents for his absence at the last meeting, honestly declaring that he had no excuse to offer. On account of absence of the principal secretary, and the want of the minutes of the preceding meeting, the society thought proper to adjourn without doing any business, except that the following gentlemen were nominated by Andrew Hagenbuch for members of this society, viz.:—Conrad Krider, and John Cramer, as honorary members, and Jacob Weaver as a residentiary member.

Adjourned.

John Moore, Sec.

Saturday Evening, January 23, 1808.

The Franklin Society met in the school-house and upon reading the roll, it appeared that the following gentlemen were absent: John Weaver, James Horner, Sr., William Randal, Tho's McKeen, and John Kerr, who stand accountable for their absence. The election of new members was then opened and the following gentlemen unanimously admitted, viz:—Capt. Michael Weaver, Abraham Wilson, Chas. Wilson and Abraham Levan, Jr. The following question was then chosen for the next meeting, viz:—Whether is agriculture, or commerce, the most beneficial to the United States? The Respondents and Opponents on this question are:—(List about the same as above).

John Rosburgh and John Moore were appointed to produce subjects of debate at the next meeting. The following gentlemen were nominated as new members, viz:—Maj. John Palmer, Honorary, Mr. Nicholas Neligh, Mr. James Clyde, Sr., and Henry Jarret, Esq., and Jacob Fatzinger.

The question that the discovery of America has been an advantage to mankind in general was debated and a majority of four votes out of twelve decided that it was an advantage.

The following motions were then made and carried by large majorities, viz:—Motion 1, that there be two pair of snuffers bought for the use of the society. Motion 2, that members who come into the society after the roll has been called shall be considered as absent members, until they make their excuses. Motion 3, that the following section be added to the Third Article of the By-Laws, viz:—That if any person shall be elected a member of this society, and shall neglect to come forward and sign the Constitution and pay his entrance money, for two meetings next succeeding that of his election, he shall be considered as having forfeited his right of membership. Motion 4, that the following section be added to the First Article of the By-Laws, viz:—That no member shall speak more than three times to the subject of debate, without the permission of the President. Motion 5, that persons proposing to become members of the society, shall have the liberty of attending the society on the evening of their nomination, and shall also have the liberty of taking an active part in the debate.

John Moore, Sec.

Allen Township, January 30, 1808.

The Franklin Society met agreeably to law, at the Academy, Jan. 30, 1808. The Secretary called the roll and the members all answered to their names except John Weaver, Andrew Hagenbuch, William Randal, John Kerr, and Charles Wilson. A motion was made and carried, viz:—that as John Weaver does not know of the law contained in the first section of the third article of the By-Laws, that a person be appointed to inform him of it, and enquire of him whether he wishes to continue in the society, and will come forward and give satisfaction for his absence or not; and Mr. John Moore was appointed accordingly. James Clyde, John Rosburgh, John Moore and John Clyde were excused for their absence at the last meeting at this house; that Thos. McKeen and D. M. MacGregor were also excused for their absence at the last meeting at the school-house.

The election was then held and the following gentlemen were duly elected members of the society, viz:—Honorary members, Conrad Krider, Nicholas Neligh, James Clyde, Sr., Henry Jarret, Esq.; Residentiary members,—Jacob Weaver and John Palmer.

The following subject was then chosen for the next meeting at this house, viz:—Whether is Republican government, such as the United States; or a Monarchical, such as the English, the most beneficial to any people or nation? 7 Respondents and 7 Opponents were appointed. . . . . .

James Clyde and James Horner, Jr., were appointed to produce each a question for the next meeting.

The following gentlemen were then nominated as new members by D. M. MacGregor: Matthias Miller, Peter Siegfried, Charles Sterling, honorary members. The question that war is the most prejudicial was then debated and decided by a majority of two votes—yeas eight, nays six. A motion was made and carried, that subjects may be postponed, for a decision, to another meeting that it may be re-debated. Adjourned.

J. Moore, Secretary.

School-house, February 6, 1808.

At the stated meeting of the Franklin Society, held at the Collosaucon school-house, Saturday evening, February 6th, 1808, the President called the roll, and the following members answered to their names, viz:—Henry Epple, Robert Ralston, John Rosburgh, James Horner, Andrew Hagenbuch; but there not being a constitutional quorum, they adjourned without doing any business.

John Moore, Sec.

Allen Township, Academy, Feb. 13, 1808.

Franklin Society. The following members met, viz., James Horner, V. President, D. M. MacGregor, James Horner, Jr., James Clyde, John Clyde, Robert Horner, Thomas McKeen, Robert Ralston and Joseph Horner. The house then proceeded to the election of new members. The candidates were Matthias Miller, Peter Siegfried, and Charles Sterling as honorary members. Matthias Miller and Peter Siegfried were duly elected. A subject of debate was then chosen, viz:—which would be the most beneficial to the United States in case of war, the Militia, or a Standing Army? Respondents and Opponents were named. . . . .

Robert Ralston and Robert Horner were appointed to produce new subjects for the next meeting. A motion was then made and carried that the Secretary record the names of the members present in the way and manner they have voted in deciding any subject of debate. The question whether a Republican form or Monarchical form of government is most conducive to prosperity and happiness of a people was debated and was decided unanimously in favor of the Republican form. Adjourned.

D. M. MacGregor, Assistant Sec.

School-house, Feb. 20, 1808.

The Franklin Society met, and the roll being called, the following gentlemen answered to their names, viz:—John Weaver, John Moore, James Horner, Joseph Kerr, Henry Epple, Thomas Horner, and Michael Weaver. The minutes were read and approved. Mr. Joseph Kerr was fined three cents for not attending the meeting of the sixth of February. J. Moore paid for absence at the same meeting, but was excused for the meeting of the sixth of January. In the case of John Weaver, J. Moore reported that he had explained the By-Law to him, and that the said John Weaver could not attend as a residentiary but would attend as an honorary member. On motion, John Weaver was admitted as an honorary member. The question, viz:—whether is Agriculture or Commerce the most beneficial to the United States? was debated, and on motion postponed to the next meeting for a re-discussion and decision. Adjourned.

John Moore, Sec.

Allen Township, Academy, Feb. 27, 1808.

The roll was called; present James Horner, V. Pres., John Moore. Sec., Thomas McKeen, James Horner, Jr., Robert Horner, Charles Wilson, Hugh Wilson, James Clyde, John Clyde, and D. M. MacGregor. By motion it was agreed that William Randal's name be erased in the books of the society, as having by his conduct entirely forfeited the confidence of mankind. Thomas Stewart was then elected an honorary member of the society. The question for next meeting is as follows, viz:—whether is the cow kind, or the sheep kind, most useful to mankind? Appointment of Respondents and Opponents. . . . .

James and John Clyde were appointed to produce new subjects at the next meeting. The subject for this evening, whether, in case of war, a militia, or a regular army raised for the purpose, would be most beneficial, was postponed for two weeks. Adjourned.

J. Moore, Sec.

School-house, Saturday, March 5, 1808.

The Franklin Society met agreeably to law. The roll being called, the following members were absent: John Rosburgh, D. M. MacGregor, James Horner, John Clyde, Thomas McKeen, Robert Ralston, John Kerr, Charles Wilson, John Wilson, Hugh Wilson. The minutes of the preceding meeting were read and approved. The absentees were examined and excused or fined as their case happened to be—James Horner, Sr., James Clyde, James Horner, Jr., Robert Horner, Andrew Hagenbuch, D. M. MacGregor, John Moore, and Joseph Kerr.

The following question was then presented and chosen, viz:—whether is the purchase of Louisiana an advantage, or disadvantage to the United States? Respondents and Opponents named. . . . .

James Clyde & James Horner, Jr., were appointed to produce subjects at the next meeting. The question concerning agriculture and commerce was decided unanimously in favor of agriculture.

D. M. MacGregor refused to vote. Adjourned.

R. Moore, Sec.

Allen Township, Academy, March 12, 1808.

The Franklin Society met. The roll being called, the following members answered to their names, viz:—James

Horner, Thomas McKeen, James Ralston, James Clyde, Hugh Wilson, and D. M. MacGregor. It was agreed that on account of the scarcity of members met the business should be postponed and accordingly adjourned to this week.

D. M. MacGregor.

Allen Township, Academy, March 19, 1808.

This evening the constitutional time of meeting for the Franklin Society, the following appeared, viz:—Henry Epple, Andrew Hagenbuch, and John Moore. As there was no quorum they adjourned without doing any business.

John Moore.

Allen Township, Academy, March 26, 1808.

The Franklin Society met agreeable to law. The roll being called, six answered to their names. A committee appointed to settle with the Treasurer and report at the next meeting, James Clyde and James Horner, Jr., were appointed. A motion made and carried that all books, money, &c., belonging to the society, be lodged in the hands of Thomas McKeen, Esq., to be safely kept by him for the society. On motion agreed to adjourn to meet in two weeks. Adjourned

J. Moore, Sec.

Allen Township, Academy, April 9, 1808.

The following members met agreeably to appointment, viz:—James Horner, Sr., James Horner, Jr., James Clyde, Robert Horner, Thomas McKeen, and John Clyde. On motion, James Horner, Sr., presided. A President and Secretary for ensuing three months were elected by ballot. Henry Epple elected President and John Moore, Secretary, and James Horner, Sr., Vice President.

Adjourned to meet at the school-room this night week.

Allen Township, April 16, 1808.

On account of excessive rain no quorum appeared. Adjourned indefinitely.

J. Moore, Sec.

Allen Township, August 20, 1808.

The Franklin Society met agreeably to public notice given by the Secretary. The roll being called, six answered to their names. The following were elected: Henry Epple, President, James Horner, Sr., Vice President, and John Moore, Secretary. The question of debate was postponed, and on motion it was agreed that the society adjourn to the third Saturday in October next, to meet in the Collosaucon school-room. Adjourned.

J. Moore, Sec.

Collosaucon, Dec. 5, 1808.

The Franklin Society being duly notified to meet on Dec. 5th, but there being no quorum, the three members present adjourned without doing any business. They regretted the lack of spirit, and on that account the society is falling into dissolution. The Secretary resigned his membership, and stood ready to deliver into the hands of any proper person, all the effects of the society.

John Moore, Sec.

It remains to add to this interesting record of the Franklin Society, that the Secretary, John Moore, submitted a detailed account of the finances of the society, of which only a summary is herewith given:

Entrance or first payments—23 members	$2.87½
Fines	.09
Monthly payments—10 members	.60
Total received	$3.56½
Expenditures, paper, candles, cord wood, blankbook, snuffers	3.06½
Balance due the society	$ .50

ANNOTATED LIST OF BURIALS

In the Scotch-Irish Settlement in Allen Township

By Wilbur L. King

Allison, James.
: There is no further inscription on this stone, which is about two feet high and one and one-half feet wide.

Andress, Jane, consort of Charles Andress, born Feb. 28, 1786, died Dec. 21, 1837, age 51 years, 9 months, 23 days.
: She was a daughter of Moses and Agnes Hemphill and had a son, Charles.

Andress, Mary, wife of Jacob Andress and daughter of Moses and Agnes Hemphill, born Oct. 9, 1778, died Aug. 22, 1853, age 74 years, 10 months, 13 days.

Barnes, Lydia H., died Oct. 12, 1835, age 11 months.
: Daughter of B. D. Barnes, who was elected a trustee of the Settlement church in 1834.

Bartholomew, Peter, born Feb. 20, 1790, died July 24, 1864, age 74 years, 5 months, 4 days.
: His wife was Elizabeth. They had a son, George.

Blair, Joseph Horner, son of James and Martha Blair, died April 6, 1865, age 1 year, 6 months.
: The brothers and sisters are John, Margaret, Robert, Keziah, Mary, William, and Martha. His mother was nee Wilson.

Bleckley, Elmira, daughter of Arthur E. and Rebecca M. Mulhallon, died Sept. 17, 1835, age 21 years, 7 months, 5 days.
: Wife of William Bleckley.

Boyd, Mrs. Elizabeth, consort of Doctor John Boyd, died Aug. 5, 1820.
: Her first husband was John Brown, a descendant of Samuel Brown.

Boyd, Doct. John, died April 5, 1837.
: His first wife was Elizabeth, widow of John Brown, and his second wife was Nancy Clyde.

Brown, Ann Fearon, daughter of Joseph and Matilda Brown, died Jan. 9, 1860, age 17 years, 5 months, 24 days.

Brown, Catharine, relict of General Robert Brown, age 91 years, 8 months, 13 days.
: Her will was proved Nov. 21, 1859.

Brown, Elizabeth Kerr, daughter of Joseph and Matilda Brown, died Aug. 7, 1847, age 2 years, 6 months.

Brown, Emma M., died June 30, 1920, age 73 years, 3 months.

Brown, James, died Sept. 8, 1800, age 16 years.

Brown, Jane, widow of Samuel Brown, died March 25, 1812, age 91 years, 8 months, 28 days.
: She was a daughter of John Boyd (?)

Brown, John, died June 2, 1798, age 38 years.
: He was the son of Samuel Brown, born 1714, died June 17, 1798, and his wife, Jane, born 1720, died March 25, 1812. His widow, Elizabeth, nee Doak, married Dr. John Boyd.

Brown, Joseph, born May 19, 1803, died May 11, 1881.

Brown, Matilda Kerr, wife of Joseph Brown, born Aug. 5, 1813, died Jan. 19, 1900.

Brown, Gen'l Robert, patriot and soldier of the Revolution, died Feb. 26, 1823, age 78 years, 2 months.
: He married Catharine Snyder and had an only son, William.

Brown, Samuel, died June 11, 1798, age 84 years.
: He married Jane Boyd (?), a daughter of John Boyd. Children: John, Robert, William, James, Esther, and Sarah.

Brown, Mrs. Susan, consort of William Brown, died March 18, 1834, age 39 years, 6 months, 6 days.
: m. n. Shimer. Her husband, William Brown, a son of Gen'l Robert Brown, died at Bethlehem, Pa., Jan. 10, 1866, in his 73rd year. She had children, Robert S. and Eliza.

Brown, Tillie Kerr, daughter of Samuel T. and Emma Brown, born July 24, 1875, died Feb. 27, 1881.

M. B., 1770.
: This is a small slab about nine by eighteen inches.

E. B., died 1828.
: A small upright stone about nine by fourteen inches with no further record.

G. B.
: A small stone about six by sixteen inches.

Carr, Mrs. Ann, wife of Capt. Wm. Carr, died April 29, 1832, in the 41st year of her age.

Carrell, Samuel, son of Samuel and Amy Carrell, died Mar. 22, 1844, age 17 years, 3 months, 26 days.

Clendinen, Adam, born July 27, 1792, died Oct. 15, 1839, age 47 years, 2 months, 18 days.
Son of Adam and Esther Clendinen.

Clendinen, Adam, died June 17, 1817, age 78 years, 2 months.
He married Esther Hall. Children: Jane 1st, died 1775; John 1st, died 1778; Jane 2nd, born 1779, married Andrew Haslett; John 2nd, born 1781; James, born 1783; Margaret, born 1784; William, born 1789; Nancy; Esther, married James Horner; Adam, born 1792; Robert, born 1795; and Thomas, born 1799.

Clendinen, Esther, wife of Adam Clendinen, died May 11, 1816, age 61 years, 7 months, and 5 days.
m. n. Hall of Philadelphia, Pa.

Clendinen, James, died March 17, 1850, age 67 years, 9 months, 25 days.
Son of Adam and Esther Clendinen.

Clendinen, Jane, died June 6, 1775.
Daughter of Adam and Esther Clendinen.

Clendinen, Jane Haslett, eldest daughter of Adam and Esther Clendinen, died April 23, 1829, age 50 years, 19 days.
Wife of Andrew Haslet.

Clendinen, John, died July 7, 1778.
Son of Adam and Esther Clendinen.

Clendinen, John, eldest son of Adam and Esther Clendinen, died Jan. 26, 1815, age 34 years, 6 months, 14 days.

Clendinen, Margaret, second daughter of Adam and Esther Clendinen, died June 30, 1827, aged 43 years, 2 months, 29 days.

Clendinen, Nancy, daughter of Adam and Esther Clendinen, died Jan. 16, 1788.

Clendinen, Robert, born Jan. 27, 1795, died Oct. 3, 1853.
Son of Adam and Esther Clendinen.

Clendinen, Thomas, born Dec. 1, 1799, died Feb. 27, 1879.
Son of Adam and Esther Clendinen.

Clendinen, Wm., third son of Adam and Esther Clendinen, died Mar. 5, 1827, age 38 years, 1 month, 8 days.

Clyde, Biddy, died Dec. 15, 1786, age 66 years.
Wife of Michael Clyde.

Clyde, Elizabeth, wife of John Clyde, died April 15, 1794.
: m. n. Hudders of Chester County, Penna.

Clyde, Elizabeth, relict of James Clyde, died June 15, 1829, in 81st year of her age.
: Daughter of James Kerr.

Clyde, Harrie, son of Rev. J. C. and M. H. Clyde, born Jan. 19, 1872, died May 14, 1872.
: He was baptized Henry Cunningham Clyde.

Clyde, James, died Nov. 3, 1827, in the 78th year of his age.
: A son of Michael and Bridget Clyde. He married Elizabeth Kerr and had issue: John, Rebecca, Jane, and Nancy.

Clyde, James, born May 20, 1783, died Sept. 6, 1866, age 83 years, 3 months, 16 days.
: A son of John and Elizabeth Clyde. His first wife was Hannah, a daughter of Joseph Horner, who is buried in Cross Creek township, Washington County, Penna.

Clyde, John, son of James and Elizabeth Clyde, died Nov. 28, 1815, in the 35th year of his age.
: He was unmarried.

Clyde, John, died Jan. 4, 1826, age 80 years, 9 months.
: He married Elizabeth Hudders, with whom he had issue: Sarah, married John McKissick; Margaret; Mary; Elizabeth and James. His second wife was Mary.

Clyde, Michael, died May 7, 1794, age 84 years.
: He and wife Bridget came from the north of Ireland and settled in the Irish Settlement probably about 1743. He owned a large tract on the Monocacy Creek in East Allen township and raised a family of four children: James, John and two daughters.

Clyde, Susan E., wife of James Clyde, died Feb. 1, 1886.

Craig, Mary, wife of Thomas Craig, Esq., died July 14, 1772, age 75 years.
: Thomas Craig died 1779.

Epple, Maria Barbara, consort of Henry Epple, died Jan. 23, 1824, age 69 years.
: Her only child married Col. Nicholas Neligh.

S. E. 1780.
: This is an uncut stone with these letters rudely carved thereon.

Gardner, Emeline, daughter of James and M. A. Gardner,

born Aug. 1, 1835, died July 19, 1840, age 4 years, 9 months, 18 days.

Gray, Martha, died June 9, 1861, age 86 years, 3 months, 4 days.
> Unmarried. Had brothers George and William.

Gregg, Margaret, widow of Robert Gregg, died April 24, 1800, age 97 years.

Gregg, Robert, died March 9, 1756, in the 40th year of his age.
> He was one of the first three commissioners of Northampton County, Pa., and was on the first Grand Jury. Children: Robert, and Margaret, wife of Dr. Matthew McHenry.

D. M. G., 1809.
> Rudely carved on an uncut stone.

Hall, Wm., born Feb. 26, 1758, died Jan. 20, 1813, age 54 years, 10 months, 24 days.
> A son of John Hall, of Philadelphia, Pa., a brother to the wife of Adam Clendinen. He was unmarried.

Hays, Barbara, died Aug. 11, 1770, age 30 years.
> The first wife of John Hays and daughter of James King. Issue: Mary, Jane, Elizabeth, John, and James.

Hays, Jane, wife of John Hays, Esq., died Dec. 15, 1825, age 78 years.
> She was a daughter of James and Jane Horner. Had son, John K. Hays.

Hays, John, died Nov. 16, 1789, age 85 years.
> He married Jane Love in Ireland and had children: William, James, John, Joseph, Elizabeth married ———— Wilson, Mary married ———— Gray, Esbel married ———— Patten, Robert, Jane married ———— Brown, and Francis.

Hays, Joseph, son of John and Jane Hays, died March 30, 1795.
> He was in his seventh year.

Hays, Mary, died Sept. 9, 1776, age 15 years.
> Daughter of John and Barbara Hays.

Hays, Mary, died Jan. 11, 1851, age 64 years, 5 months.
> Unmarried. Daughter of John and Jane (Walker) Hays.

Hays, Rebecca, daughter of John and Jane Hays, died April 10, 1840, age 48 years, 6 months.
> Unmarried.

Hemphill, Agnes, wife of Moses Hemphill, Esq., died Apr. 2, 1817, age 66 years, 2 months, 16 days.
: She was a native of Ireland. m. n. Sharp.

Hemphill, Elizabeth Mary, daughter of Thomas and Caroline Hemphill, died Nov. 29, 1844, age 12 years, 6 months, 9 days.

Hemphill, Moses, died Feb. 16, 1822, age 75 years, 3 months, 5 days.
: He married Agnes Sharp. Children: James, Joseph, Thomas, Mary, Nancy, Elizabeth married James Kerr, 1st Margaret, 2nd Margaret married Frederic Nagel, Jane, and Agnes married Thomas Wilson.

Herron, Thomas, died Oct. 4, 1772, age 63 years.
: He married Jean, daughter of Samuel Brown.

Hinkson, Mary Ellen, daughter of Dr. C. H. and Elizabeth Humphrey, wife of John Neide Hinkson, died Nov. 18, 1922.

Horner. Here lieth the body of one without name or honor, the legitimate first born son of H. E. Horner. In silent dust he sleeps entombed, age 8 weeks. Feb. 4, 1776.

Horner, Ann, died Jan. 11, 1865, age 80 years.
: Daughter of James and Ann Horner.

Horner, Ann, daughter of Robert and Jane Horner, born Oct. 30, 1820, died Feb. 3, 1879, age 58 years, 3 months, 4 days.

Horner, Elizabeth, died Aug. 11, 1826, age 36 years, 2 months, 14 days.
: Unmarried. Daughter of Hugh and Elizabeth Horner.

Horner, Elizabeth W., daughter of Robert and Jane Horner, died Dec. 29, 1834, age 12 years, 3 months, 21 days.

Horner, Elizabeth, wife of Hugh Horner, died Dec. 22, 1835, in 87th year of her age.
: m. n. Wilson.

Horner, Hannah Ann, daughter of John and Hannah Horner, of Washington Co., Pa., died Feb. 9, 1854, age 36 years.

Horner, Hugh, son of Hugh and Sarah E. Horner, died May 12, 1827, age 4 years, 10 months, 28 days.

Horner, Hugh, died April 15, 1806, in 63rd year of his age.
>Born Oct. 20, 1743, a son of James and Jane Horner. He married Elizabeth Wilson. Children: James H., Robert, William, Hugh, Jane, Elizabeth, Judith and an unnamed infant.

Horner, Hugh, died July 15, 1861, age 73 years, 2 months, 24 days.
>A son of Hugh and Elizabeth Horner; married Sarah E. Humphrey; children: John, Edward, Hugh, Elizabeth H., Sarah Jane, Harriet, Matilda, and Mary Louisa.

Horner, James, died May 1, 1793, age 82 years.
>He was one of the first Grand Jurors of Northampton County. He and his wife Jane, nee Kerr, came from Ireland in 1734. Children: Hugh, Jane, Thomas, Sarah wife of Wm. McNair, Mary, James, and John.

Horner, James H., died Oct. 28, 1823, in 45th year of his age.
>Married Esther, daughter of Adam Clendinen. Children: Henrietta, Maria, and Elizabeth.

Horner, James J., died June 27, 1848, age 78 years, 3 months.
>Son of Joseph and Sarah Horner. Unmarried.

Horner, Jane, wife of Robert Horner, born Nov. 21, 1788, died July 16, 1857.

Horner, Jane, wife of James Horner, who suffered death by the hands of the savage Indians, Oct. 8, 1763, age 50 years.
>m. n. Kerr. She came with her husband to America in 1734.

Horner, Jane J., died Nov. 10, 1859, in 87th year.
>Unmarried. Daughter of Joseph and Sarah Horner.

Horner, Jane, wife of Thomas Horner, died Sept. 9, 1835, age 74 years, 5 days.

Horner, Jane Wilson, daughter of Robert and Jane Horner, born Jan. 24, 1826, died Sept. 10, 1904, age 78 years, 7 months, 16 days.

Horner, Joseph, born Oct. 24, 1790, died Jan. 27, 1866.
>Son of Joseph and Sarah Horner. Married Margaret Wilson, daughter of John and Ann Wilson. Children: Sallie and Jane.

Horner, Joseph, died March 2, 1835, in 95th year of his age.
>He and wife Sarah, nee Allison, had children: James J., Jane J., Hannah, John, Margaret, Sarah, Samuel, and Joseph.

Horner, Judith, died Aug. 10, 1798, age 14 years.
>Daughter of Hugh and Elizabeth Horner.

Horner, Margaret, daughter of Joseph and Sarah Horner, died Dec. 1, 1844, in the 61st year of her age.
> Unmarried.

Horner, Mary Louisa, daughter of Hugh and Sarah E. Horner, died Aug. 28, 1829, age 1 year, 8 months.

Horner, Mary L., daughter of Robert and Jane Horner, died Oct. 4, 1847, age 16 years, 5 months, 7 days.

Horner, Robert, son of Robert and Jane Horner, died Jan. 20, 1825, age 4 days.

Horner, Robert, died July 7, 1844, age 63 years, 2 months, 14 days.
> Son of Hugh and Elizabeth Horner. Married Jane Wilson of Bucks County, Pa. Issue: Hugh R., Robert, Ann, Jane, Mary L., and Elizabeth W.

Horner, Samuel, son of Joseph and Sarah Horner, died June 25, 1824, age 36 years.
> Unmarried.

Horner, Sarah, daughter of Joseph and Sarah Horner, died Sept. 20, 1811, age 26 years.
> Unmarried.

Horner, Sarah, consort of Joseph Horner, died May 28, 1820, age 76 years.
> m. n. Allison.

Horner, Sarah E., wife of Hugh Horner, died Oct. 19, 1871, age 70 years, 10 months, 20 days.
> Daughter of Dr. Edward Humphrey.

Horner, Thomas, died Nov. 27, 1825, age 76 years, 27 days.
> He married Jane Patterson and had children: James, Thomas, Sarah, Jane, and Ann.

Horner, William, died May 14, 1868, age 81 years.
> Son of Hugh and Elizabeth Horner. Died single.

Humphrey, Dr. Charles H., born March 5, 1807, died June 3, 1893.

Humphrey, Dr. Edward, died Dec. 5, 1847, age 71 years, 6 months, 4 days.
> Married Elizabeth Hays. Children: John H., Sarah E., Mary K., Charles H., and Jane.

Humphrey, Elizabeth, wife of Dr. Edward Humphrey, died

Jan. 27, 1844, age 73 years, 10 months, 24 days.
  Daughter of John and Barbara Hays.
Humphrey, Elizabeth Ann, daughter of John H. and Mary A. Humphrey, died Aug. 25, 1839, age 6 years, 10 months, 6 days.
Humphrey, Elizabeth, wife of Dr. C. H. Humphrey, born Nov. 27, 1813, died March 29, 1883.
Humphrey, Mary Ann, wife of John H. Humphrey, died July 20, 1845, age 38 years, 7 months, 24 days.
Humphrey, Thomas, son of Dr. C. H. Humphrey, born Apr. 28, 1844, died June 1, 1867, age 23 years, 1 month, 2 days.
Humphrey, Dr. Wm. J., born March 25, 1852, died Oct. 19, 1919.
Irwin, Rev. John, son of Rev. Leslie Irwin and wife Mary Ann Wilson, born Aug., 1848, died June 6, 1889.
Irwin, Samuel Hays, born May 16, 1850, died Dec. 4, 1854.
  Son of Rev. Leslie and Mary Ann Irwin.
Kennedy, James, born Feb. 26, 1787, died Nov. 20, 1872, age 84 years, 9 months, 20 days.
  Was an Associate Judge of Northampton county, 1844 to 1849. Married Jane, daughter of James and Elizabeth Clyde. Had a son Clyde.
Kennedy, Jane, wife of James Kennedy, died Dec. 30, 1854, age 70 years, 5 months.
Kerr, Elizabeth, wife of James Kerr, died June 9, 1870, age 81 years, 1 month, 6 days.
  m. n. Hemphill.
Kerr, James, died Nov. 17, 1854, age 77 years, 10 months, 25 days.
  Son of James and Jane Kennedy; married Elizabeth, daughter of Moses and Agnes Hemphill; children: Caroline, Nancy, Frew, Matilda, William, John, and James.
Kerr, James, died March 23, 1827, age 83 years, 10 months.
  Married Jane McInstry. Children: Joseph, James, John, Nathan, and Mary.
Kerr, James, son of James and Elizabeth Kerr, died Sept. 6 ———, age 3 years, 7 months, 27 days.

Kerr, Jane, wife of James Kerr, died March 17, 1836, in her 83rd year of her age.

Kerr, John, son of James and Elizabeth Kerr, died Jan. 20, 1824, age 3 years, 5 months.

Kerr, Joseph, died July 23, 1833, age 59 years.
>Son of James and Jane Kerr; married Magdalena Hagenbuch.

Kerr, Magdalena, wife of Joseph Kerr, daughter of Christian and Susan Hagenbuch, died Nov. 15, 1824, age 48 years, 10 months.

Kerr, Nathan, died June 18, 1844, age 62 years, 1 month.
>Son of James and Jane Kerr; married Sarah Horner, daughter of Thomas and Jane Horner; children: Eliza, wife of Joseph Buchelm, Lavinia, Jane, Thomas H., William, Joseph, and Sarah L.

Kerr, William, son of James and Elizabeth Kerr, born Feb. 20, 1815, died Nov. 14, 1819.

King, Gabriel, died May 28, 1758, age 21 years.
>Son of James and Mary King.

King, James, died April 30, 1745, age 38 years.
>He married Mary Walker, a native of Ireland. So far as the tombstones show, this was the first burial in the settlement graveyard.

King, Mary, died Jan. 9, 1790, age 78 years.
>The wife of James King and a sister of Capt. Richard Walker.

T. H. K.
>This is an uncut yellow stone about six by eight inches.

Lattimore, Arthur, born 1710 in Ireland, died 1777, age 67 years.
>Committee of Safety 1776; County Sub-Lieutenant 1777; brother to Robert Lattimore. He and his wife Mary were natives of Ireland.

Lattimore, James, born June 19, 1788, died April 18, 1843, age 54 years, 9 months, 29 days.
>Son of William and Mary Lattimore.

Lattimore, Mary, born in Ireland, died 1780, age about 65 years.
>Wife of Arthur Lattimore.

Lattimore, Ralston Monroe, born Dec. 15, 1821, died Nov. 22, 1822.

Lattimore, Gen'l William, died Nov. 11, 1833, in the 70th year of his age.

The above Seal was used by the Allen Township Presbyterian Church of the "Irish Settlement," (known also as The English Presbyterian Congregation, 1797). (See page 265.)

WALNUT STREET PRESBYTERIAN CHURCH OF BATH, PA.
The members of the Old Allen Township Presbyterian Church erected the church in 1870, and since then hold their services in Bath. (See page 348.)

Son of Robert and Ann Lattimore. He married Mary Walker and had children: John, William, Robert, James, Samuel, Ralston Monroe (?), Christiana, M. A., and Nancy.

Likens, Mary, died June 16, 1773, age 18 years.

Loder, ————, First born son of John and Eliza Loder, born July 12, 1848.

Loder, Frederic N., son of John and Eliza Loder, born Aug. 5, 1849, died May 8, 1852, age 3 years, 9 months, 3 days.

L. L., 1797.
>This is a small rough, and uncut stone with inscription rudely carved.

McHenry, Ann, died Oct. 18, 1818, age 41 years.
>Daughter of Dr. Matthew McHenry.

McHenry, Elizabeth, died June 8, 1831, age 57 years.
>Daughter of Dr. Matthew McHenry.

McHenry, Margaret, wife of Dr. Matthew McHenry, died March 17, 1796, in the 43rd year of her age.

McHenry, Dr. Matthew, died Dec. 13, 1783, in the 40th year of his age.
>Son of Rev. Francis and Mary (Wilson) McHenry. He was appointed surgeon on board the Provincial ship Montgomery, Apr. 13, 1776. He married Margaret Gregg, marriage license being issued Oct. 17, 1770. Children: Ann, Elizabeth, and Matthew.

McNair, Christiana, wife of John McNair, died Jan. 27, 1782, age 82 years.

McNair, Senr., John, died April 5, 1762, age 72 years.
>He settled in the Irish Settlement about 1736. His wife was Christiana. Children: William, John, Robert, Andrew, Margaret, and Ann.

McNair, Margaret, wife of William McNair, Esq., died July 20, 1783, age 49 years.
>A daughter of Hugh and Sarah McNair.

McNair, William, son of John McNair, Jr., and Margaret, his wife, died Aug. 2, 1769.

McNair, Sarah, daughter of John McNair, Jr., and Margaret, his wife, died Feb. 16, 1788.

McNeill, Mary, consort of Samuel McNeill, Esq., died July 17, 1810, age 58 years.
>She was a sister of George Palmer.

McNeill, Palmer, son of Samuel and Mary McNeill, died Dec. 15, 1809, age 28 years.

Miller, E. A., born Oct. 9, 1808, died April 15, 1868, age 59 years, 6 months, 6 days.
> She was Eliza Ann, daughter of Arthur E. and Rebecca Mulhallon and wife of Alexander Miller.

Miller Eliza R., died Dec. 10, 1833, age 5 years.

Miller, Elizabeth, died April 10, 1824, in the 28th year of her age.
> Unmarried.

Moffat, Mary, died Oct. 26, 1829, age 83 years.
> Wife of William Moffat.

Moffat, William, died Dec. 25, 1831, in the 86th year of his age.

Mulhallon, Arthur E., died Sept. 18, 1826, in the 42nd year of his age.
> He married Rebecca Clyde and had children: John, William, Eliza Ann, Elmira Bleckley and Sarah.

Mulhallon, Rebecca R., died April 12, 1868, age 82 years, 6 months, 6 days.
> Daughter of James and Elizabeth Clyde and wife of Arthur Mulhallon.

Nagle, Caroline, daughter of Frederic W. and Margaret Nagle, born Feb. 15, 1826, died Sept. 14, 1838, age 12 years, 6 months, 29 days.

Nagle, Catharine, daughter of Frederic W. and Margaret Nagle, born Feb. 24, 1820, died Aug. 1, 1838, age 18 years, 5 months, 7 days.

Nagle, Frederic W., died Dec. 6, 1864, age 72 years, 4 months, 12 days.
> He married Margaret, 2nd, daughter of Moses and Agnes Hemphill. Issue: William Frederic, Nancy, Mary Jane, Catharine, Elizabeth, Margaret, Caroline, and Lucinda.

Nagle, Margaret, wife of Frederic W. Nagle, daughter of Moses and Agnes Hemphill, died Feb. 14, 1864, age 71 years, 9 months, 5 days.

Neligh, Henry, born Nov. 18, 1798, died Nov. 20, age 2 days.
> A son of Nicholas Neligh.

Neligh, Col. Nicholas, born 1768, died June 15, 1816, age 48 years.
> He was a storekeeper and married the only daughter of Henry and Maria Barbara Epple.

Oliphant, Margaret, daughter of William and Susan Oliphant, died May 12, 1778, age 16 years.

Oliphant, Susan, wife of William Oliphant, died March 11, 1778, age 38 years.

Orr, Henry, died Aug. 9, 1850, age 29 years.

Orr, John, died Jan. 26, 1883, in his 71st year.

I. M. C. O.
> This is a slate splinter with the letters rudely carved thereon.

Palmer, Charlotte, died March 20, 1810, in the 4th year of her age.
> Daughter of George and Mary Palmer.

Palmer, Debora, died April 9, 1810, in the 2nd year of her age.
> Daughter of George and Mary Palmer.

Palmer, George.
> He was surveyor-general of the State of Pennsylvania. His first wife was a sister of Col. Thomas Craig. They had children John and Eliza.

Palmer, John, died June 14, 1813, in the 35th year of his age.
> Unmarried son of George Palmer.

Palmer, Mary.
> m. n. Conrad, the second wife of George Palmer. Their children were Charlotte, Debora, Mary, Sarah, Harriet, Juliet, and Thomas.

Perry, Joseph, died June 26, 1766, age 55 years.

Price, Mary, wife of Joseph Price, died May 4, 1834.
> She was the daughter of John and Elizabeth Brown. Her husband is buried in Bucks County, Pa.

Ralston, Mrs. Eliza, consort of J. Ralston, Esq., died Feb. 13, 1808, in the 28th year of her age.
> A daughter of George Palmer.

Ralston, James, died July 26, 1775, age about 76 years.
> An elder in the Presbyterian church in the settlement. He married Mary Cummock and had issue: Mary, Samuel, John, and Jane.

Ralston, Esq., James, died Jan. 20, 1836, in the 69th year of

his age.
> Known as Squire Ralston. He was a son of Samuel and Sarah Ralston.

Ralston, John, died Feb. 17, 1795, age 60 years.
> Paymaster 1781; a delegate from Northampton county, Penna., to frame the Constitution of 1776. He was a son of James and Mary Ralston and married Christiana, a daughter of James King. Children: James, John, Mary, Lettice, Ann, Jean, Christina, Robert, and Samuel.

Ralston, Lettice, died Sept. 30, 1848, age 67 years, 6 months.
> Unmarried. Daughter of Samuel and Sarah Ralston.

Ralston, Jr., Mary, died Nov. 20, 1748, age 16 years.
> Daughter of James and Mary Ralston.

Ralston, Mary, wife of James Ralston, died July 23, 1774, age 74 years.

Ralston, Samuel, died Oct. 13, 1785, age 55 years.
> He married Sarah King and had children: Samuel, James, Isaac, Gabriel, Mary, and Letitia.

Ralston, Jr., Samuel, died Jan. 11, 1795, age 24 years.
> A son of Samuel and Sarah Ralston. He married Letitia, daughter of Rev. John and Jane Rosbrugh.

Ralston, Sarah, wife of Samuel Ralston, died Feb. 27, 1784, age 41 years.
> A daughter of James and Mary King.

Raup, Ebezena C., daughter of Henry and Margaret Raup, died Sept. 4, 1861, age 10 months, 4 days.

Raub, Henry, born Sept. 20, 1818, died Sept. 20, 1875, age 57 years.

Raup, Joseph Henry, son of Henry and Margaret Raup, born Feb. 28, 1852, died Feb. 10, 1853, age 11 months, 12 days.

Raup, Laura Jane, daughter of Henry and Margaret Raup, died Aug. 11, 1862, age 5 months, 17 days.

Raup, Nancy C., daughter of Henry and Margaret Raup, born June 12, 1855, died Feb. 13, 1865, age 10 years, 8 months, 1 day.

Raup, Samuel T., son of Henry and Margaret Raup, died Aug. 13, 1865, age 1 year, 10 months, 7 days.

Rockman, Isabel, died Dec. 3, 1802, in the 18th year of her age.

Rosbrugh, Jane, died March 27, 1809, age 70 years, relict of Rev. John Rosbrugh, formerly pastor of this congregation, who fell a victim to British cruelty at Trenton, Jan. 2, 1777.
> A daughter of James and Mary Ralston. She married John Rosbrugh in 1766 and had five children.

Russel, Margaret, consort of Rev. Robert Russel, born March 18, 1764, died April 10, 1824, age 60 years, 22 days.
> She was the daughter of Thomas Armstrong, an elder of the Presbyterian church.

Russel, A. M., Rev. Robert, late pastor of the English Presbyterian congregation of Allen township, died Dec. 16, 1827, in the 70th year of his age, and the 30th year of his ministry.
> Had children: Thomas Boyd, Susan, Sarah, and Robert.

Russel, Susan, died March 10, 1862, in the 64th year of her age.
> Unmarried: A daughter of Rev. Robert and Margaret Russel.

Russel, Thomas Boyd, died Feb. 5, 1827, age 24 years, 3 months, 13 days.
> A son of Rev. Robert and Margaret Russel.

Schaffer, Catharine, born June 13, 1797, died Jan. 1, 1884, age 86 years, 6 months, 18 days.

A. E. S.
> This is a small slab about eighteen by twenty inches low in the ground.

Scott, Jane, daughter of W. G. and N. K. Scott, died Sept. 6, 1836, age 1 year, 8 months, 14 days.

Walker, John, died June 7, 1777, in the 61st year of his age.
> Children: William, Jane married John Hays, Ann, Mary Ann, and John.

Walker, Mary Ann, died April 14, 1773, age 56 years.
> nee Blackburn. Wife of Robert Walker.

Walker, Mary, wife of John Walker, Jr., died June 15, 1793, in the 33rd year of her age.

Walker, Robert, died Feb., 1758, age 58 years.
> He married Mary Ann Blackburn and had issue: John, Jane,

Mary Ann, and a daughter.

Weidner, John, died May 13, 1821.

Weitzel, Sarah Jane, daughter of Michael and Jane W. Weitzel, died Feb. 25, 1850, age 5 years, 7 months, 20 days.

Wesselhoeft, Robert Palmer.
> A son of Dr. Wesselheoft and wife Sarah, nee Palmer.

Whiteside, ———, died Sept., 1823, 6 months, 20 days.

Whiteside, James, died April 18, 1823, age 43 years, a native of Ireland.

Wilson, infant daughter of Abram and Mary Wilson, stillborn Dec. 2, 1835.

Wilson, Abram, died Jan. 30, 1840, age 74 years, 9 months, 17 days.
> A son of Samuel Wilson. He married Mary Young and had issue: Samuel, Hugh, Osman, John, Eliza, and an infant.

Wilson, Ann, died Jan. 8, 1851, age 79 years, 7 months.
> Wife of John Wilson and daughter of John and Jane Hays.

Wilson, Charles, son of Hugh Wilson, Esq., and Sarah his wife, died Aug. 20, 1768, age 42 years.
> He married Margaret, a daughter of John and Christiana McNair. Children: Sarah, Hugh, Christiana, John, and Margaret.

Wilson, Eliza Ann, daughter of Abram and Mary Wilson, born Nov. 28, 1833, died May 10, 1834, age 5 months, 12 days.

Wilson, Esq., Hugh, born in Ireland 1689, died in autumn of 1773, age 84 years.
> He married Sarah Craig in Ireland and had children: Samuel, Charles, Francis, James, Thomas, Mary, Margaret, and Elizabeth. He was one of the first Justices in Northampton Co., Pa.

Wilson, Hugh, died Nov. 30, 1830, age 69 years, 1 month.
> Son of Samuel Wilson. His wife was Elizabeth. Children: Hugh, Abram, Thomas, Samuel, Sarah, Abigail, Mary, and Elizabeth.

Wilson, Jean, daughter of John and Ann Wilson, died Oct. 18, 1826, age 20 years, 5 months.

Wilson, John, died Jan. 1, 1857, in the 91st year of his age.
> Son of Charles and Margaret Wilson. He married Ann Hays and had issue: Charles, Jane, William, McNair, John H., Margaret, and Mary Ann.

Wilson, John Alexander, son of Charles and Catharine Wilson, Aug. 5, 1843, age 2 years, 5 months.
Wilson, Margaret, wife of Charles Wilson, Esq., died Nov. 25, 1823, age 95 years.
Daughter of John and Christiana McNair.
Wilson, Mary S., born July 25, 1826, died Feb. 3, 1828.
Wilson, Robert Steel, son of Charles and Catharine Wilson, died July 29, 1843, age 3 years, 11 months.
Wilson, Sally, daughter of Charles and Margaret Wilson, died Dec., 1778, age 21 years.
Wilson, Sarah, wife of Hugh Wilson, Esq. The date of birth and death not known.
m. n. Craig.
Wilson, William McNair, died Jan. 18, 1851, age 44 years, 6 months.
A son of John and Ann Wilson. He married Jane Britain.
Wyckoff, William B., son of Peter and Eliza Wyckoff, born Oct. 26, 1839, died Dec. 12, 1841, age 2 years, 1 month, 16 days.
S. W.
An uncut sandstone with these letters only.
Young, Robert, died March 21, 1813, age about 91 years.

THE SCOTCH-IRISH
OF THE
"FORKS OF THE DELAWARE"

(Now Northampton County, Pennsylvania)

[Founded upon a paper read before the Northampton County Historical and Genealogical Society at the annual meeting held February 5, 1907]

By Rev. John C. Clyde, D. D.

PREFACE

IN THE following pages will be found historical material pertaining to the two Scotch-Irish Settlements in the Forks of the Delaware. That pertaining to the Craig, or West Branch (Lehigh River) Settlement may seem fragmentary. It is presented in this shape because the author has published three works bearing on this part of the Forks Settlement, viz.:

"History of the Allen Township Presbyterian Church, and the Community which has sustained it, in what was formerly known as the Irish Settlement, Northampton County, Pa."

"Genealogies, Necrology and Reminiscences of the Irish Settlement, or a record of those Scotch-Irish Presbyterian Families who were the First Settlers in the Forks of the Delaware, now Northampton County, Pa." A sequel to the History of the Allen Township Presbyterian Church; and

"Rosbrugh, a tale of the Revolution, or life, labors and death of Rev. John Rosbrugh, Pastor of Greenwich, Oxford and Mansfield Woodhouse (Washington) Presbyterian Churches, N. J., from 1764 to 1769, and of Allen Township Church from 1769 to 1777; Chaplain in the Continental Army; Clerical Martyr of the Revolution; killed by the Hessians in the battle of Assanpink at Trenton, N. J., January 2d, 1777; founded on a paper read before the New Jersey Historical Society at its meeting in Trenton, January 15th, 1880, to which is added historical data of the Rosbrughs of the connection in America."

From these volumes it was felt that the reader might glean whatever further information the author had, and which might seem to be wanting in these pages.

As to the historical matter pertaining to the Hunter, or North Branch (Delaware river) Settlement, it will be found to be very largely of an ecclesiastical nature. The aim has been made to do for this Settlement substantially what was done for the Craig Settlement in the History of the Allen Township Church.

The two settlements in their early history, being associated ecclesiastically, some material here will be found similar to that given in connection with the History of the Craig Settlement.

The ecclesiastical aspect has been made predominant because it was felt the seeker after information would find it difficult to get access to the ecclesiastical records; whilst civil information as to persons and events involved could be gleaned from the county records of wills and deeds, readily accessible to all; and from tombstone and family records, together with the traditions and like sources of information.

This field is left open to some enterprising descendant of the Hunter Settlement family who may be historically inclined. The aim has been to make the Church History complete in outline mainly from official records, avoiding too much detail, so that the inquirer may know just where to dig for the hidden treasure that he may be in search of. It is hoped no one will be unduly disappointed in his expectations when perusing the pages herewith submitted.

Easton, Pa., June, 1907.

J. C. C.

The Scotch-Irish of Northampton County, Pennsylvania; Who they were? What became of them? and Who represents them now?

"We can not pause, 'tis not for human will
To check the pen or shun its solemn trust;

> But living souls, discerning good and ill,
> May leave their records beautiful and just."

Having published a History of the Craig Settlement Church in 1876; Genealogies, Necrologies and Reminiscences of this Settlement in 1879; and in 1880, the Life, Labors and Death of Rev. John Rosbrugh, pastor of this Settlement Church, together with the history of the family, it is presumed we have little historical matter, not found in these volumes which would be suited to and of interest if presented upon this occasion. The least that we can do therefore is to attempt some general statements by which the memories of the dead past may be revived and set forth in connection with the living present. In this we must not be confined exclusively to the ecclesiastical or civil aspect of the case, but be given free access to either or both as circumstances suggest. This is the more needful when we remember that to a large extent the affairs of the church and of the people were inseparably connected. The Scotch-Irish were taught that the church must be sustained whether men or women made a profession of religion or not; and this was manifested in the cases of not a few who once lived in this county who were staunch supporters of religion though not openly making a profession of faith.

The first thing to which we wish to call attention is the fact that the ecclesiastical affairs of the Scotch-Irish of the County date well back to the beginning of things Presbyterian in this country. The formation of the first Presbytery, that of Philadelphia, took place, it seems, in 1706, and it was the only one till 1716. In this latter year it was divided into four parts, and so came into existence the Presbyteries of New Castle in Delaware; of Snow Hill in Maryland, and of Long Island in New York.

There is an interesting fact connected with the immigration of the Scotch-Irish, which goes far to explain the circumstance of the division of the Philadelphia Presbytery and the formation of the Synod of Philadelphia at the same time.

It seems that "as early as 1717 no less than five vessels of immigrants from the North of Ireland arrived on the coast of New England, but forbidden to land at Boston by the intolerant Puritan, the immigrants moved up the Kennebec, and there settled. The Winter of 1717-18 being one of unusual severity, the great majority of these settlers left the Kennebec and came overland into Pennsylvania, settling in Northampton County. Hence your Irish Settlement." So writes to me Dr. Egle, of Harrisburg, author of the Illustrated History of the Commonwealth of Pennsylvania, published in 1876.

So large a number coming at this time, it is to be presumed there was a considerable stream of immigration during several years previous, and these settling to the South of New England on the Atlantic seaboard, would explain the formation of the Presbyteries mentioned in the localities designated, and also explain the inducements held out to the large number who came in 1717-'18 to remove to the southward, into the bounds of these Presbyteries.

The same influx of Scotch-Irish Presbyterians would explain the formation of other settlements besides the ones in Northampton County, by the people finding it necessary to press from the seaboard toward the interior to carve out for themselves homes in the New World.

The truth of this is shown in the necessity felt for the formation of the Presbytery of Donegal, in Lancaster County, in 1732, in addition to the four Presbyteries already mentioned. This was the year after the Craig Settlement Church in Northampton County comes to notice in the records of the Synod of Philadelphia, which goes to show that these people had arrived and taken up their abode here previous to this time.

From this it will be seen that the Craig Settlement Church dates back to within twenty-five or twenty-six years of the inception of Presbyterianism, as an organized body, in this country.

Perhaps at this distant day no feelings will be hurt if we

whisper loud enough to be heard by all, that the Scotch-Irish ancestors of some of our most highly respected families were squatters. This will appear from the civil records bearing upon the transfer of landed estates.

The Province of Pennsylvania was granted by the Crown to William Penn, in 1681. At William Penn's death in 1718, his sons John, Thomas, and Richard became the Proprietaries. On the 18th of May, 1732, by a joint warrant of the Proprietaries, made at London, the Surveyor General was directed to lay off a tract of five thousand acres for the personal use of Thomas Penn. This was done and it included lands which had been occupied by at least some of the families who originated the Craig Settlement, as transfer deeds show.

The warrant for these five thousand acres was immediately transferred to Joseph Turner, of Philadelphia, and by him to William Allen in 1735. William Allen deeded part of this tract to James Craig in 1743, he being one of the first settlers.

From this it appears there were no surveys until after 1732. But the first settlers were on the ground previous to this time. The records of the Synod of Philadelphia seem to show that Elder Thomas Craig represented the church of the Craig Settlement in Synod, in 1731. The Scotch-Irish were here, therefore, previous to this date, and family records show us that they came and squatted upon unoccupied land, in 1728. Of this Dr. Egle, in his history of Pennsylvania, says:

"The proprietary land-office having been closed from 1718 to the year 1732, during the minorities of Richard and Thomas Penn, emigrants seated themselves without title on such vacant lands as they found convenient. The number of settlers of this kind entitled them to great consideration. Their rights accruing by priority of settlement, were recognized by the public, and passed, with their improvements, through many hands in confidence that they would receive the Proprietary sanction. Much agitation was produced when the Provincial proclamation required all who had not obtained and paid for warrants, to pay to the Receiver General within four months, the sums due for their lands, under penalty of ejectment. As a consequence great difficulties arose; the Assembly sought to compromise the matter by payment of the purchase money being postponed for several years longer." Page 75.

HUNTER SETTLEMENT

IT WILL be noticed that we have thus far used the term Craig Settlement in speaking of the Scotch-Irish of Northampton County. There were Scotch-Irish families, however, in another settlement within the bounds of county. The expression "Forks of Delaware" is a common one in early secular and ecclesiastical records. Whether this expression originated from the divergence of the streams of water, or from the divergence of Indian trails, the locality designated was that lying between the Lehigh—the West Branch, and the Delaware proper—North Branch.

The Craig Settlement was on the West Branch, and broadly speaking, included the section of county from the neighborhood of Bath westward to the Lehigh River. The Hunter, or North Settlement, embraced the section of country on the Delaware, from the neighborhood of Martin's Creek northward through the Townships of Lower and Upper Mt. Bethel. That this is a correct statement of the facts may be verified by reference to various records. In the record made relative to the ordination and installation of the first pastor, Rev. Daniel Lawrence, in the "Forks of Delaware," April 2d, 1747, it was said he was to "preach two-thirds of his time at the Western Settlement, and one-third at the Northern."

On the inside of the cover of the original account book of the Craig Settlement Church, the following inscription is found, viz.:

"The account book of the Congregation of the West Branch of Delaware in the Forks, Jan. 9th, 1749. The Payments to Commence May 1st, 1749, and continue according to terms."

An Abington Presbytery record, of Oct. 4th, 1753, speaks of "Both Settlements in the Forks of Delaware," * * * "and the North Branch particularly." A Philadelphia Presbytery record, of Aug. 13th, 1761, speaks of supplies "At the Forks of Delaware" * * * "two Sabbaths at Allentown and one at Hunter's."

As near as can be ascertained, the Hunter Settlement was started about 1730, or practically at the same time as the Craig Settlement. In order to follow the fortunes of the Scotch-Irish in the Hunter Settlement, it will be well for us not to lose sight of the ecclesiastical connections because these had a bearing upon their history. The records just referred to show that the churches in the Craig and Hunter settlements were under the same ministers during their early history.

The original Presbytery of Philadelphia being organized in 1706, we must look to these records for ecclesiastical information down to 1738. They throw little light upon the situation. In the Minutes of the Synod of Philadelphia for 1731, the name of Elder Thomas Craig appears and a natural inference is that he was from the Craig Settlement, but no reference seems to be made to the Hunter Settlement.

Up to 1738, the Craig Settlement Church seems to have been in an unsettled condition, and the same perhaps may be truly said of the Hunter Settlement church, if there were enough people in the community to sustain a church organization. It is perhaps safe to assume that when "Forks of Delaware" is mentioned in ecclesiastical records prior to 1747, it means Hunter's Settlement, in conjunction with the Craig Settlement, so far as the circumstances would justify.

This brings us to a change in ecclesiastical jurisdiction caused by developments on the New Jersey side of the Delaware River, opposite to Hunter's Settlement. In 1738 the Presbytery of New Brunswick was constituted out of the Presbyteries of Philadelphia and New York. This is made apparent from the following record of the Synod of Philadelphia:

"Upon a supplication of some members of the Presbytery of New York to be erected into a district Presbytery with some members of the Presbytery of Philadelphia, overtured."

"That the petition be granted, and that all to the northward and eastward of Maiden Head and Hopewell unto the Raritan River, including also Staten Island, Piscatua, Amboy,

Bound Brook, Basking Ridge, Turkey, Rocksiticus, Minisinks, Pequelly and Crosswicks be the bounds of the Presbytery, and that the said Presbytery be distinguished by the name of the Presbytery of New Brunswick, and that the time of their meeting to be the second Tuesday of August next at New Brunswick."

Almost simultaneously with the organization of the new Presbytery we find the Hunter's and Craig Settlement Churches repairing thither for ecclesiastical help. They sought supplies from the New Brunswick Presbytery in 1738.

It appears that their application came up before the Presbytery for consideration, July 31, 1739, as they were convened at New Brunswick. In answer thereto it was agreed that Mr. Gilbert Tennent preach at the Forks some time this fall. It seems that Mr. Tennent fulfilled his appointment and visited the Forks in the latter part of 1739.

In the Spring of 1740 they again applied to the Presbytery for a supply of preaching, and the matter came up for consideration May 31st of that year. The following action was taken with reference thereto:

In compliance with the afore-mentioned supplication for supplies, the Presbytery do appoint as follows: "That Mr. Robinson supply the Forks the first Sabbath of July; that Mr. Campbell supply Tehicken half the time and Newton and the Forks the other half equally between them."

The Presbytery convened at New Brunswick again that year, August 2d, at which time it was reported that the foregoing appointments had been complied with. The same day "A call was presented from the Forks of the Delaware for McKnight's labors." This call seems not to have been accepted. Two days later, at the same meeting of the Presbytery, August 4, 1740, the people again petitioned for preaching. We find a reference made to it under that date in the following record:

"A petition from the Forks of the Delaware and Mr. Green's being presented to the Presbytery in compliance therewith, they thought proper to advise Mr. Campbell to supply them as often as he shall judge proper till our next." How often, or just what length of time Mr. Campbell continued to preach under this appointment, does not appear. He ceased, however, before the Spring of 1742.

On May 29th, 1742, we find the people petitioning again for preaching. This time it was in conjunction with Greenwich. We are unable to decide from the records whether this petition from the Forks was from Hunter's Settlement to the exclusion of Craig's; or from Craig's to the exclusion of Hunter's. It is to be presumed, however, it was from them conjointly. The minister they desired to have sent to them was Rev. Charles McKnight, presumably the same to whom they had extended a call in August, 1740. The application came up before Presbytery on the above date, as it was convened in Philadelphia. Whether Mr. McKnight was secured or not does not appear. If he did go, it was but for a short time, for Oct. 12th of this year we find the people again asking for supplies.

In answer to this application the Presbytery appointed Mr. Campbell to devote one-third of his time to them. For immediate supply of the pulpit we find the following appointments: Rev. Wm. Dean to preach the next Sabbath, next after October 13th, 1742, at Neshaminy, and then three Sabbaths at the Forks of the Delaware. After this he was to supply Cohensie and Cape May until within three Sabbaths of the next meeting of the Presbytery, which was to be held on the fourth Tuesday of May, 1743. These three Sabbaths were to be spent in the Forks of the Delaware.

With Mr. Campbell devoting one-third of his time to the Forks and Greenwich, in addition to these six Sabbaths of Mr. Dean, the Forks of the Delaware must have enjoyed a good supply of preaching from October 12, 1742, to the latter part of May, 1743.

At the meeting of the Presbytery in Philadelphia, on the fourth Tuesday of May, (May 26), 1743, three calls were presented for the services of Mr. Dean: One from the Forks of the Delaware, one from the Forks of the Brandywine, and one from Cape May.

Mr. Dean not being prepared to decide whether he would accept any one of these calls, was granted till the next meeting of Presbytery to consider the matter. In the meantime, Presbytery directed Mr. Dean to supply the Forks of the Delaware until their next meeting; at the same time preach as much as was convenient at Pequea.

The Presbytery next convened, August 12th, 1743, at which time Mr. Dean, by letter, signified that he was not yet ready to declare his acceptance of any one of the calls which had been presented to him, but was willing to continue to supply under the existing arrangement. Presbytery directed him to continue to supply in the Forks of Delaware, and instead of preaching at Pequea and Forks of Brandywine, as was intended, devote that time to preaching at Tehicken and Bethlehem.

At a meeting of Presbytery held Oct. 12th, 1743, Mr. Dean declared his non-acceptance of any of the calls that had been presented to him. It now seems his labors ceased in this locality until the next year. We find the next day, Oct. 13th, 1743, Mr. Campbell is permitted by Presbytery to supply Tehicken and Bethlehem, which had been assigned to Mr. Dean. If he had been devoting one-third of his time to the Forks of Delaware and Greenwich, as by appointment of Oct. 12th, 1742, which does not clearly appear, he now ceased to devote so much time to the Forks as formerly. Presbytery simply requested him to supply the Forks of Delaware sometimes. At this meeting of Presbytery, Oct. 13th, 1743, Rev. Charles Beatty was ordered to supply in the Forks of Delaware sometimes.

At the Spring meeting of Presbytery, in 1744, we find the people asking for supplies. The Presbytery considered their petition May 26th, and accordingly sent Mr. Dean to supply the Forks till the next meeting, which was on Sept. 12th. There being no record to the contrary, it is presumed Mr. Dean fulfilled the appointment, whether he devoted his whole time to the Forks or not does not appear.

Now emerges a significant epoch in the history of the Hunter Settlement. It was at this time, 1744, that David Brainerd, the Missionary to the Indians, located at Martin's Creek. Within recent years a monument has been erected to mark the spot where his cabin stood.

While his mission was to the Indians, doubtless, the Scotch-Irish of Hunter's Settlement often listened to his preaching in their immediate neighborhood. His diary shows a number of visits to the Scotch-Irish of the Craig Settlement; as, for instance, July 23, and 27, Oct. 13, and 14, and Dec. 29, 30, and 31, 1744. April 27, Sept. 4, and 26, 1745, and Feb. 18, 1746. He says under this latter date: "Preached to an assembly of Irish people nearly fifteen miles distant from the Indians." This was near the end of his earthly labors, as he died in 1747. If he discoursed to these white people "fifteen"—(The distance to the Craig Settlement) miles, as he says, from his lodgings, it is presumed he preached more frequently to the Scotch-Irish white people of Hunter's Settlement, in the midst of which he lived. As an evidence of this we find in his diary the following, under date of Apr. 14th, 1745. "Was disordered in body with fatigue of the late journey, but was enabled, however, to preach to a considerable assembly of white people, gathered from all parts round about, with some freedom, from Ezek. xxxiii. 11.

Aside from the presence of David Brainerd, we find Presbytery convened Sept. 12th, 1744, at which time Mr. Dean's appointment in the Forks having closed, the people reserved their application for supplies. In accordance with this application, Rev. Eleazer Wales was appointed to supply them the two last Sabbaths of Sept. and the first Sabbath of Oct. Mr. Beatty was also appointed to supply one Sabbath, and Mr. Dean as much as he could until the next meeting of Presbytery.

We find, however, that Mr. Dean did not preach in the Forks in accordance with this appointment, as he was dismissed by the Presbytery of New Brunswick, Oct. 4th of this year, to connect himself with the Presbytery of New Castle. On May 19th, 1745, the Presbytery met and the Forks people made their usual application for preaching, accompanied with a request for the administration of the Lord's Supper in their midst. From the records of this meeting we learn that Mr. Daniel Lawrence preached at the last Sabbath in June. Presbytery convened Sept. 20th, 1745, at which time two calls were brought in for the pastoral services of Mr. Daniel Lawrence. The one was from the two Bethlehems, in New Jersey; the other from Maiden Head and Hopewell. Mr. Lawrence not being present at the meeting of Presbytery, consideration of these calls was deferred until the next meeting. Under the circumstances, Mr. Lawrence was directed to supply two Sabbaths at Maiden Head and Hopewell, and then he was to repair to the Forks of Delaware. He was to supply two-thirds of his time in the Forks and devote the other third to the two Bethlehems, in New Jersey. July 21, 1746, Presbytery convened. At this meeting there was a supplication from the congregations at Maiden Head and Hopewell, requesting the labors of Mr. Lawrence until the next meeting of Presbytery, by way of trial, with a view to his settlement there, likewise a supplication from the Bethlehems for the same purpose.

Some people from Oxford Furnace also supplicated that they might share the labors of Mr. Lawrence in case he should be appointed to supply the Forks of Delaware. It seems that in the midst of this clamor, as it were, for the services of Mr. Lawrence, the Presbytery returned him to his labors in the Forks, with instructions to preach every fifth Sabbath at Tunis Quick's, in the Forks of the Delaware. Thus things seem to have survived until the meeting of Presbytery, Oct. 16th, 1746. At this meeting the people in the Forks renewed their call for Mr. Lawrence to undertake the pastoral charge among them. The matter being proposed to him by Presbytery, he signified his acceptance of the call; Presbytery thereupon appointed a committee to ordain and install him.

This committee was composed of Rev. Richard Treat, Rev. James Campbell, Rev. James Davenport, Rev. James McCrea, and Rev. Charles Beatty. Rev. Richard Treat was to "preside over the whole affair." Mr. Lawrence was given John 3:18, from which to preach a popular sermon as part of trial for ordination. He was also directed to prepare a Latin Exegesis and hand it in to the committee, in the Forks of Delaware, on the first day of April, 1747. The committee having assembled in the Forks at this time, and these requirements having been complied with on the part of Mr. Lawrence, Presbytery directed the committee to proceed to his ordination and installation, if the way should be found in all other respects clear.

The ordination and installation was to take place April 2d. The instructions of Presbytery were carried out, as we heard from the following report. "Forks of Delaware, Apr. 2d, 1747. The committee appointed by Presbytery to attend to the ordination of Mr. Daniel Lawrence, viz.: Mr. Treat, Mr. Davenport, Mr. McCrea, Mr. Campbell, (Mr. Beatty for good reasons not attending), did according to appointment meet at the place, and having yesterday heard him preach a sermon on John 3:18, and received his exegesis (upon the question assigned) both to good satisfaction, and there appearing no objection in the way, they proceeded this day according to appointment, with fasting and prayer and imposition of hands, to ordain Mr. Lawrence to the Gospel Ministry over this people. Concluded with prayer and blessing."

Then and there it was agreed by the representatives of the two settlements that they have and desire to be united; that so long as Mr. Lawrence shall continue to be minister to them both that he shall preach two-thirds of his time at the Western Settlement, and the other one-third part at the Northern, without any alteration except by judgment of Presbytery. This record is significant in that it shows the first recorded settlement of a pastor over the churches in the two Scotch-Irish settlements in Northampton County. While they had supplies of preaching previous to this time, they seem to have been united in receiving the ministrations of those sent among them. This seems to be implied in the expression: "Then and there it was agreed by the representatives of the two settlements that they have (been) and desire to be united." The absence of records to show that Hunter Settlement had previously acted separately seems to corroborate this assumption.

On account of difficulties with some of the people of his charge, as well as ill health, Mr. Lawrence spent the winter of 1747, and spring of 1748 at Cape May. At a meeting of the Synod of New York, convened at Maiden Head, May 18, 1748, we find the following record: At the sitting of the Synod in the forenoon of May 19th, "motion was made to the Synod in behalf of Cape May, and in order to have some provision made for the settlement of a minister there * * * * the Synod proceeded to consider the motion respecting Cape May, and in order to the relief of that people, the Synod doth recommend to the Presbytery of New Brunswick to send down Mr. Lawrence immediately for a few salt baths." Thus it would seem Mr. Lawrence by his sojourn at Cape May during the winter opened the way for his return there in the spring, as above indicated.

How long he remained there at this time does not appear. It was probably, however, only for the few Sabbaths indicated. Returning to the Forks of Delaware, he seems to have continued his labors until the spring of 1752. We must now take into consideration ecclesiastical changes in the Presbyterian church-at-large, to understand what influences were brought to bear upon the Scotch-Irish of the Hunter, as well as of the Craig Settlement.

There was a schism in the Presbyterian church-at-large, in 1741; and this resulted in the formation of a new Synod called the Synod of New York, in addition to the former Synod of Philadelphia. The Presbytery of New Brunswick was attached to the Synod of New York.

As a consequence, however, of the schism of 1741, there was a rivalry between the two Synods for jurisdiction in these parts. Out of this rivalry came the formation of a new Presbytery called Abington, by the Synod of New York. This appears from the following record in the minutes of the Synod for the year 1751: "A petition of a number of the members of the Presbytery of New Brunswick, praying to be erected into a distinct Presbytery, was brought into the Synod. The further consideration of it deferred till the next sederunt * * * *". The consideration of the petition of some members of the Presbytery of New Brunswick was resumed, and after hearing what they had to offer in support thereof the Synod agreed to grant said petition, and to erect that part of the Presbytery of New Brunswick that live in Pennsylvania, together with those who live in New Jersey, to the southward of Philadelphia, bordering upon Delaware, into a distinct Presbytery by the name of the Presbytery of Abington, and also appoint their first meeting to be at Philadelphia the third Wednesday in May next."

Thus the Hunter Settlement Church, as well as that of the Craig Settlement, with their pastor, Mr. Lawrence, came under the jurisdiction of the Presbytery of Abington.

The first meeting of the New Presbytery we have seen by the direction of Synod, was held on the third Wednesday of May (20), 1752, in the city of Philadelphia. At this meeting Cape May supplicated that Mr. Lawrence might be sent unto them on trial for settlement, in case he be liberated from his present charge.

The matter of dissolution of the pastoral relation between Mr. Lawrence and the churches in the Forks of the Delaware, came up for consideration in the Presbytery the next day. After hearing Mr. Lawrence and the commissioners from the charge, the Presbytery finally dissolved the pastoral relation, assigning as a reason for so doing the feeble health of Mr. Lawrence, and the prospect of his recovery by removing to some other field of labor.

Thus the Forks churches became vacant, and the first pastorate ended May 21, 1752. This was the year, it will be noticed, that Northampton County was erected out of Bucks.

After Mr. Lawrence left the Forks. the churches were supplied principally by the Presbytery till 1761. As appears from the records of Presbytery, these supplies were as follows: Immediately upon the dissolution of the pastoral relation, the commissioners from the Forks present at the meeting of the Presbytery, May 21st, 1752, asked for supplies. In answer to this request, Mr. Lawrence was to supply two Sabbaths; Mr. Charles Beatty, two; Mr. James Campbell, two; Mr. Thomas Lewis, one. Further, provisionally, Mr. Beatty, Mr. Campbell, Mr. Richard Treat and Mr. Lewis were to supply them each one Sabbath in addition.

At the meeting of Presbytery at Philadelphia September 19th, 1752, supplies were asked for. Mr. Lawrence was appointed to preach four Sabbaths; Mr. Beatty, two; Mr. Campbell, two; and if Mr. Morrison be at liberty, he is desired to supply this winter between Tehicken and the Forks.

At Presbytery in Philadelphia, May 16th, 1753, supplies were asked for. Mr. Lawrence was appointed to supply "Two or three at the Forks". June 20th of this year, preaching was again applied for, and Mr. Henry Martin was sent to preach four Sabbaths.

At Philadelphia, October 4th, 1753, "Application was also made from both settlements in the Forks of the Delaware for supplies, and the North Branch particularly desire leave to apply to the Presbytery of New Brunswick, or any other Presbytery belonging to our Synod for the same purpose.

This is a significant record in that it implies that the Hunter Settlement people had been united with those of the Craig Settlement in support of the Gospel as specified in the record of ordination and installation of Mr. Lawrence. They now ask permission to independently seek for supplies from the New Brunswick Presbytery, which had jurisdiction just across the Delaware River from them in New Jersey, and with which they had been connected prior to the formation of the Abington Presbytery.

The next month, November 21st, there was a meeting of the Presbytery in Philadelphia, at which time Mr. Benjamin

Chestnut was appointed to preach four Sabbaths and Mr. Henry Martin four. At this meeting the Presbytery said: "The Forks of the Delaware have full liberty to make application to any Presbytery belonging to our Synod for as much supply as they can afford." Thus was granted the request of the Hunter Settlement people as made the previous month.

At a meeting of the Presbytery at Newton, April 9th, 1754, Mr. Martin reported that he had preached two of the Sabbaths of his appointment at the Forks, but had failed the other two for reasons which were sustained by the Presbytery. At this meeting appointments were made for the Forks as follows: Rev. Andrew Hunter, third and fourth Sabbaths; Mr. Martin, two; Mr. Beatty, two. These appointments, as subsequently reported, were complied with.

Philadelphia, November 5th, 1754, Mr. Hunter was appointed supply, three Sabbaths, and Mr. Martin two, which were complied with.

Philadelphia, May 28th, 1755. Mr. Lawrence was sent to supply the first Sabbath of October; Mr. Martin, two; and Mr. Chestnut, two Sabbaths.

At this meeting of the Presbytery, "The Congregations of the Forks of the Delaware" asked permission to present a call to a "candidate" under the care of the Presbytery of New Brunswick, and if he did not accept, asked for what supplies the Presbytery might be able to give them.

Thus it seems the Forks congregations had been improving the permission granted the previous fall to seek supplies from the New Brunswick Presbytery, which permission had been more particularly asked for by the Hunter Settlement people. The request for the permission to present a call to a member of the New Brunswick Presbytery was acceded to, but for whom the call was made out does not appear. That it was not accepted is manifest from the fact that the congregation remained vacant for several years after.

Philadelphia, October 21st, 1755, Mr. Beatty, Mr. Chestnut and Mr. Martin were appointed to supply each one Sabbath and fulfilled their appointments.

Philadelphia, September 21st, 1756, Mr. Beatty was appointed to supply three Sabbaths; Mr. Chestnut, three; and Mr. Martin, two, before the next (May) meeting of the Presbytery.

Philadelphia, May 24th, 1757, Rev. William Ramsey was appointed to supply the last Sabbath in June and the first two in July; Mr. Martin, two before the next meeting of Presbytery; Mr. Chestnut, the first two Sabbaths in August, and Mr. Beatty, the first Sabbath in September.

Philadelphia, October 4th, 1757. Mr. Martin was appointed to preach four Sabbaths; Mr. Beatty, one; and Mr. Chestnut, the second Sabbath in November.

Philadelphia, May 17th, 1758. Mr. Chestnut was appointed to preach two Sabbaths and Mr. Martin to devote one-fourth of his time to the churches in the Forks.

At this juncture of affairs there was again a change in the matter of ecclesiastical jurisdiction with reference to the Hunter and Craig Settlement churches. The former Synods of New York and Philadelphia now united under the name of the Synod of New York and Philadelphia. They first met as a united body on the afternoon of May 29th, 1758. The next day the Presbyteries were arranged. It was agreed that the Presbytery of New Brunswick continue as it is, only that Messrs. Cowel and Guild are added to it. "Agreed that Messrs. Cross, Gilbert Tennent, Francis Allison, Treat, Chestnut, Martin, Beatty, Greenman, Hunter, Ramsey, Lawrence and Kinkead be the Presbytery of Philadelphia, to meet for the first time on Wednesday next, at four o'clock in the afternoon at the old Presbyterian church." Thus passed out of existence the Presbytery of Abington to which the Forks churches belonged, and they came under the jurisdiction of the new Philadelphia Presbytery.

Accordingly, by this Presbytery, at Philadelphia, November 30, 1758, Mr. Chestnut was appointed to preach two Sabbaths in the fall, and two in the spring; and Mr. Martin to preach four Sabbaths, two of them to be in the winter, at the Forks.

Philadelphia, May 15th, 1759. Rev. James Latta was appointed to preach the fourth and fifth Sabbaths in September; Mr. Chestnut, four Sabbaths, two of them being the last Sabbath in July and the first in August; Mr. Beatty, two Sabbaths; and Mr. Martin, "as much as he can".

Philadelphia, October 2d, 1759. Presbytery appointed Mr. Martin to preach four Sabbaths; Mr. Chestnut, four; Rev. John Simonton, two; and Mr. Beatty, two.

Philadelphia, May 14th, 1760. Rev. Joseph Montgomery was appointed to preach one Sabbath and Mr. Latta, two.

Philadelphia, August 20th, 1760. Mr. Latta was appointed to supply two Sabbaths.

Philadelphia, November 20th, 1760. Mr. Latta was appointed to supply two Sabbaths before the next meeting of Presbytery, and Mr. Chestnut two Sabbaths in March.

This completed the list of supplies for this long vacancy. In addition to these, furnished by the Presbyteries of Abington and Philadelphia, under whose jurisdiction the churches in the Forks were during the vacancy, we find from evidence preserved in the bounds of the congregation that Rev. Benjamin Hait, of the Presbytery of New Brunswick, preached in 1758; and Rev. Thomas Lewis, of the Presbytery of Suffolk, preached in 1759.

In 1757, Thomas Buckman purchased of William Allen, already referred to in connection with the Craig Settlement, seven hundred acres of land along the Delaware River, above the mouth of Martin's Creek. This tract included the church and graveyard lots.

If a visit is paid to the locality of what is familiarly known as the "Three Churches" at Martin's Creek, in Lower Mt. Bethel Township, (now Washington Township), to the property owned by Mr. Elias Hutchison in 1876, on the road from Martin's Creek to Easton, and to a point about a mile below Ackermanville, there will be found the old burying ground, where lie the ashes of many of the Scotch-Irish families who belonged to the Hunter Settlement.

Upon the tombstones will be found such inscriptions as these:

Alexander Miller, died September 5, 1765, in the 84th year of his age.

Robert Lyle, Esq., died December 9th, 1765, in the 67th year of his age.

James Martin, died May 20th, 1767, aged 57 years.

James Moody, died July 31st, 1771, aged 25 years.

These were doubtless among the early settlers. The James Martin here mentioned, it seems, was the one who gave Martin's Creek its name. The early family names were Buckman, Hutchison, Lockhard, McFarren, Moore, Nielson, and Ross.

We now approach the second pastorate in the Hunter Settlement. At a meeting of the Presbytery of Philadelphia in the City of Philadelphia, August 13th, 1761, Rev. John Clark presented his credentials from the Presbytery of New Brunswick and was received a member of the Presbytery. The same day a call was presented to him from the Forks of the Delaware. He took the matter under consideration until the next meeting.

In the meantime he was directed to supply at the Forks of the Delaware in the following manner, viz:—Two Sabbaths at Allentown, interchangeably, except two Sabbaths at Tehicken. Here, it will be noticed, the church in the Craig Settlement began to be designated by the name of the Chief Justice, Allen—as Allenstown, or Allen Township, which name it bears to this day. This was to more clearly distinguish it from the other church in the "Forks", Mt. Bethel in the Hunter's Settlement.

For some reason, no record of which has come to hand, the people in the Forks became divided upon the subject of calling Mr. Clark. Whether this opposition was from the Craig Settlement, or from Hunter's, or from both, does not clearly appear, but the presumption is that it was at least in part from Hunter's, for opposition to Mr. Clark developed there at a little later period.

At the next meeting of the Presbytery, November 17th, 1761, both parties appeared to press their views in the matter. The one party did not wish the Presbytery to permit Mr. Clark to accept the call which he had under consideration; the other insisted upon their right to call him.

The Presbytery inquired of the commissioners, who favored the calling of Mr. Clark, whether they thought they were able to support him as promised in their call, in case the opposing party declined to assist. If they thought they could, they were at liberty to prosecute their call, leaving the opposing party to act according to their own judgment. It seems the friends of Mr. Clark expressed their ability to fulfill their promises to him, as at a later hour of the same day Mr. Clark signified to the Presbytery his acceptance of the call from the Forks of the Delaware, in which they promised him during his continuance with them as a regular Gospel minister the sum of * * * pounds per annum and the use of a parsonage.

The parsonage referred to was doubtless within the bounds of the Craig Settlement as may be gathered from what the writer has said in his history of the Allen Township or Craig Settlement Church on the subject of the Parsonage Farm. At this meeting of the Presbytery, November 17th, 1761, Mr. Latta was appointed to preach at the Forks, three Sabbaths in March; and Mr. Chestnut, the last Sabbath of November.

It would seem the dissatisfied ones were not disposed to acquiesce in the settlement of Mr. Clark, as we find that at the meeting of Presbytery in Philadelphia, April 6th, 1762: "A few people in the Forks of Delaware applied for preaching." Manifestly there was a turmoil kept up among the people. The installation of Mr. Clark had been deferred up to this time, probably on account of the difficulties; now, however, a request was made for his installation. The request was acceded to by Presbytery, but the time for the installation was to be fixed at the next meeting.

Accordingly, May 18th, 1762, at Philadelphia, the Presbytery fixed Wednesday, October 13th, following as the day for Mr. Clark's installation. Rev. Richard Treat was to preside and preach the sermon; Rev. Henry Martin, Rev. James Latta, and Rev. Charles Beatty were to assist in the other parts of the service. This committee reported to Presbytery, November 9th, 1762, that they had installed Mr. Clark according to appointment. Thus the Forks churches came under the care of the second regular pastor again, October 13th, 1762. At this juncture it is well to note that in 1759, Samuel Rea purchased two hundred acres of the seven hundred acre tract which Thomas Buckman purchased, in 1757, from William Allen, and which included the church and grave-yard lots.

It seems the troubles well nigh, if not wholly, subsided after the installation of Mr. Clark. Apparently things moved along smoothly in the pastoral charge until 1766. In the meantime a slight change in ecclesiastical jurisdiction is to be noted. On the afternoon of May 28th, 1762, the Synod of New York and Philadelphia took the following action, viz.: "In compliance with a request from some members of Philadelphia Presbytery, the Synod appoint that the members of that Presbytery be erected into two Presbyteries for one year at least, and that the new Presbytery be called by the names of the Second Presbytery of Philadelphia, and that their first meeting be at the First Presbyterian Church in this city, the second Tuesday in August."

There were now the First and Second Presbyteries of Philadelphia. This arrangement continued till 1786. In the forenoon of May 22d, of this year, the Synod of New York and Philadelphia took the following action:

"That the distinction of First Presbytery and Second Presbytery of Philadelphia, shall henceforth cease, and that the members of these two Presbyteries, except those that are annexed to the Presbyteries of Baltimore and Carlisle, be united into one Presbytery to be known by the name of the Presbytery of Philadelphia, to hold their first meeting on the third Tuesday of October next in the City of Philadelphia, and the Rev. Dr. Sproat to preside, or in his absence, the senior minister present. Thus we see the Hunter Settlement Church, with that of the Craig Settlement, were under the jurisdiction of the First Philadelphia Presbytery from 1762, till they were relegated to the Presbytery of New Brunswick in 1770.

October 26th, 1766, difficulties in the Hunter Settlement, or Mount Bethel Church, were brought to the attention of the First Presbytery of Philadelphia. Mr. Clark desired to be released from his pastoral charge. This was not acceded to by Presbytery, but all parties were counseled to exercise Christian forbearance, and settle their difficulties in an amicable manner. Thus things were quieted down till the next spring. April 7th, 1767, however, the Hunter Settlement, or Mt. Bethel people asked Presbytery to appoint a committee to inquire into their affairs, and call Mr. Clark to account upon some charges which they desired to prefer against him. Mr. Clark made a satisfactory explanation to Presbytery in regard to the matters and Rev. Charles Beatty and Rev. William Ramsey were sent to Mt. Bethel as a healing committee.

Notwithstanding this, May 21st, 1767, commissioners from Mt. Bethel reported to Presbytery that there was no hope of peace and reconciliation among them; whereupon Rev. Richard Treat, Rev. Enoch Green, and Rev. Benjamin Chestnut, from the First Philadelphia Presbytery, were added to the committee already appointed, and Rev. John Hanna, Rev. William Kirkpatrick, and Rev. John Rosbrugh, of the Presbytery of New Brunswick, were invited to meet with them at Mt. Bethel on the third Tuesday of June, and endeavor to settle the difficulties.

November 3d, 1767, this committee reported that some of them had fulfilled the duties of their appointment, but as there was no quorum present, they had taken no decisive action. They had, however, endeavored to allay the existing animosity. The next day, November 5th, owing to the gloomy aspect of affairs and the bodily weakness of the pastor, Presbytery released Mr. Clark from his pastoral charge. Thus the churches in the Forks became vacant again, November 4th, 1767.

This vacancy was not of long duration. From time to time, supplies were granted by the Presbytery. The next spring after Mr. Clark left, the Presbytery, May 28th, 1768, sent Rev. Alexander Mitchell to supply two Sabbaths, and again November 23d, to supply one Sabbath. March 29th, 1769, the Craig Settlement people, apparently on their own motion, and without reference to the people of the Hunter Settlement, or the Mt. Bethel people, made a move in the direction of separation ecclesiastically from the latter portion of the Scotch-Irish people in the Forks of the Delaware. They desired to extend a call to Rev. John Rosbrugh, who was pastor of the Greenwich congregation across the Delaware River in New Jersey, opposite to the Forks, who was a member of the New Brunswick Presbytery.

Mr. Rosbrugh had been ordained and installed at Greenwich, December 11th, 1764, doubtless in conjunction with Mansfield, Woodhouse (Washington), and Oxford (the Oxford near Belvidere). Having entered upon the full work of the ministry, he felt he ought to take to himself a wife again, a first help-meet having been taken away by death. Belonging to the class known as Scotch-Irish, it was most natural for him to seek a companion from among those who were of similar origin.

To what better source could he go than to the Scotch-Irish of the Forks of the Delaware? To the Craig Settlement he looked for the object of his desire. It was not long till he found and won one who was to share his fortunes in life. He became intimate with the family of James Ralston, an Elder in the Craig Settlement Church. He married the daughter Jane of this family, and took her to his home in the bounds of the congregation at Mansfield and Woodhouse.

The time of the marriage we have not been able to learn, but conjecture it was in the early part of 1766.

The location of the three separate parts of Mr. Ros-

The Present Allen Township Presbyterian Church, built of Stone in 1813. Weatherboarded in the meantime. The first two churches were built of logs. (See page 310.)

brugh's charge, some ten to fourteen miles apart, would indicate that his labors must have been arduous aside from other discouragements. The discouraging phase of his experience is reflected in a representation which he made of his charge to Presbytery April 19th, 1768. The record is as follows:

"Mr. Rosbrugh represented to the Presbytery that Mansfield-Woodhouse, one branch of his present charge, through the removal of sundry of his members out of the congregation, and by other means were now become so few and weak as not to be able to contribute their quota towards his support, and that sundry of them had consented to his leaving them. And that seeing the other branches of his charge were not able to make up the deficiency of that now mentioned, and that as his circumstances are straitened and necessitous, these things laid him under the disagreeable necessity of asking to be wholly dismissed from his present charge.

The consideration of this matter was laid over till the next day. It then came up and the following record was made with regard to it:

"Mr. Rosbrugh's request for a removal from his present charge, came under consideration, and the Presbytery after hearing and considering the reasons for said motion, do judge that the matter is not yet ripe for proceeding to his removal, as it does not appear to us that Mansfield-Woodhouse, the branch of the congregation which it seems is most deficient in supporting Mr. Rosbrugh, have been formally notified of Mr. Rosbrugh's design at this time to sue for a dismission from them; neither is there any representative here to answer for them; neither is there any one here to represent Oxford congregation, which is another branch of his charge; and as the removal of a minister is a weighty matter, and not to be rashly done, we would proceed with all possible tenderness and caution in it. We therefore think proper to defer the matter till the fall Presbytery, and in the meantime order that Mr. Rosbrugh give due notice to the people of Mansfield-Woodhouse that unless they discharge their arrears and pay their quota as usual, his labors shall be taken from them; and should they decline to bear their part as before, then Mr. Rosbrugh is to preach one-half of his time till next Presbytery, at Greenwich, and a third part at Oxford, and the remainder at discretion."

Such was the status of affairs in April, 1768. At the same meeting of Presbytery, when the foregoing action was taken, Mr. Rosbrugh was appointed to supply one Sabbath at Smithfield and one at Allentown, or Craig Settlement Church. At the fall meeting of Presbytery, October 18th, 1768, the report was brought in that Mansfield-Woodhouse had failed to make up their quota of the salary, and that Mr. Rosbrugh had accordingly preached one-half of his time at Greenwich, and one-third at Oxford. The Presbytery adjourned to meet at Oxford on the third Wednesday of November to further consider the matter. At this meeting it seems some arrangement was made and certain conditions specified upon which he was to remain in charge of Greenwich and Oxford. At the spring meeting of Presbytery, however, April 18th, 1769, it was reported that Oxford and Greenwich had failed to comply with the conditions upon which he was to remain with them, and he was accordingly dismissed from all parts of his charge.

At the same meeting of Presbytery when he was released from his pastoral charge, a call was presented to him to take charge of the Craig Settlement Church, in connection with Greenwich. He was now called to the congregation in which his father-in-law, James Ralston, was an Elder, and his wife's family were members. This matter had been well forwarded before the meeting of the New Brunswick Presbytery which convened to dissolve the pastoral relation at Oxford and Greenwich, March 29th, 1769. The Craig Settlement people asked permission of the First Philadelphia Presbytery, to which they belonged, to present a call to Mr. Rosbrugh of the New Brunswick Presbytery; showing that they had decided at that time to call him. They were advised to secure, in connection with Mt. Bethel or Hunter Settlement people, as much of his time as they could.

Mr. Rosbrugh had expressed his willingness to accept the call to the Forks, as early as April 3d, of this year, and the following record was made in the Craig Settlement Church book, viz.:

"The Rev. John Rosbrugh accepted the call to Allentown congregation the 3d day of April, 1769; that is to allow the congregation two-thirds of his time for * * * pounds per annum." The contemplated arrangement then doubtless was to give Greenwich one-third, and the Craig Settlement people two-thirds of the minister's time. So far as the records indicate, it would seem the Hunter Settlement people were given practically the go-by. With this arrangement in view, the matter was brought before the Presbytery of New Brunswick, where it was duly considered, April 18th, 1769, and it was decided to make such arrangement, provided the Craig Settlement Church was "regularly set off to the Presbytery of New Brunswick", it having been under the care of the Presbytery of Abington from 1751 to 1758, and from that time on, under the First Presbytery of Philadelphia.

In pursuance of the stipulation of the Presbytery of New Brunswick, the Allen Township or Craig Settlement people petitioned the Synod of New York and Philadelphia, convened in Philadelphia, to set them off to New Brunswick Presbytery. The petition came up for consideration on the afternoon of May 23d, 1769, and the following action was taken, viz.: "A petition from the congregation, in the Forks of Delaware, to be taken from under the care of the First Presbytery of Philadelphia, and to be put under the care of the Presbytery of New Brunswick, was brought in and read. After the committee on behalf of the congregation and both Presbyteries concerned were heard, it appeared not expedient for the present to grant the prayer of the petition.

But the Synod ordered the First Presbytery of Philadelphia to inquire more particularly into the state and connection of that congregation, and empower said Presbytery to set them off to the Presbytery of New Brunswick if it should appear expedient; or if it should appear more expedient to set off the congregation of Greenwich to the First Presbytery of Philadelphia, the Presbytery of New Brunswick are empowered to set them off." Notwithstanding this delay, Mr. Rosbrugh doubtless devoted his time thereafter almost exclusively to the Craig Settlement and Greenwich people. This is confirmed by a record made October 19th, 1769, by the Presbytery of New Brunswick, which is as follows:

"That Mr. Rosbrugh be a constant supply to the people at Greenwich and Allentown, except 3d Sabbath, to Mt. Bethel, till our next." This would seem to indicate that the well-being of the Hunter Settlement people was not overlooked by the New Brunswick Presbytery. The expression—"Except 3d Sabbath, to Mt. Bethel" may perhaps not inconsistently be interpreted to mean that every third Sabbath was to be devoted to the Hunter Settlement. At the spring meeting of New Brunswick Presbytery, April 17th, 1770, he was appointed to supply one Sabbath at Mt. Bethel, one at Oxford, one at Basking Ridge, at Lower Hardwick (Hackettstown) one, and administer the Lord's Supper, in addition to his regular labors at Allentownship and Greenwich.

In accordance with the action of Synod in 1769, the matter of the transfer of the Allentownship or Craig Settlement Church to the Presbytery of New Brunswick came up on the afternoon of May 21st, 1770, in the Synod of New York and Philadelphia, convened in New York, when the following action was taken: "The First Presbytery of Philadelphia reported that, in compliance with an order of Synod last year, they had, in conjunction with the Presbytery of New Brunswick, inquired particularly into the state and connection of the congregation of Allentown, in the Forks of Delaware, and it is the unanimous opinion of both Presbyteries that it is at present most subservient to the interests of religion in those parts, for the Presbytery of New Brunswick to take under their care, not only the congregation of Allentown, but also the congregation of Mt. Bethel, both of which are in the

Forks of Delaware, and both of which have been under the care of the First Philadelphia Presbytery."

The Synod therefore ordered the Presbytery of New Brunswick to take both said congregations under their care for the future. Thus were the interests of the Hunter Settlement people safeguarded, and both churches in the Forks went back to the Presbytery of New Brunswick, whence they departed at the organization of the Abington Presbytery in 1752. The conditions upon which Mr. Rosbrugh was to be allowed to accept the call to the Craig Settlement Church and Greenwich were thus met. Notwithstanding this, he did not at that time express to Presbytery his acceptance of the call. This may have been owing to troubles which arose about this time in the Hunter Settlement or Mt. Bethel Church, which was doubtless to constitute a part of his charge.

In October, 1771, he was appointed to supply Mt. Bethel Church on the fourth Sabbath of that month and administer the Sacrament of the Lord's Supper, and preach three more Sabbaths at his discretion. At the spring meeting of Presbytery, April 15th, 1772, he expressed his acceptance of the call to the Allentownship or Craig Settlement Church, but for some reason no preparations were made for his installation.

On October 13th, 1772, the Allentownship people renewed their request for his installation, which was "cheerfully complied with." It took place October 28th, 1772, at twelve o'clock. Rev. John Guild presided and preached the sermon; the other members of the committee of installation were Rev. John Hanna, Rev. Jacob Van Arsdalen, and Rev. Samuel Kennedy. From the records we have been unable to determine whether Mr. Rosbrugh was installed over the Hunter Settlement Church, as part of his charge when becoming pastor at Allentownship or not. The most that seems to appear is that he preached there occasionally. It may perhaps be said that here began the parting of the ways ecclesiastically, between the Craig and Hunter Settlement people.

Foresman says: "About this time, perhaps in the fall of 1773, Mt. Bethel and Oxford Churches united in calling Rev. William Schenck. He did not accept this call."

This was a natural move upon the part of these churches. Mr. Schenck was ordained by the Presbytery of New Brunswick in 1772 (Gillette, page 156). In preaching among the churches it so happened doubtless that he was within the bounds of Lower Mt. Bethel and First Oxford contiguous across the Delaware River in New Jersey. Foresman says: "In February, 1774, these churches united in calling the Rev. John Debow. Mr. Debow accepted this call and was installed May 19th, 1775, but going to North Carolina soon after, he received and accepted a call and settled there in 1776." The minutes of the Synod of New York and Philadelphia for May, 1774, inform us that the Presbytery of New Brunswick had licensed Mr. John Debow. We presume Foresman had before him some authoritative record by which he fixed the date of Mr. Debow's installation on May 19th, 1775. There are corroborative records in the bounds of the First Oxford church as to the fact that Mr. Debow commenced to serve these churches in 1775.

In connection, however, with this fact, the minutes of Synod for 1774, wherein was reported his licensure, the following record is found, page 459: "Mr. John Debow, a probationer, under the care of New Brunswick Presbytery * * * are appointed to go to the southward as soon as they conveniently can, and supply under the direction of the Presbyteries of Hanover and Orange, each of them one whole year at least." This record was made on the forenoon of May 26th, 1774. On the forenoon of May 18th, 1775, Synod made the following record: "Mr. Debow has not fulfilled the mission to the Southern colonies; the reasons for the omission were sustained." Page 463. "The reasons for the omissions" we may infer, were that the Presbytery of New Brunswick had the previous day installed him pastor at Lower Mt. Bethel and First Oxford. Notwithstanding his engagement at Lower Mt. Bethel and First Oxford, Synod appointed him to do missionary work in the South. On the afternoon of May 23d, 1775, Synod made this record: "Mr. Debow to supply nine months amongst the Carolina vacancies before the care of the Hanover Presbytery."

On the forenoon of May 23d, 1776, Synod made the following record:

"Messrs. Debow * * * * * fulfilled their missions as appointed at our last." If in accordance with this record, Mr. Debow spent nine months in missionary work in the Carolinas, between May, 1775, and May, 1776, his term of service at Lower Mt. Bethel and First Oxford could not have been of more than three months duration. This explains Foresman's declaration that he went "to North Carolina soon after, and received and accepted a call and settled there in 1776." In 1780, Mr. Debow, as a member of the Presbytery of Orange, preached one or more Sabbaths at the Craig or Irish Settlement Church. On the forenoon of May 20th, 1784, Synod put on record the fact, reported by the Presbytery of Orange: "That Rev. Messrs. John Debow and James Campbell have been removed by death."

After the departure of Rev. John Debow, in 1776, the Mt. Bethel Church seems to have been left to its own resources largely so far as ministerial services were concerned.

An old record seems to indicate that, in 1777, Rev. Philip Stockton accepted a call to Lower Mt. Bethel in conjunction with First Oxford and Knowlton. If there was any foundation for this assumption it probably rested upon the occasional supply of the pulpit there by him. Mr. Stockton was licensed by the Presbytery of New Brunswick between May, 1774, and May, 1775. On May 17th, 1775, Synod made record as follows, viz:

"The Presbytery of New Brunswick report, that since our last they have licensed to preach the gospel, Mr. Philip Stockton." Doubtless Mr. Stockton preached, after his licensure, in various places, as he had the opportunity, and perhaps among others, at Lower Mt. Bethel. But the greater part of his time was doubtless taken up, in the early part of

1777, with ministrations at First Oxford, Knowlton, and Mansfield Woodhouse or Washington. This appears from the fact that at a meeting of the Presbytery of New Brunswick held at Amwell, October 14th, 1777, he was offered a call from these three combined charges. This was not placed in his hands, but he was appointed to supply these churches the next six months. Accordingly, on April 29th, 1778, he reported to Presbytery, met at Cranberry, that he had preached as appointed, and now accepted the call to these churches.

Mr. Harris, from Knowlton, asked that he be installed as soon as possible. The ordination and installation took place at First Oxford, August 11th, 1778. Thus it is seen Lower Mt. Bethel was disjoined from First Oxford, with which it had previously been connected. It was not associated with the Allentownship or Craig Settlement Church. This appears from the following record: The First Philadelphia Presbytery met at Deep Run, April 7th, 1778, on account of the presence of the British Army in Philadelphia at that time. At this meeting "A commission from the congregation of Allentown, in the Forks of Delaware, appeared before Presbytery and represented that the Rev. Mr. Sproat, a member of this Presbytery, in consequence of an invitation from the congregation had come into the society, and agreeably to their earnest desire, expressed a willingness to supply them till the way should be clear for his returning to his own congregation in Philadelphia. The Presbytery are well pleased with this proposal, and recommend it to Mr. Sproat to supply the said congregation as long as may be convenient for him, and on such terms as he and they can agree."

Thus it appears that the Allentownship or Craig Settlement Church was acting independently. This disjunction is manifested also in the following record of Synod made on the afternoon of May 22d, 1777, viz:

"By the committee of overtures, a supplication from the congregation of Allentown, in the Forks of Delaware, requesting that they may be set off from the Presbytery of New Brunswick, and put under the care of the First Presbytery of Philadelphia, to whom they formerly belonged, was brought in and read. The Presbytery of New Brunswick freely concurring, the Synod grant the supplicants' request, and the First Philadelphia Presbytery is ordered to take said congregation under their care."

This makes consistent the action taken with reference to Rev. Mr. Sproat which we have just referred to. Foresman says: "On the record of the second Tuesday of August, 1783, the Rev. Francis Peppard was installed pastor of the Mt. Bethel Church for a part of his time, having preached, as it would appear, for the congregation for some time previous to his installation. We presume there was some good reason, from records, for this statement, but what these reasons were we are unable to determine. As we have seen, the minutes of Synod show the transfer of the Craig Settlement church from the New Brunswick Presbytery to the First Philadelphia Presbytery; but they do not show a like transfer of the Hunter Settlement or Mt. Bethel Church. As to Mr. Peppard, we find: he was licensed to preach the gospel by the Presbytery of New Brunswick in the latter part of 1763 or the early part of 1764. He was ordained to the full work of the ministry by the Presbytery of New York in 1764-65, and continued in connection with that Presbytery till 1772-73, when he became a member of the Presbytery of New Brunswick. According to the minutes of the Presbytery of New Brunswick, he was offered a call from Upper and Lower Hardwick, that is Yellow Frame and Hackettstown, October 16th, 1764. He declined the call; the people complained, and Presbytery rebuked him.

Gillette says, (Page 153): "At Bethlehem he (Enos Ayers) was succeeded by Francis Peppard, who had charge also of the church organized at New Windsor in 1766." The minutes of Synod for 1765 say, "The Presbytery of New York report that they have ordained the Rev. Mr. Francis Peppard to the work of the ministry; and that the Rev. Mr. Enos Airs (Ayers) is dead since our last". He is reported absent from Synod in 1766; present in 1767; present as a member of the Presbytery of New York in 1768; absent in 1769; absent in 1770; present in 1771; absent in 1772. In 1773 he is marked absent from Synod as a member of the Presbytery of New Brunswick, showing that between May, 1772, and May, 1773, he had been transferred from the New York to the New Brunswick Presbytery.

It seems that subsequent to 1771 he preached one or more Sabbaths at Greenwich. In October, 1772, the people at Upper and Lower Hardwick again sought his services, each asking for one-half of his time; this notwithstanding he had declined to serve them when asked to do so in 1764. Presbytery sent him to them as stated supply for the ensuing six months. The people of these two congregations sent in a united call for his services to the Presbytery of New Brunswick, convened at Pennington in April, 1773. He accepted the same, but the time of his installation does not appear from the records.

As a member of the New Brunswick Presbytery, he was absent in 1776; absent in 1777; present in 1778; absent in 1779; absent in 1780; absent in 1781; absent in 1782; present in 1783; and in 1784 he was present in Synod as a member of the First Philadelphia Presbytery. This shows that between May, 1783, and May, 1784, he had finished his labors as pastor at Upper and Lower Hardwick and had departed from the Presbytery of New Brunswick. Very little has come down to us by way of record as to what transpired in the united charge under him. The pastorate seems to have been, in the main, uneventful. The History of Sussex and Warren Counties, New Jersey, tells us (Page 631) that on April 22d, 1775, the Presbytery of New Brunswick, in session at Freehold, appointed him to supply one Sabbath at Knowlton. A record of the First Philadelphia Presbytery made October 17th, 1780, is as follows: "A written application from the congregation of Allentown was presented by Mr. Hugh Horner, their commissioner, requesting supplies from us, and also liberty to apply to some other Presbytery for the same purpose. Presbytery cheerfully granted them that liberty, and recommended to them to apply to the Presbytery of New Brunswick, as most likely to favor their design."

It would seem the people of the Craig Settlement improved the permission granted them to apply to the Presbytery of New Brunswick for supplies, as we find them asking permission of Presbytery, convened at Neshaminy, April 17th, 1781, to present a call to a member of that Presbytery. The following record, under that date, is sufficiently explanatory: "Mr. John Ralston, a commissioner from Allen's Township, requests supplies for that congregation, and also that they may be permitted to prosecute a call before the Presbytery of New Brunswick for the Rev. Mr. Peppard, a member of that Presbytery". At a later stage of the meeting: "The congregation of Allentown are permitted to prosecute the call for Mr. Peppard before the Presbytery of New Brunswick, agreeably to their request".

The call presented to Mr. Peppard was accepted by him, but at what time does not appear. He removed, it seems, to the bounds of the Craig Settlement, but took no immediate steps for the transfer of his ecclesiastical relations. His residence in the Craig Settlement and preaching to the people there without being installed, was in due time taken notice of by the First Presbytery of Philadelphia, under whose care the church was. In the minutes of Presbytery, convened in Philadelphia, October 15th, 1782, the following record may be found: "Presbytery were informed that the Rev. Francis Peppard, a member of the New Brunswick Presbytery, has accepted a call from the congregation of Allen Township, in the Forks of Delaware, and has, for some time, resided among that people as their minister, but as the congregation has not applied to the Presbytery to have him installed, nor has Mr. Peppard offered to join himself to us as a member, the Presbytery appointed Mr. Mitchell to write to Mr. Peppard and the congregation, to know their sentiments on that affair, and make a report at our next".

At a meeting of the Presbytery, May 23, 1783, of New

Brunswick, Mr. Peppard was dismissed from the Presbytery and was received a member of the First Philadelphia Presbytery. The commissioners of the congregation, at the same meeting, applied for the installation of Mr. Peppard. Accordingly, Rev. Alexander Mitchell was appointed to preside at the installation, which was to take place on the second Tuesday of August. Rev. James Grier was to preach the sermon, and Rev. Nathaniel Irwin was to give the charge. We find the following report of this committee to Presbytery, at Philadelphia, October 21st, 1783:

"The committee appointed to install Mr. Peppard in the congregation of Allen Township, in the Forks of Delaware, report that they attended to and performed that business on the thirteenth of October. The reasons for not attending on the day appointed, sustained." The natural inference from these records is that Mr. Peppard, shortly after the meeting of the First Philadelphia Presbytery, October 17th, 1780, by invitation went over from his Upper and Lower Hardwick charge, in New Jersey, and preached for the Craig Settlement Church people. Shortly after this they offered him a call which he expressed his willingness to accept. He naturally removed to and occupied the parsonage in the Craig Settlement. This makes intelligible the First Philadelphia Presbytery record of October 15th, 1782, which says: "And has for some time, resided among that people".

The irregularity of this course being taken notice of, he naturally asked to be dismissed from the New Brunswick Presbytery to connect himself with the First **Philadelphia** Presbytery, which he did May 23d, 1783. This would imply the dissolution of his pastoral relation in his former charge. A New Jersey record says this dissolution took place May 22d, 1783. It must not be forgotten that during all this time the Hunter Settlement, or Mt. Bethel Church, was still under the jurisdiction of the New Brunswick Presbytery to which Mr. Peppard belonged, it not being transferred to the First Philadelphia Presbytery until May 21st, 1777, when the Craig Settlement Church returned to that Presbytery.

He evidently was absent from his New Jersey charge, in an irregular manner, from the latter part of 1780 till he was released in May, 1783. He may have been devoting part of this time to Mt. Bethel, in connection with the Craig Settlement Church. There would not be anything irregular in this so far as Mt. Bethel and the New Brunswick Presbytery were concerned. This may account for the delay and irregularity as is evidenced in connection with the Craig Settlement Church.

It will be noticed the date given by Foresman, "the second Tuesday of August, 1783," is precisely the date originally fixed upon by the First Presbytery of Philadelphia for Mr. Peppard's installation at the Craig Settlement Church. If Mr. Peppard was dismissed from the New Brunswick Presbytery and received by the First Philadelphia Presbytery May 23d, 1783, as the record shows, it is difficult to understand how he could have been installed at Mt. Bethel on the second Tuesday of August, 1783, over a church under the jurisdiction of another Presbytery. We give these details of the records to enable the reader to form a judgment whether Mr. Peppard was a pastor at Mt. Bethel, as stated by Foresman, or, at least, a supply, in connection with the Craig Settlement Church. Foresman apparently gives the matter away by saying: "Precisely how long Mr. Peppard continued to serve the Mt. Bethel Church does not appear. His pastorate, however, was a comparatively short one, the Rev. Asa Dunham being installed pastor of the Mt. Bethel and Oxford Churches in 1787".

This affiliation of the Mt. Bethel Church with First Oxford, on the New Jersey side of the Delaware, was a quite natural arrangement. Both churches were under the jurisdiction of the New Brunswick Presbytery. This combined pastorate extended over a period of ten years, terminating on September 18th, 1797. Little has come down to us by way of ecclesiastical record for this decade of Lower Mt. Bethel history. What is recorded may doubtless be found in the minutes of the New Brunswick Presbytery for the period. On the forenoon of May 22d, 1788, the Synod of New York and Philadelphia received the report of the Presbytery of New Brunswick, in which it was said: "New Brunswick Presbytery reported, that they have, since our last, ordained Mr. Ira Condit to the work of the gospel ministry, and in the pastoral charge of the congregation of Newton and Hardwick; and have also ordained Mr. Asa Dunham to the work of the gospel ministry, in the pastoral charge of the congregations of Oxford and Mt. Bethel".

Gillette, in speaking of Presbyterianism in Pennsylvania, from 1789—1800, mentions "Asa Dunham, at Mt. Bethel and Oxford" (Page 302). Mr. Dunham in a statistical report of General Assembly, appears in charge of Mt. Bethel and Oxford in 1789. He was a commissioner to the General Assembly from New Brunswick Presbytery in 1796. In 1798, the New Brunswick Presbytery in reporting to the General Assembly, say: "Rev. Asa Dunham, without charge". In the same report they say: "That they have dissolved the pastoral relation between the Rev. Asa Dunham and the congregations of Oxford and Mt. Bethel, September 18th, 1797". As a commissioner to the General Assembly this year (1798) Mr. Dunham's name appears as representing the Presbytery of Huntingdon. Thus it appears that between September 18th, 1797, and May 17th, 1798, he had been dismissed from the Presbytery of New Brunswick and had been received by the Presbytery of Huntingdon. Again Gillette says (Page 500): "In 1800 the Presbytery of Huntingdon numbered twelve ministers, of whom four—John Hoge, Asa Dunham, Hugh McGill, and James Johnston, were without charge". Again: "In 1811, the Presbytery of Northumberland was erected. The pastors of it, transferred from the Presbytery of Huntingdon, being Asa Dunham, John Bryson, Isaac Grier, John B. Patterson, and Thomas Hood".

Foresman says: "At a meeting of the Presbytery of New Brunswick, held at Trenton, New Jersey, September 19th, 1799, calls from Oxford and Lower Mt. Bethel Churches were presented to Rev. David Comfort, who was for many years pastor of the Church of Kingston, New Jersey. Mr. Comfort did not accept these calls, and Lower Mt. Bethel was again supplied by Presbytery. The Rev. David Barclay was called to Lower Mt. Bethel, Knowlton and Oxford Churches, and was installed pastor of the Mt. Bethel Church July 19th, 1805. It is probable that Mr. Barclay was at Lower Mt. Bethel for some time before he was installed pastor".

We are now brought to the experiences of the Hunter Settlement, or Lower Mt. Bethel Church, with Rev. David Barclay. Before considering these experiences, it may be well for us to note some things pertaining to the congregation aside from the routine of the preaching services. We have seen that in 1757 Thomas Buckman purchased land at Martin's Creek, which included the church and graveyard lots, and that in 1759 he sold lands to Samuel Rea, which included these lots. As in the case of the Craig Settlement, the church people were practically squatters upon this land, for Mr. Rea did not sell and deed this property to them till August, 1803. At this time the deed was made in trust to Thomas Beard, Alexander Miller, and Peter Simonton. The school-house lot, it will be observed, lies between the church lot and the burying ground. This lot was given in May, 1802, in trust, to Nathaniel Brittain and Thomas Beard.

A charter of incorporation was obtained from the Pennsylvania Legislature, for the congregation, in 1809. This charter is signed by the Rev. David Barclay, their minister, and by David Ayers, Robert Galloway, Nathaniel Brittain, and Jeptha Arrison, the Ruling Elders. Members of the congregation who signed it were Joseph Bowman, John Neilson, John Davison, Samuel Gulick, John Hutchison, Peter Middagh, Moses Ayers, Robert Moody, Peter Simonton, Peter Jacoby, Henry Winter, Isaac Benward, Samuel Rea, John Galloway, John Ross, William Galloway, John Neilson, James Hutchison, George Kennedy, John McCrea, William Hutchison, Robert Kennedy, Samuel Eakin, Andrew Hutchison, Thomas Middagh, Alexander Lockard, and Robert Brittain.

The lot on which the present church stands was purchased from William Lander, in April, 1815. The Trustees of the church whose names appear in the deed for this property, were William Hutchison, Moses Wallace, Samuel Loder, John Jacoby, David Beard, and Robert Kennedy.

Shortly after the close of the American Revolution, as in the case of the Craig Settlement, families began to migrate from the Hunter Settlement. A company consisting of the family names of Moore, Galbraith, Copeland, Gaston, Wilson, Martin, Boyd, and Hutton, went to East Tennessee and started a settlement there. They called their church Mt. Bethel, in memory of their Northampton County Mt. Bethel church. This Mt. Bethel church, Presbytery of Halston, Synod of Tennessee, of the Presbyterian denomination, is now ministered to by the Rev. Dayton A. Dobbs, and last year reported a membership of one hundred and twenty-eight. As late as 1867 there were among the officers of the church those bearing the Northampton County Mt. Bethel family names of Moore, Galbraith, and Wilson. As in the case of the Craig Settlement, another band from the Hunter Settlement migrated to Western Pennsylvania. These bore the family names of Benward, Mason, McFarren, Miller, Moody, Morris, and Neilson. They called this migration "Going to Fort Pitt".

Another company moved to the West Branch of the Susquehanna River. These bore the family names of Beard, Covert, Foresman, Henderson, Marr, Moore, Scott, and Silliman. The writer in his boyhood days, on the West Branch of the Susquehanna, was familiar with the names of some of these, such as Silliman, Simonton, Galloway, Marr, and others. The present Judge Marr of Schuylkill County is of this stock.

In 1812, the Elders of the Mt. Bethel Church were Robert Galloway, Jeptha Arrison, Nathaniel Brittain, John Hutchison, Samuel Gulick, and David Ayers. We may now take up the pastorate of Rev. David Barclay at Lower Mt. Bethel. As Foresman says: Mr. Barclay was installed over the three churches of Knowlton, Oxford, and Lower Mt. Bethel. The installation took place at Knowlton, June 19th, 1805. This is probably the date intended by Foresman when he says the installation at Lower Mt. Bethel took place July 19th, 1805. Mr. Barclay's advent came about in this manner: After the days of Rev. Mr. Stockton, at Knowlton, that congregation became practically disorganized. At the April and September meetings of the New Brunswick Presbytery, 1801, there were appointed as supplies at Oxford, and presumably at Lower Mt. Bethel, Rev. Messrs. Barclay, Comfort, Hanna, Sloan, and Snowden. Rev. Mr. Barclay was to administer the Sacrament of the Lord's Supper in the fall of 1801. Oxford and Lower Mt. Bethel offered a call to Rev. Matthew LaRue Perrine, whose name appears as performing some service in the vicinity about this time, but he declined it.

These two churches also, in connection with Knowlton, it seems, offered a call to Rev. Mr. Cummius, which he likewise declined, these brethren following the example of Rev. Mr. Comfort in 1799, as we have seen. At a meeting of the New Brunswick Presbytery, held April 20th, 1803, Mr. John Linn was present and designated as an Elder from Knowlton. It is to be presumed that he was one of the Elders who had been in service during the pastorate of Rev. Philip Stockton. Mr. Linn at this time asked for supplies, and five were granted. Among these was again the name of David Barclay, who was to preach on the second Sabbath of March, 1804.

The General Assembly Minutes for 1804, mentions among the vacant charges: "Oxford and Mt. Bethel united, able to support a minister". The three congregations of Lower Mt. Bethel, Knowlton, and Oxford, united in a call to Rev. Mr. Barclay. It seems that owing to the unsatisfactory condition of things in these churches, and the difficulty of getting any minister to consent to labor among them, Presbytery advised Mr. Barclay to accept the call. This he did at their meeting held April 24th, 1805. Each one of the congregations was to pay him $200 per annum salary. The installation services took place, as already stated, at the Knowlton church, June 19th, 1805. Things moved along apparently for a number of years without much to attract the attention of the outside public, notwithstanding the eccentricities of the pastor and idiosyncracies of the people.

Difficulties, however, arose in due time, which required the intervention of the Presbytery. Accordingly, a committee was appointed to settle the dispute, which had caused some of the Knowlton people to prefer charges against their pastor. The committee, consisting of Rev. Messrs. Comfort, Finley, and Woodhull, met the congregation on January 16th, 1811, to adjust matters. Foresman says: "The sympathy of the majority of the people of Lower Mt. Bethel congregation seems to have been with Mr. Barclay, as among the files of New Brunswick Presbytery have been found three petitions from the congregation to that body, in one of which they pray Presbytery not to remove Mr. Barclay; and in the other to appoint him their supply for one-half of his time".

One of these petitions is as follows:

"To the Reverend Presbytery of New Brunswick:

"The Presbyterian congregation of Lower Mt. Bethel being informed that Rev. David Barclay has desired leave to resign his pastoral charge, the session has consulted the members of this church, and do find that they are all unanimous, and wished that he may not be removed. We hope it will not be taken amiss if we inform Presbytery that since he became our pastor, his conduct among us has been such as becometh a minister of the gospel of Christ, and that his labors in many instances appear to have been crowned with success, and peace and harmony appear to prevail in this church. We therefore humbly request that Reverend Body to take our case under consideration, and if consistent, to continue his labors among us. And your petitioners as in duty bound will ever pray.

"Done at Lower Mt. Bethel, May 18, 1812."

This is signed by the Elders, Robert Galloway, Joseph Arrison, Nathaniel Brittain, John Hutchison, Samuel Gulick, and David Ayers. The labors of Presbytery's healing committee were barren of results for near the end of the year, 1812, we find the Knowlton congregation was cited to appear and show cause why the pastoral relation should not be dissolved.

Some of the people stood by the pastor and eleven commissioners were appointed to appear before Presbytery at Oxford and resist the dissolution of the pastoral relation. Notwithstanding this, Presbytery dissolved the relation.

The Lower Mt. Bethel Church brought into Presbytery on April 27, 1813, a call for Mr. Barclay's pastoral services. He took the matter under advisement. January 11th, 1814, Presbytery forbid his preaching at Knowlton, Oxford and Lower Mt. Bethel.

At the meeting of Presbytery held at Basking Ridge, shortly after, Lower Mt. Bethel and Knowlton asked that he be appointed their stated supply. This was refused. At this meeting he asked that the restrictions be removed which prevented him from preaching to the three congregations of which he had been pastor. The request was not granted. He appealed to Synod, and the case was remanded to the Presbytery, which acted upon it at a meeting held at Princeton, November 22d, 1814. The restriction so far as it applied to Lower Mt. Bethel, was removed, but he was admonished by Presbytery.

The Rev. Joseph Campbell was appointed to visit and communicate to the Mt. Bethel people, Presbytery's action in the matter. At a meeting of Presbytery in Trenton, April 25th, 1815, supplies were provided for the congregation for the ensuing six months. The way being now clear, by the action of Presbytery, in November, 1814, the Mt. Bethel people made out a call for Mr. Barclay which came before Presbytery at its meeting held October 3d, 1815, at New Brunswick. The call was not put into his hands and supplies were appointed for the next six months. They brought up the matter again at the meeting of the Presbytery at Lawrenceville, April 23d, 1816.

At this time, Elder Samuel Gulick from the congregation

submitted documents to Presbytery, bearing on the case. These were placed in the hands of a committee which reported, recommending among other things, that Dr. Archibald Alexander be appointed to draft a letter to the Lower Mt. Bethel people expressive of the views of Presbytery touching Mr. Barclay's case. At the same time supplies were appointed for the succeeding six months.

The perseverance of the saints at Mt. Bethel was manifested in their bringing in again a call for Mr. Barclay, at the meeting of Presbytery held at Cranberry in October, 1816. This call asked for one-half of his time.

At the same time, a remonstrance came against his settlement and the call was withheld from him. Not being able to have him installed as pastor, at a subsequent meeting of the Presbytery they asked for his appointment as stated supply. The request was not granted.

In order to follow the fortunes ecclesiastically of Lower Mt. Bethel Church, we must now record a change in Presbyterial jurisdiction.

The Presbytery of Newton was organized by the Synod of New York and New Jersey in October, 1817, out of the Presbytery of New Brunswick. Synod's action was as follows: "Resolved, That the Synod erect and do hereby erect a new Presbytery to be called the Presbytery of Newton, composed of those members and congregations now of the Presbytery of New Brunswick which lie north and west of a line drawn from the Delaware so as to include the congregations of Amwell, Flemington, Lamington, and Basking Ridge."

"Resolved, That the new Presbytery meet at Mansfield on the third Tuesday of November at eleven o'clock in the forenoon and that the Rev. John Boyd, or in the case of his failure, the oldest member present, preach and preside at the opening of the said meeting."

The geographical line by which the new Presbytery of Newton was separated from the New Brunswick Presbytery, started, it will be noticed, on the Delaware river, a short distance above Lambertville and held an irregular course to the northeast, through the counties of Hunterdon, Morris, and Sussex, till it reached the State line between New York and New Jersey. All the territory in New Jersey north and west of this line and a part of Northampton and Monroe counties in Pennsylvania, were included in the boundary of the Presbytery.

The churches under its care within these limits were: Smithfield in Monroe County, and Upper Mt. Bethel, Lower Mt. Bethel, and Easton, in Northampton County, Pennsylvania. In New Jersey: Amwell First, Amwell Second, Flemington, Pleasant Grove, Alexandria, Kingwood, Bethlehem, Basking Ridge, Lamington, Fox Hill, German Valley, Hackettstown, Newton, Hardwick (Yellow Frame), Marksboro, Knowlton, Oxford, Mansfield, Harmony, and Greenwich.

The first meeting was held in the Mansfield (Washington) Church on the third Tuesday of November, 1817, and was moderated by Rev. John Boyd, by appointment of Synod. The ministers present were: David Barclay, David Bishop, John Boyd, Joseph Campbell, Jacob R. Castner, Horace Galpin, Halloway W. Hunt, Jacob Kirkpatrick (elected Clerk), and Joseph L. Shafer. Absent, Garner A. Hunt, William B. Sloan, and Jehiel Talmage.

Elders present: James Dunham from Bethlehem, Thomas Kennedy from Greenwich, Alexander Finley from Basking Ridge, Ebenezer Stilson from Mansfield, John Stinson from Marksboro, and James Thomson from Hackettstown.

Thus it is seen that the Hunter Settlement, or Lower Mt. Bethel Church, became a constituent part of the new Presbytery of Newton, and Rev. Mr. Barclay was present at its first meeting.

As might have been expected, the troublesome affair of Mr. Barclay and the Lower Mt. Bethel Church came to the front easily. On November 18th, the record shows Mr. Barclay was without charge and he was appointed to preach at Greenwich on the third Sabbath of December, 1817, and the fourth Sabbath of January, 1818. At this meeting a motion was made to remove the restrictions placed upon Mr. Barclay by the Presbytery of New Brunswick with reference to his preaching at Knowlton and Lower Mt. Bethel.

Action in the matter, however, was postponed till the next meeting of Presbytery. On April 28th, 1818, the restrictions were removed and Lower Mt. Bethel presented a memorial asking for one-half of his time. This memorial was laid on the table. The next day, April 29th, appointment of supplies was made for the period between the first Sabbath of July and the third Sabbath of August. These were Rev. Messrs. David Bishop, Benjamin I. Lowe, G. A. Hunt, and Joseph Campbell.

At a meeting of Presbytery held at Greenwich, October 6th, 1818, Mr. Barclay asked for testimonials to travel abroad. The Clerk was instructed to furnish him with the same, which he subsequently did as the records show. The next day, Presbytery appointed him to supply at Lower Mt. Bethel six months at discretion. At this meeting something more was done by way of removing Mr. Barclay's disabilities with reference to Knowlton and Lower Mt. Bethel. It may naturally be inferred that he utilized his credentials in traveling abroad, for on April 25, 1819, he was dismissed in good standing to the Presbytery of Redstone. Thus he passed off the scene of action in this part of the church.

Elder Jacob Kerr, of Knowlton Church, published a book of more than four hundred pages entitled:

"The several trials of David Barclay before the Presbytery of New Brunswick and the Synod of New York and New Jersey." It is an interesting work in that it shows the mode of ecclesiastical procedure in that period of the church's history.

We must at this period take into account a new element bearing upon the Scotch-Irish of the Hunter Settlement and their ecclesiastical affairs. It is the introduction of Upper Mt. Bethel in church affairs. From what has already been said it is plain that these Hunter Settlement people were thrown largely, in church affairs, with the people on the opposite side of the Delaware River, in New Jersey, especially after the close of the American Revolution. We must therefore associate some of these affairs with them in order rightly to understand their history.

As we have seen, the Lower Mt. Bethel portion of the people were more or less associated with Knowlton. We have also seen that at the close of Rev. Philip Stockton's ministrations there the church practically became disorganized. So manifest was this that the Presbytery found it necessary to take some action in the matter.

On September 22d, 1802, Rev. Ebenezer Grant was appointed to supply the congregation at his discretion. In connection with this appointment action was taken as follows:

"On motion, resolved, that the Rev. Ebenezer Grant be required when he shall supply agreeably to appointment at Nolton to enquire into the state of the people whether they are in a situation to be organized as a congregation, and whether they desire to be considered under the care of Presbytery."

Rev. Mr. Grant's report on the subject was presented to Presbytery in April, 1803. Among other things he said: There is at this time no regularly organized congregation in the township of Nolton nor any house of worship exclusively belonging to that denomination; the officers and regular members of the society with which the Rev. Philip Stockton was formerly connected, having almost all died or removed; but that there is a very small body of Episcopalians with which the Rev. Mr. Felters was not long since connected; and a considerably numerous society of High Dutch Calvinists, among whom Rev. Mr. Linn had some time past officiated.

The Episcopalians aided by the Presbyterians (who are still the more numerous, although in an unformed state), had many years since erected a stone church near the banks of the Delaware, in which the clergy and people of each denomination were reciprocally admitted. But this house being situated on one side of the township, rendered it inconvenient for the great body of the people to attend public worship. That the three before named denominations had therefore subscribed liberally toward erecting a large and convenient building for public worship in a pleasant spot, and nearly in the center of the Township of Nolton, which is at least ten miles in length and eight miles in breadth, and it was confidently expected the house would be finished before the ensuing winter."

The congregation of the little Episcopalian Stone Church referred to, was organized about 1784, and is brought to notice again in after years in connection with Harmony and Upper Mt. Bethel Presbyterian churches under the name of St. James Church. It stood half a mile or so below the Delaware Station. It was burned June 27th, 1866, by a spark from a locomotive on the D., L. & W. R. R. Its successor is the Episcopal church of Delaware Station.

The Presbyterian element of it in early days may be perhaps represented by the present Presbyterian Church of Delaware Station. By this report we see that the High Dutch Calvinists, the Episcopalians and the Presbyterians, united in the erection of the new Knowlton church where it now stands, which it was expected would be finished before the close of 1803.

It seems apparent that the Knowlton church was not reorganized until after April, 1803, for at that time, Rev. Mr. Grant speaks of it as in a disorganized condition, but with a church building in process of erection. The name of the church as reorganized was: "The First English and German Congregation in Knowlton."

At the meeting of Presbytery, April 20th, 1803, however, Mr. John Linn was present and is designated as an Elder from Knowlton. It is to be presumed that he was one of the elders who had been in service during the pastorate of Rev. Philip Stockton. It is, however, the first time that the records mention an elder as representing the Knowlton Church since the day of Rev. Mr. Stockton. Mr. Linn at this time asked for supplies and five were granted.

April, 1804, supplies were granted for five Sabbaths during the ensuing summer. As we have seen, a new church had been erected. In the records two names appear as designating the Knowlton congregation. The "New" meant the new church at the present location; and the "Old" meant St. James Episcopal, or "Stone," Church on the Delaware.

On October 15th, 1804, there were present in Presbytery Elder J. Linn to represent "New" Knowlton, and Elder Hugh Forman to represent "Old" Knowlton. Dr. Samuel Stanhope Smith with five others were appointed to supply at "Nolton Stone Church", or St. James on the Delaware during the winter of 1804-5.

We have given these details that the associations of the Mt. Bethels with churches on the New Jersey side of the Delaware River may be better understood. By reference to the minutes of the New Brunswick Presbytery for April, 1813, it will be found that the Upper Mt. Bethel Church in the Hunter Settlement was not organized until after this date. The minutes of this date also reveal to us a "German Meeting House" in Upper Mt. Bethel, located in Williamsburg". These same minutes show us that Rev. Garner A. Hunt, pastor at Harmony, was permitted to give one-half of his time to the English Presbyterians near the German Meeting House in Upper Mt. Bethel, Pa., and St. James, N. J.

The Presbyterial records for October, 1813, tell us that at that time Mr. Hunt's time was divided thus: One-half at Harmony, one-fourth at Upper Mt. Bethel, and one-fourth at "St. James" Episcopal. In August or September, 1815, Rev. William Sloan of Greenwich preached to the Harmony people and urged them to raise $300.00 and keep their pastor, Rev. Mr. Hunt, all of his time. This they did and so he ceased his labors at Upper Mt. Bethel as well as at St. James.

A letter written in March, 1899, by Mr. James Depew, says Upper Mt. Bethel and Lower Mt. Bethel were at first united but shortly after 1813 (?) the first Upper Mt. Bethel church was built at Centreville, two miles south of Williamsburg, where it now stands, six miles north of Lower Mt. Bethel. Gillette says, in 1817: "Upper and Lower Mt. Bethel" were vacant. From the minutes of the Presbytery of Newton we learn that on April 29, 1818, Rev. Jehiel Talmage was appointed supply at Upper Mt. Bethel one-fourth of his time; and the same appointment was renewed on October 7th, at a meeting held at Greenwich, the same year. The appointments by Presbytery, April 26th, 1819, were: Rev. Mr. Talmage, fifth Sabbath in May; Rev. G. A. Hunt, fourth Sabbath in June; Rev. Samuel F. Leake, fourth Sabbath in July; Rev. Joseph Campbell, fourth Sabbath in August, and administer the Sacrament; and Rev. Jacob R. Castner the third Sabbath in September. At the fall meeting of Presbytery, October 5th, Elder David Demott was present to represent the Upper Mt. Bethel Church. The next day, October 6th, Licentiate Benjamin I. Lowe was appointed stated supply, for two years, at Upper Mt. Bethel, to give to this church one-third of his time, in connection with Lower Mt. Bethel. We last saw Lower Mt. Bethel at the close of Rev. David Barclay's labors there. April 29th, 1818, Presbytery made appointments of supplies for the church, as we have seen.

We have seen also that at the October meeting, 1818, Presbytery appointed Rev. Mr. Barclay to supply Lower Mt. Bethel for six months at his discretion. It is presumed he preached there more or less during these six months, and at the same time arranged his affairs with a view of departing to another part of the country, which we have seen he did in the spring of 1819. April 26th, 1819, Presbytery appointed the following supplies for Lower Mt. Bethel: Rev. Jacob R. Castner, second Sabbath of May; Rev. Wm. B. Sloan, second Sabbath in June; Rev. David Bishop, first Sabbath in July, and administer the Sacrament; Rev. G. A. Hunt, first Sabbath in August; and Rev. David Bishop, the fifth Sabbath in August.

At a meeting held at Harmony, June 15th, 1819, Presbytery appointed Licentiate Benjamin I. Lowe to supply the third Sabbath in July and at discretion till the next stated meeting. October 5th, 1819, Elder Carpenter McFall represented Lower Mt. Bethel in Presbytery. The next day, October 6th, Mr. Lowe was appointed Stated Supply to the church for two years, to give to it two-thirds of his time in connection with Upper Mt. Bethel. He was, by arrangement of Presbytery, ordained an evangelist, December 8th, 1819, at eleven o'clock a. m., at Lower Mt. Bethel.

At this meeting Elder Peter Melick represented the congregation. Thus we see Lower and Upper Mt. Bethel united under one minister. Following the fortunes of Lower Mt. Bethel in the records, we find that Elder Samuel Gulick represented the church in Presbytery, at Hackettstown, April 25th, 1820. Under this date the Treasurer of Presbytery received from Lower Mt. Bethel $3.00 for Educational Fund, per Rev. Mr. Lowe; also $3.00 for Missions. From Upper Mt. Bethel, for Missions, $1.50, and for Education, $1.50.

April 24th, 1821, Elder Robert Butts represented the church in Presbytery. At this meeting it was stated that the previous statistical report showed a membership of 29. During the year there had been added, on examination, 22, and by certificate, 2. One had died, leaving a total of 52. There had been baptized 17 infants and 6 adults. At Upper Mt. Bethel, the previous report of membership was 13. There had been added on examination 7, one had died, leaving a total of 19. The infant baptisms were 3. In benevolence the combined congregations had given to Missions $2.00; General Assembly, $2.00; Education, $2.00; and to Theological Seminary, $3.25.

October 2d, 1821, Elder Samuel Gulick represented Lower Mt. Bethel in Presbytery. At this meeting there was sent in what appears to be a combined statistical report for the two congregations. It shows that there had been 31 additions, with a total membership of 70; there had been 6 adult and 20 infant baptisms. There had been given for Missions $2.00; for General Assembly, $2.00; for Theological Seminary, $3.25; and for Education, $2.00. This report is found in the Records, Volume I. Page 115. It is perhaps a restatement, with slight modifications, of the report sent in the previous April. At this meeting the two congregations sent in a call for the pastoral services of Mr. Lowe. Having been previously ordained, as we have seen, the first Tuesday in November was the time appointed for his installation. Lower and Upper Mt. Bethel at this meeting were reported by Presbytery to Synod as being under the care of Rev. Benjamin I. Lowe. Presbytery met at Lower Mt. Bethel on November 6th, 1821.

This church was represented by Elder Peter Middagh. At this meeting Rev. Mr. Lowe was installed pastor over the two congregations.

April 24th, 1822, the statistical report was sent in and may be found in the records, Volume I. Page 156. It showed that at Upper Mt. Bethel there had been 3 additions, with a total membership of 21. There had been 1 adult and 1 infant baptism. At Lower Mt. Bethel there had been 9 additions, and a total membership of 60. There had been 1 infant and 8 adult baptisms. The combined congregations had given for Missions, $2.50; General Assembly, $2.50; and for Theological Seminary, $2.28. October 1st, 1822, Elder Moses Wallace represented the church in Presbytery. There had been some trouble in the congregation, and Mrs. Jane Galloway had taken an appeal from the action of session.

At this meeting Presbytery adjudicated the case, a record of which may be found in Volume I. Pages 187-188. Session's action was confirmed.

At the meeting of Presbytery, April 22, 1823, the statistical report was sent in, and may be found in the records, Volume I. Page 201. It was a combined report for the two congregations. There had been added 13, with a total membership of 59. There had been 1 adult and 19 infant baptisms. There had been contributed for Missions, $1.50; General Assembly, $1.50; Theological Seminary, $1.00; and for Education, $2.00. The church was represented at this meeting by Elder Moses Wallace.

At the meeting of Presbytery, held October 7, 1823, the

pastoral relation of Mr. Lowe with the church was dissolved. Elder John Rosenberry represented the congregation at this meeting. The pastoral relation was dissolved that Mr. Lowe might accept a call to the churches at Hardwick (Yellow Frame), Marksboro, and Stillwater, in New Jersey. Of this pastorate Foresman says: "Mr. Lowe's labors in this church continued only about four years, but in this comparatively short time he accomplished a good work. A goodly number were added to the church. He seems to have been very successful as a Bible class teacher, according to the testimony of the older members of this church.

Previous to Mr. Lowe's time, Sessional records were kept in a very careless manner, if kept at all. He procured a book, and carefully kept a record of all Sessional meetings, made out a roll of members of the church, and recorded the marriages and baptisms that he solemnized. The records of the church have been carefully kept and preserved since Mr. Lowe's time to the present."

We may now go back and take up the thread of history belonging to the other branch of the charge, Upper Mt. Bethel, where we left it at the installation of Rev. Mr. Lowe. As Foresman tells us, Rev. Mr. Lowe was careful in the matter of Sessional records at Lower Mt. Bethel. So we find he was as careful at Upper Mt. Bethel. In a letter received from Elder Jonathan Moore of the Upper Mt. Bethel church, under date of March 2d, 1899, we are informed that the records of that church, prior to 1820, have been lost. The present records, however, begin with that year. On May 27th, 1820, Session met with Rev. Benjamin I. Lowe as moderator, and elders present, David Demott, Joseph Ink, and Robert Butts.

At a meeting of Presbytery held October 3d, 1820, Elder Joseph Ink represented the congregation. At the meeting of Presbytery held April 24th, 1821, as we have seen, the statistical report was sent in, which showed that to the 13 members previously reported, there had been added on examination 7; one had died, leaving a total of 19. The infant baptisms were 3. The Treasurer's account shows that April 25th, 1820, the church contributed $1.50 to the Educational Fund, per Mr. Lowe. As we have seen, October 2, 1821, Upper with Lower Mt. Bethel sent in a call to Presbytery for the pastoral services of Rev. Benjamin I. Lowe.

At this meeting there was sent in what appears to be a combined statistical report for the two congregations. This report we have already alluded to in connection with Lower Mt. Bethel. Upper Mt. Bethel came under the pastoral charge of Rev. Benjamin I. Lowe, November 6, 1821, by virtue of the installation services held at Lower Mt. Bethel on that date. April 24th, 1822, the statistical report went into Presbytery and may be found in records, Volume I, Page 156. It is a combined report for the two congregations and has been already referred to.

On April 23d, 1823, the combined statistical report for the congregations came into Presbytery. It may be found in the records, Volume I, Page 201, and has been attended to. According to the records, at this meeting of Presbytery, April 22d, 1823, the pastoral relation between Mr. Lowe and the Upper Mt. Bethel church was dissolved, it being six months before the relation was dissolved at Lower Mt. Bethel, October 7th, 1823.

Upper Mt. Bethel having been pastorless since April, it is not surprising that we find that at the October meeting of the Presbytery, 1823, Rev. Nathaniel Conkling, as the General Association's missionary, was appointed to supply there four months, in connection with Smithfield and Walpack.

We may now go back and take up the fortunes of Lower Mt. Bethel, following upon the dissolution of Mr. Lowe's pastoral relation in October, 1823.

Licentiate John Gray was asked for by the First Church of Easton, October 1st, 1822. The request was that he be appointed as supply there for one year, and that he be ordained. The ordination took place December 3d, 1822, and was sine titulo as an Evangelist.

Being established at Easton, it was natural that Mr. Gray

should become associated with Lower Mt. Bethel. Accordingly, we find he was appointed by Presbytery, April 24th, 1823, to supply there.

October 7th, 1823, he was appointed by Presbytery to preach at Lower Mt. Bethel every other Sabbath for one year. Foresman tells us that he was to give but one service upon the days he preached there. April 28th, 1824, the statistical report was sent in. It is found in records, Vol. I. Page 233, and is as follows:

Upper Mt. Bethel is blank; Lower Mt. Bethel reported 6—added; 1—dismissed; and a total membership of 69. There had been one adult and 5 infant baptisms. October 6th, 1824, Elder William Brittain represented the congregation in Presbytery. As we have seen, Rev. John Gray had been appointed to preach the previous year, giving the people one service every other Sabbath. Now they ask for one-fourth of his time for the ensuing year. This request was referred to the committee on supplies, and supplies were granted, as we learn from the record, Volume I. Page 246.

Mr. Gray was engaged for Easton, three-fourths of his time, for one year. April 27th, 1825, the statistical report is blank, as seen by records Volume I, Pages 264 and 269. October 4th, 1825, Rev. John Gray was assigned to the congregation for one-fourth of his time, the other three-fourths being devoted to Easton. The next day, October 5th, it appears, with reference to the statistical report, that the church was vacant and unable to support a minister. (Volume I. Page 287). Rev. John Gray was appointed to preach at Lower Mt. Bethel on the Sabbath of October 3d, and at discretion. At this time the statistical report shows 10 added, and a membership of 74. There had been 8 infant baptisms.

April 26th, 1826, the statistical report is blank. October 3d, 1826, Rev. John Gray was appointed Stated Supply, one-fourth of his time for one year, the other three-fourths to be given to Easton for one year. It is presumed this arrangement continued till the fall of 1828. At this time the records for October 7th, 1828, tell us he was called to

Easton and installed pastor there the next day, October 8th. This seems to have left Lower Mt. Bethel somewhat at sea, ecclesiastically. We find that on October 6th, 1829, they were permitted by Presbytery to make such arrangements as they could with Mr. Gray for supplying them. April 28th, 1830, the statistical report was blank. At this meeting of Presbytery supplies were appointed for the pulpit. Rev. John Gray was appointed to preach the second Sabbath of May, and at discretion; and Rev. John Vanderveer the third Sabbath in May. A new arrangement was now effected. Lower Mt. Bethel became associated once more with a New Jersey church. This was with Harmony, its nearest neighbor on that side of the river. October 6th, 1830, these combined churches asked for the services of Licentiate James C. Watson, for the ensuing six months. Mr. Watson's time was to be divided equally between the two congregations. At the Spring meeting of Presbytery, April 26th, 1831, Elder Robert Brittain represented the congregation. The statistical report was blank.

Rev. Henry E. Spayd, in his MS. history of the Harmony church, says Mr. Watson ceased at this time to serve these two congregations. Consistent with this is the record of April 27th, 1831, of supplies being provided for Lower Mt. Bethel. These supplies were: first Sabbath in May, Rev. John Gray; second Sabbath in July, Rev. John Vanderveer; second Sabbath in August, Rev. Samuel Sturgeon; second Sabbath in September, Rev. H. N. Wilson. October 4th, 1831, Elder John Rosenberry represented the congregation in Presbytery. At this meeting Harmony and Lower Mt. Bethel united asked permission to employ Licentiate Robert Love, of the New Castle Presbytery, to supply the pulpits for the succeeding six months, giving to each one-half of his time. This request was granted.

April 24th, 1832, Elder Morris Morris represented the congregation in Presbytery. The congregation, in conjunction with Harmony, now had Mr. Love's services continued, as Stated Supply, for the next six months. This arrangement

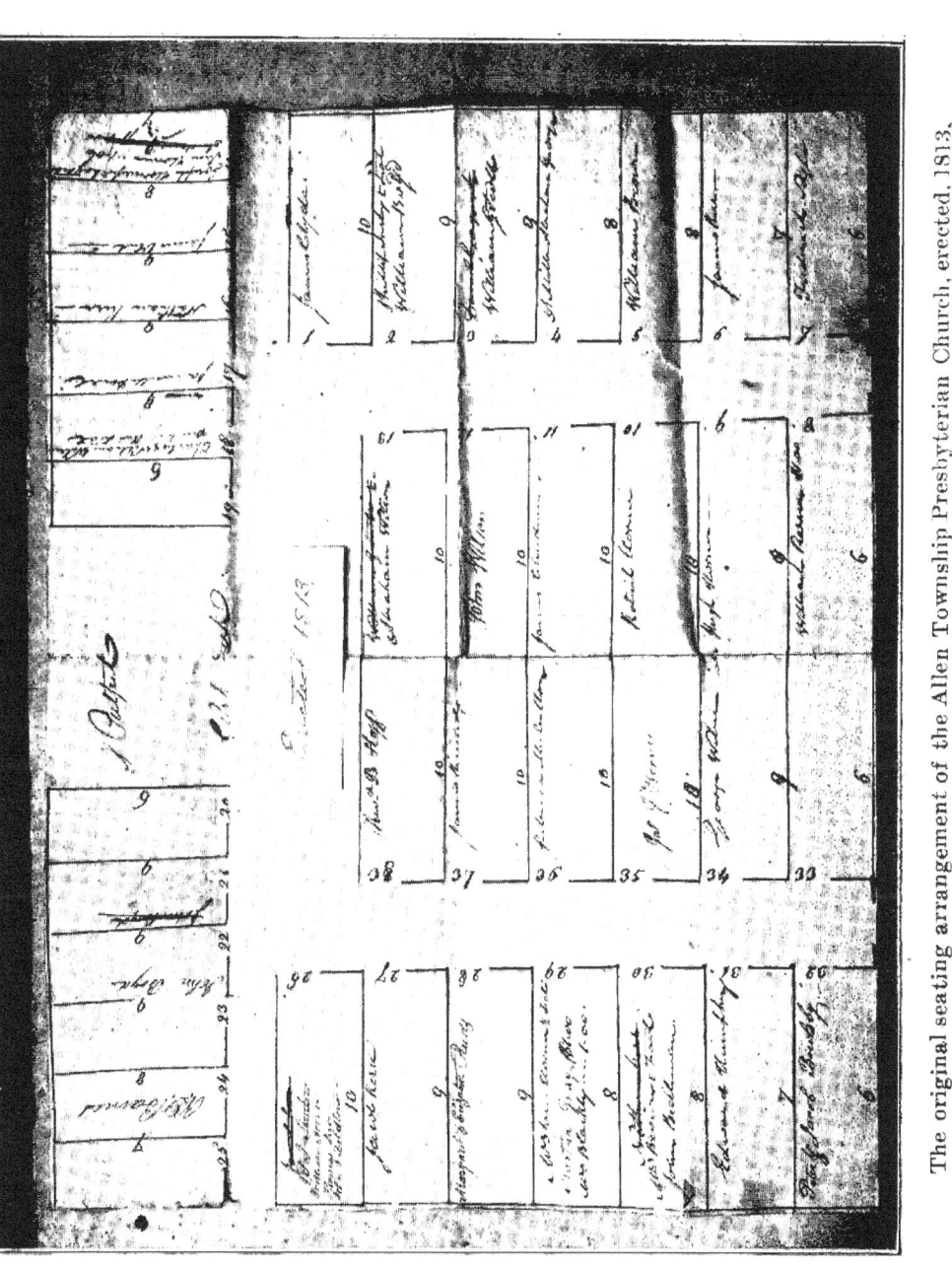

The original seating arrangement of the Allen Township Presbyterian Church, erected, 1813. (See page 310.)

The Presbyterian Burial Ground in the Scotch-Irish Settlement, near Weaversville, Pa. (See page 407.)

was renewed for another six months at the meeting of Presbytery, October 2d, 1832. Each church received half of the minister's time. This year (April 24th), the congregation contributed $21.50 for Missions. April 24th, 1833, the two churches were granted the services of Mr. Love for one year. This year $15.50 were contributed to Missions (April 23d), and $2.00 to General Assembly commissioners' fund.

April 22d, 1834, Elder Robert Brittain represented the church in Presbytery. At this meeting the church, with Harmony, was given Mr. Love again for one year, as Stated Supply.

April 27th, 1835, Elder John Rosenberry represented the church in Presbytery. At this time Mr. Love ceased to serve the Lower Mt. Bethel people but continued his labors at Harmony. Accordingly, supplies were appointed by Presbytery, at this time, for Lower Mt. Bethel. They were as follows: second Sabbath in May, Rev. Samuel Galloway; fourth in May, Rev. Benjamin I. Lowe; first in June, Rev. Joseph McCool; third in June, Rev. D. X. Junkin; first in August, Rev. John Vanderveer; third in August, Rev. John Gray; fifth in August, Rev. Samuel Galloway; second in September, Rev. J. T. Field; fourth in September, Rev. Jehiel Talmage.

October 6th, 1835, Lower Mt. Bethel was represented by Elder John Connelly in Presbytery. At this time Upper and Lower Mt. Bethel once more became united under one minister, and the Scotch-Irish of the Hunter Settlement went forward with outside influences bearing upon them. They were now ministered to by Licentiate John McCullough.

We may now appropriately go back and notice the ecclesiastical fortunes of Upper Mt. Bethel from the time it separated from Lower Mt. Bethel till the advent of Mr. McCullough. We have seen by the minutes of Presbytery of October, 1823, it was ministered to by Rev. Nathanial Conkling, in connection with Smithfield and Walpack, after the departure of Rev. Benjamin I. Lowe. April 28th, 1824, the statistical report was sent in and is found in records, Volume

I, Page 233. It showed 6 added on examination; dismissed, 1; with total membership of 69. There had been 1 adult and 5 infant baptisms. At this meeting of Presbytery supplies were appointed. These were: fourth Sabbath of May, Rev. James B. Hyndshaw; third in July, Rev. John Gray; third in June, Rev. Jehiel Talmage; third in August, Rev. Samuel F. Leake; second in September, Rev. Jehiel Talmage; first in October, Rev. Garner A. Hunt. October 5th, 1824, Supplies were asked for, one-fourth of the time for six months. The request was referred to the committee of supplies, and the request was granted. Rev. Jehiel Talmage was appointed to preach the fourth Sabbath in October and at discretion.

April 26th, 1825, supplies were again asked for and the matter referred to the committee on supplies. No record is found of the committee report. The statistical report sent in at this time is blank.

October 5th, 1825, supplies were asked for. In connection with the statistical report it is stated that the church was vacant and unable to support a minister.

April 25th, 1826, Elder David Demott represented the congregation in Presbytery. The statistical report was blank this year. The next day the matter of supplies was attended to, but what the arrangement was we have not learned.

April 25th, 1827, supplies were arranged for. Rev. Jehiel Talmage was appointed to preach the first Sabbath in May, and at discretion. Mr. Samuel F. Leake, a candidate for the gospel ministry, was transferred from the New Brunswick Presbytery to the Presbytery of Newton, April 29th, 1818, and was licensed at Greenwich, October 6th, of this year, by the latter Presbytery. He was ordained, sine titulo, at Harmony, by the Presbytery, June 19th, 1819. He preached at various times and places among the New Jersey Churches after his licensure. April 26th, 1819, he was appointed to supply Upper Mt. Bethel the fourth Sabbath of July. After rendering various services to New Jersey churches, Mr. Leake asked from Presbytery, August 8th, 1826, traveling credentials, showing that he was on the move. His pastoral relation at Harmony was dissolved April 23d, 1828.

April 24th, 1828, supplies were arranged for Upper Mt. Bethel, by Presbytery. Rev. Jehiel Talmage was appointed to preach the second Sabbath of May, and at discretion. October 8th, 1828, supplies were again provided for the church. Some one, whose name we have not learned, was to preach the third Sabbath of October and at discretion. Moore, in his letter of March 2d, 1899, says Rev. Mr. Leake began his labors at Upper Mt. Bethel, October 20th, 1827, and closed his services there, before May 30th, 1829.

This information, it is presumed, was obtained from sessional or other records within the bounds of the congregation and seems to refer to such supplying of the pulpit as was done from time to time by Mr. Leake under appointments of Presbytery. Moore also says that Rev. Jehiel Talmage began labors at Upper Mt. Bethel, May 30th, 1829, the time at which he says Mr. Leake ceased. This, too, presumably, may refer to similar labor performed by Mr. Talmage; for April 29th, 1829, Presbytery provided supplies. Rev. Jehiel Talmage was to supply the first Sabbath in May, and at discretion. The same was done October 7th, 1829.

The supplies appointed were: November 15th, Rev. Robert Love; December 13th, Rev. Isaac N. Candee; January 10th, 1830, Rev. Alexander Heberton; February 7th, Rev. John Vanderveer; March 1st, Rev. John Gray. The statistical report came in April 28, 1830, and is blank. The same day supplies were provided. Rev. Jehiel Talmage was to preach the first Sabbath in May and at discretion. Supplies were also provided October 6th, 1830; Rev. Jehiel Talmage was to preach at discretion. April 26th, 1831, Elder Henry Labar represented the church in Presbytery. The statistical report this year was blank. Supplies were arranged for. Rev. Jehiel Talmage was to preach at discretion. October 4th, 1831, Elder Samuel Kirkendall represented the congregation in Presbytery. At this time supplies were arranged for. Rev. Jehiel Talmage was to preach the fifth Sabbath of October and at discretion. April 26th, 1832, supplies were provided. Rev.

Jehiel Talmage was to preach the fourth Sabbath in April and at discretion. October 2d, 1832, Elder Henry Labar represented the congregation in Presbytery. At this meeting the services of Rev. Jehiel Talmage were secured, one-fourth of his time for six months. If Moore's statement is correct he had been serving the people more or less, if not regularly, since March 30th, 1829.

April 23d, 1833, Elder Manasseh Miller represented the congregation in Presbytery. At this meeting supplies were provided. Rev. Jehiel Talmage was to preach the third Sabbath in May, and at discretion. April 24th, 1834, supplies were appointed. Rev. Jehiel Talmage was to preach the fourth Sabbath in April and at discretion. As we have seen, October 6th, 1835, Lower Mt. Bethel was represented in Presbytery by Elder John Connelly. At the same meeting Upper Mt. Bethel was represented by Elder **Henry Labar.**

As we have seen, at this meeting the two Scotch-Irish congregations in the Hunter Settlement were united under the same minister, Rev. John McCullough, who was received as a licentiate from the Presbytery of New Castle and ordained as an Evangelist, December 22d, 1835.

At the meeting of Presbytery when Mr. McCullough was ordained, Elder John Rosenberry represented the Lower Mt. Bethel Church. We find that Mr. McCullough also preached one or more Sabbaths at the Craig Settlement in 1835.

In the records of Presbytery for October 7th, 1835, mention is made of the fact that in Upper Mt. Bethel there was in process of erection a new church building. Moore in his letter of March 2d, 1899, tells us the church building on the present site was erected in 1836. April 26th, 1836, Elder Morris Morris represented Lower Mt. Bethel in Presbytery. October 5th, 1836, Presbytery assigned Mr. McCullough to Upper and Lower Mt. Bethel for six months. This would provide preaching till April, 1837. In Moore's letter it is stated he began his labors at Upper Mt. Bethel, December 10th, 1836.

At this meeting of Presbytery, October 4th, 1836, Lower

Mt. Bethel was represented by Elder Robert Brittain. October 3d, 1837, Elder Henry Labar represented Upper Mt. Bethel in Presbytery. The next day, October 4th, the two Mt. Bethels had supplies appointed for them, showing that Mr. McCullough was on the move. Rev. Azariah Prior was to supply Upper Mt. Bethel at discretion. This is consistent with the fact that on October 18th, 1837, Mr. McCullough had travelling papers granted to him. Under date of November 17th, 1837, it is recorded that Lower Mt. Bethel had contributed $52.00 and Upper Mt. Bethel $14.00, for Missions.

Moore in his letter tells us that Mr. McCullough's labors ceased at Upper Mt. Bethel previous to March 13th, 1838. Foresman says his labors had ceased in both churches by April, 1838. The Presbyterial records show that on April 23d, 1839, he was then laboring in Texas. He was dismissed from the Presbytery of Newton October 2d, 1839.

April 25th, 1838, the two Bethels asked for the services of licentiate Azariah Prior for one year, and that he might be ordained. He had been received by Presbytery as a licentiate on August 9th, 1837.

In accordance with the request made, he was ordained June 27th, 1838. He was dismissed from the Presbytery April 23d, 1839. How much preaching Mr. Prior did in the combined field does not very clearly appear from the records.

Moore says, Rev. Leslie Irwin, who was subsequently pastor at the Craig Settlement, began to labor at Upper Mt. Bethel, May 13th, 1838, and ceased before September 12th, 1839. This statement may rest upon records within the bounds of the congregation, but we presume it must refer simply to supplies for Upper and Lower Mt. Bethel. October 3d, 1838, Rev. Thaniel B. Condit was appointed to supply the two Mt. Bethels, giving half of his time to each.

At this point Foresman gives us some interesting facts as to the church buildings at Lower Mt. Bethel. He says: "The first building was a rude structure, small and doubtless built of logs. This seems soon to have given way to a frame building. The time when this second edifice was erected can not be definitely fixed. This second building was enlarged in a very singular manner. It was sawed into two equal parts, and the parts were separated twenty or thirty feet and the intermediate space filled up, the original building being almost square.

I learned from a former respected ruling elder of this church, Mr. John Connelly, that this enlargement was made about eighty-five years ago (1791).

The present edifice was erected in the summer of 1838, at which time the Rev. Azariah Prior was Stated Supply. Its cost was $3,795.50. The congregation had at this time a fund of $1,756.41, the proceeds of a sale of a parsonage property situated near the village of Richmond. This money was appropriated to aid in paying the debt of the congregation incurred in building the church.

The site of the church was changed when the present building was erected, the old site being the northern boundary of the graveyard. For several years previous to the building of this edifice, the Lutheran and Reformed congregations occupied the Presbyterian church alternately, on the Sabbaths it was not occupied by the Presbyterian congregation.

When the proposition was made to build a new church edifice, many of the members of the different congregations were decidedly in favor of building a church to be owned jointly by the three denominations. Others, and probably a considerable majority, in the Presbyterian congregation, were as decidedly opposed to the union measure. The prospects for an amicable union of the three denominations being by no means encouraging, the Lutheran and German Reformed congregations decided to unite in building a church, and the Presbyterian congregation soon after decided to build a church of their own.

This arrangement was surely the best for all concerned, and especially so for this congregation, as in a very few years they called and settled a pastor for the whole of his time, which arrangement has been continued ever since.

April 24th, 1839, both Upper and Lower Mt. Bethel were granted supplies by Presbytery. The supplies for Upper Mt. Bethel were: fourth Sabbath in April, Rev. John Turbitt; second of May, Rev. Joseph Worrel; fourth in May, Rev. Albert Williams; second in June, Rev. Joseph Worrel; fourth in June, Rev. William B. Sloan; first in July, Rev. —— Hill; third in July, Rev. Joseph Worrel; first in August, Rev. James Scott; third in August, Rev. Joseph Worrel; first in September, Rev. Elias R. Schenck; third in September, Rev. William B. Sloan; fifth in September, Rev. John Vanderveer.

The supplies at Lower Mt. Bethel were: first Sabbath in May, Rev. Leslie Irwin; third in May, licentiate Cunningham; first in June, Dr. George Junkin; third in June, Rev. Jacob R. Castner (to administer the Sacrament of the Lord's Supper); fifth in June, Rev. John Vanderveer; second in July, Rev. William B. Sloan; fourth in July, Rev. John Grant; second in August, Rev. D. X. Junkin; fourth in August, Rev. I. N. Caudel; second in September, Rev. James M. Olmstead; fourth in September, Rev. J. G. Force.

Upper Mt. Bethel, April 24th, 1839, reported $5.37; and again October 2d, $10.00 as having been given for missions. Moore tells us that February 2d, 1839, Upper Mt. Bethel became incorporated.

Rev. Mr. Prior having been dismissed from the Presbytery at the spring meeting of 1839, it was natural for the people to seek a new man for the charge. Moore tells us that the Rev. James Clark began to labor at Upper Mt. Bethel, September 12th, 1839. Consistent with this then, we find Presbytery being met October 16th, 1839, arranged for the installation of Mr. Clark over the two Mt. Bethels on the third Wednesday of November.

A subsequent record shows that the installation took place November 20th, 1839. April 28th, 1840, Presbytery dissolved the pastoral relation between Mr. Clark and the Mt. Bethels in order that he might accept a call to the First Church in Belvidere, N. J. At this meeting of the Presbytery, April 30th, 1840, supplies were provided for the two Mt. Bethels.

They were for Lower Mt. Bethel: first Sabbath in May, Rev. Andrew Tully; third in May, Rev. Solomon McNair; fifth in May, Rev. John Vanderveer; second in June, Rev. D. X. Junkin; fourth in June, Rev. Dr. George Junkin; second in July, Rev. John Gray; fourth in July, Rev. Jacob R. Castner, (to administer the Sacrament of the Lord's Supper); second in August, Rev. Leslie Irwin; fourth in August, first in September, third in September and first in October, Rev. Andrew Tully. The supplies for Upper Mt. Bethel were: second Sabbath in May, Rev. Condit; first in June, Rev. James Clark; third in June, Rev. Jonathan H. Sherwood; first in July, Rev. McCarrel; third in July, Rev. John Vanderveer; first in August, Rev. Andrew Tully; third in August, Rev. D. X. Junkin; fifth in August, Rev. Andrew Tully; second in September, Rev. John Gray; fourth in September, Rev. Andrew Tully.

It was subsequently reported that Revs. Jonathan H. Sherwood, Thaniel B. Condit, and James Clark failed to fulfill the appointments as above made. At the meeting of Presbytery, held October 6th, 1840, the two Mt. Bethels sent in a call for the pastoral services of Rev. Andrew Tully. Mr. Tully comes to notice, April 24th, 1833, as a candidate for the gospel ministry. October 4th, 1837, he appears as received by Presbytery as a candidate. The same is said of him October 4th, 1838, and again October 2d, 1839. He was licensed at the meeting of Presbytery held October 6th, 1840; arrangements were made for his ordination and installation in pursuance of a call which had been sent in. This was to take place the fourth Tuesday of November. The services were held November 24th, 1840, at Lower Mt. Bethel.

Moore tells us his labors began at Upper Mt. Bethel, November 21st, 1840. April 28th, 1841, Lower Mt. Bethel reported $12.00 raised for Foreign Missions, and October 5th, $3.37½. At the meeting of Presbytery held April 26th, 1842, Rev. Mr. Tully was called to Lower Mt. Bethel for the whole of the time. Thus the two Scotch-Irish churches in the Hunter Settlement were once more separated, so far as their ecclesiastical arrangements were concerned. We may now follow the fortunes of Lower Mt. Bethel under the exclusive pastorate of Rev. Andrew Tully.

Foresman says: "The largest number added to the communion of the church during any year of its history, was probably for the year ending April, 1843, when sixty-seven were added to the church upon profession of their faith. The total number of communicants reported at that time was two hundred and eighteen. This large accession to the membership of the church occurred in the earlier part of the Rev. Andrew Tully's pastorate. Some of you have a very distinct recollection of the interesting meetings that were held at that time, and especially of the valuable services of the Rev. Jacob R. Castner, then pastor of the Mansfield Church."

On April 29th, 1843, Lower Mt. Bethel reported $10.00 for Domestic, and $70.00 for Foreign Missions. On April 23d, 1844, it reported $32.75 for Foreign Missions; $3.00 for General Assembly Commissioners' Fund; $1.00 for Contingent Fund; and on December 30th, $2.10 for Domestic Missions. April 22d, 1845, it reported $12.00 for Foreign Missions; $5.00 for General Assembly Commissioners' Fund; and 50 cents for Contingent Fund.

April 23d, 1845, a request from Lower Mt. Bethel came into Presbytery for pecuniary aid for the support of the Gospel, thus indicating the waning fortunes of the congregation. Consistent with this, was the granting of aid October 8th, 1845; October 7th, 1846; April 26th, 1848, and April 25th, 1849.

October 7th, 1846, the church reported $10.68 for Education. April 27th, 1847, it reported $20.00 for Domestic Missions; $2.00 for Commissioners' Fund. January 5th, 1848, it reported for Colportage 50 cents, for Contingent Fund work under Rev. Talmage, $3.00. March 15th, 1848, it reported $145.00 for Foreign Missions; $100.00 of which was to make Rev. Andrew Tully a life Director of the Board of Foreign Missions; and $7.00 for Education. April 26th, $2.00 for Commissioners' Fund, and 50 cents for Contingent Fund.

April 24th, 1849, it reported $2.00 for Commissioners' Fund and 50 cents for Contingent Fund. June 1st, $4.00 for Colportage; April 23d, 1851, it reported $7.00 for Commissioners' Fund, and 50 cents for Contingent. April 27th, 1852, it reported $4.00 for Commissioners', and 50 cents for Contingent Fund. May 18th, 1854, it reported for Commissioners' and Contingent Fund, $4.00; and October 4th, of this year, $50.00 for Foreign Missions.

At the meeting of Presbytery held October 4th, 1853, the Lower Mt. Bethel people acquiesced in the request of Rev. Andrew Tully for a dissolution of the pastoral relation in order that he might accept a call to the Harmony Church in New Jersey. The church was to be declared vacant the third Sabbath in October of that year.

Foresman says: "Soon after the dissolution of Mr. Tully's pastoral relation to the church, the congregation purchased from him a property for a parsonage, situated on the public road about a mile and a half north of the church, paying in part for this property at the time of purchase, and paying the balance in a few years. The house has been enlarged and improved and is now among the most commodious and comfortable parsonage buildings in our country congregations. Its site is a most charming one, healthful, sightly, in a peaceful and pleasant neighborhood, having almost all the advantages without the ordinary nuisances of country villages; on the thoroughfare passing through the country from Portland to Easton and the stage between these points passing and repassing."

Returning now to Upper Mt. Bethel, we find that at the same meeting of Presbytery, April 26th, 1842, at which it was separated from Lower Mt. Bethel, supplies were provided. Rev. Thomas Mack was appointed to supply the church two-thirds of his time. October 5th, 1842, the Upper Mt. Bethel church sent in a call to Presbytery for the services of Rev Thomas Mack. He had been licensed at the spring meeting, April 26th, 1842. At this fall meeting, the request was made that he be ordained and installed. This took place at Upper Mt. Bethel, December 7th, 1842.

Moore says his services there commenced October 30th, 1842. April 29th, 1843, $15.00 was reported for Domestic Missions. April 24th, 1844, the church was aided to the amount of $75.00. Aid was also granted April 23d, 1845. There was reported for Domestic Missions, April 23d, 1844, $5.00; and October 7th, 1846, $5.25. In 1846 also there was contributed to Commissioners' Fund of the General Assembly $3.00. October 8th, 1845, it emerged that there was trouble at Upper Mt. Bethel in connection with the minister. Consonant with this at this meeting, arrangements were made for providing supplies for the pulpit. The supplies were: for the third Sabbath in October, Rev. Joseph Worrel; first in November, Rev. Dr. George Junkin, and third in November, Rev. Joseph Worrel.

The church appeared to be vacant irregularly. Rev. Mr. Mack's character was questioned. Charges were preferred against him, and he was cited October 22d, to answer charges. At this meeting the dissolution of the pastoral relation was asked for. November 14th, his trial began. At another meeting, held December 22d, the charge was sustained, and he was suspended from the functions of the ministry.

Pursuant to this, at this meeting supplies were provided for the pulpit. Rev. Joseph Worrel was directed to declare the pulpit vacant and to act as Stated Supply for the church till the next meeting of the Presbytery. Moore tells us that Mr. Mack's labors ceased at Upper Mt. Bethel before March 26th, 1846. April 29th, 1846, Rev. Joseph Worrel was appointed to supply the pulpit the ensuing six months.

Mr. Mack's case was up in Presbytery, April 28th; August 4th; and October 6th, 1846; April 27th and August 4th, 1847; April 25th, 1848; August 7th, 1850, and May 14th, 1851, at which time he was restored to the ministry. October 8th, 1851, he was again referred to, and was dismissed from the Presbytery, April 27th, 1853.

April 27th, 1847, there was reported $7.50 for Domestic

Missions; $3.00 for Education, and $1.30 for Commissioners' Contingent Fund; April 26th, 1848, there was reported $12.20 for Domestic Missions; 77 cents for Education; $2.00 for Colportage; $4.69 for Presbyterial Incidental Fund; and $1.65 Commissioners' Contingent Fund.

April 24th, 1849, $5.00 was reported for Domestic Missions. April 23d, 1850, $1.00 was reported for Domestic, and $1.00 for Foreign Missions. April 23d, 1851, $4.00 was reported for Commissioners' and Contingent. April 27th, 1852, $4.35 was reported for Foreign, and $3.00 for Domestic Missions; Education, $1.06; Commissioners' and Contingent, $1.00. April 19th, 1853, $14.00 was reported for Domestic, and $12.00 for Foreign Missions; $3.00 for Education; $1.00 for Publication. April 28th, 1854, $10.00 was reported for Foreign, and $10.00 for Domestic Missions; $5.00 for Publication; and $2.00 for Commissioners' and Contingent Fund.

In the meantime, supplies were provided for the church as we have seen, April 29th, 1846. Financial aid was granted from the Board of Missions, October 7th, 1846. Moore tells us Rev. Joseph Worrel began his labors at Upper Mt. Bethel, March 26th, 1846. As we have seen, he supplied the pulpit pending the troubles with Rev. Mr. Mack, which we have seen come to the surface in 1845. We find that on April 27th, 1847, he was assigned to preach for the people three-fifths of his time. August 4th of this year, a call from the congregation was put into his hands. October 5th, a committee was appointed to install him.

April 26th, 1848, it was reported that he had been installed. At this meeting of Presbytery financial aid was granted to the congregation, and again at the fall meeting, October 4th; again April 25th, and October 3d, 1849; and April 24th, 1850. December 25th, 1850, it emerges that there were difficulties in the congregation. It is presumed that from this cause the pastoral relation between Mr. Worrel and the congregation was dissolved April 23d, 1851. He was dismissed from the Presbytery October 8th, 1851. The next day after the dissolution of the pastoral relation between Mr.

Worrel and the congregation, April 24th, supplies were granted. They were: for May 4th, Rev. Reeves; and to declare the pulpit vacant; May 18th, Rev. John A. Rilly; June 1st, Rev. William C. McGee; June 15th, Rev. Oliver St. John; June 29th, Rev. John Correll; July 13th, Rev. James G. Moore; July 27th, Rev. Thaniel B. Condit; August 10th, Rev. Andrew Tully; August 24th, Rev. Baker Johnson; September 7th, Rev. Ephraim Simonton; September 21st, Rev. J. H. M. Knox.

Revs. R. H. and Henry Reeves were members of Presbytery about this time,—which one is meant is not clear.

October 8th, 1851, licentiate Gershom Goble was appointed to supply; but how much is not clear. April 28th, 1852, supplies were appointed. They were to preach every two weeks, as follows: third Sabbath in May, Rev. Jehiel Talmage; fifth in May, Rev. Wm. C. McGee; second in June, Rev. James McWilliams; fourth in June, Rev. John A. Rilly; second in July, Rev. George C. Bush; fourth in July, Rev. Aaron H. Hand; second in August, Rev. Andrew Tully; fourth in August, Rev. Ephraim Simonton; first in September, Rev. Reeves; third in September, Rev. Oliver St. John. At this time also financial aid was granted. To equalize the appropriations to the churches helped financially, Upper Mt. Bethel's appropriation was reduced to $75.00. April 20th, 1853, licentiate Gershom Goble was received by the Presbytery and appointed to supply the church for six months. The church was also granted aid at this time.

October 4th, 1853, the supply of the pulpit was provided for, and aid Granted. Rev. Gershom Goble was appointed to supply the ensuing six months. The church was recommended for an appropriation of $100.00. May 30th, 1854, Rev. Mr. Goble was extended a call by the cogregation. D. X. Junkin says that he was a "Licentiate of Presbytery of Allegheny, though a native of Northampton County, Pa. Stated Supply at Upper Mt. Bethel for six months. Received April 20th, 1853. Continued with that church till ordained and installed pastor, May 30th, 1854." There was an adjourned meeting of Presbytery held at Upper Mt. Bethel, May 31st, 1854, at which time Mr. Goble was ordained and installed pastor there. The sermon was preached by Rev. Myron Barrett; Rev. Thaniel B. Condit presided and offered the ordination prayer; Rev. James Edwin Miller gave the charge to the people, and Rev. Dr. Wilson the charge to the pastor.

October 4th, 1854, the church was granted aid, and also again April 18th, 1855. Moore says Mr. Goble closed his labors before August 31st, 1856. Junkin says it was July 26th of that year. At Belvidere, July 23d, 1856, Rev. Gershom Goble asked leave to resign his pastoral charge on account of ill health. Commissioners were heard and the request was granted. Rev. J. E. Miller was to declare the pulpit vacant the second Sabbath after, and Rev. William C. Cattell was to supply the pulpit every other Sabbath until the next spring meeting of Presbytery.

Licentiate Smith Sturges was received by Presbytery October 19th, 1853. He labored in the First Church of Phillipsburg, where he was installed pastor April 17th, 1855. Tounsend in his MS. history of the Phillipsburg church, says the pastorate relation was dissolved there September 3d, 1856. Moore says Mr. Sturges began labors at Upper Mt. Bethel August 31st, 1856. He says the labors there ceased before December, 1857. He says Rev. P. W. Mellick began labors December, 1857, and closed before May, 1862. April 23, 1856, $2.50 was reported for Commissioners' and Contingent Fund; April 28th, 1857, for the same, $2.00; April 7th, 1858, for same, $4.00. October 5th, 1859, $25.00 was reported as a contribution to the Phillipsburg church. Rev. Solomon McNair was received by Presbytery, May 12th, 1853, from the Presbytery of Donegal, and duly installed pastor at Mansfield or Washington. His pastoral relation there was dissolved in 1860. Moore says he began labors at Upper Mt. Bethel, May, 1862, and closed there before June, 1865. Junkin says Theron Brittain preached for six months in 1864. Moore says Rev. Tees began labors June, 1865, and closed before April,

1866. He says Rev. Edwin Town began labors at Upper Mt. Bethel, April, 1866, and closed before November 28th, 1868.

He tells us that in 1868 the church at Portland was erected, but that the two congregations remained as one till 1880. November 28th, 1868, Rev. William B. Darrah began labors and closed before September, 1871. This, it will be noticed, brings us down to the union of the Old and New School churches in 1870. We may now return and bring down the fortunes of Lower Mt. Bethel to the same point. We last saw this church at the close of Rev. Andrew Tully's pastorate, the third Sabbath of October, 1853. Foresman says: "From October, 1853, to April, 1854, the church was supplied by members of Presbytery appointed, and by other ministers invited by sessions.

This brings us to the long pastorate of Rev. Robert B. Foresman. He came to the Presbytery of Newton, April 18th, 1854, as a licentiate, from the Presbytery of Luzerne. He accepted the call from the Lower Mt. Bethel church. As to this pastorate he says: "He began his labors in the church on the first Sabbath of April, 1854, and was ordained and installed at a meeting of Presbytery held in the church May 30th, 1854. In the ordination and installation services, the Rev. John A. Reiley presided and offered the ordination prayer; the Rev. Solomon McNair preached the sermon; the Rev. George C. Bush gave the charge to the pastor, and the Rev. Andrew Tully charged the people.

My pastoral relation to this church continued until the last Sabbath of December, 1872, when I left to take the pastoral charge of the Yellow Frame Presbyterian church, in Warren County, New Jersey."

Thus it is seen Mr. Foresman's pastorate practically closed with the Union of 1870. During this pastorate, John Connelly, John Roseberry, Morris Morris, and Merari Gulick were in the eldership of the church. April 23d, 1856, $4.50 was reported for Commissioners' and Contingent Fund; and April 20th, 1857, $3.00 for the same. October 22d, 1857, $71.00 was reported as a contribution to the Phillipsburg church.

April 7th, 1858, $10.00 was reported for Commissioners' and Contingent Fund; and April 27th, 1859, $5.00 for the same.

As coming within the purview of the present generation, it might be said, Rev. Prof. J. W. Scott, D. D., of Hanover College, Indiana, was the son of Rev. William Scott, whose wife was the daughter of Samuel Rea, of the congregation. Others who entered the ministry from the congregation were: Samuel Galloway, Ephraim Simonton, who recently lived and died at Hackettstown, N. J., Samuel Ayers, John Brittain, Theron Brittain, and George C. Pollock, who graduated from Lafayette College in the class of 1861.

Foresman says: "During my pastorate of this church, two interesting services occurred: one during the year ending April, 1861, when thirty-nine were received into the communion of the church upon profession of their faith; and the other during the year ending April, 1871, when thirty were received. The Bangor church was, in part, formed from members belonging to the Lower Mt. Bethel church. Of this Foresman says: "At the earnest solicitation of a number of persons residing in and near the village of Bangor, some of whom were members of the Lower Mt. Bethel church, the pastor of this church began to hold, at first monthly, and in a short time after, semi-monthly, Sabbath afternoon preaching services in the winter of 1869 and 1870. The encouragement was such, that at the stated meeting of the Presbytery of Newton in April, 1870, request was made for the organization of a Presbyterian church at Bangor.

"A committee was appointed by Presbytery, authorized to organize a church, as petitioned for, if the way should be clear. This committee met in the Mennonite church at Bangor, June 14th, 1870, and organized a church named the First Presbyterian Church of Bangor, consisting of nineteen members, four of whom were members of the Lower Mt. Bethel Church, and continued to supply the Bangor church by appointment of Presbytery at discretion until the termination of his pastorate in December, 1872."

We may now return and note the fortunes of the Upper

Mt. Bethel church, from the time Rev. William B. Darrah closed his labors prior to September, 1871. In 1871 the statistical report shows the church to be vacant. It had added two on examination and three by certificate during the previous ecclesiastical year. Its total membership was eighty-seven. The Sabbath school membership was one hundred and ten. It raised for use in the bounds of the congregation $936.00, and for the benevolent and other causes outside of the congregation, $93.00.

September, 1871, Rev. Chester Bridgeman commenced his labors. It seems he was elected to the pastorate, but it does not appear that he was ever installed. He terminated his services before January, 1874. During the year there were added on examination nineteen and by certificate five. In 1873 there were added by examination two, and by certificate two. The membership in 1872 was one hundred and ten and in 1873 one hundred and seven. The membership of the Sabbath school of the two years stood at one hundred and fifty.

In 1872, money raised for home purposes, $2,937.00, and for outside purposes, $60.22. In 1873, money for home purposes, $800.00, and for outside purposes, $81.60. The preponderance of money raised for home purposes in 1872, $2,937.00, over the amount raised in 1873, shows there must have been some special reason for the difference.

January, 1874, the former pastor, Rev. Andrew Tully, began his labors. In 1853, as we have seen, Mr. Tully had left Lower Mt. Bethel to accept a call to Harmony, N. J. The history of Sussex and Warren Counties, N. J., says he closed his pastorate at Harmony April 6th, 1861. It says that from December, 1866, he was pastor at Second Wantage, or Beemerville Church, in New Jersey; also that during 1872 he supplied at Knowlton, New Jersey; also that his pastorate at Beemerville closed in 1873.

This allowed him to return to labor in his former charge, as Moore tells us, January, 1874. He died in the bounds of the Upper Mt. Bethel congregation at Portland, April 5th, 1880.

There were added in 1874, on examination, five; by certificate, five; membership, eighty. Sabbath school membership, one hundred and fifty. Moneys for home use, $700.00; for outside purposes, $39.49.

In 1875, added on examination, two; by certificate, one; Sabbath school membership, two hundred. Money for home use, $3,036; for outside purposes, $201.30.

In 1876, added on examination, sixteen; by certificate, six; membership, eighty; Sabbath school membership, one hundred and sixty-nine; money for home use, $790.00, and for outside purposes, $60.00.

In 1877, added on examination, seven; by certificate, seven; membership, one hundred; Sabbath school membership, one hundred and seventy-five; money for home use, $700.00; for outside purposes, $75.00.

In 1878, added on examination, four; by certificate, one; membership, ninety; Sabbath school membership, two hundred; money for home use, $600.00; for outside purposes, $72.00.

In 1879, added on examination, eight; by certificate, three; membership, ninety; Sabbath school membership, one hundred and sixty; money for home use, $700.00; for outside purposes, $73.30.

Thus it is seen that during Mr. Tully's pastorate there were constant accessions to the membership of the church both on examination and by certificate; the highest in one year, 1876, on examination, being sixteen, and the lowest number in 1875, being two; the highest number by certificate in 1877, being seven; and the lowest number in 1875 and 1878, being one.

The fluctuation in membership being from forty-five in 1875 to one hundred in 1877. The fluctuation in the Sabbath school membership was from one hundred and fifty in 1894 to two hundred in 1875 and 1878. The gross amount of money raised for home uses was $7,526.00, the fluctuation being from $700.00 in 1874, 1877, and 1879, to $3,036.00 in 1875. The gross amount of money raised for outside purposes was $521.09. The fluctuation being from $39.49 in 1874 to $20.30 in 1875.

The very large preponderance of money raised for both home and outside purposes in 1875, shows there must have been special reasons for the same, though these do not appear on the records.

The Rev. Mr. Tully having died, as we have seen, April 5th, 1880, the church became vacant, and so appears in the statistical report of that year. There was added on examination this year, one; by certificate, five; the membership was one hundred and fifty; money for home use, $750.00; and for outside purposes, $111.45.

Now comes a change in the status of the Upper Mt. Bethel church. As Moore tells us, it was depleted by the organization of the Portland Presbyterian church within its bounds. Although there were two organizations, the people continued as one in the support of a minister.

Moore tells us that Rev. J. Bailie Adams commenced his labors in the combined field, March, 1881, as Stated Supply. This year there were added at Upper Mt. Bethel, on examination, two; the membership was fifty-five; the Sabbath school membership was eighty; money for home purposes, $200.00; for outside purposes, $4.95. There were three elders in the congregation at this time.

At Portland this year there were added on examination, two; by certificate, three; making in the two congregations, four on examination, and three by certificate. The membership was forty-four, making with the other church, ninety-nine; the Sabbath school membership was seventy-seven, making with the other church, one hundred and fifty-seven. No money was reported for home use at Portland, but $100.00 was reported for outside uses. The church started with two elders.

In 1882, there were added at Upper Mt. Bethel, on examination, eight; the membership was fifty-eight; and the

Sabbath school membership, seventy-five; money for home purposes, $400.00; and for outside purposes, $69.50.

At Portland there were added on examination, three; or for the two churches, eleven; by certificate, seven; the membership was forty-six, or with the other part of the charge, one hundred and four; the Sabbath school membership was ninety-seven, or with the other part of the charge, one hundred and seventy-two; money for home use, $182.00, or with the other charge, $582.00; for outside uses, $56.40, or with the other charge, $125.90. Portland this year reported but one elder.

In 1883, there were added at Upper Mt. Bethel on examination, two; by certificate, five; membership, sixty-two; Sabbath school membership, one hundred and ten; money for home use, $465.00; for outside uses, $86.09. Eldership reported, four.

At Portland in 1883, the report seems not to have been made, except that the membership of the church, forty-six, was copied from the previous year; and $75.00 was reported for outside uses.

In 1884, Upper Mt. Bethel reported as added on examination, six; by certificate, six; membership, sixty; Sabbath school membership, one hundred and three; money for home use, $325.00; for outside uses, $77.51. The eldership was three.

At Portland in 1884, there were added on examination, one, or with the other church, eleven; membership, forty-six, or combined, one hundred and six; Sabbath school, ninety-eight, or combined, two hundred and one; money at home, $345.00, or combined, $670.00; money for outside uses, $42.83; or combined, $120.34. Portland this year reported one elder.

In 1885, Upper Mt. Bethel did not report any additions on examination or by certificate; the membership was fifty-nine; Sabbath school membership, one hundred and twenty-four; money for home use, $3,000.00; for outside uses, $58.00. The eldership was three. The large amount of money for home use indicates that there was some special work on hand among the people.

At Portland, in 1885, there were added on examination, eighteen; by certificate, one; membership, fifty-nine, or combined, one hundred and eighteen; Sabbath school, ninety-five, or combined, two hundred and nineteen; money for home use, $357.00, or combined, $3,357.00; for outside uses, $36.60, or combined, $94.60; Portland this year reported four elders.

During the ecclesiastical year 1885-6, Rev. J. Bailie Adams closed his labors in the combined field, and in 1886, Upper Mt. Bethel appears as having a pastor elect; and Portland appears as vacant.

This year, 1886, Upper Mt. Bethel added on examination, two; and by certificate, two; the membership was fifty-eight; Sabbath school, eighty-five; money for home use, $1,310.00; for outside purposes, $47.07. The eldership was three. Again the large amount of money for home use shows the special work on hand. This year, 1886, at Portland, there were added by certificate, one; or combined, three; membership, fifty-nine, or combined membership, one hundred and seventeen; Sabbath school membership, seventy-five, or combined membership, one hundred and sixty; money for home use, $347.00, or combined, $1,657.00; for outside uses, $7.08, or combined, $54.15. This year Portland reported three elders and three deacons.

In 1887, Rev. David B. Rogers appears on the combined field, but whether as Stated Supply or pastor elect is not indicated. Moore tells us he began his labors September, 1886. This year Upper Mt. Bethel received on examination, one; by certificate, one; membership, fifty-seven; Sabbath school, eighty; money for home use, $455.00; for outside uses, $27.96. Eldership, three. At Portland, there were received by certificate, three, or combined, four; membership, sixty-seven, or combined, one hundred and twenty-four; Sabbath school, one hundred, or combined, one hundred and eighty; money for home use, $444.00, or combined, $899.00;

money for outside use, $28.08 or combined, $56.04. The eldership was three.

In 1888, at Upper Mt. Bethel, there were received on examination, one; by certificate, two; membership, fifty-one; Sabbath school, seventy-two; money for home use, $315.00, for outside uses, $59.27. The eldership was three. Rev. Mr. Rogers appears this year as pastor elect. At Portland this year, there were received on examination, eight; or combined, nine; by certificate, eight, or combined, ten; membership, seventy-eight, or combined, one hundred and twenty-nine; Sabbath school, one hundred and fifteen, or combined, one hundred and eighty-seven; money for home use, $933.00, or combined, $1,248.00; money for outside uses, $21.37, or combined, $80.64. Eldership, three. Here also Mr. Rogers appears as pastor elect.

In 1889, at Upper Mt. Bethel, there were received on examination, two; membership, forty-five; Sabbath school, seventy; money for home use, $300.00; for outside uses, $72.61. The elders were two. Mr. Rogers is this year reported as pastor. At Portland this year there were added on examination, one, or combined, three; by certificate, one; membership, seventy, or combined, one hundred and fifteen; Sabbath school, one hundred, or combined, one hundred and seventy; money for home use, $503.00, or combined, $803.00; for outside uses, $27.50, or combined, $100.11. The eldership was three. Here also Mr. Rogers appears as pastor.

In 1890, both churches are reported vacant. Moore tells us Mr. Rogers' labors ended before August, 1890. This year there were added at Upper Mt. Bethel on examination, two; membership, forty-two; Sabbath school, seventy; money for home use, $250.00; for outside purposes, $6.95. The eldership was two. At Portland there were no additions; membership was fifty-six, or combined, ninety-eight; Sabbath school, eighty-five, or combined, one hundred and fifty-five; money for home use, $317.00, or combined, $567.00; for outside uses, $25.00, or combined, $31.95. Eldership, three.

In 1891, Rev. Robert Long Adams appears as pastor of

the united congregations. Moore tells us he began labors in August, 1890. This year there were added at Upper Mt. Bethel on examination, two; membership, thirty-eight; Sabbath school, seventy-five; money for home use, $280.00; for outside use, $68.62. The eldership was two. At Portland there were added on examination, seven, or combined, nine; by certificate, seven; membership sixty-two, or combined, one hundred; Sabbath school, seventy, or combined, one hundred and forty-five; money for home use, $606.00, or combined, $886.00; for outside use, $65.16, or combined, $133.78. The elders were three. In 1892, Rev. Mr. Adams is reported as pastor of both churches, showing that his installation had taken place.

This year at Upper Mt. Bethel there were added on examination, nine; by certificate, two; membership, forty-two; Sabbath school, sixty; money for home use, $280.00; for outside use, $30.18. The eldership was two. At Portland there were added on examination, thirty-two, or combined, forty-one; by certificate, four, or combined, six; membership, eighty-eight, or combined, one hundred and thirty; Sabbath school, ninety-four, or combined, one hundred and fifty-four; money for home use, $720.00, or combined, $1,000.00; for outside use, $50.82, or combined, $81.00. The eldership was three. The large number added this year to each church, and especially at Portland, indicates that there had been a revival of considerable proportions.

In 1893, there were added at Upper Mt. Bethel on examination, thirteen; membership, forty-seven; Sabbath school, sixty; money for home use, $290.00; for outside uses, $73.62; the eldership was two. At Portland there were added on examination, one, or combined, fourteen; by certificate, two; membership, eighty-four, or combined, one hundred and thirty-one; Sabbath school, seventy-five, or combined, one hundred and thirty-five; money for home use, $540.00, or combined, $830.00; for outside use, $86.68, or combined, $160.30. Eldership three. Here it will be noticed the large number received on examination took place at Upper Mt.

Bethel, as against the larger number received at Portland the year before.

In 1894, there were received at Upper Mt. Bethel on examination, one; and by certificate, one; membership, forty-two; Sabbath school, sixty; money for home use, $290.00; for outside use, $63.70. The eldership was two. At Portland there were received on examination, two; or combined, three; membership, seventy-six, or combined, one hundred and eighteen; Sabbath school, eighty-three, or combined, one hundred and forty-three; money for home use, $653.00, or combined, $943.00; for outside uses, $76.40, or combined, $140.10. Eldership three.

In 1895, there were received at Upper Mt. Bethel, by certificate, one; membership, forty-one; Sabbath school, sixty; money for home use, $300.00; for outside use, $43.78. The eldership was two. At Portland there were received on examination, two; by certificate, two, or combined, three; membership, sixty-seven, or combined, one hundred and eight; Sabbath school, one hundred and forty-seven, or combined, two hundred and seven; money for home use, $355.00, or combined, $655.00; for outside use, $80.94, or combined, $124.62. Eldership three. The few additions during the latter two years indicates the usual state of religion after the revival of the previous two years.

In 1896, both congregations are reported as having a pastor elect. Moore tells us Rev. R. L. Adams closed his labors in the field before April, 1896. At Upper Mt. Bethel this year there were no additions reported. The membership was forty; the Sabbath school, forty-five; money for home use, $150.00; for outside use, $37.10. The eldership was two. At Portland also no additions were reported for the year. The membership was fifty, or combined, ninety; Sabbath school, one hundred, or combined, one hundred and fifty-five; money for home use, $500.00, or combined, $650.00; for outside use, $58.00, or combined, $95.10. The eldership was three.

In 1897, Rev. John Thompson appears as pastor of each

of the churches. Moore tells us he began his labors, April, 1896. This year also no additions were reported at Upper Mt. Bethel. The membership was thirty-eight; Sabbath school, seventy-one; money for home use, $275.00; for outside use, $50.60. The eldership was one. At Portland the additions were six by certificate; membership was sixty, or combined, ninety-six; Sabbath school, eighty-six, or combined, one hundred and fifty-seven; Money for home use, $750.00, or combined, $1,025.00; for outside use, $109.50, or combined, $160.10. Eldership was four.

In 1898, there was one addition on examination. The membership was thirty-eight; Sabbath school, seventy; money for home use, $335.00; for outside use, $58.42. Eldership one. At Portland the additions were on examination, two, or combined, three; by certificate, three; membership, sixty-three, or combined, one hundred and one; Sabbath school, fifty-eight, or combined, one hundred and twenty-eight; money for home use, $395.00, or combined, $730.00; for outside use, $125.40, or combined, $183.82. Eldership four.

In 1899, both churches appear as having a pastor elect. At Upper Mt. Bethel there were added on examination, two; by certificate, one; membership, thirty-nine; Sabbath school, sixty; money for home use, $330.00; for outside use, $44.66. Eldership, one. At Portland there were added by certificate, two, or combined, three; membership, fifty-seven, or combined, one hundred and twenty-three; money for home use, $384.00, or combined, $714.00; for outside use, $50.41, or combined, $97.07. Eldership four.

In 1900, Rev. Francis H. Laird appears as pastor of each of the churches. By this we know that Rev. John Thompson had closed his labors in the field. This Moore tells us occurred March, 1899. It will be observed we have continuously quoted from a letter written us March 2, 1899, by Elder Jonathan Moore. At this time he was the only surviving elder in the congregation at Upper Mt. Bethel.

This year, 1900, there were added at Upper Mt. Bethel on examination, twenty-one; by certificate, thirteen; membership, seventy-one; Sabbath school, seventy-six; money for home use, $400.00; for outside use, $87.29. The eldership was one. At Portland there were added on examination, fourteen, or combined, thirty-five; by certificate, seventeen, or combined, thirty; membership, eighty-three, or combined, one hundred and fifty-four; Sabbath school, seventy-five, or combined, one hundred and fifty-one; money for home use, $670.00, or combined, $1,070.00; for outside use, $111.27, or combined, $198.56. Eldership four. By the largely increased additions, both on examination and by certificate, in each part of the field, it is manifest there was at this time a considerable revival or ingathering.

In 1901, both congregations appear as vacant, showing that Rev. Mr. Laird had concluded his labors. This year there were added at Upper Mt. Bethel on examination, three; by certificate, two; membership, sixty-nine; Sabbath school, eighty; money for home use, $530.00; for outside use, $74.10. The eldership was one. At Portland there were added on examination, thirteen, or combined, sixteen; membership, ninety, or combined, one hundred and fifty-nine; Sabbath school, eighty, or combined, one hundred and sixty; money for home use, $690.00, or combined, $1,220.00; for outside use, $77.30, or combined, $151.40. The eldership was four.

In 1902, Rev. Henry S. Welty appears as pastor of both churches. This year there were added at Upper Mt. Bethel on examination, one; by certificate, one; membership, sixty-six; Sabbath school, seventy-nine; money for home use, $400.00; for outside use, $79.90. The eldership was one. At Portland there were added on examination, one, or combined, two; by certificate, two, or combined, three; membership, ninety, or combined, one hundred and fifty-six; Sabbath school, ninety, or combined, one hundred and sixty-nine; money for home use, $506.00 or combined, $906.00; for outside use, $88.00, or combined, $167.90. Eldership three.

In 1903, there were added at Upper Mt. Bethel on examination, two; membership, fifty-nine; Sabbath school, sixty-five; money for home use, $400.00; for outside use, $89.60.

The eldership was one. At Portland there were added by certificate, two; membership, eighty-nine, or combined, one hundred and forty-eight; Sabbath school, one hundred, or combined, one hundred and sixty-five; money for home use, $500.00, or combined, $900.00; for outside use, $67.00, or combined, $156.60. Eldership two.

In 1904, there were added at Upper Mt. Bethel, on examination, five; membership, sixty-two; Sabbath school, seventy; money for home use, $400.00; for outside use, $109.90. The eldership was one. At Portland there were added by certificate, three; membership, ninety-one, or combined, one hundred and fifty-three; Sabbath school, one hundred, or combined, one hundred and seventy; money for home use, $600.00, or combined, $1,000.00; for outside use, $66.90, or combined, $176.80. The eldership was two.

In 1905 there were added at Upper Mt. Bethel, on examination, one; by certificate, one; membership, sixty; Sabbath school, seventy-four; money for home use, $400.00; for outside use, $69.20. At Portland there were added on examination, three, or combined, four; by certificate one, or combined, two; membership, eighty-six, or combined, one hundred and forty-six; money for home use, $725.00, or combined, $1,125.00; for outside use, $70.10, or combined, $139.30. The eldership was two.

In 1906 there were added at Upper Mt. Bethel on examination, two; membership, fifty-nine; Sabbath school, sixty; money for home use, $400.00; for outside use, $79.00. The eldership was one. At Portland there were added on examination, five, or combined, seven; by certificate, ten; membership, eighty-nine, or combined, one hundred and fifty-eight; Sabbath school, one hundred, or combined, one hundred and sixty; money for home use, $600.00; or combined, $1,000.00; for outside use, $73.60, or combined, $152.60. The eldership was two. Rev. Mr. Welty was still in the pastorate.

This resumé will enable us to note at a glance what had been done in the upper part of the Hunter Settlement ecclesiastically since the union of 1870.

It remains for us to give a resumé of Lower Mt. Bethel for the same period, and in this way we will have brought before us in review the ecclesiastical status of the whole Hunter Scotch-Irish Settlement in the "Forks of the Delaware".

We last saw Lower Mt. Bethel at the close of the pastorate of Rev. Robert B. Foresman, December, 1872; and when the church at Bangor was just starting upon its career.

In 1871, at Lower Mt. Bethel, there were added on examination, thirty-six; by certificate, four; membership, one hundred and seventy-one; Sabbath school, ninety; money for home uses, $900.00; for outside uses, $85.00.

In 1872, added on examination, one; by certificate, one; membership, one hundred and seventy; Sabbath school, one hundred; money for home use, $1,449.00; outside uses, $122.26.

In 1873, there were no additions either on examination or by certificate; the membership of the previous year, one hundred and seventy, was reported; money for outside purposes, $10.20. Rev. Alpheus H. Holloway appears as the pastor elect. Foresman tells us that Rev. Mr. Holloway preached the first time March 16th, 1873; administered the Sacrament of the Lord's Supper March 30th. The first Sabbath in April he took charge of the congregation; June 18th, he was installed as pastor. In this service, Rev. Frank E. Miller, D. D., preached the sermon; Rev. James W. Wood gave the charge to the pastor, and Rev. J. Thompson Osler gave the charge to the people.

In 1874, there were added by certificate, two; membership, one hundred and thirty-seven; Sabbath school, sixty-five; money for home use, $1,200.00; for outside purposes, $174.90. Rev. Mr. Holloway appears as pastor, showing that he had been installed during the year.

In 1875, there were no additions; membership, one hundred and thirty; money for home use, $1,179.00; for outside use, $177.59.

In 1876, there were added on examination, two; membership, one hundred and twenty-five; Sabbath school, sixty; money for home use, $1,200.00; for outside use, $160.00. At this time (1876) the elders were Joseph Galloway, William McIlhaney, Morris Rosenberry, Robert L. Ross, and Joseph Ross. The trustees were—William E. McIlhaney, Pres, Charles Keifer, John Rosenberry, Thomas Lockart, Sec'y., Hon. Elias Shull, Treas., Marshal B. Ross, Castner Carhart, and Henry Rasley.

On October 1st of 1876, the former pastor, Rev. Robert B. Foresman, delivered his memorial sermon in the church at Lower Mt. Bethel. (Reprint of sermon in a later section).

In 1877, there were additions on examination, five; by certificate, four; membership, one hundred and thirty-two; Sabbath school, seventy; money for home use, $1,115.00; for outside use, $97.25.

In 1878, there were added on examination, two; by certificate, one; membership, one hundred and thirty-two; Sabbath school, eighty; money for home use, $1,100.00; for outside use, $87.60.

In 1879, there was added on examination, one; membership, one hundred; Sabbath school, eighty; money for home use, $1,026.00; for outside use, $75.24.

In 1880, there were added on examination, two; by certificate, one; membership, ninety-two; Sabbath school, seventy-five; money for home use, $765.00; for outside use, $69.00.

In 1881, there were added on examination, four; membership, ninety; Sabbath school, eighty; money for home use, $960.00; for outside use, $55.44. Elders seven.

In 1882, there were added on examination, six; by certificate, two; membership, ninety-five; Sabbath school, eighty; money for home use, $750.00; for outside use, $63.04. Elders seven. This year the church appears as vacant, showing that Rev. Holloway's services had terminated.

In 1883, there were no additions; membership, ninety; Sabbath school, fifty; no money is reported for home or outside purposes; elders five; church vacant.

In 1884, there were added on examination, fourteen; by certificate, nine; membership, one hundred and twenty-four; Sabbath school, eighty; money for home use, $770.00; for outside use, $58.45. Elders six; church vacant.

In 1885, there was added on examination, one; by certificate, four; membership, one hundred and twenty-four; Sabbath school, eighty; money for home use, $900.00; for outside use, $48.00. Elders five. Rev. J. I. Campbell appears this year as pastor elect, which fact doubtless accounts for the ingathering, and evidences of prosperity otherwise as seen in the report of 1884.

In 1886, there were added on examination, six; by certificate, five; membership, one hundred and thirty; Sabbath school, eighty; money for home use, $1,000.00; for outside use, $60.88. Elders five. Mr. Campbell now appears as pastor.

In 1887, there were added on examination, two; membership, one hundred and thirty; Sabbath school, eighty; money for home use, $900.00; for outside use, $103.60. Elders five; church vacant, showing that Mr. Campbell's labors had ceased.

In 1888, there were no additions; membership, one hundred and five; Sabbath school, fifty; money for home use, $725.00; for outside use, $21.30. Elders five. Now Rev. J. B. Clark appears as pastor elect.

In 1889, there were added on examination, ten; by certificate, four; membership, one hundred and five; Sabbath school, one hundred; money for home use, $914.00; for outside use, $29.55. Elders five. Rev. Mr. Clark now appears as pastor.

In 1890, there were added on examination, twenty-seven; membership, one hundred and ten; Sabbath school, one hundred; money for home use, $921.00; for outside use, $39.55. Elders seven. The large number of additions this year shows that there had been considerable religious interest in the congregation during the year.

In 1891, there were added on examination, five; membership, one hundred; Sabbath school, one hundred; money for home use, $800.00; for outside use, $57.20. Elders six.

In 1892, there was added on examination, one; by certificate, three; membership, one hundred and two; Sabbath school, one hundred; money for home use, $600.00; for outside use, $48.00. Elders seven. The church is now reported vacant, showing that Mr. Clark's labors had ceased.

In 1893, there were three additions by letter; membership, eighty-five; Sabbath school, one hundred; money for home use, $347.00; for outside use, $62.10. Elders six. Rev. Joseph H. Doremus now appears as pastor.

In 1894, there were added on examination, four; membership, eighty-six; Sabbath school, one hundred; money for home use, $755.00; for outside use, $109.50. Elders six.

In 1895, there was added on examination, one; membership, eighty-two; Sabbath school, one hundred; money for home use, $625.00; for outside use, $104.74. Elders five.

In 1896, there were no additions; membership, eighty; Sabbath school, ninety-three; money for home use, $550.00; for outside use, $88.20. Elders five.

In 1897, there were no additions; membership, seventy-five; Sabbath school, eighty; money for home use, $705.00; for outside use, $62.20. Elders five.

In 1898, there were no additions; membership, seventy-five; Sabbath school, seventy-two; money for home use, $502.00; for outside use, $81.75. Elders five.

In 1899, there were no additions; membership, seventy; Sabbath school, forty-seven; money for home use, $400.00; for outside use, $48.25. Elders five.

In 1900, there were no additions; membership, sixty-eight; Sabbath school, forty-seven; money for home use, $400.00; for outside use, $54.70. Elders five.

In 1901, there were no additions; membership, sixty; Sabbath school, forty; money for home use, $400.00; for outside use, $50.80. Elders five.

In 1902, there were no additions; membership, fifty; Sabbath school, thirty; money for outside uses, $6.00. Elders five. The church is now reported vacant, showing that Rev. Mr. Doremus had closed his labors in the field.

In 1903, there were no additions; membership, forty; elders four. Vacant.

In 1904, there were added on examination, four; membership, forty-two; money for outside uses, $4.00. Elders five. Vacant.

In 1905, there was added by certificate, one; membership, thirty-eight; money for outside purposes, $4.20; elders, four. Vacant.

In 1906, there were no additions; membership, thirty-seven; money for outside purposes, $16.00. Elders three. Vacant.

Thus in brief is told the story of Lower Mt. Bethel. This with what has been given with reference to Upper Mt. Bethel and Portland, will give an ecclesiastical bird's-eye view of the Scotch Irish in the "Forks of the Delaware".

In bringing to a close this latest attempt to put into permanent form historical facts pertaining to this section of the country, it will not be inappropriate to insert a few items of correspondence which we have had in connection with the matter. It will be noticed we have referred to James Depue and Jonathan Moore. The valuable information furnished by them came to hand as a sequence of a correspondence we opened under date of January 27th, 1899, with the late Mr. Josiah Ketcham, editor of the Belvidere Apollo.

Under date of March 21, 1899. Mr. Ketcham wrote:

My Dear Mr. Clyde:

Enclosed please find a note in regard to the church you wrote about some time since. Here is a letter that was handed to me. I waited, hoping to get some information. If I get more I will hand it to you or send it.

Yours truly,

Josiah Ketcham.

The "Note" spoken of is as follows:

"The Presbyterian Church of Upper Mt. Bethel, Pa.,

Near the spot where this Monument stands Missionary Brainerd built his House, not far from Martin's Creek, Pa. (See page 539.)

The Scotch-Irish Presbyterian Burial Ground, at Three Churches, Lower Mt. Bethel, Pa. Methodist Church Shown at Rear. (See page 576.)

(Northampton County) was at first united with the Presbyterian Church of Lower Mt. Bethel. The first church building was at Centreville about two miles south of Williamsburg, where it now stands, and was six miles north of the Lower Mt. Bethel Church. Rev. Leake preached at the two Bethels and Oxford and Harmony, N. J. Rev. James Clark preached a short time at the two Bethels and was called to Belvidere in April (1840), and was the Rev. James Clark, D. D., who died at Philadelphia a few years ago.

The Mt. Bethel churches were separate during the ministry of Rev. Andrew Tully, his whole time being called for at Lower Mt. Bethel. I remember when young hearing of records of Upper Mt. Bethel church being lost and advertised —think they were never found—were the first record the church had.

(Signed) James Depue.

The "letter" referred to by Mr. Ketcham is as follows, and is self-explanatory:

Mt. Bethel, Pa., March 2d, 1899.

Mr. James Depue,

Dear Sir:—

As regards the history of the Upper Mt. Bethel Presbyterian church, asked for in your letter some days ago, I would say that records we have date back as far as May 27, 1820, and no farther.

The organization of the church, however, I am told, was some years prior to this date. The church building first erected on the site now occupied, was in 1836. The church became a corporate body February 2d, 1839. I find on the earliest record now in possession, that the Moderator, May 27, 1820, was Rev. B. I. Lowe, and members of the Session as elders—David DeMott, Joseph Ink, and Robert Butts. Ministers who have served the church following B. I. Lowe up to the present date, according to records, are as follows:

October 20, 1827, Rev. Mr. Leake.

May 30, 1829, Rev. Talmage.

December 10, 1836, Rev. McCullough.
May 13, 1838, Rev. Leslie Irwin.
September 12, 1839, Rev. James Clark.
November 21, 1840, Rev. Andrew Tully.
October 30, 1842, Rev. Thomas Mack.
March 26, 1846, Rev. Joseph Worrel.
April, 1852, Rev. Gershom Goble.
August 31, 1856, Rev. ——— Sturges.
December, 1857, Rev. P. W. Mellick.
May, 1862, Rev. Solomon McNair.
June, 1865, Rev. Teese.
April, 1866, Rev. E. Town.
November 28, 1868, Rev. W. D. Darrah.
September, 1871, Rev. Chester Bridgeman.
January, 1874, Andrew Tully, died in the charge.
March, 1881, Rev. J. B. Adams.
September, 1886, Rev. D. B. Rogers.
August, 1890, Rev. R. L. Adams.
August, 1896, Rev. John Thompson, who now, March, 1899, resigned the charge.

During the year 1868, a church edifice was erected by the congregation of Upper Mt. Bethel Church at Portland. The two congregations remained as one organization until 1880, when the Portland congregation became a separate and distinct organization. The two churches remained still under one pastorate, supporting jointly one minister.

The elders of the Portland Church at the present time are A. F. Hauser, James I. Cline, Ephraim Bellis and Wm. Ward.

I am the only surviving elder of the Mt. Bethel Church, at present. If these few items are of use to the parties writing up the history of this part of Pennsylvania, they are cheerfully submitted.

Respectfully,
(Signed) Jonathan Moore.

The foregoing facts with others obtained from the writers, have been given their proper place in the narrative.

Another communication is as follows:

> Bath, Pennsylvania, January 30, 1907.

Rev. J. C. Clyde, D. D., Easton, Pa.

Dear Sir,—

The invitation to attend the annual meeting of the Northampton County Historical and Genealogical Society, has just reached me. I regret that circumstances are such that I will not be able to be present, for I certainly would like to hear your lecture on "The Scotch-Irish in Northampton County". Hope, however, that arrangements will be made by the Society to have your address published. As a member, I am satisfied to pay for my copy.

I am a descendant of one of the original Scotch-Irish families in this county, my ancestor settling in the Hunter Settlement in Mt. Bethel Township, long before the American Revolution, and it is one of the few Scotch-Irish names still remaining there.

By 1768, this ancestor of mine, Wm. McIlhaney, possessed 373 acres of land in what is now Lower Mt. Bethel, just across the Delaware from Belvidere, N. J. It joined lands of the McIlroys, McCrackens and the McDowells and close to that of the McNeils, McFerrens and the McEwens.

Why these Macs were bunched so closely together, I cannot say. This information I got from old and original property drafts which are in my possession. In the assessment list of taxables of Northampton County for 1780, his son James McIlhaney is assessed at 1469 pounds, the name here being spelled McKelhaney. By that time he (James) owned 503 acres; this included the island in the river, north of Belvidere, and was known as McIlhaney's Island up to 1840. I find it so named in the Colonial Records. My father, John McIlhaney, came to this locality, Bath, in 1860, and since that time has resided here. He was born in Lower Mt. Bethel seventy-one years ago.

Hoping your article will appear in print, and that I may secure a copy, I remain,

>Very respectfully,
>(Signed)   Asa K. McIlhaney.

Still another communication is as follows:

>46 Woodlawn Av., Middletown, N. Y.,
>February 27, 1907.

Rev. John C. Clyde, D. D., Easton, Pa.

Dear Bro,—

Through the kindness of my friend James Edmiston, of Lower Mt. Bethel, Pa., (or Martin's Creek), I have the "Easton Argus" of February 6, containing a report of your address at the Annual Meeting of the Historical and Genealogical Society of Northampton County. I enjoy it much. If you have it in pamphlet form, I would like to have one or two copies at my own expense.

When I was a chap of seventeen years, my sister Jane (now eighty-seven and living, well preserved in Tallula, Ill.,) was the wife of William Wilson, brother of the wife of Rev. Leslie Irwin, all of whom I met those days. I also saw 'Squire Clyde, your father or grandfather; Dr. McIlhaney, &c.

John M. McIlhaney, elder of the Bath Church, was an old schoolmate of mine in the old schoolhouse by the side of the old grave yard at the "Three Churches". I do not believe there is an old tombstone there I am not familiar with.

Part of our devotion to the grave yard was due to an old apple tree whose little apples were toothsome to the hard students we boys were in those days. I grew up within one-fourth of a mile of that grave yard, and my church life for my first twenty years was in that Presbyterian Church under the ministry of Rev. Andrew Tully and Rev. R. B. Foresman. One of my most prized friends is Jonathan Moore of Mt. Bethel Church. He needs no introduction to you. This week I received two copies of the printed minutes of Lehigh

Presbytery. I am surprised at the amount I find there that interests me. Pardon this outbreak onto you by

Yours fraternally,

(Signed) Theron Brittain.

And now our task is done. We have endeavored, as intimated at the outset, to bring up some reminisences of the dead past and associate them with the living present. How well we have succeeded we must leave it with the reader to decide.

We trust, however, that no decendants of the old families will feel that in the brief space at our command, we have purposely slighted them. We could not do justice to all under the circumstances, and must ask pardon for anything that may be amiss. If further light is desired on this interesting subject, it may be obtained from original records. From Foresman's Memorial Discourse delivered in the First Presbyterian Church, Lower Mt. Bethel, Pa., October 1, 1876; from the writer's published works; and from his unpublished History of Presbyterianism in Northern New Jersey.

"Here sleeps their dust, 'tis holy ground;
And we the children of the brave,
From the four winds are gathered round,
To lay our offering on their grave."—Pierpont.

SCOTCH-IRISH SOLDIERS
In the American Revolution from Mount Bethel

Compiled by Asa K. McIlhaney

Lieut.—Samuel Rhea
    Peter Middaugh
    Joseph Martin
    John Lyle
    John Connelly
    Ephraim Simonton
    Robert Moody

Capt.—John Neilson
    Timothy Jayne
    Alexander Foresman
    Wm. Scott
    Alexander Patterson
    Hugh Gaston
    Patrick Campbell
    John Long

Sergt.—Robert Wilson
    Robert Scott
    James Simonton
    James McCartney
    Wm. Connelly
    Samuel McCracken

Corp.—Elijah Crawford

Private—Samuel McCracken
    John McFarren
    Alexander Miller
    Thomas Connelly
    Andrew Bowman
    Andrew Nye
    John Crawford
    Robert Matheson
    Henry Campbell
    John Kerr
    Alexander Lockhart
    David Lockhart
    Wm. Hammon
    Thos. Moore
    Robert McCracken
    Joseph Orr
    James Silliman
    James Matheson
    Wm. Matheson
    Robert Lyle
    Aaron Lyle
    Thomas Silliman
    Alexander Silliman
    James Thompson
    David Lyle
    Hector McNeal
    Robert Galloway
    Andrew Oliphant

Private—Neal Campbell
   William Gaston
   James Beard
   Patrick Burns
   James Scott
   Charles Brown
   Hugh McCracken
   Thomas Ross
   Peter Simonton
   Samuel McFarren
   John McCollum
   George Scott
   Nathaniel Brittain
   Samuel Patton
   Wm. Lockhart
   James McIlhaney
   David Ross
   George Baird
   David Ayres
   Joseph Foresman
   Samuel Foresman
   Benj. Simonton
   Wm. Rea, Jr.
   John McFarren
   John Kirkpatrick
   James Gaston

Private—John McEwen
   Thos. Beard
   John Hutchison
   Anthony Moore
   Joseph Wallace
   Wm. McFarren, Sr.
   Samuel Nye
   Thos. Craig
   Hugh Foresman
   Robert Scott
   Thos. Martin
   James McCartney
   John Connelly
   Joseph Henderson
   John Neilson, Sr.
   Leboeth Brittain

Drummer—
   Wm. McFarren

From:—
"Penna. Archives, Fifth Series, Vol. VIII.

A certificate of names to be taxed in Mount Bethel Township. By Jacob Woods, Constable.

Return of Mount Bethel Township for County Tax, January, 1775.

From the original manuscript in possession of Asa K. McIlhaney.

	Acres of land	Cleared	Sowed	Horses	Horned cattle	Sheep	Mills	Inmates	Negroes	Bond servants	Trades
Nelson, John	150	50	9	2	2	1	0	0	0	0	
McCracken, Hugh	100	20	7	2	2	0	0	0	0	0	26 age
Martin, Joseph	200	70	15	3	5	7	2	1	0	1	Carpenter
Moore, Thomas	70	26	10	2	3	1	0	0	0	0	
Hood, Robert	0	0	0	1	2	0	0	0	0		Weaver
Moor, James	200	60	20	3	2	6	0	0	0	0	
Loycker, David	80	20	8	1	4	0	0	0	0	0	
Moor, Anthony	200	100	15	3	3	7	0	1	0	0	
Crawford, John	190	90	20	3	3	5	0	0	0	0	
Crawford, John, Jr.	0	0	1	0	1	0	2	0	0	0	
Jones, John	0	0	6	2	1	0	0	0	0	0	
Patterson, Hugh	150	70	10	4	3	7	0	0	0	0	
Moody, Adam	200	70	25	3	4	12	0	0	0	0	
Miller, James	200	80	10	9	3	0	0	0	0	0	
Moor, William	200	60	20	3	4	8	0	0	0	0	
Hamon, William	0	0	0	0	1	0	0	0	0	0	Weaver
Allen, David	200	60	11	5	5	0	0	0	0	0	
Hutchison, James	130	40	15	2	4	10	0	0	0	0	
Miller, Alexander	100	70	12	2	4	3	0	0	0	0	
Miller, Alexander, Jun.	15	15	4	2	2	5	0	0	0	0	
Miller, Samuel	0	0	2	1	2	4	0	0	0	0	
Miller, John	106	70	12	2	4	5	0	0	0	0	
Sharp, John	40	3	1	2	0	0	0	1			Servant
Shuck, Philip	100	30	1	2	3	4	0	0	0	0	
Miller, Samuel	47	8	0	2	3	8	1	0	0	0	
Kester, Michael	90	50	10	4	4	6	0	0	0	0	
Nelson, Jonathan	150	40	7	2	2	10	0	0	0	0	
Pell, Nicholess	100	8	2	2	2	0	0	0	0	0	
Kirkpatrick, Alexander	80	9	2	2	3	0	0	0	0	0	

Beard, George	150	50	10	2	4	4	0	0	0	0
Dunn, Patrick	115	7	2	1	2	1	0	0	0	0
Taylor, Samuel	100	20	6	1	3	0	0	0	0	0
Campble, Neals	4	4	0	0	0	0	0	0	0	0
Oliphant, James	100	30	15	0	3	0	0	0	0	0 Cordwinder
Hess, Michael	50	12	7	2	1	0	0	0	0	Ditto
Painter, Christopher	50	12	6	1	2	0	0	0	0	Ditto
Ramble, George	100	40	10	2	2	0	0	0	0	
Hilyard, Francis	100	20	5	2	2	0	0	0	0	
										14 years
Teeter, Jacob	10	5	4	4	1	0	0	1	0	0 Taylor
Smith, Henry, Jun.	100	10	5	2	1	0	0	0	0	0
Smith, George	100	10	5	2	1	0	0	0	0	0
Piper, Samuel	50	10	5	1	1	0	0	0	0	0
Cornequa, Widdow	180	40	10	0	0	0	0	0	0	0
Tebrick, John	114	40	15	2	3	4	0	0	0	0
Long, John, Jun.	150	30	10	2	2	5	0	0	0	0
Eilenberger, Christian	100	25	12	3	4	4	0	0	0	0 Cordwinder
Mitchel, Robert	0	0	0	0	0	0	0	0	0	0
Schoolmaster										
Lomerson, Low	200	60	40	3	3	13	0	0	0	0
Meddagh, Peter	200	100	30	3	7	4	0	0	0	0
Meddagh, Garrit	0	0	0	2	4	7	0	0	0	0
Standly, Peter	1	0	4	0	0	0	0	0	0	0
DePue, Benjamin	280	120	40	5	5	0	0	0	0	0 Deeded
DePue, John	285	120	30	6	5	0	0	0	1	Ditto
Scott, John, sch'master	150	20	10	3	1	0	0	0	0	0
Scott, William	150	0	0	0	0	0	0	0	0	0
Smoke, Daniel	200	100	18	2	0	0	0	1	0	0
										9 years old
Mason, William	118	50	15	2	3	3	0	1	0	0
Mason, Henry	230	60	20	4	4	10	0	0	0	0
McFerrin, Wm.	294	80	20	3	4	12	0	0	0	0
Ruckman, Thomas	300	150	50	5	6	20	0	0	0	2
										17 years old
Otter, Adrian	200	80	20	3	4	6	0	1	0	0
Rhea, Samuel	200	80	20	4	6	8	0	0	0	0
										18 years old
Amre, Jacob	150	70	30	4	4	6	0	1	0	0
Johnston, Samuel	60	30	7	2	2	0	1	0	0	0
Nye, Michael	116	60	10	3	4	0	10	0	0	0 Deeded
Jacobe, Henry	200	100	20	2	3	0	4	0	0	0 Ditto
Weever, Christian	100	50	12	2	2	0	3	0	0	0
Lemmons, Jacob	0	0	15	3	2	0	1	0	0	0

Dildine, Henry	200	80	20	3	3	0	6	0	0	0	Deeded
Dildine, John	50	10	5	0	0	0	0	0	0	0	Do
Dildine, Andrew	0	0	0	2	1	0	0	0	0	0	17 years
Bowman, Christopher	250	60	23	2	5	0	10	1	0	0	
Scott, John	350	100	40	4	5	0	0	0	1	0	
Englert, Casper	0	0	0	0	1	0	0	0	0	0	
Turn, Casper	100	20	0	1	2	0	0	0	0	0	Weaver
Teeder, Elias	0	0	8	2	3	0	3	0	0	0	
Labare, George	100	12	8	2	2	0	6	0	0	0	
Young, George	50	7	4	1	2	0	2	0	0	0	
Long, Elias	0	0	8	2	3	0	2	0	0	0	
Long, John, Sen.	200	60	20	4	5	0	5	1	0	0	
Peck, Jacob	0	0	12	1	1	0	0	0	0	0	
Peck, George	200	30	0	1	2	0	2	0	0	0	
Snyder, Jacob	80	10	5	1	2	0	3	0	0	0	
Long, Joseph, Sen.	0	0	20	2	4	0	8	0	0	0	
Long, Joseph, Jun.	0	0	0	0	1	0	0	0	0	0	
Ramble, Jacob	63	20	15	2	3	0	7	0	0	0	
Foresman, Robert	300	40	20	3	6	1	10	2	2	0	Miller
Marr, John	0	0	0	0	0	0	0	0	0	0	
Williams, John	0	0	0	1	1	0	0	0	0	0	
Smith, John	127	30	10	2	2	0	3	0	0	0	
Whiteman, Henry	200	35	16	3	5	0	7	0	0	0	
Whiteman, Jacob	200	8	0	0	0	0	0	0	0	0	
Gaston, William	235	35	3	1	4	0	0	0	0	0	
Gaston, John	100	23	7	3	7	0	2	0	0	0	
Gaston, James	70	6	6	1	2	0	0	0	0	0	
Waggener, Mathies	300	20	6	1	10	0	7	0	0	0	
Gerris, Philip	150	30	15	3	2	0	3	0	0	0	
Durham, James	150	30	8	0	8	0	2	0	0	0	
Marr, Thomas	50	10	10	2	2	0	0	0	0	0	
Marr, William	50	20	5	2	2	0	3	0	0	0	
Marr, David	50	15	0	0	2	0	0	0	0	0	
Santee, Valentine	100	4	4	1	2	0	0	0	0	0	
Mordan, Ralph	100	10	5	2	3	0	0	0	0	0	
Potman, John	100	2	0	2	3	0	0	0	0	0	
Colvert, Joseph	100	4	3	3	3	0	0	0	0	0	Shoema'er
McNeal, Hector	100	2	0	0	2	0	0	0	0	0	
Beer, William	250	50	20	2	3	0	8	0	1	0	Deeded
Beer, Robert	150	0	0	0	0	0	0	0	0	0	
Otter, Darick	149	82	30	5	3	0	9	0	0	0	Deeded
Cample, Patrick	215	50	20	2	2	0	4	0	0	0	Deeded

Name									Notes
Mack, William	120	0	0	0	0	1	0	0	0	0	Deeded
						18 years old				
Goodwin, Benjamin	192	60	0	2	2	0	0	0	0	0
Mack, George	0	0	10	2	2	1	5	0	0	0
Mack, John	0	0	10	2	2	0	6	0	0	0
Hamilton, James	250	48	10	2	4	0	2	0	0	0
Eviret, Sarah	250	60	23	2	2	0	2	0	0	0
Everit, Zeanis	150	40	12	2	5	0	18	0	0	0
Britton, Zebulon	100	3	3	2	1	0	0	0	0	0
Everit, Asa	100	30	15	2	2	0	0	0	0	0
Covert, John	60	20	10	2	2	0	0	0	0	0
Chapman, James	0	2	1	1	1	0	0	0	0	0
Brown, John	200	10	6	0	2	0	0	0	0	0
McCracken, Thomas	85	42	7	2	3	0	0	0	0	0
Ross, Thomas	200	60	20	3	3	0	7	0	0	0
Patten, Samuel	0	30	10	2	2	0	0	0	0	0
Muckelhany, Widdow	450	60	20	2	0	0	0	0	0	0	Deeded
Beard, James	300	150	30	4	5	0	5	0	0	0	Do
Johnson, William	200	10	6	2	2	0	0	0	0	0
Muckelroy, Alexander	200	0	0	0	0	0	0	0	0	0
Scott John	100	0	0	0	0	0	0	0	0	0
Stackhouse, Thomas	50	10	0	1	2	6	0	0	0	0
Rumich, Casper	110	20	7	2	2	3	0	0	0	0
Bailey, William	100	30	5	2	2	4	0	0	0	0
Scott, James	150	30	10	3	9	13	0	0	0	0
Labare, William	150	25	10	2	4	5	0	0	0	0
Labare, Charles	140	20	15	3	3	3	0	0	0	0
Gaston, Joseph, Esq.	415	50	21	2	9	11	0	0	0	1
Scott, Henry	200	30	7	2	4	0	0	0	0	0
Stackhouse, Jos., Sen.	100	20	10	2	2	1	0	0	0	0	Hunter by Trade
Scott, Charles	0	0	0	0	3	0	0	0	0	0
Marr, Joseph	50	20	20	2	1	0	0	0	0	0
											ages 20,25,31
Stackhouse, Benjamin	100	40	10	2	4	0	0	0	0	3
Beraker, Jacob	200	15	6	2	1	2	0	0	0	0
McKoun, (?) John	79	20	10	1	2	2	0	0	0	0
Fox, Christopher	100	30	7	2	3	5	0	0	0	0	Deeded
Fox, Jacob	0	0	0	0	0	0	0	0	0	0
Plummer, William	197	40	18	2	6	0	0	0	1	0
Richert, Robert	150	25	10	2	4	0	0	0	0	0
Richert, James	0	0	0	1	1	0	0	0	0	0

Richert, William	80	50	15	2	3	0	0	0	0	0
Humes, Archibald	30	5	4	1	1	0	0	0	0	0
Shearer, James	150	30	15	1	2	0	0	0	0	0
Shearer, George	50	5	0	1	1	0	0	0	0	0
Barton, Elisha	0	0	0	1	3	1	1	0	0	0
Field, Andrew	118	56	20	2	1	0	0	0	0	0
Simenton, Robert	225	100	40	3	3	5	0	0	0	0	Deeded
Simenton, Robert	100	0	0	0	0	0	0	0	0	0	No deed
McCracken, Robt., Jun	60	10	5	1	1	3	0	0	0	0
McCracken, Samuel	0	0	0	2	0	0	0	0	0	0
Moore, John	180	40	12	3	3	5	0	0	0	0	20 years old
Smith, Henry	173	30	10	3	4	7	0	1	0	0
Templer, Philip	100	40	3	1	1	4	0	0	0	0
Connoly, John	50	70	2	0	2	0	0	0	0	0
Connoly, Thomas	100	30	8	1	2	0	0	0	0	0
Britton, Nathanael	100	40	10	3	2	0	0	0	0	0
Taylor, James	50	6	4	2	2	0	0	0	0	0
Dildine, Harmon	100	30	10	2	2	4	0	0	0	0
Herrin, John	240	20	3	1	4	4	0	0	0	0
Miller, Henry	130	40	10	4	5	6	1	0	0	0
Rea, William	0	0	0	1	0	0	0	0	0	0	Blacksmith
Ker, Lenard	100	30	0	0	0	0	1	0	0	0
Audid, Flory	100	4	3	2	1	0	0	0	0	0
Loycker, Alexander	130	16	14	1	3	1	0	0	0	0
Miller, Adam	100	5	3	1	2	0	0	0	0	0
John, Nelson	0	0	2	2	1	0	0	0	0	0

Names of Young Men.

John Van
Hugh Foresman
John Hindman
Matthies Waggener
Philip Caress
Thomas Stackhouse
John Alexander
Moses Morden
Joseph Stackhouse
John Humes
Anthony McClanen
Obediah Everit
David Ross
Joseph Orr
Henry Weaver
John Meddagh
James Simonton
John McFerrin, Jun.
John McFerrin, Sen.
James Thomson
Thomas Mason
James McCartney
Robert Marshele
Hugh Hill
John Rice
Jacob Kester
Niegel Campbell
Math. McCleanen
William Scott
John Sharp
Jacob Beeracker
Robert Bear
John Dildin
Daniel Smoak
Jacob Whitman

A FEW SCOTCH-IRISH FAMILIES OF OLD MOUNT BETHEL

By Asa K. McIlhaney, Bath, Penna.

NEAR the Lower Mt. Bethel Presbyterian church and along the public highway is the old graveyard which is surrounded by a well-built stone wall four feet high. Within the enclosure everything is fairly neat and in good order. We approach this isolated resting place of the dead. Near the entrance a beautiful weeping willow throws its shade on the graves of the writer's paternal grandparents and stands sentinel to many more of his name and blood. Their sacred dust has long since mingled with the common clay, but the chiseled tombstones remain to tell "their short and simple annals." Here can be read the names of Ayres, Baird, Beard, Bowman, Brittain, Connelly, Cyphers, Drake, Davison, Deats, Depue, Eakin, Edmiston, Foresman, Galloway, Gulick, Hutchison, Johnson, Ketchledge, Keifer, Lowrey, Lyle, Lockard, Loder, McCollum, McCracken, McCrea, McFall, McFarren, McIlhaney, McKibben, Miller, Morris, Martin, Moody, Middaugh, Norton, Patton, Rea, Ross, Rosenberry, Stocker, Scott, Simonton, Silliman, Taylor, Winters, and other North Irishmen. Most of these names are on record in the Colonial and Revolutionary Wars, where they were active in the struggle for American Independence.

Samuel Rea, whose tombstone gives the information that he died September 19, 1813, at the age of 81 years, was prominent in the Revolutionary struggle as an officer of militia in active service, County Lieutenant and Agent for Forfeited Estates. He was born in New Jersey in 1732, his parents having emigrated from Ireland, and they located in Lower Mt. Bethel in 1759, and were the owners of a great deal of the territory lying between Martin's Creek and the Three Churches. The ground on which the Presbyterian Church is located once belonged to Samuel Rea. He served for a time as Coroner of the county and Justice of the Peace.

Samuel Rea married Ann McCracken, daughter of Robert, and had eight children. Their daughter, Ann Rea, married Rev. George McElery Scott, son of John Scott and Jane Mitchell, who emigrated to the west. Their son, Rev. John Witherspoon Scott, D. D., married Mary Potts Neal, and their daughter, Caroline Scott, married Benjamin Harrison, twenty-third President of the United States.

Other descendants were Mrs. Rutherford B. Hayes and the Hon. Wm. G. Scott, who from 1823 to 1827 represented Northampton County in the House of Representatives, where he introduced the memorial and documents of the committee of trustees for the incorporation and aid of Lafayette College.

Mr. Wm. G. Scott was born in Lower Mt. Bethel, where his father and grandfather had resided many years before. He entered the army early in 1812, as an ensign in the Fifteenth United States Infantry.

In October, 1812, he was promoted to a Lieutenancy, in which capacity he served until the following year, when he resigned by reason of ill health. He took part in the Battle of Fort George and received the approbation of General Boyd in person on the field for his conduct.

In the same community with 'Squire Rea lived Henry Winter, the village blacksmith, who though a generation his junior, was associated with him in church and secular affairs, for they were both members of the Presbyterian Church and of the Democratic party.

About the close of the eighteenth century Henry Winter began to take an active interest in military affairs, and he attained to the colonelcy of a regiment of infantry. In politics he served in the Assembly from 1811 to 1814, and as State Senator from 1819 to 1825. He was a Presidential elector in 1828 and cast his electoral vote for Andrew Jackson. He was appointed a courier to deliver the report of the electoral vote of Pennsylvania in Washington and made the trip on horseback. In 1825, he presented to the Senate the petition for the incorporation of Lafayette College. He died in 1849, and his remains are buried near those of Col. Rea. For some years previous to his death he also served as a Justice of the Peace.

Col. Winter's parents were Peter Winter and Margaret Haynes, of New Jersey, who for a time resided in Northampton County, Pa., whence they removed to Luzerne County, where both are buried in the old Cooper burying ground near Wilkes-Barre. Col. Winter was over six feet in height, a man of commanding appearance, a fluent speaker, and frequently presided at the meetings of the local Democracy and military assemblages. He married Susan Bowman, daughter of Peter Bowman and ——— Barnes, his wife, of New Jersey, and had children. Of these: a daughter (Susan Winter), married Joseph Baird, who emigrated to the west in 1839; their son, John Baird, (born in Northampton County in 1822, and who died at Lincoln, Neb., May 3, 1905), married Lovina Dexter, daughter of Col. Darius Dexter, of Dexterville, N. Y.

The Dexter and Haynes families are of early New England origin. The only child of John and Lovina Dexter Baird is Mary Baird, the talented wife of Hon. William Jennings Bryan.

Peter Winter, his only son, was for many years the collector for the Delaware Bridge Company and then resided on North Front street, adjacent to the bridge, and latterly in Phillipsburg, N. J., where he died in 1858, leaving two daughters, Mrs. William Mott Patterson and Mrs. Sylvester A. Comstock, both now deceased. One of Mrs. Patterson's daughters was Mary Patterson Weaver, the wife of Ethan Allen Weaver, of Germantown, the well-known Northampton County historian, to whom the writer of these lines is indebted for much of the information given herein.

From the McFarren family has descended Col. Warren S. Dungan, ex-Lieut. Gov. of Iowa, and from the Bowman family Bishop Thomas Bowman, for many years the oldest Bishop of the M. E. Church, whose home was in Orange, N. J. His mother was a Brittain.

Other prominent descendants of Mount Bethel families

were the Rev. Prof. J. W. Scott, D. D., of Hanover College, Indiana, and the Reverends Samuel Galloway, Ephraim Simonton, Samuel Tyers, John Brittain, Theron Brittain, and Geo. C. Pollock, who graduated from Lafayette College in the class of 1861.

Dr. Zachariah Drake, born 1785, and died 1851, was the village poet, and some of his poetic productions are still in the hands of friends of the Drake family.

The McIlhaneys

The McIlhaney family is one of the oldest in Northampton County, being identified with its interests for over a century and a half. It is one of the few original Scotch-Irish families that have descendants still living in the county. Though it is not certain, the probability, however, is that the ancestor of the McIlhaneys came originally from Milford in the County of Ulster, in the northern part of Ireland. There has been some question as to the original spelling of the name, but a cursory examination shows that most of the members of the family spell it as above written.

The first of the family to settle in Northampton County was William McIlhaney, who came with the Ulster-Scot immigrants and settled, about 1730, in the Township of Lower Mount Bethel, known as Martin's Creek Settlement. We find by the records that in 1768 he possessed three hundred and seventy-three acres of land in two tracts, one of which, containing three hundred and forty-eight and one-half acres, was his homestead. He died intestate in 1773, leaving a wife, three daughters and a son, James McIlhaney, the heir-at-law. As the partition of the two tracts could not be made without prejudice, the court ordered a jury to make a just and true partition of the same, value and appraise the real estate. The property was appraised at £615 9s., whereupon James McIlhaney appeared in court and declared himself ready to accept the same, giving good securities. In the assessment list of taxables of Northampton County for 1780 he is assessed at £1,469, and the records show deeds for five hundred and three acres of land taken out by him between 1768 and 1805.

This big tract of land was situated in Lower Mount Bethel Township, just across the Delaware River from Belvidere, New Jersey. It included an island in the river just north of the Belvidere bridge, known up to 1840 as McIlhaney's Island.

James McIlhaney was a soldier in the war of the American Revolution. He served as a private under Capt. John Neilson of the 3rd Company and under Col. Jacob Stroud of the 6th Battalion of Militia in the County of Northampton, State of Pennsylvania. He had a son William who came into possession of a part of the original tract. The latter's son William was born in the old homestead, Sept. 9, 1799. Besides being engaged in agricultural pursuits, he followed the trade of tailor, and lived at what was known as the "Three Churches," near the Lower Mount Bethel Presbyterian Church. He served as Postmaster at Martin's Creek, under the administrations of Jackson, VanBuren, Harrison, and Polk, after which he was elected Clerk of the Orphans' Court of Northampton County. He married Catharine Shultz, of Holland Dutch extraction, who was born May 5, 1805, and died March 14, 1864. William McIlhaney died January 24, 1881, completing a service of forty years as ruling elder in the above named church. The children of William and Catharine (Shultz) McIlhaney were: 1—Thomas M., born May 13, 1823, died December 15, 1885; for many years he was a prominent citizen and attorney of Stroudsburg, Penna., serving for eighteen years as Prothonotary of Monroe County; at the time of his death he was president of the Stroudsburg National bank. 2—Peter, born December 12, 1824, was engaged in farming, and lived for many years in Lower Mount Bethel Township. 3—James, born August 22, 1826, died January 25, 1883; was engaged in teaching near Easton, Pennsylvania. 4—Hiram, born August 14, 1828, died May 19, 1886. 5—Mary, born December 8, 1830, married Henry Rasley, died December 17, 1880. 6—Jane, born January 5, 1833, died May 24, 1890. The two sisters lived during the greater part of their life on their father's homestead at the "Three Churches." 7—John M., of whom further. 8—William H., born in 1840, and died in 1918, at Cornwall, New York.

John M. McIlhaney, son of William and Catharine (Shultz) McIlhaney, was born April 25, 1836. In 1860 he became a resident of Bath, Pennsylvania, served as Justice of the Peace, Notary, and was Postmaster during Cleveland's second administration. He died May 30, 1911, in Bath. He married Mary Kinney, a native of Belvidere, New Jersey, January 10, 1863. To this union six children were born: Jesse D., died in infancy; Asa K., of further mention; Harry E., Ella M.. Anna C., and Frank T., who died young.

Asa K. McIlhaney, son of John M. and Mary (Kinney) McIlhaney, was born March 12, 1867, in Upper Nazareth Township, Northampton County, Pennsylvania, and for thirty years was a teacher. In religious affiliation he is a Presbyterian. He married at Bath, Penna., February 8, 1888, Maggie H., daughter of Samuel E. and Harriet (Stout) Cole, and they were the parents of three children: Samuel J., who died young; Ruth B., of further mention, who married Alexander Newton Gish, and Marion F.

Ruth B. (McIlhaney) Gish was born October 3rd, 1889, and died November 12th, 1918. Their children are Dorothy McIlhaney Gish, born October 16, 1916, and Alexander Newton Gish, Jr., born November 30, 1917.

Mr. Asa K. McIlhaney, of Bath, well known educator, historian, and nature lover, has the credit of compiling and publishing an autograph treasure: "Tributes to Nature," to which more than a hundred eminent men and women of America and Europe have contributed letters of prose and poetry pertaining to Arbor Day, Trees and Flowers. Among the contributors are the well-known names of Rudyard Kipling, Thomas A. Edison, Gene Stratton Porter, Woodrow Wilson, Benjamin Harrison, John Burroughs, W. D. Howells, Oliver Wendell Holmes, Henry Van Dyke, Harriet Beecher Stowe, and Frank Hill Phillips, &c. These have been collected and published under the title "Tributes to Nature," in 1922.

Mr. McIlhaney's proposition to have the mountain laurel accepted as the State Flower has received hearty endorsement throughout the State of Pennsylvania. As an ardent lover of nature, his choice of the mountain laurel has sentiment, history and patriotism to support it for such a purpose.

Beside his interest in nature, he is a historian of the first rank in matters pertaining to local history, especially the Scotch-Irish Settlement and Bath. He has proved his interest in the Northampton County Historical Society by supplying a number of valuable documents and papers for the Society's first publication "The Scotch-Irish of Northampton County."

While principal of the schools he instituted the historic Arbor Day, 1888, in Bath, Pa. By this means, a grove known as "Authors' Grove" has gradually been established, in which each tree is a living monument to the great men and women in literature. Thus the pupils not only learn to love trees, but also become interested in the lives and writings of distinguished authors. The authors honored by the planting of a tree in recognition of their worth, brought messages filled with beautiful sentiments and graceful diction.

The town of Bath, the history of which he has written so informingly, the Northampton County Historical and Genealogical Society, of which he is a charter member, and the Scotch-Irish of Northampton County, of whom he is a descendant, owe Mr. Asa K. McIlhaney a debt of gratitude for the contribution he has made to their better understanding.

Albert Drake McIlhaney, a teacher of commercial studies in the Easton High School for many years, was a son of the above named James and Mary Morris McIlhaney and was born at Martins Creek in 1851. In 1872 he moved with his parents to Easton and taught school in Williams Township but in the fall of 1873 began teaching in the schools of Easton. He married Sallie K. Transue of Easton.

In 1895 he was placed in charge of the commercial department (which he organized) and taught until June, 1914, when he was elected as assistant teacher in the Allentown Preparatory School, remaining there until June, 1918. He was an elder in the Brainerd Union Presbyterian Church, and a charter member of the Northampton County Historical and Genealogical Society. He died in Allentown, May 27, 1921.

Dr. Wm. H. McIlhaney was a son of the above named Hiram and Rachel Hummer McIlhaney and is also a native of Lower Mt. Bethel. In his youth he attended select school in New Jersey, where he prepared to teach. He rose rapidly in his profession and when a young man, was elected Principal of the South Easton High School.

After serving as principal for several terms, he began the study of medicine and graduated in due time from the Jefferson Medical College, Philadelphia, and practiced for many years in Easton, Penna. He married Sallie Merrill, daughter of Judge Merrill of Lower Mt. Bethel. He served for many years as elder in the Presbyterian Church, South Side, Easton. Died, March, 1921, age 66 years.

In connection with the history of the "Hunter Settlement" the following letters will be of interest:

William J. Bryan,
Lincoln, Nebraska.   Nov. 18th, 1897.

Mr. Asa K. McIlhaney,
    Bath, Pa.

My Dear Sir:—

I am in receipt of your favor of Nov. 12th. The clipping which you enclosed is correct. My father makes his home with me and when I told him of your letter, he said he remembered the family. When he was a little boy a Mr. McIlhaney kept the post-office about a quarter of a mile east of the Lower Mount Bethel Presbyterian Church. The church stood in the cemetery, but he thinks it has since been taken down. He remembers a young son whom he thinks was named James.

He also would be very glad to have the address of any of the family whom you may locate in your investigations.

His father and mother moved west in 1839 when he was fifteen and he has lost all trace of the family. If you have occasion to write again, he begs me to ask you if there are any of the John DePue family still in the county. Father is now seventy-four years old and was greatly pleased with this message from his boyhood home. With thanks for your interest and with best wishes, I am,

Very truly yours,

Mary B. Bryan.

William J. Bryan,
Lincoln, Nebraska.   Sept. 20th, 1898.

Mr. Asa K. McIlhaney,
    Bath, Pa.

My Dear Sir:—

Your favor of last January was duly received and we were very glad to hear from you. Father was greatly interested in the facts you wrote and told me who the people were whose graves your uncle had visited. He bids me tell you that the Bairds and Beards are really one family. When he came west in 1839, he had the misfortune to lose his father a few weeks after arriving. Father remembered that he wrote his name sometimes Beard. He did not think this was the correct spelling as he thought he remembered seeing Baird in his grandmother's Bible. And so certain was he that he was correct that he wrote the name Baird from that time on. Some fifteen years after his father's death, he visited his grandmother and to his astonishment found in the Bible the name was properly Beard. But as he was known by the name of Baird, had conveyed property in that name, etc., he decided it was best to hold to that name. The James Beard of whom you speak was my father's grandfather. David Baird was my father's great uncle, as was also Benjamin Baird, whom father remembers to have been an old bachelor.

The farm upon which my father lived was situated as

follows:—Leaving the McIlhaney post-office, follow the road leading to old Mr. Hoover's farm, to the farm rented by Benjamin Taylor on the Delaware River (father says your father will remember this farm as it was quite a large one). Just across the road from this farm, was the farm father's grandfather owned and upon a part of this, his father lived. It contained iron ore and your uncle may remember seeing the teams go past the office taking the ore to Matthew Henry's furnace.

George Snyder, he thinks, taught school in Miller's school house. Father remembers him very well. His mother and family lived west of Martin's Creek and he went to school with him for one year.

When father reached long division in his arithmetic, George took his seat beside him and explained the work to him thoroughly. If he is still living father wishes to send his regards to him and would be glad to hear from him. Let me ask, is his sister Mary living?

Father's mother's brother, one Peter Winter, son of Col. Henry Winters, married George Snyder's half-sister, Mary Davidson.

At any time that you have leisure, we shall be pleased to hear from you if you care to write. We are glad to know that the ancestors were loyal to their country. With best wishes,

Very truly yours,
MARY B. BRYAN.

THE VILLAGE POET

HOW old Doctor Drake of the Hunter Settlement is impressed by the coming of young Doctor Deichman, c. 1830.

"There is a thing come to our town,
    As big as a college Proctor;
His name's Tom Thumb of high renown.
    He calls himself a doctor.

Tom soon made cures with drops and pills
    Beyond all calculation.
Knocked all complaints head-over heels,
    Checked death's sad desolation.

Tom told the folks with learned address,
    Their lives he would insure all;
On his big words they laid such stress
    They called him doctor cure-all.

Acourting sometimes Tom would go,
    Neglected oft his duty.
He scoured the country high and low,
    In quest of wealth and beauty.

At last he suited his big self,
    Not long could Tommy tarry,
That he might quick secure herself
    He coaxed his dear to marry.

The damsel quick gave her consent.
    Tom in his arms close locked her.
To marry Tommy she was bent
    Because he was a doctor.

Her parents next Tom asked, 'tis said,
    They both did recommend it.
Her mother cried and was afraid
    Her daughter could not stand it.

The wedding day was quickly set—
    They bought her nuptial dresses,
And all the time they could get
    Was spent in sweet caresses.

Tom to the tailor quick did dash,
    Quite sick with love's sweet passion.
Says Tom—"I'll pay you ready cash
    To make my suit best fashion."

The *tailor went to work in haste
    With shears and needles speedy,
To make Tom's coat to suit his taste,
    That all things might be ready.

The workmanship few could surpass,
    Neat finished was each border,
Instead of cash this stupid ass
    Paid Muckle with an order.

Now Tom Thumb's fine blue wedding coat
    Cost many a hard dollar;
'Twas made in style and nice set out
    With fine black velvet collar.

The wedding day the guests sat close,
    Quite loaded was each carriage;
All hastened to the bride's white house
    To celebrate Tom's marriage.

Tom's got a wife we now suppose.
    They say she's quite a dandy;
With freckled face and crooked nose
    And hair a little sandy.

Now Tom's wife's dad loves land and cash,
    Her mother rum most dearly,
They care for naught but this world's trash,
    Obtained e'er so unfairly.

Tom's room is fixed up quite neat
  With curtains fine and fringy.
But when folks call, Tom will not treat,
  He is so cussed stingy.

Tom sometimes tends the bar
  And deals out gin and brandy;
Sees all his patients near and far,
  And shoots at mark on Sunday.

Tom Thumb's as large as life
  On tiptoe lightly treading,
Says Tom—"I'm glad I've got a frau,
  And had a merry wedding."

Tom Thumb is a boasting lad,
  He puffs his deeds with splendor;
In garb of innocence he's clad,
  And struts just like a gander.

* Wm. McIlhaney is reported to have been the tailor.

TEMPERANCE DEDICATION HYMN

By Z. Drake

Sung at the Dedication of Temperance Hall at Bath, Dec., 1848

"To temperance, so good and great,
This Hall, today we dedicate;
To check destruction's sweeping flood,
We interpose this moral good.

Let all who use strong drink beware,
It is a dang'rous fatal snare;
The sparkling poison in the bowl,
Destroys the body and the soul.

The drunkard's course oft leads to where
Lost spirits howl in dark despair;
In those foul dens, where vice is rife,
He often ends his wretched life.

Strong drink sinks thousands in despair,
All this, no temp'rance man need fear;
For temp'rance shuns such vice and wrath,
And helps to smooth life's rugged path.

When temp'rance is right understood
It is productive of much good;
It will contribute to our health,
Respectability and wealth.

Oh! may it ever be our aim,
Poor wretched drunkards to reclaim,
With heaven's aid, we may do this
And pave their way to endless bliss.

Since temp'rance lessens vice and crime,
Then onward speed its march through time,
Until its banner be unfurled
In ev'ry land throughout the world.

DAVID BRAINERD

From Dr. Clyde's "Reminiscences"

IT seems to be the prevailing impression that Mr. Brainerd pursued his labors among the Indians in a howling wilderness, where he never had the opportunity of beholding the face of a white man. To dispel such an impression, the attention need only be directed to the fact that he went to the Forks of the Delaware in 1744, sixteen years after the Irish Settlement had been started within fifteen miles of his location, and fourteen years after the starting of the Hunter's Settlement at a point still much nearer to him. This will account for the repeated references made by him to the white people, in his diary.

We give here from the "Memoirs of the Rèv. David Brainerd," New Haven edition, 1822, a number of references by him to his visits in the Settlement.

1744, Monday, July 23. "Rode to a settlement of Irish people, about fifteen miles southwestward; spent my time in prayer and meditation by the ways. Near night, preached from Matt. V. 3: 'Blessed are the poor in spirit, &c.' God was pleased to afford me some degree of freedom and fervency. Blessed be God for any measure of assistance."

Wednesday, July 25, he preached to Indians about seventeen miles westward of the Settlement, whither he had gone on Tuesday, "and then returned to the Irish Settlement and there preached to a numerous congregation. There was a considerable appearance of awakening in the congregation." (Page 158.)

Saturday, October 14. "Was much confused and perplexed in my thoughts; could not pray; and was almost discouraged, thinking, I should never be able to preach any more. Afterwards, God was pleased to give me some relief from these confusions; but still I was afraid, and even troubled before God. I went to the place of public worship, lifting up my heart to God for assistance and grace in my great work, and God was gracious to me, helping me to plead with Him for holiness, and to use the strongest arguments with Him drawn from the incarnation and sufferings of Christ for this very end, that men might be made holy. Afterwards, I was much assisted in preaching. I know not that ever God helped me to preach in a more close and distinguishing a manner for the trial of men's state. Through the infinite goodness of God, I felt what I spoke; He enabled me to treat on divine truth with uncommon clearness; and yet I was so sensible of my defects in preaching, that I could not be proud of my performance, as at some times; and blessed be the Lord for His mercy. In the evening I longed to be entirely alone, to bless God for help in a time of extremity; and longed for great degrees of holiness, that I might shew my gratitude to God". Page 165.

Saturday, December 29. On Saturday he rode to the Irish Settlement, about fifteen miles from his lodgings, in order to spend the Sabbath there". Page 187.

Lord's Day, December 30. "Discoursed both parts of the day, from Mark VIII. 34: 'Whosoever will come after me, &c.' God gave me very great freedom and clearness, and in the afternoon especially, considerable warmth and fervency. In the evening also, had very great clearness, while conversing on divine things. I do not remember ever to have had more clear apprehensions of religion in my life; but found a struggle in the evening with spiritual pride".

"On Monday he preached again in the same place with freedom and fervency". Page 187.

1745. Saturday, April 27. "The next day he went to the Irish Settlement, often before mentioned, about fifteen miles distant, where he spent the Sabbath, and preached with some considerable assistance". Page 197.

Wednesday, September 4. "Rode 15 miles to an Irish Settlement and preached there from Luke XIV. 22: 'And yet there is room'. God was pleased to afford me some tenderness and enlargement in the first prayer, and much freedom as well as warmth in the sermon. There were many tears in the assembly; the people of God seemed to melt; and others to be in some measure awakened. Blessed be the Lord, who lets me see His work going on in one place and another". Page 230.

Monday, September 9. "Left the Indians at the Forks of the Delaware, and set out on a journey toward the Susquehanna River; directing my course toward the Indian town more than a hundred and twenty miles westward from the Forks. Traveled about fifteen miles, and there lodged". Page 232.

Friday, September 26. "Was still much disordered in body, and able to ride but slowly (on return journey from Susquehanna). Continued my journey, however. Near night arrived at Irish Settlement, about fifteen miles from mine own house". Page 239.

1746. Tuesday, February 18. "Preached to an assembly of Irish people, nearly fifteen miles distant from the Indians". Page 279.

If the reader will go to the old town of Northampton, in Massachusetts, and take the street leading from the center of the town to the bridge crossing the Connecticut River, he will soon arrive at the resting place of the ashes of David Brainerd. Entering the old burying ground to the left of the street, and walking less than a hundred yards, beneath an arch of shade trees, to his right hand, near the carriage-way, surrounded by murmuring pines and beneath a solitary New England elm, he will find the following inscription:

"Sacred to the memory of the Rev. David Brainerd, a faithful and laborious missionary to the Stockbridge, Delaware and Susquehanna Tribes of Indians, who died in this town Oct. 10, 1747, Æ 32."

"The sunny slope of a green hill" is the spot where David Brainerd often preached to congregations of white settlers and Indians. This was a few yards from the present Presbyterian Church at Martin's Creek.

A marble tablet erected on another spot in the vicinity of

Martin's Creek on land of the late Abraham Shimer, bears this inscription:

> "A few rods north of this spot David Brainerd erected his missionary cabin, Dec. 6, 1744. Where much of his diary was written".

On the other side of the tablet is:

> "Erected by the Brainerd Missionary Society of Lafayette College, December 6, 1884."

The identification of the spot where Brainerd did his preaching is interesting. In his diary Brainerd wrote under date of February 17th, 1745, that he preached all day on the sunny slope of a green hill at the Forks of the Delaware. Many whites were present. Among them came on horseback from Bath Jane Wilson, a girl fifteen years old. When eighty years of age, in 1810, she described the spot where Brainerd stood to Rev. Mr. Moody, who was then preaching in this county. Shortly before his death, he showed the spot in question to Rev. Andrew Tully, who was for many years pastor at Harmony, N. J., and Mt. Bethel. Before Mr. Tully's death he showed the place to Professor Coffin, remarking as he drove the stake into the ground, "This is the exact spot".

MEMORIAL DISCOURSE
Delivered in
The First Presbyterian Church.
Lower Mt. Bethel, Pa.
October 1, 1876
By
Rev. Robert B. Foresman, a Former Pastor
Phillipsburg, N. J.
R. S. Brittain

Warren Democrat Print

PRESENT CHURCH ORGANIZATION

PASTOR
Rev. Alpheus H. Holloway

RULING ELDERS
Joseph Galloway, Wm. McIlhaney, Morris Rosenberry, Robert L. Ross, Joseph Ross

---

TRUSTEES
Wm. E. McIlhaney, President, Charles Keifer, John Rosenberry, Thomas Lockhart, Secretary, Hon. Elias Shull, Treas., Marshal B. Ross, Castner Carhart, Henry Rasley.

SUCCESSION OF PASTORS.

Rev. Daniel Lawrence	1747
Rev. Rosebrough	1769–1777
Rev. Joseph Treat	1800
Rev. David Barclay	1805–1811
Rev. Benjamin I. Lowe	1820–1823
Rev. John Grey, D. D.	1824–1831

Rev. Robert Love	1832–1835
Rev. John McCullough, S. S.	1836–1837
Rev. Azariah Prior	1838–1839
Rev. James Clark, S. S.	1839–1840
Rev. Andrew Tully	1840–1853
Rev. Robert B. Foresman	1854–1872
Rev. A. H. Holloway, installed June 18, 1873	

NOTE.—First preached in Lower Mt. Bethel Presbyterian Church in 1868. Revised and repeated by request on the first Sabbath of October, 1876. Some facts and data credited to "The History of the Allen Township Presbyterian Church" by John C. Clyde.

MEMORIAL SERMON

> "For thy servants take pleasure in her stones and favor the dust thereof." Psalm 102:14.

It is not at all strange that the people of God have always manifested a very deep interest in everything pertaining to Zion's prosperity. The church of God is dear to him "as the apple of his eye"; his love toward it is unbounded. For God so loved the world that he gave his only begotten son, that whosoever believeth in him, should not perish but have everlasting life. John 3:16.

The church is the purchase of the Redeemer's blood. "Take heed therefore unto yourselves, and to all the flock over the which the Holy Ghost hath made you overseers, to feed the church of God, which he hath purchased with his own blood." Acts 20:28.

It is the object of His peculiar love. "Husbands love your wives as Christ also loved the church and gave himself for it." Ephesians 5:25.

The love of the devout Jew for Zion is proverbial. How often does the pious Psalmist give expression to his ardent love for her, and he exhorts others: "Walk about Zion and go round about her; tell the towers thereof. Mark ye well her bulwarks, consider her palaces, that ye may tell it to the generation following." Psalm 48:12-13.

This was not a love simply for the external worship in which the pious Jews engaged; it was a love to the church, the sanctuary and its services because of their relation to God. The true Israelite loved the fellowship of his brother because they were interested in the same covenant; heirs to the same blessed inheritance, and partakers of the same spirit.

The church of God as the society of men; the building in which the people of God assembled for worship; the communion table around which they met to commemorate the death of their once crucified Lord; the hallowed spot where believers sleep in Jesus, all are full of interest to the child of God because of their relation to his Father and Saviour.

The sweet singer of Israel sang of Zion's excellency and beauty, and the saints of all the ages have echoed his song. "Beautiful for situation, the joy of the whole earth is Mount Zion on the sides of the north, the city of the great King." Psalm 48:2.

Can it be otherwise? Can the child of God be indifferent to the interests of his Father's kingdom? He cannot, but with Israel's prophet and bard he again exclaims: "If I forget thee, O Jerusalem, let my right hand forget her cunning; if I do not remember thee let my tongue cleave to the roof of my mouth; if I prefer not Jerusalem above my chief joy." Psalm 137:5-6.

Under the Jewish dispensation, the central point of interest was Jerusalem, where for a time, the tabernacle was pitched, and where, afterward, the temple was built.

It was there that God had recorded His name, and where especially, He manifested Himself unto His people, and hence Jews from all parts of the world flocked to this city, there to present their offerings.

At stated times in the year, the roads leading to Jerusalem were thronged with devout Jews, and the city crowded with strangers.

The time has long since passed, however, when the prophetic words of Jesus to the woman of Samaria were fulfilled that "the hour cometh when ye shall neither in this mountain, nor yet in Jerusalem, worship the Father." John 4:21.

While it is true, however, that the ceremonies peculiar to the Jewish system of worship have ceased to be observed under the dispensation of the Spirit, it is nevertheless true that the Christian worshipper does "take pleasure in the stones of Zion, and favor the dust thereof".

Hallowed associations cluster around these sacred spots, where our fathers in past generations have worshipped, and where their precious dust now reposes.

I need scarcely say that, as we now recount the dealings of God's providence with this particular church, it is to you, my Christian brethren, an occasion of the most tender and solemn interest.

Early in the eighteenth century a little band of devout worshippers sat together for the first time in a small building of rude structure, standing in yonder graveyard, and there reverently worshipped the God of Israel.

Soon after a settlement was made in Mt. Bethel, as it is well known, the sainted Brainerd broke the bread of life to the untutored Indian, not far from the spot where we now worship. These hills and ravines witnessed his agonies of soul as he wrestled with the angel of the covenant in behalf of the poor Indian, and have echoed the sound of the invitation of the gospel as they fell with so much unction from his lips. It was a source of much pleasure to some of the older members of this church to say that they had heard David Brainerd preach.

The precise time when the church of Mt. Bethel (or as it was originally called, Forks North), was organized, or when the first building was erected, has not been ascertained. The early Sessional records of this church have been lost, if such records were kept. In consequence of this its early history cannot be very satisfactorily gathered.

Many facts pertaining to its early history were obtained several years ago from the late Rev. Richard Webster, of Mauch Chunk, Pa., who had both taste and talent for gathering up incidents connected with the early history of the Presbyterian Church in the United States, and I am indebted to him for many facts embodied in this discourse.

The tract of land which lies between the Delaware and the Lehigh Rivers and the Blue Mountains was named "The Forks of the Delaware".

After the Indian walk, by which William Penn's purchase from the Indians was measured, a large portion of this tract was sold to Wm. Allen, of Philadelphia, his purchase including the ground afterward occupied by this congregation as a burying ground and church lot.

About the year 1734, a settlement was made within the

bounds of what is now Lower Mt. Bethel, which has long been known as Hunter's Settlement. A settlement made on the Lehigh about the same time was called Craig's Settlement. The people of these two settlements were mostly from the North of Ireland, and there was for many years a most pleasant intimacy between them.

Among the names of the early settlers in Mt. Bethel are found those of Miller, Moore, Lockard, Lyle, Moody, Martin, Nielson (Nelson), Buckman, Hutchison, Ross, McFarren, McIlhaney, Sullivan, Galloway, Foresman, McCollum, Dunn, McCracken, Beard, Brittain, Scott, Hanna, Winters, Barton, McEwen, Gulick, Nye, Gaston, Kennedy, Rhea, Gordon, Taylor, Martin, Syllaman, Campbell, Patterson, Robinson, Craig, McElroy, Oliphant, Lemmon, Stackhouse, Anderson, McNeil, Bruce, Galbraith, Richie, Crawford, McGarrick, Tripp, Peck, Goodwin, Eggleton, Stinson, Mathewson, Tompson, Carr, Ayres, Barnhill, Ketchledge, Sherlock, Beatty, McComb, Burns, McCall, McFall, McKibben, Edmiston, McCrea, Patton, Rosenberry.

In September, 1738, the Forks of the Delaware asked New Brunswick Presbytery for supplies, and the Rev. Gilbert Tennent was directed to go there in the fall. On hearing Gilbert Tennent preach on a certain occasion, Whitfield said: "Never before heard I such a searching sermon. He went to the bottom indeed, and did not daub with untempered mortar. He convinced me more and more that we can preach the gospel no further than we have experienced the power of it in our own hearts. I found what a babe and a novice I was in the things of God. He is a son of thunder, whose preaching must either convert or enrage the hypocrites".

And again he says of him: "Indeed he is a good soldier of Jesus, and God is pleased in a wonderful manner to own him and his brethren. The congregations where he has preached have been surprisingly convicted and melted down."

This is Whitfield's estimate of the man who was among the first to plant the standard of the cross in Mt. Bethel.

Mr. Tennent was directed to preach in both Hunter's and Craig's Settlements.

It is probable that this church was organized about this time (1738) and the church is about 138 years old, i. e., in 1876.

In May, 1740, the Rev. James Campbell, of Tehichen (Tinicum), was sent to the Forks by the New Brunswick Presbytery, and also about the same time the Rev. William Robinson, who was distinguished as an eminent and successful evangelist in his day.

In May, 1742, Mr. Campbell was directed to give one-fourth of his time to the Forks, and in the fall one-half.

It cannot be ascertained definitely as to the time given, by the supplies, respectively, to the Forks North and Forks West, as the term Forks is used without any designation, quite frequently, in the record of the appointment of supplies by Presbytery.

The Rev. John C. Clyde in his History of the Allen Township Presbyterian Church, says: "On May 29, 1742, we find the people petitioning again for preaching. This time they petitioned in conjunction with Greenwich. We are unable to decide from the records whether this petition from the Forks was from the Mt. Bethel people, to the exclusion of the Settlement, or from the Settlement, to the exclusion of Mt. Bethel, or from both conjointly."

It is more probable that the request for preaching at this time was from the churches Forks West and Forks North conjointly, as they seem as yet to have been supplied for the most part by the same ministers, being both within the territory designated "The Forks".

The Mt. Bethel Church was served by supplies of Presbytery, probably every second or third Sabbath, until the spring of 1746.

The Rev. David Brainerd began his missionary labors among the Indians of the Forks of the Delaware early in the summer of 1744. In his journey from Massachusetts to the designated missionary field, he traveled by way of Fishkill and Goshen, in New York, passing through the settlement of Irish and Low Dutch people, called the Minnisinks. This settlement was on the Delaware River, about twelve miles above the Forks.

"On the 13th of May, 1744, he came to Lakhauwootung (Lehigh) within the Forks, and was respectfully received by the king, and preached most of the summer at his house. This was near the Settlement of Hunter, at Mt. Bethel, and Craig, in Allen Township." (Webster's History of the Presbyterian Church in America, page 517.)

In October, 1744, Brainerd, accompanied by Eliab Byram, minister at Mendham, New Jersey, visited an Indian settlement on the Susquehanna River, near Berwick, and preached to them four days, the Indians listening attentively. Webster says: "On the way back, both he and Byram preached at the Irish Settlement, where was a numerous congregation, and then returned to his dwelling. His abode was at Lower Mt. Bethel, where his house still remained at the beginning of the present century."

In Brainerd's diary, for the Lord's Day, February 17, 1745, the following record is found: "Preached in the wilderness on the sunny side of a hill, to a considerable number of white people, many of whom came near twenty miles, from Kreidersville to Martin's Creek. Discoursed to them all day from John 7:37: 'In the last day, that great day of the feast, Jesus stood and cried, saying, if any man thirst, let him come to me and drink.' I think I was never enabled to offer the free grace of God to sinners with more freedom and plainness. Afterward I was enabled earnestly to invite the children of God to come renewedly to this fountain of water of life, from which they had heretofore derived unspeakable satisfaction. There were many tears in the assembly, and I doubt not but that the Spirit of God was there convincing poor sinners of their need of Christ."

Brainerd labored at the Forks of the Delaware about a year, having accomplished in this comparatively short time, a great work, both among the Indians and the white people.

He was truly "a burning and a shining light," and the happy influence of his eminently devoted life and faithful teachings, contributed much to the edifying and strengthening of the little band then composing the Mt. Bethel Church.

From 1742-1746, as has been remarked, the church was supplied by members of the Presbytery, conjointly with the church at the Irish Settlement. Among the persons supplying these churches during this time, were Rev. William Dean, who afterward became pastor of the Forks of the Brandywine, and who died there July 9, 1748, and the Rev. Charles C. Beatty, the grandfather of the Rev. Charles C. Beatty, D. D., of Steubenville, Ohio. Mr. Beatty was afterwards called to the Forks of the Neshaminy. At the request of the Forks of the Delaware, the Rev. Daniel Lawrence was sent May 26, 1746, to supply them for a year, with a view to settlement.

At a meeting of Presbytery, in October, 1746, a call was presented to Mr. Lawrence by the Forks of the Delaware, which he accepted. Presbytery appointed a committee, consisting of Rev. Richard Treat, Rev. James Campbell, Rev. James Davenport, and Rev. Charles Beatty, to ordain and install Mr. Lawrence. April 2, 1747, was fixed as the time for these services.

The committee performed the duty assigned, as appears from the following minute:

Forks of the Delaware, April 2, 1747.

"The committee appointed by Presbytery to attend to the ordination of Mr. Lawrence, viz: Mr. Treat, Mr. Davenport, Mr. McCrea, and Mr. Campbell, (Mr. Beatty for good reasons not attending), did, according to appointment, meet at the place, and having yesterday heard him preach a sermon on John 3:18, and received his exegesis, (upon the question assigned), both to good satisfaction, and there appearing no objection in the way, they proceeded this day, according to appointment, with fasting and prayer, and imposition of hands to ordain Mr. Lawrence to the Gospel ministry ovei this people. Concluded with prayer and the blessing. Then and there it was agreed by the representatives of the two

Settlements that they have and desire to be united and so long as Mr. Lawrence shall continue to be minister to them both, that he shall preach two-thirds of his time to the Western Settlement, and the other one-third to the Northern, without any alteration except by judgment of Presbytery."

I quote again from Webster's History: "The Forks North and the Forks West have been favored with a portion of Brainerd's labors, and were by no means an unpromising field, having many excellent, pious families, but it was a laborious field; a wide, dreary, uninhabited tract of fifteen miles lying between the two meeting houses. Lawrence was not a robust man, and was directed to spend the winter and spring of 1751 at Cape May, New Jersey, then in very necessitous circumstances."

In his absence, these churches were supplied by the Rev. Benjamin Chestnut, of Woodbury, New Jersey. Mr. Lawrence soon after settled at Cape May.

Forks had now for supplies, successively, the Rev. Benjamin Hait, afterward settled at Connecticut Farms, New Jersey, and Rev. William Kirkpatrick, of Amwell, New Jersey.

"In 1751, those members of the Presbytery of New Brunswick, who resided in Philadelphia, and in New Jersey, to the southward of that city, were formed into a new Presbytery, and called the Presbytery of Abington." (Hodge's History of the Presbyterian Church, Volume II. page 310.)

Forks North and Forks West came under the care of this Presbytery about this time. Full liberty was given to these churches to apply for supplies to any Presbytery belonging to the Synod.

From May, 1752, until August, 1761, the church was served by supplies appointed by the Presbytery, among whom were Revs. Charles Beatty, Richard Treat, Benjamin Chestnut, and Andrew Hunter.

In May, 1758, the Synods of Philadelphia and New York called, respectively, the Old and New Sides, united. Upon this union, a re-arrangement of the Presbyteries, to some extent, became necessary. The Presbytery of Abington was now merged in the Presbytery of Philadelphia, and Forks North (Mt. Bethel) came under the care of Philadelphia Presbytery.

At the meeting of the Presbytery of Philadelphia, held in Philadelphia, August, 1761, the Rev. John Clark was received from the Presbytery of New Brunswick, and a call was put into his hands from the Forks of the Delaware which he asked and obtained leave to take into consideration until the next meeting of the Presbytery, being directed by Presbytery, in the meantime, to supply "at the Forks of the Delaware" in the following manner, viz: two Sabbaths at Allentown (Allen's Town), one at Hunter's Settlement, interchangeably, except two Sabbaths at Tehicken. The reason of Mr. Clark's asking to hold the call for consideration seems to have been that opposition was made to his settlement.

At the ensuing meeting of Presbytery, held in November, 1761, his friends, by permission of Presbytery, agreed to settle him without the aid of those opposing him, offering him a salary of eighty pounds sterling and a parsonage. The parsonage was on the West Branch, or what is now called the Allen Township congregation.

Mr. Clark signified to Presbytery his acceptance of this call, but in consequence of the existing difficulties in the congregation, he was not installed until October, 1762. The Rev. Richard Treat presided and preached on the occasion. Revs. Henry Martin, James Latta and Charles Beatty are named as appointed to take part in the installation services.

In October, 1766, the Mt. Bethel people laid a complaint before the Presbytery against their pastor, Mr. Clark, and were advised by Presbytery to drop it. Mr. Clark now asked leave of Presbytery to resign his charge of the Mt. Bethel Church, but Presbytery refused to grant his request. In the spring of 1767, Mt. Bethel asked to have Mr. Clark put on trial, but Presbytery refused, and sent the Rev. Mr. Ramsey, of Fairfield, New Jersey, as a healing committee. The committee did not succeed in healing the difficulties, the disaffected party persevering in their opposition to Mr. Clark. Commissioners from the congregation, reported to Presbytery in May, 1767, that there was no hope of a reconciliation.

Upon hearing this report, the committee of Presbytery was enlarged by the appointment of the following additional members, viz: The Revs. Richard Treat, Enoch Green, Benjamin Chestnut, John Hanna, William Kirkpatrick, and John Rosbrough were invited to meet with them at Mt. Bethel on the third Tuesday of June, to endeavor to adjust the existing difficulties.

The committee failed in their efforts to settle the difficulties, and Mr. Clark, in view of the opposition manifested toward him and on account of failing health, asked to be released from his charge in November, 1767. Presbytery granted his request, and Mr. Clark afterward settled in Hartford County, Maryland.

The church now being vacant, was supplied for a time by supplies appointed by Presbytery. The Allen Township and the Mt. Bethel congregations were transferred by the Synod of Philadelphia, from the First Presbytery of Philadelphia to the Presbytery of New Brunswick, in May, 1770. A short time before this, early in the summer of 1769, the church of Mt. Bethel began to be served for a portion of his time by the Rev. John Rosbrough. What proportion of his time was given to Mt. Bethel, or how long these services were continued has not been ascertained. His residence was within the bounds of the Allen Township congregation, to which he gave a portion of his time, and where he remained until shortly after the commencement of the revolutionary struggle, and served for a time as Chaplain. A few days after the battle of Trenton he was brutally murdered by a body of Hessians, near Pennington, New Jersey.

About this time, perhaps in the fall of 1773, Mt. Bethel and Oxford Churches united in calling the Rev. William Schenck. He did not accept the call. In February, 1774, these churches united in calling the Rev. John Debow. Mr. Debow accepted this call and was installed May 19, 1775, but going to North Carolina soon after, he received and accepted a call and settled there in 1776.

For a time again Mt. Bethel was dependent upon Presbytery for occasional supplies. On the second Tuesday of August, 1783, the Rev. Francis Peppard was installed pastor of the Mt. Bethel Church for a part of his time, having preached, as it would appear, for the congregation for some time previous to his installation. Precisely how long Mr. Peppard continued to serve the Mt. Bethel Church does not appear. His pastorate, however, was a short one comparatively, the Rev. Asa Dunham being installed pastor of the Mt. Bethel and Oxford churches in 1787. Mr. Dunham was released from the pastoral charge of these churches September 18, 1797.

At the meeting of the Presbytery of New Brunswick, held at Trenton, New Jersey, September 19, 1799, calls from Oxford and Lower Mt. Bethel churches were presented to the Rev. David Comfort, who was for many years pastor of the church at Kingston, New Jersey. Mr. Comfort did not accept these calls, and Lower Mt. Bethel was again supplied by Presbytery.

The Rev. David Barclay was called to Lower Mt. Bethel, Knowlton, and Oxford Churches, and was installed pastor of the Mt. Bethel Church, July 19, 1805. It is probable that Mr. Barclay preached at Lower Mt. Bethel for some time before he was installed pastor.

With the history of Mr. Barclay some of the older members of this church are familiar. The Rev. Dr. Junkin, in his discourse delivered on the semi-centennial anniversary of the organization of Newton Presbytery, says "Mr. Barclay was a man of decided ability, quick, earnest and energetic in his motions and his speech, but of impetuous and imprudent temperament." A Mr. Jacob Kerr, an elder of the Knowlton Church, published a volume of more than four hundred pages, entitled "The several trials of David Barclay before the Presbytery of New Brunswick, and the Synod of New York and New Jersey."

While this old book exhibits the patience, care and wisdom of the church courts in conducting these trials, the facts put upon record in its pages are lamentably illustrative of the doctrine of total depravity, and had better never been printed. Mr. Barclay was evidently not a wise man, nor were his prosecutors. No serious criminality was proved against him, but such indiscretion was shown as induced Presbytery to restrict him from preaching in Knowlton, Lower Mt. Bethel and Oxford, January 11, 1814.

The sympathy of the majority of the people of Lower Mt. Bethel congregation seems to have been with Mr. Barclay, as among the files of New Brunswick Presbytery have been found three petitions from the congregation to that body, in one of which they pray Presbytery not to remove Mr. Barclay, and in the other two, to appoint him their supply for one-half his time.

It may be interesting to many to hear one of these petitions:

"To the Reverend Presbytery of New Brunswick:

The Presbyterian congregation of Lower Mt. Bethel being informed that Rev. David Barclay has desired leave to resign his pastoral charge, the Session has consulted the members of this church and do find that they are all unanimous and wishes that he may not be removed. We hope it will not be taken amiss if we inform the Presbytery, that since he became our pastor, his conduct among us has been such as becometh a minister of the Gospel of Christ, and that his labors in many instances appear to have been crowned with success, and peace and harmony appears to prevail in this church.

We therefore humbly request that Revd. Body to take our case under consideration, and if consistent, to continue his labors among us. And your petitioners as in duty bound will ever pray.

Done at Lower Mt. Bethel, May 18, 1812.
                        Robert Galloway
                        Jeptha Arrison
                        Nathaniel Brittain
                        John Hutchinson
                        Samuel Gulick
                        David Ayers
                                      Elders."

At a meeting of the Presbytery of New Brunswick held in New York City, October 20th, 1812, Mr. Jacob R. Castner, then a licentiate, and afterward and for many years the faithful and beloved pastor of the First Mansfield Church, was appointed supply for Lower Mt. Bethel Church for the third Sabbath of October, and at discretion.

At a meeting of Presbytery, in Trenton, New Jersey, April 27, 1813, John Hutchinson being present as Elder from Lower Mt. Bethel, a call from this church is put into the hands of Rev. David Barclay, which he asks permission to hold for consideration.

At the meeting of Presbytery held at Hackettstown, New Jersey, January 11, 1814, Mr. Barclay was forbidden to preach at Oxford, Knowlton and Lower Mt. Bethel.

At a meeting of Presbytery held soon after at Baskingridge, New Jersey, application was made by Knowlton and Lower Mt. Bethel for Mr. Barclay as stated supply. This request was not granted. At this meeting of Presbytery, Mr. Barclay asked to have the restriction from preaching in Lower Mt. Bethel, Knowlton, and Oxford removed. His request was denied. He appealed to Synod, and the case seems to have been referred back to the Presbytery by the Synod as a special meeting of the Presbytery was held at Princeton, November 22, 1814, to consider Mr. Barclay's case.

At this meeting of the Presbytery the restriction from preaching in Lower Mt. Bethel was removed. Mr. Barclay was admonished by Presbytery, and the Rev. Joseph Campbell was appointed to visit Lower Mt. Bethel Church and make known the action of Presbytery in Mr. Barclay's case.

At a meeting of Presbytery held in Trenton, New Jersey, April 25, 1815, supplies were appointed for Lower Mt. Bethel for six months.

At a meeting of Presbytery, held in New Brunswick, N. J., October 3, 1815, a call was laid before Presbytery from Lower Mt. Bethel for Rev. Mr. Barclay. This call was not put into Mr. Barclay's hands and supplies for Lower Mt. Bethel were appointed until the next stated meeting of the Presbytery.

At the meeting of Presbytery held at Lawrenceville, New Jersey, April 23, 1816, Elder Samuel Gulick from Lower Mt. Bethel Church, laid papers before Presbytery relating to Mr. Barclay's case, which were referred to a committee, and this committee in their report recommended among other things, that the Rev. Dr. Archibald Alexander write a letter to the church of Lower Mt. Bethel in behalf of the Presbytery, and supplies were appointed for Lower Mt. Bethel until the next stated meeting of the Presbytery. The congregation presevered in their efforts to secure the pastoral services of Mr. Barclay, as we learn from the records, that at a meeting of Presbytery at Cranberry, New Jersey, in October, 1816, a call was again laid before Presbytery for one-half of Mr. Barclay's time. This call was accompanied by a remonstrance, and the call was not put into Mr. Barclay's hands.

At a subsequent meeting of Presbytery, a petition from the Lower Mt. Bethel church was presented asking that Mr. Barclay be appointed their stated supply. He was not appointed.

On the third Tuesday of November, 1817, the Presbytery of Newton was organized, having under its care at its formation the following churches, viz:

Alexandria, Amwell First, Amwell Second, Baskingridge, Bethlehem, Flemington, Fox Hill, German Valley, Greenwich, Hackettstown, Harmony, Hardwick, Kingwood, Knowlton, Lamington, Mansfield, Marksboro, Newton, Oxford, and Pleasant Grove, in New Jersey; and Easton, Lower Mt. Bethel, Upper Mt. Bethel and Smithfield in Pennsylvania.

In all twenty-four churches.

In the records of the Presbytery of Newton for April, 1818, mention is made of supplies having been appointed for Lower Mt. Bethel. In October, 1818, Mr. Barclay was appointed stated supply for Lower Mt. Bethel Church for the third Sabbath of July and at discretion until the next stated meeting of Presbytery.

June 15, 1819, Mr. Benjamin I. Lowe, a licentiate, was appointed to supply the Lower Mt. Bethel Church on the third Sabbath of July, and at discretion until the next meeting of Presbytery; and October 5th, 1819, he was appointed stated supply of the church for two-thirds of his time for two years. He was ordained as an Evangelist at the meeting of Presbytery held at Lower Mt. Bethel, December 8, 1819, and was installed pastor of the Upper and Lower Mt. Bethel Churches, November 6, 1821, and continued to serve these churches acceptably and faithfully until October, 1823, when the pastoral relation to them was dissolved, with a view of his taking charge of the churches of Hardwick, Marksboro, and Stillwater in New Jersey. Mr. Lowe's labors in this church continued only about four years, but in this comparatively short time he accomplished a good work. A goodly number were added to the church. He seems to have been very successful as a Bible class teacher, according to the testimony of the older members of this church.

Previous to Mr. Lowe's time, Sessional records were kept in a very careless manner, if kept at all. He procured a book, and carefully kept a record of all Sessional meetings, made out a roll of the members of the church, and recorded the marriages and baptisms that he solemnized. The records of the church have been carefully kept and preserved since Mr. Lowe's time to the present.

In October, 1823, the Rev. John Gray, for many years pastor of the First Presbyterian Church of Easton, Pa., was appointed stated supply of the Lower Mt. Bethel Church for one service for every other Sabbath during the succeeding year. Mr. Gray continued to serve the church according to this arrangement probably until October, 1828, when he was installed pastor of the church of Easton.

The church seems now to have been supplied for a time by members of Presbytery.

In October, 1830, Mr. James C. Watson, then a licentiate of the Presbytery of Philadelphia, was appointed supply for the churches of Lower Mt. Bethel and Harmony for six months. The Rev. James C. Watson is now and has been for several years, pastor of the Presbyterian Church of Milton, Pa.

The Rev. Robert Love served the churches of Lower Mt. Bethel and Harmony as stated supply from October, 1831, to April, 1835. Mr. Love was installed pastor of Harmony Presbyterian Church in 1836 and continued in this relation until his death, in 1838. Although stricken down, when just having fully entered upon his chosen work, he yet accomplished much for the honor of our blessed Master, and is remembered still by many in both the Harmony and the Lower Mt. Bethel congregations, as a truly devoted and faithful servant of God.

Mr. McCullough was stated supply of Upper and Lower Mt. Bethel Churches from October, 1835, to April, 1838. He resided in Texas for many years and as I have been informed, has been without charge.

The Rev. James Clark served the churches of Upper and Lower Mt. Bethel as pastor from November, 1839, to April, 1840.

The Rev. Andrew Tully was pastor of Upper and Lower Mt. Bethel churches from November, 1840, to October, 1845, and of Lower Mt. Bethel alone from October, 1845, to October, 1853, when he accepted a call from the Presbyterian Church of Harmony, N. J.

Mr. Tully's labors were greatly blessed in this congregation. Large numbers were added to the church during his pastorate, and a more liberal spirit was developed among the people, both as regards contributions for the support of their pastor, and in aid of the benevolent operations of the church, and a commendable interest was manifested in family religion and in maintaining Sabbath School, Bible Class and prayer meeting services. Previous to Mr. Tully's pastorate the church had always been associated with some other church or churches in the support of a pastor or stated supply.

Mr. Tully, as has already been stated, was pastor of the united churches of Upper and Lower Mt. Bethel, from 1840 to 1845. In October, 1845, he resigned his pastorate of the Upper Mt. Bethel Church, and became pastor of the Lower Mt. Bethel Church for the whole of his time. The congregation now more promptly and cheerfully, with the aid of a small appropriation, for a short time, from the Board of Domestic Missions, supported their pastor for the whole of his time, than when contributing for his support for one-half of his time.

From October, 1853, to April, 1854, the church was supplied by members of the Presbytery appointed, and by other ministers invited by the Session.

The Rev. Robert B. Foresman, a licentiate of the Presbytery of Luzerne, was now called to the pastorate of the church. He began his labors in the church on the first Sabbath of April, 1854, and was ordained and installed at a meeting of Presbytery held in the church May 30, 1854. In the ordination and installation services, the Rev. John A. Reily presided and offered the ordaining prayer; the Rev. Solomon McNair preached the sermon; the Rev. George C. Bush gave the charge to the pastor, and the Rev. Andrew Tully charged the people. My pastoral relations to this church continued until the last Sabbath of December, 1872, when I left to take the pastoral charge of the Yellow Frame Presbyterian Church in Warren County, New Jersey.

Soon after the dissolution of Mr. Tully's pastoral relation to the church, the congregation purchased from him a property for a parsonage, situated on the public road about a mile and a half north of the church, paying in part for this property at the time of purchase and paying the balance in a few years. The house has been enlarged and improved and is now among the most commodious and comfortable par--sonage buildings in our country congregations. Its site is one of the most charming ones, healthful, sightly, in a peaceful and pleasant neighborhood, having almost all the advantages without the ordinary nuisances of country villages; on the thoroughfare passing through the country from Portland to Easton, and the stage between these points passing and re passing daily. My pastorate of this church covered a period of eighteen years and seven months, which is the longest pastorate in the history of this church, and while much less was done for the honor of the Master during this time than ought to have been accomplished, there is abundant reason for thankfulness, that the labor expended was not altogether unfruitful.

Very many changes took place during this pastorate; a number of the aged and not a few of the younger members of the congregation, have finished their work and ended their pilgrimage, among whom were four venerable and beloved members of the Session, viz: John Connelly, John Rosenberry, Morris Morris, and Merari Gulick.

After the union of the two General Assemblies of the Presbyterian Church, the United Assembly at its meeting in Philadelphia, in May, 1870, rearranged the boundaries of the Synods. In this rearrangement, the church of Lower Mt. Bethel, together with the other churches belonging to the Presbytery of Newton and lying in Pennsylvania, were included in the Synod of Philadelphia.

The Synod of Philadelphia, at its meeting held in Philadelphia in June, 1870, in dividing its territory into Presbyteries, formed the Presbytery of Lehigh to be composed of the ministers and churches in Northampton and some other counties of Pennsylvania. The Lower Mt. Bethel Church by this arrangement came under the care of the Lehigh Presbytery.

At the earnest solicitation of a number of persons residing in and near the village of Bangor, some of whom were members of the Lower Mt. Bethel Church, the pastor of this church began to hold, at first monthly, and in a short time after semi-monthly, Sabbath afternoon preaching services in the Mennonite Church of Bangor, in the winter of 1869 and 1870. The encouragement was such that at the stated meeting of the Presbytery of Newton, in April, 1870, request was made for the organization of a Presbyterian Church at Bangor.

A committee was appointed by Presbytery, authorized to organize a church, as petitioned for, if the way should be clear. This committee met in the Mennonite Church at Bangor, June 14th, 1870, and organized a church, named the First Presbyterian Church of Bangor, consisting of nineteen members, four of whom were members of the Lower Mt. Bethel Church.

The pastor of the Lower Mt. Bethel Church continued to supply the Bangor Church by appointment of Presbytery, at discretion, until the termination of his pastorate, in December, 1872.

The Rev. James M. Salmon was installed pastor of the Bangor Church for the whole of his time in the summer of 1873. The present membership of the church is thirty-eight, and its prospects for growth are very encouraging. I feel a peculiar gratification in the encouraging growth of this young church, having been an humble instrument in beginning and for a time fostering the enterprise.

The present pastor of the Lower Mt. Bethel Church, the Rev. Alpheus H. Holloway, occupied the pulpit for the first time on March 16, 1873; administered the Sacrament of the Lord's Supper, March 30; took charge of the church on the first Sabbath of April, and was installed June 18, 1873. In the installation services the following persons took part: the Rev. Frank E. Miller preached the sermon; the Rev. J. Thomson Ostler delivered the charge to the people, and Rev. James W. Wood charged the pastor. It has been stated that the precise time when the first church edifice was erected has not been ascertained.

"The Meeting House" in the Forks North is first mentioned in the minutes of Presbytery in 1755, but as the settlement was made about 1734, and the early settlers were many of them pious people, it is not probable that they would have been satisfied to be without a house of worship for so many years, and we have already seen that supplies were sent them by Presbytery in September, 1738. Rev. Dr. Junkin, in his history of the Presbytery of Newton, says: "A house must have been built at Lower Mt. Bethel as early as 1747."

The first building was a rude structure, small and doubtless built of logs. This seems soon to have given way to a frame building. The time when this second edifice was erected cannot be definitely fixed. This second building was enlarged in a very singular manner. It was sawed into two equal parts, and the parts were separated twenty or thirty feet, and intervening space filled up, the building being originally almost square.

I learned several years since from a former respected Ruling Elder of this church, Mr. John Connelly, that this enlargement was made about eighty years ago. The present edifice was erected in the summer of 1838 at which time the Rev. Azariah Prior was stated supply. Its cost was $3,795.50.

The congregation had at the time a fund of $1,756.41, the proceeds of the sale of a parsonage property situated near the village of Richmond. This money was appropriated to aid in paying the debt of the congregation incurred in building the church.

The site of the church was changed when the present building was erected, the old site being near the northern boundary of the graveyard. For several years previous to the building of this edifice, the Lutheran and Reformed congregations occupied the Presbyterian Church alternately on the Sabbaths that it was not occupied by the Presbyterian congregation.

When the proposition was made to build a new church edifice, many of the different congregations were very decidedly in favor of building a church to be owned jointly by the three denominations; others, and perhaps a considerable majority in the Presbyterian congregation, were as decidedly opposed to the union measure.

The prospects for an amicable union of the three denominations being by no means encouraging, the Lutheran and German Reformed congregations decided to unite in building a church, and the Presbyterian congregation soon after decided to build a church of their own.

This arrangement was surely the best for all concerned, and especially so for this congregation, as in a very few years they called and settled a pastor for the whole of his time, which arrangement has been continued ever since.

It has been supposed that William Allen, of Philadelphia, of whom mention has already been made as having purchased a large tract of land early in the eighteenth century, including the land now owned and occupied by this congregation as a burying ground, that this William Allen gave the congregation a title for this ground, but the records of the Register's Office, at Easton, show that a deed was not given for this land until August, 1803, when the land was purchased by the congregation from Samuel Rea, Esq., for a small sum, and a deed obtained for it.

Thomas Ruckman purchased seven hundred acres of land from William Allen, in 1757, lying along the Delaware River, from the mouth of Martin's Creek, and extending four hundred rods up the river. This purchase included the church lot and burying ground.

In 1759, Mr. Ruckman sold two hundred acres of this tract, including the land above named, to Samuel Rea, Esq, and Mr. Rea sold the church lot to the congregation, in August, 1803, and gave a deed for it in trust to Thomas Beard, Alexander Miller and Peter Simanton. Previous to this time, the congregation had no title for the church lot, and held possession of it only by sufferance of its owners.

The deed for the school house lot, lying between the church and the burying ground, was given in May, 1802, and was given in trust to Nathaniel Brittain and Thomas Beard,

It may be interesting to many to hear an extract from the deed for the old church lot and burying ground. After describing the boundaries of the lot, the deed says: "On which the Protestant religious society or congregation of said Township and its neighborhood have erected a house or place of worship, called the Mt. Bethel meeting house, and part thereof used by them as a burial place for their dead. In trust nevertheless to and for the interests and purposes hereinafter mentioned, limited and described of and concerning the same, that is to say for a site of a meeting house or place of public worship, and a burial place for the members of the said Protestant, Presbyterian religious society or congregation professing the doctrines set forth in the Confession of Faith of the Presbyterian Church in the United States of America, under the direction of the Synods of New York and Philadelphia."

This congregation was incorporated and a charter obtained from the Legislature of Pennsylvania, in February, 1809.

The charter is signed by David Barclay, minister; David Ayers, Robt. Galloway, Nathaniel Brittain and Jeptha Arrison, Ruling Elders; and by the following members of the congregation, viz: Joseph Bowman, John Neilson, John Davison, Samuel Gulick, John Hutchison, Peter Middagh, Moses Ayers, Robert Moody, Peter Simanton, Peter Jacoby, Henry Winter, Isaac Benward, Samuel Rea, John Galloway, John Ross, William Galloway, John Neilson, James Hutchison, George Kennedy, John McCrea, William Hutchison, Thomas Middagh, Robert Kennedy, Samuel Eakin, Andrew Hutchison, Alexander Lockard, and Robert Brittain, not one of whom now lives. The lot upon which the church edifice now stands was purchased of William Lander, in April, 1815.

The Trustees of the congregation at that time, and whose names are mentioned in the deed, were William Hutchison, Moses Wallace, Samuel Loder, John Jacoby, David Beard, and Robert Kennedy.

At a comparatively early day after the settlement of Mt.

Bethel, the spirit of emigration began to manifest itself to a very considerable extent, and this spirit has continued to prevail to a greater or less extent until the present time. This spirit seems to be characteristic of the Scotch-Irish people. We see it manifested in their coming to America in large numbers at an early day.

This was wisely ordered of Providence in the early settlement of the British colonies, for they were a pious people, being especially strict as it regards the observance of the Sabbath, and the maintenance of religious worship. One result of the working of this spirit of emigration in Mt. Bethel was that the names of some originally large families have become extinct, and these families have been lost to this congregation.

It is a pleasure, however, to know that while they have been lost to us, they have not been lost to the cause of Christ. The Master has had a work for them to do in other parts of the great field, and has sent them out from us to accomplish that work.

Soon after the Revolutionary War, several families emigrated from Mt. Bethel to Eastern Tennessee and formed a settlement there. In the month of February, 1867, as some of you perhaps remember, an article appeared in the Presbyterian, written by the Rev. William B. Rankin, at that time a Professor in Tusculum College, near Greenville, in Eastern Tennessee, in which he spoke of a colony having emigrated from Mt. Bethel, Pa., to Eastern Tennessee, and stated that a church was soon organized where they settled, which was called Mt. Bethel, in remembrance of the church which they had left in Pennsylvania.

Upon seeing this article in the Presbyterian, a letter was written to Mr. Rankin asking further information as to these emigrants, and the following is his reply, written June 6, 1867:

"Dear Brother: Your kind favor of March 12th is before me. My absence from home and the press of duties, I trust will be sufficient apology for the delay in writing.

The names of the men and families, who emigrated to Eastern Tennessee from Mt. Bethel, on Martin's Creek, Pennsylvania, are as follows as near as I can ascertain, viz: Anthony Moore, James Galbraith, Daniel Copland, Alexander Gaston, Thomas Wilson, ——— Martin, Boyd, and Hutton.

I am pastor of the Mt. Bethel Church in East Tennessee, and the names of Moore, Galbraith and Wilson are still in my Session. I am the great-grandson of the above-named Anthony Moore, who, I think, was an Elder in Mt. Bethel, Pennsylvania, and one of the first Elders of the Mt. Bethel Church in East Tennessee. He owned and lived on the farm at the mouth of Martin's Creek.

My grandmother, Sarah Moore (Rankin), was fifteen years old when her father, Anthony Moore, moved from Mt. Bethel, Pa., to Eastern Tennessee. I know nothing of the history of the Mt. Bethel Church, Pennsylvania, only by tradition from my grandmother, who died some eighteen years since.

I have often heard her speak of a large apple tree under which the Rev. David Brainerd preached to the Indians. I think it stood on her father's farm. The Rev. Mr. Debow was pastor of the Mt. Bethel Church in Pennsylvania during the Revolutionary War. He was my grandmother's minister. She often spoke of him as an excellent man. Debow was the man and not Robinson that I intended in my article of February 9th in the Presbyterian.

The impression was made and left on my mind by my grandmother, that Mr. Debow was murdered by the Hessians. These were the circumstances.

Their neighborhood was threatened by the enemy. The neighbors assembled and formed themselves into a company to go out and drive them back. Their minister was with them, leading the company. After traveling a few miles they halted and held a council, and decided that their minister should go back. as it was thought not best to thus hazard his life. He did so, and while on his return, he met with some of the enemy—was chased into a cellar, and while endeavoring to conceal himself among some empty barrels, was killed with bayonets.

My father, who is still living, aged seventy-three years, says that he recollects well hearing the old people who came from Mt. Bethel, Pa., talk about what a solemn time it was when Rev. Mr. Debow preached the funeral sermon of the Rev. Mr. Rosbrough, in their old church. They spoke of the affecting scene, when the widow entered the church, carrying a child in her arms, followed by two little sons, each carrying a Bible under his arm. The impression is left on the minds of the present generation here, that both were murdered, Rosbrough first, and Debow, then pastor of Mt. Bethel Church, preached his funeral sermon and was afterward murdered himself in the manner above mentioned.

My mind had never been called to these things until after I wrote my article of February 9th. It was from mere accident, (I should rather say providential) that I mentioned the relationship between Mt. Bethel in Eastern Tennessee and Mt. Bethel in Pennsylvania.

I am very much interested in their histories, and am much obliged to you for your letter.

I trust this is but a beginning of an acquaintance between yourself and your people, and myself and my people, that may grow into a near and warm Christian love and sympathy.

Fraternally yours,
Wm. B. Rankin."

This letter has been given just as written by Mr. Rankin, although it contains some inaccuracies. Of these inaccuracies I need not speak, as they will readily be detected.

It was doubtless felt to be a great loss to this church when these families removed from Mt. Bethel; but it now appears that they were to be honored of God, as standard-bearers in His great army in Eastern Tennessee and we now have Christian greetings from a descendant of one of these pious families of the fourth generation. and our hearts are cheered by the tidings of the good work which they have already accomplished, and which is still in progress, and which promises so much for the good of Zion in the future.

Soon after this emigration to East Tennessee, a number of families removed from Mt. Bethel, Pa., to Western Pennsylvania. This emigration was at that time called going to Fort Pitt. Among names of families removing to Fort Pitt were those of Moody, Morris, Miller, McFarren, Mason, Neilson, and Benward.

A little later several families removed from Mt. Bethel and settled along and near the West Branch of the Susquehanna River, in the region of Milton. Among the families removing to this region were those of Marr (Carr), Beard, Sillaman, Scott, Henderson, Covert, Moore, and Foresman.

It is a matter of much interest to me, that in the providence of God I have been brought back to Mt. Bethel, where my ancestors for many years lived and worshipped God, after the name had been extinct in Mt. Bethel for nearly fifty years.

More recently, many have emigrated to Ohio and Michigan, and to other Western States. Many have feared that in consequence of this constantly prevailing spirit of emigration in the members of this congregation, this church would at no very distant day become extinct. There is perhaps as little of the spirit of emigration among us now as there ever has been, and the ability today to support the gospel in this congregation, will compare favorably with what it has been at any former period in its history.

The names of those who have been connected with this church and who have become ministers of the gospel are, as far as has been ascertained, as follows, viz: William Scott, son of John Scott, who formerly owned and lived upon the property where Mrs. Susan Hazen now lives. This Rev. William Scott was the father of the Rev. J. W. Scott, D.D., lately a professor in Hanover College, Indiana, who visited Mt. Bethel a few years since, and was much interested in visiting our graveyard. The Rev. Wm. Scott married a daughter of Samuel Rea, Esq., of whom mention has already been made.

The names of others who have entered the ministry, and who have been members of this church, are Samuel Galloway, Ephraim Simanton, Samuel Ayers, John Brittain, Theron Brittain, and George C. Pollock.

Several others, descendants of those formerly members of this church, have entered the ministry of reconciliation. It is an interesting fact, and well worthy to be mentioned in gathering up the history of this church, that most of those who have entered the learned professions from the families of this congregation, have chosen the ministry of the gospel.

What the number of church members was at the organization of the church or for many years after, has not been ascertained. The earliest statistical report of this church which has been found, was made to the Presbytery of Newton, in April, 1821. The number of church members reported at that time was fifty-one.

The early records of the church having been lost, but little can be learned as to accessions to the church during the earlier period of its history.

It is more probable that accessions were made mostly from the families of the church, and by certificate from families moving within its bounds. Additions were perhaps not made in large numbers. Much attention was given to catechetical instruction and pastoral visitation, and accessions were perhaps more steady and uniform.

The church has been blessed with several interesting seasons of refreshing, when many precious souls have been gathered into the fold.

Twenty-two are reported as having been added to the church in 1821, which would seem to indicate a more than the usual degree of interest in the church.

The largest number added to the communion of the church during any year of its history, was probably for the year ending April, 1843, when sixty-seven were added to the church upon profession of their faith. The total number of communicants reported at that time was two hundred and eighteen. This large accession to the membership of the church occurred in the earlier part of the Rev. Andrew Tully's pastorate.

Some of you have a very distinct recollection of the interesting meetings that were held at that time, and especially of the valuable services of the Rev. Jacob R. Castner, then pastor of the Mansfield Church.

Thirty-three years have passed since, and but a few, comparatively, of those gathered into the church at that time, are now with us. Many have gone the way of all the earth, and others have gone out from us and are now connected with other churches.

During my pastorate of this church, two interesting revivals occurred—one during the year ending April, 1861, when thirty-nine were received into the communion of the church upon profession of their faith, and the other during the year ending April, 1871, when thirty were received, most of whom remain with us until this day, but some have fallen asleep.

As it regards membership, it may be said that this church has held on its way remarkably well in view of the drain upon it by emigration, of which mention has already been made.

The oldest inscription that I have been able to find in the graveyard, is that which marks the resting place of Mrs. Jean Miller, who died June 13th, 1763, in the 27th year of her age. This was twenty-five years after the Rev. Gilbert Tennent was sent as a supply to the Forks of the Delaware, by the New Brunswick Presbytery.

It is probable interments were made in this graveyard about the time Mr. Tennent first preached here—1738.

In the early settlement of Mt. Bethel, there were three burial places in Lower Mt. Bethel: one connected with this church, one on or near the farm now owned by Mr. Elias Hutchinson, on the old road leading from Martin's Creek to Easton, and another on the farm of Mr. John Young, about a mile south of the village of Ackermanville. This last was called Thompson's burying ground, and was not as old as either of the others. Which of the other two is the older, I am unable to say.

It may be interesting to give some more of the older inscriptions in our grave yard:

"Robert Lyle, Esq., died Sept. 5th, 1765, in the 67th year of his age."

"Alexander Miller, died Sept. 5th, 1765, in the 84th year of his age."

He was perhaps one of the first settlers, and not improbably a ruling elder.

"James Martin, died May 20, 1767, aged 57 years." He was also doubtless one of the original settlers. From his family, Martin's Creek took its name.

"James Moody, died July 31, 1771, aged 25 years."

Could we have spread before us the names of all the members of this congregation who have died since the organization of this church, what a lesson we would have of death's doings among us.

Five generations have passed away. "We are strangers before Thee and sojourners as were all our fathers; our days on the earth are as a shadow, and there is none abiding."

We have seen that this church in the earlier years of its existence, enjoyed the ministrations of eminently devoted and able servants of God. Tennent, Brainerd and Robison, who preached for this people, were men well known and greatly beloved and honored in their day for their fidelity, zeal and success in the Master's cause, and their memories are still cherished with much respect and veneration by pious people.

Others might be named who have ministered in holy things at this altar, whom God has honored, as instruments in His hand for the accomplishment of much of His glory and for the good of precious souls.

And then again how many of the fathers and mothers, and of the younger members of this church, of the generations that have lived and died have given evidence of devoted piety, and whose prayers may be regarded as our richest legacy. These prayers are now being and yet to be answered as the truth of God as proclaimed from this pulpit, and spoken in the families of this congregation is made effectual to the edification of believers and to the conversion of impenitent sinners.

Have we not seen in this hasty and imperfect review of God's dealings with this church, abundant reason for thankfulness to Him? And have we not great reason to be encouraged to go forward in the faithful discharge of duty, in view of what the Lord has done for us in the past?

We believe that this church has not yet accomplished her mission. We believe the Lord has still a work for her to do; and for the performance of this work, every true soldier of the cross must gird himself, putting on the whole armor of God.

My Christian brethren, members of this time-honored church, is there reason why you should not be intensely interested in its prosperity? How is this interest to be shown? I answer in especially and always by earnest prayer and effort for the promotion of the spiritual prosperity of the church. If you do your duty, dear brethren, as members of this church, you cannot be indifferent to its spiritual welfare. And let us remember that the spirituality of the individual members of any church determines the measure of spirituality for that church as a body of believers. The spiritual prosperity of the church being secured, you need have no fears as to its temporalities. The love of the spiritual-minded church member will be shown by the manifestation of the deepest interest in everything pertaining to Zion's temporal prosperity, "For thy servants take pleasure in her stones and favor the dust thereof." "The Lord hath done great things for us whereof we are glad."

"Hitherto hath the Lord helped us." For a period of almost a century and a half, His hand has been over us for good. He has not in anger removed our candlestick. Blessed be His name."

"We will rejoice in His salvation and in the name of our God we will set up our banners."

Former Members of the Session.

John Rosenberry. He studied the welfare of the church and gave of his means as God had prospered him.

Morris Morris. A brother-in-law of Mr. Rosenberry, gave what he could for the cause of Christ.

John Connelly. A man of more than ordinary intelligence. A good theologian for laymen. "These limbs of mine in my younger days," he says, "have often carried me to the house of dissipation, and now, as long as they are able, they must carry me to the house of prayer." He was a rigid disciplinarian and died in the full hope of a blessed immortality.

Merari Gulick. He was a man of God, faithful in his day and generation. He lived near God and gave liberally to the church and to missions.

THE SCOTCH-IRISH PRESBYTERIAN BURIAL GROUND

At Three Churches, Lower Mt. Bethel Township, Northampton County, Pennsylvania

[Copy furnished by Horatio Gates Shull]

This burial ground, beautifully located in the hills of Lower Mt. Bethel, seven miles north of Easton, on the old stage road from Martin's Creek to Portland, and distant from the Delaware River one-half mile across the fields, is the oldest public burial ground in the township, the earlier burials taking place in the years 1730-1750, the graves being marked by field stones, from which the inscriptions, if any, have entirely disappeared.

The yard is enclosed by a substantial stone wall of unknown age, but to the writer's knowledge, at least seventy-five years old. In the northeast corner of the yard stood the first house of worship in the township. Rev. Gilbert Tennant preached in this house as early as 1738. A few loose stones, that marked the spot, have been removed. For many years the yard was a mass of fallen stones, weeds and briars. Recently, those whose forbears rest amidst its quiet surroundings, removed all unsightly growths, leveled the graves and graded the ground. Grass seed was sown, the stones firmly reset, and what was formerly an abomination to the eye is now a place of beauty.

The hill on which this burial ground is located is known as "Church Hill," it being the site of three churches, in which worship the Presbyterian, the old and the new Lutheran congregations.

Available space for burial purposes having become exhausted, a new burial ground was established on an adjacent hill and named "Church Hill" Cemetery. In it the descendants of those who founded Hunter's Scotch-Irish Settlement, along with their neighbors, of many nationalities, bury their loved ones.

In the old yard are found more than three hundred stones, on which the inscriptions are legible, seventy per cent of the names found, indicating the Scotch-Irish ancestry of the deceased.

Before their existence is forgotten through the lapse of time, it may be well to call attention to two private Scotch-Irish burial places in the township: one found in the corner of a field on the west side of the junction of the old Easton and Stumptown roads, one-fourth mile north of the Black Hill. In it were buried those who were prominent in the membership of Hunter's Scotch-Irish Settlement at its founding. All stones have disappeared and field crops are grown on the graves of those who sleep beneath.

The other of the two was the burial ground of related people, Ketchledges, Thompsons, and Millers. It is located in a field on what was the farm of a man known as "Honey" Young, opposite the junction of the Wind Gap and Ackermanville-Martin's Creek roads, at the southern end of a small village named Factoryville. The ground covering those buried here is also cultivated. Headstones in a good state of preservation stand against four apple trees that mark the spot. Others probably may be found sunken by their own weight far beneath the surface soil.

August 20th. 1925.

Scotch-Irish Presbyterian Burial Ground at Three Churches, Lower Mt. Bethel

1—Robert Galloway, died April 9th.
2—Elizabeth, wife of Robert Galloway, died Dec. 20, 1846, aged 85 years, 10 mo., 11 days.
3—Mary Galloway, died June 29, 1859, in her 55th year.
4—Nancy Ross, daughter of Robert Galloway, born Sept. 19, 1785; died Feb., 1810.
5—Agnes Thompson, died April 11th, 1814, in her 77th year.

6—John Davison, died Oct. 9, 1825, aged 61 years.
7—Christianna, wife of John Davison, died Aug. 2, 1863, in her 90th year.
8—Andrew Lomison, born Nov. 18, 1781; died Aug. 28, 1827.
9—Christeen Carhart, born Aug. 12, 1793; died Jan. 2, 1880.
10—George Mack, died April 10, 1823, in his 49th year.
11—William Stinson, died Sept. 4, 1840, in his 83rd year.
12—Anna Stinson, died June 7, 1817, in her 88th year.
13—Elizabeth Stinson, died April 11, 1831, in her 64th year.
14—David Lockhard (see numbers 33 and 34), died Mar. 25, 1813, in his 88th year.
15—Zachariah Lockhard, born Mar. 1, 1798; died April 12, 1861.
16—Hannah, wife of Zachariah Lockhard, born Oct. 16, 1803; died Sept. 23, 1881.
17—Josiah, son of Zachariah and Hannah Lockhard, born May 25, 18_2; died Oct. 24, 1848.
18—Ann Lockhard, born May 18, 1801; died Dec. 29, 1872.
19—Samuel Lockhard, born May 3, 1773; died Aug. 30, 1850.
20—Rachel, wife of Samuel Lockhard. born Mar. 3, 1776; died Nov. 19, 1841.
21—Jane, wife of Ephraim Lockhard, died Nov. 11, 1869, aged 58 yrs., 5 months.
22—Mary M. Kirkendall, daughter of James and Nancy Lockhard, wife of David Kirkendall, born Nov. 14, 1795; died Mar. 6, 1852.
23—Zachariah Drake (a physician), died Feb. 9, 1851, aged 66 yrs., 9 mo., 9 days.
24—Martha, wife of Zachariah Drake, born Feb. 21, 1789; died Jan. 27, 1875.
25—Anna Maria, wife of Aaron Sandt, died Sept. 2, 1888; aged 72 years.
26—Joseph Keller, died April 26, 1850, in his 40th year.
27—Sarah A., wife of Joseph Keller, born June 8, 1814; died Oct. 6th, 1864.

28—John Evans, died Feb. 1, 1852, aged 88 yrs., 4 mo., 19 days.
29—Jane Evans, died May 16, 1858, aged 85 yrs., 11 mo., 1 day.
30—James Edminson, died April 27, 1855, in his 65th year.
31—Elizabeth, wife of James Edminson (she was daughter of Gerret Middagh), died Feb. 12, 1857, in her 65th year.
32—Agnes McSwinea, died Sept. 6, 1808, in her 85th year.
33—Alexander Lockhard (see No. 14), died April 25, 1804, in his 59th year.
34—David Lockhard (see No. 14), died Dec. 12, 1788, aged 28 years.
35—William McFarren, died April 2, 1804, aged 15 years.
36—Isabel, wife of William McFarren, died Aug. 2, 1809, in her 86th year.
37—Joseph Bowman, son of James Bowman, died Sept. 27, 1761, aged 1 year, 11 mo., 6 days.
38—Joseph Bowman, died Oct. 12, 1859, aged 35 years, 2 mo., 27 days.
39—Joseph Bowman, died April 20th, 1836, in his 69th year.
40—Elizabeth, wife of Joseph Bowman, died May 5, 1849, in her 50th year.
41—Catherine, wife of Andrew Bowman, born April 1, 1796; died April 3, 1865.
42—Robert Lyons, died Oct. 27, 1848, in his 71st year.
43—Anna Lyons, born Mar. 15, 1785; died July 24th, 1827.
44—Isaac Lyons, son of Robert Lyons, born Nov. 1, 1821,
45—David Ayres, Esq., (see numbers 59 and 60), died Jan. 25, 1835, in his 91st year.
46—Elizabeth, wife of David Ayres, died Feb. 13, 1815, in her 78th year.
47—David Ayres, died Dec. 30, 1883, aged 87 years, 4 mo., 19 days.
48—Margaret, wife of David Ayres, (born Ketchledge), died May 2, 1856, aged 61 years, 5 mo., 7 days.
49—Moses Ayres (father of No. 53), died June 8, 1851, aged 81 years, 24 days.

50—Mary, wife of Moses Ayres (see 89), died June 7, 1840, in her 65th year.
(was daughter of Nathaniel Brittain)
51—Philip Datesman, died Jan., 1840, aged 50 years.
52—William Mason, died Feb. 1, 1794, in his 53rd year.
53—John, son of Moses and Mary Ayres, died Oct. 13, 1795, aged 7 months.
54—E. Dunfield, (Elizabeth, wife of Joseph Dunfield,) died June 7, 1798, aged 27 years, 3 months.
55—Robert Cole, born Oct. 3, 1801; died Mar. 13, 1832.
56—Catherine, wife of Robert Cole, died April 12, 1851, aged 45 yrs., 5 mo., 7 days.
57—David, son of Robert and Catherine Cole, died Feb. 3, 1851, aged 19 years, 11 mo., 27 days.
58—Ann Hornung, wife of Henry Hornung, born June 10, 1780; died June 13, 1823.
59—Elizabeth, daughter of David and Elizabeth Ayres, died July 6. 1777, in her 6th year.
60—Mary, daughter of David and Elizabeth Ayres, died July 10, 1777, aged 2 years.
61—Sarah Snyder, wife of John K. Snyder, died Dec. 28, 1851, aged 55 years, 10 mo., 15 days.
62—James Hutchison, died Jan. 12, 1814, 100 years of age.
63—Agnes, wife of James Hutchison, died June 1, 1803, aged 86 years.
64—Sarah Hutchison, died Dec. 26, 1869, in her 63rd year.
65—Rachel Nyce, wife of William Foresman, died June 30, 1809, aged 29 years, 2 mo., 5 days.
66—Robert Foresman, died June 2, 1805, in his 82nd year.
67—Jane All, wife of Robert Foresman, died Jan. 10, 1810, aged 82 years.
68—Philip Foresman, died Jan., 1811, aged 50 years.
69—Samuel Eakin, born April 17, 1777; died April 18, 1864.
70—Sallie, wife of Samuel Eakin, born June 22, 1788; died Jan. 23, 1862.
71—Elizabeth, daughter of Samuel and Sallie Eakin, born April 11, 1816; died Aug. 7, 1839.

72—Elizabeth, wife of John Eakin, daughter of Zachariah and Martha Matilda Drake, died Aug. 18, 1854, aged 35 years, 6 mo., 26 days.
(See number 23)
73—James McFall, died Aug. 29, 1880, aged 72 years, 1 mo., 12 days.
74—Francis McFall (father of 102 and 296), born April 1, 1774; died April 2, 1840.
75—Sarah, wife of Francis McFall, died July 28, 1862, in her 82nd year.
76—Thomas McFall, died Mar. 11, 1824, aged 47 years, 9 days.
77—Ann, wife of Thomas McFall, died May 6, 1866, aged 84 years, 8 mo., 5 days.
78—Calvin, son of Peter Winters and Mary Matilda McFall, born Oct. 29, 1839; died Mar. 6, 1842.
79—William, son of Peter Winters and Mary Matilda McFall, born Mar. 24, 1844; died Oct. 10, 1847.
80—Hugh McFall, died July 7, 1848, aged 57 years, 7 mo., 25 days.
81—John McFall, born Nov. 6, 1803; died April 15, 1863.
82—Margaret, daughter of Jesse and Mary McFall, died Jan. 12, 1852, aged 4 years, 1 mo.
83—Elizabeth McFall, died April 3, 1877, aged 76 years, 4 mo., 8 days.
84—Sarah, wife of George Fox, born Dec. 29, 1792; died May 9, 1835.
(George Fox, buried in cemetery at Three Churches)
85—Andrew Smock, died April 28, 1773, aged 23 years.
86—Adam Moody, died Nov. 19, 1781, aged 67 years.
87—Anna, wife of Adam Moody, died April 22, 1802, aged 87 years.
88—James Moody, died July 31, 1771, aged 25 years.
89—Nathaniel Brittain, died Oct. 2, 1817, in his 73rd year.
90—Nathaniel Brittain, died Mar. 8, 1799, in his 49th year.
91—John Brittain, died Nov. 4, 1808, in the 6th year of his age. (Born the 2nd day of September, 1802, the only son

of his mother and the youngest son of my old age, his father, Nathaniel Brittain.)

92—Robert Brittain, born Dec. 25, 1771; died Feb. 12, 1857.

93—Sidney, wife of Robert Brittain, died Dec. 31, 1846, aged 53 years, 5 mo., 4 days.

94—William Brittain, died Oct. 30, 1847, aged 68 years, 7 mo., 12 days.

95—Catherine, wife of William Brittain, died Oct. 17, 1847, aged 66 years, 6 mon., 23 days.

96—James Brittain, born May 20, 1804; died June 26, 1858.

97—Sally Ann, wife of James Brittain, born Dec. 8, 1803; died Nov. 24, 1851.

98—William, son of James and Sally Ann Brittain, born Aug. 12, 1827; died Feb. 10, 1850.

99—William Brittain, died Sept. 24, 1847, aged 32 years, 8 mo., 26 days.

100—Samuel Brittain, died Feb. 10, 1837, aged 34 years, 1 mo., 20 days.

101—Henry G. Brittain, born Mar. 20, 1807; died Aug. 21, 1884.

102—Sally Ann, wife of H. G. Brittain, born April 20, 1808; died March 2, 1842. (Daughter of No. 74, sister of 124).

103—Eleanor, wife of H. G. Brittain, born April 3, 1805; died Oct. 4, 1878. (Sister of No. 102).

104—Garret Middaugh, joined Patriot Army 1776, born 1732, died 1810.

105—Peter Middagh, died Oct. 28, 1829, in his 82nd year.

106—Thomas Middagh, died May 27, 1841, in his 59th year.

107—Rebecca, wife of Thomas Middagh, died Aug. 31, 1852, aged 60 years, 7 mo., 8 days.

108—Thomas Middagh, died Dec. 12, 1868, aged 46 years, 3 mo., 26 days.

109—Cornelia, wife of Thomas Middagh, died Feb. 2, 1890, aged 60 years, 9 mo. (Born Cronk.) (See No. 116).

110—Peter Jacoby, died Sept. 7, 1814, in his 49th year.

111—Mary Jacoby, died Jan. 20, 1889, aged 70 years.

112—Henry Jacoby, died Nov. 12, 1809, aged 76 years.

113—Eleanor, daughter of Peter and Mary Jacoby, died May 18, 1827, aged 15 years, 6 mo., 18 days.
114—Matilda W. Larison. (no dates)
115—Joseph Patton, died Aug. 26, 1793, in his 21st year.
116—Mary, wife of James Middaugh, died Nov. 24, 1851, aged 58 years, 6 mo., 28 days.
(Should follow 109).
117—Jane Shuck, born July 3, 1825; died Oct. 21, 1865.
118—Jonathan Nielson, died Feb. 9, 1787, aged 79 years.
119—Sarah, wife of Jonathan Nielson, died July 17, 1791, aged 83 years.
120—Margaret Albright, born Feb. 23, 1804; died April 22, 1867.
121—Samuel McCracken, died Sept. 8, 1794, in his 48th year. (See No. 132)
122—Jerusha McCracken, died Oct. 4, 1794, in her 50th year.
123—Peter D. Kiefer, died July 3, 1875, aged 66 years, 6 mo., 15 days.
124—Jemima, wife of Peter D. Kiefer, born June 11, 1807; died April 26, 1865.
(Daughter of 74, sister of 102 and 103).
125—Francis, son of Peter D. and Jemima Kiefer, born Jan. 25, 1840; died Dec. 1, 1841.
126—Elizabeth, daughter of Peter D. and Jemima Kiefer, born Dec. 14, 1837; died Dec. 27, 1844.
127—Sarah, daughter of Peter D. and Jemima Kiefer, bapt. April 1, 1836; died March 6, 1837.
128—Catherine Kiefer, born Feb. 11, 1757; died Feb. 11, 1825.
129—Samuel Kiefer, born May 8, 1793; died Feb. 11, 1865.
130—Sarah, wife of Samuel Kiefer, born Jan. 4, 1806, died Aug. 30, 1865.
131—Mary, daughter of Joseph, Sr., and Sarah Kiefer, born Jan. 30, 1810; died May 13, 1827.
132—Robert McCracken, died Feb., 1786, aged 77 years.
133—Mary, wife of Robert McCracken, died Nov., 1781, aged 73 years.
134—Elias, son of William and Christina Shuman, born Dec.

4, 1806; died Aug. 24, 1807.

135—Charity, daughter of Philip and Margaret Shull, died Mar. 4, 1819, aged 4 years.

136—George Kennedy, died Mar. 3, 1835, aged 82 years.

137—Jane Kennedy, consort of George Kennedy, born a Nelson, died Nov., 1830, aged 75 years.

138—Robert Kennedy, born April 15, 1776; died Mar. 5, 1826.

139—Marthy Keannedy, died Aug. 1, 1812, in her 27th year.

140—Elizabeth, wife of Isaac Stocker, born Kern—two children—born Dec. 1, 1797; died Oct. 1, 1820.

141—George Stocker (father of Isaac), died Mar. 21, 1811, aged 40 years, 7 months (should be 50 years 7 months).

142—Peter W. S. Major, son of Thomas and Mary V. Major, (she was born Shull), born Dec. 8, 1832; died June 28, 1833.

143—Peter O. Major, Co. B, 51 Pa. Infantry. No dates.

144—James Beard (see No. 150), died Mar. 5, 1802, aged 72 years.

145—Isabel Beard, died Aug. 13, 1819, aged 82 years.

146—James Beard, born April 21, 1765; died Oct. 7, 1831.

147—Elizabeth Beard, died Oct. 18, 1794, aged 27 years.

148—Joseph Beard, died July 30, 1791, aged 17 years.

149—Rebecca Beard, died April 7, 1774, aged 2 years.

150—Sarah, daughter of James and Isabel Beard, born June 18, 1761; died Oct. 5, 1832.

151—Matthew Beard, born April 4, 1808; died Sept. 11, 1831.

152—Benjamin Baird, born June 28, 1778; died Jan. 22, 1818.

153—David Baird, born Dec. 9, 1780; died May 23, 1853.

154—Sarah, wife of David Baird, born Mar. 1, 1793; died June 19, 1852.

155—Philip Deats, died May 19, 1881, aged 71 years 20 days.

156—Caroline, wife of Philip Deats, born Mar. 23, 1822; died Feb. 24, 1883.

(Born Ross)

157—John Deats, born April 6, 1759; died Oct. 12, 1836.

158—Elizabeth, wife of John Deats, died June 17, 1856, aged 74 years, 10 mo.

159—Peter Deats, born Jan. 5, 1782; died Sept. 25, 1857.
160—Christina, wife of Peter Deats, born Dec. 25, 1788; died Jan. 13, 1868.
161—Julia Deats, wife of John Ketchledge, born Mar. 31, 1812; died Aug. 8, 1899.
162—John Ketchledge, born Sept. 30, 1815; died Mar. 25, 1877.
163—Maria Deats, wife of John Connelly, born Jan. 6, 1808; died Oct. 30, 1882. (See No. 314).
164—Emma R. Resh, daughter of John and Julia Ketchledge, born Jan. 14, 1854; died Oct. 10, 1882.
165—John Connelly, born Sept. 15, 1789; died June 17, 1858.
166—Elizabeth, wife of John Connelly, born Aug. 20, 1785; died Mar. 30, 1865.
167—Jeremiah Connelly, died May 31, 1844, in his 27th year.
168—Mary Shull, wife of Joseph Deats, born Feb. 26, 1850; died Jan. 16, 1873. (See No. 183).
169—Anthony Ketchledge, born Nov. 1, 1816; died July 14, 1876.
170—Mary, wife of Anthony Ketchledge, died Oct. 12, 1873, aged 53 years, 3 mo., 3 days.
171—Samuel Virgil Wolfslear, born June 30, 1820; died Sept. 9, 1823.
172—Thomas Searl, born Jan. 28, 1784; died June 12, 1846.
173—Elizabeth, wife of Thomas Searl, born April 18, 1788; died June 2, 1852.
174—John Johnson, born Nov. 1, 1761; died Jan. 19, 1815.
175—Jerusha, wife of John Johnson, born Feb. 18, 1764; died Sept. 8, 1822.
176—William Johnson, born Feb. 17, 1800; died Jan. 15, 1862.
177—Margaret, wife of William Johnson, died Dec. 31, 1882, aged 82 years, 10 mo., 25 days.
178—John Johnson, born May 26, 1805; died Dec. 17, 1852.
179—Caroline, wife of John Johnson, died May 19, 1861, aged 54 years, 10 mo., 21 days.
180—Euphama Osmun Johnson, born Feb. 9, 1822; died Oct. 24, 1823.

181—Mary Smith, died Jan. 13, 1854, aged 61 years, 9 mo., 25 days.

182—Margaret, wife of John Ackerman, died April 10, 1854, aged 59 years, 2 mo., 19 days.

183—Arlington, son of Joseph and Mary Deats, born June 26, 1872; died Dec. 12, 1872. (See No. 168).

184—Samuel Reaser, died Sept. 9, 1815, in his 81st year.

185—Ann, wife of Samuel Reaser, died Mar. 27, 1781, aged 44 years.

186—Thomas Ruckman, died Mar. 20, 1790, aged 49 years.

187—Rachel, wife of Thomas Ruckman, died June 27, 1774, aged 26 years.

188—Isaac, son of John Grafford, died Dec. 23, 1765, in his 17th year.

189—John Simonton, died June 5, 1848, aged 33 years, 5 mo., 20 days.

190—Thomas Morris, died April 13, 1814, aged 69 years.

191—Ann, wife of Thomas Morris, died June 26, 1834, aged 81 years.

192—Butler Morris, born April 19, 1791; died Dec. 25, 1875.

193—Rachel, wife of Butler Morris, died July 21, 1854, in her 59th year.

194—Morris Morris, born April 9, 1787; died June 18, 1872.

195—Martha, wife of Morris Morris, born June 21, 1787; died June 7, 1868.

196—Sarah, wife of Robert Morris, died Jan. 12, 1816, in her 25th year.

197—Susan Morris, wife of William J. Scott, relict of John Vanatta, died Feb. 22, 1889, aged 66 years, 10 mo., 13 days.

198—William L. Scott, born May 28, 1828; died Feb. 21, 1868.

199—Susan, wife of William Scott, died Aug. 14, 1859, aged 27 years, 5 mo., 10 days.

200—Ann, wife of Henry Winters, born Dec. 3, 1781; died Jan. 4, 1854.

201—Henry Winter, died May 5, 1849, in his 76th year.

202—Christian D. Winter, born Dec. 25, 1815; died Oct. 3,

1855.

203—Susanna Winter, died May 30, 1854, in her 58th year.

204—Maria Theresa Fradeneck, born Aug. 11, 1826; died Jan. 16, 1846.

205—John Depue, died April 19, 1777, in his 51st year.

206—Abraham Depue, born Sept. 28, 1764; died Oct. 21, 1851.

207—Susanna, wife of Abraham Depue, died May 3, 1854, aged 83 years.

208—Abraham, son of Abraham and Susanna Depue, born Sept. 19, 1819, aged 13 years, 11 mo., 12 days.

209—John Depue, died Mar. 2, 1845, aged 69 years, 2 months.

210—Elizabeth, wife of John Depue, died Oct. 28, 1859, aged 75 years, 2 months.

211—John Depue, died Dec. 21, 1874, aged 63 years, 3 mo., 24 days.

212—Margaret, wife of John Depue, died Oct. 23, 1870, aged 41 years, 3 mo., 7 days.

213—Adam Depue, born Aug. 27, 1808; died Aug. 2, 1847.

214—Mercy, wife of Adam Depue, born Oct. 15, 1807; died Nov. 15, 1845.

215—Moses Depue, born July 20, 1802; died July 31, 1871.

216—Margaret, wife of Moses Depue. born July 21, 1805; died Mar. 6, 1872.

217—Philip Depue, born April 12, 1806; died June 2, 1836.

218—Abraham, son of Philip and Susan Depue, born Oct. 24, 1829; died June 3, 1832.

219—Jacob Depue, born June 24, 1810; died Nov. 4, 1838.

220—James, son of Abraham and Susanna Depue, born Aug. 18, 1794; died May 11, 1843.

221—Elizabeth, daughter of John and Elizabeth Depue, died June 20, 1842, aged 26 years, 8 months.

222—Sarah, daughter of Benjamin Boyd and Catherine Depue, died July 28, 1833, aged 51 years, 7 mo., 10 days.

223—Jemima, wife of William Bitters, born Sept. 14, 1801; died Sept. 9, 1837.

224—Richard Zink, died April 24, 1848, aged 32 years, 16 days.

225—Susanna, wife of Andrew Durling, born July 2, 1790; died Oct. 5, 1827.

226—Rebecca Lee, died Aug. 23, 1844, in her 69th year.

227—Jane Lowry, born May, 1774; died Mar. 18, 1839.

228—John McCollom (perhaps husband of 229), died Dec. 10, 1792, in his 29th year.

229—Rachel McCulah, (perhaps McCollom), died April 8, 1852, aged 87 years, 6 days.

230—Sarah Jamison, died April 16, 1861, aged 65 years, 11 mo., 19 days.

231—Samuel Gulick, died May 22, 1825, aged 69 years, 12 days.

232—David Allen, died June 20, 1776, aged 66 years.

233—F. G. (June, 1766, aged 27 years).

234—Robert Lyle, Esquire, died Dec. 9, 1767, aged — years.

235—Thomas Moore, died Sept. 25, 1791, aged 53 years.

236—Mary, wife of Henry Snyder, died Mar. 6, 1856, in her 67th year.

237—Jacob B. Mershon, died June 14, 1848, aged 39 years, 8 months.

238—Elizabeth, wife of Jacob B. Mershon, died Dec. 30, 1843, aged 32 years, 7 mo., 24 days.

239—Mary, wife of Jacob B. Mershon, died June 23, 1874, aged 64 years, 7 months.
(Born Middagh)

240—James Martin, died May 29, 1767, aged 57 years.
(Progenitor of the Martin family of Lower Mt. Bethel)

241—Ann, widow of James Martin, died June 24, 1799, aged 71 years.
(Daughter of Thomas Miller, L. Mt. B.)

242—Col. Joseph Martin (son of 240), died Mar. 10, 1798, in his 39th year.

243—Alexander Miller, died Sept. 5, 1765, in his 84th year.
(Named Sanders Miller in his will and bequeathed 5 shillings to niece, daughter of Alexander Miller; lived in Bedminster township at time of death.)

244—Mary, wife of Alexander Miller, died Dec. 12, 1765, in her 62nd year.
245—James Miller, died Dec. 26, 1803, aged 71 years.
246—Jean, wife of James Miller, died July 13, 1763, in her 27th year.
247—Robert Miller, died Mar. 20, 1848, aged 70 years, 11 mo., 5 days.
248—Jane, wife of Robert Miller, born Oct. 11, 1785; died Oct. 26, 1870.
249—Peter Miller, died Dec. 1, 1859, aged 41 years, 9 mo., 23 days.
250—John Miller, died Jan. 1, 1865, aged 40 years, 7 mo., 13 days.
251—Henry Miller, born July 15, 1773; died May 24, 1850.
252—Olivia, wife of Henry Miller, born Mar. 20, 1772; died Oct. 10, 1858.
253—Matilda, wife of Jacob Miller, born April 9, 1815; died Jan. 20, 1854.
254—James Thompson, died Oct. 5, 1791, aged 52 years.
255—Here lie the remains of Jennet Sullyman, wife of Alexander Sullyman. (Dates not legible—It is one of the very old ones, as shown by character of stone).
256—John Rosenberry, died Sept. 8, 1860, aged 81 years, 10 mo., 4 days.
257—Susanna, wife of John Rosenberry, died Jan. 13, 1811, in her 36th year.
258—Morris Rosenberry, born Feb. 10, 1813; died Feb. 18, 1895.
259—Isabella, wife of Morris Rosenberry, born May 10, 1819; died Sept. 15, 1865.
260—Jane Rosenberry, born Feb. 27, 1819; died June 21, 1887.
261—Levi Loder, born Nov. 1, 1800; died Nov. 27, 1876.
262—Mary, wife of Levi Loder, born Dec. 16, 1800; died Dec. 24, 1853.
263—Mary Hummer, born July 7, 1804; died Feb. 24, 1850.
264—Thomas Ross, died Dec. 12, 1798, aged 73 years.
265—David Ross, died Jan. 26, 1811, in his 59th year.

266—James Ross, born Oct. 10, 1755; died Mar. 4, 1832.

267—Abigail, wife of John Ross, born Oct., 1776; died Mar. 22, 1833.

268—Catherine Ross, died July 6, 1818, aged 69 years.

269—Joseph Ross, Sr., died April 6, 1862, aged 71 years, 3 mo., 7 days.

270—Susanna, wife of Joseph Ross, Sen., died Jan. 5, 1845, aged 55 years, 3 months.

271—James Ross, born April 11, 1845; died Mar. 4, 1875.

272—William McIlhaney (see No. 294), born Sept. 7, 1799; died Jan. 24, 1881.

273—Catherine, wife of William McIlhaney, born May 5, 1805; died Mar. 14, 1864.

274—Baltzar Steel, born 1779; died Jan. 12, 1852.

275—William Norton, Sen., born July 16, 1796; died July 3, 1864.

276—Ruth, wife of William Norton, born May 17, 1801; died Aug. 11, 1880.

277—Enoch G., son of William and Ruth Norton, died Oct. 14, 1855, aged 32 years, 6 mo., 9 days.

278—Sarah Ann, wife of Peter Mixsell, daughter of William and Ruth Norton, born July 13, 1827; died Dec. 1, 1849.

279—John Gardner, died April 18, 1870, aged 76 years, 3 mo., 4 days.

280—Sarah, wife of John Gardner, died Dec. 30, 1872, aged 67 years, 7 mo., 25 days.

281—Aaron Kester, born Mar., 1816; died Jan. 5, 1843.

282—Jane, wife of Jacob Kooker, died Aug. 24, 1854, in her 73rd year.

283—Charles Tidd, born May 2, 1774; died Oct. 22, 1836.

284—Catherine, wife of Charles Tidd, born Feb. 9, 1782; died June 23, 1854.

285—Rebecca, wife of Peter Cyphers, died June 2, 1860, in her 67th year.

286—Benjamin Taylor, died Mar. 8, 1855, aged 71 years, 9 mo., 6 days.

287—Mary, wife of Benjamin Taylor, died April 8, 1868, aged 80 years, 11 mo.. 22 days.

288—Susan, wife of Conrad I. Taylor, died Aug. 19, 1852, aged 26 years, 7 mo., 5 days.

289—Samuel Reed, Esq, died Sept. 9, 1815, in his 81st year.

290—Ann, wife of Samuel Reed, died Mar. 27, 1781, aged 44 years.

291—Mary, wife of John Clark, died June 2, 18—8, aged 66 years, 6 mo., 11 days.

292—Richard Merrill (born in France), born June 28, 1767; died Feb. 3, 1850.

293—Mary, wife of Richard Merrill, born Nov. 7, 1772; died Mar. 3, 1848.

294—Hiram McIlhaney (son of 272), born Aug. 14, 1828; died May 19, 1886.

295—Rachel, wife of Hiram McIlhaney, born Aug. 3, 1824; died June 6, 1897.

(She was born Hummer)

296—Hannah, wife of John Farrow, died May 12, 1851, aged 35 years, 1 mo., 5 days.

(She was daughter of No. 74)

297—Mary, wife of Jeremiah Rockafellow, died (no date), aged 51 years, 11 mo., 21 days.

298—Caroline, wife of Jeremiah Rockafellow (second wife), born Feb. 27, 1827; died July 14, 1887.

(He had third wife, named Elizabeth Garren—no issue.)

299—John, Jr., son of Jeremiah and Mary Rockafellow, died Sept. 15, 1875, aged 21 years.

300—Morey Field, died Aug. 21, 176— (4th figure of year obliterated). (May have been Mercy.)

301—Esther VanKirk, died April 10, 1847, aged 85 years.

302—John Ussington, died April 12, 1855, aged 79 years, 7 mo., 2 days.

303—Abigail, wife of John Ussington, died Sept. 20, 1832, in her 70th year.

304—Susan Laning, wife of Elijah Laning, died Feb. 20, 1825, in her 32nd year.

305—Christiana, daughter of Jeptha and Isabella Adison, died April 21, 1804, in her 8th year.
(Isabella Adison was born Rea)
306—Francis Oblinger, died July 27, 1854, aged about 50 yrs.
307—Catherine, wife of Francis Oblinger, born June 18, 1803; died Aug. 4th, 1854.
308—John Oblinger, born May 28, 1837; died July 29, 1854.
309—John McCrea, died Sept. 10, 1847, in his 69th year.
310—Elizabeth, wife of John McCrea, died Aug. 19, 1846, in her 69th year.
311—Nancy, daughter of John and Elizabeth McCrea, died Oct. 20, 1855, aged 15 years, 1 mo., 30 days.
312—Jane McRea, died Mar. 10, 1851, in her 27th year.
313—Emaline, daughter of James and Martha McCrea, born Feb. 9, 1832; died Jan. 9, 1852.
314—John Connelly (husband of No. 163), born Feb. 4, 1804; died Sept. 22, 1889.
315—Andrew Vanvliet Middagh, died April 3, 1846, aged 21 years, 6 mo., 19 days.
316—Amanda Drach, died Dec. 2, 1849, aged 16 years, 1 mo., 25 days.
317—John, son of George and Sarah Fox, born Dec. 5, 1813; died Aug. 12, 1826. (Son of 84)
318—Rebecca Rush, born Dec. 3, 1847; died April 20, 1905.
319—William H. Resh, born July 29, 1852; died Aug. 8, 1921. (Husband of 164)
320—Nancy, daughter of Joseph and Eleanor Steele, died Dec. 7, 1850, aged 6 mo., 25 days.
321—John Scott, died June 24, 1792.

Maiden Surnames of Women Buried in the Presbyterian Burial Ground at Three Churches, Lower Mt. Bethel

See Nos.
63—Agnes Kelso, wife of James Hutchison, born in Ireland.
103—Eleanor, daughter of Francis and Sarah McFall, wife of H. G. Brittain.
124—Jemima, daughter of Francis and Sarah McFall, wife of Peter D. Kiefer.

HUNTER SETTLEMENT IN MT. BETHEL TOWNSHIP 593

130—Sarah Everitt, wife of Samuel Kiefer.
156—Caroline Ross, wife of Philip Deats, sister of Jos. Ross.
182—Margaret Deats, wife of John Ackerman.
241—Ann Miller, daughter of Thomas and Isabella Miller, wife of James Martin (a judge).
109—Cornelia Cronk, wife of Thomas Middagh.
170—Mary, daughter of Andrew and Jane (Brittain) Hutchison.
295—Rachel Hummer, wife of Hiram McIlhaney.
259—Isabella, daughter of Butler and Rachel Morris, wife of Morris Rosenberry.
70—Sarah, daughter of Nathaniel and Jean (Simonton) Brittain, wife of Samuel Eakin.
197—Susan Morris, wife of Wm. J. Scott, relict of John Vanatta.
4—Nancy, daughter of Robert and Elizabeth Galloway.
31—Elizabeth, daughter of Gerret Middaugh, wife of James Edmiston.
48—Margaret, daughter of Anthony and Mary (Hutchison) Ketchledge, wife of David Ayres.
50—Mary, daughter of Nathaniel and Jean (Simonton) Brittain, wife of Moses Ayres.
72—Elizabeth, daughter of Zacharias and Martha Matilda Drake, wife of John Eakin.
102—Sally Ann, daughter of Francis and Sarah McFall, second wife of H. G. Brittain.
137—Jane Nielson (Nelson), wife of George Kennedy.
140—Elizabeth, daughter of Leonard and Catherine Kern, 1st wife of Isaac Stocker.
161—Julia, daughter of John Deats, wife of John Ketchledge.
164—Emma Ketchledge, daughter of John and Julia (Deats) Ketchledge, wife of Wm. H. Resh.
163—Maria, daughter of John Deats, wife of John Connelly.
166—Elizabeth, either sister of Charles Tidd or sister of Charles Tidd's wife.
168—Mary, daughter of James B. and Elizabeth (Frey) Shull, 1st wife of Joseph Deats.

239—Mary Middagh, wife of Jacob B. Mershon.

22—Mary M., daughter of James and Nancy Lockhard, wife of David Kirkendall.

278—Sarah, daughter of William and Ruth Norton, wife of Peter Mixsell.

293—Mary Nye—as widow of ——— Bitters, married second Richard Merrill.

296—Hannah, daughter of Francis and Sarah McFall, wife of John Farrow.

305—Christianna, daughter of Jeptha and Isabella Adison.

270—Susanna Fox, wife of Joseph Ross.

310—Elizabeth, daughter of Nathaniel and Jean (Simonton) Brittain, wife of John McCrea.

128—Catherine Kiefer, daughter of Andreas Engleman, the immigrant, married Oct. 29, 1782, Peter Küfer, son of Johan Küfer, of Tinicum Township, Bucks Co., Pa.

ADDENDA

Scotch-Irish Presbyterian Burial Ground at Three Churches, Lower Mt. Bethel.

322—Henry Rasley, born Jan. 26, 1830; died June 28, 1904.

323—Mary Ann, wife of Henry Rasley, born Dec. 8, 1830; died Dec. 17, 1880. (She was born McIlhaney.)

324—Jane. (No inscription, also born McIlhaney, sister of Mary Ann and second wife of Henry Rasley.)

325—Catherine Louisa, daughter of Thomas and Catherine McIlhaney, died Feb. 19, 1852, aged 2 years, 6 months, 1 day.

326—Elizabeth, daughter of Peter and Mary McIlhaney, born May 6, 1852; died Apr. 23, 1855.

327—Jesse, son of John and Mary McIlhaney, born Feb. 16, 1865; died Mar. 28, 1866.

No. 300—Morey Field, should read Marcy Field.

www.ingramcontent.com/pod-product-compliance
Lightning Source LLC
Chambersburg PA
CBHW020630300426
44112CB00007B/71